From:

To: my favorik
!

Marilyn

juicy & adoring

love

D1376840

2010

"You can't help feeling sorry for guys like Newman. They have too much to lose if they make one false step. Look what *Confidential* did to Tab Hunter. Whenever Joanne Woodward came up, Newman became all macho. He was sad in many ways. Having to pretend to be what he wasn't. But most of us Hollywood hunks in the 1950s had to do that."

Matinée heartthrob **Jeffrey Hunter**

"Hell, guy, you just can't seem to realize what's happening. You're the new kid on the block. Every gay and every horny broad in Hollywood wants to go to bed with Paul Newman. You're doing pretty well for a married man. I've always had this belief that if a married man played it right, he can have more fun than single blokes."

Rod Steiger

"Paul Newman has the potential of becoming a magnificent actor if he ever gets through this complex he has about playing boy-macho."

Joan Crawford

"Even Newman's baby blues couldn't lure the women away from those TV boxes. We should have stripped him down more and shot the film with him half naked. That day will come for movies, I predict."

Robert Wise, lamenting the failure of the
Paul Newman film he directed, *Until They Sail*

"Mr. Newman, Mr. Newman! Would you like to see my body?"

Sandra Dee, at 14

"I never got around to screwing Paul Newman, although I certainly intended to. He had as much sex in the 50s as I did, but whereas he got away with it, I didn't"

Rock Hudson

"Newman is just as much of a narcissist as Gore Vidal, but he disguises it completely, and, like the most skilled of actors, puts up a mask to confuse the world. I suspect he will go far in an industry that is all about illusion. There is no self-awareness in this handsome young man at all. He is an obvious homosexual, but does not dare admit that to himself. He's a selfish rogue while pretending to be benevolent, supporting all the right causes. He has a facile charm but no depth. In spite of the hot sun out here, he already knows that California is a cold, harsh land. He does not want it to hurt him. So what will he do? What must he do? He will inflict emotional pain on others, therefore avoiding the pain of having the blows strike him first. I predict Newman will turn into a cardboard figure. There will be no reality to him. He can't be real. A tragedy, really. But, this is, after all, Lotusland."

Anaïs Nin

PAUL NEWMAN

"I'm really a very ordinary guy. Sure, I drank whiskey a lot. For a while, it really screwed up me up. There are periods in my life in which I don't take any particular pride. I'm not very good at revealing myself. I cover for it by telling terrible dirty jokes."

OTHER BOOKS BY DARWIN PORTER

Biographies
Merv Griffin, A Life in the Closet
Brando Unzipped
The Secret Life of Humphrey Bogart
Katharine the Great: Hepburn, Secrets of a Life Revealed
Howard Hughes: Hell's Angel
Michael Jackson, His Rise and Fall (What Really Happened)

And Coming Soon:
Steve McQueen, King of Cool (Tales of a Lurid Life)

Film Criticism
Blood Moon's Guide to Gay & Lesbian Film (Volumes One & Two)

Non-Fiction
Hollywood Babylon-It's Back!

Novels
Butterflies in Heat
Marika
Venus
Razzle-Dazzle
Midnight in Savannah
Rhinestone Country
Blood Moon
Hollywood's Silent Closet

Travel Guides
Many editions of *The Frommer Guides* to Europe, the Caribbean,
California, and parts of America's Deep South

PAUL NEWMAN

The Man Behind the Baby Blues

HIS SECRET LIFE EXPOSED

Another Hot, Startling, and Unauthorized Celebrity Biography by

Darwin Porter

BLOOD MOON Productions, Ltd.

PAUL NEWMAN, THE MAN BEHIND THE BABY BLUES

Manufactured in the United States of America

ISBN 978-0-9786465-1-6

First Edition, First Printing, July, 2009

Cover designs by Richard Leeds (Bigwigdesign.com)
Distributed in North America and Australia
through The National Book Network (www.NBNbooks.com)
and in the UK through Turnaround

THE AUTHOR DEDICATES THIS BOOK TO THE SOURCES WHO CONTRIBUTED TO ITS COMPILATION:

Janice Rule
Eartha Kitt
Sal Mineo
Anthony Perkins
Robert Francis
Tennessee Williams and Frank Merlo
William Inge
James Leo Herlihy
Lana Turner
Maila Nurmi
Shelley Winters
Geraldine Page

and countless others.

Gone, but not forgotten

A world class American Icon

Paul Newman 1925-2008

CONTENTS

CLIMBING THE LAVENDER LADDER
Paul Newman's Secret Life as a Bisexual

In the opinion of many of his fans, Newman's emotional and sexual involvements with the women in his life (Monroe, Crawford, Taylor, Grace Kelly, Audrey Hepburn, and perhaps most importantly, Joanne Woodward) are more compelling than the equivalent relationships he shared with men.

But according to Darwin Porter, the full story of what Newman did as a means to his end in Golden Age Hollywood hasn't ever been fully revealed—until now.

During a span of more than 50 years, insiders on Broadway and in Hollywood have spoken of Paul Newman's closeted life. Details about the megastar's bisexual history have been among the entertainment industry's worst-kept secrets.

For decades, the underground press has included Paul Newman on their list of bisexual or gay stars, a list that included Rock Hudson, Roddy McDowall, Richard Chamberlain, Farley Granger, Tab Hunter, Burt Lancaster, Marlon Brando, James Dean, Montgomery Clift, and countless others. "WAS PAUL NEWMAN GAY?" ran one headline. Yet another proclaimed: "DEEP INSIDE THE HOLLYWOOD CLOSET: RUMOR MILL IMPLICATES PAUL NEWMAN."

Even during Newman's lifetime, Larry Quirk, the dean of Hollywood biographers, wrote about Paul Newman's "homosexual panic" and how he maneuvered his way "up the lavender ladder." Quirk was making veiled references to his casting couch interludes with playwrights Tennessee Williams (author of *Cat on a Hot Tin Roof*--its film adaptation propelled Newman to stardom) and William Inge (author of *Picnic,* the play that launched Newman's legend on Broadway).

According to Darwin Porter, the secret life of Paul Newman reached the peak of its exposure and speculation during the 1970s, when Newman acquired the film rights to *The Front Runner,* a best-selling novel about a homosexual coach who falls desperately in love with his star (male) athlete.

In his role as the film's producer, Newman originally offered the role of the athlete to Robert Redford, who refused to play a gay character, fearing that it would harm his image at the box office. Consequently, Newman negotiated with Cal Culver, America's leading gay porn star of the 1970s, to interpret the role. Cal, a friend and confidant of Darwin Porter, later revealed to the gay press that he had had an affair with Newman. Additionally, Darwin's best friend, novelist James Leo Herlihy, had an affair with Newman when he was trying to persuade him to star as Joe Buck in the film version of his novel, *Midnight Cowboy.*

Many of Newman's personal friends, particularly those from the Actors Studio, spoke privately over the years about Newman's sexuality. They included actress Janice Rule (who later became a psychotherapist, with a respected practice in New York City), Rod Steiger, Geraldine Page, Eartha Kitt (who was introduced to Newman via her best friend, James Dean), and "Vampira," (aka Maila Nurmi), TV-land's first Goth, and a famous personality of the 1950s.

Tony Perkins, a friend of Herlihy's, privately admitted that he'd sustained a sexual affair with Newman when they both lived at the Château Marmont in Los Angeles in the 50s. The self-admittedly gay writer Gore Vidal spoke openly about his near-obsessional fixation on Newman during Newman's appearance in Gore's teleplay of *Billy the Kid.* And during one particularly complex point in their relationship, Paul Newman and his then "mistress," Joanne Woodward, shared a Malibu beach house with Vidal and his "husband," Howard Austen. Throughout that chapter of their lives, all four members of the ménage remained "artfully nonspecific" as to the direction of the emotional links going on within that beach house.

Sal Mineo, another friend of Darwin's, confessed to having sustained a sexual affair with Newman that began on the set of *Somebody Up There Likes Me.* Sal confessed his undying love for Paul to yet another author, Larry Quirk, who published this then-first-time news in a book released by Taylor Publishing Company. Later, an unauthorized feature story on Newman revealed that Jackie Witte (Newman's first wife) threatened to leave him when she learned about his affair with James Dean.

Brooks Clift, another of Darwin's friends, revealed the details of an affair that his brother, Montgomery Clift, had had with Newman. And actor Frank McHugh, a close friend of Spencer Tracy and a member of the hard-drinking "Irish Mafia" of Hollywood, claimed that he accidentally walked in on Newman and the recently deceased actor Jack Lord, catching them together "in an embarrassing position." Newman, Lord, and McHugh were each at the time filming a teleplay together.

For more on the startling details associated with the bisexual side of the actor whom no one seemed to be able to get enough of, Blood Moon hereby presents Darwin Porter's newest biography.

Best wishes to all of you, and many thanks.

Danforth Prince
President, Blood Moon Productions

Paul Newman's Passions

Marlon Brando

Jackie-O

Montgomery Clift

Marilyn Monroe

Steve McQueen

Grace Kelly

Robert Redford

Elizabeth Taylor

Joan Crawford

Tom Cruise

Audrey Hepburn

James Dean

Chapter One
Born on the Right Side of the Tracks

"Over my dead body will a son of mine go into the theater. An actor? Are you out of your fucking mind? Do you want to lie on a casting couch for every cocksucker from Broadway to Hollywood? I'll tell you what will happen to you. The same thing that happens to every pretty boy sentenced to prison in Ohio."

In Shaker Heights, Ohio, a young Paul Newman had finally confessed what his mother had known all along. One day he'd go to New York to become an actor.

Arthur S. Newman was to die in 1950, never living to see his son become one of the legends of motion pictures. His father had predicted failure for his son, warning him that he'd end up in the gutter, walking the streets of New York's Bowery, begging for a handout.

The elder Newman would have failed as a prophet. It was his son, Paul Newman, the actor, who in the decades to come would distribute millions of dollars worth of food for homeless, starving children.

***

On January 26, 1925, Paul Leonard Newman was born in Cleveland Heights, an affluent suburb of Cleveland itself.

"It was cold as all three tits on a witch the day my son was born," Arthur Senior later said. He arrived at the hospital in black leather boots, having plowed through snow more than three feet deep. It was fourteen degrees below freezing, the weather made even worse by the cruel winds blowing off Lake Erie.

In bed, Theresa presented her husband with an eight-pound baby boy. "Here is our incredibly beautiful son with the loveliest blue eyes God gave a

1

man since Adam walked on the face of the Earth. My dream was to have a blond-haired, blue-eyed baby boy."

Most babies have cloudy eyes, but Paul's reportedly were a piercing shade of blue from the moment he popped out of the womb.

Arthur Senior looked at the baby more skeptically. "I don't know who he takes after. The men in my family all had black eyes."

A year later the family moved into a spacious, eleven-room home at 2983 Brighton Road in neighboring Shaker Heights, a suburb even more affluent than Cleveland Heights. A German Jew, Arthur Senior was a second-genera-tion American. His wife, Theresa, had arrived at Ellis Island in New York at the age of four, coming from Hungary. The year before Paul was born, she'd given birth to another son, Arthur Newman Junior.

Theresa told her new neighbors in Shaker Heights that her younger son was "my pride and my joy. I love my older child too. But he's daddy's boy. Paul belongs just to me."

Sarah Cohn, a distant relative of Arthur Senior, was harshly critical of the way Theresa was bringing up her younger son. She frequently complained to Arthur. "Theresa is trying to make a girl out of him. She won't let him get one spot of dirt on his clothes before she bathes him and dresses him in finery. She even perfumes him. Didn't perfuming babies go out of style with Louis XIV? I must admit, though, that he's cute as a button."

"I'll make a man out of him if it's the last thing I do," Arthur Senior vowed. "Compared with how I grew up, the kid lives in the lap of luxury. I

Arthur S. Newman and **Joseph Newman**
Newman's father (left) and uncle (right)

never really knew my father. He died when I was only a baby. I came up through the school of hard knocks. But look where I am today."

Even in the middle of the Depression that fell on the world in 1929, Arthur Senior provided generously for his family, giving them not only a luxurious home in an upmarket neighborhood, but seeing that they had meat on the table every night when much of America was waiting in breadlines.

As a teenager, Arthur Senior had been a pioneer in radio broadcasting. In 1917, he joined with his older brother, Joseph Newman, to found Newman-Stern, a retail sporting goods business.

Even though sales were down in the early 1930s, the store still made a reasonable profit at the end of every year. In later life, Paul would deny his rather affluent early life, claiming he was the son of poor immigrants, which he was not, of course.

Sarah recalled that both Arthur Junior and Paul were the best-dressed boys in Shaker Heights. As they grew older, their father gave them fifty cents a week in allowance. But Theresa supplemented their income by presenting each of her children with a crisp five-dollar bill, which she took from the family's food budget. Many families in those Depression-laden days didn't even have five dollars a week to spend on groceries.

Paul had at least thirty different shirts, each of them starched and pressed. He wore a different one for every day of the month, beginning the wardrobe shift when a new month arrived. "With his blond hair and those blue eyes, he was a sight to behold," Sarah said. "Every woman wanted to pick him up and kiss him. The men restrained themselves, pinching his cheeks instead. Perhaps that's why his cheeks looked rosy red all the time."

"As a kid, I was split into two different personalities," Paul once told playwright Tennessee Williams in Key West. "Dad wanted me to be a tomboy, a great athlete, a commercial gent. My mother appealed to my sensitive side—the artist, the poet. She was the one who urged me to read every book I could find and to expand my mind. The character of Brick in *Cat on a Hot Tin Roof* was

perfect for me. All my life I was split into two different directions. One side of me wanted to live life with my dead friend Skipper in the play, the other side was tempted to fuck the living shit out of Maggie the Cat and be the heterosexual stud most of my fans wanted me to be."

"Dad liked to deny things to my brother and me or make us work hard for them," Paul said. "Take baseball mitts. The boys at school had shiny mitts purchased from the Newman sporting goods store. Arthur didn't get a new baseball mitt until he turned ten. Dad made me wait until I was eleven."

Years later, Paul and his older brother, Arthur Junior, were rivals competing for their father's affection. "At night over dinner, I heard nothing but praise for Junior's accomplishments," Paul said. "His prowess on the athletic field. He had more muscles than I did. He was a great swimmer. Good at football. A baseball hitter from hell. He could outrun me. He was everything in a son my father wanted. I got no praise at all from my dad. He was cold and distant. He once said at the dinner table that my mom should dress me like a girl, since that's what I was growing up to be."

Although Arthur Junior and Paul got along in later life, and even worked together, Paul once claimed that when they were growing up, their sibling rivalry was belligerent.

"Even though I was a short, scrawny, ninety-eight pound weakling in the ninth grade, I had my brother beat by an inch or two—at least in one department," Paul once confided to actress Shelley Winters one drunken night in Greenwich Village. "That is, to judge from the look of things. I never took measurements, of course."

Theresa, who had been born a Hungarian Catholic, had converted to Christian Science when Paul was five years old. She converted Paul to her religion before he entered the first grade, but her husband, as a German Jew, remained hostile to Christian Science.

She was hardly a fanatic and, unlike the tenets of her faith, allowed both her sons to have proper medical care. Later in life, his religious training seemed to have had little effect on Paul: "Most of it sounded like a lot of crap to me," he said.

It was Theresa who instilled in Paul the vision of becoming an actor. "Nothing would thrill me more than taking a train to Broadway to see my son's name

Attending his first movie

4

in lights," she said. "I think he has the possibility of becoming the next John Barrymore—and even better looking."

"Whatever you do, don't tell the world you've got Jewish blood," she warned her son. "Most of the world hates Jews. Your real name is spelled N-E-U-MAN. But I got your father to change it to Newman."

Paul did not take her advice. When he first arrived in Hollywood, he let his associates know he was Jewish. "It's nothing to be ashamed of," he told friends. "I'm proud of my heritage." Of course, he did not take out ads in newspapers, and many of his co-workers never knew he was Jewish. In fact, when Otto Preminger cast Paul in *Exodus*, several news accounts noted that the director had hired a "non-Jewish actor" for the role.

"I like the name of NEW MAN," Theresa told Paul. "It's poetic and symbolic of your bright future in America. My secret nickname for you is going to be 'Numie.' It'll be just something we use in private. Our little secret. You can share all your secret desires with me. Never your father. He doesn't understand you have the sensitive soul of a poet. Men like him are concerned only with commerce. They treat their sons and especially their wives with brutality. I have to endure sex with him. It feels like a knife stabbing me in the gut. The only good that ever came out of sex was God's gift of you."

Theresa had a lot of spare time because her husband hired a combination maid and cook. Often she'd take a bus to downtown Cleveland and the Hannah Theatre where she attended matinees. She was reluctant to admit it, but Sarah Cohn claimed that Theresa wanted to be an actress herself. "She read all the fan magazines—Greta Garbo was her favorite," Sarah said. "She dreamed dreams that could never be."

Whenever Theresa returned from a stage production in Cleveland, she described in minute detail every scene to her young son. Amazingly, for reasons not known, she did not invite him to go with her to the theater.

When his mother wasn't attending the theater, she prepared elaborate Hungarian specialties for her family. "She made the world's greatest goulash," Paul later claimed. "It was dear old mom who gave me my love of food. She even taught me how to cook. I learned all her secret recipes, some of which I would one day publish in a book."

"Dad took me on fishing trips," Paul said. "He encouraged me to go out for sports in spite of my small size. He taught me to swim. One time when he caught me

The cutest kid in Shaker Heights

5

cooking with mom, he shouted at her. 'You're raising a son, not a god damn girl! Get that fucking apron off that kid. A kitchen is no place for a boy.'"

"But the world's greatest chefs were and *are* men," she protested.

"She also wanted me to be a musician," Paul said. "I took piano lessons. I failed. I tried the violin. I failed, never becoming a virtuoso like Jack Benny." As he said that, Paul flashed his famous grin to suggest he was joking.

"In the early years I told each of my parents what they wanted to hear," Paul said. "Dad learned that I wanted to grow up to be a baseball player. Mother believed that I wanted to go on the stage, even though I had not committed to acting."

***

Encouraged by Theresa to join *The Curtain Raisers*, a children's theater, Paul made his stage debut at the age of seven, playing a court jester in *The Travails of Robin Hood*. In that play, he yodeled a song composed by his uncle, Joseph Newman. His father's brother was a journalist and poet. "He was the artist in the family—not me," said Arthur Senior. Joseph, like Theresa, felt that a kid with Paul's stunning looks belonged on the stage.

By the age of twelve, Paul was playing Saint George in *St. George and the Dragon*. The dragon was actually a placid old bulldog, and Paul's job was to pour salt on its tail and vanquish him. "My legs were shaking on opening night," Paul later said. "They've been shaking on opening night ever since. I'll let you in on a secret. These skinny legs never shook more than when I had to go out and face the critics as the curtain went up on *Sweet Bird of Youth*."

After witnessing his performance as Saint George, Theresa told her son, "You have such beauty. Too bad it has to be wasted on a boy."

Years later he confided a secret to his mother after he returned from his first job in Hollywood. "Believe you me, that beauty has not been wasted."

Paul recalled that "it was Uncle Joe who defined the rewards awaiting a young man who devoted himself to the artistic life. He became my surrogate father."

When Paul was only sixteen, Uncle Joe had told him, "Your mind is a flame to be kindled."

There is a certain irony in the fact that the man who would grow up to become a sex symbol around the world did not early in life fill out the potential of his frame.

When he attended local elementary schools, he was frequently beaten up by older bullies. Since most of these boys were not too familiar with homosexuality, they referred to Paul as a sissy. One day after school a group of six bullies attacked him and hauled him off into the bushes. There Paul was restrained while one of the boys pulled down his pants. One of the boys later claimed, "We wanted to see if pretty boy was really a boy. All of us had to look at his jewels just to make sure."

At Shaker Heights High School, Paul wanted to be a football player but didn't have the build for it. I did get offered the job of a male cheerleader, though. I also wanted to play baseball. But I was no good at that either. The coach told me I pitched like a girl."

"I worked in some school plays as an actor and stage manager," Paul recalled, "but I had no real interest in becoming an actor. Early in life I learned a bitter lesson about the theater. An actor doesn't always get the role he wants. In a school production, I tried to get the role of first grave-digger in *Hamlet*. It went to another guy."

When he told his mother of his loss, she comforted him. "Forget about playing a grave-digger. That's not for you. My dream is to live long enough to see my son starring in *Hamlet* on Broadway."

"My father just assumed I was going to join him in the sporting goods business," Paul said. "I worked there after school and on Saturdays. He paid me less than he did his other employees. But he promised both Junior and me that one day he'd give us the family business. I wasn't looking forward to selling footballs and baseball mitts for the rest of my life."

In his final years of high school, Paul's height shot up four inches. His exact height would remain a lifelong debate. His most generous appraisers claim that at his peak he stood five feet, ten and a half inches tall. His critics countered that he "towered" no more than five feet, six inches.

In 1986 Paul's height, or lack thereof, became a nationwide debate. *The New York Post* launched a campaign that promised to pay $1,000 in charity donations for every proven inch the actor measured over five feet, eight inches.

Appearing on the TV program, *Live at Five*, Paul responded to *The Post* in anger. "For a newspaper that makes ten million a year, a thousand dollar bet is chicken feed. I'll write a check to *The New York Post* for a half-million dollars. If they're wrong, though, then it's time to start playing hardball. Let's not make it one thousand dollars an inch. Make it one hundred thousand an inch, or one hundred twenty-five thousand a quarter-inch for anything above five

Saint George
Paul's first starring role

7

feet, eight inches." *The Post* backed down and refused to take Paul up on his offer.

Like his future friend, Tom Cruise, Paul was extremely sensitive about his height, claiming he stood five feet, eleven inches. Many co-workers in the film industry doubted that. One in particular, Sandi Burton, posed with him for promotional pictures for *A New Kind of Love*. She claimed that she measured five feet nine inches, and "I remembered looking down at him."

The *London Mail* hired a policewoman, the city's expert on body height. She used an elaborate trigonometric formula on a photograph of him walking down Piccadilly in London. The *Mail* announced her scientific conclusion. "Paul Newman measures exactly five feet, seven inches tall."

When Paul shot up in height, he also began to fill out, becoming more muscular, although his well-defined body would always be taut, not massively developed like that of Arnold Schwarzenegger.

"There was no contest," Mary Schribner, a classmate said. "Paul Newman was the best good-looking guy in school. He wasn't just handsome but strikingly good looking, the most beautiful boy I'd ever seen. But girls didn't want to date him. He was always pulling pranks on girls, always up to some mischief. He once put a dead snake in a girl's lunchbox. He was a cut-up, the class clown. He liked to play gags. He sat right behind me in class and was always annoying me. Once when I sat down, it sounded like I'd let out a big fart. He'd put some rubber contraption under my seat. The whole class laughed at me. I felt so embarrassed I cried. What girl in her right mind would want to date Mr. Tomfoolery?"

Eventually, the school bullies stopped calling him a sissy and began wanting to hang out with him, especially one friend named Ralph Sage. His wild nights out with the boys led to a serious accident in 1940. Paul had borrowed his father's car to go on a joyride with his friend Ralph. Losing control of the wheel, Paul crashed the vehicle into a big oak tree, almost totaling it.

Miraculously both he and Ralph escaped with only minor injuries. As punishment for this, for a full eleven months every day after school ended, Paul was confined to the house unless he was otherwise needed to help out in the sporting goods store.

Paul might not have been popular with the girls at his high school, but as he grew into manhood he attracted attention from one of his neighbors—let's

Media frenzy and a question of size

8

call her Jane Doe. She'd first met Paul when he had a paper route along Brighton Road and had watched him grow up. Back when he was nine years old, she used to invite him inside her home for freshly baked cookies.

Jane's husband had died in the Japanese attack on Pearl Harbor, and the neighbors reported that she was the loneliest, saddest woman in Shaker Heights. Even after Paul gave up the paper route and went to work for his father, he still saw Jane on occasion.

Following the car accident, when his father refused to let him drive the family car, Paul secretly borrowed Jane's car "whenever I needed wheels," as he later admitted. Arthur Senior had no knowledge of this. The car had belonged to Jane's sailor husband, and she almost never used it.

Details are lacking, and Paul told only a few close friends, including one Chris Chase, but at some point in their relationship, Jane attempted to seduce the handsome sixteen-year-old. From all reports, the sexual encounter was a disaster, and Paul had been too nervous to perform adequately with the older woman. That ended their years-long friendship, and Paul avoided her house from then on and was no longer seen driving her car.

The experience may have turned him off girls, and especially older women, for years. While appearing on Broadway in William Inge's *Picnic*, he confessed to the playwright that, "It took me years to decide which direction I wanted to go in. I was very confused at the time, and I let a lot of people, especially in the Navy, take advantage of me. Even back then, I knew one thing, and that was I did not want to live the life of a homosexual. It was too limiting, too degrading. I wanted to spend my life making love to beautiful women, but I just didn't know how to go about it. A lot of boys my age were getting girls pregnant without meaning to—and being forced to marry them. I didn't want to be forced into anything like that. I was also a growing boy with needs, and those needs were very sexual. My hand came into intimate contact with a certain part of my body night after night. But I wanted more."

***

Part of Paul Newman's legend is that he was a "romantic loner" while growing up in Ohio. He always appeared to be dreaming "the impossible dream," Arthur Senior said. His mother had the opposite point of view. "He will do great things, accomplish much. He can do whatever he sets his mind to do, only he's not sure what that is yet."

When he was just thirteen, Paul began his long, rambling walks around Greater Cleveland, discov-

Braving the winter winds of Ohio

ering hidden beauty spots. He was also attracted to tawdry scenes, and was fascinated to see female prostitutes soliciting their trade in the seedy parts of Cleveland. Once he walked for miles, just following the railroad tracks, as if that would lead him out of the Cleveland area and into a new life. He explained to Theresa that, "I need time to think, to get away, be myself, and figure things out." He never explained exactly what he was figuring out.

His distant relative, Sarah Cohn, had always observed the young boy closely, and she was filled with opinions. "Behind those blue eyes was a bubbling cauldron," she said. "Paul never invited anyone, not even his mother, to look inside his head. There were things going on there that we could not even conceive. Those penetrating eyes of his only told you that something was going on, but you didn't know what. I suspected that he was dangerous. I knew he'd started drinking beer, and a lot of it, when he was only fifteen. He managed to conceal this from his father, but Theresa found out. She forgave him. He could have been exposed as a serial killer, and that woman would have pardoned him his sin. If anyone knew what was going on with Paul, it was Chris Chase, who became his buddy. I think he attended another school. For a time, Paul and Chris became inseparable."

Every high school in the country had a hunky stud like Chris Chase. Many girls avoided him out of fear, but others clustered around him. The guys sought him out too. Blond and blue-eyed, he was handsome in a menacing sort of way.

Although he was only seventeen, he looked much older. He was the most physically developed of all his classmates, with on most occasions a day's growth of beard, when the other boys needed only one shave a month, if that. His chest hair was always visible above the neckline of a white T-shirt.

The circumstances of how he met Paul, who was enrolled in another school, aren't known. But soon they were going everywhere together, attending football games and going for long rides in the Ohio countryside in Chris's hot rod.

Paul may have been honored that such a sought-after student wanted to spend time with him instead of joining in the more usual pursuit of available girls.

"There was a chemistry there," said Betty Cally, who attended school with Chris. "I saw them having an ice cream soda one afternoon, and though they were the center of attention, these guys didn't even know anyone else existed. When they met each other, Chris stopped dating girls and Paul gave up

Forbidden to drive:
Paul in Shaker Heights

10

that rough gang of guys he used to pal around with. In those days, it wasn't unusual for a boy to spend more time with his best pal than he did with his girlfriend. Boyfriends were an everyday affair. Being with your girl was a special occasion—dressing up for a date to the movies, or on rare occasions a visit to a cheap restaurant, perhaps attending some school event together."

Chris was also a guitar-picking singer of limited talent. He was a dime-store Elvis Presley long before that singer swept the nation. Thanks partly to Chris' good looks and dynamic sex appeal, he got a few weekend bookings at bars and nightclubs in downtown Cleveland.

Paul was given permission to spend a weekend in the city with Chris. The lie told was that they were going to stay at the house of Chris's uncle. In fact, Chris had booked them into a seedy hotel a block from The Blue Note, where he was appearing as a singer. Chris, who looked far older than his actual years, had presented a fake ID when he was hired. Chris then persuaded the club's manager to allow (the underaged) Paul into the club as well.

The night Chris took him out was Paul's first exposure to a night club. He didn't know what to expect. Chris told him to stand at the bar where he'd cleared it with the bartender that Paul was allowed to order beer. Excusing himself, Chris went backstage to change into his costume for the night.

As Paul waited for Chris to go on, he found himself the center of attention from a lot of older men, one of whom asked him, "Are you skipping your boy scout meeting tonight?" Paul was too terrified to speak and tried to ignore the men's lewd propositions. As he scanned the bar, he could not see one woman in attendance.

When the beer consumption led to the inevitable, a tipsy Paul headed back to the men's room. Chris still hadn't made an appearance. On the way to the toilet, Paul was groped two or three times. He struck at the hands that felt him up.

Standing at the urinal in the men's room, he found it impossible to urinate with so many eyes fastened on his crotch. He slipped into a private stall and locked the door. By the time he emerged from the toilet, Chris was on the stage. Paul was shocked at his appearance.

Chris was the original Naked

"The worst actor in Ohio"
Rehearsals for better
things to come

11

Cowboy, pre-dating the famous iconic image in Times Square. With his guitar strapped on, he wore only white boots and a tight-fitting and very revealing bikini. Paul didn't think he was much of a singer, but he enthralled the audience. His signature song was "You Are My Sunshine."

At the end of his act, which met with roaring applause, Chris removed his ten-gallon hat and passed it around the audience. The men filled it with dollar bills.

A waiter came and ushered Paul backstage to Chris' dressing room, where he was changing into street clothes. He ordered Paul to count the money in his hat. As Chris dressed, Paul counted out one-hundred and eleven dollars. He'd never held that much money in his life.

"Let's get some grub," Chris told him. "After that, I'll rent us a hot whore for ten bucks. We'll enjoy her together."

Two hours later Paul found himself in bed naked with an equally naked Chris and a much older hooker who seemed bored with the two young boys. Chris went first, as Paul watched in fascination. When it came time for his turn, he was reluctant to mount the prostitute but was urged on by Chris.

"I began to rub my hands over Paul's body until it produced the desired effect," Chris later claimed. "He finally did the job. I really believe if I hadn't been rubbing and fondling him, he'd never have gone through with it."

Chris also claimed that a month later, when Paul obtained permission from his parents for another nocturnal excursion to downtown Cleveland, he seduced Paul. "I figured if he'd let me feel him up, he wouldn't resist my next moves. This time no whore. I had him all weekend in that flea trap. I taught the kid everything he knows about man-on-man sex. He took to it like a pig in shit. He was a natural. He ended up doing everything I wanted, and I'm a God damn demanding guy in bed."

Paul's affair with Chris did not last long. There was a scandal that was whispered about in Shaker Heights. It seemed that Chris, for pay, had gotten sexually involved with one of his high school teachers, who had taken pornographic

Senior Class
of
Shaker High School

pictures of him. Somehow this became known to the police who moved in. The scandal was hushed up but the teacher was fired and disappeared from town.

Without a final good-bye to Paul, Chris also left town.

His involvement with Paul might never have been known if Chris didn't surface a year later in Greenwich Village. For a brief moment of glory, his Naked Cowboy act drew several hundred gay men into whatever club he was appearing in.

Years later, after Paul had became a famous movie star, Chris "dined out" at such Village restaurants as the San Remo, telling tall tales of his seduction of Paul to such figures of the literati as Jack Kerouac, Edward Albee, and a young novelist, James Leo Herlihy, who'd later write *Midnight Cowboy*. It was because of Chris that rumors of Paul's homosexuality spread through the Greenwich Village underground long before they surfaced in Hollywood.

***

After Chris's scandal with his teacher and their sudden departures from Cleveland, rumors and gossip spread through the school. Because of his close ties with Chris, Paul became the victim of unwanted speculation.

As if to erase the memory, Paul devoted himself to pursuing debate and became the most skilled in his class. He was articulate, with a charisma that grabbed the attention of his audience. "It was not that his points were so valid," said William Walton, his English coach. "It's that he knew how to sell them so effectively that you wanted to believe everything he said. He also had a keen intelligence. In addition to being a good debater, he became interested in serious drama."

During this period, it isn't known why he quit working for his father at the sporting goods store. Perhaps they'd had an argument. But Paul was soon seen hustling sandwiches at Danny Budin's Corned Beef Palace. He no longer wanted to depend on an allowance from his parents, but preferred to make money on his own.

"He was stubborn and defiant," Sarah Cohn said. "Of course, many young boys go through a rebellious period like Paul did. He was so independent. He didn't want anybody telling him what to do. It was the beginning of his restless years, where he would wander aimlessly from job to job. He even took a job selling encyclopedias from door to door. He told me he wanted to see if he could sell himself to people. He made several hundred dollars. Frankly, I think a lot of bored housewives bought the encyclopedias from him because he was so handsome and charming."

Somewhere along the way he became involved with a somewhat plain but

13

remarkably intelligent sixteen-year-old girl, Betty Roberts. "Many of the girls were afraid of Paul," she said. "There were a lot of rumors about him. He was often moody and wouldn't speak to you. On other days, he could be absolutely charming. I pursued him. For weeks, he didn't pay attention to me. Then one day he invited me out and after that, we began to date. I was serious. He wasn't. But he told people I was his girl. He'd give me a good night kiss and that was that. I guess I would have done more but he never asked me."

"When we were alone, he never put the moves on me," she claimed. "But when we were with others, he always put his arm rather possessively around me. I began to feel that he was saying, 'I'm Paul Newman, and I like girls.' I found our relationship very confusing. I could never figure it out. I wanted him to talk to me about our future. Maybe our getting married one day. Every morning when I woke up, I never knew if I was still his girl or not. He would sometimes go for days without even speaking to me. Then he'd show up with that wonderful grin of his, and he'd be just as charming as ever. I almost said he could charm the pants off a person, but that never happened between us."

After he was graduated in 1943, Paul immediately dropped Betty without a farewell and enrolled in the U.S. Navy for flight training. He would not be called up right away, so he signed up for courses at Ohio University in Athens. "My subject was Lager 101," he'd later recall. "I drank enough beer to sink a tanker." If drinking was his major, economics and business were his minor. Arthur Senior still had hopes of Paul coming back from college and taking over the sporting goods business.

When sober, Paul appeared as a boxer in the university's theatrical production, *The Milky Way*, showing off his newly muscular physique in scarlet-covered trunks. In this play by Lynn Root and Harry Clark, Paul was cast as Speed McFarland, a middleweight boxing champion, foreshadowing his eventual, much bigger role in his first hit film, the 1956 *Somebody Up There Likes Me*, where he played the role of middleweight champion Rocky Graziano.

Working on that production of *The Milky Way* was Janet Holsom, whose parents had settled in Ohio after years of braving the winters of Manitoba. "She's the sexiest gal I've ever met," Paul wrote a buddy, Ralph Sage, a member of his former gang of pals back in Shaker Heights. Ralph was serving at the time in the U.S. Navy, as he'd signed up in December of 1941, right after the Japanese attack on Pearl Harbor. Paul wrote to Ralph during a period of several months while he himself was in the Navy. Perhaps Paul wanted to counter those rumors that had spread among his contemporaries about Chris Chase and himself.

In contrast to his restrained behavior with his girlfriend, Betty, Paul became sexually intimate with Janet, perhaps even on their first date—that is, if his letters to Ralph are to be believed. Paul's letters were almost pornographic, as were those of thousands upon thousands of other young men in the 40s, writing to pals about their conquests, often in foreign ports. He called her breasts "melons," and referred to her vagina as "a dark blueberry bramble." He confessed to Ralph, perhaps exaggerating, that "I nearly choke her when I come. She calls the big vein on my dick 'the come canal.'"

In 1958, after Paul had become a world-famous movie star, Ralph would attempt to sell Paul's steamy letters to *Confidential* magazine, but was turned down. Even so, mimeographed copies of these scalding letters would circulate through underground Hollywood, challenging rumors of Paul's alleged homosexuality.

It remains somewhat of a mystery why Ralph even bothered to save Paul's letters in the first place, since Paul was not famous at the time and their friendship back in Shaker Heights hadn't been particularly intimate. It has been speculated that Ralph may have had a secret schoolboy crush on his "pretty boy friend."

Paul's studies at Ohio University ended abruptly when the Navy called for him to report for duty. Two days before he was called up, Janet informed him that she was pregnant. Although Paul promised to marry her when he got out of the Navy, Janet wasn't so certain. She'd heard that a lot of servicemen all over America were making such promises to abandoned girlfriends on the homefront with no intention of "carrying through with their sweet talk." She demanded that Paul get the money "from your rich parents" for an abortion.

He had no intention of letting his parents know he'd gotten a girl pregnant. He still had one thousand dollars in the bank, money he'd earned when selling encyclopedias from door to door.

With that money, Paul rented a car and drove Janet across the U.S./Canadian frontier to an abortion clinic that had been used by many other students at Ohio University. In a letter to Ralph, Paul claimed that following the abortion, Janet had cried all the way back to Athens. Apparently, at one point, she had screamed at him, "You killed my baby!" She seemed to forget that the abortion was her idea. In spite of the tensions between them, Paul still called Janet "my girl," and promised to return to her and settle down at war's end.

"We'll see how all this comes out," she reportedly told Paul. "What if America loses the war and the Nazis invade Ohio? The soldiers will probably capture me and send me to some prison camp as a sex slave."

He assured her that "there is no way the United States is going to lose, and I'll be back."

***

Paul was ordered by the Navy to report to the grounds of Yale University, where he signed on for training in the V-12 program of the Navy Air Corps. "I'll be a flying ace and shoot down twenty, maybe even thirty, of the *Luftwaffe*," he told his mother back in Shaker Heights.

But during his first week at Yale, his hopes of becoming a Navy pilot were dashed. All recruits were subjected to an eye test. Paul's results revealed that those incredibly blue eyes of his could not determine the difference between red and green, a skill he'd need as a pilot.

He was dismissed from the air corps and sent to boot camp, little knowing that he would have his first intimate encounter with a movie star, thereby beginning a parade of conquests that would continue throughout most of his life.

Paul had heard stories from other recruits about how brutal the conditions were at boot camp. He'd seen enough movies to know what to expect from his drill sergeant, anticipating a bully of an officer—the kind Ernest Borgnine would play years later, tormenting poor Frank Sinatra in *From Here to Eternity*.

But when he met his instructor, to Paul's astonishment, he encountered a man of almost stunning beauty, Robert Stack. He'd seen Robert give singing sensation Deanna Durbin her first on-screen kiss in *First Love* (1939), the actor's debut movie. Paul had been captivated by Robert and had seen his other movies, including his turn as Frank Morgan's Nazi son in *The Mortal Storm* (1940).

In the fan magazines, Paul had read that Robert had been born into a wealthy family and was both a polo player and the world's greatest skeet champion. He was known as "The Swinging Bachelor" of Hollywood, and he'd had affairs with Judy Garland, Ingrid Bergman, and countless others.

His father, an advertising executive, had created the slogan, "The beer that made Milwaukee famous." What the fan magazines didn't know, or at least didn't report, was that Robert was also a bisexual, having had affairs with both Tyrone Power and Howard Hughes. In the summer of 1940 he'd shared his small double bed in the Hollywood Hills with a libidinous new buddy of his, John F. Kennedy, the son of the former ambassador to England.

Even though Robert was an officer and Paul an enlisted "swabby," the attraction between the two men was electric, enough so that Paul's fellow sailors became aware of it. Both Robert and Paul tried to keep their ongoing affair a secret, but in that they did not succeed. Apparently, none of the officers ever found out about the time Robert and Paul spent together off base, but Paul's comrades in the barracks knew and gossiped about the clandestine relationship.

The exact details of Paul's involvement with the dashing movie star will

16

never be known. What is known is that when Paul left the base he'd walk for half a mile to a point where Robert was waiting for him in his private car.

Paul had been merely color blind, but a Navy optometrist had pronounced Robert "practically blind." Even so, he'd been allowed to enlist as a gunnery officer. "It pays to be a movie star when you want something," Robert later said.

Paul never became an aerial gunner during the war, but he was taught air-to-air gunnery by Robert in case he ever had to face Japanese Zeros with 20mm automatic cannons. Robert warned Paul and the other men that in a crash, the pilot often walked away, whereas the poor gunner in the rear was usually hauled off in a meat wagon. "The mortality ratio is something like three to one, gunners to pilots," Robert claimed.

It can be assumed that Robert instilled fear in Paul, but used the upcoming danger he might face in the war as a seduction tool. Later, in Hollywood, Robert told his friends that since he might have died in the war, he'd been "determined to live life to the fullest in case it was blotted out by the Japs."

"I think Paul developed some very strong feelings for Robert," said another Paul, Paul Reiner, who served with Newman. "Stack wasn't interested in any school-gal romance," Reiner claimed. "He was a love 'em and leave 'em kind of guy. You know the type. A girl in every port—or, in Stack's case, a girl or a cute boy in every port. The bastard pursued the thrill of the moment, and seemed always open to some new sexual adventure. On the other hand, Paul took their relationship seriously. When Stack eventually was reassigned, Paul took it real bad. I think Paul thought he meant more to Stack than he really did."

After training the recruits, Robert was assigned to tour naval bases in America along with five other men, seeking to sign up volunteers as gunners. There was a shortage of gunners, as not many men wanted to take such a high-mortality job in what they called a flying coffin.

Years later, in his memoirs, Robert claimed that the bus assigned to his men was no more than a "portable cat house. I was put in charge of a bunch of swingers that put Hollywood's best to shame. When I arrived at each destination, there would be complaints from outraged mothers whose innocent daughters had been misused or had run away with sailors in official Navy vehi-

Robert Stack:
Drilling Paul

17

cles. My men also left a trail of demolished bars and unpaid bills."

Even through his tumultuous and later heart-breaking affair with Robert, Paul continued to write love letters to the girl back home. "He talked about this Janet all the time," Reiner said. "She must have been a regular Betty Grable. He tried to convince us how much he was in love with Janet, but his true love seemed to be Robert Stack. Those two male lookers could have had any girl within a radius of fifty miles, and they wanted each other."

Reiner later claimed that Robert had had a profound influence on the more innocent Paul. "After Stack dumped him, Paul went into a kind of lovesick mourning, although he tried to conceal it. He drank all the beer he could hold and adopted this devil-may-care attitude. 'We gotta live for today,' he told me, 'because tomorrow we die.'"

"Even though he talked about this Janet creature all the time, he became the wildest one of our bunch," Reiner said. "When we went carousing, drinking and chasing whores in clipjoints, the bitches flocked to Paul in droves because he was so good looking. He didn't' turn them down either. One whore told me she'd do Paul for free. Beneath it all, I suspected he was lonely, depressed, and a bit heartsick. He still wasn't sure who to be. One side of him seemed to want to go back to Ohio, marry Janet, have eight kids, and run the family business. But there was also a wild streak in him. One drunken night, Paul told me that Stack had promised to take him to Hollywood after the war was over and make a movie star out of him."

"I just might go to Hollywood on my own and become a movie star without his help," Paul told Reiner.

As far as it's known, this was Paul's first admission that he was even considering trying to become a movie star. Robert had been the first to plant that idea in his beautiful head. There would be many others who would also promote that dream.

***

After boot camp, Paul was assigned as an aviation radioman, third class, aboard torpedo planes, and flown to stations in the Pacific that included Guam, Saipan, and Hawaii.

In spite of studio publicists who, years later, tried to present Paul as a great naval hero along the lines of John F. Kennedy, he really wasn't. He saw no combat. His most dramatic moment during World War II involved a quirky coincidence which, if circumstances had been different, would probably have killed him. Paul's plane had been scheduled to join five other aircraft aboard an aircraft carrier somewhere in the Pacific Ocean. Unexpectedly, on the morning of the mission, the pilot in charge of Paul's squadron developed a severe ear infection, and the mission on which Paul was to have flown was aborted. A substitute plane was sent instead, and Paul, along with the rest of the crew, was grounded until their pilot recovered.

The substitute plane landed, mid-ocean, aboard the carrier, where it was positioned in "The Ready Room" for takeoff. Suddenly, roaring out of a dense cloud cover, came a Japanese *kamikazi* pilot, his plane loaded with explosives. He plummeted from the sky onto the deck of the aircraft carrier, careening into The Ready Room where the substitute plane exploded. Everyone aboard was killed.

Two hours later, Paul heard about the fatalities. He later recalled the experience to his family and friends, referring to it as "the most terrifying news I'd ever heard in my life. My heart is still beating today because of my pilot's earache. After I heard the news, I developed the shakes. I couldn't sleep that night. I lay in a pool of my own sweat. I was still shaking the next morning."

After that incident, Paul retreated into a womb, not having contact with any of his fellow sailors except when necessary. He recalled reading ten to fifteen books a week, from Willa Cather to Margaret Mitchell's *Gone With the Wind*. "I'd be better playing Ashley Wilkes than Rhett Butler," he once said. He still drank as much beer as he could get, and looked forward to shore leave in Honolulu when his ship would arrive, loaded down with horny sailors.

En route to Saipan, Paul received a "Dear John" letter from Janet. She told him that she was marrying the divorced father of three children who had a good business going in Cleveland.

"I will always love you, but you are far too unpredictable for me to consider as a marriage partner. It's more than the drinking. It's something else that bothers me. What drives you to drink so much in the first place? Please don't answer this letter.

Eternally,
Janet."

Feeling great remorse, Paul became moody. When his fellow sailors approached him, he snapped at them. He didn't like being rejected by anyone. He'd once told his mother, Theresa, "In my life, I'll be the one doing the rejecting. When it's time for me to move on in a relationship,

Hellcat in the Navy

19

I'll be the decider."

Janet's "Dear John" letter had made a mockery of that boast, and Paul felt defeated, wondering what was wrong with him. All of the homosexual sailors aboard his troopship hit on him, and when he landed in port, the available girls flocked to him, each making themselves available.

Noticing the sudden change in Paul's usually genial disposition, the handsome chaplain aboard Paul's troopship approached him one afternoon as he was reading Nietzsche. Throughout their time in the service together, the chaplain had always been excessively friendly with Paul, putting his arm around him on many occasions and offering to meet with him privately to discuss spiritual matters. Paul had never taken him up on those offers.

That afternoon, however, was different from the rest. Years later, Paul told his friend, the author Gore Vidal, that the chaplain came on strong to him, openly soliciting him for sex. "Now *that* really put me off," Paul told Vidal.

"Did that put you off Christianity or homosexuality?" Vidal asked.

"Neither," Paul said flippantly. "Nietzsche."

In years to come, Paul told a completely different version of the incident to his close friend, the gay actor Anthony Perkins. Paul said that he followed the chaplain to his cabin where he allowed him to perform an act of fellatio on him. "I was feeling completely rejected, and somehow the chaplain made me feel wanted, desirable. It was a harmless arrangement. The chaplain got his sexual thrill, which he'd wanted since he first laid eyes on me, and I got a relief from my tensions. No one was harmed."

Paul also confided to Anthony that he visited the chaplain's cabin frequently during their time in the service together. "It was a hell of a lot better than jerking off. He was crazy about me, and I got my jollies. And I knew that the moment I sailed into port, I'd be chasing girls again."

When Paul's troopship arrived in the port of Honolulu, he joined many of his sailor buddies and lined up to sample the girls at Pearl's Garden of Delights, just one of the many whorehouses that flourished here during World War II. Newsreel footage of that era showed sailors lined up around the block waiting for their chance with a prostitute.

The working girls in any house were limited, but the horny sailors numbered in the hundreds. To combat this problem, the madam of Pearl's bordello came up with a rather startling solution: Every sailor would be allowed only one minute on top of a woman.

The madam had hired a beautiful Hawaiian in a blond wig to stand at the door and be "the fluffer," long before that term came into vogue decades later. The fluffer masturbated the young men and got them close to an eruption before they were ushered into a cell to mount a prostitute. The sailors were processed as in a factory.

20

Paul allowed himself to be fluffed into readiness by the skilled masturbator before his turn inside the room where he faced a mulatto prostitute who was part black, part Hawaiian.

The fluffer's wrist never seemed to tire. In 1948, an underground mimeographed memoir circulated on the back streets of Honolulu. It sold for a dollar and was called "The Adventures of Fifi." In it, Fifi claimed, "I jerked off half the sailors in the Pacific fleet. I was so skilled at what I did that many of the sailors made dates with me. Even when some of them discovered that I was a beautiful young man in drag, pretty as any girl, they didn't kick me out of bed but enjoyed all the pleasures I could provide for them. I was very, very good at my work. In fact, I'm living today with one of the blond gods I was introduced to when I masturbated him. He's corn fed. From Kansas, and he loves me."

It is not known if Paul were one of those men who later dated the very talented "Mr. Fifi."

***

Discharged from the Navy in April of 1946, Paul returned to a post-war Ohio and enrolled on the GI bill in the all-male Kenyon College in the town of Gambier, a rural area some ninety miles southwest of Cleveland. For the moment at least, he had no intention of getting hooked up with another woman after his rejection by Janet in Athens.

After his return home, he found that nothing had changed very much in Shaker Heights. Arthur Senior still regarded his son as a lightweight, praising instead the achievements of his older son. He told his relative, Sarah Cohn, that "all Paul did for the war effort was lie in a bunk reading Tolstoy's *War and Peace*. He was no hero. America won the war without him."

His father ordered Paul to study economics in college so he'd be prepared to work in the family sporting goods business. He obeyed his father, but found his business studies boring. In spite of his weight of only 150 pounds, he dreamed of becoming an athlete. He did make the second-string football team, "but I was no Saturday's Hero," he later confessed.

At this point in his life, he was still turned off by women. "I got the clap from some whore

In Honolulu, a good-looking sailor boy meets "The Fluffer"

21

in Honolulu," he told his team members, who seemed to view this as a badge of honor, not a disgrace. It seemed to prove that Paul was a real man and at the age of twenty-one had had more experience than the late teens he hung out with.

Paul broke his "fast" from women when he agreed to go with five of his teammates for a night of skirt-chasing, hell-raising, and beer drinking at The Rusty Nail, a seedy beer joint in neighboring Mount Vernon, where Hank Williams—not Bing Crosby or Frank Sinatra—was king of the jukebox.

The club was patronized by the good ol' boys of Mount Vernon and a lot of horny young women whose husbands were away. "The suds flowed and the girls were the kind of whores who didn't charge," Paul later said.

What exactly happened that night remains cloudy. It seems that a young husband from Mount Vernon had come into the beer hall looking for his errant wife, finding her in the arms of the football captain from Kenyon. After a few blows were exchanged, a full-fledged fight erupted between the males of Mount Vernon and the "invading" college boys from Kenyon. In the melee, Paul was hit over the head with a beer bottle, but the blow did not knock him out and he kept on fighting.

When the police arrived, they found the club in shambles. Many of the patrons had fled, but Paul, lying unconscious in a corner, was discovered by a policeman. His forehead was bleeding, but he was not seriously injured, although hopelessly drunk. One of his teammates had been slashed across his shoulder blade with a knife and had to be rushed to the hospital.

In the Mount Vernon Police station, Paul was locked up in a cell with four of his other teammates. He remembered waking up the next morning "with a volcanic headache lying in a pool of my own vomit, slime green in color, or so I was told. I don't see green."

Arthur Senior read about his son's exploits on the front page of *The Cleveland Plain Dealer*. Two students were expelled from Kenyon, the other four, including Paul, placed on suspension. As a final blow, he was kicked off the football team.

Even though Theresa told her husband that "boys will be boys," Arthur Senior went two months before speaking to his "bad boy" son. When Paul came home from college breaks, he was forced to eat alone in the kitchen and not at the family table.

Back at college, Paul resumed his heavy beer drinking, seemingly forgetting about his time in jail. His classmates predicted he'd graduate from Kenyon "Magnum Cum Lager."

To redeem himself in his father's eyes, and to show what a keen sense of business he had, Paul opened a laundry off campus. He'd saved up a few hundred dollars and could afford the rent. It was the first laundry in the area ever run by a student.

He came up with a scheme to lure students away from the competing laundries nearby. Two kegs of beer were on tap at all times. Paul offered the brew free to his classmates. Even though he pulled in sixty dollars a week from this enterprise, he grew bored with "being the Chinaman of Kenyon." He sold his new business to two of his classmates for six-hundred dollars.

The two young men who took over were not successful, even though they continued to offer the kegs of beer. One afternoon one of the college men, who'd arrived with a bag of smelly underwear, had too much of the brew. He wandered onto the nearby square and tried to masturbate a tied-up horse.

The animal bolted, but the student hung on to the horse's penis. A policeman not only reclaimed his horse but tossed the student in jail, charging him with bestiality. The beer kegs were hauled away, and the laundry shut down.

***

Years later, Paul's drama professor, James Michael, recalled, "I had trouble not casting him as the lead in every play we put on. He had such stage presence." Nine plays followed, ranging from the riotous *Charley's Aunt* to the more classic *The Taming of the Shrew*.

Paul didn't agree with his professor's assessment of his acting talent. "I just learned my lines by rote and spoke them in a monotone. I didn't really react to my fellow cast members. I could have phoned in my performance. I didn't know a horse's piss about acting until I joined the Actors Studio in the summer of 1952."

Years later, Paul told another actor, Karl Malden, "from the very beginning, acting scared the shit out of me. It's like going on stage, pulling down your pants and flopping your dick at the audience so they can appraise its size. I felt vulnerable and I still do every time I face a camera or a live audience."

"Magnum Cum Lager"

When Professor Michael returned from a field trip to Broadway, along with eight senior drama majors, he raved to Paul about the quality of post-war theater in America, singling out one performance in particular, that of

Kenyon College

Marlon Brando in *A Streetcar Named Desire*.

"He will change acting for all time. Brando is a genius. If you want to be an actor, you've got to go and study his performance, his technique. It is nothing sort of sensational. He dominates the stage even when he is standing silently by and Jessica Tandy is going into her Tennessee Williams theatrics."

With money from the sale of his laundry, Paul made a solo journey by train to New York "all by my lonesome," he'd later recall. His parents objected, but in a show of independence, he made the trip East without their permission.

With the six hundred dollars stuffed into his pants, Paul arrived at Grand Central Station. Armed with a street map, he walked to the YMCA to save the taxi fare. He wanted to spend his money only on theater tickets, planning to survive on hot dogs until he returned to Shaker Heights.

Ever since December 3, 1947, when the curtain rose at the Ethel Barrymore Theater on *A Streetcar Named Desire*, Marlon Brando had been the sensation of Broadway. The play was sold out when Paul tried to buy a ticket, but standing room was available.

"From the moment Brando walked on that stage," Paul later confided to Geraldine Page at the Actors Studio, "I was mesmerized." In a sweaty, tight-fitting red T-shirt, and even tighter jeans, Brando was like an animal in heat. Some of the women in the audience swooned.

"He was raw meat up there on that stage," Paul told Geraldine. "Vulgar, a pig really, but what a pig. He was violent, crude, and I was completely hooked. As for myself, I realized that I'd merely been standing on the stage, delivering lines. I'd put no emotion in them. I'd never inhabited a character like Brando did. I mean he dug under his skin like a parasite sucking for blood. Brando inhabited the soul of Stanley Kowalski. He was not play-acting. He was real. All the acting I'd seen up to then had been phony shit."

A bit shy, Paul summoned his courage to go backstage and congratulate Brando. About a hundred other people, mostly women, had the same idea. The stage manager controlled the crowd.

Months later at the Actors Studio, Shelley Winters told Paul that she'd been dating Brando at the time until she found out that he was simultaneously seducing some of the biggest names in Hollywood. Many of these fabled stars, including Joan Crawford, had gone backstage ostensibly because they were intrigued at the prospect of playing Blanche DuBois in the play's much-anticipated film version. "Even a broken-down old whore like Crawford knew she'd be wrong cast as Tennessee's delicate moth," Shelley said. "Crawford came backstage for one reason, and one reason only. She wanted Brando to fuck her."

After seeing Brando's performance, Paul decided he didn't want to waste his money going to any other Broadway plays, not even *All My Sons*, by Arthur Miller, which had also been recommended to him by his college professor. He planned to spend every evening of those remaining in New York attending performances of *Streetcar,* watching Brando.

"There was so much to see and study in his performance," Paul later told Geraldine. "You couldn't take it all in with just one viewing. Brando was a hard book to read, one with many pages, each turn of the page more enigmatic than what you'd read on the previous page. But I was determined to figure him out."

Buying better seats, Paul showed up for each of his remaining nights in New York. On the second and third nights, he continued to go backstage but was turned away by the stage manager, although he noticed that some young pretty women were allowed access to Brando's dressing room.

After watching yet another of Brando's mesmerizing performances, Paul came up with an idea. He'd read in a magazine that Brando rode his motorcycle through the streets of New York after every performance. Paul figured the motorcycle had to be parked in the alleyway outside the theater.

He left the theater through the main entrance and walked around to the alleyway. Indeed, there was a motorcycle parked there, bright, shiny, and locked for safekeeping. He must have waited for an hour until the crowd backstage had departed. Finally, the theater's back door opened, and he heard Brando's recognizable voice. "Good night, Charlie. Keep those pussies coming, and nothing ugly, okay?"

Alone in the alleyway with Brando, Paul confronted the actor. What happened next depends on the veracity of Carlo Fiore, Brando's longtime companion. The dialogue reported by Fiore was allegedly said by Brando.

Apparently, Paul knew instinctively that if he rushed Brando for an autograph, he'd be brushed aside. He'd worked all night on his opening line to attract Brando's attention. "Mr. Brando, you're the greatest thing since God granted men the right to come."

At first Brando looked startled before bursting into laughter. "You're okay, kid," he said. "What a beauty! You're almost as good looking as I am."

"You're not just good looking,

Marlon Brando
An object of desire

you've got sex appeal," Paul is reported to have said. "I'm an actor too, but I don't know how to project sex appeal."

"You've got to act from your crotch," Brando said.

"I wish you'd teach me how to do that," Paul said.

Brando walked over to his motorcycle and unlocked it. He turned to Paul again. "First, you've got to have lowdown, rotten sex. I mean the type of sex that would make a hardened old whore puke. That kind of sex. Now get your fucking cute little ass over here and plop it down on my cycle. I'm going to take you on a tour of the midnight sights of Manhattan."

Paul apparently was afraid, but joined Marlon on his bike for a ride through the canyons of New York.

Fiore later claimed that Brando boasted that "I fucked the kid in all known positions. He even inspired me to some new positions. The kid resembles me. He looks a bit like I used to look, but I'm different now. I know this is the strangest thing to say. It was as if I was fucking my younger self, even though I'm only about a year older than the guy. Of course, by the time he got on that train for Cleveland, he'd fallen madly in love with me."

"That kid has something I can't put my finger on, but it's there," Brando told Fiore. "I think when all the semen from my noble tool permeates his blood stream, it'll be the beginning of his liberation. Mark my words. He's got something. There's a star quality lurking deep within his bowels."

"Do you think you'll ever see him again?" Fiore asked. "Invite him to New York. You're planning to go to Paris after your contract is up. Maybe take him to Paris. He is one cute guy. And those blue eyes. I could go for him myself and I'm completely straight."

"Yeah, right," Brando said sarcastically. "No, what do you take me for? A lovesick puppy. You should know better. No pretty boy or beautiful woman can get enough of my horny tool. I like to walk out just when they're begging for more."

Back at school, Paul wrote Brando a fan letter every week. None was answered. When Brando's contract with *Streetcar* was up, and he bowed out of the play, Paul's letters to Brando were returned, not forwarded.

He fully expected never to encounter Brando again, but he planned to watch all his hero's future movies, studying his every nuance. "If I ever become a movie star," he told his mother, Theresa, "I want to be known as the second Marlon Brando."

Paul would live to regret uttering those words.

***

Back at school, Paul switched his major from economics to English and speech. "That didn't last long," he said. "I grew bored with Keats, Shelley, and especially Lord Byron." Using Brando as his role model, he changed his curriculum to drama.

It was a long jump, but acting soon replaced football playing as a fixation in his life. "I went from being the worst football player on the team to becoming the worst actor in the history of American colleges," he later recalled.

"I tried to be Brando, but couldn't get there," he said. "In trying to imitate Brando I came off as a big ham. I even took to muttering. It wasn't until I joined the Actors Studio in New York in the months ahead, that I truly learned what Brando was all about."

That was Paul's own negative self-assessment. His early audiences back in the Middle West saw great talent in the aspirant actor, enough so that he was cast in the lead role of ace reporter Hildy Johnson, a part played on the screen by Pat O'Brien in the 1931 film adaptation of *The Front Page*.

The play by Ben Hecht and Charles MacArthur had been a hit on Broadway in the 1920s. "Even if Paul couldn't act all that great by then, he could still mesmerize an audience by his sheer male beauty," said cast member Stella Broggan, who had to drop out of rehearsals when she learned about her unexpected pregnancy. "No, Paul wasn't the daddy. How I wished he was."

Paul later called *The Front Page* "a corker of a play that had a lot of mileage still left in it. On opening night I took five separate curtain calls. The wild applause went to my head. It was my first real taste of adulation."

In spite of his self-assessment as an actor, in 1948 he was offered a job in summer stock at the Priscilla Beach Theater in Plymouth, Massachusetts. Almost nothing has ever been written about the summer of his junior year, and years later, Paul himself refused to talk about it.

Since its establishment in 1937, the oldest barn theater in America had become one of the country's best known venues for the training of young actors. Not just Paul, but many future stars got their start here, including Bob Reiner, Sandy Dennis, Pat Carroll, even Monte Hall.

Paul drew a salary of eighteen dollars a week. To make ends meet, his mother, Theresa, enclosed a twenty dollar bill in many of her letters.

Terry Lewis, a young actress in the company, recalled that Paul felt embarrassed whenever he was complimented on his good looks, especially those baby blues. He told her he wanted to be cast in character parts, not as a handsome matinee idol.

"I don't want to be known as a pretty boy with all the implications that label carries," Paul said. "I'd even be willing to disguise myself with makeup and appear as a hunchback, or at least hide my face behind a long beard.

27

Instead, I look like Goldilocks."

"When I wasn't chasing after him," said actor Barry Ritter, "I felt sympathy for him. Here was this incredibly beautiful boy from the Middle West suddenly thrown into a viper's nest of homosexuals. I think he got propositioned by every guy in the cast. Well, almost. Girls found him a hottie and were after him too. For the first time in his life, Paul Newman learned what it was like being a sex symbol. From what I've heard, that summer was just the beginning of what would go on for the rest of his life. From the New York islands to the California coast, Paul Newman would be pursued. He couldn't even go to the bathroom without being followed by guys."

Ritter revealed that Paul claimed he had sex with two or three young women in the cast, but he didn't follow up on a subsequent date with any of them. He didn't seem to want to get involved. "I plotted to seduce him to no avail," Ritter said. "He took great care not to get undressed in front of me. He shared the upper bunk, and sometimes I could hear him jerking off at night. Finally, one night he gave in to me. We'd been drinking heavily. Lots and lots of suds. When we got back to our room, I made my moves on him. I started giving him a blow-job. At first he resisted but then he gave in to me. Although I brought him to a climax, he was as responsive as a dead fish. He just lay there and endured it. It wasn't that great for me, and I didn't come on to him after that. But in the gay bars of my future, I always bragged about sucking off Paul Newman. Since my acting career didn't pan out—I went into the insurance business—giving Paul Newman that blow-job became my claim to fame."

***

At two o'clock on the afternoon on June 13, 1949, Paul was graduated from Kenyon College with a Bachelor of Science degree. With a contract in his pocket, and accompanied by his father, he waited for two hours at the local train station as his father urged him to abandon his summer plans and work instead in the family business. Paul adamantly refused, waving goodbye as the train headed for Williams Bay, Wisconsin. There, he had a "room-and-board" deal for a

Paul as ace reporter in *The Front Page*

28

season of summer stock at the Brecksville Little Theatre.

Paul made his stage debut in Williams Bay in a play called *John Loves Mary*, playing the role of a soldier named John. The film version of the play, starring Ronald Reagan in the same role, was being shown at the same time on movie screens across the country. "I was far better than Reagan," Paul later claimed. He was beginning to have a higher opinion of himself as an actor, although he admitted, "I was miles from being in Brando's league."

Cast as Mary, the role played on screen by Patricia Neal, Jackie Witte was a Wisconsin native. She was an attractive, brown-eyed blonde with charm, personality, and as much wit as her last name implied. Soon, Paul was smitten with her and began to date her, becoming more and more involved as the summer deepened. He hadn't been seriously involved with a woman since Janet Holsum had dumped him. At first their dating was casual, and Paul continued to have sporadic and brief sexual encounters with both men and other women.

When Jackie and Paul co-starred together in *Dark of the Moon*, they spent more time kissing behind the curtains than in front of them.

Jackie and Paul met at a time when young girls across America were dreaming of romantic love, the theme of which blared constantly over jukeboxes playing the hits of, among others, Pat Boone. In addition to their role as generators of romance, these women expected their future husbands to be good providers.

Jackie was different. She urged Paul to pursue a highly unreliable career in the theater and "to take chances. Life's an adventure and has got to be lived to the fullest. You're an artist, not some dull businessman working in a Cleveland suburb."

No woman had ever talked to him like that before. "Jackie urged me to pursue my dream, even though I wasn't sure I knew what that dream was at the time," Paul said. "I still had hopes of returning to Kenyon and becoming a drama professor. But Jackie convinced me I was more than that. I later gave credit both to Marlon Brando and to Jackie for turning my head around and getting me to pursue a career as an actor, although I fully expected at the time that I'd starve to death."

Paul's role as a soldier was followed by his portrayal of The Gentleman Caller in Tennessee Williams' *The Glass Menagerie*, which had been a huge hit on Broadway. Having seen Tennessee's other play, *A Streetcar Named Desire*, on Broadway with Brando, this was Paul's second and more intimate introduction to the work of a playwright who would loom large in his future.

At the time it would have been inconceivable that Paul would star on the screen in two of the playwright's most famous plays, *Cat on a Hot Tin Roof* and *Sweet Bird of Youth*. It was perhaps even more inconceivable as well that one day he'd direct his future wife in *The Glass Menagerie*.

Just as his relationship with Jackie was heating up, along came Richard Casey, an extraordinarily handsome young actor who bore a striking resemblance to Robert Wagner as he appeared in the 1956 film, *A Kiss Before Dying*. Ironically that film co-starred Joanne Woodward, Paul's second wife to be.

Paul, at least according to Richard, was torn between Jackie and him. "I was just as good looking as he was, and I knew from the first day we met that he was attracted to me. When we got together, it was like plugging something into an electric socket. I went after him big-time, and I don't know if Jackie was even aware of it. It seems she had stars in her eyes and couldn't see straight. I think she fell in love with Paul long before he fell in love with her. I was determined to have him, and it didn't take long for me to win the prize. I was a prize myself. One prize meeting another prize. The results were explosive."

Richard later claimed that one or two guys in the cast had already "had" Paul and had found him unresponsive. "I kindled his fire. We had sex in every position, and he came on strong to me, wanting to try everything he'd done in the sack with Brando. He told me all about that. It's a wonder we had enough energy left after a night together to appear on stage. I don't know if he was also making it with Jackie, because when Paul left my bed I didn't think there was much left for her."

Uncertain of where to go in his future, Richard mapped out the road for both of them. They'd both work in stock as actors until they got their big break on Broadway. "I told him my name would be up on the marquee starring in a hit play on Broadway. At the same time I promised him he'd also have his name up in lights at the theater across the street, appearing in another hit play. For a time, we believed this fantasy. Actually, it was only half a fantasy. For him, the dream came true. For me, it didn't."

The big break came for Richard when he was spotted by a theatrical agent

Summer love: Meeting actress **Jackie Witte**

showcasing summer stock productions, looking for the male stars of tomorrow, many of whom he'd sample on the casting couch before agreeing to find jobs for them. He saw Richard's performance and went backstage to introduce himself. He was immediately mesmerized by Richard's sex appeal and good looks, completely ignoring Paul.

The agent promised he'd get Richard work on Broadway if he'd come to New York. Foolishly believing the agent, Richard agreed to follow him. He urged Paul to go to New York with him. That is when Paul experienced what one of his biographers, Lawrence J. Quirk, called "homosexual panic."

It was a turning point in Paul's life. He decided he didn't want to pursue life as a homosexual. Richard remembered Paul sobbing when he had to tell him goodbye at the train station. "I knew he wasn't just telling me goodbye, but saying goodbye to a whole way of life. He was a very macho guy and just didn't want to be known as a pretty boy queer. He told me he didn't want to end up like another Farley Granger."

Both actors had gone to see pretty boy Granger in Alfred Hitchcock's experimental *Rope*, in which he played John Dall's fellow killer and nervous lover. "I watched Paul fade in the distance at the train station," Richard claimed. "Our paths never crossed again. I saw all of his movies and wondered what might have been."

***

Eventually, Jackie and Paul opted to leave the Brecksville Little Theater in Williams Bay, Wisconsin, in favor of an autumn season with the Woodstock Players in Woodstock, Illinois. They were intrigued by the idea of appearing jointly in plays together while living the domestic life of a married couple even though they were unmarried.

As the autumn leaves began to fall, Paul found himself also falling, this time in love and for the first time. Never before had any relationship in his life, male or female, been called love, infatuation perhaps.

At least for a short time in his life, he gave up all other relationships and devoted himself to Jackie. Their love had become sexual, and he felt fulfilled with another person. He may still have harbored other desires—and no doubt he did—but like many men of his time he tried to suppress them.

Their talk was of marriage. On his forty-five dollar a week salary, he bought a used 1937 Packard. He managed to keep up payments on it, because their modest little apartment cost only ten dollars a month in rent.

Apparently, Paul never confided to any friends or associates at the time his exact feelings about his upcoming marriage. There must have been a part of him that wanted to flee to New York, hook up with Marlon Brando, and become a glamorous actor on the Broadway stage. But he held back.

Jackie may have sensed the inner turmoil raging within him. Unexpectedly, he's sometimes become irritable and hostile among people who wished him well. "I could tell that Paul was unhappy," said John Bremmer, who worked at the theater. "But when he was with Jackie, he seemed happy and very much in love. Even so, I sensed she was not enough for him. He wanted more. Without knowing it, and like most of the other young men of his age in the Middle West at the time, he was slowly drifting into something he didn't really want—marriage and fatherhood. His father constantly wrote him to come home and join the family business, something Paul vowed he'd never do."

"I didn't know Jackie very well, but I observed her from a distance," Bremmer said. "I could understand why Paul went for her. She was no prom queen or empty-headed bottle blonde. She seemed to have opinions about everything, and they made sense. She was very sensitive to other people, and the cast liked her. She was a very talented actress and probably would have gone far in the theater if Paul hadn't turned her into a housewife. She was not only smart, but very well spoken, very articulate. She seemed to meet Paul passion for passion. I once spotted the two of them during a break in rehearsals, and they seemed to have their tongues down each other's throats."

By December of 1949, Jackie had convinced Paul to marry her. "It wasn't much of a honeymoon," he later recalled. "Like I had the money to fly her to Bermuda." In fact as the marriage progressed, he found money so tight he took a temporary job as a worker on a nearby farm.

Jackie wanted to have a child with Paul, although he warned that their life was too unsettled, their future uncertain. Nonetheless they began to have unprotected sex. By the spring of 1950, she was pregnant.

Their lives changed in significant ways. An urgent letter arrived from Theresa, urging Paul to return to Shaker Heights. At the age of fifty-seven, his

Jackie Witte onstage:
The career she abandoned for Paul

McHENRY COUNTY THEATRE GUILD
presenting
THE WOODSTOCK PLAYERS

chronically ill father had taken a sudden turn for the worse. His mother admitted to him her greatest fear. "The doctor privately told me Arthur has only weeks to live."

Closing down their operations in Woodstock, Paul and Jackie, with their possessions stored either inside their dilapidated Packard or roped down on top of its roof, drove to Shaker Heights.

Knowing the clock was ticking, Paul went in for a reunion with his father. Even though Arthur Senior was in a weakened condition, Paul talked to the dying man for more than an hour. Later he told Theresa and Jackie, "Dad was always disappointed in me, and I know that. But I promised him that I'm gonna make something of my rotten life. I begged him to hold onto life. I told him I wanted him to live so he could be proud of his son one day."

Five days later, a doctor summoned to the Newman household came out of the bedroom. He told the family, "He's gone. I couldn't save him."

In frustration, Paul pounded the wall. "I never got a chance to show him." Jackie and Theresa looked on in astonishment. Paul's brother, Arthur Junior, said what might have been on everybody's mind. "That's a pretty selfish way to look at Dad's death."

Despondent over his father's untimely death, Paul buckled under, giving in to Theresa's demands to fulfill his father's last wish. Paul agreed to help run the family's sporting goods business. He spent long hours at the store, sometimes working two or three hours after its 5pm closing. He wanted to be a success.

Jackie waited impatiently for him at the Newman household. A son was born on September 23. Paul named him Alan Scott Newman.

Since they couldn't afford to buy a home in Shaker Heights, Paul and Jackie purchased a modest home in neighboring Bedford. "My life in the suburbs has begun," he lamented to Arthur. "Just like thousands of other young men who returned from the battlefields. A wife, a family, a kid, a house with a mortgage, a lawn to mow, maybe more kids in the future. The prospect of getting old and never having made something big out of my life."

He grew increasingly alienated and bitter and started taking those day-long walks whose patterns he'd established when he was much younger. Sometimes he'd disappear for long stretches at a time, not telling Jackie or his family where he went. On some of those excursions, he'd drive into Cleveland, where he'd absent himself for an entire weekend.

No one knows exactly what he did during those periods away from home, or who he saw. In almost every case, he chose not to talk about them after his return to Bedford.

For eighteen months, he'd been a dutiful son, competently running the sporting goods store, succeeding at it, and generating a quite good profit at the end of every month.

But one Sunday, he excused himself for an early morning drive to a nearby lake. He didn't return home until late that evening. He claimed he'd gone fishing, although he hadn't taken his equipment with him. Apparently, he spent the day staring into the lake.

That evening, back home after his day at the lake, he called his brother, at first neglecting to tell Jackie what he planned to do.

Friday, May 19, 1950

OBITUARY

ARTHUR S. NEWMAN

Arthur S. Newman, who was secretary-treasurer of the Newman-Stern Co. here for 35 years, passed away on Thursday, May 11 at the age of 56.

A native Clevelander, Mr. Newman entered the newspaper business shortly after his graduation from Central High School, serving as advertising solicitor and later as reporter for the Press.

Speaking to Arthur in a very determined voice, he said, "I've had it! I will not relive my father's life. You've got to run the store yourself. Sell those baseball bats. As soon as I sell the house, I'm heading east to pursue a dream."

"Are you taking Jackie and Scott?" Arthur asked.

"Sure, why not?" he asked. "They can come along if they don't mind living through some hard times."

Arthur decided that without Paul he didn't want to operate the family business either. The brothers put it up for sale. In the meantime, to earn money with his extra two mouths to feed, Paul took a temporary job on a golf course range. He searched for lost balls, digging them out of the mud and washing them in cold water for later re-use. His hands remained constantly chapped.

He also broadcast radio commercials as a spokesman for the Ohio Bell Telephone Company, and he was hired by the McCann-Erickson Advertising agency for voice-overs because of his theatrically trained baritone voice.

When the sports goods store sold three months later, Paul had his nest egg to head East with Jackie and Scott. His day of flirting with other occupations was over. He was going to live in New Haven and work for a master's degree in drama at Yale University. Even more important, he'd pursue a career as an working actor in the theater.

From behind the wheel of his Packard, with his wife in the front seat and baby Scott in the back, he drove in the direction of New York City. Four thousand dollars in cash were concealed in a black leather pouch in the glove compartment.

At one point during the trip, he lowered the window and yelled out at a passing car, "Broadway, here I come!"

Chapter Two
Crotch Acting

Enrolling in the Yale School of Drama, Paul moved his family into a cramped top floor apartment in New Haven in the autumn of 1951. He knew that even if he failed as an actor on Broadway, he might still qualify to teach speech and drama one day at a college like Kenyon, his alma mater.

As his savings were meager, he supplemented his income by selling Colliers Encyclopedias in New Haven, finding many bored housewives willing to purchase a set from such a handsome huckster.

His first role at Yale was in a production of *Saint Joan* by George Bernard Shaw. The part called for him to cry. "I tried and tried but my eyes were dry," Paul said. "When my fellow cast members started making fun of me, I began to sob. I was filled with frustration. When the waterworks came, I couldn't turn them off. Somehow I got through opening night. After that, I concentrated more on studying to become a director, thinking that might be my true calling."

Jerry Morgan worked for a modeling agency in Manhattan. Every season he arrived on the Yale campus to photograph young men who wanted to earn extra money modeling, usually as a clothes mannequin. Among his recruits that sunny afternoon was Paul, who agreed to pose for him, as Jerry had assured him it was a quick and easy money. At one point, Jerry asked Paul to remove his shirt. So far as it is known, this was the first professional photo ever taken of Paul without his shirt. There would be many more such pictures in his future.

The photo shoot ended in disappointment for Paul when Jerry asked him

Straight Arrow

35

to return with him to his motel. Paul refused, thinking he'd never see Jerry again. He suspected the photographer didn't even work for a modeling agency.

Two weeks later Paul got a call from Jerry, who told him he'd landed him his first gig, modeling white shirts for a Macy's photo layout. The pay was one hundred dollars for an afternoon. Putting on his one and only suit, a gray-and-white seersucker, Paul rode the train into Manhattan.

Two women in the modeling agency seemed impressed with Paul's good looks and flirted with him when he was signing a contract. That same afternoon, Jerry took the photos, and Paul had to change into five different shirts in front of Jerry's devouring eyes.

At the end of the day's work, Paul accepted Jerry's invitation for a drink at the bar of the New Yorker Hotel. When Jerry tantalizingly held back the check that had already been made out to Paul, Paul eventually submitted to Jerry's request for a blow-job. The act of fellatio was committed later in Jerry's apartment two blocks away.

"He didn't even take his pants off," Jerry later told his gay colleagues, "but I enjoyed him. I got three other jobs for him in the next three months, and passed him around to other photographers. That Newman kid got quite a lot of blow-jobs, but male models in those days were used to that, viewing it as part of the job."

Out of sheer boredom, Paul joined the local campaign headquarters to elect Adlai E. Stevenson, who was running on the Democratic ticket for president of the United States. He was up against the popular general, Dwight David Eisenhower, running on the Republican ticket. Although Paul realized that Ike had been a brilliant commander during World War II, he did not want a military man in the White House.

Paul's involvement in the campaign had begun casually, his duties consisting mainly of stuffing envelopes, but the Stevenson campaign marked the beginning of Paul's lifelong commitment to politics.

Paul's New Haven apartment, which rented for sixty dollars a month, was in a decaying clapboard-sided structure that was rotten in places. The floors sagged, and two families lived downstairs. "Their babies screamed at night," Paul recalled. "Scott screamed all day. The place drove me crazy. I hated to come home to face all those hollering children, even one of my own."

At night he preferred to walk the streets of New Haven, still a relatively small town back then. He'd stop into a tavern or two, having a few beers before bracing himself to return home to Jackie and Scott.

As he neared his twenty-seventh birthday, he told Jackie, "Even if a director casts me in something, I'll be too old for the part."

Frank McMullan, a professor teaching Paul how to be a director, prided himself on spotting stars of tomorrow. Paul had a charismatic aura about him and his looks on stage were dazzling. He told Paul, "You don't belong on the stage but in movies, where the camera can zero in on those blue eyes of yours." Paul thought he was coming on to him.

In the spring of 1952, McMullan cast Paul in the role of Karl in an original play, written by a student at Yale, about Beethoven. Paul felt uncomfortable in the role of Beethoven's nephew, complaining, "I should be cast in modern pieces, not period dramas."

On *Beethoven's* opening night, word reached the student actors backstage that Audrey Wood and William Liebling were in the audience. She was the literary agent for both Tennessee Williams, the hottest playwright on Broadway, and William Inge, the Kansas-born dramatist. During the 1950 season, his play, *Come Back, Little Sheba* had earned him a reputation as the most promising playwright on Broadway. Audrey's husband, Liebling, was one of the most successful theatrical agents in America, having represented at various times both Marlon Brando and Montgomery Clift.

Both agents were always on the lookout for new talent, and New Haven was a place where, in the past, they had often found it. Backstage, Audrey encountered the hopeful student playwright. Although on some previous occasions she'd been gentle and indulgent with emerging talent, she was curt with the student. "Not even a rewrite can save this play."

Audrey and her husband had headed backstage to introduce themselves to Paul Newman. Facing hostile stares from the other jealous student actors, Paul greeted the agents. "Liebling appraised me like I was a piece of meat," Paul recalled. "Even though with wife in tow, I took him for another casting couch agent. I thought he wanted to get into my pants more than he wanted to get me a part on Broadway. I was wrong, as I later learned."

Liebling gave Paul his card and asked him to call him after he'd finished his studies at Yale, but only if he decided to move to New York. "Thinking it was a come-on, I almost threw away his card that night," Paul told Professor McMullan. "But for some reason I held onto it. I carried it around in my wallet but months would go by before I was desperate enough to call on this short, ugly—yes, repulsive—little guy with the beady eyes. He'd practically salivated over me that night at Yale, and I was sure he couldn't wait to get my cock in his mouth."

In the weeks ahead, Paul admitted that he "walked up and down every street in New Haven, trying to figure out what to do." Stopping at a tavern, he ordered beers until he ran out of money. Staggering back to his family's apartment, he decided to drop out of Yale and check into an uncertain future in New York.

As he climbed the steps to his studio, he heard the screams of his two-year-old son. Inside, he learned from Jackie that Scott had been crying all day.

"Nothing will pacify him," Jackie told Paul.

"A change of scenery will do the brat good," he told her. "We're moving to New York. I've decided to shit or get off the pot. I'm going to become a full-time actor."

***

In a rented truck and en route to Manhattan, Jackie delivered a stunning piece of news. She was pregnant with their second child. "That hit me like a ton of bricks," Paul recalled. "Here I was with little money, a wife, and a growing family, and I was heading for New York with no prospects, only a dream. I felt trapped. I should be a bachelor arriving in the city, not a family man nearing the ripe old age of thirty. As I approached the city, I felt as if a hunk of lead as big as a baseball had settled permanently in my stomach."

Jackie's aunt lived on Staten Island, and she'd secured an apartment for them near Curtis High School on the island's North Shore.

Although the rent, sixty dollars a month, was the same as in New Haven, the Ambassador Apartments at 30 Daniel Low Terrace were a vast improvement. These six stories of cream-colored brickwork with black accents represented Art Deco at its best. Paul felt he'd come up in the world and always admired the metalwork on the entrance doors, done in a peacock pattern, before he entered the building.

"We were still poor as church mice," Paul recalled, "but we had a touch of class after moving from that baby factory ghetto in New Haven."

"The summer we moved to Staten Island was the hottest on record," Paul claimed. "The apartment was a cauldron. I stripped off my clothes the moment I entered. On some days, Scott screamed so loud the neighbors complained."

From Monday to Friday, Paul put on that seersucker suit and, in the stifling heat, walked the 12-minute downhill slope to the Staten Island Ferry and boarded it, heading across the murky waters of New York Harbor to the canyons of New York. He carried with him a baloney sandwich for his lunch.

Once in Manhattan, he made the rounds, one casting agent after another. The results were always the same. No jobs available. Back on Staten Island at three o'clock, he went door to door, selling encyclopedias. One week he got lucky and made five hundred dollars. But there were lean times too.

Although some casting agents had complimented Paul on his "striking male beauty," his first role was that of an extra, playing an old man applauding the inauguration of President William McKinley. The play was called *The March of Time*.

Paul's stunning looks were disguised by a makeup artist. For three hours of work, he was rewarded with a seventy-five dollar paycheck, enough to pay the rent and electric bill for the month. When no other jobs came in, Paul summoned his courage and reached for that business card that he'd been carrying around in his wallet. Without an appointment, he arrived at the cluttered offices shared by Audrey Wood and William Liebling. He figured if Liebling could get him a job on Broadway, he could always shut his eyes and imagine it was the beautiful young actress, Marilyn Monroe, giving him a blow-job.

Liebling not only remembered Paul from Yale, but agreed to see him. First, Paul had to spend more than an hour sitting on a bench without a cushion in the agent's outer office. In times past, or in the future, many future stars would get their start by warming this same bench, including Cloris Leachman, Eli Wallach, Julie Harris, Cliff Robertson, and even the great Montgomery Clift, who'd gone on to stardom in Hollywood.

Fifteen minutes into the interview with Liebling, Paul realized the agent didn't have seduction on the brain but was serious about finding work for him. "I deal only in star parts," Liebling told Paul. "I don't book walk-ons for actors. There's nothing that I know of for you right now. But William Inge has written what I think will be the hit of the coming season. A play called *Picnic*. I think I can get you something juicy in it. Let's stay in touch."

"In the meantime, I've got mouths to feed, including my own and one on the way," Paul said.

"I suggest television," Liebling said. "It's booming. There are tons of jobs for handsome actors. I'll get you an appointment with my friend, Maynard Morris. He discovered Gregory Peck and Barbara Bel Geddes. Maynard gets work for actors in television. I'm a stage agent."

With a warm handshake, Liebling wished Paul well, and said he'd call him when he set up the appointment. "Who knows? You may become a big-time TV star before that Broadway role comes through. I'm no bullshitter. I'm going to pull something out of the hat for you and it's going to be on Broadway."

***

True to his word, Liebling arranged an appointment for Paul with Maynard Morris of MCA, Inc. The interview was successful, and Paul signed with the agency. He was turned over to John Foreman, who would eventually become Paul's business partner. Going to work at once, Foreman found work almost immediately for his new client, whom he described to casting directors, especially the gay ones, as a "Greek god."

Paul was cast in a live broadcast, *Tales of Tomorrow*, playing an army sergeant. He was given about two dozen lines to speak. "I survived shaking like a leaf in the wind," he later recalled. Offstage the sound of menacing ice creaking and crackling could be heard. "It was supposed to be scary," Paul said, "but it really wasn't."

This was one of television's first attempts at science fiction. At that time in media history, the movies handled the genre much better.

Paul's debut into live television came during that medium's launch of its golden era, when writers who included Paddy Chayefsky and Rod Serling were churning out first-rate dramas. Paul followed his venture into science fiction with appearances in teleplays called *The Mask*, *You Are There*, *Danger*, and *The Web*, the costs of which were underwritten by such companies as Philco, US Steel, and Playhouse 90.

"I was an untuned piano being hauled out to play in various TV productions," Paul said.

The most visible of these was an ongoing role between 1952 and 1953 in a TV soap-opera series known as *The Aldrich Family*. Based on Clifford Goldsmith's play, *What a Life*, it originated as a popular radio series focusing on a teenager, Henry, a bumbling adolescent whose "Coming, Mother" catchphrase opened each episode. The radio series had been followed by eleven Henry Aldrich movies, each released by Paramount between 1939 and 1944, the first two featuring Jackie Cooper in the title role.

For his role in the TV version of this ongoing ode to Americana, Paul was paid $200 a month for a part which in his words, "sucked."

Paul would later tell Shelley Winters that, "I knew I was getting cast for my body and my looks, and not for any Marlon Brando acting technique. But it didn't matter so much. I was working, supporting my family, and learning more about acting every day. In my gut, though, I felt something big was about to break for me. For a while, at least, there was a temporary reprieve from those casting couch blow-jobs, but they resumed when I broke into the Broadway theater."

Sometimes, when he couldn't face the idea of another late-afternoon sales pitch for encyclopedias, Paul would avoid rushing downtown for the ferryboat back to Staten Island. Actor friends, at least those with jobs, were usually willing to buy the handsome hunk a drink in an Irish bar on Third Avenue or a cheap meal in the theater district along 44th Street. He may have shared more than food and drink with some of these actors. A few years later, when Paul became famous as a Hollywood star, many of these actors boasted of having had brief affairs with Paul, although these reports can't be verified.

Some nights Paul walked alone through the theater district, hoping and dreaming. "It was one of the greatest moments in the American theater," he later recalled. "Not just Tennessee Williams and Arthur Miller, but all sorts of emerging playwrights were turning out masterpieces. It was a dynamic time, and I wanted to be a part of it. I imagined it was like Elizabethan London at the time of Shakespeare. I knew if I could just hold out, my time would come."

In September Paul had a brief flirtation with a young actress, Sally Beckham, while his wife on Staten Island tended to Scott. Sally's good looks made up for her lack of talent on the stage. Her big hope rested on her auditioning for the Actors Studio. Three days before, the actor who was to appear with her came down with the flu.

In desperation, she asked Paul to play a scene with her from *Battle of Angels*, an early play by Tennessee Williams. He readily agreed, wanting to enter the august precincts of the school that virtually every actor on Broadway had praised. The Actors Studio had given the world Marlon Brando, who was still Paul's role model. Having received no responses from his letters to Marlon, Paul had stopped writing.

Watching Paul emote were other actors climbing the ladder to fame. They included Karl Malden, Rod Steiger, Eli Wallach, and Kim Stanley. Sitting by himself in the corner, and looking sullen, was a handsome, rather intense young actor, James Dean.

Although many of these actors had already gone through their initial training, they'd shown up that particular afternoon because Lee Strasberg had announced a party for them that evening at his home.

Paul thought he gave a dreadful performance, but, nevertheless, he was asked to join the Actors Studio. Heartbroken, Sally was rejected. She fled the premises, and Paul never saw her again.

He was introduced to burly Rod Steiger, who seethed with intensity both on and off the stage. He had already appeared on the screen in the 1951 film *Teresa*, in which he'd played John Ericson's therapist. "You've got something, kid," Steiger told Paul. "You just don't know how to express it yet."

Paul later told Geraldine Page, "If I had known all those more talented actors were sitting out there judging me, I would have passed out." Geraldine herself was on the dawn of one of her greatest successes. She was soon to win the role of the Southern spinster in Tennessee Williams's

"In Elizabethan London"

41

Summer and Smoke. At the time, Paul could not have imagined that one day he'd co-star with her in both the stage and later, in 1962, the movie version of another Tennessee Williams play, *Sweet Bird of Youth*.

Paul was awed to meet Karl Malden, who didn't need acting lessons but often dropped into the Actors Studio. He made no comment about Paul's acting, but accepted the young actor's congratulations on his performance, both on stage and on the screen, in *A Streetcar Named Desire*. "Perhaps we'll appear on the stage together one day," Malden told Paul, suggesting he might be a prophet. That play, *The Desperate Hours*, lay in both of their futures.

Eli Wallach seemed like an actor dedicated to his craft. "If you join up with us," he told Paul, "be prepared to take a lot of ribbing. You'll hear it all. 'Be like a snake! Don't bathe! Mumble your lines! Wear torn T-shirts.'" He walked into the afternoon, uttering the pained cry "Stella! Stella!"

Paul recognized the actress walking toward him as Kim Stanley. Instead of reaching out to shake his extended hand, she kissed him on both cheeks and congratulated him on his performance in *Battle of Angels*.

"She was one of the most intense women I'd ever met," he later told Marlon Brando. "There was a turbulence in her face, like a woman who'd known trouble all her life." All traces of her New Mexican accent had been lost when she first spoke to Paul.

He took in the beauty of this blonde, who was glamorous but not in the fake, campy way of Marilyn Monroe. Kim's beauty seemed to come from

At the Actors Studio:
"Keeping my mouth shut"

within. Weeks later, he'd tell Shelley Winters, "I think I fell in love with Kim the first day I met her. I know it sounds like I had a schoolboy crush, but she made me feel that I'd married the wrong woman. Kim seemed to be the gal I'd been waiting for all my life. In many ways, Kim—and to some extent Geraldine Page—was but a mere rehearsal for the real girl of my dreams, Joanne Woodward."

Impulsively, Paul asked her to "go have a Coke with me." She laughed. "No boy's asked me out for a Coke since I took the bus from Tularosa with twenty-one dollars stuffed in my bra." She kissed him again on the cheek. "Can't make it today. Got another date. What about meeting me here tomorrow at three o'clock? Then I'll belong just to you."

"Lady, I can't wait."

"Now don't you go jerking off in your dreams about me tonight," she cautioned. "I want you to save it all for me tomorrow."

He watched in stunned disbelief as she headed out of the studio, still not believing his ears. Had she really said that? Surely she was joking. But, then again, maybe not. Perhaps that's how women at the Actors Studio talked. Maybe talk like Kim's was what "The Method" was all about.

"She turned you down, too?" came a soft voice from behind him. "When I came on to her, she told me to go home and grow up, and then she'd give me a roll in the hay."

Paul turned around to stare into the face of a broodingly handsome young man with an appealing vulnerability. On closer look, he seemed dangerous. Perhaps psychotic.

"Hi, I'm James Dean," he said. "Loved your performance. But you need to find your fire. If you'd get up there on stage with me, we could play a love scene in front of all these fuckers. You and me, emoting together, would set this whole studio on fire."

"I usually play love scenes with girls," Paul said defensively.

"That's like going through life with your right hand tied behind your back."

"Hey, pal, let's slow down," Paul said. "First, Kim Stanley. Now you, Mr. James Dean himself. I've heard of you. I'm just a country boy from Ohio. Back where I come from, we

"I'm James Dean, the guy to break you in."

43

like to work up to things. First, a few harmless dates. Get to know each other a bit."

"Life's too short for all that shit." He lit a cigarette and offered one to Paul. "A smoke? Shall I nigger-lip it for you?"

"No, I light my own."

"Stubborn little fucker, aren't you?" Dean said. "I love a challenge. I want to be the guy who breaks you in."

"Let's cool it a bit," Paul said. "The temperature's rising."

"Yeah, and that's an impressive hard-on rising in your pants. Somebody, and I know who, wants to fuck James Dean." He possessively linked his arm with Paul's. "Let's hit the sidewalk and give all the queens a treat. The two prettiest boys in New York parading down the avenue. We'll have them salivating, but we'll have eyes only for each other. C'mon, Blue Eyes, let's get the hell out of this joint."

***

It was six o'clock the following morning when Paul finally boarded the Staten Island Ferry for transit back to his apartment. He'd been out all night with Dean and hadn't called home. Whatever reception he got from Jackie is lost to history.

What isn't lost is the tortuous relationship that Paul launched with Dean in the few years that remained before his death.

The young actor, perhaps in a sadistic way, insisted in sharing news of his sexual trysts with his sometimes lover and patron, Rogers Brackett, a TV producer. It is only because Rogers in later life revealed the details of Dean's private life that we know of the actor's link with Paul.

Paul may have been shocked when Dean took him back to an apartment on Fifth Avenue at West 38th Street, an elegantly furnished retreat within a relatively posh neighborhood. Perhaps Paul thought the struggling young actor would be living in a seedy hotel room. "I'm a kept boy," Dean explained to Paul. "It's not something I'm proud of, as I'm the independent type. But it's what I'm doing for now. Hanging out with an older man is a learning experience for me in case I ever have to play a male whore on the screen."

"I can play many roles, but I'd never accept the part of a male whore," Paul said with conviction. Apparently, he'd changed his mind when he was eventually cast in *Sweet Bird of Youth* by Tennessee Williams.

"It's safe to assume that Dean was like no other lover Paul had known before or would know again," Rogers said. "When the Indiana farm boy with the angelic face in the faded blue jeans met pretty boy with the intense blue eyes from Shaker Heights, a volcano erupted. At least for three weeks. Jimmy

44

could never sustain such intensity for a longer period, although he would continue in ongoing relationships. It's just that the love-making became more casual, a sometimes thing instead of a burning passion. If Jimmy is to be believed, Paul Newman fell madly in love with him. From what I hear, Newman is a level-headed guy and would eventually come to his senses, but not before he took that perilous journey as Jimmy's lover. I could only sympathize with Newman. Following Jimmy around like a lovesick puppy is a journey into hell. I should know!"

From the very beginning of his relationship with Paul, Dean wanted to be in charge. On the second day of their affair, Dean gave Paul a copy of *The Little Prince* by Antoine de Saint-Exupéry. Dean claimed he'd read it eighteen times—"and it changed my life." Crossing to Staten Island on the ferry, Paul read the first chapter and found it silly and ridiculous, tossing it into the sea.

During the period when their love affair was still torrid, Paul and Dean would meet in the late afternoon at the Blue Ribbon Cafe, an actors' hangout in the Broadway district. Paul had made the casting rounds that morning, and Dean had often finished some minor role in a television production, a part that his patron, Rogers Brackett, had secured for him.

One afternoon when Paul walked into the café, he found Dean sitting in the corner, nursing a coffee and wearing a red baseball cap. On the table rested another red baseball cap. "Put it on," he ordered. Paul tried on the cap, finding it a perfect fit. "From now on, I want us to walk around New York in matching red baseball caps. It'll be a bond between us. Let people think what they will."

Paul not only wore the baseball cap that day, but was soon seen on the streets of New York walking with Dean with his matching cap. Paul was seen on the West Coast wearing that red baseball cap even after Dean's untimely death. And then one day he no longer wore it.

When Rogers returned from Chicago, Dean sadistically pointed out the stains of semen he'd exchanged with Paul on Rogers' bed. Dean seemed to take delight in describing in minute detail the sex he'd enjoyed while Rogers was away. "I fucked him; he fucked me, and I taught him to swallow my spit just like you do," Dean claimed.

Rogers was always hurt and jealous to learn of Dean's affairs, but at that point in their relationship he was willing to hang on. "It was the price I paid for keeping Jimmy in my life."

"I am liberating that boy from Ohio," Dean told Rogers. "One night I got him to fuck me in the doorway of an abandoned building in the meat-packing district. Sex is all the more exciting when it's done in a dangerous public place."

Dean and Paul had endless long walks and deep, intense talks in the coffee houses of Greenwich Village where they dared to dream impossible dreams. At one point, Dean suggested that Paul desert his family.

According to Dean's plan, both of them could set out hitchhiking from New York to Los Angeles. "I want to leave without a cent in our pockets," Dean claimed. "We'd be on the cutting edge. Live off the land, or as Tennessee Williams says, 'depend on the kindness of strangers.' Remember one thing: A pretty boy never has to go hungry."

"Are you suggesting we hustle?" Paul asked in astonishment.

"Why not? Everybody in life, from the President of the United States to some housewife preparing dinner for her husband, is a hustler."

Apparently, Paul went through a period of enormous guilt about his neglect of his growing family. At some point it was rumored that Jackie found out about his relationship with Dean and demanded that he give it up.

Presumably, Paul agreed to her demands and promised to drop Dean, but he never did. If anything, he became more secretive than ever.

The relationship continued even, or especially, when they reached Hollywood, each of them arriving there through very different means.

***

The Actors Studio changed Paul's life and brought him into contact with some of the stellar lights in the American theater, especially the Method Acting visionary Lee Strasberg, director Elia Kazan, and producer Cheryl Crawford.

"I meet all of you young actors, and I have nothing but sympathy for you," Kazan told Paul. "All of you waiting for that *one part* that will make you a star. In your case, you're probably hoping for a defining role like Marlon had when he played Stanley Kowalski. Year after year I see actors living the illusion and growing older as their dreams don't come true. Don't let that happen to you. Take the work you're offered. Chances are you won't be as lucky as Marlon. Become a working actor instead. But maybe around 1964 'the part' will hit you like a ton of bricks. Who knows? Maybe I'll be the guy who directs you in your defining role."

In later life, in reference to his successes at the Actors Studio, Paul referred to it as a case of

Kim Stanley
"The sexiest woman I've ever met."

"Monkey see, monkey do. I just sat there and watched how actors like Julie Harris and Maureen Stapleton pulled it off. I had enough sense not to open my big mouth. In truth, I never became a true Method actor like Brando," Paul said. "I was more of a cerebral actor. Even so, Lee Strasberg taught me to become the part I was playing, drawing upon memory of past experiences. Of course, that caused a lot of inner turmoil and pain in me. I came to realize I'd buried certain parts of my life, things I didn't want to face. Going to the Actors Studio was like lying on a headshrinker's couch."

In years to come, Paul would have only the highest praise for the Actors Studio, and he contributed financially to it. "I learned everything I know about acting at the Actors Studio."

***

That "homosexual panic," as labeled by Paul's biographer, Lawrence J. Quirk, set in almost immediately after his night of "dirty sex" with Dean.

Although a bit battered, Paul headed out the following afternoon from Staten Island for his three o'clock rendezvous with Kim Stanley. It seemed important to his sense of self that he quickly re-establish his heterosexual credentials.

Meeting Kim at the Actors Studio, Paul went for a walk with her in Central Park. Like himself, she had been involved in an affair with Marlon Brando, who had left her for other lovers, both male and female. "At least Marlon worked with me to get rid of my Southwestern drawl," she told Paul.

Kim was not the world's most beautiful blonde, but there was a loveliness to her and a warmth that drew him close to her. She smelled delicious, fresh and fragrant, as if she'd just emerged from a bath. In the park, she closed her eyes and stood still for a long minute looking into the sun. "I come from the land of the sun," she said, "New Mexico. New York is often cold and gray. I miss all the rattlesnakes slithering about."

"Why are you here, trying to be a famous actress, if you just want to go home?" he asked. "I have no intention of returning, except perhaps for a visit, to Shaker Heights."

"I can't answer that," she said. "I've got these battles going on inside myself. It's as if there are two Kim Stanleys. One wants to spend the rest of her life in an adobe hut in the desert making tortillas. The other wants to be a Marilyn Monroe of the stage." She stopped abruptly, looking into his intense blue eyes. "Tell me the truth: Do you think I'm sexy?"

He moved closer to her, bending over to lick the salt from her neck. There was a growing excitement in him. "You may—just may—be the sexiest woman I've ever met. Not in an obvious, fake way like the glamour gals of the screen. But like a real woman should be." He stood back from her, looking into her face. "I bet you have creamy tits."

"Does your wife have creamy tits?" she asked.

"Not that I ever noticed," he said. "But what is that question leading up to? Are you getting around to the fact I'm a married man?"

"Hell, no," she said. "I don't care whether a man is married or not. Do you think Marlon Brando worries about such matters? Why should I, just because I'm a woman?"

"That's fine with me," he said. "I find marriage restricting. I should never have rushed into it. I think actors should be free and independent, experiencing life as it comes along, and not becoming some henpecked guy rushing home at night to a screaming kid and a nagging wife. What kind of life is that for an artist?"

"If you're trying to convince me to go to bed with you, don't," she commanded. "Even before we set off on this walk, I'd already determined to surrender my creamy tits to you and a lot of other good stuff ."

The details of this encounter between Kim and Paul appeared in the unpublished memoirs of Brooks Clift, brother of Monty. He too took Kim as a mistress, and, to judge from his book, he shared his love affairs in great detail during pillow talk with her, and she did the same with him.

If Brooks is to be believed, the two-week affair between Kim and Paul fizzled out for one major reason. One afternoon when they were in bed, making jungle animal noises, she called out "MARLON" as Paul penetrated her. Apparently, that made Paul's erection deflate, and he got out of bed and put on his clothes. "I'm not Marlon Brando, and I'll not be his replacement in your life. My name is Paul Newman, and I'm a very different man."

"Don't judge me," she said. "When Marlon moves into your life, he takes over your soul. He possesses you. I'm trying to get over him. You look like him. You can help me get over him. You don't know what it's like to get fucked by Marlon Brando."

Stepping into his pants, he looked at her with a certain disdain. "You're wrong about that. I am one of the many who knows exactly what it feels like to get fucked by Marlon Brando." In anger, he stormed toward the door. "Baby, it's over between us. Kim Stanley does not exist for me."

He looked back one final time to see her standing naked by the bed. "Don't go," she managed to say. "Please don't leave me alone."

***

Late in 1952, after only two months of training at the Actors Studio, the call Paul had been waiting for materialized. William Liebling had arranged for him to read for William Inge, who had finally finished his Broadway-bound play, *Picnic*. The play would change Paul's life for all time.

On his way to Inge's apartment, insecure and nervous, he encountered a woman on the street who stopped him and asked for his autograph. "You're Marlon Brando, aren't you?" she asked. "I loved you in *A Streetcar Named Desire*. Could I have your autograph?"

This was just the beginning of such requests from fans who, throughout the 50s, mistook him for Marlon Brando. He dutifully signed Brando's name and headed into the apartment building and up the elevator where Inge waited for him.

He checked his appearance in a tiny mirror near the elevator buttons. Author Charles Hamblett described what he looked like at that time in his life. "His eyes could have come straight from an identikit (sic) picture of Monty Clift, his mouth was a refinement of Vic Mature's Magyar leer, and the shade of John Garfield hovered around the thrust of his jaw."

Kansas-bred Inge came from the same Midwestern roots that had given birth to Paul. As a former teacher of high school English and drama, Inge was familiar with the nervousness of an aspirant young student actor. He offered Paul a drink. "I've already had five drinks in the past two hours, so you need to catch up with me."

The drink put Paul at ease. As a prelude to Paul's reading from the script, Inge spoke of his hometown. "I'll always remember Independence, Kansas. A beautiful little town with enormous shade trees and lots of fine spacious homes. I've been to Shaker Heights. Our towns have much in common. I recall the celebrations of Halloween and the city park. We had a sad old river there. There was an old wives' tale that the Indians had left a curse on the river and that it would take one life a year in vengeance on the white man for having usurped their land."

When Paul was sufficiently at ease, Inge asked him to read the part of Hal, the leading male role. Paul later claimed, "I was awful but Inge was very indulgent."

In Key West years later, Inge told Tennessee Williams, "Paul messed up bigtime, but I found him exciting. First, he was a beautiful man. I just wanted to strip off his clothes and tongue him from head to toe. I'd never seen an actor with this particular type of male beauty. And he was also a nice guy with unbelievably nice manners. I was determined to have him at all costs."

At the end of Paul's bad reading, Inge congrat-

William Inge:
"Please take off your shirt."

ulated him. "You're very talented as an actor," he said, not meaning it. "Forgive me, but I must ask you to pull off your shirt. On stage Hal appears shirtless in a pivotal scene, and the actor who plays him has to have a certain build."

Without being asked again, Paul stood in front of Inge and pulled off his shirt and underwear top. "Inge asked me to walk around while he devoured my chest," Paul later told Kim Stanley after they'd reconciled. "I felt like a piece of meat being inspected. But I'd do anything to get cast in a Broadway play. Inge knew just how far I'd go."

With the passage of years, the story of just how Paul parlayed his good looks into success as an actor became widely known on Broadway, but because of the fear of libel, it couldn't be described in print at the time. In 1996, writing while Paul was still alive, biographer Lawrence J. Quirk cited Paul's "climbing the lavender ladder" en route to success on Broadway.

"I knew what Inge wanted, and he was going to get the prize," Paul later confided to Kim. "We song-and-danced each other that day. Or should I say that the cat toyed with the mouse? When he invited me for a romantic dinner the following night, I knew what was coming, and I proved to be the man for the job. God damn it, Inge was like a suction pump. I don't think there was one orifice left unexplored. When I got on the 2am ferry to Staten Island, I was drained dry. But Inge had promised to arrange an audition for me with Joshua Logan, who was to direct *Picnic*."

The next day, Liebling called Paul and wanted to meet with him shortly before noon in his office. He'd received a call from Inge praising Paul's talent, although warning that the producers might give the role to a bigger star like Marlon Brando should he become available. "I'll personally lobby for Paul," Inge assured Liebling. "Even if Paul loses out on the role of Hal," Inge promised, "I'll do what I can to get him one of the other parts."

As Paul was leaving Liebling's office that day, he had a chance encounter with one of the agent's former clients. It was Montgomery Clift, who had recently flown in from Los Angeles. Paul seemed dazed by the actor's stunning beauty. He'd seen him in *Red River* opposite John Wayne, and had been mesmerized by his screen image. He'd also been enthralled watching Monty in the screen's most clinging embrace, the goodbye scene between Elizabeth Taylor and him in the 1951 *A Place in the Sun*.

Like many of the actors Paul was meeting,

Joshua Logan:
"In search of the unobtainable"

50

Monty was very direct, making his intentions known. "Where has God's gift been hiding all my life?"

In spite of himself, Paul blushed. Monty took his hand and did not release it for the longest time. "You're the greatest," Paul managed to mumble. He was clearly awed and could have cursed himself for appearing like some gangly schoolboy fan in front of Monty. "I . . . I . . . don't know what to say."

"I've got to run now," Monty said. "Just give me permission to get your phone number from Liebling. Let me call you. It's not every day I meet up with a man who's more beautiful than I am." Monty kissed Paul gently on the lips. There was just a flicker of tongue.

That afternoon, on the way back to Staten Island, one would have to imagine just what was dancing through Paul's brain. Surely he thought that being in New York at that particular moment in the history of the theater was the most exciting place he could be on the planet. To complicate matters, Liebling told him that he'd received a call from Marlon Brando that morning, wanting to know Paul's address and phone number. Marlon was coming back to New York. "I thought Marlon had forgotten all about me," Paul said. "Gone Hollywood."

"Don't fool yourself," Liebling told him. "No one who links himself with Paul Newman is likely to forget him. You're unique and I feel the world is about to discover that sooner than later."

***

A closeted homosexual, Joshua Logan suffered from frequent bouts of manic-depression. On the day he met Paul, Logan was in an uncharacteristically ebullient mood.

Paul was immediately impressed with this man of the theater who had emerged out of Texarkana, Texas to become president of the drama group at Princeton. Its players included Henry Fonda, Margaret Sullavan, and James Stewart. In the 1930s Logan had actually visited Constantin Stanislavsky in Moscow.

In 1958, when Logan was directing *Blue Denim* on Broadway, a play by gay author James Leo Herlihy, Logan confided to the playwright, "I not only wanted to direct Paul in *Picnic*, I wanted to sample what was actually in his picnic basket. As you know, I've had many actors in my day, but Paul was exceptional and that was immediately apparent when he walked into my apartment. His arms and legs moved in perfect rhythm. The fact that he was a bit shy made him all the more adorable. Long, lean, and muscular, his body radiated a power that back then he hadn't yet tapped. His nose was well formed and aquiline, as if he had patrician ancestry. His hair was thin but the kind you

51

wanted to run your fingers through. He was extraordinarily handsome with clear blue eyes, bluer than an alpine lake in summer. He had perfectly formed lips. And when he smiled, he revealed strong white teeth. There was just a stubble of beard, which appeared like golden flecks against his perfect skin."

"Sounds like you fell in love," Herlihy said.

"I did indeed," Logan said. "I always go for the unobtainable. That way I can revel in my depression at the inevitable rejection."

Paul read for Logan that day, and, overcome by the moment, the director promised Paul the lead role of Hal, a juicy part that would have been ideal for Marlon Brando. The role of Hal was that of a drifter, an uninhibited stud who was "Inge's jerk-off fantasy," in Paul's view. Entering into a small Kansas town where women were deprived of men, leading lives of strained sexual relations and quiet desperation, the character of Hal was like a firecracker, igniting long-suppressed emotions.

That night when Paul arrived back on Staten Island, he told Jackie, "I'm going to be a Broadway star. It's happened at last!"

Based on Logan's promise to star him in *Picnic*, Paul moved Jackie and Scott out of Staten Island and into a two-bedroom apartment in Queens Village on Long Island. The plan involved Paul's daily transit by car from there into the heart of Manhattan to star in the play.

Lost in the fantasy of overnight stardom, Paul got a jolt of reality when Liebling called him with the bad news. Apparently, Ralph Meeker had become available, and Logan, having changed his mind, had cast him in the role of Hal instead.

The brazenly macho Meeker was obviously more suited for the part than Newman. Logan had worked with him on *Mr. Roberts*, for which he'd received a Theatre World Award, and he'd taken over the role of Stanley from Marlon Brando in *A Streetcar Named Desire*. He also had a number of screen credits under his belt.

Paul was bitterly angered at both Logan and Inge, but promised Liebling he'd conceal his fury. "Losing the role of Hal was one of the hundreds of disappointments I would eventually experience in my long career," Paul later said.

The news from Liebling wasn't all bad. For a salary of one-hundred and fifty dollars a week, Logan would hire Paul as Meeker's understudy and also give him a one-line walk-on role. Paul would play "Joker," a slightly menacing gas station jockey who would make a pass at Madge, the play's heroine, which would be played by the very beautiful Janice Rule.

Even after he'd signed to join the *Picnic* cast, Paul continued to pursue additional work with his new MCA agent, John Foreman. Paul referred to his performances in teleplays as, "the best thrill in town, a totally new experience for me. I was able to play all kinds of roles, since I hadn't been categorized."

In July of 1953, Foreman landed Paul a TV role in "The Bells of Damon." In September of the same year, a part in another teleplay, "One for the Road," would also be presented to him.

One morning at the offices of MCA, Paul's meeting with Foreman ran longer than an hour, even though the agent had a young blonde-haired actress waiting outside to see him as well. As Foreman opened the door to his office to let Paul out, Joanne Woodward jumped up from her seat. Foreman introduced her to Paul, who apologized for "eating into your time. We got carried away."

"Oh, that's okay," she said in a cornpone Southern drawl. "I've spent all my life waiting for one man or another."

There were no great sparks, no love at first sight.

"My introduction of these two was a historic moment in theater and film history," Foreman recalled. "They couldn't have seemed less interested that day. Who could have predicted what was to come?"

***

"I hated him on sight," Joanne Woodward later recalled. "He was pretty and neat like an Arrow Collar ad. He looked like a snobby college boy type in an unimpressive seersucker suit, the kind insurance salesmen wore in summer making the rounds in my native Georgia."

Like Paul, Joanne had been born a winter baby but not into freezing weather. When she entered the world on February 27, 1930, it was 70 degrees Fahrenheit in Thomasville, Georgia, a town that had once flourished as a winter resort, lying only ten miles north of the Florida border.

With her blonde hair and pixie face, she looked at the world through inquisitive green eyes. By the age of five, she had become an avid movie-goer. She told her parents, Wade Woodward and Elinor Trimmier Woodward, that she wanted to grow up to become an actress like Bette Davis and Joan Crawford. Ironically, at the time of her birth, her mother had wanted to name her after Joan Crawford, but after prolonged wheedling, her Southern relatives succeeded in getting the child named Joanne instead. A brother, Wade Jr., had been born earlier.

When Elinor took Joanne to see Laurence Olivier playing the melancholy Heathcliff in *Wuthering Heights*, Joanne developed her first serious crush.

That same year of 1939, when the newspapers announced that the premiere of *Gone With the Wind* was to be held in Atlanta, Joanne begged her mother to take her.

In Atlanta, she even convinced her mother to wait outside the hotel where

Olivier was staying with Vivien Leigh, who played Scarlett O'Hara in the film. When the door to their limousine opened, Joanne, aged nine, jumped inside, landing on Olivier's lap.

In school it was revealed that Joanne had a high I.Q., and she excelled in her grades. Life seemed so happy in the Woodward household that she later said she was devastated when her parents announced that they were divorcing. "It took years for me to adjust to that," she said. Her father went to New York, where in time he became vice president of Scribner's, the publishing house.

When Joanne and her mother moved to Greenville, South Carolina, the future actress had not abandoned her dream of life in the theater. She began to attract attention in high school productions. Weighing 117 pounds, she had measurements of 32-24-34, which attracted the interest of some of her male classmates. She generally ignored their glances, and continued to do so during her two years at Louisiana State University

Returning to Greenville, she appeared in a local production of Tennessee Williams's *The Glass Menagerie*—ironically, the same play in which Paul had appeared during his own school years in Ohio. Years later, Joanne would star in a film version of that same play, directed by none other than Paul himself.

Persuading her mother to let her go to New York, Joanne arrived there by train at the age of twenty-one. Until she got work in the theater, she planned to support herself on the sixty dollars a month her father gave her. Almost immediately she enrolled in the Neighborhood Playhouse, which, like the Actors Studio, trained the aspiring stars of tomorrow.

At the playhouse, she studied under the great dramatic coach, Sanford Meisner, who warned her to "get rid of that Southern drawl, or you'll appear only in plays by Tennessee Williams."

Like Paul, Joanne signed with MCA, under whose management she pursued roles in live television dramas. She appeared in an original teleplay, *Penny*, which aired on June 9, 1952. Other live television roles followed.

Between jobs, Joanne liked to hang out with her fellow actors, talking about the theater. She had long cups of coffee with Rod Steiger, a newly made friend of Paul's. She even befriended a young aspiring actor, James Dean, hardly know-

Joanne Woodward with **Paul**
"I hated him on sight."

54

ing that he was sleeping on occasion with her future husband.

Her big goal involved starring on the Broadway stage, and she avidly followed casting calls. As a result of attending a cattle call, she was summoned to appear before Joshua Logan, who asked her to read a scene from the upcoming play he was directing, *Picnic*. Amazingly, he liked her reading and hired her to understudy both Janice Rule, playing Madge, and also Kim Stanley playing Millie, Madge's younger sister.

When Joanne reported for work the next day, Logan introduced her to Paul. "We've met before," she said.

Paul claimed he didn't remember their initial encounter in John Foreman's office. "I meet so many aspiring actresses," he said. That remark didn't endear Paul to her and confirmed her earlier impression that he was a conceited snob.

"I had all the lovers I could handle at the time," Paul later confided to Rod Steiger. "I wasn't about to take on another, even though I could tell that Woodward was attracted to me. Besides, I had a wife at home, a son, and a baby on the way. Maybe Jackie thinks that by becoming a baby factory she can hold on to me. Or else my rubbers had big leaky holes. I'm practically a walking sperm factory."

Paul wasn't exaggerating about all those lovers. According to Rod Steiger, "He should have kept his pants unzipped for convenience. In those days, he was one busy boy."

***

Backstage, Logan introduced Paul to a relative newcomer, character actress Eileen Heckart, who was cast in *Picnic* as a schoolteacher named Rosemary. Eileen and Paul chatted amicably until Logan tapped him on the shoulder. "There's another cast member here. She says she knows you and is waiting for you in her dressing room." For some reason, Logan was being mysterious. Walking up to the dressing room, Paul knocked on the door.

"Come on in, it's open," came a voice that sounded familiar, though he wasn't sure.

Opening the door, he encountered Kim Stanley in bra and

Paul's dream come true, grainy and gritty :
Checking out the signage on Broadway
for his role in *Picnic*

panties, with her feet propped up on her dressing table. "Come on in, big boy," she said to him, "and lock the door behind you. We've got some unfinished business. Now come over here and take care of momma."

As *Picnic* went on the road, opening in such cities as Cleveland, Joanne began to look at Paul with a different eye. "He wasn't conceited at all. In fact, I found him rather modest for such a good-looking boy. He had a protective wall around him when I met him, but deep down he was a sensitive man with the soul of an artist. He just didn't want the world to know that."

On the road, Paul began to "date" Joanne in a casual way. They often met for a cheap lunch in some dreary coffee shop or treated themselves to a late-night dinner together after the evening's performance. They talked about the weakness of the play's third act and how Logan was fighting with Inge to rewrite it. Sometimes Paul didn't tell Joanne good night until two o'clock in the morning.

In the beginning of their relationship, Paul claimed he did not view Joanne as a romantic attachment but as a good and like-minded friend. They talked about books they'd read, Method acting, movies or plays they'd seen. When not performing in *Picnic*, they often attended a movie matinee together.

"I have no doubt but that they were sexually attracted to each other, but weren't admitting it, not even to themselves," said Kim Stanley, who seemed jealous of Joanne.

"Kim was looking for a series of good fucks during the long run of *Picnic*," Logan later said. "She told me that her greatest fantasy was to have a three-way with both Newman and Brando. I don't know if Paul was paying secret visits to Joanne's hotel room—or not. But it wasn't a question of if they'd start fucking, but when."

***

Paul's lucky break came when Logan decided that the actor playing Alan Benson, Hal's roommate in college, was dull and slowed down the action of the play. Firing him, Logan hired Paul to play Alan, the rich boy who loses his girl (Janice Rule) to the more seductive jock, Hal, as played by Meeker.

After rehearsing Paul for three days in the role of Alan, Logan began to feel that he'd made a mistake. "Paul has no fire either," Logan confessed to William Inge. "He's pretty and has a sexy body, but doesn't know how to use it."

"Let's seek an outside opinion," Inge told Logan. "We're both hung up on Paul and can't be objective."

Called in to watch Paul's performance as Alan were Tennessee Williams, Elia Kazan, and Dorothy McGuire, who had scored such a box office hit in the film, *Gentleman's Agreement*, in 1947.

After Paul's performance, both Kazan and Tennessee congratulated Paul, although McGuire remained noncommittal.

"You are not just beautiful," Tennessee exclaimed, embracing Paul, "but spectacularly beautiful. Up to now I thought Marlon was the most beautiful man I'd ever seen on the stage. Now you come along, making my fickle heart waver. With you on the stage with Ralph Meeker, all homosexuals will have a difficult choice. Do they want to see sexual menace or do they want to worship at the altar of male beauty?"

Paul was embarrassed at Tennessee's adulation, but he returned the compliment. "It's an honor to get a seal of approval from America's greatest playwright."

"With a compliment like that," Tennessee said, "all you have to do is blow in my ear and I'll follow you anywhere. One of these days, I'm going to write a role for you, one so great you'll always be remembered for it."

"A promise I'll hold you to, Mr. Williams."

After Kazan and Tennessee had approved of Paul for the role of Alan, Logan decided to head to Broadway with Ralph Meeker and Paul as his male stars. Even so, Paul complained to Logan. "I'll do what I can with Alan. But he's an unreconstructed square. Meeker eats me alive on stage in his juicy part. I play Madge's boyfriend, but it's obvious to the audience I'm going to lose her to Meeker's more threatening sexuality. Alan is a thankless role for any actor."

"All of us must start somewhere," Logan told him.

Paul also complained to Inge. "Could you rewrite Alan a bit? I mean, he's without depth or resonance. Give me a chance." Inge turned a deaf ear to him, as he was angry with Paul, who had refused to become the playwright's off-duty stud.

Meeker was Paul's rival both on and off the stage. The more experienced actor had virtually ignored Paul during tryouts on the road. One day he called Paul to his dressing room, where he was relaxing in his boxer shorts while drinking a beer. He offered Paul one, which he gladly accepted.

Paul sat down next to Meeker, who carefully evaluated his understudy. "So you think you're man enough to replace me as Hal in case I get sick or go on vacation?"

"You're great in the part," Paul said. "I couldn't really replace you. Of course, I'd try

Ralph Meeker,
"There's no sock stuffed into *my* crotch!"

to give an adequate performance. Perhaps I'd feel the same way you did when you replaced Brando in *Streetcar*."

"That faggot," Meeker said with contempt. "Brando's a big fucking ass-hole. I was much better in the role of Stanley than he was. But he got all the credit."

"Who said life is fair?" Paul took a big gulp of his beer.

"I've called you here to give you one acting tip, and only one," Meeker said. "And you'd better listen and listen good. When you walk out on that stage, you've got to make every faggot in the audience dream of sucking your big dick. You've got to make every horny bitch in the audience want to get plowed by your whopper. If you don't have a big dick like I do, you've got to convince the audience you do."

"That beats everything I've ever learned at the Actors Studio," Paul said. "I'll heed your advice."

"Ever since you've met me, you've been salivating every time I come around," Meeker said. "Tonight's your lucky night. I didn't get any pussy last night, and I'm horny as hell." He reached inside his shorts and pulled out his penis. "Try this on for size."

"You've got the wrong bitch," Paul said. "I'll summon Kim Stanley for you." Paul slammed down his beer and headed for the door.

"Fuck you, faggot," Meeker called after him.

Years later Paul told Shelley Winters, "Meeker gave me a hot acting tip. But I don't think I ever followed his advice until I made *Hud*."

The following afternoon Logan decided to rehearse his two under-studies, both Paul and Joanne, in a slow jitterbug to the tune of "Moonglow." "This was the sexiest moment in the play," Logan told his actors. "While Hal is dancing with Madge, I want him to virtually fuck her—symbolically, that is."

After Joanne and Paul had gone through the routine three times, Logan grew frustrated. "With Meeker and Janice Rule, I get sizzle. With Woodward and Newman, I get fizzle. Let's do it again."

Paul still didn't please Logan, who urged him to "do some dirty

Ralph Meeker and **Janice Rule**
Sexual menace

58

dancing. Wiggle your ass more." The director put his hands on Paul's buttocks and moved them in rhythm to the music. "I had almost given up on them, and then all of a sudden they got it. They moved into each other like some sort of erotic mating dance. They were falling in love just like in Inge's script. But it wasn't play-acting. This was for real. After that dance that afternoon, I knew that Jackie had lost her husband."

Over a drink that night, Joanne confessed the truth to Logan. "I've set my hat for that guy. Married or not, I'm gonna get him."

***

Thanks to his promotion to the status of a featured player, Paul earned two hundred dollars a week. With trepidation, he approached the Broadway opening night for the Theater Guild's production of *Picnic*, which premiered on February 19, 1953. Although Meeker, Kim Stanley, and Janice Rule stole the night, Paul's role as Alan did not go unnoticed. The critic, Richard Watts, Jr., cited his "excellent work" in the Inge play. *Picnic* would run for fourteen months and 477 performances, eventually winning the Pulitzer Prize.

After only two nights of appearing in *Picnic*, an emergency call came in for Paul backstage. He learned that Jackie had been rushed to a hospital, where she'd given birth to a baby girl.

After the curtain closed, Paul sped along in his Volkswagen to Long Island where he met a beaming-faced Jackie, holding a little baby whom she'd already named Susan Kendall Newman. Paul was allowed to hold her in his arms, although he appeared so nervous Jackie feared that he might actually drop the baby.

"Instead of being a proud father like I should have been," Paul later confided to Kim Stanley, "I felt I was still trying to find my own way in the world, and here I was responsible for a wife—and now two kids. I didn't want to become a typical suburban husband of the Fifties."

In spite of his newborn baby, Paul spent the rest of 1953 and the years to come devoted to his career and his newly minted friends in the theater. The self-image he retained as a "family man" seemed less and less appropriate. When he and Geraldine Page were voted two of the "Most Promising Personalities of 1953," the actress whispered to him, "It's hard being a husband, father, and full-time actor, isn't it?" He agreed.

During the run of *Picnic*, Paul had been seeing more of Joanne than Jackie. Officially Paul assured fellow cast members that he and Joanne were "just friends." But no one, especially Kim Stanley or Logan, believed that. It was suspected that Paul had occasional sleepovers at Joanne's apartment on Fifty Sixth Street and Madison Avenue in New York. It was a five-flight walkup.

A female cast member recalled that one day when she dropped in on Joanne, she found both Paul and Joanne stark naked, and painting the ceiling and walls of her cheap rental. Joanne wore a shower cap to protect her hair.

As Paul hurried to the bathroom for his clothes, Joanne claimed that they didn't want to spill paint on their street clothes.

How Paul explained these sleepovers to his wife Jackie is not known. He learned what breakfast at the Woodward household was like. It meant walking down to the street and purchasing two hot dogs from a street wagon vendor and carrying them back up those five flights.

When Rod Steiger learned about Jackie's second child, he said that Paul wanted to keep his wife "barefoot and pregnant," and stashed safely out of sight in Long Island while he pursued his stage career and various affairs in Manhattan. Paul told Steiger that Jackie had "abandoned forever" her dream of becoming an actress. With Paul away from the house most of the time, Jackie had become a full-time housewife and mother.

Even though he'd grown older, Scott was still screaming. "I feel my son has an outrage against the world," Paul claimed to Steiger. "Like he didn't want to be born, and he hates me for bringing him into such a fucked-up world."

***

In addition to his many affairs, Paul still avidly pursued roles in live tele-plays as a means of supplementing his income from *Picnic*. Along the way he met director Sidney Lumet, who in 1982 would helm *The Verdict*, starring Paul. Impressed with the young actor, Lumet cast him in three episodes of the CBS series *You Are There*. Paul recalled, "I remember playing everybody from Nathan Hale to Julius Caesar."

Even though he was appearing on Broadway, Paul still showed up regu-larly at the Actors Studio, where Lee Strasberg and Elia Kazan continued to guide and encourage him as an actor. One day Strasberg introduced him to one of the studio's famous alumni, Shelley Winters.

Blowsy, effusive, and brassy, the star latched onto Paul like a *Tyrannosaurus rex* who'd sunk its teeth into a tasty smaller dinosaur for lunch. She could appear drab or sexy on the screen, as exemplified by *A Place in the Sun* (1951), in which Montgomery Clift drowns her so he'd have a chance at Elizabeth Taylor. She could also be sexy and vampish as she was in *Cover Girl* (1944). She invited him to her favorite Italian trattoria in Greenwich Village, where he drank beer and she devoured her favorite dishes, a scene eerily evocative of the 1966 movie, *Harper*, in which they'd appear together.

She was filled with remarkably candid stories about Hollywood, which greatly amused Paul. He'd never met a woman so full of personal revelations regardless of how embarrassing. One amusing incident concerned a dinner party Yvonne De Carlo had invited her to. "In the powder room, she bluntly asked me, 'Which one do you want tonight—Clark Gable or Errol Flynn?' I went with Flynn. Now I know what 'in like Flynn' means."

She had Paul laughing and feeling wonderful. "You're my kind of broad," he told her.

Before that night was over, Shelley became another woman in whom he could confide, even the dark secrets that he'd told no man or woman. "Don't worry, sweetcheeks," she told him. "Marlon has told me everything about the two of you. We have that kind of relationship."

He flushed with embarrassment.

"Don't be shy," she said. "All actors do it. Me, too. When Marilyn and I roomed together, we sometimes got each other off when there were no men around. There's nothing to be ashamed of."

She jumped up. "Speaking of Marlon, I've got to get to the phone. I was supposed to meet him tonight to get fucked."

When she came back to the table, she asked for more wine. "I told Marlon I was dining with you. He's on his way here. He wants to see you again."

"He's not jealous that I'm out with you?" Paul asked.

"Don't worry. He wants to be a part of it. Call it a double date."

"But I always thought a double date was a man and woman going out with another couple."

"Kid, you've got a lot to learn. In Hollywood a double date is when I take on two men at the same time, or a horny male like Sinatra goes for two women in the same bed."

Later when Marlon joined them in the restaurant, he was all charm and smiles. "I went over on my motorcycle to visit you on Staten Island, but found out you'd moved. I was terribly disappointed."

"I wished you'd tracked me down," Paul said.

"Hey, fellows," Shelley said. "Don't forget I'm the girl sitting here. I'm the star of this picture, remember?"

Marlon turned to Shelley. "Everybody is telling me that Paul looks like me. Another Brando."

"Just what the world needs," she said sarcastically, "Paul's his own man and has his own face and style." She slammed down her wine glass. "I've got other plans for the two of you tonight. Enough of you lovesick puppies sitting here staring at each other to see who's the most gorgeous. I've got needs too. In fact, I plan to take *A Streetcar Named Desire* to a *Picnic*, and I want both of you to imagine I'm Marilyn Monroe for the night."

61

If Shelley Winters is to be believed, she had a three-way that night with Marlon Brando and Paul Newman.

As she once told her lover John Ireland and four other dinner guests, at a table at Downey's Restaurant in New York, "In the Forties I had the two hottest men on the screen, Clark Gable and Errol Flynn. In the 50s I sampled the two hottest actors in the American theater, Paul Newman and Marlon Brando. I wonder what the 60s or even the 70s and 80s will bring for me. I can't wait."

***

When Ralph Meeker announced he was leaving on a two-week vacation, Josh Logan came to Paul and said, "Here's your big chance. At last you get to play Hal."

Paul was elated about his first big break on Broadway, until Logan punctured his balloon. "Frankly, I don't think you're sexy enough for the part. Meeker is very sexy on stage or off, from what I hear. But you're an uptight college boy, which is okay for the role of Alan, but not for Hal. Meeker acts from his crotch. You move across the stage like you don't even have a dick. Brando in *Streetcar* was a crotch actor. For this role you've got to be white, trashy and sleazy—a low-down sexual menace."

"I can do that," Paul said. "Give me a chance. I'll study. I'll work with you. I'll do anything."

"Okay, I'll take you out to my house for the weekend, but you've got to do everything I tell you to do. If you'll learn and cooperate, I'll mold you into Hal. I might even let you play Hal in the road show version."

Logan drove Paul to a friend's house in Connecticut, where they could be alone and undisturbed for the weekend. Details of what actually happened on that weekend are sketchy, the only surviving account being what Paul later confided to Shelley Winters. Reportedly, Logan insisted that Paul strip naked for the entire weekend, presumably to "get in touch with your crotch." Completely nude, Paul was rehearsed in how to walk like a stud, stand like a stud, and move like a stud. In spite of his initial reluctance to appear nude before Logan, he grew more comfortable under the director's tutelage. "Even though you're wearing pants, I want the audience to be aware of your crotch at all times."

Paul told Shelley it was "a boot camp initiation. I wasn't happy satisfying the voyeuristic pleasures of a closeted homosexual, but I knew he could teach me something—and he did. I know I've got a lot to learn. I just can't do sexual menace like Meeker and Brando. Maybe it'll come to me."

Of course, Shelley asked the obvious question. "Did you guys get it on?"

"In a very one-sided way," Paul said. "I figured if I could give it to Inge, I might as well pump it to Logan. He had such praise for my dick that when we drove back to New York that Monday morning, I felt it was fourteen inches long."

Years later, Paul gave a highly edited version of his experience with Logan to a reporter from *The New York Times*. "At that time in my career, I probably wasn't a sexual threat like Logan suggested. When he told me to get in shape, I thought he meant spend six hours in the gym every day. I went to work to build up a muscled physique, which I've been working on ever since and certainly have shown off plenty of times on the screen. That lack of sexual threat comment still rankles me, though. I've been chewing on that one for almost thirty years."

***

Word had gone out along Broadway and had even reached Hollywood that a hot new star was appearing on Broadway, taking over for Ralph Meeker in *Picnic*. "It didn't match the excitement that Brando had generated," Shelley Winters said, "during his performance in *Streetcar*, but the word was out to catch Newman's act."

Movie studios, even potential stars wanting to play one of the parts, arrived nightly. Paul didn't need to make any phone calls to alert potential producers or directors. The New York papers widely publicized his appearance.

Just before one of his performances, during his second week as Hal, he was alerted by Logan that both Frank Sinatra and Marilyn Monroe were in the audience. "I wasn't just nervous that night, I had butterflies coming out of my asshole," Paul told Geraldine Page. "I wasn't so afraid of Marilyn, but of Sinatra. For some reason, I thought he'd make fun of me. I knew he hated Method actors like Brando."

Backstage, Marilyn chose not to be herself that night, but appeared as all that was good, bad, glamorous, and phony about a movie star. "She was beautiful and tacky at the same time," Paul later told Shelley, her former roommate.

With that breathy voice and

Frank Sinatra
"Suicidal over Ava Gardner"

Marilyn
Tinseltown's glam star meets the most beautiful boy on Broadway

exaggerated sexuality, she came on strong, kissing Paul on the lips as part of Paul's introduction to Sinatra. "She was playing the bubble-headed innocent number she did in *Gentlemen Prefer Blondes*, but I knew right from the beginning that she was one smart cookie," Paul said.

Sinatra was still depressed and almost suicidal over the recent breakup of his marriage to Ava Gardner. But, in spite of Paul's fears about meeting him, he warmly extended his hand and congratulated Paul on his performance. "You're great, kid," Sinatra told him. "Originally Logan wanted Brando for the part. That jerk would have fucked it up big time."

"Now, now Frankie," Marilyn said. "Marlon has his nice side."

"Yeah, right," Sinatra said.

Paul accepted their invitation for an après-theater dinner. Every head in the restaurant turned to watch Marilyn slither across the restaurant floor. Paul and Sinatra were virtually ignored by the rubber-neckers.

Over drinks and dinner, Paul deciphered the real purpose of the visit. Marilyn was lobbying for the role of Madge in the movie version of *Picnic*. "Janice Rule would be okay," Marilyn said, "but no sex appeal. In the movies, you've got to have sex these days to lure them away at night from The Box."

"If you say so, sugar," Paul said, feeling tipsy from the wine. Being in the presence of two fabled stars, and accepted by them as an equal, was going to his head even more than the wine.

Shortly after midnight the party was over, and Sinatra suggested they go back to his hotel suite for a nightcap. Marilyn giggled and Paul readily accepted.

En route to Sinatra's hotel, Marilyn whispered in Paul's ear that Sinatra was so horribly depressed over Ava that she was trying to help him get over her.

"You're the gal to do it," Paul assured her.

Back in Sinatra's suite, the champagne flowed. Marilyn didn't like the hard stuff. She gave them a detailed description of how she'd play Madge differently from Janice Rule's interpretation. Shortly after 1:30am, Sinatra rose to his feet. "I'm going to leave you kids alone for some fun while I hit a late-night spot with some buddies of mine." He leaned over and kissed Marilyn, patting Paul's cheek. "Take good care of our gal," he told Paul. "For this, you're gonna owe me big time."

When he was gone, Marilyn giggled and snuggled up close to Paul. "Now I want to know something."

"Ask me anything," he said.

"What does the most beautiful boy on Broadway do with the most glamorous star in Hollywood when they're alone together?"

"I can answer that," he said, as his lips came down on hers.

No one knows exactly what Marilyn and Paul did that night. The only after-the-fact "review" came from Marilyn's friend, Shelley Winters. At the Actors Studio, the loud-mouthed actress told Paul, "Marilyn said you were better than Brando. A more considerate lover. She said she likes a man who is kind and takes into account a woman's needs. She prefers that to brute sex."

"I hope that's a good review, but I want people to stop comparing me to Marlon Brando. We're different."

"That's true," Shelley said. "Your cocks are certainly different, but you do look like him a bit."

Before the curtain went up on *Picnic* the following night, Paul dropped off a thank you note at Sinatra's hotel. He expressed his gratitude for the hospitality and the introduction to Marilyn.

He never expected to hear from him again. One evening, days after Meeker returned to take back the role of Hal, Sinatra called the theater, inviting Paul to come by his hotel for drinks after the show.

Paul was eager to see Sinatra again, rushing over to the hotel and arriving in a breathless condition. Sitting in his suite in his underwear, Sinatra welcomed Paul. It appeared that he'd been drinking all day.

"And how was Marilyn?" he asked. "I assume she took good care of you before flying back to the coast."

"I think I'm in love," Paul said. "She's the best."

A frown crossed Sinatra's brow. "Don't get hung up on any chick regardless of how gorgeous she is," he said. "Marilyn will fuck you unknowns one day and forget you the next—that is, unless you're a big star, and I think you're heading there."

Sinatra said he hadn't been out all day and wanted to go for a walk. The day had been balmy. Once the two men hit the streets, it started to rain. Paul wanted to dart for cover, but Sinatra restrained him. He wanted to continue to walk the lonely streets of New York, even though both of them were getting soaked. "I wasn't about to chicken out," Paul told Shelley.

Later, Sinatra, with Paul in tow, arrived back at his hotel where he asked Paul to strip down. "I remember thinking, 'Oh, no, don't tell me Sinatra is gay, too,'" Paul later said. "It wasn't like that at all. He called room service to come and get my clothes to dry. We sat around in the hotel's terrycloth robes getting drunk."

According to Paul, Sinatra looked him up and down. "You like girls, don't you?" he asked. "I get mixed reports on you."

"Yeah, I'm a pussy man," Paul claimed. "Just ask Marilyn herself."

"She's not a reliable witness," Sinatra said. "Even gay men like to fuck her." Getting up, he went over to the phone and dialed someone. After he'd put down the receiver, he came back to join Paul. "I called a pal of mine. He's arranging for two hot showgirls with big tits to come over tonight and take care of us."

In about half an hour, two showgirls—one a shapely blonde, the other a leggy brunette—arrived at Sinatra's suite. Paul remembered seducing the blonde on the carpet in the living room, with Sinatra reserving his bed for the brunette.

After that night of intimacy, Paul assumed he'd become a member of Sinatra's inner circle. He began to doubt that when there was no follow-up call from the singer. Two weeks went by before he heard from Sinatra calling from Mt. Sinai Hospital, in New York City's borough of Queens. He wanted Paul to come over to slip him a bottle of liquor, which, of course, was against hospital rules.

With a bottle concealed under his trench coat, Paul came into the hospital where Sinatra had pre-cleared him through security for a trek upstairs to his private room. The singer had checked incognito into the hospital.

In bed, Sinatra looked as if he'd lost weight and his eyes seemed sunken into his head. "Pal, did you bring the good stuff?"

"Indeed I did, my man." With an eye out for the nurse, Paul poured Sinatra a drink. As he reached for it, Paul noticed that his wrists were heavily bandaged. "What happened?" Paul asked.

"I tried to slit my wrists," Sinatra candidly admitted. "I've tried to kill myself before. My buddy, Jimmy Van Heusen, found me on the floor of the elevator in his apartment house on Fifty-Seventh Street. I was bleeding heavily. He called an ambulance and they rushed me to this hospital."

At that point, the phone rang. "Get it for me?" Sinatra asked. "Take a message."

"Hello," came that familiar breathy voice over the phone. "Frankie, you don't sound like yourself."

"This is Paul Newman," he said. "I'm taking messages for Frank."

"Oh, Paulie," she said. There was an awkward pause. "I like the sound of that name. You do such nice things to a girl. I want to see you again. But right now we've got to save Frankie. Got a pencil?"

"I'll get one." He found a pencil on a nearby table and came back on the phone.

"Tell Frankie I've arranged for him to see Dr. Ralph G. Greenson when he gets back to Los Angeles. I call him Romy."

Paul wrote down the data.

Realizing who it was, Sinatra said, "I'll take the call."

Paul excused himself and stood in the corridor until Sinatra and Marilyn had finished a private conversation. Called back, Paul walked into the room, where he noticed that Sinatra was finishing off another glass of Scotch. "Marilyn and I agree you're one cute guy. I told her I'd fuck you myself if I were into boys. Ava accuses me of sleeping with boys."

"You, Frank Sinatra!" Paul said in astonishment. "The greatest lady-killer in the history of Hollywood?"

"Even the Caesars liked a little diversion," Sinatra said.

"You're joking, of course," Paul said.

"I don't know," he said, cracking a smile. "I slipped a peek and saw your naked ass bobbing up and down on the sofa in my suite while you banged that two-bit whore. It looked mighty tempting."

"I'll pretend I never heard that," Paul said.

Sinatra had another week in New York, and he hired Paul as his "babysitter," paying him two hundred dollars a week. What his first wife might have known about this deal can't be ascertained.

"I strolled Fifth Avenue with him," Paul said when he later confided to Shelley Winters. "I got a haircut if he wanted a haircut. I sat with him when he got his shoes shined. I went and had massages with him, Frankie insisting that the girls be bare breasted and give blow-jobs at the end of the session. I even drove him down to a joint in New Jersey where he sang. The pain of Ava seemed to make his ballads more soulful, especially when he sang of 'a gal that got away.' I even fucked with him. I'd moved up in his world. I was no longer on the floor, but on the bed with him, pounding away at some broad, meeting Frankie thrust for thrust. Every now and then he'd look over at me. 'How's it coming, kid?' he asked."

"And then he was gone," Paul said. "It was the fastest week I'd ever spent in my life. In one week, Frank lives what most people do in a year. He was off to Hollywood, to Marilyn, and countless others. I never expect to hear from him again."

***

Janice Rule, cast as the female lead, Madge, in *Picnic*, began her career as a dancer but broke her ankle during the Broadway run of *Miss Liberty* in 1949. Before that happened, she'd been spotted by a scout for Warner Brothers, who had signed her to a supporting role in the 1951 film *Goodbye, My Fancy*, which starred Joan Crawford.

During the run of *Picnic*, many of Hollywood's biggest stars, both male and female, came to see the production, some of them eager to be cast in one of the roles. By 1953, Joan Crawford knew that she was far too old to play the leading role of Madge. But when she came backstage to congratulate Janice, she had another motive. She actually wanted to meet Paul Newman. Tennessee Williams, who was superficially acquainted with Crawford, had told her that the actor was "divine."

In a pattern well known to Hollywood insiders, Joan Crawford always wanted to be among the first to seduce whatever new boy happened to be in town. "Town" in this case usually meant Hollywood, but in some cases the geography extended to New York.

Previously, as this rule applied to Brando, Crawford had already joined a long line-up of leading ladies going backstage, expressing their hopes to play Blanche DuBois in the film version of *A Streetcar Named Desire*. But in most cases these women had one single-minded goal: To seduce the dynamic, sexy young Brando.

Crawford had even seduced child star Jackie Cooper when he was only seventeen. Before meeting Paul, she'd also seduced Jeff Chandler, Rock Hudson, and countless others. She definitely wanted to add another notch in her garter belt by sampling Paul's sexual goodies.

Backstage, she congratulated every member of the cast, but focused primarily on Paul. He seemed flattered by her attention. After all, she was one of the grandest of all movie stars, even though her glory days as the queen of cinema were fast fading.

Her casting couch technique involved the suggestion that she wanted to use a young actor as her co-star in a future movie project. She'd been given a script, and she told Paul he'd be ideal playing one of its leading men.

When Crawford invited Paul for dinner the following night after the show, she told him she'd like to discuss the role further with him.

A telegram for Paul arrived the next day from Crawford, claiming that he'd given "one of the most riveting performances I've ever seen on Broadway."

He told Logan, "Can you imagine, Joan Crawford all to myself. A date with a movie legend. Out of all the young studs on Broadway, she picked me. I may be starring with her in her next film."

Logan looked at Paul skeptically. "You've got a lot to learn, kid, both about Crawford and about Hollywood in general." He walked away.

Before the curtain went up on *Picnic* that night, a messenger delivered a rented tuxedo to Paul and a note from Crawford. He was

Joan Crawford:
"We Texas gals eat beefcake."

68

instructed to change into the tux, and that after the show she'd be waiting out-side in a rented limousine to take him for dinner at the 21 Club.

Janice Rule and Paul had not really bonded during the stage run of *Picnic*. The development of their close but rather secretive friendship wouldn't evolve until later. Paul was learning fast, however, that beneath her rather prim and proper façade, Janice nurtured a secret passion. She loved Hollywood gossip, even though she pretended to hold it in disdain. It's because of what she called "my loose lips sink ships" revelations that we know so much about Paul him-self.

Janice's "loose tongue," as she called it, got her into occasional trouble. After her involvement in *Picnic,* she became romantically involved with Farley Granger, a popular cinematic heartthrob. After the abrupt termination of their engagement, she told many of her friends, "Farley prefers hot men to a doll like me." It was partly because of Janice and her passion for gossip that word spread throughout Hollywood that Granger was actually a homosexual. Later in life, moving on to other interests, Janice abandoned her acting career and became a successful psychotherapist in Manhattan.

After his highly visible date with Joan Crawford, and consistent with her hunger for gossip, Janice sent Paul a note, asking him to come to her dressing room. "Oh, God," Paul told director Logan. "Another horny broad for me to service. At least this one's a looker."

Paul had never really appreciated Janice's beauty until he was called into her dressing room. In her slip, she was a leggy and long-waisted young red-head with the clearest skin he'd ever seen on a woman. Up until then, he'd noted that she was feisty and especially competitive around Kim Stanley.

Janice welcomed him into her dressing room, and soon they were talking, laughing, and joking. He loved her deep throaty laugh. She was having a vodka and tonic before curtain and offered him one, which he gladly accept-ed. "I came from an Irish family from New Jersey. My father taught me how to drink when I was a kid."

As it turned out, Paul was wrong about Janice's intentions of summoning him to her dressing room. She didn't intend to seduce him, but wanted instead to learn the gory details about his tryst with Crawford.

He confided to Janice that the aging star was the "most take-charge woman I've ever met. For the benefit of the limousine driver, she even defined the best route to take to 21."

In those days photographers—they weren't called paparazzi then—wait-ed outside the popular joint to take candid shots of visiting celebrities, many of whom derived from Hollywood.

From the back of her limousine, the regal movie queen spotted the photographers from afar. She checked her face in a compact mirror and applied a finishing touch before turning to Paul. "You darling boy, you want to see how a star makes an entrance?"

As the photographers snapped away, she emerged from the limousine draped in mink and wearing a white turban. It was an elaborate ritual, carefully rehearsed, with Crawford showcasing her famous legs during her exit from the vehicle. Just before she glided out of the car, she turned back to Paul, who was still inside. "I gotta show the boys that Crawford still has her gams."

Every photographer captured her glittering image that night.

Every celebrity at the club came to Crawford's table to pay homage to her that night, including Milton Berle, her former lover Glenn Ford, and even Porfirio Rubirosa, the playboy from the Dominican Republic. He'd already been famously married to two of the world's wealthiest women, Woolworth heiress Barbara Hutton and tobacco heiress Doris Duke.

After Rubirosa had departed from their table, Crawford, now on her fifth vodka, confided to Paul, "That octoroon dick of his is three times the size of Clark Gable's."

"Joan," he whispered to her, "if we make it together tonight—and I suspect we're heading there—you're not going to broadcast my dick size all the way to LA, are you?"

"No, dear boy, your secrets will be safe with Mother Joan," she said. "I trust, however, I won't be dealing with any deficiencies here."

"Rest assured," he bragged, "I'm all man."

When columnist Walter Winchell came by, Crawford gave him an item for his morning column. She claimed that it was all but certain that Paul would be the leading man in her next movie.

"News to me," Paul said after Winchell had left.

"Don't worry," she assured him. "I still have a lot of clout, especially when it comes to selecting my leading men. Picture it. Joan Crawford with Paul Newman."

"Joan directed everything," Paul confided to Janice the next day. "Even what I had to eat. She ordered me a rare steak."

"I'm from Texas, darling, and we Texan gals know how to eat meat," Paul quoted Crawford as saying.

"She obviously was going for *double entendre* there," Paul told Janice.

She wanted a blow-by-blow description, but Paul was a bit shy in revealing all the details. He did tell Janice that the moment they entered her suite, Crawford pulled off her gown, dispensing with such preliminaries as offering him a nightcap.

"Her body was still quite firm," Paul claimed. "Rather beautiful as a matter of fact. Great legs. I took her on her white carpet right by a TV set broadcasting the night's news."

"Did you satisfy the insatiable?" Janice asked.

"I did my job," Paul claimed. "That's for sure. Even got a compliment. She said I was real clean, telling me she liked men without a lot of hair on their chest. She told me that Steve Cochran was a great lover and packed a magnificent pistol, but he had just too much body hair."

"I didn't know what to do when it was over," Paul told Janice. "She still hadn't invited me for that drink, and I could sure have used one at that point. Then I came to realize that the dirty deed was done, and that she expected me to leave. She told me she had to pack for an early morning flight to the Coast and that we'd stay in touch. It was goodbye. I did get a long, lingering kiss with tongue, and then I was out the door, back home to Jackie and the kids, having fucked one of the biggest stars in the history of Hollywood. I just hope that in my future there will be a lot of other big name stars who'll want to fuck me. I get off on doing the real big ones, even if they're past their prime."

Janice assured him that if he ever found success in Hollywood, all the big stars would want a piece of him. "Your phone will be ringing day and night. And it won't matter one God damn bit if you're married or not."

***

A few minutes after Paul accidentally met Montgomery Clift outside Liebling's office, the handsome young star—at the time the hottest property in Hollywood—had promised to call him. He never did.

When Monty learned that Paul was filling in for Ralph Meeker in the role of Hal in *Picnic*, he showed up unexpectedly to see the performance. Going backstage, he asked to be directed to Paul's dressing room.

In his boxer shorts, Paul opened the door and was astonished to see the drunken Monty standing outside. He quickly invited his screen favorite inside.

"Got a drink?" Monty asked.

"I'm a drinking man myself," Paul said, "and I always keep something stashed away." He reached underneath his dressing table and produced a bottle. As he finished dressing, he was nervous, perhaps fearing a critique of his performance from this gifted actor.

Montgomery Clift:
"Don't I get a kiss?"

"You played the role of Hal just as I would," Monty said.

"Considering that you're the most powerful, sensitive, and magnetic actor on the screen, I take that as high praise," Paul said.

"Don't I get a kiss for my appreciation of you?" Monty asked.

A bit taken back at first, Paul leaned over for a brotherly kiss on the cheek. Monty was having none of that. He pulled Paul to him, and soon his tongue was exploring Paul's mouth. This incident and the subsequent role Monty was to play in Paul's life were revealed in the unpublished memoirs of Monty's brother, Brooks Clift, who wrote about Monty after his untimely death in 1966.

Although details are lacking, it is presumed that Monty invited Paul back to his underfurnished duplex, where they had sex. At any rate, Paul didn't leave Monty's studio until eight o'clock the following morning.

"It was the beginning of a very complicated relationship," Brooks said. He claimed that he first met Paul when he went backstage to pick up Kim Stanley, with whom at the time he was having an affair. "Monty had already told me he was involved with Paul, and Paul knew that I was aware of all the details. So we didn't play cat-and-mouse with each other. Instead, Paul spoke openly of his relationship with Monty, both the good times and the bad times. I feel the bad times outweighed the good."

One evening when Brooks invited Paul to dinner, and both of them had had sufficient alcohol, Paul told Brooks, "Your brother is a sadistic bastard. He likes it rough, and I'm more vanilla. When Monty kisses, he doesn't do it with love, but to hurt you. His victim comes away with a bloody mouth."

"Rather vampiric, I'd say," Brooks shot back. "But you love him, right?"

"You got that right," Paul said. "Just when you want to kick him out of your life forever, he looks up at you with those soulful eyes, and you melt. He's a great actor, but a self-destructive one."

"I know about those eyes," Brooks said. "He uses them as his secret weapon. Elizabeth Taylor compares Monty's eyes to green diamonds. When he looks at me, he seems to be probing into my soul with his X-ray eyes. I'm sure he does the same with you."

"It's not the eyes, but the other shit," Paul said. "When I wake up in bed with him, I find myself battered and bruised. He sure likes to be the dominant one."

"Monty's just high-strung and filled with nervous energy," Brooks told Paul. "You need to restrain him a bit. He doesn't know what limits are. Don't let him dominate you. You should be the controlling factor. I love my brother dearly. Help him! He's disturbed."

Years later, reflecting on the early days of Paul's career, Brooks said, "When I first met him, he was still struggling for his own identity, both as a

72

man and as an actor. After a few weeks with Monty, he began to pick up some of my brother's mannerisms, which translated into his acting style. He tried being Brando. He tried being Monty. I later learned he'd also taken up with James Dean. I think he wanted to draw upon the talent of all three of Hollywood's bad boys. It must have been so difficult for him."

"When he went to Hollywood, Paul was referred to as 'the second Brando,'" Brooks said. "After a few pictures, he was referred to as the new Montgomery Clift. In just a short time, he was even competing with James Dean for parts. And aside from the professional rivalry, there was the private thing going on between these guys. I fear that Monty, Brando, and Dean took our squeaky clean Ohio boy down a murky road unlike any he'd ever traveled before."

***

Monty and Paul spent long hours discussing acting and scripts. Whenever Paul visited Monty's duplex, he found the actor deluged with scripts. In the wake of Monty's phenomenal 1953 success in *From Here to Eternity*, it seemed that every director in Hollywood wanted Monty to star in an upcoming movie.

Paul noted with alarm that Monty had taken to drinking, sometimes heavily, in the daytime. He seemed to be held prisoner by his own nerves. "I'm going to send all these scripts back," Monty told Paul one day. "They're all shit. Nothing exceptional." He picked up one script after another and dropped it on the floor in front of Paul. "Nothing exceptional," he kept repeating.

"Man, I wish some director would offer me just one of these scripts," Paul said. He picked up a discarded script called *East of Eden*. "How about this one? I read the John Steinbeck novel. I think it would make an *exceptional* movie."

"It sucks," Monty said. "Nothing exceptional about it."

"Since you're turning it down, could you ask the director to test me for a part in it?" Paul said.

Monty looked at him skeptically. "Okay, pal, if that's what you want. But why make your Hollywood debut in a film that I know will be a dud?"

The next day Paul encountered Brooks backstage. "Monty is turning down some real hot shit," Paul told Brooks. "He's going to try to get some good parts for me. Call it sloppy seconds. But I think I can really do some big stuff with Monty's rejects."

"Sounds like you're turning this relationship into a sing-for-your-supper type of thing," Brooks said. "Is this becoming a male version of *All About Eve*, Eve Harrington lusting for the roles of Margo Channing?"

"Not at all," Paul claimed. "My feelings for Monty are genuine. I can learn from him, though. Let's face it, he brings more intensity to the screen than Brando. And, in Monty's case, it's coupled with a romantic vulnerability."

"You should be a movie reviewer," Brooks chided him.

Paul lit a cigarette after offering one to Brooks. "Back to what you said before. I want to be honest with you. All of us sing for our supper in one way or another. The only problem we're having at the moment is when I have to go into that bedroom of his. He's draped it in black velvet to block out all daylight. It's like making love in a coffin."

"At least Monty doesn't lie there like a zombie," Brooks said. "We used to make it together when we were teenagers. I know firsthand about what a live wire Monty is in bed."

Even if I don't get off on the sex so much," Paul said, "I genuinely like and admire the actor I'm performing it with."

"Stick with Monty," Brooks said. "I know it sounds cynical, but it'll be worth your while. I also feel you're a good steady influence on him. Are you planning to follow him when he returns to Hollywood? You'd be the most beautiful thing on the screen."

"Yeah, so people tell me, but I'm nervous about what parts a studio might offer me."

Brooks laughed. "Most actors are worried about a studio offering them *any* part, especially in these days of television. But I think you might do well if you don't mind the pecking order?"

"What does that mean?" Paul asked.

"In Hollywood, you'll have to learn your proper place in the food chain," Brooks said. "First, the best roles will be offered to Monty. If he turns down the script, Brando will be the second choice. If he turns it down, and a director is still looking for a Method actor, you'd do well to position yourself as third in the line. That's what I call the pecking order."

Paul seemed to consider that for a moment. "If that's how they play the game, I might as well learn the rules."

"Both you and Dean are lining yourself up to become the heir apparent to Monty and Brando," Brooks said. "Good luck."

"Hell, man, I haven't completely decided that I even want to be a movie star," Paul said.

"Cut the shit!" Brooks told him. "Every loser at the Actors Studio expresses a disdain for Hollywood. But just offer one of the fuckers a movie contract, and I bet you those Method farts will start salivating."

***

74

James Dean called Paul one afternoon and asked him to go with him to the Actors Studio. When Paul met Dean, he found him draped in a scarlet matador's cape. He told Paul that he was going to perform a solo piece at the Actors Studio. He'd culled a script from a novel, *Matador*, by Barnaby Conrad, the story of an aging bullfighter facing his last hurrah or "moment of truth" in the bullring.

Up to now, as Paul had noted, Dean had never performed at the studio, but had sat watching the other actors emote, silently judging them.

When it came time for Dean to walk onto the stage, he entered awkwardly, still shrouded in his flamboyant cape. As he moved through the motions of his performance, Paul scooted down in his seat in embarrassment for his friend. Paul could not be certain, but he felt that Dean had cut off his performance only halfway through his material. Perhaps he realized how bad it was.

As Dean sat down, Lee Strasberg came on to critique what he'd just seen. Dressed haphazardly in baggy clothes, the head of the studio was a small man, looking more like a college professor than the master of the Method and a role model for both Marilyn Monroe and Marlon Brando.

Strasberg had an uncanny ability to determine what was artistically true on stage and what sounded false.

"In the history of American theater, Dean's exhibition—I wouldn't call it a performance—has to rank as the worst," Strasberg charged. "He mumbled his lines; he had no power of conviction. Another clone of Marlon Brando we don't need. Why did he choose a fading toreador? Dean has no experience as a bullfighter, much less an old one staging his last fight in the ring. What does Dean know about aging? At best, he could be cast as a confused and not very articulate juvenile. We did not feel this bullfighter's angst. All we saw on stage was a very conceited and arrogant punk who thought he could master material completely foreign to him. He cannot. He did not. A miserable failure."

Elia Kazan was in the audience that afternoon. He remembered Dean "sitting in a sort of poutish mess in the front row, scowling as Lee delivered his tirade, which was cruel even by his standards."

Wrapping himself in his cape, Dean rose to his feet and walked rapidly out of the studio, with his head held high. Paul followed him to offer what comfort he could.

Out on the street, Dean turned to Paul. "That fucker is trying to castrate me. He wants to suck my blood and destroy my uniqueness. He attacked me like some mad scientist in a lab dissecting a rabbit. I won't stand for it. I felt he was removing my skin, exposing me raw and bleeding to the other actors, each one a jealous bastard."

Dean asked Paul to go with him on a long walk through Central Park. "I once had this diamondback rattler as a pet. When he grew too big, I released him behind that bush over there. Let's go over and see if he's still there."

"I don't cotton to diamondbacks," Paul said. Nevertheless, he followed Dean behind the bush.

Concealed from the trail, Dean grabbed Paul and pulled him close. "Kiss me," he commanded. Paul obliged, although he wasn't comfortable with this display of man-to-man love in a public park. Dean was an exhibitionist, Paul was not.

"I'd prefer to do this in some other place," Paul said. "Like in private."

"But I need it now," Dean protested. "I need to feel that somebody out there loves me after that fucking take-no-prisoners attack on me by that damn little Jew."

Back on the park's main trail, Paul bought Dean a hot dog for lunch. After eating it, he impulsively turned to Paul, tugging at his arm. "Let's leave this afternoon," he urged. "Drop everything. Leave everybody behind. I want to hitchhike with you back to my home in Indiana."

"Your last hitchhiking proposal was to Hollywood," Paul said.

"Fuck, Hollywood!" Dean claimed. "I'll never go there. I've changed my mind. I want out of the theater. Not that I was ever really in it. I want you with me. I know this old farm we can buy real cheap in Indiana. Make our living from the land. Be our own men. We won't have to listen to any more assholes telling us how to act."

"No way!" Paul said. "I'm not ready for that. I want to stay here and face the perils of a life in the theater. I want to put my talent on display and let the world judge me. Sure, I'll make mistakes and be ridiculed, but I want to stay in the ring, keep on fighting."

"Your choice," Dean said with despair. "Maybe I'm being impulsive. Maybe I should follow your example. Stay here and become such a big success that Strasberg one day will lick the dingleberries off my crack."

Later that afternoon Dean invited Paul to join him for his dance lessons. Paul splurged on a taxi that took them to the studio of Eartha Kitt, who had become a success on Broadway because of her appearance in *New Faces of 1952*, where she'd scored a hit with her song, "Monotonous." In 1950, when she'd appeared on stage with Orson Welles in an adaptation of Christopher Marlowe's *Dr. Faustus*, playing Helen of Troy, the actor had bitten her in front of the audience, claiming that she was "the most exciting woman alive."

After meeting the sultry singer and dancer, Paul agreed with Welles' assessment. Eartha had trained with the Katherine Dunham Dance Company, and, as a skilled dancer herself, was giving twice-a-week lessons to Dean, whom she called "Jamie."

Ushering Paul and Dean into her studio, she hugged Dean and kissed him before planting a kiss on Paul's lips. Then she stood back and, with her cat-like eyes, surveyed the full figures of both men. "The two most beautiful white boys in New York, and Eartha's got 'em." When she spoke, her words had a purring intonation.

Embracing Dean again, she turned to Paul, "This is my soul brother. I'm his soul sister. Jamie and I can sit for hours without talking to each other, and we'll know what each other is thinking. Sometimes we burst into laughter at the same time, because we're both thinking about something that happened to us that was funny."

"She's my voodoo priestess," Dean said, hugging her tightly. "She even knows when I need to take a piss before I do."

To rehearse his dance numbers with Eartha, Dean stripped down to his underwear. Paul sat on the sofa, enjoying a cold beer.

She moved with panther-like grace in the dance. Dean tried to stay with her, but he was awkward, not getting the rhythm of the steps.

After the dance lessons, both Dean and Eartha played a pair of conga timbo drums, treating Paul to a concert. He concluded that Dean was better on the drums than on the dance floor.

"Great concert, guys," Paul said when they'd finished.

Eartha rose to her feet, reaching for Dean's hand. She walked over to Paul and stared down at him. He rose to his feet. "At the end of our bongo music, Jamie and I like to adjourn to the bedroom."

"I got it," Paul said. "I'm out of here. But thanks for the entertainment."

"You don't get it," Dean said, reaching for his arm to detain him. "Kitt here and I aren't opposed to a little company in bed."

"You aren't against a little poontang, are you?" she asked.

"It'd be a new thing for me," Paul said. "I'm ready to give it a try."

"Come along then," she said, taking his hand.

In the late 1970s, when Eartha was in Key West starring as Lola La Mour in a movie, *The Last Resort,* based on a novel *(Butterflies in Heat)* by Darwin Porter, she spent several long weekends with the writer. He was particularly interested in all the juicy details she'd left out of her autobiographies. Although she talked of many things, her most tender moments were reserved for Paul and Dean.

"I had both of them that afternoon, and I came to the conclusion that white boys are so

Eartha Kitt:
"White boys are so delicious."

delicious," she recalled. "I spread the word. The creators of *Hair* stole that line from me and put it in their hit musical. In the future, I would seduce Paul and Jamie on other occasions, but always separately, never together. That afternoon back in my studio in New York ranks as one of the most celestial experiences of my life. Those two beauties transported me to heaven. I never knew that lovemaking could be that wonderful. Not bad for a yalla gal born in the cotton fields of South Carolina."

***

Had not both Paul and Joanne been cast in *Picnic*, their long-enduring love affair might never have blossomed. Years later, Joanne told an interviewer that, "Paul and I tried to run away from each other for five years."

The outspoken Rod Steiger called that remark "pure bullshit! They were like two drivers in hot rods playing chicken as they rushed toward each other for a head-on crash. They came together in a fiery explosion of emotions. Once Joanne had decided that she wanted Paul more than any other man, she set out to get him. That he had a wife stashed away somewhere didn't really seem to matter. But it mattered to Paul."

"I knew him well at the time," Steiger claimed. "The man had a conscience and a strong feeling of responsibility about his kids. Of course, that didn't stop him from having affairs with everybody else. From James Dean to Eartha Kitt, Paul tumbled head-on into an extremely complicated life. He was the Golden Boy of Broadway. Hell, he was so fucking beautiful. Everybody wanted him, and he was willing to share the goodies with both men and women, not just Joanne and Jackie. Paul was so pretty I would have fucked him if he'd asked me to, and I'm about the straightest actor in the business. Marlon confided to me that he'd pounded Paul's beautiful ass on many an occasion. At one point Paul was more in love with James Dean than he was with either Joanne or Jackie."

"One day the Bitch Goddess of them all, Hollywood Herself, knocked on his dressing room door," Steiger said. "She'd come to claim our boy as one of her victims. Few could resist her allure, not even old Rod Steiger himself. Paul was a tasty morsel waiting to be devoured."

Knocking on that door was Stephen Brill, an agent from Warner Brothers. He made an offer a cash-strapped actor could hardly refuse: a five-year contract at one thousand dollars a week.

Although tantalized by the money and fame of becoming a movie star, Paul cringed when he heard what was in store for him. "We at Warners think you can be groomed to be the second Brando."

Chapter Three
Skinny Legs in a Cocktail Dress

Paul did not immediately rush to sign the five-year contract with Warner Brothers that had been offered to him during the run of *Picnic*. He needed time to think it over.

He also remained confused about his personal life—Jackie or Joanne? He told Rod Steiger, "Why do both women have to have names that begin with a J? It just makes it all the more confusing."

In 1953, at this point in his life, three roads lay before him, and he didn't known which one to travel. There were those who hailed him as "The Golden Boy of Broadway," and offers were coming in for future roles on the stage.

Other friends told him that he could become "The Golden Boy" of television—"the little box," as he called it. His TV roles, their scope and variety, were so daunting a challenge that he felt they were better opportuities for his growth as an actor than the Actors Studio itself.

The third possibility involved the biggest challenge of all: How to become the new golden boy of Hollywood, where the competition was much keener? He was tempted by the money Warners was offering, and he was not immune to the glamour of Hollywood, but he feared he'd be trapped in a long-term studio contract and forced to "make God-awful movies."

As he pondered his career choices, yet another possibility emerged before him. Instead of signing the contract with a studio, he could freelance and go after the roles that both Marlon Brando and Monty Clift were turning down. As a freelancer, he'd probably have greater control over his own destiny.

In the meantime, he had to earn a living. His agent presented him with a script that intrigued him for an episode ("One for the Road") within a television series called *The Web*. The teleplay would costar Wally Brown and Grace Raynor.

Although at the time, Grace was just breaking into television, she eventually became a familiar face on such future series as *Perry Mason* and *77*

Sunset Strip before she disappeared from the radar screen in 1964.

Wally Brown, whose career dated back to the days of vaudeville, was already familiar to Paul. In the 40s, RKO tried to emulate the comedy *schtick* of Abbott and Costello by pairing Brown with Alan Carney. Their broad slapstick style wasn't commercially successful, although one of their films, *Zombies on Broadway (1945)*, co-starring Bela Lugosi, eventually evolved into a camp classic. The wannabe duo lost their contracts in 1946.

Brown gave Paul some unwelcome advice. "The mistake Alan Carney and I made was in trying to imitate Abbott and Costello. They say you're the new Brando, but be yourself. Your own man. With that pretty face of yours, you'll go over big."

***

Montgomery Clift, who continued a routine of heavy drinking, kept his promise to Paul about recommending him for film scripts he'd rejected. One such script was entitled *On the Waterfront*. Monty had already achieved acclaim playing a boxer in *From Here to Eternity*, which had been released in 1953, and did not want to be cast as a fighter again. But he felt the role of Terry Malloy would be an ideal vehicle to introduce Paul to movie audiences. Monty called Elia Kazan, the project's director, who agreed to give Paul a screen test, and arranged for him to receive a copy of the script.

As soon as Paul received it, he read it nine times in one night, believing not only that this would be a fantastic part for him, but that the movie itself had a chance of becoming a classic *film noir*.

But before Kazan moved ahead with his decision to cast Paul in the role, he received a call from Sam Spiegel, the producer of the film, who demanded that the role be offered to Brando. "I know there's bad blood between the two of you," Spiegel told Kazan. "But I'm the boss around here and I want you to do it."

Reluctantly, Kazan sent a copy of the script to Brando. The actor had already told the press that he'd never work with Kazan again because "he turned canary and exposed all his commie friends." Brando was referring to Kazan's notorious 1952 appearance before the House Committee on Un-American Activities, where he submitted the names of eleven of his Broadway and Hollywood co-workers, accusing them of having supported Communist platforms and ideals.

Although Brando quickly realized that the role of Terry Malloy would be ideal for him, he called Kazan and told him, "I like the part but I can't work with a traitor like you." Then he slammed down the phone.

After rejections from both Brando and Monty, Kazan decided to take a chance on a newcomer, Paul Newman. "Monty had more or less convinced me that Newman could play the part, and I knew him and had seen his work. I thought he'd be convincing as a young fighter." Ironically, the director was predicting Paul's breakthrough role when he'd play a fighter in *Somebody Up There Likes Me*, released in 1956.

Kazan called Karl Malden and asked him to coach Paul, grooming him for the screen test. Malden had already been promised the role of the priest in *Waterfront*. "I've got to have something really hot to show Sam Spiegel. You select the girl to work with Newman."

Malden had been impressed with the acting of Joanne Woodward, and he asked her to rehearse with Paul. She gladly accepted. "There was a definite chemistry between the two," Malden recalled.

He worked tirelessly with both Joanne and Paul until he felt they were "camera ready." Then he called Kazan. "I've found your stars," Malden said. "Newman and Woodward as a couple will sizzle on the screen. You can give them a screen test and shoot the results over to Spiegel." Kazan seemed delighted with the test and sent it to Spiegel. Weeks went by and there was no response from the producer.

"Paul was nervous," Malden said. "He knew there was a lot at stake."

When word came in from Spiegel, it was a devastating blow to Paul. The producer had promised the role of the young fighter from Hoboken to Frank Sinatra, who was virtually claiming "native son status," being the most famous man to ever emerge from this then-grimy New Jersey port city. Spiegel told Kazan that "Frankie would give his left nut to play Terry Malloy."

There were more surprises awaiting both Kazan and Paul. "Who knows why, but Marlon finally changed his mind without anyone twisting his arm," Malden wrote in his autobiography, *When Do I Start?* "I had to wonder if all this talk about Paul Newman or Frank Sinatra playing the part that Marlon knew in his heart belonged to him was all it took for him to put his political ideals aside and follow his actor's heart. It was simple really: How could he pass up that part?"

As for Joanne, perhaps she never thought that she had a serious chance to play the female lead. Instead, the role went to another blonde, Eva Marie Saint.

The day Paul learned that Brando was back in the picture, he received a call from the actor himself. Although at first he was reluctant to accept, Paul agreed to come over that night and be with Brando.

Karl Malden
Getting Paul camera-ready

Shelley Winters later claimed that Brando seduced Paul that night. "Marlon had this sick thing about fucking his male competition. He'd even seduced Burt Lancaster when Burt—my former lover—was seriously considering appearing on Broadway as Stanley Kowalski in *Streetcar*. I'm not a psychologist, but maybe Marlon felt that by inserting what he called 'my noble tool' into his rival, he showed his dominance over them both as an actor and as a man. When it comes to Marlon, one can only speculate what goes on in that beautiful head of his."

"The more interesting question," Shelley said, "is why Paul allowed himself to be used like that. It must have been humiliating for him. But he was mesmerized by Brando. In my opinion, he wanted to be Brando. Yet he hated those comparisons between Brando and himself, even though they were deserved at the time. Paul told me, 'Some day, dammit, they're gonna say Marlon Brando looks like *me*.'"

When Brando finally accepted the role, Spiegel dropped Sinatra, who threatened to sue him. "The reason is money," Spiegel told Kazan. "I can get my investors to double the bankroll with Brando instead of Sinatra."

After watching Brando win the Oscar for *On the Waterfront*, Paul later revealed that he received a call from Monty. "We got together and pulled the biggest drunk of our lives. For Monty, that was really saying something. The vodka flowed like a river. He cursed himself for turning down the part, and I drank for the role that got away."

***

While filming *On the Waterfront*, director Elia Kazan plotted his next feature film, *East of Eden*, eventually released in 1954. His fantasy cast included Montgomery Clift and Marlon Brando, playing brothers, even though physically the two actors did not look alike. Both Clift and Brando turned down the parts of a modern-day Cain and Abel, as portrayed in the best-selling John Steinbeck novel.

During the casting of *On the Waterfront,* Kazan had considered Paul and Joanne Woodward for the leading players.

Now, although he remained secretive about the casting of *East of*

Rod Steiger with **Brando**
"I could have been a contender!"

Eden, he once again considered Paul teamed with Joanne. But seemingly every other day, he thought James Dean and Julie Harris would bring more sensitivity to the roles.

Kazan was also considering Richard Davalos, a New York actor of Greek-American ancestry, for the lesser role of the brother Aron, with either James Dean or Paul playing the more prominent role of Caleb Trask.

In a bizarre move, Kazan decided to bring both Dean and Paul together for a joint screen test. He wanted to analyze whatever chemistry existed between the two actors if he cast them as brothers.

When Paul got a call to go to a Brooklyn studio for the screen test, he thought that once again Monty was looking after him, letting him have a chance at the bigger star's "rejects."

Eager to be cast in the role of Caleb in the movie, Paul was startled to encounter James Dean in the studio testing for the same picture. Paul was alarmed when he learned that their screen test would be together.

For the occasion Paul looked pretty, having dressed in a white shirt with a spotted bowtie. To give himself more of a rogue-like appearance, he placed a cigarette behind his left ear. In a casual blue sports shirt, Dean appeared more relaxed, with his glasses tucked into his shirt pocket.

Kazan didn't show up for the test but delegated it to a young, inexperienced director.

Part of the original sound track and film clips from that actual test remain today.

In the background you can hear the off-camera director calling to the actors, "Hey, you two queens, look this way."

"I don't want to look at him," Paul said. "He's a sourpuss."

"I don't like him either," Dean said.

The director then called for the men to look right into the camera. Paul and Dean followed instructions. Then the director called out for them to look at each other. At this point, both Dean and Paul broke into laughter as they stared at each other face to face.

Dean moved toward Paul and said, "Kiss me!" "Not here," Paul shot back. Impulsively, he pinched Dean's ass instead.

The director called out to Paul. "Do you think Jimmy will appeal to bobbysoxers?"

Paul appraised Dean from

The James Dean/Paul Newman screen test
"Kiss me!"

head to toe. "I don't know. Is he going to be a sex symbol? I don't usually go out with boys. With his looks, sure, I think they'll flip for him."

The test was completely unscripted. Writing about that test years later, Dean biographer David Dalton said, "What determined the winner was the face: Both Jimmy and Paul Newman were nascent icons, with features that were to become as easily recognizable as Christ, Mao, or Mickey Mouse. But in this test, Jimmy's entire countenance rippled with expression while the signals in Newman's eyes and mouth were almost vaudevillian numbers restricted to isolated parts of his face. Newman's expressions were typecast into smile, frown, and cool stare, but Jimmy's face resisted and relaxed in alternating currents."

On leaving the studio, Dean seemed to realize the role of Caleb was his. "Maybe we'll be cast as brothers," he told Paul. "It's a lesser part, but Aron is a strong role."

As both Dean and Paul headed back to Manhattan that day, Dean turned to him and smiled. "The day is not completely lost. Let's go to this brownstone where I'm living on West Sixty Eight Street. You can fuck me for the rest of the day. That's gotta mean something."

En route to his brownstone, Dean told Paul, "I ran into Marlon the other day. He asked about you. I told him that on some days I'm in love with him. On other days I'm in love with you. But I claimed you and I never made it. Marlon told me that he'd never made it with you either. Both of us knew we were lying."

Two days later Kazan called Paul with the bad news. "I've decided to go with James Dean in the part of Caleb. He came out better in the screen test."

"What about me playing Aron?" Paul asked, barely concealing his disappointment.

"I've given the part to Richard Davalos," Kazan said. "He's ten years younger than you."

"Are you saying I'm too old for Aron?" Paul asked. "Then give me the father role. But, I'm warning you, you'll have to age me. I'm not *that* old."

"You're out of luck there too," Kazan said. "I gave the part of Adam to Raymond Massey."

"Okay," Paul said sarcastically, "I'll play Aron's girlfriend in drag."

"Julie Harris has the part," Kazan said. "Your girlfriend, Woodward, would have been terrific in the part, but Harris will be great. By the way, I saw Julie yesterday at the Actors Studio. She said she adores you."

"Not my type," Paul said, putting down the phone.

***

At that point in her life, Joanne had not committed to Paul. "How could I?" she asked Rod Steiger. "He's still married with a wife that's pregnant again." She was thrilled to have been accepted at Actors Studio. Like Paul, she was starting out getting experience in live television.

Teleplays kept coming Joanne's way, and in 1954 she could be seen on "the box" in such dramas as *The Dancers, Stir Mugs, Unequal Contest, Interlude, Five Star Final, Segment, Welcome Home,* and *Homecoming.*

It was her role in *Interlude* that brought her to the attention of Fox executive Buddy Adler. He promised her a film contract, which was slow in coming. In letters, she kept Paul posted, promising that she'd soon be joining him in Hollywood.

Paul was up for yet another movie role in 1954 during the casting of *Battle Cry*, based on the Leon Uris novel of marines in World War II, which had a key role for a young soldier, that of Danny Forrester.

Bill Orr, the son-in-law of Jack Warner, conducted a joint screen test of both Paul and Joanne. "They came in with a preconceived idea of what they wanted to do in the scene," Orr said. "First they rolled around on a mattress and on the floor, and then they jumped up and engaged in a boxing match. Then they rolled around on a blanket. There were other sundry peccadilloes. It had to be the worst screen test in the history of motion pictures. I suggested to Jack that he give the role of Danny to James Dean. Dean could pull this one off. Newman came off as a jerk."

On hearing the bad news, Paul said, "Losing out to Dean I understand. But the world must never know that I lost the role to Tab Hunter. How could I ever live that down at the Actors Studio? Another God damn humiliation from Hollywood. Too fucking bad. My baby blues in CinemaScope would have lit up the screen."

Joanne also lost the role of the love-hungry Navy wife, the part going to Dorothy Malone.

After the bitter disappointment of losing out on three consecutive movie roles, Paul decided "to become another hired hand at Warner Brothers." He signed the contract, even though Geraldine Page warned him, "Hollywood will destroy you."

He made another major decision. He was going to leave Jackie, Scott, and Susan stashed behind. It was a painful decision, and he knew the risk he was taking. Going to

Janice Rule
Confidential

85

Hollywood as a "bachelor" could well lead to the dissolution of his marriage.

Janice Rule later revealed that Paul practically wept when he learned that Jackie was pregnant with another child. "Unless you want to produce eighteen offspring," Janice warned him, "there are precautions a couple can take."

In saying goodbye to Eartha Kitt, Paul told her, "Something tells me I've got to be free as a bird in Hollywood. It's not that I'm completely ducking my responsibilities. I told Jackie I'll send her a generous portion of my earnings. After all, I'm going to be making one thousand big ones a week."

In telling Rod Steiger goodbye, Paul told him, "I'm not sure I'm the type of guy who wants to come home to face an angry wife every night, especially one who wants to know what I was doing until four in the morning. I like to come home when roosters are crowing. Do you know how many propositions I get in the course of one day, mostly from women, but a ton from men too? Some of these offers are so tempting I can't resist. Maybe I'm more like Marlon Brando than I thought. He told me he believes in sharing 'my noble tool with the world.'"

Steiger later speculated that it was far more difficult for Paul to say goodbye to Joanne than to Jackie. "I don't know what really happened on their final night together," Steiger said. "But I bet the sheets caught on fire."

Paul may have told Joanne and he certainly told his comrades at the Actors Studio, "I'll be more like Humphrey Bogart in Hollywood. He never sold out to any studio, and I won't either."

"Good luck," Eartha Kitt had told him after a final visit in her boudoir. "Those directors will treat you like another piece of meat to devour. They'll suck you dry. They are, after all, carnivores."

"Tell me something I don't know," he told her. "Paul Newman knows how to take care of himself."

"On the way to Hollywood, I had anxieties about my age," Paul later told Geraldine Page one night in Los Angeles. "Hell, Marlon made *The Men* before he was twenty-five, and James Dean is on the dawn of a big film career at an unripe age. Here I am pushing thirty. Some men in their thirties have daughters near the marrying age. Fortunately, I still look fifteen. I imagine that Dorian Gray portrait of mine in the closet is showing a wrinkle or two. I know how youth-obsessed America is, and here I am, 'Daddy Newman,' trying to become the next hot stud. Who knows, if Joan Crawford keeps her promises to me, I'll end up her new leading man. Of course, that means I'll have to keep plowing it to the bitch."

"Brando inspires me," Paul said to Geraldine. "Also Dean, to an extent. I want to be as wild as those rebels, Hollywood's new bad boy. For the first time, I want to shake Shaker Heights out of my blood stream. A man like me would be a sucker not to live to the fullest, wife or no wife. Jackie was so hot for me, she insisted on marriage. She pushed me into that dubious institution before I was ready."

***

Arriving in Hollywood for the first time, Paul checked into a seedy hotel near the Warners lot. "It was filled with hustlers, hookers, and drug dealers," he later recalled. "I didn't get much sleep. There were knocks on my door all night with offers. He quoted some of the temptations placed before him.

"Hey, man, I give the best blow-job in Hollywood," came a high-pitched voice. "I've sucked off Peter Lawford and Burt Lancaster."

"Honey," came the sultry voice of a woman. "I've got the tightest pussy in Hollywood. I've had it surgically altered."

"I've got good stuff, *hombre*, fresh from Tijuana."

On his first day at the studio, he was told he had to take a screen test before winning the role of a slave, Basil, in *The Silver Chalice*, a toga epic that Warners hoped would make as much money as did *Quo Vadis?* with Robert Taylor or *The Robe* with Richard Burton.

His test with the star of the picture, Virginia Mayo, the former Samuel Goldwyn leading lady, was a disaster. Although Paul photographed beautifully, his acting was wooden.

When his screen test was shown to cigar-chomping executives at Warners, Paul was ordered to report to the Studio Hairdressing Department. "Mr. Kenneth," in charge of operations, already had his instructions in the form of a memo. "Make his hair blonder—not exactly Marilyn Monroe, but a cross between Alan Ladd and Tab Hunter."

Mr. Kenneth was a gossip, and he informed Paul that James Dean had been the first choice to play the young Greek sculptor, Basil. Dean said he told Jack Warner it was a piece of shit and turned it down. Wise choice. He's supposed to be terrific in *East of Eden*."

Studio chieftains asked Virginia to work seven days a week with Paul to get him ready for another try at a screen test.

At her home in Thousand Oaks, California, shortly before her death, Virginia recalled that working with Paul "wasn't exactly a hardship. He was extremely handsome and gifted. But he'd never done any classical pictures, and this one was simply too difficult for him. He was still a novice in the movie business, after all, and they probably shouldn't have expected this of him. He should not have agreed to do the film, but he was young and eager to make a name for himself."

She claimed she spent two entire weeks working with him and "I would have fallen in love with him if it had lasted any longer." On her second test

87

with Paul, she said he had vastly improved, and this time the studio chiefs countersigned the contract that he'd originally signed in New York.

"Paul was off on that rocky road to becoming a movie star," Virginia said, "and I warned him about some of the pitfalls. Frankly, I misjudged him. I thought he'd end up on that long list of pretty boys who emerged in the 50s never to be heard of again. Working with him during his first picture gave me no clue that he'd become such a big star—and a legendary one at that."

"This is religioso shit," Paul wrote to Joanne back in New York. "I was horrified, traumatized appearing before the camera in a cocktail dress to show off my skinny legs."

This dull, confused, and muddled film was shot against cheesy sets with the actors clad in bargain-basement wardrobes. The plot was based on a best-selling novel by Thomas B. Costain. But Paul felt that Lester Samuels, writing the screenplay, had been inept.

"How can I recite such laughable dialogue?" he asked Virginia. He quoted a typical line to her: "Helena, is it really you? What a joy!"

Virginia Mayo was cast as Helena, with vampiric eyebrows. She played Paul's *inamorata*.

Pier Angeli, as Deborra, was to be Paul's other love interest. Also dyed blonde, Natalie Wood, with whom Paul would become involved in the future, played Helena as a child.

The character actor, Jack Palance, gave the most show-stealing performance as Simon the Magician.

"Palance had the only good moment in the film," Paul recalled. The magician is convinced he could fly. Mounting a tower, he jumps off. And, of course, movie-goers could predict the consequences once Palance was air-

The virginal **Pier Angeli** (left); and the vampiric **Virginia Mayo**
Torn between two lovers and a *Silver Chalice*

borne. In the picture, Paul, artisan turned slave, was ordered to craft the silver chalice that Jesus Christ drank from at The Last Supper.

Paul wanted out of his contract, but was forced to complete the film, which was directed by Victor Saville, a British expatriate. Despite his illustrious past in the film industry, *The Silver Chalice* was the wrong film for Saville. Between 1927 and 1954, he'd directed 39 movies, and between 1923 and 1962, he produced 36 films. They included *Goodbye, Mr. Chips* (1939), *A Woman's Face* (1941), *Above Suspicion* (1943), and *Green Dolphin Street* (1947).

"Saville didn't like me, and I didn't like him," Paul said. "I accurately predicted that *Chalice* would be the last film he'd ever direct. He'd have to spend the rest of his life living it down, as would I."

Nothing Paul did seemed to please Saville. The director later said that, "Newman was just one of those troublemakers, anarchists, and eccentrics being shipped over like cattle from New York."

"Saville was a difficult bastard to put up with," Paul said.

"I introduced Paul to his co-star, Pier Angeli, at ten o'clock one morning on the Warners lot," Saville said. "By three o'clock that afternoon, I think he was hopelessly in love. As for Pier, I think she was still in love with Kirk Douglas, or perhaps Marlon Brando."

Frail, tiny, and undeniably lovely, this Italian actress—called "The Little Garbo"—had appeared in a pair of films in her native Italy before gaining prominence in the role of a war bride in *Teresa* in 1951. The tabloids created a ballyhoo of a big romance between Pier and Kirk Douglas during their time together in 1952 shooting *The Story of Three Loves* with an all-star cast.

Unlike the hardened, career-driven "bitches" he'd met on Broadway and at the Actors Studio, Paul was enchanted by Pier's infectious laugh. He called her "virginal" and referred to her "refreshing innocence."

Actually she wasn't all that virginal. The Italian director, Vittorio De Sica, had introduced Pier—then known as Anna Maria Pierangeli—to Brando, hoping to cast the pair of them in his upcoming movie. Pier had confided to Virginia Mayo that she'd fallen in love with Brando, and that he'd "deflowered" her on a grassy knoll near Rome's Colosseum. "He went back to America and dumped me," Pier told Virginia.

Cast as Deborra, the Christian girl Paul marries in *The Silver Chalice*, Pier "looked radiant in Madonna blue with a gold circlet in her hair," in the words of her biographer Jane Allen. Forgetting about his wife or even Joanne, Paul fell hard for Pier, at least according to Virginia.

Although the singer Vic Damone was still a presence in Pier's life, she began to date Paul secretly. She even invited him to her family's home for an Italian Sunday dinner.

Paul at first enchanted Pier's overly protective mother, Enrica Pierangeli. But the day turned sour when Enrica learned that Paul "is not a Catholic. Not only that, but he has the Jew's blood in his veins." That night Enrica forbade her daughter ever to see Paul again, except on the set of *The Silver Chalice,* where she'd be forced to say lines to him in front of the camera.

After that, Paul was never seen in public with Pier outside of the movie lot. Virginia noted that Pier spent long hours in Paul's dressing room, and "I could only assume they were having sex. Brando had already broken in this angelic-looking little creature."

"I don't think there was any great love affair going on between these two," Virginia claimed. "I know that seems to contradict what I said earlier about Paul falling hopelessly in love with Pier. Perhaps he did, but I think that spell she cast over him lasted for only a few days. Paul was a very sensible young man, and he soon returned to reality."

"For the rest of the shoot, their romance was relatively harmless in spite of the sex," Virginia said. "She always seemed to have the giggles around him, and he was always playing tricks on her. Of course, there was the inevitable touching. They couldn't seem to keep their hands off each other. But I think even these two little lovesick puppies knew that theirs was an affair only of the moment. Nothing serious would come of it."

To complicate matters even more, James Dean, who was shooting *East of Eden* on a neighboring set on the Warners lot, strolled over to see Paul work. He introduced Dean to Pier.

"A romantic Romeo and Juliet legend was born that day between James Dean and Pier Angeli," Virginia said. "From what I observed, Pier and Dean were smitten with each other for about three weeks. The press and all those Dean biographers made far too much of this romance. If James Dean was in love with anybody on the set of *The Silver Chalice*, it was Paul Newman himself."

***

If Paul ever resented Dean taking Pier from him, he apparently never revealed this to anyone. "What could he say anyway?" Virginia asked. "He was a married man with two kids back in the East somewhere."

Actually, during the shooting of *East of Eden*, Dean saw a lot more of Paul than he did of Pier. Whereas Enrica found Paul objectionable, she came to loathe Dean, who was rude and even

Pier Angeli dumps Paul for a bored **James Dean**

downright hostile to her. "My daughter forced that horrible young man upon us until I put my foot down and ordered him out of our house forever," Enrica said. "But he was head over heels in love with my Anna Maria, although I began to hear stories about a wild homosexual streak in him."

Many biographers have suggested that the romance between Dean and Pier was platonic. Elia Kazan, the director of *East of Eden*, disagreed. "My dressing room was across the hall from Dean's. I could actually hear them making love through the thin walls. Dean was very vocal. Not a sound could be heard from Pier. The sex would usually end in a big argument. After one of these blow-ups, Dean always got drunk. I don't know how I ever finished the picture with him."

For his dates with Paul, Dean preferred some hamburger joint near a beach. He might be photographed in a tuxedo with Pier, but when he was with Paul he wore casual tight-fitting jeans, a T-shirt, and a black leather jacket, evocative of Brando's appearance in *The Wild One*.

A Sunday afternoon in Hollywood might find Paul and Dean riding horses in Griffin Park. At one point, Dean purchased matching gold friendship rings, and offered one to Paul. According to Rogers Brackett, Paul wore the ring for only a few days, before putting it away somewhere.

"When Hollywood wasn't gossiping about Pier and Dean, they were even more secretively gossiping about the strange friendship between Dean and Newman," Elia Kazan said. "I'm sure word got back to Joanne in New York. Even more devastating, I was told that word had also gotten back to Paul's wife, Jackie, and that she'd threatened to leave him and take his children if he didn't end his friendship with Dean."

"Paul refused to end the friendship, and the marriage puttered on," Kazan said. "But the bells were tolling, signaling the end of that marriage. Even so, it took a long time to die. I think the marriage ended long before the divorce finally came."

While he was making *The Silver Chalice*, Paul received a letter from Jackie. She told him that she was leaving the New York area and taking his son and daughter back to Wisconsin to live with her parents. His reaction to that move has never been revealed. "He had James Dean," Kazan said. "What did he need with a wife and kids? Paul was enjoying every moment of his bachelorhood, and wilder days were on the way when he moved over to the Chateau Marmont."

Sometimes Pier would defy her mother and ask Dean to take her to his favorite restaurant, the Villa Capri, a Los Angeles rendezvous for celebrities such as Frank Sinatra. Photographers and autograph seekers staked the place out.

Dean's patron, Rogers Brackett, said that Dean specifically patronized the

Villa Capri, usually with an attractive female in tow, because he'd been ordered by Jack Warner to be seen dating starlets. One of these was Terry Moore, the so-called secret "wife" of Howard Hughes.

In one of the rare instances he talked to the press, Dean spoke of his involvement with Pier. "Nothing complicated. I'm dating a nice girl for a change. One I can talk to. One who understands me. A good friendship. I respect her. She's untouchable, a Madonna. We move in different circles. Anyway, marriage is out of the question. Her old lady is the boss, and she doesn't like me. Not that I blame her."

The booze, the marijuana, the sudden outbursts of violence became too much for Pier. Without Dean's knowledge, she'd been dating Vic Damone. One night she suddenly broke off with Dean, telling him of her impending marriage. He beat her severely that night, or so he confessed to Elia Kazan. "I went crazy, I guess. Imagine marrying a singer who can't even sing. I sing better than Damone."

When Paul wasn't needed on the set of *The Silver Chalice*, he strolled over to visit Dean on the *East of Eden* set. Increasingly, Dean was feuding with both Kazan and the co-star of the picture, aging character actor Raymond Massey, who played his father.

Paul feared that Dean was becoming more and more anti-social. One afternoon when Kazan was showing some VIPs from New York around the set, Dean pulled out his penis and relieved his bladder right on the floor in front of an audience. "He didn't even bother to turn his back on us," Paul later said.

After urinating, Dean stormed off to his dressing room. When the VIPs had departed in shock from the set, Kazan walked over to Paul and put his arm around him.

"I made a big mistake in not casting you for the lead in this picture," Kazan told Paul. "As a result, you're filming that shit next door. I don't know if I'm going to survive this film with Dean. And I thought Brando was difficult to work with. Dean is highly neurotic. Is psychotic the word? Yesterday it got so bad I kicked his ass. He won't speak his lines clearly. He questions my direction. He may not even be an actor at all. I turn the camera on him and what I get is this obviously sick young man coming apart right on film. He is so stupid, so very stupid. His face is that of a poet, so very beautiful. It registers his pain and desolation. Maybe the Academy will take that for great acting and award him an Oscar."

***

When he reported to work on the set of *The Silver Chalice*, Paul heard a knock on his door. It was a studio messenger summoning him to the office of the director, Victor Saville. "So, he's on to me," Paul told the messenger. "My gut tells me I'm getting fired today. I wonder what fucker—or should I say sucker?—Saville has hired to replace me in this turkey?"

In Saville's office, Paul was stunned to encounter Joan Crawford once again. He hadn't seen her since that torrid "audition night" in New York. He'd later tell Virginia Mayo that "Joan was dressed as if she were about to assume the office of the first female President of the United States."

Joan walked over and kissed Paul on the lips. I've missed you, darling," she said. "Welcome to Hollywood." She turned and smiled at Saville. "Victor and I go way back. Don't tell him how long, dear heart."

Saville had produced *A Woman's Face* in 1941, a picture directed by George Cukor, and he'd also produced one of Joan's lesser films, *Above Suspicion*, in 1943, in which Joan starred opposite the wooden Fred MacMurray.

Rising from his chair, Saville discreetly removed himself from his office. "I know Joan has some private business to discuss with you."

Once the door was shut behind him, Joan moved toward Paul to give him a more thorough kissing. He responded with equal ardor.

"Stop, darling," she said, backing away. "Let's save those commando activities for tonight. A star never wants to mess up her makeup, especially when she's walking around a studio."

She walked over to Saville's liquor cabinet and poured both of them a vodka, even though it was only ten o'clock in the morning. "I'm not a bull-shitter. In New York I promised we'd be working together, with you as my leading man. The deal's come through. Yes, yes, I know it's for Republic Pictures, but let's don't go into that. Nicholas Ray is going to direct, and he's the hottest in Hollywood."

"I'm under contract," Paul said.

"Please, don't you think I still have pull at Warners?" she asked. "For years I've been the virtual Queen of Warners."

Over drinks she informed him that she'd acquired the rights to a Western called *Johnny Guitar*. It was a novel by Roy Chanslor. "Peggy Lee's going to sing 'Johnny Guitar.' I'm sure it'll be a hit. There are two strong women's roles. I'm urging Republic to hire Bette Davis for the other female lead. Can you just imagine the box office with Bette Davis and I starring in the same movie?"

"That I've got to see," he said in astonishment. "You and Bette Davis in Western drag?"

"Not only that, but at the end Bette and I will square off in a duel to the death."

"My God, I'm buying the first ticket."

"Here's where you come in. I want you for the role of Dancin' Kid. I'm cast as Vienna, a saloon keeper. Bette and I will be fighting over you. *Johnny Guitar* will make you one of the biggest stars in Hollywood. Not *The Silver Chalice*. Even Victor knows that picture's a bust before it's released."

"I'm for it," Paul said, almost without reservation. "To appear on the screen with Bette Davis and Joan Crawford, I'd do anything! I mean anything!"

"Darling, I'll hold you to that promise later tonight," she said. "By the way, you got that billing wrong. Republic has already agreed. It's Joan Crawford and Bette Davis in that order. Don't make that mistake again."

The next day Paul told Virginia Mayo that Joan Crawford "has fallen madly in love with me. What a night! What a woman!"

Wiser in the ways of Hollywood, Virginia warned him "don't get your hopes up until the ink dries on the contract. Even then, you can't be sure."

Johnny Guitar taught Paul a valuable lesson. Most pictures don't necessarily end up with the first cast mentioned. Two weeks later Joan called Paul at Warners with the bad news.

Herbert J. Yates, the owner of Republic, had decided that the combined billing of Joan Crawford with Bette Davis would be too expensive. "He told me my name along could carry the picture," Joan said. "As for the role of the Dancin' Kid, Yates has cast Scott Brady. But, as I told you, I'm not a bullshitter. I will virtually guarantee you that you'll get the lead in my next picture."

After hearing that bad news, Paul turned down Joan's invitation to come to her home for a nightcap that evening.

A few days later, a columnist floated the item that Scott Brady and Joan Crawford were having a torrid affair.

The ruggedly handsome Sterling Hayden, who eventually played the other male lead in *Johnny Guitar*, later lamented that Joan's fantasy cast didn't work out. "It would have become the camp classic of all time. The gays alone would have made it a box office bonanza. Hell, each one of those fellows would have gone to see the thing forty times each. Picture it. Bette Davis and Joan Crawford as cowgals battling over pretty boy Newman."

Joan Crawford in *Johnny Guitar* rated Paul better in the sack than John Wayne

"If there were any jealousy over the mutual involvement with Pier Angeli, it didn't manifest itself. In the weeks that followed Dean's breakup with Pier, Paul and Dean grew even closer together, the most intimate they would ever become during the short history of their friendship.

With his $1,000-a-week paycheck, Paul could afford a motorcycle to match the one Dean rode up and down the southern coast of California.

Laguna Beach was their favorite spot for overnighting. One of Dean's favorite waterfront joints was called "The Point," and the two of them could be seen there every weekend. Sometimes late at night Paul, at Dean's urging, would strip naked and jump with him into the surf, where the waves crashed around them. After a midnight swim, Dean would make love to Paul on the moonlit sands.

It is only because of Rogers Brackett that we know of this secret period in Paul's life. Perhaps in a sadistic mode, Dean liked to give Rogers a detailed account of his sexual adventures, either one-on-one encounters or else his participation in orgies. He knew this would hurt Rogers, who was very jealous.

"Jimmy always felt he'd prostituted himself in front of me, and that I'd taken advantage of him when he was a struggling actor," Rogers said. "He felt he had to pay me back for that. I thought that once he became a movie star and was financially independent, I'd seen the last of him. But he always came back. The reason is simple: Perhaps without Jimmy really realizing it, I'd become the father figure he never had."

Dean invited Paul to spend many "wild, wild" weekends with him in Tijuana. One of Dean's favorite cafes had a Western name, The Last Chance Saloon. A battered neon sign outlining the figure of a cowboy in chartreuse flickered invitingly over the door.

Instead of songs of Old Mexico, the café played country and western music. A long wooden bar ran the entire length of the saloon. On a small stage behind the bar, three nude women, each quite busty and overweight, performed lascivious dances.

As the lead dancer gyrated her massive hips, Dean told Paul, "Look at her squeezing those jugs like *maracas*." At the end of the number, the patrons, mostly men from California, shouted "Ole!" Pesos were thrown at the nude uglies.

The act was followed by the appearance of two brown-skinned twins who looked no more than fourteen years old. They didn't dance but mostly rubbed their bodies together rotating their pelvises, eventually leaning backwards as they rubbed their young vaginas together.

When the pesos landed on the floor, each girl turned the coins on their sides. Straddling the money, they seemed to suck the coins into their bodies.

"We want those two," Dean instructed the manager. He turned to Paul. "We're gonna rent a room upstairs for an hour or two."

"Don't you think they're a bit young?" Paul asked.

"Nothing is too young for this cowpoke."

On another tequila-soaked weekend, Paul attended an orgy with Dean, at least according to the account told to Rogers. Marijuana smoke competed with incense in a candlelit upstairs room painted a garish purple.

There must have been eighteen people at the orgy, almost equally divided between men and women. Four of the visitors were German tourists. "It was a night of gliding hands, shifting bodies," Dean claimed to Rogers. "If there was an empty orifice, something was plunged into it. Paul and I were the star attractions. Everybody had us that night."

"What a hot, pornographic movie that would have made," Rogers said, masking his pain.

En route back to Los Angeles, Dean and Paul stopped at a café for cold beers. "We don't have to go down to Tijuana for an orgy. You can always find one going on at the Chateau Marmont in Hollywood. I'll help you move there this weekend."

Years later, in summing up his own experiences with Dean, Paul left out the graphic details. "Brando was originally offered the lead in *Rebel Without a Cause*," Paul said, "but Jimmy was the true rebel. Brando could be outrageous in his behavior, but Dean was beyond outrageous. He was in orbit. As he entered the last months of his life, his amusements and diversions became more and more bizarre. Ordinary sexual diversions no longer held his attention. He began to move toward a dangerous new sexual frontier for his excitement. It was as if he knew he was going to die, and he wanted to squeeze decades of life into his final precious months."

***

"It was love at first sight," Paul wrote his wife, Jackie, the day Dean checked him into the Chateau Marmont, a *faux* Loire Valley castle above the Sunset Strip in Los Angeles. Paul's favorite novel about Hollywood, *The Day of the Locust*, had been written while Nathanael West holed up in a room here.

The assistant manager who showed

The Chateau Marmont
"The best place in Hollywood
for an orgy"

96

Paul to his room claimed that "Garbo once occupied this very same room."

When he'd gone, the scent of his perfume still lingered in the air. Dean told Paul, "He tells every new guest they're occupying the room where Garbo lived."

After Paul had checked in with his meager luggage, Dean told him he had to go as he was late for an appointment. "It's with Ronald Reagan, that has-been actor. He wants me for a TV show. If he's like most aging actors in Hollywood, he'll probably want me to fuck him."

Dean was referring to a teleplay for General Electric Theater, of which Reagan was the host.

"Are you dressed for the part?" Paul asked, noting Dean's dirty clothes, his trousers held together with a safety pin.

"Reagan will have to take me as he gets me," Dean said. "I'm not gonna put on a suit and tie for that fucker, the star of *Bedtime for Bonzo*. How could he criticize anyone after that piece of shit?"

With co-stars Eddie Albert and the teenage star, Natalie Wood, Dean was appearing in *I'm a Fool*, which was adapted from a Sherwood Anderson story about an imprudent young farm boy who takes refuge in role-playing when he falls in love.

With the day off and nothing to do, Paul put on his swimming trunks and wandered down by the pool, hoping to meet some aspiring young movie stars like himself. Dean told him everybody from Tab Hunter to Peter Lawford hung out by that pool.

On this particular afternoon, there was only one guest by the pool, a tall,

Lovers **Tony Perkins** (left) and **Tab Hunter** at the peak of their male beauty.
For Tony, Paul was "a sometimes thing"

97

lithe young man, who looked extraordinarily handsome in a sensitive, poetic way. Perhaps the overcast gray day had made others stay away. Paul placed his towel on a chaise longue and settled in. The young man called to him, "Hey, come over and keep me company. I don't bite."

Within minutes, Paul was shaking the hand of Anthony Perkins, who immediately became "Tony." As it turned out, he was the son of the famous stage and screen actor Osgood Perkins. He was in town to film *Friendly Persuasion*, playing a gentle pacifist farm lad, the Quaker son of Gary Cooper and Dorothy McGuire. Paul had heard of him when he played the gay student on Broadway in *Tea and Sympathy*, but had not gone to see his performance.

Tony explained to Paul that he was normally very shy, but a director warned him he had to learn to be more aggressive in Hollywood. "Otherwise, I would never have called to you like that. I would have stretched out, showed off my body like bait, and waited for you to come to me."

"What makes you think I'm interested?" Paul asked. "I'm a married man with kids."

"Tallulah Bankhead once told the press, 'Show me a married man with three kids, and I'll show you a homosexual.'"

"Well, I am out here without my wife," Paul said, "and I'm young, handsome, and horny. A guy has needs."

Tony reached for his hand, squeezing it hard. "Let's go across the street and get better acquainted."

"You mean you don't live here?"

"I will when I get my next paycheck from the studio," Tony said. "In the meantime I'm living in this janitor's room across the street. Right now the building has no janitor, and the owner is renting me the room. It's not much but come on over to see where I live."

"I don't mind a little entertainment this afternoon," Paul said.

On the way across the street, Tony put his arm around Paul. "I read in the paper you're making *The Silver Chalice* with Mayo. Some columnists call you the boy next door, and others say you're the new Brando. Which is it?"

"That's for you to find out this afternoon," Paul said, smiling.

Tony met his smile with an even wider grin. "I think this is going to be the start of a beautiful friendship."

And so it was.

***

What we know about the friendship and decades-long love affair between Paul and Tony Perkins comes from "Vampira," who was not only Tony's dear friend but an off-again, on-again lover of James Dean as well.

This Finnish-American actress was really Maila Nurmi. She claimed to be the niece of the legendary Finnish athlete Paavo Nurmi, who broke long-distance running world records in 1921, the year before her birth. In 1944 Mae West, fearing Maila was upstaging her, booted her from her Broadway play, *Catherine Was Great.* Arriving in Hollywood, she supported herself posing for pin-up photographs in men's magazines such as *Gala.*

Maila became famous on *The Vampira Show* at KABC-TV. Running for 16 episodes in 1954, with frequent reruns during the years that followed, it provided a campy format wherein she introduced movies after making a ghoulish entrance amid dry-ice fog. As the camera zoomed in on her vampire-like face, she'd let out a piercing scream before introducing the movie of the night, as she reclined seductively on a skull-encrusted Victorian couch.

Like a Zombie-like mate of Bela Lugosi, she had heavily painted long fingernails in blood red, with a mane of raven-colored hair, and a slim-waisted black-as-night outfit.

After their session in the janitor's room, Tony was hungry and invited Paul to his favorite haunt, Googie's, at the corner of Crescent Heights and Sunset Boulevard. It was a favorite stopover for up-and-coming actors like James Dean and Jack Nicholson.

"I can still remember Tony walking in with this beautiful young man," Vampira later recalled. "Like everyone else, I fell in love with his blue eyes. I think I met Paul while he was still hot from having fucked Tony. He had the smell of sex on him, or did I just imagine that in my fantasy?"

She said that, "I adored him at once. He and Tony made such a beautiful young couple. I had the same feeling about Tony and Tab Hunter, another beautiful young man Tony had just launched an affair with. James Dean had told me about Paul, although I'd never seen him act in anything. In those days all 'the boys,' as I called them, were sleeping with each other. My friend Rock Hudson was making the rounds, and Joan Crawford seduced virtually every hot trick that arrived in Hollywood."

Vampira claimed that she was surprised that Paul formed lasting friendships with both Tony and Dean. "They were wild boys. Both of them should have been put away somewhere. They

Finnish actress **Vampira** (Maila Nurmi)
The female Bela Lugosi.
In the 50s, all the pretty boys confided
their secrets to her.

were such tormented souls. Paul seemed only mildly disturbed. It was a difficult time for him. He hated working on *The Silver Chalice*, which he made abundantly clear."

"The afternoon I met him I was shocked to learn that he had a wife and kids stashed somewhere," she said. "But he didn't seem to let that influence the alternative lifestyle he was pursuing in Hollywood. After I got to know Paul better, I made a play for him myself. But he never gave me a tumble."

"I dated Tony too but he always took me home at nine o'clock, and I had to settle for a kiss on the cheek," she said. "With Jimmy, I saw some action, but I don't think his prick was really up for it most of the time. Oh, did I tell you? I was married at the time. To a guy named Dean Reisner. At least I think that's what his name was."

Vampira was only pretending that she didn't remember the name of her first husband. Reisner was a former child actor in silent films, and he later became an acclaimed screen writer. He, in fact, was the screenwriter for *Dirty Harry*, which, ironically, was a role offered first to Paul Newman before going to Clint Eastwood.

"Throughout his life, Tony kept me in the loop on all his secrets, especially his sexual ones," Vampira said. "He was a tormented soul who really wanted to go straight. It was a hopeless undertaking. I think Paul was basically straight, and had a great love for women, but there was a wild streak in him as well. I think he wanted to suppress that dark side. But in the years I knew him I was convinced that he could be had."

"He had this sense of adventure which came out later in life when he became a race car driver," she said. "Instead of racing cars in his youth, he pursued sexual adventures, as I did."

Vampira was convinced that even though Paul and Tony appeared to have an intense sexual attraction for each other, "They never had any intention of becoming a couple. Both of them were going through a period of sexual experimentation. Nobody was being faithful to anybody in those days. Certainly not Miss Vampira."

"From that afternoon in Googie's, Tony and Paul started hanging out together," Vampira said. "They would continue to do so for all the years left to them. At that time, Paul also had Jimmy when he wasn't engaged with a dozen others. As for Tony, he was about to embark on a hot, torrid romance with Tab Hunter that became the talk of Hollywood."

"I'll let you in on a secret," Vampira said. "Another hot specimen of American manhood, Robert Francis, a true Apollo, was also in Tony's life at the time and was about to enter Paul's orbit as well. That is, when Robert wasn't involved in being the plaything of Howard Hughes. What an incestuous time the 50s were back in Hollywood. And I loved every minute of it. My only regret is that I didn't get to seduce *all* of those pretty boys. But they were too busy fucking each other."

***

During the white heat of their relationship, Paul managed to see Tony almost every day. How Tony also worked ongoing affairs with Tab Hunter and Robert Francis into his life remained a puzzle to Vampira. "You couldn't prove it by me, but Tony must have been insatiable back then," she said.

Tony even convinced Paul to walk barefoot with him from the Chateau Marmont for the entire length of the Sunset Strip to Doheny. "Those two love-birds were before their time," Vampira said. "In the late 60s, thousands of hippies could be seen walking barefoot on The Strip, but Tony and Paul, it could be said, launched the fad."

"Jimmy Dean and I often ended our night at Googie's just as Paul and Tony were beginning their day," Vampira said. "We would be wasted and Paul and Tony would come in all bright eyed and bushy tailed. Tony would order a dozen prunes and a glass of freshly squeezed orange juice, but Paul wanted the works, bacon and eggs. On some mornings, he even ordered a greasy cheeseburger for breakfast."

"Even though I knew they were bed-hopping like rabbits in those days, they seemed totally in love, totally devoted to each other when they were together," Vampira said. "Tony would tell us goodbye and then hitch a ride down Sunset Strip. He always got picked up right away. No sooner did that sexy young stud stick out his thumb than we could hear the screech of brakes from some gay male eager to pick him up and give him a ride to the studio . . . or whatever."

One evening Vampira remembered when Dean, Tony, and Paul all went with her to Googie's. "Paul and Jimmy were up on a soapbox that night. Jimmy said he was not going to become some performing monkey for the studio machine. Paul also claimed that he was not going to be turned into some paper doll created by a studio. 'Surface glamour doesn't interest me at all,' Paul said. 'These Hollywood stars can have all the false glamour they want. The estates in Beverly Hills. The swimming pools. Their fancy cars. Of course, the easy sex isn't bad.'"

"Tony shocked Jimmy and Paul when he took a different view," Vampira claimed. "'I'm going to climb the ladder of success out here,' Tony vowed. 'Go to the right parties, meet all the VIPs. I want to be a movie star and enjoy all the trappings. You guys can ride your motorcycles into the desert and hang out with rattlesnakes. Not me. I want to drink champagne with the big boys.' At that point, Jimmy took his glass of freshly squeezed orange juice and slowly drizzled it over Tony's head."

Dean was a frequent visitor to Paul's room at the Chateau Marmont. Nicolas Ray, who was directing Dean in *Rebel Without a Cause*, was also living at the Chateau Marmont. Dean confided to Paul how Ray came to select Sal Mineo for the role of Plato, the closeted gay teenager smitten with Dean's character in *Rebel*. In spite of the fact that young Sal had seduced Ray, the director still claimed, "I don't see any chemistry between you and Jimmy."

One Sunday afternoon Ray invited both Dean and Sal to his bungalow in the hotel's gardens for a script reading.

"We showed Ray we had chemistry," Dean told Paul, snickering.

"You mean you guys had sex in front of Ray?" Paul asked.

"We went at it like gangbusters, and must have carried on for an hour," Dean said. "Talk about chemistry. After that session, Sal got the part of Plato. The downside of it all is that the kid from the Bronx has fallen hopelessly in love with me. I'll have to introduce you guys and take the heat off myself."

"Thanks, but no thanks," Paul said. "I'm busy enough as it is."

***

Tony brought Paul gossip from the set of *Friendly Persuasion* where he was working with Gary Cooper. "He's quite the ladies' man," Tony said, "in spite of his rumored bisexual past. He told me he's still having an affair with Grace Kelly. Let's face it: They were terrific together in *High Noon* in spite of the nearly three decades that separate them."

"From what I hear," Paul said, "Grace likes older men. I don't have a chance with her."

"She respects older men if they're big-time stars," Tony said. "The list is long. Oleg Cassini. Bing Crosby, Ray Milland. William Holden. Clark Gable. But I hear for fun she likes hot, good-looking young guys who can still get it up."

"I've already struck out with her," Paul claimed.

"Spill the beans," Tony said.

"When I first got to New York, I was invited by some friends to attend this party in an apartment. It turned out to be Grace's apartment. I think she was a model at the time. I thought she was the most gorgeous piece of ass I'd ever seen."

"So did you make it?" Tony asked.

Paul to **Grace Kelly:**
"God had a talent for creating exceptional women."

102

"I was the last guest to leave," Paul said. "I asked her if she'd mind if I stayed behind and read for her from a scene in *The Glass Menagerie*. I wanted to know what she thought about my acting. She listened politely and issued her verdict. 'I suggest you pursue some career other than the theater,' she said."

He claimed that even though he felt terrible at the professional rejection, he wanted to try to see if he could provide some other services for her that evening. "She completely rejected me. 'You're not my type,' she told me as she showed me to the door. I agree with those who call her The Ice Queen. Even so, I'm still smitten."

In one of those coincidences that often occur in Hollywood, Paul was lying by the oval-shaped pool waiting for Tony when he saw Grace leave from one of the bungalows in the gardens. She walked past him, but not before she checked out his trim, muscular physique. He wasn't going to speak to her unless she addressed him, which she did.

"Don't I know you from somewhere?" she asked. "New York, no doubt. I know that is the oldest pickup line in the books, but your face does look familiar."

He reminded her of that party in her apartment in New York.

"Oh, I was so cruel," she said. "It just goes to show you. Jack Warner knows more about talent than I do. I hear you're making a big Biblical epic that's going to be the hottest film of the year."

"Your scouts have misinformed you," he said. "A loser."

"All actors must face a dud from time to time," she said.

"But not for their Hollywood debut."

She thought for a second. "You're right. Not for a film debut. If you bomb the first time out, this town doesn't believe in giving second chances—at least not always."

"When I met you in New York, I thought you were the most beautiful woman I'd ever seen in my life," he said. "Seeing you today, I want to revise my opinion."

She brushed her hair nervously. "I must look an awful mess." As she said that, she glanced at the distant bungalow. "A rough-and-tumble afternoon."

"You misunderstand me," he said. "You're more than the most beautiful woman. A regal princess. The Helen of Troy of Hollywood. God had a talent for creating exceptional women. Take Marlene Dietrich for example. And now we have Grace Kelly herself."

"You're such a bullshitter," she said, "but I love hearing you talk. Are you free tomorrow at three o'clock?"

"Not a thing in the world to do," he said. "No studio work at all."

She glanced at her watch and looked back once more at the bungalow.

"Knock on that bungalow door over there. I've got to go. Until tomorrow."

"I'll count the seconds," he said.

She paused and looked back at him with admiration. "Eat your Wheaties," she cautioned before racing off.

"God knows what other deep-dicking she had lined up," Paul later told Vampira over breakfast the next morning at Googie's. "Yesterday afternoon and for most of the early evening, I fucked Grace Kelly. The little shit, Paul Newman, from Shaker Heights, Ohio, got the goddess herself. Gary Cooper told Tony that Grace 'looks like a cold bitch before you take her pants down—and then she explodes.' Truer words were never said."

"Is this going to be an ongoing affair?" Vampira asked.

"I doubt that very seriously," he said. "Of course, she claimed I was the best and most beautiful man she'd ever seduced. I'm not that flattered, considering that she usually sleeps with men over a hundred. Maybe she'll call, maybe she won't. I'm a small fish in the sea. She's looking for a big whale, at least in terms of money and fame. I may have a chance to become the beach boy in her life."

"Where does the beach come in?" she asked.

"I hear that rich women on the French Riviera hire beautiful French beach boys for an afternoon of sex. When they're finished with them, they pay the dues and show them to the door, the way Grace did with me that night in New York."

"I don't know," Vampira said. "I'm not advising that you sit by the phone waiting for her to call. But I hear that even though she's promiscuous, she's terribly lonely and frustrated in her life. Looking for love that she's never found. If you settle for being a sometimes playtoy, there might be a role for you in her life. Perhaps the role of a leading man in her next picture."

"Yeah, right," he said. "I'm still waiting for that call from Joan Crawford."

"Crawford's yesterday," Vampira said. "Grace is the Hollywood of tomorrow. Fuck future Oscar winners, not the Academy winners of Hollywood's past."

"Based on what I experienced last night, I'd follow Grace Kelly to the ends of the world for another session like that. It was the best sexual experience of my life." He paused, sipping his coffee. A frown crossed his brow.

"What's the matter?" she asked.

"I just had this God-awful feeling in my gut," he said. "What if my time with Grace was the best sex I'll ever have in my entire life, the biggest high, the grandest thrill?"

"Don't worry," Vampira said. "That sexual high will only be realized, big boy, when you come to your senses and take on Vampira herself. If Grace Kelly is The Ice Queen, I'm Zorita, Princess of the Tropics. I feel a tropical heat wave coming on."

"Forget it," he said, getting up and kissing her lightly on the cheek. "I gotta go."

Years later she remembered the look of his back racing out of Googie's, and the look of something else. "Great ass!" she said to herself.

***

The following morning, Paul went down to the next floor and knocked on Tony's door. It was time for their Saturday morning barefoot walk along Sunset Strip. Tony called out to him but there was a long delay before he actually opened the door. He was stark naked. "Come on in," Tony said, flashing a wicked smile. "Hustle your ass, boy. I don't want to stand here in the doorway putting on a show for all the faggots in this seedy joint."

Sitting up in bed, a sheet covering the lower half of his body, was one of the handsomest men Paul had ever seen, Robert Francis, who was relatively new to the Hollywood scene. As the trade papers had it, he was playing the coveted role of Ensign Willie Keith in *The Caine Mutiny*, a role he might have won by having a torrid affair with Van Johnson, who used his influence to get him the part. When not with Van or Tony, Robert was rumored to be the kept boy of Howard Hughes.

Robert jumped out of bed to shake Paul's hand. He too was stark naked, impressively so. "I've heard great things about you from Tony," Robert said.

"You're the hot new kid on the block, and I can see why," Paul said. "You—not me—were voted one of *Screen World's* Promising Personalities of 1954."

Both Tony and Robert dressed and joined Paul for the walk over to Googie's for breakfast with Vampira, who would just be ending her night as they were beginning their day.

As Vampira recalled years later, "I got there before them, and as I looked up I thought Paul, Robert, and Tony were the three most beautiful men I'd ever seen. Each one was an Adonis, a true Greek God. For the first time in my life, I wished I'd been born a handsome, good-looking gay male so I could join in on the fun."

"Robert and I became fast friends that morning," she claimed. "He had a great swimmer's build on him. He was very clean-cut. His barber had given him the faddish brush-cut at the time. I

Actor **Robert Francis:**
Cooling off after flying too close to the sun

105

thought he'd have a career in Hollywood playing loyal, flag-waving military types. Robert was at least five years younger than Paul, but he and Paul looked exactly the same age."

Vampira claimed that even though Tony had made a date to be with Paul, he had cancelled it without explanation. "Frankly, I think Tony was racing off to hook up with Tab Hunter, preferring that blond heartthrob that day over Paul or Robert. That was his choice. It wouldn't have been mine. He brought Robert and Paul together, hoping Paul would accept Robert's invitation to go flying with him. Robert was a student pilot at the time."

Driving to the airport with Robert at the wheel, Paul was astonished to learn that the pilot teaching Robert to fly was Howard Hughes. Not only that, but Paul was en route to the airport to meet the famous aviator himself.

"He's crazy about me," Robert candidly confessed. "I've replaced Guy Madison and Jack Buetel in his life. When we're together, there's no part of my body that goes unattended, even my big toe. Howard is very oral."

"Are you sure you want me to tag along today?" Paul asked. "Sounds like three's a crowd."

"No, Howard wants me to introduce him to hot young guys, especially those as good looking as you. That's part of our deal. He likes women too, although most of the broads he has stashed away in the Hollywood Hills are just for show."

Meeting Howard Hughes for the first time, Paul was impressed, although somewhat surprised by his sloppy attire. For such a world-famous aviator and movie producer—not to mention one of the world's richest men—Hughes seemed shy. Robert had warned Paul to speak loudly around Hughes because he was hard of hearing.

With very little conversation, Hughes invited Paul into his two-engine plane. Paul took a back seat as Hughes eased into the pilot's seat. Robert sat beside him as the student co-pilot.

Not even asking where they were going, Paul settled into his seat to take in a bird's eye view of the Southern California coastline. Hughes flew south, eventually heading out over the Pacific. He couldn't wait to get back to Hollywood to tell his friends that he'd been piloted by Hughes. It was only when the plane began to descend after the most scenic flight of Paul's life that Robert yelled back that they were landing on Catalina Island.

Howard Hughes: The Aviator crash-lands with Paul on Catalina.

Once on land, Paul thanked Hughes for the flight and told him how much he'd enjoyed it. All three of them got into a waiting car, with Hughes the driver. He steered them to a beachfront, avant-garde modern house overlooking the crashing rocks below.

Paul found himself invited to spend the night, and Robert showed him to his room, as Hughes had some important calls to make to the mainland. "I didn't know this was going to be an overnight thing," Paul whispered to Robert in his bedroom.

"It'll be just fine," Robert assured him. "Howard told me he likes you a lot."

"I'm not a male prostitute," Paul told Robert. "I'm not for sale."

"You don't understand," Robert said. "This man has power, wealth. He's already promised to make me the biggest male star in Hollywood. Play along. Maybe he'll make you the second biggest star in Hollywood."

"I don't know," Paul said. "I'm not into this."

Hughes called for them from the living room where he invited them for a late lunch at this little eatery he knew along the coast. "Best food in Catalina," he promised Robert and Paul. Paul enjoyed the seafood platter and began to warm to Hughes, who told them fascinating stories about his failed attempt to launch the Spruce Goose, his gigantic wooden plane built during World War II. He even claimed that several prominent Republicans had asked him to run for President of the United States against Harry S. Truman on the Democratic ticket in 1948.

After a tour of Catalina, Hughes drove both men back to their beachfront house. It was siesta time. Robert and Hughes retired to the master bedroom, but Paul wasn't sleepy. He walked along the rocky coast, communing with the seagulls. Back at the house, he noticed that Hughes and Robert were still locked away in their bedroom.

Feeling tired, he too retired but was awakened by Robert around eight o'clock. Hughes wanted to take them to dinner. As Paul would later tell Vampira, "The dinner and the conversation were just fine, just like it'd been at lunch. But I feared Hughes was going to put the move on me when we got back to the house. Perhaps a three-way with Robert. That didn't happen. We sat out and drank in the moonlight and then Hughes got up and told Paul good night. Robert followed him back into that bedroom. I guess I'd misjudged him."

As Paul would confide to Vampira two days later, he was awakened around three o'clock in the morning by some presence in his bedroom. When he bolted up, he noticed Hughes standing in the light in the doorway, lit from a lamp in the living room. He was clad only in his underwear.

"He said he was lonely and couldn't sleep," Paul told Vampira. "He asked me if he could join me in bed. There was no way I could make it with Hughes. I don't know why. I just couldn't do it. I'd hustled my ass to get launched on Broadway, but I just couldn't pull off that stunt in Hollywood. I got up and walked over to the door, indicating I was ready to close it on him. 'You've got Robert,' I told him. 'You don't need me.' He didn't say one word but turned and went back to his bedroom. I not only shut my door, I locked it."

Paul claimed that when he finally fell asleep, it was almost dawn. He woke up to find the house empty. Hughes and Robert had apparently flown back to the mainland without him. There was no note. He had to sail back to the mainland on the public ferry and make his way by bus back to the Chateau Marmont.

Vampira said that although Paul and Hughes failed to form a relationship, he continued to see Robert and Tony. "Apparently, Paul didn't blame Robert for Hughes taking French leave."

"For the next few weeks, I saw Paul spending a lot of time with both Robert and Tony," Vampira said. "I think it wasn't long before all three of them started sleeping together. The three-way with Robert and Hughes didn't work out, but Paul seemed to go for a three-way with Tony and Robert. God, did I envy those boys. Today they would surely have made a sex tape, so we could at least enjoy their romps vicariously. Sigh."

After the completion of *The Silver Chalice*, and before Paul flew back to New York, another blonde, even more famous than Grace Kelly, checked into the Chateau Marmont late at night. She wore no makeup and had sunglasses on, her hair hidden under a large scarf.

The Silver Chalice was in the can, and Paul was due at the studio at one o'clock for some publicity shots. He decided to sleep until noon. Around eleven o'clock that morning, there was a knock on his door.

Thinking it was Tony or perhaps James Dean, Paul staggered to the door in his underwear. When he opened the door, he encountered Marilyn Monroe.

"My, you look good enough to eat," she said, appraising his almost nude figure. She carried a bottle of chilled champagne with her. "Why don't you invite mommy in and give her a big, sloppy wet one to welcome her back to Hollywood. After all, I'm the reigning queen of this dump."

Marilyn Monroe: Chateau Marmont's newest resident. "Is she as frigid as rumor has it?"

***

It is mainly through Shelley Winters and Rod Steiger that we know of the ongoing relationship between Paul and Marilyn. Steiger was fascinated by Marilyn and "dug" most of the secrets of the relationship from Paul. Marilyn herself confided all her romantic trysts to Shelley, her former roommate. Although she kept most of Marilyn's secrets during her short lifetime, after Marilyn's early death Shelley became more outspoken.

From scattered, fragmented accounts revealed over the years, a rather touching love story emerged between Paul and Marilyn. When she'd flown back to Hollywood from New York, Marilyn was still hoping to play the lead in *Picnic*, starring opposite Paul.

But career moves were hardly on Marilyn's mind when she came knocking on Paul's door that long-ago morning back at the Chateau Marmont. He would later tell Steiger that it was Marilyn's voice more than her body that he "found the most seductive tool I've ever known. No one has a voice like hers."

"It was the perfect voice to sing 'Bye, Bye Baby,'" he would recall. "She almost whispers at times, luring you closer to her," he told Steiger. "She could raise that voice to make a point, then it would become a whisper again, almost a coo. There was the obvious sensuousness in her voice that sound engineers captured so brilliantly, but in person that voice was even more erotic, even though it carried a hint of desperation at all times. It also made a man feel that his *cojones* were bigger than they were. It made you want to protect Marilyn, perhaps save her from her own self-destruction."

Shelley claimed that in Paul Marilyn "found a safe port. There was no lusty pounding like you read in a pornographic novel. It wasn't that kind of a relationship. Marilyn knew that he was going through a sexually confused period of his life. Personally, I think she felt he could have gone completely gay at this point, and she wanted to lure him back to the warmth and comfort of a woman's breast. Both of them knew what a failed marriage was. Until the final day of her life, she had a tender feeling for Paul and always regretted never having appeared in a film with him. 'The two of us would have brought magic to the screen,' she once told me."

Shelley wanted to emphasize the tender and more romantic side of Paul's secret relationship with Marilyn, but Steiger in his man-to-man talks with Paul preferred to get down to basics. "Is Marilyn as frigid as rumor has it?"

"Not at all," Paul said. "She's loving and giving of herself. Not an acrobat like Joan Crawford. Marilyn's legs, like those of Elizabeth Taylor, are too short. Her stomach's a bit pudgy. Many younger and even more beautiful women have firmer breasts and more shapely thighs. It's hard for me to define exactly what it is that makes Marilyn so special. It's a luminous quality, I guess, the aura she carries with her, a radiance I've never known in any other woman. She has such a wistfulness about her. When she's with me, she seems to have this yearning thing that only I can satisfy. She immediately sucks you into her life, her problems, her love, her desires. No wonder she's America's sex symbol. Just compare Marilyn Monroe on the screen to Mae West, and you'll see how far America has come since the 1930s in its so-called sex symbols."

"Among women, Marilyn is the sex symbol," Steiger concurred. "She made Jane Russell in *Gentlemen Prefer Blondes* look like a truck driver in drag. As for the men, I hear you're about to replace Brando as the male sex symbol of the 50s."

"If only that were true," Paul said. "Marilyn and I aren't sex symbols, far from it. We're both two lonely people drawn to each other to share our desperate insecurities. We find comfort in each other."

After Paul had made love to Marilyn in his bed at the Chateau Marmont, the same bed that had been warmed by Robert Francis only hours before, he forgot all about his publicity photo session at Warners with Virginia Mayo and Pier Angeli.

"I remember her sitting in my armchair after we'd made love," Paul told Steiger. "She just sat there staring out the window at the blinding sunshine of the day. She'd washed off all that makeup and her hair was a bit matted. She didn't feel the need to talk, but huddled in that chair almost like a little girl. It was like she was waiting for some message to invade her mind. She was waiting for some answer. But an answer to what question?"

To break the silence, he said, "A penny for your thoughts."

Her eyes widened in a bewildered expression, as if she'd become aware of his presence for the first time that day. "I'm thinking of what I'll be on the day I'm no longer pretty anymore. When beautiful guys like you will no longer want to make love to me and when my only male companions will no longer be straight guys but homosexual men who will still be worshipping and adoring me when I'm eighty-five."

"That day will never come," he assured her. "You'll grow more beautiful as the years go by."

She suddenly rose from the armchair and stood before him, dropping the bathrobe he'd lent her and appearing stark naked. Her pubic hair was blonde, but he suspected she'd dyed it.

Thirty minutes later in his bathing suit, he was driving her to the crashing waves of the Pacific, where she wanted to frolic in her own skimpy white bathing suit. She splashed his chest with water. "Your chest is so beautiful. Especially your tits."

"You've got great tits too, babycakes," he said, splashing her back. "By the way, you're the first woman who's ever appreciated my tits. Up to now, women have ignored them."

"I've known men with more powerful physiques, but your chest is taut, sexy, and hard, not like that of an overly developed gorilla at Venice Beach, all muscle and beef except where it really counts. Yours is a real man's chest, not like some hairy ape rubbing against my tender breasts."

After nearly an hour frolicking in the waters, she sat with him on the sands staring out at the sea. "Sometimes I can sit for hours watching the Pacific Ocean," she told him. "It's not like the Atlantic. All I've seen of that ocean is from some industrial site. As a little girl growing up in California, I would come to the shore and sit for hours looking out at the sea. I know how dangerous it can be in a storm, and how many people it's killed. After all these years in Hollywood, I also know about shark-infested waters. But somehow I've always had this warm, cuddly feeling looking out at the sea because I associate it with freedom. That's something I've never had."

"It's something I don't have either," he told her. "I'm chained. To my family. To the studio. Even to my own sex drive that has taken some bizarre twists, especially after meeting James Dean. I want to be a faithful family man, a devoted father and loving husband bringing home the kisses and bacon every night. But that's not me. Deep down and late at night my true character comes out. I'm a bad boy just like Dean and Marlon Brando. I think I'm going to be a bad boy for the rest of my life. But I don't intend to let the world know me as such. I'm not going to live a life exposed in blaring headlines in tabloids."

"You and I are kindred spirits," she told him. "But it's too late for me to project the perfect image. There's no way at this point that I'll ever be squeaky clean again. I heard that Elia Kazan nailed me. He told Lee Strasberg that I was 'just a simple, decent-hearted kid whom Hollywood brought down, legs parted.' Don't let that happen to you. I've sucked many a cock on the way to my horizon."

"It's different for men," he said. "We have it easy. All we have to do is stand there while some balding fart gets down on his knees and sucks our dick."

She laughed in that funny little way she had of expressing surprise and delight, and then she leaned over and kissed him tenderly on the lips. "Let's make a deal right today," she said. "Let's always be lover and friend to each other. Never to chain one another down. Only coming together when we need to, without any sense of obligation. Just two grownups loving and trusting each other until the end."

"You've got yourself a deal," he said. "Let's seal this pact with a kiss."

That would be the first of thousands of kisses exchanged between Marilyn and Paul in their futures. Bonded together, both of them would see many a sunrise light the Pacific, but also many a sunset.

***

Fortunately, Paul's contract with Warners allowed him to do Broadway plays and even appear in teleplays. During the last week of the shoot on *The Silver Chalice*, he besieged his agent to "get me back on Broadway and make sure it's a god damn good play." He must have already made at least a hundred phone calls urging this. "I'm now finishing what will be the worst film made in the Fifties. I've got to find something great to save my fucking career."

To complicate an already-complicated life, Joanne Woodward flew into Los Angeles. She had signed a contract to film an episode, *Interlude*, starring Dick Powell, as part of a presentation on TV for the Four Star Playhouse.

The American singer, producer, actor, and director, Dick Powell, was her co-star. He was famously married to June Allyson, MGM's fading sweetheart of the 1940s. On meeting Joanne, he told her that "the best thing about switching from being an actor to being a director is that you don't have to shave or hold in your stomach anymore."

Joanne knew Powell from his 1940s tough guy roles at RKO and less so for his 30s musicals, often starring Ruby Keeler, including *42nd Street*.

In *Interlude*, Joanne played a young woman in love with an older man. Throughout the shoot, Powell had high praise for her acting talent. At the show's wrap, he sent a print of her work to Buddy Adler, who had only recently won an Oscar for the 1953 film *From Here to Eternity*, starring two of Paul's friends, Frank Sinatra and Montgomery Clift. At the time Adler previewed Joanne's work, he was hoping to replace Darryl F. Zanuck as head of production at Fox.

Adler, like Powell, was so impressed with Joanne's screen work that he showed clips to Zanuck, who was still his boss. The cigar-chomping studio boss wasn't impressed. "No tits, no talent, no looks, and no tail."

"What do you mean by no tail?" Adler asked. "Her ass looks fine to me."

"I mean I can't fuck her," Zanuck said. "She won't put out from what I hear. Besides, I hear she dates only fags like Newman and that writer, Gore Vidal. Sign her up if you want to. But if she fucks up, you're to blame. Fox isn't into losing money."

Joanne Woodward:
Losing out to Marilyn

Chapter Four
Live Fast, Die Young

Back in New York, Paul had a reunion with Jackie, who was nearing term with their third child. Several months earlier, she'd left her parents' home in Wisconsin and moved back to Long Island.

The next day, Paul met once again with Geraldine Page. He spoke of his marriage, but didn't relay any details associated with what actually happened the night he got together with Jackie after their long absence.

After their class at the Actors Studio, he and Geraldine Page adjourned to a little actors' pub in the Broadway area near Ninth Avenue to catch up with each other. He spoke of his disintegrating marriage and his rapidly increasing family.

Over drinks, he confessed to her that he had fallen in love with Joanne and out of love with Jackie. "But I can't leave a pregnant wife. What kind of heel would that make me? I've got to hang in there and try to make it work." She remembered his being near tears. Finally, he blurted out the truth. "I'm torn apart."

Geraldine gave only romantic advice. "The heart has its way," she said, "and we must follow our hearts. We're artists and artists can't be bound by conventional morality. The goal of the artist is self-fulfillment. I'm not suggesting you abandon your family. Take care of them. See to their needs. But, for God's sake, don't become the family man from Long Island with three brats in tow."

"Even though I'm in love with Joanne, I can't be faithful to her," Paul said. "Marilyn told me that she always wants to be faithful to her husband or lover of the moment, but can't. It is physically and emotionally impossible for her, as it is for me. I can be seduced by a beautiful woman."

"Or a beautiful man," Geraldine said provocatively.

"That too," he said. "But I don't want to go into that."

"Don't worry about being faithful," she advised. "Have you ever heard of an actor who was faithful to anyone?"

"Come to think of it, I haven't."

"Then go for it!" she urged. "Do what is needed and wanted to make Paul Newman a star. Give love when you feel it and withdraw love when it's not real."

Paul did not necessarily follow Geraldine's romantic advice, at least not at once. Back with Jackie, he promised to give up Joanne but refused to discuss James Dean. "I'm finished in the movies," he proclaimed, saying that in the future he would pursue work in the theater and live in the New York area as they awaited the birth of another baby.

Jackie, or so it is believed, fell for that line, although Paul may have momentarily meant it. His wife seemed convinced that the birth of another child would somehow hold the marriage together.

While waiting for Paul to make up his mind, Joanne began to date other men, including James Costigan, the actor and playwright. Right before his death in December of 2007, Costigan spoke of his role in the lives of Paul and Joanne. He had retired to Bainbridge Island in the state of Washington where he lived as a recluse.

"I came into the life of Joanne Woodward when she was dating Paul on the sly," he claimed. "We were said to be in love but that wasn't the case. She wasn't in love with me, and I certainly wasn't in love with her. She was using me actually. She felt that by going out with me, she'd make Paul jealous. Her words, 'Surely he'll come to his senses and divorce Jackie and marry me. She's all wrong for him. I'm Miss Right. I could make him happy.'"

"I think in many respects that was true," Costigan said. "Time, or at least the longevity of the Woodward/Newman marriage, proved her right. The press even went so far as to print rumors of Joanne's engagement to me. Both of us got a chuckle out of reading that fiction. I think ever since their work on *Picnic*, Joanne was determined to get Paul Newman one way or another. I never quite understood it. His prick must have been made of solid gold."

Was playwright **James Costigan** (top photo) a serious contender for Joanne Woodward's hand?

"Joanne had heard that Jackie was prettier than she was, and this infuriated her," Costigan claimed. "Jackie was also said to be sexier, although I would think dumping three kids didn't improve that figure. Joanne kept repeating what she'd said so many times in the past. '*That one* trapped Paul, first with her good looks and then with all those babies.'"

"At one point, Joanne told me, 'Paul is my best friend. I can't stand to see him so miserable. I'll never let him go. I'm determined to have him, and I don't much care how I get him. It's going to be harder than I thought, but in the end I'll prevail. I want that man. When a Georgia gal like me goes after a man, she usually gets him.'"

"Yes, Miss Scarlett O'Hara," Costigan said mockingly. "Always in pursuit of Ashley Wilkes when you could have a far sexier Rhett Butler."

Paul was already a familiar figure to Costigan. In 1953, they had appeared together in "The Bells of Damon," an episode within the TV series *The Web*, as produced by Mark Goodson and Bill Todman. "The Bells of Damon" was aired on July 19, during the hot summer of 1953.

"I don't think Paul and Joanne were even sleeping together," Costigan claimed. "Paul was still banging his wife, Jackie. He had to be. Or else those babies weren't his."

"I wasn't certain about Paul at the time," Costigan said. "The scuttlebutt along Broadway was that he had only married to mask a homosexual streak in him. I'd heard rumors that he was carrying on with both men and women, which turned out to be true. So all that talk that Paul and I were fighting over Joanne's hand was moronic. We actually became friends. Don't forget that both Paul and Joanne would star in my 1964 Broadway comedy, *Baby Want a Kiss*."

"Paul and I actually shared more in common than Joanne," Costigan said. "His parents wanted him to take over their sporting goods business in Ohio. I was born in East Los Angeles. My parents wanted me to take over the family hardware store. We both told our parents to go fuck themselves, but ever so politely."

***

Stewart Stern was born into Hollywood royalty as the nephew of Adolph Zukor, the founder of Paramount Pictures. The young writer would become a key player in Paul's career. Stern is best known today for writing the 1955 film, *Rebel Without a Cause*. But prior to that, Stern chugged out some made-for-TV teleplays, one of which featured Paul Newman.

The script written by **Stewart Stern** for James Dean made him a legend.

But the one he wrote for **Paul** (pictured behind sunglasses on the left in the photo above) was a box-office failure.

115

Broadcast on November 21, 1954, *Thunder of Silence*, written by Stern, was sponsored by the Goodyear Television Playhouse. Paul co-starred with Herbert Berghof and Inga Stevens in this drama of a troubled teenager and her father who wind up moving in with a farmer and his family.

From this telecast, a friendship developed between Stern and Paul that would last for years. At the time of their meeting, Stern was not only working on *Rebel Without a Cause*, but writing another feature film, *The Rack*, for Glenn Ford. Paul had no clue that he would ultimately become the star of *The Rack* or that in years to come Stern and Paul would collaborate on the 1968 movie, *Rachel, Rachel*, starring Paul's future wife, Joanne Woodward.

***

When Paul was working almost night and day in rehearsals for *The Desperate Hours* on Broadway, it was announced that the premiere of his long dreaded *The Silver Chalice* would take place in the small resort town of Saranac Lake in the Adirondack Mountains in Upper New York State. This remote town was selected because it had sold the most Christmas seals in a nationwide competition.

At the film's gala premiere in Saranac Lake's Pontiac Theater, Art Linkletter welcomed the stars of the film—all except one, Paul Newman himself.

After the premiere, and after its opening in theaters across the country, the film received a flood of disastrous reviews. Its dialogue elicited gasps, giggles, and embarrassed cringing from movie audiences.

The New Yorker pounced on Paul, its reviewer claiming that "Paul Newman delivers his lines with the emotional fervor of a Putnam Division conductor announcing local stops."

It was humiliating to Paul for reviewers to call him "the second Brando," especially when 1954 saw the original Brando release two archetypal movies, *The Wild One* and *On the Waterfront*.

The New York World Telegram, as did most newspapers, hammered home the Brando link. The *Telegram* reviewer noted Paul's "astonishing resemblance to Marlon Brando, an excessively sullen Brando."

Joanne didn't like the movie either, claiming, "Paul didn't lift his head. Perhaps he kept it buried in shame. You couldn't even see those baby blues."

In 1963, when Paul was one of the major stars of Hollywood, Channel 9 in Los Angeles announced that it was running *The Silver Chalice* for one entire week. In horror, Paul took out an ad in the *Los Angeles Times*. Encased in a black, funereal border, it proclaimed PAUL NEWMAN APOLOGIZES EVERY NIGHT THIS WEEK.

Instead of frightening viewers away from this multimillion-dollar flop, the ad had the opposite effect. TV watchers by the thousands tuned in to see the disaster, and *The Silver Chalice* scored one of the highest ratings in the annals of TV in Southern California.

***

For months, from the West Coast, Paul had told his wife that he needed to be alone in Hollywood to concentrate on his role of Basil in *The Silver Chalice*. Now back in New York, with a Broadway opening scheduled at the Ethel Barrymore Theatre for February 10, 1955, he told her he needed all of his days and most of his nights to focus on his lead role in *The Desperate Hours*. Except on most of those nights, he wasn't alone.

Director Josh Logan thought Paul was horribly miscast in this chiller-diller, a play adapted from a suspense novel by Joseph Hayes, telling the story of three escaped convicts who break into a house in Indiana and terrorize the Hilliard family. Paul's friend from the Actors Studio, Karl Malden, played the lead as the family man whose home is invaded, with film actress Nancy Coleman cast as his wife.

In a wild departure from the role of the innocent boy of *Picnic*, Paul was cast as Glen Griffin, a swaggering psychotic gangster, evocative of Humphrey Bogart's performance with Bette Davis in the 1936 *The Petrified Forest*. Under a close cropped skull, Paul played the grinning gunman, giving a splashy performance. Paul's rival, Cliff Robertson, had been slated for the role but had to drop out.

Even before he went on the Broadway stage, Paul knew he wouldn't get the lead role in the film version. *The Desperate Hours* had been filmed in Hollywood between October and December of 1954, starring Humphrey Bogart, who was far too old for the role but still had star power. According to the terms of the agreement, the Bogie film could not be released until the Broadway play had had its run.

A handsome young actor, George Grizzard, was cast as Paul's brother, Hank, in the play. Paul bonded with George on the first afternoon they met and began hanging out with him almost immediately.

Robert Montgomery, a fading actor from the 1930s and 40s, was assigned to direct. After his movie career wound down, he'd successfully switched to television and directing, hitting it big beginning in 1950 with his *Robert Montgomery*

George Grizzard
Paul's onstage brother
and offstage lover

117

Presents TV series, which ran for five years.

"When George and Paul met, it was apparent to all the cast that there was a strong sexual attraction there," said actress/writer Mary Orr, who appeared as Miss Swift in the play. "Even back in the 1950s, all the actors in our cast were sophisticated about such matters. But not our director. Robert Montgomery was the biggest homophobe I've ever met in the theater."

"Once Montgomery found out that George and Paul had become lovers, he made it really tough on them," Mary said. "Away from the other actors—he didn't want Karl Malden to know—he tore into the performances being given by George and Paul, leaving no flesh on their bones. George gave in to Montgomery, but Paul stood his ground. He fought constantly with the director. Before opening night, I thought either Paul or Montgomery would bolt the play."

"George and Paul made a lovely couple," said Patricia Peardon, cast as the daughter in the play. "I often went with them to Sardi's after the show. I was their beard. There were rumors on Broadway that we were having a three-way. I could be so lucky."

"George lost his heart to Paul," Patricia claimed. "It was obvious to me from the beginning that Paul was only using George for a sexual adventure. In a few months, I was certain that Paul would be back in Hollywood screwing James Dean, Tony Perkins, or whomever. He was very promiscuous in those days."

"I heard that he had a wife and kids," Patricia said, "but he never mentioned them. When Joanne Woodward came around, Paul would become very straight indeed. He didn't want Joanne to find out he was painted with the lavender brush. Of course, no one calls it lavender brush anymore."

Nancy Coleman was also very accepting of the hot romance going on between Paul and George. She also hung out with the two lovers, entertaining them with stories of her days in Hollywood and her many affairs with her co-stars. Even though he was married to Jane Wyman at the time, Ronald Reagan seduced her when they'd filmed *Kings Row* together. She'd also had scandalous affairs with Paul Henreid and Errol Flynn, and she said that her former co-star, Barbara Stanwyck, had made lesbian advances to her.

Montgomery had been badly stung by his only known venture into homosexuality. "It occurred during World War II with his friend Douglas Fairbanks Jr.,"

Nancy Coleman
"Reagan committed adultery with me."

Nancy claimed. "When we went out together at night, both Paul and George attacked Montgomery and told me how much they hated him. From what I heard, Montgomery and Fairbanks were blackmailed when someone discovered their affair. Since that time, Montgomery seemed to have a chip on his shoulder about homosexuals, and he took it out on poor George and Paul during our pre-Broadway rehearsals and trial runs."

Paul returned to his old stamping grounds of New Haven in January of 1955 for the pre-Broadway run-through. After opening there, the play moved to Philadelphia. While in that city, another actor in the play, James Gregory, convinced George and Paul to go with him to see *The Silver Chalice*.

"Of course, George and I had to get Paul drunk before he'd go into the movie house," Gregory said. "Even drunk, Paul squirmed through the entire movie. He loathed his appearance on the screen."

Bronx-born Gregory usually played tough cops, but he liked George and Paul. "I knew they were carrying on but that was no one's business but their own. I don't know what happened. Paul abruptly dropped George. I mean he wouldn't even speak to him backstage. Paul had moved on, but lovesick George was hopelessly smitten. You could feel the tension between the two of them backstage."

In February of 1955, Paul flew his mother to New York for the Broadway premiere of *The Desperate Hours*. "At last I've lived long enough to see my son become a big Broadway star," she told him backstage. "But why did you have to be so mean to that nice family in the play?"

Every night, teenage girls surrounded the backstage entrance of The Ethel Barrymore Theater, clamoring for an autograph from Paul, a man who found it silly and foolish to give autographs.

Not only that, but Paul had become the poster boy of gay New Yorkers. "For a while there, you wouldn't be considered gay unless you listened to Judy Garland sing 'Over the Rainbow' every night, had seen Gloria Swanson in *Sunset Blvd.* at least three times, and thought Paul Newman was the hottest thing since bare-backing," Merv Griffin claimed.

"Paul was off and running to challenge Brando as the male sex symbol of the 1950s," said Malden. "The adulation that would follow him around for decades began with his stage role in *The Desperate Hours.*"

The New York critics raved about Paul's performance. "They restored my confidence as an actor," he told a reporter. "My ego would soon be battered again, but for a few good months I felt like I was the King of Broadway."

Two weeks after the play opened, Jackie presented Paul with his second daughter, which she named Stephanie. "To me, Paul didn't seem all that interested in the birth of a new daughter," Patricia Peardon said. "I think by the time Stephanie came along, her mama and papa were no longer rolling around in the hay."

During the run of the play, Richard M. Nixon, then a Wall Street lawyer, intervened. He represented the family of James J. Hill of Philadelphia, who was suing, claiming that the events in the play were based on an actual hostage situation that had befallen his own family. The case went all the way to the Supreme Court, where the judges ruled against Nixon's arguments.

Perhaps this was the beginning of what became a famous feud between Newman and Nixon.

Like many plays on Broadway, *The Desperate Hours* did not survive the dreaded heat wave that descended on New York in the summer of 1955. After Karl Malden pulled out of the play and ticket sales slumped, the play closed down. When Bogie opened in the movie version, *The Desperate Hours* became one of his least attended films.

Montgomery won a Tony as the Best Director on Broadway that year, *The Desperate Hours* garnering another Tony as Best Dramatic Play of the Year.

Even during the eight-month, 212-performance run of *The Desperate Hours*, Paul became one of the brightest stars on television, appearing in one teleplay after another.

"On the verge of big stardom in Hollywood, in spite of *The Silver Chalice*, Paul was the Golden Boy of the Golden Age of Television," Josh Logan recalled.

***

In the TV series, *The Mask*, Paul co-starred with Patricia Breslin and Jo Van Fleet in an episode called "The Party Night." One episode or another within the series was broadcast on ABC-TV twice a week. Each show was expensive to produce, and ABC could not find a sponsor, so the series was dropped after four months.

But while it lasted, Paul got to work with Van Fleet before she went on to win an Oscar opposite James Dean, playing his brothel madam mother in *East of Eden*. After flickering across TV screens, "The Party Night" would fade from memory, but in 1967, Van Fleet and Paul would later immortalize themselves in film history when they co-starred together in *Cool Hand Luke*.

In New York-born Patricia Breslin, Paul met a new kind of actress. With her green eyes and brunette hair, she was a beauty but not in a flashy way. Five years younger than Paul, she was a new

Jo Van Fleet
Paul's "Party Night" with her led to *Cool Hand Luke*.

120

breed, a true television actress who would specialize throughout the 1950s in guest roles in series ranging from *The Twilight Zone* to *Robert Montgomery Presents*.

For a brief while, Paul too considered becoming only a television actor with an occasional stage appearance. "Before TV pitched itself to the brainless," Paul said, "it gave me a chance to be almost any character I wanted to be. Within a year in TV, you could play such a wide range of parts it would take thirty big screen movies to cover such a stretch. Patricia was a talented young woman who appeared in serious meaningful dramas. We would work together again the following year."

He was referring to an episode, "Five in Judgment," that was part of a series called *Appointment with Adventure*.

In September of 1954, Paul got a chance to work with first-rate talent when he was cast opposite Fay Bainter in *Guilty Is the Stranger*, part of the Goodyear Television Playhouse. The aging actress had become the first performer to be nominated in the same year (1938) for both Best Actress for her role in *White Banners* and Best Supporting Actress for her role in *Jezebel*. She took home the prize for *Jezebel* in which she had played Bette Davis's kindly Aunt Belle.

The teleplay also starred Pat Crowley, who became a leading lady or character actress in a number of 1950s TV series, including *Maverick*. She also became familiar in the 70s and 80s when she appeared in 10 episodes of the hit TV series, *Dynasty*.

"Pat was romantically linked to the gay actor Tab Hunter, but I knew there was no romance," said Tad Mosel, who wrote the teleplay's script. "It was just a ruse to trick impressionable gals who read movie magazines. I thought Paul might make a play for Pat, but he didn't. Too occupied with other affairs, I guess. Frankly, I wanted Paul just for myself, but I was smart enough to know he was out of my league. I did get to see him in his jockey shorts, however. He amply filled out the pouch, and it is a memory I have treasured for the rest of my life."

That life ended in 2008, as would Paul's. But Paul always cited Mosel as one of the leading dramatists of TV's Golden Age, and was delighted to learn that he'd won the Pulitzer Prize for his drama, *All the Way Home*, in 1961.

Paul told Ted, "I find Pat perkily pleasant, the girl next door. But if I wanted the girl next door, I'd go next door. After Grace Kelly and Marilyn

Tab Hunter and **Pat Crowley**
The romance that never was

Monroe, how can you keep Paul Newman down on the farm?"

In 1950, *Danger* was launched as a TV series. One such episode written by Rod Serling was "Knife in the Dark," which aired on December 7, 1954, starring James Gregory and Paul. Paul had appeared on Broadway with Gregory in *The Desperate Hours.*

Paul enjoyed working with the Bronx-born character actor with his deep, gravelly voice. Although many movie stars still shunned television at the time, Gregory spoke to Paul of what a "respectable medium" it was for an actor.

Paul stayed in touch with Gregory and admired his endurance. "My god, the fucker set a record for live performances. He once performed in five different TV dramas in just ten days."

***

Columbia bought to rights to *Picnic*, and the word was out that the studio was "testing unknowns" for the key roles. For some reason, Ralph Meeker had turned down the lead role of Hal in the film.

At the Actors Studio, Paul had met Jack Garfein, a Holocaust survivor and director. He was dating a blonde beauty, Carroll Baker, at the time. With her finely chiseled features, she evoked Jean Harlow and supported herself and paid her tuition at Actors Studio by dancing at night in a club.

Both Paul and Carroll were clients of MCA, the talent agency. Paul called Garfein and asked his permission to phone Carroll. He wanted to rehearse a scene from *Picnic* with her and ultimately make a screen test.

"He was such a gentleman," Garfein recalled. "He wanted my permission to call Carroll. I thought it was very touching. He didn't want me to think he was moving in on my woman."

"We had wonderful chemistry together," Carroll said after making the screen test with Paul. "I thought he was the most attractive man I'd ever met. But Harry Cohn obviously didn't think so." She was referring to the studio chief at Columbia.

Reportedly, Cohn had "the hots" for Carroll, but was unimpressed with Paul's acting. "Just what Hollywood needs: another pint-sized Jewish actor."

When Josh Logan was signed to direct the film version of *Picnic*, Paul went to him and tried to convince him he was right for Hal. "I learned my lesson well from you," Paul said. "Everything I need to know about crotch acting. I can do that part."

Logan, who had always been sexually attracted to Paul, momentarily agreed with him. But then one

Baby Doll **Carroll Baker**
She got a movie contract,
Paul got the boot.

122

afternoon, he got a call from Cohn at Columbia. "William Holden wants the role."

"But he's too old for the part," Logan protested. "It's got to be played by a hot young kid like Newman."

"Holden has something Newman doesn't, and that's star power," Cohn said before slamming down the phone. For his performance in Billy Wilder's *Stalag 17* in 1953, Holden had won the Oscar as Best Actor of the Year.

Actually Holden at first didn't want the role of Hal, knowing he was too old for the part of a charismatic bare-chested drifter, who dazzles the women of a small town in Kansas. But Cohn was very persistent, even after Holden initially told him he could "stuff Hal up your ass."

Although Carroll won a movie contract based on her screen test with Paul, she ultimately lost the female lead in *Picnic*, the role going to the icy lavender blonde, Kim Novak. Veteran actress Rosalind Russell was also signed.

Even though he'd lost out, Paul called Logan once again, asking to be cast as Alan, the role he'd played for so many months on the stage. Once again, Cohn ruled him out, casting a newcomer from Broadway, Cliff Robertson, in the part.

"I think Paul and I would have made a great screen team," Carroll said. "It almost happened."

In 1958, Carroll was being seriously considered for the lead in Tennessee Williams' *Cat on a Hot Tin Roof*. But she'd feuded with her studio by refusing to act in a series of movies based on novels written by Erskine Caldwell, the Southern pulp fiction writer who'd achieved notoriety with the publication of *Tobacco Road*.

Not only that, but she'd lost the lead in *The Three Faces of Eve* in 1957. That role went instead to Joanne Woodward, who won an Oscar the following year for Best Actress for her portrayal of that film's schizophrenic heroine.

Ironically, on a trip to Hollywood, Paul was lying nude on a wood rack in a steam bath, which he had all to himself. Suddenly, another nude man entered. Paul looked up immediately to stare into the steamy face of William Holden. A flicker of recognition came across Holden's face.

Kim Novak with **William Holden**. A jaybird-naked encounter with Paul

"Here I was jaybird naked in front of this middle-aged actor who'd taken my role," Paul recalled. "After checking out each other's dicks, we evaluated each other's bodies. No contest. I won that round as I was in tip top condition. He was a heavy drinker and was beginning to show his age. His breasts sagged a bit. He was no longer Barbara Stanwyck's *Golden Boy* of 1939."

"It was embarrassing for both of us," Paul said. "I waited a discreet three minutes so as not to be that obvious, then made a hasty retreat from that God damn bath."

Ironically, the situation between Paul and Holden would happen in reverse in another steam bath, this one at the Universal Studio gym. Holden had wanted the coveted role of Jordan ("Bick") Benedict in *Giant*, which had gone to Rock Hudson. A naked Holden, at the age of thirty-seven, encountered a thirty-year-old, heavy hung Rock, standing six feet, four inches tall. Rock won out over Holden in more ways than one. "I didn't gloat," Rock later said. "By then I knew the ways of Hollywood. When I became fifty, I knew I'd enter some steam bath somewhere and stare at the young, buffed chest of some hot actor who'd just got a star role I wanted for myself."

***

While trying to launch himself professionally, Paul's "love life seemed going in all directions," according to Lee Strasberg. "Forget the men. I'd settle for all those gorgeous women flocking to him. I had known Paul for months as an acting coach before I learned he had a wife and kids living in Queens Village or some such place," said Strasberg. "He was carrying on with everybody. All sorts of sexual preferences. I think a wife and brats were the last things on his mind."

"I don't know how much time he spent with his family," Strasberg said. "But it couldn't have been that much. He was gone from home all the time. I could only hope that his young wife had a lover on the side up in Queens. She didn't seem to be getting that much from her husband, except for that odd pregnancy here and there."

"Paul was sharing that male charm and flash of his with many of our students, both male and female, at the Actors Studio," Strasberg said. "Shelley Winters told me it was the smell of him that attracted him. 'He was the cleanest man I've ever known,' she claimed. 'So sweet smelling, especially his breath. Not smelly and stinky like Brando, although a girl needs that brute on occasion too.'"

Lee Strasberg
"Paul's love life took in all sexual preferences."

***

Back in Hollywood, Paul had a reunion with James Dean on the set of *Rebel Without a Cause*, finding him more reckless and irresponsible than ever. *Rebel* had been based on a book written by Robert M. Lindner in 1944, a property acquired by Warner Brothers in 1946. In the late 40s, the studio had tried to launch it as a film to star Marlon Brando, but plans fizzled. Brando didn't want "to play a teenager with angst."

Director Nicholas Ray revived interest in the film in 1954. He'd already scored such hits as *Knock on Any Door* in 1949, with Humphrey Bogart and John Derek. Stewart Stern, with whom Paul had worked on the teleplay, *Thunder of Silence*, produced the final shooting script for *Rebel*.

Appearing on the set to see Dean work, Paul first encountered Natalie Wood, whom he hadn't seen since they'd appeared together in the ill-fated *The Silver Chalice*. Back then, he'd found the teenager had a "marvelous sense of mystery."

On the set of *Rebel*, she appeared far more sophisticated than her years. "I have ambitions to don a frilly gown by Don Loper and a silver blue mink and embrace Cary Grant in my arms before the camera," she told Paul. "I desperately feel I'm ready to play sexy parts. Instead I wound up playing the *younger* version of Virginia Mayo in *Chalice*. In *Rebel*, I'm a teenager."

"And indeed you are," he told her, "but growing up very fast in front of my eyes." She seemed flirtatious with him. Later, he learned from Dean that he was not only seducing Natalie, but so was the film's director, Nicholas Ray.

On the way to see Dean, Paul met Ray who introduced him to Sal Mineo, the former delinquent youth from the Bronx who in 1951 had co-starred with Yul Brynner on Broadway in *The King and I*.

In a phone call to Paul, Dean told him that "Sal is a very sexy young man, very pretty, and mature for his age." Dean had already told Paul how Sal had gotten the role of Plato in *Rebel* by "auditioning" for the director at the Chateau Marmont.

Years later in an apartment in Chelsea, in New York City, Sal said, "at the time I met Paul, I was crazy in love with Jimmy, very sexually confused. I hardly paid attention to Paul that day, although I couldn't help but notice what a beautiful man he was. I heard he was married but dating Joanne Woodward. I naïvely assumed that Paul was hopelessly straight. How wrong I was. Frankly, I didn't think I would ever run into him again. But, wow, what an important role he'd play in my future."

Once Paul made it to Dean's dressing room, "those two guys picked up right where they left off," according to Eartha Kitt. "I'd bet my right nipple that Jamie had Paul's pants off in less than ten minutes. He told me that his passion for Paul was still as strong as before."

"But Jamie also told me that he was being pulled in a million different directions sexually," Eartha claimed. "He had his regular affairs at the time, especially with a young actor named Jack Simmons, for whom Jamie had gotten a small part in *Rebel*."

"Even so, he was still out on many a night searching for something new and different," Eartha said. "While shooting *Rebel*, his behavior became even more bizarre. One night he picked up a girl with one leg and seduced her. On another occasion he met this very sexy hustler who had only one arm. They were seen driving away in Jamie's new Porsche Speedster."

"On another occasion he told me that five of the biggest names in Hollywood—all legends and all family men—had sucked his cock. I pressed him for details but he refused to divulge who they were. He did say the names of these fellatio artists were as big as Clark Gable or Humphrey Bogart."

While on the set of *Rebel*, Paul learned that *East of Eden* had opened to strong box office. Warners had made a decision to exploit Dean more in *Rebel*, deciding it would go from a black-and-white B picture to an A picture in color. Dean told Paul that in the early footage he'd worn a black leather jacket but had switched to a red nylon windbreaker for the color version.

Somehow Dean managed to fit Paul into his schedule when not sleeping with Natalie Wood, Sal Mineo, Nicholas Ray, and Jack Simmons, with an occasional call on his older mentor, Rogers Brackett.

Dean was also dating starlets, on orders of the studio. "There's a homosexual panic going on out here," he told Eartha. "Homosexual stars are being exposed. Rock Hudson is definitely not careful. He's getting too blatant. Word is reaching Jack Warner about my private life. Warner is insisting that I be seen out with girlfriends. Not just seen, but photographed."

"I saw a picture of you in the paper," Paul told Dean in the presence of

Rogers Brackett
"If I were a father symbol to Dean, it was incestuous."

The doomed stars of *Rebel Without a Cause* (left to right) **Sal Mineo, James Dean,** and **Natalie Wood.**
"Everybody was sleeping with everybody."

126

Eartha. "You were out with Ursula Andress, the so-called female Brando. That takes some of the heat off me in the press, who's still calling me the second Brando. You and Ursula look so much alike I thought you were brother and sister. Are you fucking her?"

"Come on, man, I can cum just so many times a day," Dean said. "Half of Hollywood wants my juice. They're sucking me dry out here. These blow-job artists make it hard for me to save up enough sperm for fucking."

"But you manage, don't you?" Paul said, smiling.

Dean flashed his own wicked grin. "You know me too well, man."

During the filming of *Rebel*, Dean told Paul that the censors were trying to remove all hints of homosexuality in the movie. "Sal's Plato is in love with me," Dean said. "In the movie. In real life. In one draft of the screenplay, we actually kiss. But when the top brass at Warners heard about this, that scene had to go. But Sal and I decided to play our roles homoerotic anyway. In our scenes together, Sal looks at me with moonglow eyes. It's obvious that Plato's in love with me."

Dean claimed that he was "lobbying" to get Sal cast in his upcoming film with Elizabeth Taylor. Edna Ferber's *Giant* was to be shot on location. "I've got to have a fuckmate with me if I'm going to Texas. I can't take chances on finding something on the hoof down there."

"Don't you think Sal is a bit young?" Paul asked.

"Haven't you heard of childhood sexuality?" Dean asked. "Hell, I once fucked a twelve-year-old boy time and time again. Kids shouldn't have to wait to have sex. When they want it, need it, they should have it."

"But there are laws," Paul protested.

"Still the boy from Shaker Heights," Dean said. "Loosen up. It's a new day out here. Just wait until you see *Rebel*. Then you'll understand."

Dean invited Paul to join him in May to watch him compete in the Santa Barbara Races with his Porsche. Before leaving, he had dinner with Paul and Eartha telling them, "I know I'll never be able to fly, but racing is the next best thing. Like a man in the future on a space flight to Mars. Racing is more powerful than any drug I could take. What a high. It's only when I'm speeding that I feel I'm not of this earth. I feel like a man. I answer to no one. I'm in control of my own universe."

Dean's infectious love of speeding may have influenced Paul's future hobby.

In Santa Barbara, Dean was given a bad starting position but tried to make up for lost time by accelerating. Two minutes into the race, another car swerved in front of him. To avoid ramming the car, Dean careened to the side of the road, hitting two bales of hay. Straightening out his Porsche, he was back in the race, moving up to fourth position. Suddenly, his engine dropped a valve, and he had to coast off the track out of the way of other speeding cars.

This would be the last race of his life.

"I'll try and try again," Dean told Paul. "I'm a natural to win all the prizes. My dream is not to become a movie star but a race car driver."

Those exact words one day would be uttered by Paul. But at the time he watched Dean, he hadn't yet developed what would become a deep passion for racing.

Paul and Dean spent a drunken night in a roadside motel where Dean made an extravagant promise. He claimed that he was going to do "everything in my power" to get Paul cast as Bick Benedict opposite his character of Jett Rink in *Giant.* "We'll both end up fucking Elizabeth Taylor," Dean promised.

"But I heard that Rock Hudson has already been signed," Paul said.

"Don't worry about that," Dean said. "The shit's about to hit the fan. Rock will be fired from the picture before it begins shooting. Trust me, as I know about these things. You're the same age as Rock and a better actor. The part will make your career. Mine too."

As far as Paul and Eartha could later figure out, Dean knew in advance that Rock was about to be exposed as a homosexual in *Confidential* magazine. The editors had even obtained nude pictures of Rock and his friend, actor George Nader, at an all-male pool party.

At the last minute the article was suppressed and Rock's career was saved. He kept the role of Bick in *Giant.*

"I would never want to become a star because of some tragedy in the life of an actor," Paul told Eartha.

Ironically, Paul's first great breakthrough in films came about by doing just that.

***

James Dean in his death-trap Porsche

Warners had tied Paul into an iron-bound contract, which Metro-Goldwyn-Mayer later bought a share of. After the failure of *The Silver Chalice,* Warners didn't know what to do with Paul. But MGM came calling after Glenn Ford bolted from *The Rack* at the last minute.

Paul eagerly read the screen-

128

play by his newly acquired friend, Stewart Stern, who was still basking in the glow of his success with *Rebel Without a Cause*. Stern had based his movie script on a teleplay by Rod Serling.

The Rack was a drab drama, depicting the life of a troubled young officer accused of collaboration with the Communists while being brainwashed in a North Korean prison camp. In the film version, which depicted flashbacks of torture in these "camps of hell," Paul had been "broken" by his captors, after which he tried to convince other U.S. soldiers that they were fighting an unjust war. When he returned to America, he faced a court martial on a charge of treason.

Producer Arthur M. Loew Jr. and director Arnold Laven had assembled an all-star cast, including that 1940s co-star with Greer Garson, Walter Pidgeon, playing Paul's stern father. Wendell Corey and Edmond O'Brien also headed a cast that included good roles for Anne Francis, Lee Marvin, and Cloris Leachman. As a footnote, Leachman would later become one of Joanne Woodward's best friends.

"There were a lot of Hollywood bad boys in that cast," Paul said. "Especially Lee Marvin. I'd heard that he and Brando duked it out on the set of *The Wild One*."

Paul played the boy-man, Captain Edward W. Hall Jr., more effectively than the more mature Glenn Ford ever could. The most sensitive scenes in the movie were between Paul and Pidgeon, cast as his cold and distant father, who suggests that his son would have been better off had he died in action than return home to face a court martial for being a coward.

Paul Newman in *The Rack* playing a troubled young officer, brain washed and broken in a prisoners' camp from hell.	**Wendell Corey** (top photo) went from tormenting Joan Crawford to prosecuting Paul	Paul's onscreen defender, **Edmond O'Brien** (bottom center photo), was married to **Olga San Juan**, a Carmen Miranda clone

According to the plot, Paul broke under emotional pain because of his own damaged relationship with his father, a bit of a stretch.

The Rack marked the emergence of a new kind of hero, or anti-hero, on American screens, with Paul in the vanguard of movie actors of this genre.

The new hero, as evoked by Paul, was an alienated loner standing up against the world, vulnerable, yes, but masking it with a cynical face and a hard-boiled spirit. He was just as macho as Cooper and The Duke, but he could also express fragile, sensitive emotions, heretofore depicted on the screen by women.

Paul could even appear as a mama's boy, expressing regret that he had not experienced that "moment of magnificence" that so many American soldiers did in various wars, including Senator John McCain in the Vietnam conflict. Many soldier heroes endured torture and did not bend. Just the threat of more pain had caused Paul's character in the movie to break.

Wendell Corey, as Paul's prosecutor in the film, was ideally cast as Major Sam Moulton, maintaining that Paul gave in to his captors while under no legally accepted or unduly harsh torture or the infliction of emotional terror. The prosecutor raises the question in court as to why Paul broke under pressure, when so many other brave American soldiers did not.

Critic Philip Koffman, in appraising Paul's anti-hero role, claimed that "Newman showed us that the new American hero could be masculine though articulate, civilized, caring, feeling, yet a man of good character in spite of a flaw here and there. There is even a suggestion that a tragic flaw is what it takes to make a real man."

Although Paul would fight with future directors, he got on well with the cast and crew.

New Englander Wendell Corey, with his ice cold blue eyes, prosecuted Paul on screen, but was friendly off screen. He'd appeared with such screen divas as Barbara Stanwyck and Joan Crawford, and had recently starred in a big hit, Alfred Hitchcock's *Rear Window*. "I pursued Grace Kelly all during the picture, but she went for James Stewart instead," Corey told Paul. "All in all, he was the big star. Grace doesn't fool around with unknowns."

"I'm not so sure," Paul said enigmatically. "Wendell and I never became friends. After all, he was a Republican. The year *The Rack* was released, he even introduced Dwight D. Eisenhower at the ball for his second inauguration."

Rough looking Edmond O'Brien played Paul's defense counsel, Colonel Frank Wasnick. In 1954, he had received an Academy Award for Best Supporting Actor for his role in *The Barefoot Contessa*, with Ava Gardner and Humphrey Bogart.

At the time, O'Brien was married to the fiery Olga San Juan, the "Puerto

Rican Pepperpot," who had danced in 1940s musicals with Bing Crosby and Fred Astaire.

In a salacious story spread around Hollywood at the time, Lee Marvin claimed that "Olga gave nearly all of us guys in the cast, including Newman, a blow-job. She was tiny, tiny, and didn't have to get down on her knees. For most of us, she came to our beltline, which made it convenient for quickies."

Deserved or not, Olga became known as "the fellatio queen of Hollywood," following the abdication of that niche by starlet Nancy Davis after her marriage to Ronald Reagan.

Marvin had met Paul's sometimes lover, Robert Francis, when he'd played the ship's cook in *The Caine Mutiny* in 1954. "I learned from Van Johnson that Robert was having an affair with Newman," Marvin said. "Until I worked with him in *The Rack*, I always thought Newman was gay. But after I saw Olga making a few trips to his dressing room, I changed my mind about him. Of course, Olga was very discreet. She timed her quickie visits when hubbie was busy elsewhere."

Despite the indiscretions of his wife, or perhaps because he never knew about them, O'Brien got along well with Paul. The New York City actor later predicted big-time stardom for Paul. While waiting between takes, off-camera, O'Brien sometimes performed vaudeville-derived tricks for Paul and other members of the cast, many inspired by the style of Harry Houdini. Early in his career, O'Brien had billed himself as a stage magician, "Neirbo the Great"—O'Brien spelled backward.

Paul was pleased with most of the reviews of *The Rack*, except those which referred to him as "a Brando clone" or a "monotonous sub-Brando." By now, he was getting used to that comparison.

"Unlike that atrocity, *The Silver Chalice*, *The Rack* was a very good movie except it had one big problem. No one went to see it."

***

Her studio finally found a role for Joanne Woodward, casting her in the 1955 *Count Three and Pray*, opposite veteran actor Van Heflin, who could always be counted on to deliver an earnest, dependable performance even though he didn't possess conventional leading man looks.

Their co-stars included the gay actor Raymond Burr and the dashingly handsome Philip Carey, whom Paul was about to meet. Paul would get to know Carey far more intimately than Joanne ever did.

For her appearance in *Count Three and Pray*, Joanne received good reviews as the rambunctious Lissy in this redemptive story of a former drinker and womanizer who returns home from the Civil War as a newly converted

131

preacher.

It is said that Paul slept through part of the movie, but Joanne was later quoted as saying that *Count Three and Pray* was the only movie of hers that she "really liked—that I really, really enjoyed," but that may have been overstatement, not an accurate assessment of her own view of her film roles.

As part of the TV series, *Appointment with Adventure*, Paul appeared in an episode, "Five in Judgment," which aired on April 10, 1955. In this teleplay, he was reunited with Patricia Breslin and James Gregory.

Paul later recalled, "This adventure drama had an array of talent greater than the script. I was up against some stiff competition."

One of the actors, Jeff Harris, would in the future distinguish himself as a behind-the-scenes player in Hollywood, becoming, for example, executive producer of thirty-four episodes of *Roseanne* in 1989 and 1990.

Paul was impressed with the work of Frank McHugh, another of the co-stars. In time, he would appear in 150 films and TV productions. As a contract player at Warners in the 1930s, McHugh had been everything from a lead actor to a sidekick, often playing comic relief. By the time he met Paul in the mid-50s, his career was in decline.

McHugh had been part of the famous "Irish Mafia" of the 1930s in Hollywood, a group of Irish American actors that hung out together to talk and drink. This Mafia consisted of such members as James Cagney, Pat O'Brien, and Spencer Tracy. "You think a six pack of beer a day makes you a drinker?" McHugh chided Paul. "We didn't just drink glasses of Irish whisky, we drank it by the quart."

Also cast in "Five in Judgment" was the son of a Louisville drama critic, Henry Hull. He'd already scored his biggest successes before he met Paul, including creating the role of Jeeter Lester in the long-running Broadway play, *Tobacco Road*, in 1933.

Paul had seen him in the first werewolf movie, Universal Picture's classic *Werewolf of London* in 1935. His last movie would be with two of Paul's friends, Robert Redford and Marlon Brando in *The Chase* in 1966.

A reed-thin actor with a furrowed brow, Hull specialized in playing practical oldsters and crotchety geriatrics. "I'm the granddaddy of all lycanthropy *[i.e., the study of werewolves]* movies," Hull told Paul.

He also claimed that the best reason for being an actor on Broadway or in Hollywood "is that you can get more pussy in this business than any other. It's always there if you want it. I fucked Tallulah Bankhead when we did *Lifeboat* together. I also fucked Katharine Hepburn but she's mostly dyke. Even Tyrone Power offered me his pussy when we did *Jesse James*, but I turned him down."

At least one of Hull's so-called conquests denied his claim. Hepburn once said that she admired Hull as an actor, but that he was "sexually repulsive." She had appeared with him in a summer stock production of *The Man Who Came Back* at the Ivoryton Playhouse in Connecticut.

Paul promised Hull that he would fuck as many of his leading ladies as he could get. "If they'll let me take off their panties, I'll do my job, and, dare I say, do it more competently than most men. As a lover, I'm good on and off the screen."

One of the actors in *Five in Judgment*, Jack Lord, was known to Paul from the Actors Studio, where the handsome rising star had been propositioned by Marlon Brando. Allegedly at least, he'd also had a one-night stand with Marilyn Monroe. Since 1949, Lord had been married to his faithful wife, Marie, but he still had a roving eye.

"For a brief time in their careers, Paul and Jack seemed bonded at the hip," said Frank McHugh. "One day Jack was late for rehearsals, and we couldn't get him on the phone. I went to his hotel and knocked on the door. He answered it jaybird naked. Paul was lying in a double bed, still half asleep. I assumed he was naked under the sheets too. I just figured these two studs were making it, or else they liked to sleep naked together. Both of them had other beds to sleep in since both of them were married at the time."

McHugh claimed that Jack and Paul were practically "soulmates as well as bedmates," since both of them were liberal political activists. A man of culture, Jack read poetry out loud on the set and was also a very skilled painter, "a regular Leonardo," McHugh called him. Many of his paintings hang today in museums. As a merchant marine, he had painted landscapes from the decks of freighters as he sailed by Africa, the Mediterranean, and the China coast.

A rupture in the friendship between Paul and Jack came when Jack replaced Ben Gazzara on Broadway in *Cat on a Hot Tin Roof*. At the time, Paul was angling to star in the film version of that play by Tennessee Williams.

Wanting the role for himself, Paul had seen Gazzara perform in the drama three times. When Lord took over, he'd gone to see his friend and sometimes lover perform. When Lord found out that he'd been in the audience one night, and hadn't gone backstage to see him, he was furious. "I'll never speak to that shithead again," he told a cast member. Lord was doubly hurt a few years later when newspapers announced that the producers of the film version of *Cat* had cast Paul in the lead role opposite Elizabeth Taylor.

Lord rose from the ashes of this loss and went on to become a big success in television, performing in

Henry Hull
The *Werewolf of London* making outlandish claims of A-list seductions

133

the CBS series, *Hawaii Five-O* from 1968 to 1980. Along the way he accumulated forty million dollars before his death in Honolulu in 1998. Cast as Lt. Steve McGarrett in *Hawaii Five-O*, Lord became famous for his catchphrase to his sidekick, James MacArthur, "Book 'em, Danno!" Those words have entered TV history.

In the short years that remained before his casting in the film version of *Cat on a Hot Tin Roof*, Paul would find that Lord wasn't the only dragon actor he'd have to slay before playing the role of Tennessee's repressed homosexual.

***

The first film version of *Billy the Kid* was released in 1911, starring the forgotten actor, Tefft Johnson, who appeared in 131 films between 1909 and 1926.

Over the decades, many other actors would play the notorious outlaw. Oddly, most of them who were cast as the teenage Billy were middle-aged men, as exemplified by Robert Taylor in 1941. In the early Forties, Buster Crabbe almost made a career out of playing Billy the Kid in ridiculous stories that had nothing to do with the outlaw's life.

The most notorious film about Billy the Kid was *The Outlaw*, first released by Howard Hughes in 1943, who cast his reluctant lover, Jack Buetel, as Billy. Arguably, Buetel was the sexiest of all actors in this role. *The Outlaw* also introduced the large bosom of Jane Russell to world audiences.

The nadir of all Billy the Kid movies was the 1972 release of *Dirty Little Billy* starring Michael J. Pollard. The Kid is portrayed as a moronic wimp and "yellow-belly" coward, who looks up to a pimp as a role model.

While performing on Broadway in *The Desperate Hours*, Paul accepted the lead in Philco Television Playhouse's *The Death of Billy the Kid*, which would be aired on July 24, 1944. The drama of William H. Bonney (1859-81) or Henry McCarthy, his real name, was written by Gore Vidal. At the time, newspapers were referring to Vidal as the "beau" of Joanne Woodward.

Impressed with Paul, Fred Coe, a producer at NBC, gave him the role. Coe had first considered Brando, but the actor had no desire to appear in a live TV drama. James Dean was also approached and seemed interested but had other commitments. Finally, Coe turned to Paul. To direct him, he hired

Jack Lord
Naked in a hotel room with Marilyn Monroe, and naked in a hotel room with Paul

Robert Mulligan.

For the first time, Paul came face to face with Vidal, who was "engaged" to Joanne at the time. Instead of viewing the homosexual Vidal as a rival in love, Paul became one of the playwright's best friends.

Born in West Point, New York, Gore was the son of Eugene Luther Vidal Jr., who was a lieutenant in the military. Eugene was the son of the famous Thomas Gore, a Democratic senator from Oklahoma.

Gore's mother was Nina S. Gore, an actress and socialite who would later marry Hugh D. Auchincloss, the stepfather of Jacqueline Kennedy Onassis. Nina also became known for her long-running off-and-on affair with Clark Gable.

At the time Paul came together with Vidal, the writer was notorious, having published his third novel, *The City and the Pillar*, in 1948. It outraged mainstream critics, including those at *The New York Times*, because it prominently featured homosexuality.

The fact that Paul and Vidal bonded as friends meant that Paul did not take those rumors about an "engagement" or "romance" between Vidal and his Joanne seriously. A mutual friend, Bill Gray, had introduced Vidal and Joanne at a cocktail party in Manhattan in 1953.

She admired his mind and found him "almost beautiful." But as an intelligent, intuitive woman, she almost certainly knew from the beginning that he was a homosexual. Far more hip and sophisticated than Joanne, Vidal was aware that he was being "dangled" in front of Paul to make him jealous, perhaps to motivate him more strongly to divorce Jackie and marry Joanne.

Vidal told Paul that he wanted his teleplay to be "not so much about Billy himself, but the people who created the myth of Billy the Kid." Paul seemed uncertain about how to interpret that. Approaching Coe, Vidal complimented him on his choice of Paul for the role, claiming that the actor "has both vulnerability and strength."

Vidal's fixation on Billy the Kid began when he attended the ballet performance of John Kriza appearing in the title role of Eugene Loring's *Billy the Kid* in 1953. It was hailed as the most erotic ballet ever performed in New York, with Kriza dancing in chaps with bulging genitalia showing in his white briefs. Vidal became smitten with Kriza, and the two men soon were lovers.

In the course of his career, Kriza would dance for John F. Kennedy in the White House and for Krushchev in the Kremlin. But Kriza's life ended in 1975 when he drowned while swimming in the Gulf

Author **Gore Vidal** writes a gay *Billy the Kid* for Paul to play on TV of Mexico.

For some reason, Vidal, an American blueblood, identified with the character of Billy the Kid. The image of The Kid haunted him for years. In Billy, he found a character who is "forever young, undyingly loyal to personal bonds, resolutely insistent on individual freedom, and hostile to all injustice, especially from the government."

On the set of *Billy the Kid*, Paul worked with such veteran actors as Jason Robards Jr., cast as Joe Grant. Robards, son of a famous actor, would go on to greater fame and even step into Humphrey Bogart's shoes after Bogart's death in 1957 when, in 1961, he married Lauren Bacall.

Robards told Paul that he worked in films and on TV "so I can grab the money and get back on Broadway as fast as my ass will carry me. Once you're on stage, no fucking director can yell, 'Cut it!' You're out there on your own, and there's always the thrill of a live audience. Don't sell out, Newman. Don't go Hollywood." He smiled. "Except for the money, of course."

Both Vidal and Paul felt that the teleplay of *Billy the Kid* could be "turned into a great movie." Indeed, in time it would be filmed, but not exactly as Vidal had envisioned it.

On seeing Paul perform on TV, Vidal claimed that *Billy the Kid* was his favorite of all his plays for television. But then he added enigmatically, "though by no means the most admired of all my teleplays."

After the telecast, Paul's life would move closer into the orbit of Vidal. A quartet, known in Hollywood as "The Unholy Four," was formed. The only woman in that household was Joanne Woodward. Depending on your point of view, she was either Paul's mistress or Vidal's fiancée. To the stew pot, Vidal added his lover, Howard Austen.

"When the four of them started living together in Hollywood, they were the hottest topic of gossip in Tinseltown," said Tony Perkins. "All sorts of kinky rumors abounded about what the four of them were actually doing after midnight."

Paul in Gore Vidal's teleplay for *Billy the Kid*. Offscreen, he gunned down Joanne's "beau."

Deep in the throes of a hot romance with Tab Hunter in Hollywood, Tony Perkins had little time for Paul. But according to Vampira, they did get together at the Chateau Marmont on at least three different occasions to intimately connect.

Paul was shocked to learn that fans were mistaking Tony for Elvis Presley. The singer from Memphis was in town for his film debut. He'd been signed by Hal Wallis to star in *Love Me Tender*.

When Paul had his first reunion dinner with Tony, he learned that Jerry Lewis had encountered him on the Paramount lot and had spent thirty minutes talking to him before he realized he was not carrying on a conversation with Elvis Presley.

Ironically, Tony would be offered the starring role in Harold Robbins' *A Stone for Danny Fisher*, but he turned it down. Retitled *King Creole*, the role became a vehicle for Elvis.

"I don't think you look like Presley at all," Paul told Tony. "He's a greaser. You're not. Frankly, I think the King of Rock 'n' Roll stole his coiffure from Tony Curtis. Incidentally, have you seduced Curtis yet?"

"Not yet," Tony said. "He's on my list. As for Presley, he may have to watch out for me. I'm taking singing lessons, and I'm going to record. I've decided to become a singer/actor."

"You're joking!" Paul asked in astonishment.

"Hell no! My producers think I may have a hit with a little number called 'Moonlight Swim.' Tab also plans to record. I'm sure both of us will have hit records."

"God damn and hot pussy momma," Paul said. "Brando's singing and fighting with Sinatra on *Guys and Dolls*. Does that mean Paul Newman had better find a vocal coach before the Hollywood sun sets on my ass?"

Meeting with Vampira later that day, Paul told her that, "Tony seems full of himself.

"He's having his moment," she said. "Up for a Supporting Oscar in *Friendly Persuasion*, playing a mentally tormented baseball player in *Fear Strikes Out*. I bet he'll get another Oscar nomination for that role."

"And what am I?" Paul asked. "Chopped liver?"

She leaned over to give him a reassuring kiss on the lips. "Your day will come."

Both Vampira and Paul commented on the coincidence of having Tab do *Fear Strikes Out* as a teleplay before Tony was cast in the film version as the star of the Boston Red Sox who has a nervous breakdown.

"Here's what I don't understand," Paul said. "How can we guys suck each other's dicks at night and the very next day be up for the same parts? Where's the jealousy factor? I don't really feel jealous of Monty, Marlon, Tony, our friend Jimmy, or even Tab Hunter. Well, maybe Tab a little bit. He's pretty damn good looking. In a town where a guy's looks mean everything, I think he's got me beat. If I come up against him for the same role, I think he's got it over me. After all, who walked off with the role of Danny Forrester in *Battle Cry*?"

"Don't worry about it," she assured him. "There will be plenty of roles for everybody, enough to go around. Guys like you and Tony are the new breed. I'd call you guys The Inheritors. Have you seen the latest movies with John Wayne, Gary Cooper, Clark Gable, Tyrone Power, Errol Flynn? They are no longer fathers. They're granddaddies."

"Speaking of Tyrone Power," Paul said, "I'm having dinner with him tonight."

"That darling Ty has fallen for you?" Vampira asked.

"No, the dinner's also with Robert, our dear Robert Francis. Power has stolen Robert from all of our nests. It's a secondary romance. Howard Hughes still has Robert in his clutches."

"Play it right tonight," Vampira advised, "and you lucky devil you, you might end up in a three way."

"I could be so lucky."

***

In Hollywood, Paul picked up on his sometimes affair with Robert Francis, who was disappointed at the way his films had been received by the public. He was especially bitter about *The Bamboo Prison* in 1954, a prisoner-of-war drama in which he'd co-starred with E.G. Marshall, playing a Communist posing as a priest so he could gather information from American prisoners of war. "I should have won an Oscar for my performance," Robert immodestly told Paul. "But, no, nothing, just attacks from the critics."

When Robert had been cast as the lead in *They Rode West* (1954), he'd starred opposite Donna Reed, who became his friend. In that film, he played Dr. Allen Seward, a surgeon assigned to a western cavalry post. "The only good thing that came out of that was Philip Carey," Robert told Paul. "The first day I met him, I had to have him, even though Joan Crawford kept him busy on many a night."

"Howard Hughes does the same for you," Paul countered.

"I'm not exactly sure what was going on," Donna Reed, years later, recalled. "Phil and Robert were definitely having an affair. One night I saw them dining in a restaurant together with a third party who turned out to be

Paul Newman. I had my suspicions about that threesome."

"I befriended Robert, but he never completely told me everything," Donna said. "I know for a fact that Howard Hughes was keeping Robert, and they often piloted planes together. Both Robert and Newman reminded me of kids in a candy store when they first arrived in Hollywood. Everyone was after them, and since all their pursuers were gorgeous—and often rich and powerful stars—they weren't turning down many offers. Robert was strictly homosexual and Paul obviously bi, so that one was getting twice as many offers. Newman apparently settled down in later years, or so I hear, but when he first hit town, he wanted to sample everybody's goodies, both male and female. That was one busy boy. I met him on a few occasions, but he never gave me a tumble, so I can't report from first-hand experience."

"Even though Robert really enjoyed dating Paul, I always had the feeling that he'd drop Paul in a minute if that Phil Carey called," Donna said. "The former Marine stood 6 feet 5 inches and when he dropped his pants those five inches, so to speak, were doubled. At least that's what Robert claimed. I heard that even Phil's leading ladies, including Arlene Dahl, Doris Day, and Anita Ekberg developed crushes on him, but I don't think anything came of that. I know that Raymond Burr fell madly in love with Phil when they made *Count Three and Pray* in 1955, but Burr was rejected."

An outspoken **Donna Reed** was amazed at how her male friends played musical chairs with each other at night.

"Phil and Robert also appeared together in *The Long Gray Line* in 1955, but Robert had to spend more time with the star of that picture, Tyrone Power," Donna said. "I know that the female star of the film, Maureen O'Hara, walked in on the director, John Ford, who had his tongue down Power's throat. It's hard for me, a mere straight woman, to keep track of all those guys back then. They were in and out of each other's beds as fast as a revolving door. But I think they had great fun. I envied them their freedom."

"A woman has to be more careful unless she's Jayne Mansfield, Mamie Van Doren, Barbara Payton, or even Marilyn Monroe," Donna said. "And in those cases, it doesn't matter since they don't have any pristine reputation to uphold like that Grace Kelly, who was probably the biggest slut of them all, although the American public didn't know

The handsome former Marine, **Phil Carey**, was an object of desire chased by everyone from Doris Day to Paul himself.

that at the time."

***

Paul met Tyrone Power in the waning years of his life. The movie idol was to die in 1958 of a heart attack on the set of *Solomon and Sheba* during a dueling scene. Paul had always admired Tyrone's movie star handsomeness, with one of the most classic profiles in the history of cinema. Paul had first seen Tyrone emoting onscreen way back in the late 1930s when he was a kid growing up in Shaker Heights.

When he actually met Tyrone for the first time, Paul noticed a remarkable change in the real man as opposed to his screen image. Although he was still handsome, Tyrone's face showed telltale signs of decay, including bags under his eyes and a certain jowly condition around his cheeks and throat.

Robert Francis seemed like he had a serious case of hero worship whenever Tyrone was in the room. Paul found the movie idol personable, articulate, well educated, and a gracious host.

Paul had driven to an address in the Hollywood Hills. Recently divorced from Linda Christian, Tyrone explained to Paul that he was temporarily renting someone else's house. "I need a hideaway. Smitty arranges these things for me." He was referring to Smitty Hanson, his longtime "trick."

In the early part of the evening, both Robert and Tyrone spoke of their experiences in shooting John Ford's *The Long Gray Line* at Columbia studios. Both of them had been filming interior shots with the understanding that they'd soon be heading East for the bulk of the filming at West Point.

During the course of the evening, Paul learned that director Ford was making it with both of his handsome stars, the younger one and the more vintage beauty.

"I thought Ford was the most macho male in Hollywood," Paul said.

"Those are the kind to watch out for," Tyrone cautioned. "Hell, Ford used to throw John Wayne on his casting couch back in the Stone Age."

At the point when Paul entered Tyrone's life, the star was throwing caution to the wind, whereas he'd led a life of discretion up until then. Many of the scandal magazines were hovering over him like vultures. With Smitty Hanson's help, Tyrone was staging orgies— many of them bisexual, others exclusively

The fading matinee idol of the 1930s, **Tyrone Power,** liked the smell and sexual excitement of other males at his orgies.

140

homosexual. It was the underground talk of Hollywood.

Van Johnson, Tyrone's friend, was a frequent guest at these orgies, as was Errol Flynn, who had been Tyrone's lover in the 1930s. Sometimes beautiful, young, aspiring actresses were brought in, most of them eager to meet Tyrone. Often the young men invited were well-built hustlers, who'd come to Hollywood to become movie stars but had ended up selling their bodies to the highest bidder.

At these orgies, Tyrone, in the words of his biographer Hector Arce, would have "to see and smell the sexual excitement of other males before he too could become aroused."

And now the screen grows black.

"Paul told me about meeting Tyrone and the early part of the evening," Vampira said. "But he didn't tell me how the night went. I know he stayed overnight. I just assumed he had a three-way with Tyrone and Robert. Not only that, I think Paul and Robert started to attend Tyrone's orgies—indeed, I'm sure those two good-looking boys were the star attractions. Paul seemed too embarrassed to talk about it."

"Maybe he'd hung out with James Dean too long, but Paul was shaking off those Midwestern morals and getting deep into the shit of Hollywood," Vampira said. "In later years he'd become more respectable, but 1955 was a year to let it rip. He was still young and full of piss, and he didn't want to miss out on a thing. I think he was really enjoying himself until tragedy struck that year. Like lightning, it struck twice."

***

Paul awoke on the morning of July 31, 1955 with a bad cold. He'd been scheduled to fly to Catalina Island with Robert, but called him and told him he couldn't make it. Originally, Howard Hughes himself had been slated to fly with Robert, but some emergency at his office at 7000 Romaine Street prevented him from accompanying Robert, who then called Paul to "fly with me."

With both Paul and Hughes unavailable, Robert called another male friend to be his co-pilot. Still inexperienced in the air, in spite of taking lessons from Hughes, Robert set out on that clear, bright summer day.

Up in the air, something went wrong with the plane's single engine. It sputtered and then went dead. Trapped in the doomed plane, Robert and his friend hurtled to their deaths. When the plane hit the ground, it exploded, killing both men.

That afternoon, Paul heard the news over the radio. Robert's death brought on a morbid depression and a bout of heavy drinking.

According to Vampira, "Paul was not only mourning Robert's untimely death, but how his own life might have been violently snuffed out. Both Robert and Paul were on the dawn of what each of them hoped would be a spectacular career in Hollywood. Paul lived to see his dream come true. Poor Robert did not. I went with Paul on at least three visits to Robert's grave site at Forest Lawn. And, then, as might have been predicted, Paul seemed to place Robert in a far and distant corner of his brain and move on with his life. In just a few weeks, he'd be facing another untimely death of a friend and lover, and this would have a far greater impact on his life."

***

All actors are curious to see how another actor will interpret the role they originate. Such was the case when Paul went to see Richard Jaeckel perform in the West Coast version of *The Desperate Hours*, the same play that Paul had starred in on Broadway.

After slipping in to see the play once the curtain had gone up, Paul went backstage at the Carthay Circle Theater to congratulate Richard on his performance. "You did far better than I did," Paul graciously told him. "You were more menacing, more believable. We pretty boys have a hard time convincing audiences we're killers at heart."

Meeting Paul in his dressing room, Richard was "charmed" by him, as he later told Van Johnson, whose seduction of Richard led to his getting cast in the 1950 film, *Battleground*.

Short, stocky, and ruggedly handsome, blond-haired Richard, a year younger than Paul, had graduated from Hollywood High. While working in the mailroom of 20th Century Fox, a gay casting director spotted him and arranged for him to audition for the role of Private Johnny Anderson in *Guadalcanal Diary* (1943), one of that studio's major war epics.

Richard's film career was interrupted by a four-year stint in the United States Navy from 1944 to 1948. When he returned to films, and based on his debut in *Guadalcanal Diary*, directors thought of him as ideal for war movies, casting him in *Battleground* with Van Johnson and *Sands of Iwo Jima* with John Wayne.

Bisexual Richard was not averse to having affairs with better-established actors who were

Robert Francis invited Paul to "fly with me" on that fateful morning in July, 1955.

142

either gay or bisexual themselves. Hollywood was filled with rumors of the affair that Van had sustained with Richard during the filming of *Battleground*. The Duke liked Richard so much during the filming of *Sands of Iwo Jima*, that he invited him to share his dressing room, and no star ever did that.

Richard really came to the public's attention in 1952 when he played the role of Turk, Terry Moore's athletic boyfriend in *Come Back, Little Sheba*.

During the filming of this movie, Richard had an ongoing affair with Burt Lancaster. The star of the film, Shirley Booth, was well aware of this, as perhaps was Terry Moore playing Richard's girlfriend. After the film was wrapped, and perhaps to make him jealous, Richard revealed details of his affair with Burt to his longtime companion and lover, actor Casey Sullivan, "Lancaster and Wayne are both big, big stars," Richard said. "But off the screen, when I take off my pants, *I'm* the star. I've got three times more than either of them. Van's pretty well hung, though."

On the first night of their meeting, Paul invited Richard to join him for a night of drinking. "One thing led to another," Casey said, "and those two hotties ended up in bed together at a Laguna motel for the weekend. I always envied Richard for getting to seduce Paul Newman. He was my favorite."

After their initial meeting, Paul, at least according to Casey, continued to see Richard on and off for a number of years.

As the years went by, according to Casey, Paul kept holding out the promise of casting Richard in a picture opposite him. "Richard went along with these promises," Casey said, "but considered them empty. He liked Paul and continued to see him, but he didn't think he'd do anything to advance his career the way Van Johnson, Burt Lancaster, and John Wayne had. Then one day, surprise of surprise, it happened. But it was a long time in coming."

***

Suddenly, Frank Sinatra came back into Paul's life. Behind the scenes, after he was cast as the narrator in Thornton Wilder's *Our Town*, he had been instrumental in getting the thirty-year-old Paul cast as a sixteen-year-old high school student in the same play. In 1944, the play had starred a young Montgomery Clift at the City Center in New York.

Our Town was Wilder's sentimental tribute to small-town America, and had netted him a Pulitzer Prize. Cast as George Gibbs in the play, Paul learns about love, loss, mourning, and death in Grover's Corners, New Hampshire. The rehearsals would

Richard Jaeckel,
Sleeping his way
to the top

143

last for two weeks before a live transmission on TV.

Cast opposite was the lovely Eva Marie Saint, who had just completed *On the Waterfront* with their mutual friend, Marlon Brando. In years to come, Paul and Eva would again be cast together in *Exodus*. "Here I was playing this lovesick teenager opposite Eva," Paul said. "She'd just won an Oscar for playing opposite Brando in *On the Waterfront*. It was unfair considering how different the roles were, but I just knew the critics would once again compare my performance opposite Eva with Marlon's performance opposite Eva. Indeed they did, and I came out the fucking loser. I loved Marlon dearly, at least on that rare occasion when I got to see him, but sometimes I wanted to cut off his dick. Symbolically speaking, that is."

For the broadcast, Sammy Cahn wrote the lyrics for "Love and Marriage," Jimmy Van Heusen the music. Sinatra's version hit the charts in 1955, as did a competing version by Dinah Shore.

Even though he'd secretly gotten Paul cast in the part, Sinatra did not greet him like a friend. On the first day of rehearsal, he came over to him. "Listen, kid, I've got a monopoly on blue eyes. I fear if you become a star, like people are saying, we'll be competing for the title of blue eyes. You may have to start wearing glasses."

"I wouldn't dare to compete against you for anything," Paul said.

"Stick to that plan," Sinatra said. "I'd win in any competition with you, especially if we measured each other's dicks. Now get me some fresh coffee. Make it fresh or I'll snip your balls off—that is, if you've got any."

"Working with Sinatra is like defusing a ticking time bomb," Jimmy Van Heusen said to Paul the day he first appeared on the set.

After starring with Paul, Eva had only the highest praise for him, calling him "one of the most sensitive actors I'd ever seen on the screen."

Paul told Sinatra that he found Eva "ethereally lovely, but I think she's aptly named. She's too much of a saint to mess around with my tool, although I'd whip it out for her at a moment's notice if she'd only give me the look."

"She's too decent a girl to get mixed up with us," Sinatra told Paul. "Both of us had better stick to Hollywood whores. Speaking of Hollywood whores, I've got a date with one tonight at her suite at the Plaza. She knows you and wants you to have dinner with us in her

With Marlon Brando in *On the Waterfront*, **Eva Marie Saint** faced a sexual dynamo. With Paul Newman in *Our Town*, she confronted a lovesick teenager.

suite."

Paul was intrigued, thinking Sinatra had arranged another one of his busty showgals for a night of fun and games.

They rehearsed until eight that night and took a cab to the Plaza. When the door to the suite was thrown open, Paul was startled to see Grace Kelly in a white gown meant more for lounging than the street.

She kissed both men on the lips and invited them in for a dinner catered by room service. "I'm in town for some shopping," she told Sinatra and Paul, "and I wanted to see some dear friends." She looked with a certain enchantment at both men. Paul seemed flattered that Grace numbered him among her friends.

Sinatra and Grace had become close when he'd accompanied Ava Gardner to Africa for the shooting of *Mogambo*. Grace had co-starred in the movie with Ava and Clark Gable. During that time, Grace had a brief affair with Gable.

Over dinner, Grace and Sinatra enthralled Paul with stories of their adventures during the shoot in Africa. "There were all these tall Watusis in the film," Grace claimed. "Rather beautiful men in a primitive sort of way. All of them were hired as extras and they wore breechclouts. We were walking along by a row of them. All of a sudden, Ava said to me, 'I wonder if their cocks are as big as people say. Have you ever seen a black cock?' I turned various shades of red. Then Ava reached out and pulled up the breechclout from one of the Watusis. His face was filled with pride as his mammoth cock flopped out. By then my face was beyond scarlet. Ava let the pouch drop. She turned to me and said, 'Frank's bigger than that.'"

Paul burst into laughter but Sinatra did not seem amused.

The rest of the evening Sinatra and Grace spent discussing their upcoming picture, *High Society*, a musical remake of *The Philadelphia Story*, which had marked the comeback of Katharine Hepburn to the screen in 1940.

Around one o'clock, Sinatra turned to Paul. "Grace and I have some private business to conclude. In other words, the party's over. Scram, kid."

Grace graciously showed Paul to the door where she secretly slipped him a note. On the elevator going down, he read it. BE HERE AT TEN O'CLOCK TOMORROW MORNING FOR BREAKFAST.

Paul found that three's a crowd after dining with **Frank Sinatra** and **Grace Kelly**. But Grace was not opposed to a morning tryst the next day with Paul.

145

The next day at the Actors Studio, he told Rod Steiger, "I've become a call boy."

"Selling it by the inch, huh?" Steiger asked.

"No, I'm Grace Kelly's call boy," Paul said. "Every time she's in town, she calls me, and I come running to paradise."

***

An unexpected call came in from Fred Zinnemann, the director, who was still basking in the glow of his success with *From Here to Eternity*. "I want you to play the part of Curly, the cowboy, in my upcoming *Oklahoma!* I don't have to tell you it's the role of the year."

"A musical?" Paul was flabbergasted.

"Of course, we'll have to dub your voice, but we do that all the time. Of all the actors around today, you're the perfect vision of Curly, the right physical specimen. We'll have to test you, naturally."

"I can do it if you'll take care of the singing," Paul assured him. "I sing only in the shower, but I sound great. The boy from Ohio can play a boy from Oklahoma. It's a bit of a stretch, but I can do it."

A week later Paul felt that he had performed poorly in the test, but Zinnemann assured him that "you photographed beautifully. I think you're going to be our Curly."

Paul later claimed that he felt he'd "queer the deal" if he mentioned the upcoming film to anyone before a contract was signed. Finally, however, Zinnemann's silence became deafening. Paul called Rod Steiger, who had been cast as Jud, the sinister hired man in the film, and told him that Zinnemann wanted him for the role of Curly.

"Not so fast," Steiger said. "I just made a test with James Dean in New York. Zinnemann said it was 'the best screen test' he'd ever shot. Zinnemann raved about our 'Poor Jud Is Dead' number. James did his own singing."

"I've been fucked!" Paul said before putting down the phone. He decided to "booze it up" for a few days to get over his disappointment.

When he finally called

Dean and arranged to get together, he found that his actor friend was also wallowing in depression. "After practically assuring me of the role of Curly in *Oklahoma!*, Fred Zinnemann fucked me. I was out of the picture the moment Frank Sinatra wanted the role. As far as I'm concerned, I sing better than Frank Sinatra."

"If you say so, pal," Paul told him.

"Two weeks later both Dean and Paul read in the trade papers that Sinatra had bolted. Zinnemann had apparently come to his senses and cast Gordon MacRae in the part. Paul took the news philosophically. "What the hell? Let's face it: MacRae has that baritone voice needed for the role. When Hollywood-style movie musicals fade in the dust, MacRae when he's seventy-five will probably be in some roadside inn somewhere singing 'Oklahoma!' to a bunch of drunks."

Paul got the age wrong, but his prediction came true.

***

It was ironic that in the weeks right before his death, Dean was rehearsing during the day with Paul and making love to him at night. At long last their dream of co-starring together had come true. Both of them had been cast in *The Battler*, a teleplay based on an Ernest Hemingway story.

Producer Fred Coe, who rose out of the depths of Alligator, Mississippi, to become a prolific television, theater, and film producer, came up with the idea of casting both Dean and Paul in the same teleplay. Coe was one of the major players in the Golden Age of television, having begun his career in 1945 when virtually no one had a TV set. He often relied on literary classics as a starting point for his teleplays.

Coe had been impressed with the dramatic potential of Ernest Hemingway's autobiographical "Nick Adams" stories, and his best friend, A.E. Hotchner, had agreed to write the teleplay for one of those stories, *The Battler*. In another touch of irony, Hotchner became Paul's best friend long after "Papa" had committed suicide.

The Battler was set to be aired on October 18, 1955 as part of NBC's *Playwright '56* series. Coe hired Arthur Penn as the director. He'd been a member of Joshua Logan's stage company and had attended the Los Angeles branch of Actors Studio. In time, Penn would direct eight different actors in Oscar-nominated performances, including Anne Bancroft, Warren Beatty, and Faye Dunaway.

Paul looked forward to working with Penn, although he soon realized that the director was not a sycophantic admirer of Lee Strasberg. "That guy ruined an entire generation of actors with that sense memory crap of his," Penn told

147

Paul.

With his horn-rimmed glasses and a cigar perpetually in hand, Penn showed great sensitivity in working with Dean and Paul. "He knew how to handle an actor," Paul said. "He was not just a director, but a philosopher and an artist. He knew how to let whatever limited talent I had breathe and develop at its own pace. He wasn't a dictator like Otto Preminger with whom I'd regrettably work in the future."

Paul was set to play Hemingway's Nick Adams as a young man. The character was Hemingway's literary alter ego. Dean was miscast as an aging boxer with a damaged eye and that inevitable cauliflower ear.

One night around three o'clock in the morning, Dean woke Paul up. "What's the matter?" Paul asked, groggy with sleep.

"I just had a golden dream," Dean said, jumping out of the bed and dancing around the room. "It was great! I dreamed that you and I are about to become the two hottest shits ever to hit Tinseltown. James Dean and Paul Newman. We're going to win more Oscars, make bigger pictures, than all the farts who came before us. Years from now when everyone's forgotten Bogie as the fag in *Casablanca*, the world will be talking about James Dean and Paul Newman."

"Come back to bed," Paul said.

***

Marlon Brando did not seek out the press and did not like to talk to reporters. But when he did, his remarks were invariably controversial. He was particularly incensed when some critic, after seeing *East of Eden*, called Dean "not just another Elia Kazan actor, but one with far more depth and sensitivity than Brando himself."

Speaking on record, Marlon said, "Dean and I worked together at the Actors Studio. He has a certain talent. However, in *East of Eden*, he seems to be wearing my last year's wardrobe and using my last year's talent."

Dean's ego was weak and vulnerable, and his sense of self-esteem was always shaky and so fragile he could collapse emotionally at only the slightest provocation.

Such was the case when Marlon's remarks were told to him. Working with Dean in rehearsals for the Hemingway teleplay, *The Battler*, Paul claimed that "Dean practically had a nervous breakdown. He couldn't concentrate in rehearsals. At one point, he was shaking like a leaf in the wind. Marlon was a very bad boy. He must have known how devastating his remarks about Dean's talent would be. Maybe Marlon was trying to get back at some dumb critic and didn't consider how much Dean loved and worshipped him."

"Marlon wanted both Dean and me to be our own men, our own style of actor," Paul said. "Maybe this was the way he had of cutting the umbilical cord with Dean. After all, Dean had been pursuing Marlon for years like a lovesick puppy. Thank God Marlon didn't spill his bile over my body. I was too weak and vulnerable back then. An attack from Marlon on my own acting abilities would have shattered me."

"I must say Marlon always treated me with a certain respect, something he didn't always show Dean or another one of his rivals, Monty Clift," Paul claimed. "Even though they called me 'the second Brando,' and this must have pissed him off, he never made me the butt of his practical jokes. I also never became the victim of his sadism. As for practical jokes on another actor, that would lie in my future when I met my fellow actor, Robert Redford."

Meeting with Dean at Googies in Hollywood, Eartha Kitt and Paul had never seen him so bitter about Hollywood, "*Giant* is my last picture," he proclaimed. "I've decided this incestuous cesspool called Hollywood is not for me. Marilyn Monroe is the perfect personification of Hollywood. All false glamour. There is no reality to her. A man can go crazy here."

"Fuck Hollywood!" Dean said in a voice loud enough to be overheard at the next tables. "Fuck Jack Warner and his studio. So he made movies with Bette Davis and Joan Crawford. Big fucking deal. Who are they anyway? Davis was all about overacting and exaggerated mannerisms and Crawford is nothing but a self-created illusion. My greatest thrill in life would be to tie Warner down in a desert and crap over his face. Then I'd leave him to die in the desert, food for ravenous wolves."

"The best thing that could happen to Southern California is for an earthquake to come along and topple the whole fucking place into the Pacific Ocean like the lost continent of Atlantis," he said. "The whole town is filled with nothing but cocksuckers. I've stuffed my pecker into the mouths of some of the biggest producers and directors in Hollywood before those fuckers went home to give their wives and kids a big sloppy wet kiss. Those losers probably had my semen still in their rotten mouths."

"Rock Hudson couldn't get enough of my ass," Dean claimed, "when we started filming *Giant*. "He fucked me so much I thought his dick was going to fall off. Then he turned on me. Hudson is nothing but a piece of shit. There's nothing real about him. Like Marilyn, he's the perfect example of a Hollywood product. If Hollywood did not exist, Hudson would have been a truck driver getting blow-jobs at seedy truck stops."

That night Dean invited Paul to go with him for a midnight ride in the Hollywood Hills in his souped-up Porsche. Paul had another date and turned him down, but Eartha volunteered to go.

The next day she called Paul. "I wish I hadn't accepted Jamie's invitation.

It was the nightmare ride of my life. I felt that he was committing suicide and trying to take me with him."

After she'd escaped from that death trap, she stood on the sidewalk, warning Dean. "This Porsche is going to be your coffin. I just feel it."

That was the last time she ever spoke to him or saw him again.

On September 30, 1955, Eartha called Paul. She'd just heard over the radio that Dean had died in a car crash. "That Porsche did indeed prove to be his coffin," she said sadly. "I'll never forgive Jamie for cheating me out of his presence in my life. No one else in the world understands me." She put down the phone.

Almost immediately another call came in. Still in shock, Paul picked up the phone. At first he thought it might be Eartha calling back, as she'd ended the call rather abruptly.

It was someone from Warner Brothers. Years later he tried to recall that phone call, but couldn't remember the name of the person calling. He thought it might have been Jack Warner himself, but he wasn't sure. "I was out of my mind at the time."

"Dean's gone but you're here, kid," the voice said. "Some actor has to fill his shoes. You probably didn't know this, but Dean was about to sign to do nine pictures in a row with us. All of those movies could star you. You'd be perfect. Here's the chance of a lifetime. It's a sad fact that Dean is dead, but we the living have to go on. Fuck all that talk about you being 'the second Brando.' If you're smart and play all the angles, and if you lick enough asses, you could be the next James Dean."

Paul put down the phone.

Hollywood's hottest star, **James Dean**, came to a mangled end in September of 1955 on a lonely stretch of California back road.

His untimely death held many implications for the career of Paul Newman.

Chapter Five
A Tumbling Tumbleweed

Based on the flood of public emotion which followed in the wake of Dean's death, Paul assumed that plans for the teleplay, *The Battler*, would be scrapped. But Fred Coe wanted it to be aired on schedule within three weeks of Dean's fatal crash. And he wanted Paul to take over Dean's role as the star of the teleplay.

Coe called Paul. "I have no one else who can learn the part at this late hour. It would be easy to get another actor to play the secondary role you were originally assigned, but at this point, only you can be the star. Let's face it: You know Dean's part better than he did."

Paul didn't want to change roles. "I can't do it emotionally," he told a mourning Eartha Kitt, who was suffering greatly at the loss of her soulmate. "If I accepted the lead, I'd be advancing my career at Jimmy's expense. Both of us loved him dearly. I can't—I *won't*—fill his shoes. Coe and Penn will have to get someone else."

Yet somehow, Eartha managed to convince Paul that filling in for their departed friend would be a way to honor his memory. "That heavy makeup that the role calls for will help everyone forget your reputation as a pretty boy." she said. "You'll have to survive purely on your acting skills, 'cause their makeup artists will make you look like a battered pug."

A.E. Hotchner, the teleplay's author, felt he had to apologize to Hemingway for pushing Paul into the lead role at the last minute. In a letter to Hemingway, he wrote, "We were forced to fill the part by risking young Newman in the lead." Papa Hemingway's reaction to Paul's performance that night in October is unknown.

"Suddenly, I agreed to play this punch drunk wreck of a man at fifty-five, a lean and hungry former champ," Paul said. "Since I was at the height of my so-called male beauty, it took the makeup boys hours to disfigure me."

In 1962 Paul would again portray *The Battler* when 20th Century Fox cast

151

him in a big screen adaptation of that play, retitling it *Hemingway's Adventures of a Young Man.*

After the telecast, Fred Coe took Paul out for a drink to congratulate him on his fine performance. A drunk in the bar had just seen Paul's TV portrayal of a boxer and challenged him to a fight. At first Paul tried to shrug him off, but the drunk was persistent. A brawl erupted, and Paul ended up with a black eye.

Two other industry insiders were watching the TV debut of Paul's telecast. One was the director, Robert Wise, the other a producer, Charles Schnee. These two men had recently received an agreement from Dean to star as Rocky Graziano in his life story, *Somebody Up There Likes Me.* Both Wise and Schnee were devastated by the death of their potential star. But after watching Paul in *The Battler*, both the director and producer decided that Paul would be ideal in the role of Graziano.

Wise called Paul and arranged a meeting. Paul showed up with his black eye. "You didn't have to get makeup to give you a boxer's black eye," Schnee said.

"By the way," Wise said, "that's the best black eye I've ever seen the makeup department create."

"That's no black eye makeup," Paul said. "That's the real thing. I got into a bar fight."

"With that shiner, you've almost got the role," Wise said. "We know you can act. All we want you to do at this point is strip down and try on these." He held up a pair of scarlet boxing trunks with large gold bands on the sides. "We want to see how you're built," Wise said.

Hesitant to strip down to his underwear, Paul eyed Wise skeptically. "You're not gay, are you? I don't have to put out to get this part, do I?"

"I'm a pussy man myself," Wise said. "So is Schnee here."

Paul stripped down, and both Wise and Schnee found his physique well defined.

Robert Wise
Orders Paul to strip.

"You could be beefier, so go to the gym and puff yourself up every day," Wise said. "You've got the part, though."

"It'll make you a star," Schnee promised.

"We've also got great news for you," Wise said. "We've cast Pier Angeli as the girl. I heard you used to bang her before Dean moved in to take her away."

"Something like that," Paul muttered. He felt reservations about Pier entering his life again.

He called Eartha and told her the news. "I

152

think people are going to stop calling me the second Brando. Now they'll be calling me the second Dean. When will I ever become Paul Newman?"

"Don't worry, sweetcakes," Eartha said. "You'll need to worry only when some younger stud is billed as the second Paul Newman."

***

To Paul's dismay, Tony Perkins, his sometimes lover and friend, was undergoing a career move at Paramount. Noting the public hysteria that developed in the wake of Dean's tragic death, the "suits" at Paramount decided they needed a young actor as a direct replacement for Dean. Tony was their candidate for the job.

When Paul returned to Hollywood and called Tony for a "session," as he put it, he was shocked. Although he'd never mentioned any involvement before, Tony was mourning a relationship with Dean that had never existed. He not only maintained that he'd lived with Dean as his roommate at Sunset Plaza Drive, but that he had been "the love of Jimmy's life."

Not wanting to accuse his self-enchanted friend of lying, Paul said, "Jimmy was one busy boy."

"There are 365 days in a year," Tony said. "I know a guy who has sex with at least two different men a day. That's 730 men a year. If you look at it that way, Jimmy didn't set the world's record for seduction."

"I've been reading about you and Dean in the fan magazines," Paul said.

"Of course, in public I talk about living with Dean as his roommate, not as his lover. One has to be discreet about these things. The fans can draw their own conclusions about how close we were."

Before the night ended, Tony had proclaimed himself "the new James Dean." Ironically, Tony didn't seem to realize that it was Paul himself who was being hailed as the new James Dean.

Competing with lovers such as Brando had always made Paul feel uncomfortable. But whereas Tony was openly trying to profit from Dean's death, Paul had been the unwilling actor who'd had Dean's roles thrust upon him, both on TV and in the movies. He didn't want to be the new Dean. He resented that comparison as much as he did his label of a Brando clone.

"When will these newspapers stop making these stupid comparisons?" he asked Rod Steiger.

"When the next Paul Newman comes along," Steiger told him.

Paul had never felt so distant from Tony as he did the night of their reunion. He'd later relate this to Eartha Kitt. "Tony's making a big mistake," he said. "He's not James Dean. Nor was he his dearest friend and lover. That's all bullshit."

"I have an equally awful story to tell you," she said. "Rock Hudson, who knows what a good friend I was of Jamie, came up to me at a party. He told me that he'd always resented Jamie's meteoric rise in the business. 'I'm glad he's dead,' Hudson said. 'That fatal car crash removed serious competition from me.' I slapped the fucker's face."

A struggling young actor, Jack Simmons, emerged to refute Tony's charges. He claimed that he had been Dean's live-in lover at the apartment on Sunset Plaza Drive. He also told biographer Charles Winecoff that, "No one can ever be a new Jimmy Dean. Jimmy was all internal and driven, while Tony Perkins was sort of mechanical, physically plotted and contrived. There is no comparison."

Simmons had met Dean when they appeared together on *The Dark, Dark Alley* for General Electric Theater. Dean had also been instrumental in getting him cast as a gang member in *Rebel Without a Cause*.

A few weeks after Dean's death, Simmons contacted Paul with a proposition. He very accurately claimed, "I did everything for Jimmy. I was with him on the set. If he wanted a cup of coffee, I got it for him. Hungry? I brought him his favorite sandwich. At night my ass was always available to him. I hated it, but I even let him burn my butt with cigarettes. He liked to do that and have it done to him. It was awful painful, but I let him put his fist up me. He jerked off while I screamed in pain."

"Why are you telling me all this crap?" Paul asked. "I don't want to hear it."

"I'm out of a job," Simmons said. "I could be your personal assistant just as I was for Jimmy. I think you're going places in this business, and I've decided I'll never be a star myself."

"My God, man, you weren't a personal assistant," Paul said. "You were a slave." Anger rose in his voice. "I don't buy slaves." He slammed down the phone.

***

Deep into his preparation for the role of Rocky Graziano, Paul received a stunning setback. Brando called Wise and Schnee, telling them that he wanted to play the role of Rocky Graziano in *Somebody Up There Likes Me*. Not only that, but he then called Paul and asked him to be his sparring partner in preparation for the role.

Stunned at his reversal of fortune, Paul agreed to box with him, but failed to tell him that Wise and Schnee had first offered the role to him.

At the gym the next day, a buffed Brando told Paul that, "I don't much like the idea of filling in for James Dean, but I've been studying Rocky and I want to go for it."

While they were working out in a gym together in Brooklyn, Brando told Paul that he used to box with Karl Malden while waiting backstage to go on in *Streetcar*. "One night I asked this fireman to go a few rounds with me," Brando said. "We squared off, circling each other. All of a sudden, he winds up throwing a haymaker at me. I saw it coming but it was too late. Next thing I know I was flying ass over heels into a pile of wooden crates. I saw stars and began bleeding from the nose like a stuck pig. I put some cold compresses on my beak but couldn't stop the bleeding. I had to rush out onto the stage with blood gushing from my nose."

Brando also claimed that when he was later taken to the hospital he encountered a doctor—"a sadist and butcher"—who set his nose badly.

"Your new look gives you character," Paul said. "If someone asks, now that your nose is set crookedly, I'm the pretty one. But put up your dukes, kid. In the ring they call me killer."

After three weeks of working out together in the ring, Brando told Paul, "I called Wise. I told him to get some other thug to play Rocky. I'm not going to make the picture." Then he delivered a shocker. "He told me you wanted to play Rocky. Go for it! Bring home an Oscar."

***

As part of a loanout to Metro-Goldwyn-Mayer, and as a means of getting into shape for the role of Rocky Graziano in *Somebody Up There Likes Me*, Paul worked out every day at the Hollywood YMCA. When he went to the showers, he was followed by admiring homosexuals who wanted to see him in the nude. As he later told Vampira, "I decided it was okay to give them a show, providing that none of them made a grab for the package."

"I've got to make good this time," Paul told his director, Robert Wise. "Maybe Hollywood will forgive me for *The Silver Chalice*, but if I fuck up Rocky, I'm a goner."

Before working with Wise, Paul had made it a point to view a copy of *The Set Up*, another boxing movie that Wise had made in 1949 starring Robert Ryan.

He was a skilled director and seemed to know

Marlon Brando
"A sadist and a butcher"

155

how to bring out the best in Paul. "Day by day we forgot all about Paul Newman," he said. "Paul became Graziano up there on the screen. He had his speech down perfect, his walk, everything. He even learned to box like Graziano."

On the set, Paul enjoyed his reunion with Eileen Heckart, who had been cast as the mother of the character he played in *Somebody Up There Likes Me*. Both of them recalled their earlier roles on Broadway in *Picnic* when he had played Janice Rule's boyfriend, and when Eileen had been cast as one of the town's sexually repressed older women. Both Paul and Eileen lamented that Hollywood had not granted them the opportunity to repeat their roles in the film version of *Picnic*.

During their reunion, Paul congratulated Eileen on her Oscar-winning performance in *The Bad Seed* (1956). Years later, she ruefully told the press, "One night you're winning the Oscar and receiving those air kisses. The next day, you're photographed standing in the unemployment line."

Working for the first time with veteran character actor Everett Sloane, Paul came to admire his ability too. An original member of Orson Welles' Mercury Theater troupe, Sloane had been acting since the age of seven when he portrayed Puck in *A Midsummer Night's Dream*. Sometimes Paul worked secretly with Sloane on some of his difficult scenes before testing them out with Wise himself.

"He was one of the great pros of *film noir*, and I'll miss him," Paul said when he learned of Sloane's suicide from an overdose of barbiturates at the age of 55 in 1965. "I'd seen him three months before, and he told me he was going blind because of glaucoma," Paul said. "Everett told me he couldn't stand the thought of living in darkness."

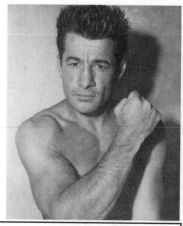

Rocky Graziano
Teaching Paul the ropes.

Paul Newman
With a *Noo Yawk* accent.

Still mourning the death of his lover, James Dean, a very young Sal Mineo approached Paul one day on the set. Sal had been cast as Graziano's friend, Romolo, in *Somebody*.

Fourteen years older than the Bronx-born Sicilian American, Paul congratulated him on his Oscar nomination for *Rebel Without a Cause*. "I thought you and Dean were terrific. I'm sorry he's gone."

"Not as sorry as I am," Sal said. He appeared on the verge of tears. "I noticed you work out every day. I'd like to join you at the Y."

Wise to Sal, Paul warned him, "Okay, but working out is all we're going to do. I don't intend to replace Dean in your life."

Sal's lip quivered, and Paul became aware of how insensitive he'd been. "Of course, you can work out with me. C'mon, get your stuff, kid. Just how old are you anyway?"

"I'm plenty old enough to know what I'm doing," Sal said. "Jimmy thought so."

"Yeah, but he had an affair with a twelve-year-old, so we can't cite him as a source," Paul cautioned. "As for me, I'm not a child molester."

At the gym and after a workout that stretched on for an hour and a half, Paul was keenly aware that Sal was, at least visually, devouring his body. Strangely, it didn't make him uncomfortable. He began to warm to the young actor, who seemed far older and more experienced than his years.

Sweaty and a bit tired, Paul finally announced, "I've had it for the day. Hustle your ass, kid, and join me in the shower. That way you can determine how I stack up against your buddy—and mine—Mr. James Dean."

That dying afternoon was the start of a beautiful friendship, most of it conducted in secret during the years to come.

***

Paul once again came together with Pier Angeli, but their love affair, launched on the set of *The Silver Chalice*, had grown cold. She was distant, yet very kind and respect-

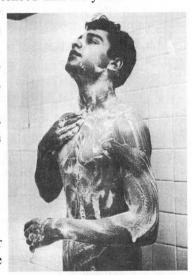

Sal Mineo
"Hustle your ass, kid!"

ful of him. "We both loved James Dean, and we both lost him," she said to him privately. "Now I have Vic Damone and you have Joanne Woodward." He couldn't help but notice that she'd failed to mention his wife Jackie.

Both of them found it ironic that he was Jewish playing an Italian-American in the movie, and she, a bona fide Italian, was playing his Jewish girlfriend.

When he first encountered her, Pier was suffering from a broken ankle but mending quickly. She'd fallen down the stairs at her house. Until she recovered, he carried her in his arms to lunch and back. It was somewhere along the way that she seemed to fall in love with him again.

Their passion was rekindled when Wise flew them to New York to film scenes together on the East Side. "I'd never seen New York this cold before," Wise said. "In only a day or two, Paul was warming Pier's bed. Her plaster cast had been removed."

Paul introduced Pier to Graziano, saying, "Rocky, meet your wife."

The former champ took them on a tour of what he called "the landmarks of my life," including the Caponzzelle Bar and the tough streets where he'd fought in gang wars.

When Vic Damone flew into New York to reclaim Pier, Paul found another place to spend the night. "Paul had to go back to fucking the Mineo kid," Wise claimed.

Back on the West Coast, Pier became upset by a blonde-haired woman who kept appearing on the set and staring at her. "I can't work when she looks at me like that," she told Wise. Pier had never seen Joanne Woodward in a film and didn't really know what she looked like. But Joanne obviously knew who Pier was.

"I told Wise I couldn't act with this scary lady staring at me," Pier later claimed. "He asked her to stand out of my sight line. She must have thought I was stealing her boyfriend. But isn't that calling the kettle black, as you Americans say? It was Joanne Woodward who was stealing someone's husband."

Pier Angeli, Paul, and Everett Sloane
"I can't live in darkness."

Back on the West Coast, and with his putty nose and *Noo Yawk* accent, Paul was delivering a "Star-Is-Born" performance, the most effective in his young life. Wise was impressed with how he'd gotten all those *deez* and *dems* in the right place, with his marbles-in-the-mouth stammer.

In a statement uncharacteristic of Wise, he told Paul, "I think you're going to win an Oscar for playing Rocky, and I've never said this to an actor before. You're giving a *tour-de-force* performance. You're on your way, kid."

In spite of such praise from his director, Paul later recalled, "I was the most miserable guy in Hollywood." He was drinking more whisky than ever. "I'm screwed up but I don't want help," he told Vampira. He seemed guilt ridden about his rapidly dissolving marriage and his turning his back on his family, except to offer financial support. Yet he wasn't ready to commit to Joanne either.

"Somehow I've convinced myself I can screw my way out of the trap I'm in," he confessed to Vampira. "I forget my troubles only when I'm fucking, and I fuck a lot. I'm not particular who I plug these days just so long as it's a live body."

"Just who are the lucky recipients of your guilt?" Vampira asked. "I'm certainly not the beneficiary."

"The usual suspects," Paul said. "Joanne, of course. Tony's still around. When Pier and I teamed up again, our reunion was a bit chilly, but I ignited the flame again, at least when Vic Damone's not around. He's a bit young, but I'm helping Sal Mineo get over the love of his life, our beloved Jimmy. There's even a new kid on the block," Paul said. "Steven McQueen. I advised

Rocky Graziano with Paul Newman
"A frontrunner for the Oscar"

There's even a new kid on the block," Paul said. "Steven McQueen. I advised him to drop the 'n' and call himself just Steve. Believe it or not, he too had an affair with Dean in New York and fell madly in love with him. How did Dean get around to all these people?"

"You seem to be following in his footsteps," Vampira said.

"*Touché*," he said. "I think this McQueen kid is going to go far. He's a wild fucker, though. Just when you think you've done it every which way, he comes up with a new twist to the old game."

"Tell me all about it, and don't leave out any sordid details," she urged.

***

On the West Coast, his friend, Geraldine Page, was shocked to see how miserable Paul was. In spite of the pain it would cause his family, she urged him to divorce Jackie and marry Joanne. "Otherwise, you'll self-destruct, and then where will you be?"

When Sinatra flew into town and invited him out, even that hardened drinker was shocked at how much booze Paul could consume in an evening. "Fuck, kid," he said, "are you using me as a role model? Get that monkey off your back. Drink in moderation. Never more than a quart in one night. I also hear you're fucking everything that walks, just like Papa here," Sinatra said. "That's okay, but I'm still alarmed by those queer rumors about you. Tell me they're not true. What in hell are you up to? Trying to become another Peter Lawford? Another Monty Clift?"

"Frank, you know how Hollywood makes up shit," Paul said. "I'm no fucking queer, man. In fact, I'm off to meet a hot blonde right now."

"Glad to hear that, boy," Sinatra said. "We straight guys don't want to diminish our already diminishing ranks by losing a stud like you."

Paul lied to Sinatra about his sexual preferences that night, but at least told the truth in one regard. He was indeed meeting a hot blond.

Steven McQueen.

***

It was on the set of *Somebody Up There Likes Me* that he had first met Steven McQueen, according to Janice Rule, Paul's "secret" confidante, during extended dialogues which Paul had with her in Los Angeles.

Paul was approached by a young actor with curly blond hair. He was wearing a plaid sports jacket, dirty jeans, and a beanie cap. "Hi, I'm Steven McQueen. Can I talk to you or have you gone Hollywood?"

"I'm the last person in Tinseltown who will ever go Hollywood," Paul

160

said, reaching for McQueen's hand. At first Paul thought he was a greaser, until he realized he'd been cast as a blade-wielding punk member of Graziano's street gang in the movie.

"So, how does it feel, starring in another of these Hollywood fairy tales?" McQueen asked.

"This isn't Walt Disney," Paul said. "This is gritty *film noir*."

"Bullshit!" McQueen said. "Poor kid grows up on the East Side. Shithead father. Weak mother. Joins a gang. Becomes The Thief of Brooklyn. Gets sent up. Trouble in the military. Crawls out of a gutter using his fists—not his brain. Turns out a winner. Rags to riches. Meets a girl. Happy ending."

"Maybe it's a fairy tale after all," Paul said. "I never thought of it that way, kid."

"Don't call me a kid," McQueen said. "I'm just as much of a man as you are. Maybe more so."

"I wouldn't be so sure about that," Paul said.

"You want to check into some seedy motel with me, so I can prove it," McQueen said.

The two men seemed to circle each other for a silent moment, like two roosters sizing each other up before combat. "I don't go that route. You have nothing you need to prove to me."

"Don't kid a kidder," McQueen said. "I know you want it. Everybody on the set knows you're pounding pretty boy Mineo every night. Why not take on someone more experienced?"

"So what if I am?" Paul asked. "That's none of your God damn business. And if I'm so satisfied with Mineo, that would leave nothing left over for you."

"That's not a problem," McQueen said. "Even if you're worn out, we still could get it on. You see, I'm the pounder, not the poundee."

"My ass is strictly off limits," Paul said. "Don't even dream about it."

McQueen lewdly grabbed his crotch. "Within a week, I'll have you begging for it."

"Not bloody likely," Paul said. "With every hole in Hollywood spread before me, what makes you think I need to hook up with a cocky bastard like you?"

"There's a chemistry between us," McQueen said. "I could feel it the first time I saw you on the set. It's strange. I'm a man for the ladies, but when I saw you I said to myself, 'Self, I'm gonna fuck that handsome boy one day.

Steve McQueen
in one of his earliest
(legitimate) film roles
"A fairy-tale after all"

Sooner than later."

"That will never happen, but I must tell you, I admire your approach. I've been hit on by any number of guys, but your way of propositioning me is completely original. Believe it or not, I like you, in spite of your crude technique."

"Believe it or not, we're gonna be friends," McQueen said. "It'll be more than liking me. You'll end up loving me."

"You know, I would like to hang out with you," Paul said, "and I can't believe I'm saying this. But you're one of the most interesting characters I've ever met. Maybe if I get to know you, I'll find out if you're real or not."

"I'm all flesh and blood, red blood that is," McQueen said. "You'll find out just how real I am, man. One night when I'm plowing into your ass, and you're begging for me to stick in the final two inches, you'll know how real I am."

"That will never happen," Paul said.

"I've got to go," McQueen said. "I'm due on the set. Now gimme a kiss until we meet up again."

"A peck on the cheek is all you're gonna get from me," Paul said.

McQueen leaned into him. Before Paul realized what was happening, McQueen's lips seemed locked onto his, as his tongue explored Paul's mouth. Breaking away, and within an inch of Paul's ear, he said, "I just pretend to be a tough guy. After midnight, I'm an adorable, cuddly love machine."

Without saying another word, McQueen sauntered off. Paul did not wipe his mouth on his shirt sleeve. Instead he licked his lips, or so he claimed to Janice Rule, when he related this story to her.

***

It happened during the fourth time Paul went out with Steve McQueen, who sometimes still called himself Steven. In spite of McQueen's posturing, nothing intimate had yet transpired between them. Meeting McQueen at his favorite hangout, a joint called Pete's, Paul settled into a booth opposite the young actor.

Paul found that he could talk and drink with McQueen for hours, during which he had no sense of time. They were forming a friendship, but it was tinged with rivalry. Their mutual competition would dominate their careers for years, as future directors would often propose both of their names for the same roles. Yet in spite of a slight jealousy, Paul found himself attracted to McQueen and wanted to spend as much time with him as he could.

"He was a liar, but such a charming one," Paul later told Janice Rule. "For example, he told me that Robert Wise had originally promised *him* the role of Rocky. Wise did no such thing. Steve just made it up."

McQueen didn't stop with the lie about Wise. He also maintained that during the course of his affair with James Dean, Dean had promised to maneuver McQueen into each of the many roles being offered to him at the time, claiming that within a few months, he intended to abandon the film industry altogether. Although that was also a lie, McQueen seemed to have convinced himself that every aspect of it was true. "One day, Wise will star me in a picture," McQueen predicted. Ironically, that forecast became true when Wise cast McQueen in *The Sand Pebbles*, after which McQueen was nominated for an Academy Award.

McQueen seemed deeply interested in how much money Paul was pulling in for his work on *Somebody*. Paul bluntly told him. In a voice filled with resentment, he said that Warners was paying him $1,000 a week but had lent him out to MGM for a one time fee of $75,000.

"You're making more than I am on this piece of shit," McQueen said. "I get nineteen big ones a day unless I'm speaking a line. Then I get fifty bucks."

It would sometimes take eight to ten beers before McQueen lost his tough guy image and became a vulnerable human being. He confessed to Paul that, "Just like the next guy, I'm looking for a little love and understanding. Hollywood is a cold place. Sometimes, I need to hold someone by a fire. Someone who can turn a tough street kid like me into a lover. Someone like you."

"You're barking up the wrong tree, kid," Paul said. "I'll be your friend. But let's keep it at that. I don't want to venture beyond that."

Somehow, however, that night at Pete's was different from the others. "There was so much sexual tension in the air between us that you could cut it with a knife," Paul told Janice Rule. "I was too drunk to even think straight, much less act straight. As the night wore on, Steve kept looking better and better."

"With my defenses down—blame it on the *cerveza*—I agreed to go back to his place. I knew what was going to happen. I can't pretend to be some college boy who wakes up the next morning and claims, 'I was so drunk he took advantage of me.' Back at his place, a smelly hole, we had a little fun, but we were pretty wasted. It was ten o'clock the next morning before we really got it on."

Steve McQueen
"Now gimme a kiss"

He leaned back in his chair in the café where he'd been relaying this information to Janice. "I'm seeing the fucker again tonight, and this time I'm gonna try to remain at least a bit sober so I can enjoy it more. Steve's got this fabulous technique. He licks you all over until you're hotter than a firecracker. Then, while he's got you all worked up and panting, he comes on like gangbusters. Sexually, we're pretty evenly matched. Even our dicks are about the same. We could be brothers."

"Sounds like you're having fun," Janice said.

"I am," he answered, "but I'm uncomfortable as hell with the idea that I've stepped directly into each of Dean's professional acting roles, and acquired each of his lovesick puppies as well—Pier Angeli, Sal Mineo, and now Steve McQueen. What would Dean think of that?"

"Wherever he is tonight, he'd probably be enjoying a good belly laugh. But how does Joanne Woodward fit into this picture?" she asked.

"I'm in love with her, and when I'm with her, I forget about all those other puppies," he said. "These experiences are teaching me one very important lesson: A man is a complicated creature, with many facets and multiple personalities, and Paul Newman intends to discover who he is regardless of what road he has to travel."

"In other words, you're embarking on a road of self discovery," she said, sounding like the psychotherapist she would eventually become. "I'm with you. One man will never be enough for me. Even if I'm in a marriage, my husband will never be enough. I just know that."

"You mean that?" he asked, looking startled. "You know, Janice, you're looking pretty good. Perhaps you and me sometime?"

"That's certainly an option, and I'm sure it'll happen sometime in our future, but right now you've got plenty of other places to shove it. Who's the lucky one tonight?"

"Sal," he said. "Steve's picked up this hot little number—female, that is— and they're shacked up tonight. Pier is in bed with Vic Damone. So Sal won me by default."

"Worse fates can befall you," she said. "He's one cute kid."

"What I like about Sal is his willingness to do anything you command," Paul said, "and I mean *anything*."

***

Paul worked out daily with Sal Mineo in the gym, which was usually followed by a session of love-making. "The kid is hot, hung, and fuckable," Paul confided to Vampira. "Far older than his actual years."

Sal was quickly becoming known as the "Switchblade Kid," and indeed he'd committed street crimes in the Bronx before making it to Broadway. There, he had appeared in Tennessee Williams' *The Rose Tattoo*. Later, he won a Broadway role in *The King and I* with the bisexual actor, Yul Brynner.

He was vainly proud that he'd received an Oscar nomination for playing the supporting role of Plato, the soulful teenager in *Rebel Without a Cause*. He told Paul that the director had actually filmed a scene of him kissing Dean in the movie. "Of course, it was cut from the final version."

If Paul's lovemaking with Sal ever reached a low point, it was when Sal, at the moment of climax, called Paul "Deano, baby." But Paul quickly forgave him for that, because he, too, missed the presence and lovemaking of Dean.

Since the release of *Rebel,* Sal had appeared to be on his way to major stardom. This dreamy-eyed, baby-faced rising star was frequently stalked by teenage girls, some of whom seemed to desperately want a lock of his hair.

He tried to lure Paul into taking pep pills, which he consumed at the rate of a dozen per day. Noting his habits, Paul said, "We can take the Catholic boy out of the Bronx, but he's still a Catholic in Tinseltown." He was referring to Sal carrying a rosary with him at all times, and refusing to work without a Saint Christopher medal around his neck.

"The kid is one of the most intense young men I've ever known," Paul told Rod Steiger. "He lives a feverish lifestyle. He's going to go Hollywood big time. Already, a manufacturer wants Sal to endorse its switchblades and zip guns."

Even before he matured to drinking age, Sal was seen sipping cocktails at Chasen's, the Brown Derby, and the Ambassador Hotel's Cocoanut Grove nightclub. There, he was photographed sitting at a table with Frank Sinatra and Lana Turner.

"I know how to bring Sal down to earth when he gets too carried away, bragging about how those red vel-vet ropes always come down for him," Paul told Janice. "He speaks of the fancy cars he'll own, the suits he'll have tailor made in Beverly Hills, and fans who trail him wherever he goes. I let him go on and on while I'm lying impa-tiently with him in bed. Finally, when I've had enough, I tell him, 'Get over here, kid, and eat out my ass.' That brings him back to Earth."

Sal Mineo (left)
Falling in love with **James Dean**

Before Paul had to fly back to

the coast, Sal confessed to him that he'd fallen madly in love with him. Years later, in an apartment in New York's Chelsea district, Sal admitted, "I thought I'd never love again after Jimmy died, but what I felt for him I transferred onto Paul."

To Paul's astonishment, Sal wanted him to move in with him and live together as a couple. "Give up Woodward. Give up all the others. I'm man enough to satisfy every need you have."

"That you are," Paul said. But before the night ended, he knew he'd have to tell Sal that they could be no more than "fuck buddies," and that he had another agenda to pursue that didn't revolve exclusively around him.

By midnight Paul lowered the boom and gave it to Sal straight. The young man looked devastated. He took it worse than Paul had expected. Perhaps Sal was in love with him after all.

He ran from the room and into the night. Paul didn't know where he was going. He went to sleep that night, thinking Sal would eventually accept the reality of what he was saying and come back.

Sometime before dawn, Paul fell asleep. Around five o'clock that morning, Robert Wise called Paul and told him to meet him at a hospital in South Los Angeles. It was an emergency.

Arriving at the hospital, Paul encountered Wise who told him that Sal had checked in under an assumed name. He was resting peacefully but had slit his wrists around three o'clock that morning.

The hospital staff would not admit Paul as one of Sal's visitors. Paul agreed to come back during visiting hours the following afternoon.

Around five o'clock the following day, Paul was led in to see Sal, who was sitting up in bed with his wrists bandaged.

"You foolish, foolish kid," Paul scolded him. "What were you thinking? You're on your way to becoming a major heartthrob of the 50s. Do you really want to throw away your life?"

Sal just stared at him, waiting for a long time before speaking. "I want to hear the words coming from your own mouth."

Paul hesitated, but finally managed to say, "I'll always be there for you, kid."

***

For a brief period, Gore Vidal lived with his lover, Howard Austen, at the Chateau Marmont, as did the married Paul Newman with his mistress, Joanne Woodward.

As *The Los Angeles Times* put it, "No wonder people come here to have affairs—it's got that air of history, where you know a lot of people did things they weren't supposed to do." Indeed if details about the shack-up of Joanne and Paul had been known to the general public, it could have seriously damaged their promising careers.

Paul remembered overhearing Harry Cohn, founder of Columbia Pictures, telling Glenn Ford and William Holden, "If you're going to get into trouble, do it at the Chateau Marmont." Although that advice had not been directly aimed at him, Paul took it seriously.

Nicholas Ray had told Paul, "If you're a novelist or actor from New York, you'll feel at home in this dark, rambling old French castle. It's not part of the state of California. If you want to pick up a garage mechanic with dirty fingernails, you can hustle him up on the elevator directly from the garage to your hotel room. Chances are, no one will see your comings and goings. After he's spurted, slip him a twenty and send him on his way. On the way up in the elevator, you can unzip him and cop a feel to make sure he's worth the twenty before you actually get him up to the room and undress him."

It was at the Chateau Marmont that Paul and Gore Vidal had plotted to convince Warner Brothers to film a movie version of *Billy the Kid*, the role Paul had originally played on TV. Gore had agreed to turn his teleplay into a full script ready for the cameras.

Without Joanne or Howard, Gore and Paul were often involved in intense discussions about Billy the Kid and were often seen alone together for hours at a time. That led to speculation around the chateau, and later among Hollywood insiders, that Gore and Paul were having a torrid affair.

The source of many of those rumors was Tennessee Williams, who had sustained a decade-long crush on Paul, and who was perhaps jealous that Paul had become "best friends" with Gore.

Gore seemed to take these rumors in stride. He once wrote, "There is a strange compulsion for journalists to reveal that stars of every sort and in every field are either homosexual or anti-Semitic or both. Most young men, particularly attractive ones, have sexual relations with their own kind. I suppose this is still news to those who believe in the two teams: straight, which is good and unalterable; queer, which is bad and unalterable unless it proves to be only a preference, which must then, somehow, be reversed, if necessary by force."

It was around the pool at the Chateau

Howard Austen
Known as "Mrs. Gore Vidal"

Marmont that Joanne and Paul began to read Gore's novels, including *The City and the Pillar*, which had almost ruined the author's promising career before it had even started. Critics, including those at *The New York Times*, objected to how he'd written openly and without apology about homosexuality.

"I'd like to live to see the day when Hollywood has advanced to the point that it will make a movie based on *The City and the Pillar*," Paul said.

"I doubt if that day will ever come," Howard said. "Not in my lifetime."

Sometimes the English writer Christopher Isherwood would drop by to visit Joanne, Paul, Gore, and Howard. With him was a young Californian, Don Bachardy, a handsome, blond-haired painter who looked fourteen. The distinguished author of *The Berlin Stories* had met Bachardy on the beach one day and had taken him home. They'd been living together ever since.

Speaking privately one day with Paul, Isherwood confessed, "Since I'm seen with Don all the time, they call me a chicken hawk." In a soft voice, almost a whisper, the author said, "I'll lend you Don for the night if that would please you. Of course, you'd have to agree to let me watch you, the two most beautiful boys in Hollywood, making love to each other." Paul thanked Isherwood but turned down "your generous offer."

Sometimes all four of what had become known as Hollywood's most notorious quartet were seen gathered beside the pool. Sometimes, when Paul was away working, Joanne maintained intense discussions in private with Gore about the future of his race for the Presidency of the United States.

"Of course," Gore cautioned, "the specter of homosexuality might rear its ugly head during the campaign." Presumably, it was Joanne herself who volunteered to consider marrying him as a means of providing "cover."

"I wouldn't mind playing the role of First Lady," she said. "It'd be a hell of a lot better than this stinking part I've got in *A Kiss Before Dying*. And it also might be a hell of a lot more interesting than sitting around this pool waiting for Paul to make up his mind to divorce Jackie and marry me."

There remained another question. "What to do about Howard?"

"Perhaps we could let Howard permanently occupy the Lincoln Bedroom rent free," Gore said mockingly.

Fred Kaplan, in his biography of Gore,

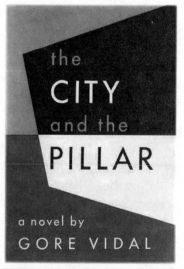

the
CITY
and the
PILLAR

a novel by
GORE VIDAL

Banned from The New York Times

quotes Joanne as saying, "I think if we had gotten to that point and Gore had said, 'Let's get married,' I might very well have done so. Because I was very fond of him. Many people have had that sort of marriage. I can't imagine how long it would have lasted. I would have driven Gore crazy, or he would have driven me crazy."

Both Paul and Joanne configured themselves as Gore's celebrity supporters, as did Eleanor Roosevelt, when he unsuccessfully ran for Congress in a Republican district in New York State in 1960.

Joanne played a pivotal role in the *film noir*, *A Kiss Before Dying*, released in 1956. It had a stellar cast which included Hollywood heartthrobs Robert Wagner and Jeffrey Hunter.

In that film, Mary Astor was cast as Robert Wagner's mother. An iconic screen great at the time, she had become famous in her portrayal of the calculating Brigid O'Shaughnessy, playing opposite Humphrey Bogart in *The Maltese Falcon* (1941). Robert was cast as a psychopathic but well-groomed college student who's scheming to marry the unsuspecting Joanne as a means of inheriting her father's Kingship Copper Mines. When he learns that she's pregnant out of wedlock, he takes her to the top of the City Hall building in Tucson and pushes her off the roof, hoping that her murder will look like a suicide. He then reaches out romantically to her sister, Ellen (Virginia Leith), in the hopes of marrying her to ingratiate himself with her conservative tycoon father.

After the release of the film, Joanne described it as "the worst picture ever made in Hollywood. It's my *Silver Chalice*." It's true that critics dismissed the film at the time as lurid melodrama, but over the years it has developed a cult following and is a far better thriller than reputation has it.

At the time of its release, its star, Robert Wagner, was dismissive of the film, referring to it as "a small bomb." But in later years he had a kinder appraisal, especially when latter-day critics lavished praise on the movie and cited his performance as Bud Corliss as the greatest of his life.

The film was based on a chiller novella by Ira Lewin, who would later write the horror classic, *Rosemary's*

Vidal, Woodward, and Newman
Two bucks vying for the lady's affection

Baby. Ironically, Paul read the script before Joanne. An early version of *A Kiss Before Dying* was sent to Montgomery Clift, who read it and rejected it as "cheap melodrama."

But he suggested to Paul that "you might do something with this character. You have the clean-cut image needed to hide a calculating black heart. Let's look at your own life, for instance. You live a life of betrayal, deceit, and lies. I bet Joanne Woodward, as smart as she is, doesn't have a glimmer of what you're up to most of the time. She understands only what you present to her."

Paul was not offended by Monty's remarks. "You're right. Secretly I'm a devil. I can be a very, very bad boy. But so can you."

"It was around this time that Paul met Robert Wagner," said Jeffrey Hunter, the film's co-star. "I saw lust in Paul's eyes. He found Robert's looks mesmerizing, and it was obvious that he was attracted to the gorgeous young man, who had narrowly escaped from the clutches of both Clifton Webb and the gay mega-agent, Henry Willson, only to land in the bed of aging actress Barbara Stanwyck."

"Robert Wagner was Paul's first serious crush," Janice Rule later said. "There would be two other serious crushes in his life. Robert Redford and later Tom Cruise. Robert Wagner gave him a bad case of unrequited love. This was a new emotion for Paul. Until he met Wagner, and later Redford and Cruise, Paul had managed to seduce practically any man or woman he wanted. If Paul is to be believed, he never went to bed with Wagner, but he sure had the hots for him. He just didn't dare face possible humiliation by making a play for him. He suspected that Wagner, because of his previous associations with Henry Willson, might be fair game, but Paul was afraid to risk a direct come-on."

"There was more to it than that," Janice claimed. "Paul not only wanted to bed Wagner, but he wanted to look like him. Ever since Paul had seen him on the screen playing the bit part of a soldier in *With a Song in My Heart*, with Susan Hayward, he'd found his looks dazzling. Even though Paul was called beautiful, one of the greatest looking men in the movies, he always felt he was too ethnic.

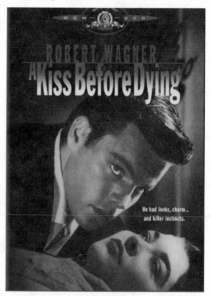

"He **(Robert Wagner)** had looks, charm,and killer instincts"

He feared at times that he looked 'too Jewish.' To him, Wagner represented the dreamy idol of WASP good looks and charm. 'I'm a better actor than he is,' Paul told me, 'and if I had his looks I could be the King of Hollywood. If I got that pretty boy in my bed, I'd send him to paradise. He can put his shoes under my bed any night. In this movie, he's supposed to have gotten Joanne pregnant. He could get me pregnant any night he wanted, and I don't know nothin' 'bout birthin' babies.'"

***

Columnist Hedda Hopper was actually a far more sophisticated woman than she appeared to be. To appeal to her readership in small town America, she pretended to be narrow minded, "a provincial" as she called it.

Prior to the release of *Somebody Up There Likes Me*, a Warner Brothers' publicist arranged for Paul to visit Hopper at her home, presumably for a "get-to-know-you" chat and interview. Robert Schaffer, a member of Warners' publicity department, told Paul, "Hedda and Louella Parsons don't have the power they used to, but they can still make or break stars in this town."

Less rebellious than Marlon Brando or Monty Clift, Paul dutifully drove over to Hopper's home to pay his respects to the aging journalist. He realized how crucial it was to cater to Hopper and her vanity, yet simultaneously, he feared that by granting an exclusive interview to Hedda Hopper, he'd deeply offend her arch-rival, Louella Parsons. Such was Paul's "Judgment of Paris" when he rang Hedda Hopper's doorbell.

Over drinks in her living room, Hopper at first amused Paul with her highly subjective stories from the Golden Age of Hollywood. He laughed when she told him, "Errol Flynn was seriously pissed off about something I wrote in my column, and rang my doorbell. The moment I opened the door, he began masturbating, while standing on my stoop and facing me. I began laughing, and continued laughing until he finished with a dramatic flourish all over my doorstep. I'll

Left to right:
Jeffrey Hunter, Joanne Woodward, and **Robert Wagner.**
RJ: "Paul's first serious crush"

say one thing for Errol. He's the only man I know who can ejaculate in front of a fully dressed woman who's laughing derisively during the entire process."

Finally, Hopper moved in for the kill. "Do you suck up?" she asked Paul bluntly.

"I'm not sure if I follow you, Miss Hopper."

"I consider you one of the bad boys of Hollywood from what I hear, and I want to know how you plan to play me," she said. "Brando practically gave me the finger when he saw me. But Dean knew how to suck up. Once I encountered him in a restaurant and he came over and talked to me for an hour, leaving his boyfriend at table alone. Would you do that for me?"

"That sounds pretty rude to one's guest," Paul said. "I don't know if I'd leave my partner alone, but I would meet with you at the appropriate time if you wanted to interview me."

"That's not exactly a suck-up, but I guess it'll do. I'll be frank. Our relationship can go two ways. I know enough shit on you to ruin your career before it even gets started. I've been told that you had a fling with Dean, as well as one with that dreadful Marlon Brando. And I know you're married to some spineless clinging vine back East, and that out here, you're shacked up with Joanne Woodward and hanging out with that sissy queer, Gore Vidal. Such news could be very bad for you, and I'm the gal to spill the beans. If you don't want me to do that, how about giving me some good copy and for the moment, at least, we'll declare a truce. That is, unless you piss off Hedda the way I pissed off Flynn."

"Whatever happens," he said, "you won't find me masturbating on your doorstep."

"That's okay," she said. "Errol Flynn would be a tough act for one of you youngsters to follow."

"Other than the scandals you've suggested, what kind of red meat do you want from me?"

"First, I want to know if you've got balls. You see Robert Montgomery on the screen, and you can figure out he has balls. When Clark Gable came on with Carole Lombard, or whomever, you knew that he not only had balls but knew how to clank them. Which are you?"

"Given that choice, I'd follow in Gable's footsteps." He managed to get

Hedda Hopper
"You have to suck up to me."

172

through the rest of the afternoon. He didn't exactly give Hopper red meat. As he later told Gore Vidal, "It was more like grilled hen."

At the door, Hopper, a little drunk, decided to give Paul some unwanted advice. "If you are as queer as some people say, I want you to stay away from my son and don't corrupt him. The other night I caught him in bed with Van Johnson going down on him."

"Miss Hopper, as a gentleman, I give you my word of honor. You'll never find me going down on William DeWolf Hopper Jr."

"At least you got his name right." She slammed the door in his face, but then suddenly reopened it. "If you marry that Woodward creature, make sure you give me the scoop. Don't let that bitch Louella know about it until I print it. Got that?"

"My God, I'll make you my best man if you want me to. Speaking of balls, you've got them, Hedda."

"That's Miss Hopper to you." She slammed the door a final time.

***

Paul's appearance opposite Elizabeth Taylor in the 1958 release of *Cat on a Hot Tin Roof* was preceded by a bizarre sequence of casting sagas. Among others, they involved Tennessee Williams, Vivien Leigh, Grace Kelly, and Elvis Presley.

The dramas began in 1954 while Tennessee was still working on the play. Actually, he didn't complete the third act of the play until three days before opening night at the Morosco Theater on March 24, 1955. Even so, months before its premiere, there were undercurrents of speculation about the play. *The Los Angeles Times*, in an embarrassing bit of misinformation, even labeled it a "comedy."

Paul's involvement in what was to become one of his most celebrated movies began with a mysterious phone message that came in to a publicist at Warner Brothers. The message was from a "G.K." The publicity department was savvy enough to know that the woman calling was Grace Kelly. The person who took the call recognized her voice.

Later, Paul, who was with Vampira and Tony Perkins that day, said, "Once again I'm Grace Kelly's call boy. But what man with red blood in him would turn down an invitation from that goddess?"

"Speaking of goddesses, even those of yesterday, how are you doing on your game plan to fuck all the fading beauties of the 1940s?" Vampira asked.

"It's slow going," Paul said. "So far, only Joan Crawford. But we'll see. How about you, Tony?"

"The love goddesses of yesterday don't appeal to me," he said. "I'd rather

173

fuck those male matinee idols of the 30s that I used to swoon over in the movies. I've got to move quickly before they expire."

"Who do you have in mind?"

"Clark Gable, Robert Taylor, Errol Flynn, and Tyrone Power."

"Better hurry up," Paul urged him. "I think you'll have no trouble with Taylor, Flynn, and Power, but I heard Gable gave up the gay life during the early 30s. From the looks of those screen idols today, their time on Earth is very limited."

Later that night, when Paul arrived at a secluded hideaway in the San Fernando Valley, he was ushered into a backroom where Grace was waiting at table with a man.

To his surprise, Paul quickly learned that the man was Tennessee Williams. She rose from the table with the grace of a swan to kiss him gently on the mouth. Tennessee also slowly rose to his feet, kissing Paul on both cheeks. "I've never forgotten you since Bill Inge and I saw you audition for *Picnic*."

After very routine chatter and congratulations on the recent accomplishments of each of these artists, Grace assumed a rather business-like aura. "Tennessee has the most divine proposal. He's at work on a Broadway play. It's called *Maggie the Cat*. He's proposing that I open the play on Broadway, run with it for 85 nights, then turn it over to—say, Kim Stanley. During this time, I'll sign a contract to appear in the movie. I'm crazy for the idea of the movie but appearing on Broadway frightens me."

"Grace Kelly in a new Tennessee Williams play," Paul said. "What a dynamite idea. How do I fit in? The guy who gets Maggie the Cat purring?"

"Like a true Hun, you get right to the point," Tennessee said. "You'd be cast in the male lead, and you don't get the frustrated Maggie purring at all. You'd be playing a homosexual."

Remembering his recent talk with Hedda Hopper, Paul said, "I've got the balls to do that if I don't have to wear pink."

"Actually, it's a very masculine role from what Tennessee has told me," Grace said. "Like me, you'd agree to appear in the stage version, followed by the movie."

"In the play Maggie has a foul mouth and is very earthy," Tennessee said. "In other words, Grace would be playing against type. I like that kind of casting."

"And me?" Paul asked.

"You'd be in your pajamas for most of the play," Tennessee said. "We'd naturally have to have some scenes to show off that sculpted Davidesque chest of yours, arguably the most beautiful in Hollywood. God created your chest for silken tongues to lap." He turned to Grace and smiled. "How I envy Grace for having sampled the world's tastiest specimen. As for me, an aging queen can only dream of what a delight that must be."

Showing a slight embarrassment, Grace laughed to mask her feelings. "It seems that you've gone through your Brando fixation and turned to more modern stars. Paul is the embodiment of the new breed taking over Hollywood."

"You're known for appearing with older stars," Paul told her. "Gary Cooper. Clark Gable, Ray Milland, James Stewart. It might be fun for you to work with someone closer to your own age."

"It'd be more than fun," she said. "We'd burn up the screen."

"There is a great role for a character actor," Tennessee said. "Big Daddy. I have Orson Welles in mind."

"He's certainly big enough," Paul said. "If the arrangements can be made and those who hold us in bondage approve, I'll go for it. I don't have to read the play. Knowing that Tennessee wrote it is good enough for me. I'm sure it'll be a masterpiece."

At the end of dinner, a rather handsome young man with a slight growth of beard appeared in the rear of the restaurant to escort a drunken Tennessee back to his car. The playwright didn't bother to introduce his driver. "I was writing all my roles for Brando," Tennessee said, rising on wobbly legs. "But he's getting too beefy to play a Tennessee Williams leading man. Today I'm creating characters like Brick who are lean, mean, and astonishingly beautiful. Men who inspire sexual fantasies regardless of the viewer's persuasion."

He looked his driver over skeptically. "Right now I'm studying the world

(Left to right): **Newman, Grace Kelly, Tennessee Williams**
"The Dream That Never Came True"

175

of hustlers. Someday I'll cast you as the lead in one of my plays where you'll play a hustler. I envision Tallulah Bankhead playing an aging, has-been actress opposite you." He gently kissed Paul on the lips before heading off into the night with his paid companion.

When Paul sat back down at table, he felt Grace place her delicate hand on his thigh. "I've booked us a room upstairs at this sleazy joint."

"Isn't this cockroach palace pretty poor digs for the glamorous Grace Kelly, used to sleeping only on satin sheets?"

"Perhaps it is," she said rather demurely. "But tonight I'm taking off the white gloves. I want you to treat me like some slut you picked up on the most dangerous street in South Los Angeles."

"Tonight you'll get your wish, sweetheart."

***

On the day he woke up to film a pivotal scene in *Somebody Up There Likes Me*, Paul stared into the doe-eyed eyes of Sal Mineo. It had been a rough night. Sal had a direct way of talking. "I bet my rosebud is hotter than Joanne Woodward's pussy," he said. Paul turned over and headed for the bathroom. He didn't like talk like that.

Director Robert Wise was waiting at the studio to direct Paul in a crucial scene, his on-film match with Tony Zale. Zale was a former middleweight champion who was playing himself in the movie. "Think of this match as a dance number," Wise instructed Paul.

As the morning lengthened, Wise was disappointed with the match. "Newman was gun-shy with Zale," Wise later claimed. "He was afraid that if he accidentally clipped Tony, Tony—in a fighter's reflex reaction—would cold-cock him. I've never forgotten the experience of seeing Paul pull back from Tony. Maybe Paul was also trying to save that pretty face of his."

In spite of the difficulty Wise had in filming his *faux* boxing match, after the film was released, Paul was praised for this climatic scene with Zale. In fact, the bout between Zale and Paul is still ranked as one of the greatest boxing scenes ever filmed. Bosley Crowther of *The New York Times* called the match "one of the whoppingest slugfests we've ever seen on the screen." *Collier's* was more impressed with Paul's chest and biceps, claiming they measured up to the "brawniest of Hollywood's beefcake actors."

In a touch of irony, right before the film was released, Monty Clift told Paul that Dean had not been the first choice to play Rocky. Originally Wise had offered the role to Monty, because he'd been impressed with his portrayal of a boxer in *From Here to Eternity*. Monty turned him down. "I don't want to become known for boxing roles," Monty said.

The second choice, Dean, had accepted the role even though he was not muscular like a professional boxer. His face was far too sensitive to convince audiences that he was a street fighter and an inarticulate pugilist.

Even though *Somebody Up There Likes Me* was Paul's breakthrough role, he was disappointed at the flood of reviews comparing him once again to Brando.

"Ersatz Brando," claimed many a reviewer, although there were those perceptive enough to know that in *Somebody Up There Likes Me*, Paul had charted his own path as an actor. "I don't want to be doomed forever to walk in Brando's shoes."

Privately, Paul knew that it was a question of who was imitating whom.

Brando had not only briefly considered playing the role of Rocky Graziano himself, but he'd "ripped off Graziano" for his interpretation of the character of Stanley Kowalski in *A Streetcar Named Desire*."

"Before I opened on Broadway, I spent weeks with the lug," Brando confessed to Paul. "I watched him like a hawk getting ready for a spring chicken dinner. I studied his speech patterns, the way he walked, his every mannerism. I understand you did the same damn thing. Except in your case you were studying to play the *real* Rocky. I was trying to form a character created by Tennessee Williams. No wonder people compare our performances. When I gave Rocky tickets to go see *Streetcar*, he knew that was himself up there on the stage raping the pathetic Blanche DuBois."

Paul put up a brave front for Brando, telling him that he'd picked up two bad habits from the boxer. "Graziano taught me to spit in the streets and say fuck every third word."

But privately he complained to friends such as Tony Perkins and Rod Steiger. "I had every right to rip off Graziano's character because I was playing him on the screen. Brando was playing Stanley Kowalski, an entirely different character. Life isn't fair. Hollywood's not fair. Critics aren't fair. I'm going out tonight with Steve—yes, it's Steve now, not Steven—and pull the drunk of my life."

Paul went by himself to see *Somebody* at a movie house on Hollywood Boulevard so he could study his performance better without having to respond to the reactions of accompanying friends. As he emerged from the theater, a boy about fourteen years old came up to him.

Tony Zale
Man of Steel

177

"May I have your autograph, mister?" he asked.

Paul, who hated to sign autographs, gave him one anyway. The boy studied it carefully. "Oh," he said, "you're not Marlon Brando. You're Paul Newman. Can I have another autograph?"

"Sure," Paul said, granting his request. "This one for your mother?"

"No, I need two of yours to trade for one of Brando."

***

For months, Robert Wise and his associates kept circulating the rumor that it was almost certain that Paul would be nominated for an Oscar as Best Actor of 1957. Joanne Woodward, even Gore Vidal, joined in this chorus of approval. One friend of Rocky's wrote Paul a fan letter from Brooklyn. "That was our boy Rocky Graziano we saw up there on the screen, not pretty boy Newman." Paul was a fairly modest guy, but eventually he came to believe that he was indeed going to break out and win the Oscar after having already made two box office failures.

Then one night, months later, a call came in from Brando at about two o'clock in the morning. "I've been nominated for an Oscar for *Sayonara*," Brando told him with pride, years before he'd eventually shun such an award. "The smart money in Vegas is on me. I'm the frontrunner."

Paul was too proud to ask him who else had been nominated. It wasn't until he read the papers the following morning that he learned he hadn't even been nominated. In the "Best Actor" category, Brando was up against Anthony Quinn for *Wild Is the Wind*, Charles Laughton for *Witness for the Prosecution*, Anthony Franciosa for *A Hatful of Rain*, and Alec Guinness for *The Bridge on the River Kwai*. Guinness walked off with the prize, much to Paul's disappointment.

"Fuck Hollywood, fuck their Oscars," he told McQueen over the phone. "Tonight, let's drink up all the booze in town."

"You're on, kid," McQueen said.

"Now who's the kid? I'm old enough to be your father."

"Yeah, right," McQueen said. "Your dick wasn't big enough at the age of five in 1930 to have fathered a stud like me."

***

Over the years Paul had many affairs, either with beautiful women or with handsome men with whom he was cast. Even so, he never tried to match Steve McQueen's record of "fucking every one of my leading ladies."

Bang the Drum Slowly was shot in New York, and aired on September 16,

1956 on *The United States Steel Hour*. During the shooting of the teleplay, in which Paul had a leading role, he became involved with the bisexual and closeted actor, George Peppard.

Bang the Drum Slowly was based on Mark Harris's baseball novel, which was first published in 1956 as a sequel to his other famous novel, *The Southpaw*, first published in 1953. In the teleplay, Paul was cast as Henry Wiggen, a celebrity pitcher, who relates the saga of a baseball season with the New York Mammoths, a fictional team loosely based on the New York Yankees.

The title of the teleplay was derived from the song, "The Streets of Laredo," which contains the lyrics, "O bang the drum slowly, and play the fife slowly. . . ."

In the teleplay, it's revealed that the starting lineup of the Mammoths will have to be altered by the worsening Hodgkin's disease of their catcher, Bruce Pierson, as played by actor Albert Salmi. George Peppard's role in the teleplay was that of Piney Woods, a slightly crazed backup catcher who's also ambitious, Southern, a hayseed, and ruthless. In the teleplay, Piney is plotting to replace Pierson (the official, not-very-bright catcher).

As part of the teleplay, the character of Pierson entrusts the secret of his worsening disease to the character played by Paul, who struggles with the moral implications of his loyalty to his team versus his loyalty to his friend.

The novel encompassed some wide-ranging geographies, but the set decorator had to compress all of them onto a single sound stage, and all of its chronologies into a span of less than fifty minutes.

The end of each scene was punctuated with blackouts, wherein the actors raced from one set and time frame to another. During each of the blackouts, a spotlight focused only on Paul, who functioned within the teleplay as the narrator. At the beginning of his performance, Paul warned the audience, "There's not much room in the studio here. You have to use your imagination."

The broadcast was a great success. Forty years after the telecast, *TV Guide* would vote *Bang the Drum Slowly* as one of the 100 Most Memorable Moments in the history of television, citing Paul's appearance at "the peak of his blue-eyed beauty."

Ironically, in some respects, the action behind the scenes was more intriguing than what went on in front of the camera. During rehearsals, Paul established two secretive and rather bizarre relationships with his co-stars.

Before being cast in the same drama, Paul and George had had only a passing acquaintance with each other from the Actors Studio. During one of his dinners with Janice Rule, Paul told her, "George is almost as handsome as I am."

As a budding psychoanalyst, Janice speculated that Paul actually wanted to look like George, just as previously, he had wanted to look like Robert Wagner. "Although Paul became the male sex symbol of the 1950s, he actually wasn't that pleased with his body," Janice said. "He believed he was too short. And he always wanted to have more meat on his legs."

George's second wife, actress Elizabeth Ashley, to whom he was married from 1966 to 1972, aptly described his appearance after her first meeting with the former Marine. "George Peppard looked like some kind of Nordic god— six feet tall with beautiful blond hair, blue eyes, and a body out of every high school cheerleader's teenage lust fantasy."

Paul's reaction, at least according to Janice, was similar to Elizabeth's. "Even though they knew each other, Paul's affair with George didn't burst into bloom until they worked together on that baseball play. I wouldn't exactly call it a love affair. But I bet they had great sex together. What male beauties they were."

"One night I went out with both of them together," she said. "I'd never seen two men drink so much. I thought each of them would become an alcoholic. Paul didn't. George did. He was also a smokestack. No sooner would one cigarette go out than he'd light up another one. Paul, who was always very open with me, jokingly said, 'It's hard to give George a big gooey wet one because he's always got a cigarette in his mouth.'"

Except for Janice's observation, details about the relationship between Paul and George are sparse. However, the two actors knew each other for years. Author Truman Capote came to know George when in 1961 he was cast in his most famous role, that of Paul Varjak in *Breakfast at Tiffany's* opposite Audrey Hepburn.

"During the filming, Paul came onto the set to see both Audrey, whom he knew casually, and George," Capote said. "He departed for the weekend in New England with George. I just assumed they were having a little fling. It certainly appeared so to the rest of the cast. I wish those two hunks had invited me as their chaperone. At least they could have asked me to watch."

"Each of those actors should have been arrested for being so good looking," Capote said. "Looking at the two of them together would give a queen an orgasm. If some studio ever remakes *Gone With the Wind*, the director should cast George as Rhett Butler and Paul as

George Peppard
"Sexy but ruthless"

180

Ashley Wilkes. I couldn't quite pull off Scarlett, but in blackface I could do the Butterfly McQueen role."

George would continue to have an occasional fling with a man, mostly young actors enamored of his screen image. He'd have a very brief affair with Rock Hudson when they co-starred in *Tobruk* in 1967. But, for the most part, he "loved the ladies," as his fellow students at the Actors Studio claimed. "From what I heard, he sampled the charms of many of them, including a number of famous actresses of his day," Janice said. "I would have gone away with him, but he never asked me."

Years later, in 1973, Michael Moriarty and Robert De Niro would bring *Bang the Drum Slowly* to the big screen. But many critics preferred the simplicity of the original teleplay. In the words of one critic, "Newman's and Salmi's basic warmth comes across better than Michael Moriarty's rather diffident performance and Robert De Niro's intense Method acting performance."

When Paul was asked if he'd seen the De Niro version, he snapped, "No, and I don't plan to, as I prefer to keep the memory of the original."

There were a lot of memories to keep. Out of respect for one of those memories, Paul called George when he learned he was dying in Los Angeles of lung cancer in 1994. All those years of heavy smoking had finally caught up with him. "I was my own worst enemy," George told Paul as he'd told so many others. "Mine isn't a string of victories. It's no golden past. I am no George Peppard fan."

"But I am!" Paul assured him.

***

Albert Salmi, with his tall, brawny physique, was a Method actor taught by Lee Strasberg himself, the same way that Paul was.

"I think Paul and Salmi spent the early part of their friendship either in a Turkish bath or a Finnish sauna checking each other out," said Rod Steiger. "Salmi was always trying to convince Paul that Finnish saunas were superior to Turkish baths."

"I don't really know if those two hunks bumped pussies in the night or not," Steiger said. "I came to suspect that Paul was playing Eve Harrington to Salmi's Margo Channing, even though Salmi was three years younger than Paul."

Steiger, of course, was referring to the scheming character that Anne Baxter played in the 1950 *All About Eve* where she plotted to fill the stage shoes of Margo Channing (Bette Davis).

One night, perhaps in a Finnish sauna, Albert revealed to Paul that he was

181

under consideration for *Bus Stop*, the new play by William Inge. There was a juicy male role, Bo Decker, a brash young cowboy with boorish manners, who falls for a stripper.

Years before, Inge had promised Paul that he'd make him the biggest star on Broadway, tailoring all his male roles for him. But when Paul learned there were sexual strings attached, he rejected Inge, who had never forgiven him.

Paul volunteered to rehearse Albert before he faced an audition with Inge himself and the the play's director, Harold Clurman. As it happened, Albert had not been given a script and would have to go into the reading cold turkey. Perhaps hoping that Albert would fail in his audition, Paul advised him to wear a suit and tie instead of the Levis, cowboy boots, and plaid shirt that was called for as part of the role.

During the plays previews in Philadelphia, the role of Bo was being played by Cliff Robertson, but Clurman wanted to fire him and bring in a new actor better suited to the part. Robertson, of course, was the same actor who had replaced Paul as the boyfriend in the movie version of *Picnic*.

Albert called Paul to tell him that he'd pulled off the audition. Both Clurman and Inge wanted him to play Bo, in spite of his appearance at the audition in a business suit. While there, he learned that Kim Stanley had been cast in the coveted role of Cherie, the stripper.

Finally, Albert was delivered a copy of the script for *Bus Stop*. Paul was almost as eager to read it as Albert was. He promised to work with Albert in his role before he had to go on stage with Kim.

"The moment Paul read that script, he could see PAUL NEWMAN written on every page," Steiger said. "The character's not housebroken. He's an innocent with a combustible element. When he meets this hot pussy, Cherie, he wants her and is determined to have her at all costs. He's got an unbridled lust for life."

Paul had confided to Shelley Winters that, "I'm destined to play the role of Bo."

"Destined is a pretty big word for a stage actor to use, but I think I understand why you said that," she said.

"I use the word and I mean it," he said. "I want that part, and I don't care who I have to fuck to get it."

"Even Bill Inge?" she asked provocatively.

"Even that, if I have to," he said.

Albert Salmi and Newman
in *Bang the Drum Slowly*.
"A lot of time in the sauna"

182

"That is, if I can get it up again for him."

Setting aside past differences, Paul braced himself and called Inge again, urging him to reject Albert for the part and cast him instead.

"As *Picnic* clearly showed, you don't have that wild streak in you to play Bo," Inge said.

"I've got a god damn wild streak in me, and I'll fucking show you," he told Inge.

The playwright slammed down the phone. Paul had been his crush of yesterday. New and younger game lay in his future, notably Warren Beatty.

"Paul was working hard behind Albert's back to get the role of Bo," Steiger claimed. "But to Albert's face, he pretended to be his best friend. I think that if that heavy drinking Finn had ever learned about this double cross, he'd have beaten the shit out of Paul."

In a final, desperate maneuver, Paul even resumed, at least temporarily, his on-again, off-again affair with Kim Stanley. She told Paul he was right for the role, and she promised to secretly lobby for him.

Brooks Clift, her other lover, claimed she didn't lobby very hard, because she believed that Paul was too pretty and not rough enough around the edges. "He is just too polished a gentleman to play a hayseed like Bo Decker. Paul has 'class' written on his face."

Before going to Philadelphia, Albert worked with Paul on the script until two or three o'clock each morning for an entire week. Paul assumed the role of the beautiful showgal, Cherie.

"He deliberately gave Salmi bad advice," Steiger said, "although I don't know that for sure. Frankly, I think Paul wanted Salmi to bomb in Philadelphia, the way that Cliff Robertson had bombed. If Salmi also got fired, then Paul could step into the role. He knew every line of the play. He could even dress up in drag and play Cherie's part in an emergency."

Brooks claimed that Paul and Kim had another tiff when he learned that she didn't really back him for the role. Not only that, but Albert had claimed that Kim appeared at his hotel room one night in a robe, carrying a bottle of champagne and a couple of glasses. "She told me she was lonely," Albert told Paul. "I found her very attractive, and she convinced me we should make love off the stage so that we'd have more chemistry on the stage."

Later Albert claimed he'd turned down Kim's late-night proposition, but perhaps he said that as a means of protecting her reputation, since she was married at the time to actor Curt Conway.

Not knowing of Paul's own involvement with Kim, Albert told him of his private seduction of the star. This made Paul doubly jealous of his rival, although he managed to conceal that.

Produced by Roger L. Stevens and Robert Whitehead, *Bus Stop* opened to rave reviews on May 2, 1955 at the Music Box Theater in New York.

At this point, Albert had not yet learned of Paul's attempt to steal the role from him. Tenaciously Paul was still clinging to his dream of playing Bo. He was certain that a movie of *Bus Stop* would be made, and he told Steiger that "Albert is not photogenic. His rough looks are okay on stage, but not in a close-up."

Kim and Albert were hailed as the toast of Broadway, and *Bus Stop* was voted the best play of the season. Despite that high praise, Albert told a national-al magazine that this "boy-meet-girl play is just a piece of fluff, nothing more, nothing less." His widely circulated observation enraged Inge.

After hearing about that, Paul once again called Inge and found him more receptive to his playing Bo, at least on the screen. Furious at Albert's remarks, Inge promised Paul that he'd lobby for him to bring the role of Bo to the big screen.

One night, Paul received a call from Marilyn Monroe, who had arrived mysteriously in New York. She wanted to dress up incognito and be taken to see *Bus Stop*. He agreed to have a reunion with her, and he accompanied her to the Music Box Theater. When the house lights dimmed, she entered the theater with him, taking an out-of-the-way seat. It was obvious what her designs were. She wanted to play Cherie in the movie version.

At the theater, Marilyn seemed to delight in the show, squeezing Paul's hand repeatedly. At the end of the play, she wanted to go backstage to meet Albert. But Paul discouraged the idea, claiming that Kim Stanley would find out and would be furious, thinking she was trying to steal the role from her. He told Marilyn that Kim had her heart set on playing Cherie in the film.

That night Paul took Marilyn back to her hotel where he made love to her—that is, when they weren't talking about the changes that they would make in Inge's play when it was filmed.

The next morning, Paul encountered Steiger at the Actors Studio and swore him to secrecy about what he was to tell him about his night with Marilyn. "My dream is about to come true," he said. "Paul Newman and Marilyn Monroe starring in *Bus Stop*. I can see our names linked in movie marquees across the country."

"Perhaps," Steiger said skeptically. "But you've got the billing wrong. Any actor will always have to play second fiddle

Kim Stanley
"Torn between two lovers"

184

to Marilyn."

Twentieth Century Fox purchased the rights to the play and began to fashion it into a showcase for Marilyn's talents. The film's director, Josh Logan, called Albert to tell him that Fox was interested in having him test for the role of Bo.

Three days later, Albert told Paul he'd met with Logan, who was still touting the theory of crotch acting he'd articulated so well, years before, to Ralph Meeker.

When Albert invited Logan to join him in a Finnish sauna, and when the director saw firsthand how well endowed Albert was, he came up with a suggestion. For the film, Logan proposed that Albert "wear skin-tight jeans and show basket. John Barrymore always claimed that when he appeared on stage in green tights, he stuffed a sock in there and that ticket sales among the ladies and homosexual males soared."

Albert told Logan that, "I can go for that since I'm right proud of what I've got. We Finns are gods among men."

To Paul's surprise, he learned that Elvis Presley had appeared in the audience to see *Bus Stop*. Like Marilyn, he had arrived incognito and was not recognized by his fans.

"I heard through Logan that Elvis wants to play Bo," Albert said. "If he's really serious, he'll get the part. Let's face it: Elvis Presley and Marilyn Monroe would be the box office attraction of the decade."

Paul warned Albert "not to worry. There's no way in hell that Colonel Tom Parker will let his moneymaker do a straight dramatic part."

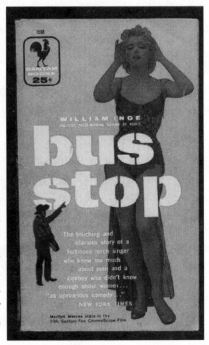

The prediction came true. Colonel Parker completely rejected the idea of *Bus Stop* for Elvis. Parker's exact words were, "I'm not gonna let my star appear in some play by a queer. The next thing I know, Elvis will be wanting to do a Tennessee Williams play."

Albert had contracted to star in the road tour of *Bus Stop* with former child actress, Peggy Ann Garner. Between 1938 and 1949, she had appeared in eighteen films. But by 1955 her star was dimming.

Taking time out from the play's road tour, Albert took the train to New York for a screen test with Logan. Back on the road, his relationship with Peggy Ann heated up. Albert later said, "I bedded Peggy Ann—or did she bed me?" Whatever, the couple got married in 1956, a union that lasted until 1963.

A week after his screen test, Albert heard from Logan. "The suits at Fox don't feel you're right for the movie role."

When that news reached Paul, he called Logan and practically demanded that he get the part. "I can play Bo. Marilyn and I have great chemistry together. Besides, you owe me one."

"I don't owe you a God damn thing," a drunken Logan told him. "Just because you let me suck your cock doesn't give you any claim to shit. Do you know how many actors' cocks I've sucked? Hell, back in the Thirties, I used to suck off both Henry Fonda and James Stewart."

One afternoon at the Actors Studio, Kim encountered Paul, managing to be gracious about her loss. "Marilyn had other commitments, and I got the role of Cherie. Logan even came backstage and told me it was definite. But now her schedule's clear, and she's available to take the role, and I'm the loser. I'm horribly disappointed. But Marilyn is such big box office, and she is right for the role. You and I have seen her act at the studio. We know how good she is. None of us believe that she's the lightweight her adoring fans seem to think."

Backstage that night at *Bus Stop*, Paul felt Kim's despair. Hoping to cheer her up, he stripped down and pulled off her robe. On the floor of her dressing room, he was making love to her when he heard a loud pounding on her locked door. It was her husband, actor Curt Conway. He was calling out for Kim.

Throwing her robe around her, she hustled Paul into her tiny bathroom before opening the door to greet her husband. She told her husband that she was alone, although he'd learned that she was having affairs with other men.

Months later, when the filming of *Bus Stop* began, Kim wired Marilyn in California. "I send you my best. You have a lovely, lovely play to film."

Paul told Steiger, "I'm glad Conway didn't have to take a leak that night." In a way, Paul was rehearsing for his upcoming madcap performance in *Rally 'Round the Flag, Boys!*

Conway and Paul would not meet until both of them were cast in the 1963 *Hud*.

Elvis Presley
"Missing the bus"

***

Back in Hollywood, Paul hooked up with Marilyn for a one-night stand, still hoping he had a chance to play Bo opposite her. She had more or less convinced him that she had persuaded Logan to cast him in the part.

After their lovemaking, she kissed him on the mouth. "Sorry, honey, I've got bad news. Logan, that bastard, has cast Don Murray."

Paul was crushed, especially by the way Marilyn had chosen to tell him the bad news.

"Murray's got no fire," he said. "He's a nice-looking boy-next-door type."

Even so, Murray got an Oscar nomination that year as Best Supporting Actor.

"Marilyn led me on," Paul raged to Vampira the next day. "She fucked Albert, and then she screwed Elvis. She was flirting and fucking with all the potential Bos."

"At least you got a few good screws out of the deal," Vampira said. "Fucking Marilyn was your consolation prize."

In time, Albert learned about Paul's behind-the-scenes maneuvering to grab the role of Bo from him. Although they would work together in the future, he never really forgave him.

***

For the *Kaiser Aluminum Hour* on television, Paul was cast as Danny Scott in *The Army Game*, a teleplay directed by Franklin J. Schaffner. It aired on July 3, 1956.

The cast brought Paul into contract with Sydney Pollack, an actor who would become even more famous as a director.

As a Hollywood footnote, Pollack would be far more significant in the career of Paul's future friend, Robert Redford, than he would in Paul's filmography.

Long after appearing on TV with Paul, Pollack would be cast in Redford's film debut, the 1962 *War Hunt*. They became friends and would later collaborate on seven films, including *The Way We Were* in 1973 and *Out of Africa* in 1985. In time, Pollack would finally work with Paul when they filmed *Absence of Malice* in 1981. However, Al Pacino had been the director's first choice of a star.

Years later Paul with a smirk commented on the Redford/Pollack films, "I guess Sydney went for Redford's puss and that blonde hair instead of my baby blues and buffed chest. Because he fell for Redford's male flash, I lost out on

187

a lot of good parts. I'm only joking, fellows. As far as I know, Redford and Pollack are straight arrows."

Also appearing in the cast of *The Army Game* was George Grizzard, whom Paul had dropped so abruptly when they were appearing on Broadway in *The Desperate Hours*.

In 1977, at Ted Hook's Backstage restaurant in New York, George spoke to actress Barbara Baxley and author Darwin Porter about his reunion with Paul. George and Barbara were discussing co-starring in *The Last Resort*, a film version of Porter's novel, *Butterflies in Heat*.

"When we came together again, I wasn't sure if Paul would even speak to me," George confided. "But he walked right up to me in the studio and embraced me. We started up with our love affair where it had left off. I couldn't believe the change in his attitude from the last time I'd seen him. I fell madly in love with him all over again. And, guess what? Once again, after two torrid months, he abandoned ship like before. After that, I'd had it with Paul. I still loved him dearly, but I had to move on for the sake of my sanity."

***

Also as part of *The Kaiser Aluminum Hour* series, Paul starred with Don Gordon and Silvio Minciotto in *The Rag Jungle* which aired on November 20, 1956. Paul had little contact with Gordon, a Californian who was his same age. Gordon would become one of the best friends of Paul's future rival, Steve McQueen, appearing with him in *Bullitt*, *Papillon*, and *The Towering Inferno*. The latter film would also star Paul, of course.

Years later, whenever the subject of the close bond between McQueen and Gordon would come up, Paul tended to be dismissive. "I'm tired of hearing all this crap about what blood brothers they are, riding off into the hills on their fucking bikes. Lovebirds like to flock together."

"I had the chance to become Steve's biker buddy, riding off in the middle of the night in the pissing rain," Paul claimed. "Sleeping buck-ass naked with the buck-ass naked Steve in a scalding hot motel room with bedbugs in a desert

Robert Redford (left) with **Sydney Pollack**
"Falling for the hunk's male flash"

188

where if you walked ten feet outside the door you stepped on a rattlesnake. Steve wanted me above all others. He liked to go away with men while keeping his wife of the moment home barefoot and pregnant. I know the same charge has been leveled against me. It's not true in my case. It was true in Steve's case. A man's man. Women for sex, men for company, or whatever."

Janice Rule always claimed that she felt Paul was jealous of McQueen's ability to bond with other men. "In spite of his protests, I think Paul wanted to be out there riding in the moonlight on his bike alongside Steve. Discovering the world that way."

"The subject of the strange relationship between Steve McQueen and Paul Newman could fill an entire book," Janice said. "Frankly, I think the two of them, in spite of being such rivals, had the hots for each other. One time I told Paul that I thought he and Steve should get married and settle down on a sheep farm in Australia. He never spoke to me again for a month."

During rehearsals for *The Rag Jungle*, Paul spent more time talking to the aging actor Silvio Minciotti than he did with Gordon. Born in Italy in 1883, Minciotti had played Papa D'Amato in the 1952 film, *Clash by Night*, starring Barbara Stanwyck and Marilyn Monroe.

"Paul was fascinated to learn that Marilyn had a lesbian streak in her," Minciotti claimed. "I told him that when Marilyn wasn't fucking her good-looking co-star in the movie, Keith Andes, she was screwing Barbara."

"I think Babs could have really fallen for Marilyn but blondie cut her off at the end of our film," Minciotti said. "She had other fish to fry. Paul was like a sponge absorbing all I knew about Marilyn and Barbara shacking up. I secretly suspected the image of those two pussies making it together provided a jack-off fantasy for him."

"He told me that he'd seduced Stanwyck's best friend, Joan Crawford, as indeed Marilyn had herself," Minciotti said. "Paul said that like Marilyn, he, too, planned to seduce some of his dream girl fantasies of the Forties. He even named his specific target victims, each a wet dream of his. Lana Turner, Ava Gardner, Judy Garland, and Rita Hayworth. I was absolutely certain that before the Fifties came to an end, and before each of these bitches got too old, Paul would have them."

"He seemed very determined, and I can't imagine one of those aging movie queens kicking a young stud like Paul Newman out of their beds," Minciotti said. "Stanwyck was never a serious consideration for seduction. 'I hear she likes to control the fuck,' Paul told me. 'I could never go for that. When I fuck, I like to be the man. The one in charge.'"

***

189

More and more television viewers came to know the name of Paul Newman during the mid-50s. Critics hailed his performance in such teleplays as *The Five Fathers of Pepi*, which first aired in 1956 as part of *The United States Steel Hour.* "Live television was a great learning tool for me," he said. "You had guys like Tad Mosel and Max Shulman writing for the medium. It was a very creative time, even though some critics dismissed our work as 'kitchen sink.' It was a glorious period to be a young actor. I preferred the stage, but teleplays were my next favorite goodie. At that time, I had utter contempt for films on the big screen, which was getting even bigger at the time with CinemaScope."

"Of course, there were hazards," Paul recalled. "I remember in some military drama, I had to salute my superior officer. My fly was unzipped and my shirt tail was hanging out. Fortunately, that was all that was hanging out."

Years later, Paul would hardly remember his appearance in *The Five Fathers of Pepi*. Playing an Italian named Giorgio, he briefly befriended his co-star in the teleplay, Phyllis Hill, who had divorced Oscar-winning actor Jose Ferrer in 1953.

Paul took this classically trained ballet dancer out on a couple of dates, but all that he remembered was Phyllis lamenting "what a philandering louse Jose was." She told him that women who marry actors are fools. "Too much temptation is thrown at them. They are only men , after all, and they can't resist the next pretty girl. You marry an actor and he always comes in at four o'clock in the morning and never tells you where he's been."

***

In 1956, Joanne Woodward returned to Broadway to star in the Leslie Stevens play, *The Lovers*, opposite actors Hurd Hatfield and Darren McGavin at the Martin Beck Theatre. The play opened in May of 1956, but closed after four performances. Some reviewers inaccurately hailed it as her Broadway debut, forgetting that she had filled in for both Janice Rule and Kim Stanley during the run of *Picnic.*

At this time Paul was going through one of the most difficult and troubled periods of his life. "He drifted from bimbo to bimbo, or whatever,

Janice Rule
"Why don't you marry Steve McQueen?"

but his real love was for the bottle," claimed Rod Steiger. "One day he wanted to run off with Joanne. The next day he was overcome with guilt and wanted to return to Jackie and his three kids. He was completely messed up."

Geraldine Page also noted that "Paul never got so wasted that he missed a day's work. He always showed up cold sober the morning after. He knew his lines and gave a role, usually on TV, his best. He was a professional in every sense of the word. It was after six o'clock in the evening that he became a total mess."

Night after night, he drove home drunk, wherever that home happened to be. He escaped police detection until the night of July 5, 1956, when he pulled the drunk of his life. He was very despondent because he and Joanne had agreed never to see each other again.

He'd left the Jolly Fishermen Restaurant on Main Street in Roslyn, Long Island, and was heading to the home he shared with Jackie and his family in Fresh Meadows. Losing control of his car, he plowed into some shrubbery until he hit a fire hydrant. He could still maneuver the car, so he backed up and fled the scene of the accident. A policeman on patrol spotted him running a red light and gave chase, with dome light flashing.

Forcing Paul from the car, the policeman told him he was under arrest.

"Get out of my way," Paul shouted at him. "I'm acting for Rocky Graziano."

"Meet another Rocky who's hauling you off to jail." The officer's name was Rocco Gaggiano.

Handcuffed to the officer, Paul was taken in a squad car to the Mineola jail where reporters and photographers were waiting. At first he thought the police had tipped off the press, but he later learned that they were waiting for new developments in a local kidnapping case. One of the photographers recognized Paul and snapped his picture, which landed on the front page of *The New York Daily News*. Paul spent the night in jail, driving home stone sober the following morning.

The arrest and the publicity that ensued had no effect on his career. In the 1950s drunk driving wasn't viewed in the same way it is today. The public was long used to drunken celebrities like Frank Sinatra making a scene. Paul seemed to be living out the character of Rocky Graziano that he had played in *Somebody Up There Likes Me*.

Paul, however, took it more seriously. He knew he could destroy his career if he didn't stop drinking. Janice Rule arranged for him to go to an analyst. He went only three times before not showing up for his fourth appointment. He turned to Janice instead, who to some degree functioned as his psychotherapist long before she earned the credentials to become one professionally.

She advised him to face the inevitable reality. "You know you've got to live with your guilt and go through the pain of divorce. You'll probably have to give Jackie custody of your children. You're making good money and can provide for them. The children may also suffer emotional scars, and you have to be prepared for that. Even so, at some point you've got to abandon your dreams of the past and go forward into the surprises of the future. You may not even end up with Joanne. Most likely it will be somebody else. In your case, it might be a woman or even a man."

"I need the security of a home and marriage…I know that about myself," he told her. "But deep down and until I get too old, I know, and you know, I'll be a tumbling tumbleweed."

Our Hero Meets Rocky:
Arrested on a DWI in Long Island.

Chapter Six
What Becomes a Legend Most?

"This Newman?" came a heavily accented Hungarian voice over the phone. "How are your balls hanging?"

"Who in the fuck is this?" Paul demanded to know.

"Michael Curtiz, you prickless faggot. Bogie, *Casablanca*. Don't tell me you don't know me. I'm the best thing in Hollywood since God invented the pussy."

"What can I do for you?"

"Jack Warner, the fuck, gave me the KO to cast you opposite cunt Doris Day in a new musical."

It took a moment for Paul to realize KO meant OK. "Bitch can sing but can't fuck," Curtiz said. "In this movie, Virgin Day must sing and get fucked by you. Do you think hairs on pussy are really blond?"

"So, I hear," Paul said, "unlike Marilyn, who bleaches." He paused a moment. "Did you say musical? I don't sing."

"If that faggot, Brando, can sing in *Guys and Dolls*, so can you. You don't have to sing in picture. Day for singing, you for fucking the bitch. You play shithead boyfriend. A real louse. You beat cunt and then rape her."

"Sounds like a great part for me," he said sarcastically. "I'll get back to you. And, by the way, my balls are hanging just fine."

Feeling he was getting nowhere with the illiterate Curtiz, Paul called Warner Brothers and got connected with the producer of the film, Martin Rackin. The son of a silk mill owner, he would in a few short years become head of production at Paramount Pictures.

Rackin explained that in 1942, Warners had acquired the screen rights to Helen Morgan's life story and had begun plotting another boozy biopic about the torch singer to "The Lost Generation." He claimed that during the previous decade some 40 actresses, including Jane Wyman, had been considered for the role.

Rackin wanted Paul to play Larry Maddux, the fast-talking, double-dealing heel Helen Morgan falls in love with. "I can see it now," Rackin said. "Helen, as played by Day, perched atop that piano, plaintively warbling sad songs about men, especially you, Maddux, who mistreated her. In her torch song style, she'll be singing 'Can't Help Lovin' That Man.'"

When the script was delivered to Paul, he found it a sudsy melodrama that had been worked over by twenty writers since the war years. "Too many cooks have spoiled the broth," Paul told Joanne. "I play a love 'em leave 'em type."

"Typecasting, if you ask me," she said.

Hollywood likes to imitate success. *The Helen Morgan Story* was inspired by two previous box office hits: *Love Me Or Leave Me* (1955), where Doris Day starred as singer Ruth Etting, and *I'll Cry Tomorrow* (also 1955), in which Susan Hayward played the tragic Lillian Roth. Forever imitative, the producers had turned first to Doris, wanting to cast her as Helen Morgan, a doomed singer, in a similar story.

Even though Doris had already been the focal point of *Love Me Or Leave Me*, the so-called story of singer Ruth Etting (1896-1978), she at least momentarily considered depicting yet another singer, Helen Morgan (1900-41). In the Etting story, a gangster called "Gimp," played by James Cagney, would dominate her life. In *The Helen Morgan Story*, a gangster called Maddux, to be played by Paul, would play a similar role. Paul planned to let James Cagney inspire his portrayal of this Prohibition-era gangster who seduces and then exploits Morgan.

Curtiz told Jack Warner, "Compared to Cagney, Newman might come off as girl. Maybe we should call Newman Pansy in the movie."

When the Morgan story was first presented to Doris, the script was called *Why Was I Born*. Morgan, like Etting, had a lot of links to the Mob.

Evoking the Lillian Roth character that Susan Hayward had played, Morgan, according to her fans, always sang better drunk than sober. It was rumored that between acts she swallowed an emetic which let her drink more liquor again before she went out once more to face a live audience. "After a good vomit," Morgan said, "I always sing better."

Doris wasn't happy that Curtiz would

Michael Curtiz
"You prickless faggot"

be directing the movie. She hadn't forgotten when he called her "a sexless bowl of goulash," but appeared willing to work with him again.

After two weeks of mulling it over, Doris called Jack Warner and told him to find another star. "My fans would never accept me playing such an unsavory character. It would offend them."

What she didn't tell the studio chief was that she was getting thousands of letters protesting her proposed appearance in the film. "It's against the will of God," wrote one irate Kansas housewife. There were rumors that Doris had even received death threats. Many of her fans said they'd stayed away from *Love Me Or Leave Me* because they didn't want to see her play a drunken prostitute.

Reportedly Doris later said, "My only regret in turning down the movie is that I wouldn't have a chance to work with that hunk Paul Newman."

In spite of a jealous husband, Marty Melcher, Doris was said to have been previously involved with actors, often her leading men, including Jack Carson, Tyrone Power, Ronald Reagan, and Steve Cochran.

***

After the fiasco casting of Doris Day, Curtiz told anyone who'd listen that "cunt Day is not the only blonde bitch in this town."

Paul was summoned to the director's office around three o'clock one afternoon where he was introduced to Miss Peggy Lee, the singer Duke Ellington had dubbed "The Queen."

In person, she had that platinum cool and inimitable whisper she presented in front of a live audience.

Curtiz had directed Peggy in a remake of *The Jazz Singer* in 1953, and Paul had sat through only half of the film, finding it "so schmaltzy." Even so, he had only the greatest admiration for Peggy as an artist, and had been one of the millions who'd adored her recordings of "Golden Earrings" and "Mañana."

"Newman, meet the new Helen Morgan," Curtiz said. "Fuck Day. How could she play drunk? Probably never had drink stronger than Kool-Aid."

"I'm not a stranger to a drink," Peggy said, shaking Paul's hand and looking into his blue eyes. "My God, you're even better looking than my second husband, Brad Dexter. When I married the bastard, I thought he was the handsomest man in Hollywood. Obviously, I'll have to revise that."

"Your kindness is only exceeded by your beauty," Paul said. "That and your talent. Forget your pals Frank Sinatra and Bing Crosby. No one can wrap themselves around a song like Peggy Lee. I read the other day that you're Albert Einstein's favorite singer."

"I was flattered by that, but found it a little creepy when I learned that Josef Stalin likes to jerk off while listening to me sing."

After more than an hour of listening to Curtiz and Peggy talk about the picture and Helen Morgan, Paul was ready to go. Before midnight, he had to work both Sal Mineo and Joanne into his busy schedule.

Even though Curtiz had agreed to send Peggy home in a studio limousine, Paul volunteered to drive her. She readily accepted.

She made it clear on the drive there that she might be very willing to have dinner and accept an invitation for a sleep-over. Bowing out because of prior commitments, he asked permission to call her next week.

"I've been a nomad since I divorced Brad," she said, speaking with a candor that surprised him. "Lonely, but looking, searching. It's like I'm trying to piece together the puzzle that is myself. Some of the pieces are missing."

"I have that feeling too," he said.

As he drove into her driveway, a man was sitting on her stoop waiting for her.

"My God," she said, "That's Brad himself. I forgot I had an appointment to see him. We have some financial problems to work out."

Getting out of the driver's seat and opening the passenger's door for her, Paul turned to meet Brad Dexter. Square-jawed like Charlton Heston, broad-shouldered and handsome, Brad had been labeled "the sweetest meanie to ever slug a hero or tussle with a lady." Perhaps Paul imagined it, but Brad seemed to hold his hand for thirty seconds longer than necessary. He didn't seem in the least jealous that Paul had shown up with his former wife.

Paul congratulated him on his appearance in the film noir, *The Asphalt Jungle* (1950), in which he was rumored to have had a torrid affair with Marilyn Monroe. He'd also been known to supply stud service to Mae West when she'd cast him in *Diamond Lil*.

"I loved you in *The Silver Chalice*," Brad said to him. "Great legs."

Top photo and insert **Miss Peggy Lee.** Above, with husband Brad Dexter on their "Wedding Day in Hell"

196

Paul chuckled as he winked at Brad. "Keep that up and I'll blow in your ear."

"I don't want to break up this fling between you two lover boys," Peggy said, "but I'm the star. Get in the house," she commanded Brad. "We've got some unfinished business."

Brad shook Paul's hand again, as Peggy leaned in to give him a quick brush kiss on the lips. "The promise of more to come," she whispered into his ear. "Call me."

As he'd later tell Rod Steiger during the description of his encounter with Peggy Lee, "I decided that very day that I was going to have to employ a social secretary."

"Hell, guy, you just can't seem to realize what's happening," Steiger said. "You're the new kid on the block. Every cocksucker and every horny broad in Hollywood wants to go to bed with Paul Newman. You're doing pretty well for a married man. I've always had this belief that if a married man played it right, he can have more fun than single blokes."

***

Paul did not call Miss Peggy Lee. Instead he showed up drunk at her doorstep around one o'clock one morning. She'd been wandering her lonely house that night, listening to music. After determining who it was, she opened the door for him.

"He was wasted," she later told Frank Sinatra, who passed the comment along to Paul. "But I'd never seen such a sexy bastard before."

"I'm horny," Paul ungallantly told her.

"You've come to the right place," she said, reaching out to guide him inside her door.

That was all he remembered until the next day, or so he claimed to Vampira and Tony Perkins. He said he woke up nude and alone in her master bedroom. "It was like a fantasy room and, in spite of my headache, I felt like a king. All blue velvet and white carpeting. *Trompe l'oeil* paintings of vines on all the walls." Getting up from the bed, he immediately sat down in a Louis XIV chair, trying to decide what to do and what had happened.

Finally, he went into her bathroom and showered, brushing his teeth with her toothbrush. He looked around the bedroom but didn't find his clothes. He must have discarded them downstairs.

Throwing a towel around himself, he headed downstairs and followed the smell of freshly brewed coffee into a garden with a carp-filled pond. He had to cross a Japanese bridge that led to a pagoda where he found her sitting in a white robe, her blonde hair glistening in the late-morning sun.

"My Prince Charming, awake at last," she said.

"I swear I don't remember a thing from last night," he said, sitting down opposite her and taking the coffee she offered.

"I remember last night," she said. "But I'll never tell you what happened, except to say that I had the thrill of my life exploring every inch of the Golden Boy of Hollywood."

"You've had your memory, and I want mine," he told her, putting down his coffee cup. He looked up at the sky. "It must be noon already. Do you believe in *Love in the Afternoon*?"

"Isn't that the name of Gary Cooper's latest movie?"

"It is indeed, and I've seen a preview of it," he said. The cameraman had to use extreme shading to disguise Coop's features in his scenes as an aging Casanova with that angelic Audrey Hepburn." He held his face up to the sun. "Look at me. A man in his prime. No shading necessary."

"I never answered your question," she said.

"And what was that?" he asked.

"About *Love in the Afternoon*," she said. "Us gals from North Dakota believe in love in the morning, love in the afternoon, and love at midnight."

"I don't know what you did to me last night," he said. "But here's my chance to level the playing field."

The next day he learned from Vampira that Peggy was a married woman. She'd wed a handsome young actor, Dewey Martin, who climbed out of a cockpit in the South Pacific and made it to Hollywood and into her bedroom.

"Thank God he must have been out of town last night," Paul said. "I didn't notice any husbands running around. Too bad about the marriage thing." He had a smirk on his face. "I was hoping to become the next Mr. Peggy Lee. All is not lost. When we do the Morgan thing, I'll be spending a lot of time in her dressing room."

That was not to be. The next week Paul learned he wouldn't be appearing opposite Peggy Lee in *The Helen Morgan Story*.

***

On the morning of May 13, 1956, tragedy struck. Paul was awakened around two o'clock by an urgent call from Mira Rostova, Monty's acting coach and confidante. She was calling all the actor's closest friends with the

Paul Newman
"Exploring every golden inch"

grim news.

After attending a dinner party at the home of Elizabeth Taylor and Michael Wilding, at which Rock Hudson was a guest, Monty took off in his Chevrolet down a hill following a dangerously curvy road. Actor Kevin McCarthy, one of his closest friends, was driving a separate car in front of him on that foggy night.

Disoriented by drugs and alcohol, Monty lost control of his car, which jumped over the curb and plunged down the hill.

In panic, Paul demanded that Mira tell him if his friend were dead or alive. Apparently, he was alive, but Mira seemed more concerned with his appearance than his life. "That beautiful face," she told Paul, "is gone forever. I just know in my heart that the beauty butchers will never be able to restore it." She broke into uncontrollable weeping.

When she pulled herself together, she promised Paul that she'd keep him abreast of Monty's condition. She also said that she'd arrange for Paul's access to the hospital as soon as he was able to receive visitors.

Years later, Mira shared with the author her memories of how helpful Paul had been during the process of easing Monty into the second phase of his life with a much altered face.

When Paul was allowed to visit Monty, he drove to the hospital with Mira. En route, she blasted Elizabeth. "It's all the fault of that beautiful witch. Monty had told her the afternoon of the party that he was too tired to drive up that mountain. He never liked to drive at night, and he knew that the access road to her house was treacherous. She called him at least three times that afternoon, urging him to come because she really wanted him there. He relented and agreed to come. He should have gone to bed instead. They were shooting *Raintree County*, and the role was sapping all his energy. He desperately needed rest."

Mira remembered that when she entered Monty's room at the Cedars of Lebanon Hospital, his head was swollen "as big as one of those pumpkins at Halloween. His face was a total wreck. Actually, you couldn't even make out his face in that mass of swollen flesh. A broken nose, a broken jaw, a cracked upper cheekbone, a gaping split in his upper lip, and cuts and bruises all over his face. I wanted to scream."

Mira remembered Paul as going

Monty Clift's near-fatal crash
The night he lost his beauty

199

into shock. "He was holding back tears as he viewed the wreckage of what had been the world's most beautiful man. Poor Monty could not see the tears in Paul's eyes. At that point, he didn't even know who we were."

Throughout the ordeal, Mira had only praise for Paul for being such a loyal, devoted friend. "He didn't even tell his closest friends about our secret visits with Monty. In no way did he want to appear that he was generating personal publicity for himself and capitalizing off Monty's misfortune. When Monty finally could sit up and talk, both of his jaws were wired together. He was being fed a liquid diet through a straw. We could hardly understand what he was trying to say through clenched teeth."

"The only time I got mad at Paul was when he did a terrible thing," Mira said. "While I went to the toilet, Monty apparently asked Paul to slip him martinis into the hospital, which he could drink through a straw. As anybody knows, alcohol was about the worst thing for him at this time. I think Paul also slipped him Demerols. Once when I came into the room, Monty was walking around, half supported by Paul. The doctors had forbidden him to walk at all, because the cracks in his facial skeleton might come loose. It was just like Monty not to listen to a soul."

When Monty was able to go home after more than two weeks in a hospital bed, Paul and Mira drove him to his dingy little house on Dawn Ridge Road. At least it had a swimming pool. Paul came to visit as often as he could. On several occasions, he encountered Libby Holman, the famous chanteuse who'd been accused of killing her husband, the twenty-year-old tobacco heir, Zachary Smith Reynolds.

Sometimes Paul came alone to see Monty; at other times he was accompanied by Mira. He told her what she already knew, that Monty was drinking heavily and taking morphine-based painkillers.

"I can't bear to look at him sometimes," Paul said. "He was so beautiful. You know, and I know, and as sure as hell Monty knows, that his beauty will never be restored."

As if to demonstrate the truth of that, Monty once took his hand and rubbed it across the contours of Paul's face. "I was once young and beautiful like you."

"And you'll be again," Paul assured him. "But, first, you've got to get well."

"That's bullshit and you know it."

Mira knew all of Monty's secrets, including his intimate relationship with Paul. Paul confessed to her that on one afternoon when he came to visit, he found Monty lying out by his pool, taking in the sun and trying to recover to go back to the set of *Raintree County*. "He was in the nude and I was astonished when he asked me to give him a blow-job. 'I want to feel that I'm still desirable,' Monty told me. I obliged but I wasn't into it."

Already an expert on nutrition, a field of expertise he'd develop even further later in life, Paul often prepared meals for Monty. He'd go to the Farmers Market in Los Angeles and find the lushest avocados and papayas, Monty's two favorite foods. He'd then make delicious, creamy shakes in a Waring blender which Monty would consume through a straw.

Eventually, Paul shopped for soft foods such as squash, bananas, and potatoes which Monty could slip into his mouth, taste only briefly at the roof of his palate, and then swallow. "It caused me pain to watch him try to eat, and it caused him pain to eat," Paul said. "He winced every time he swallowed."

Although both Mira and Libby Holman urged Monty not to return to work, he did not take their advice. "I owe it to Bessie to finish the film," he told Mira and Paul. He was referring, of course, to Elizabeth Taylor.

Back on the set, Monty managed to finish the film with his damaged face, but it became a personal disaster for him. He really was in no condition to work.

When he flew back to Hollywood and checked into the Chateau Marmont, he called Paul to come over for a visit.

Paul later confided in Mira what had happened. "When I came face to face with him in his room, I stared into his eyes," Paul said. "They looked like they were made of glass. Monty Clift was no longer there for me."

As if sensing Paul's reaction, Monty turned on him in anger, shouting, "Get out of here, pretty boy! I never want to see you again."

***

Michael Curtiz called to tell Paul that Jack Warner had nixed the casting of Peggy Lee in *The Helen Morgan Story*. "I want an actress, not a nightclub singer," Warner shouted into the phone at Curtiz. The director had to return to his casting couch.

No sooner had Curtiz arrived one morning at his office than he received a call from Jennifer Jones. He picked up the phone because she was still a big name in Hollywood, having married David O. Selznick. To his astonishment, he learned that she'd joined the chorus of other actresses wanting to play Helen Morgan. Privately, although he knew her voice could be dubbed, he felt she would be miscast as the torch singer. "I think I'd rather cast Joan Crawford in the part," Curtiz told his producer, Martin Rackin.

Through the studio grapevine, Paul heard of a possible change in casting. During his stint in the Navy, he'd seen Jennifer in her 1943 *The Song of Bernadette*, for which she'd won an Oscar. It was hard to imagine that an actress who looked so young, innocent, and virginal could play Morgan.

But Monty Clift had assured Paul that Jennifer over the years had undergone a remarkable change of personality—and "not for the better." Monty had had nothing but horror stories about working with the star in the 1954 release of *Indiscretion of an American Wife*.

Paul did not look forward to working with her, especially after Rackin introduced the star to him at the studio. She had never seen one of his movies, and didn't really know who he was, although she said his name sounded familiar. "Clark Gable, Gregory Peck, I know. Who can keep up with all these new stars?"

"Before the movie ends, Jennifer Jones will have Paul Newman tatooed onto her pussy," Paul told Tony Perkins. Just as he was gearing up to appear opposite her, following in the ill-fated footsteps of Monty, Michael Curtiz told him that "Jones is off the picture. The bitch with the red pussy, Susan Hayward, is now Helen Morgan. You still in my picture. Bogie would have been better choice."

Even though Paul never connected with Jennifer, he met her on other occasions in the years ahead. "After seeing your latest work, I'm still determined to make a movie with you one day," she told him one night at a party.

"Let's see if that happens," Paul said, thinking such a casting event would never come to be. But it did when Jennifer made her last screen appearance in his 1974 *The Towering Inferno*.

Over the years, he and Jennifer exchanged an occasional note. These greetings were usually from her, congratulating him on a role he'd recently played.

In early November of 1967, he sent her a note at a hospital where she was recovering. She'd checked into a Malibu motel and had taken an overdose of sleeping pills. Instead of dying in her room, she was discovered unconscious on the beach and rushed to a hospital where doctors worked overtime to save her. "Hang in there," Paul wrote in his note. *"Beat the Devil."*

He was, of course, referring to her 1953 film, *Beat the Devil*, in which she'd co-starred with Humphrey Bogart.

He'd send her another note in May of 1976, two years after appearing with her in *The Towering Inferno*, when he read in the papers that her daughter and her only child with Selznick,

Monty Clift and **Jennifer Jones**
Performing Indiscretions

202

Mary Jennifer Selznick, had killed herself.

He wondered why these two women, who seemingly had all that the material world could offer, would want to kill themselves. But Jennifer, in one of her cards to him, wrote, "My mother told me never explain, never complain."

In the weeks leading up to the first shot of *The Helen Morgan Story*, Susan Hayward insisted on approving her leading man. The studio, at the instigation of Curtiz, arranged for Paul to visit the fiery redhead at her home.

From the slums of Brooklyn to the stenographers' pool to a modeling agency, Susan was an actress he admired, although he considered her a dime store version of Barbara Stanwyck. He'd found her portrayal of Lillian Roth in *I'll Cry Tomorrow* a stunning *tour de force*, but he was surprised that she'd agreed to play the disturbingly similar role of Helen Morgan.

A passionate firebrand, Susan was not unlike some of the tempestuous women she'd played on the screen. Sitting in her living room, he accepted the Scotch and soda she'd generously offered. It was obvious that she was at least three drinks ahead of him.

"I went after the role of Lillian Roth," she said. "Knocked June Allyson on her ass. That bitch is a nympho. Fucks every grip on the set of every one of her movies."

She looked him up and down. He'd later claim that he felt the Oscar-winning actress was undressing him. "At least I'm still enough of a money-maker to retain approval of my leading man. What makes you think you're enough of a man to handle a woman like me? You're not a fag, are you? I was married to that fag, Jess Barker. I caught him in bed with Howard Hughes. When I called him a queer, he ripped off my clothes and beat the shit out of me. Threw me naked into the pool. You're not a fag, are you?"

"I think you've asked that before?" he said.

"You never answered."

"You didn't give me a chance," he said. "No, I'm not a fag. But I don't condemn those who go in for that stuff."

"I'll buy that," she said. "Live and let live, I always say. Besides, you couldn't work in this business unless you had a tolerance for fags. I don't know about you, kid, but I've been through some tough times. Horrible depressions, the low of lows. A suicide attempt. When a beautiful woman like

Susan Hayward
"You're not a fag, are you?"

203

me reaches her mid-thirties in Hollywood, she's got a lot to worry about. I've been trying everything lately to escape my fears. Booze, of course, even sexual experimentation. My ten-year marriage has ended. I'm fighting to keep my kids from perverts. All my close friends are dying. I'm out there on a limb of a rotting tree dangling in the wind." Ending her monologue abruptly, she looked at him again, as if for the first time. "What's happening to you?"

Since she'd been so personal, he related to her on the same level. "My marriage is coming to an end. Like you, I've got kids, three in all, a boy and two girls. I'm doing some sexual experimentation on the side too."

"I hear you're shacked up with that *A Kiss Before Dying* gal," Susan said. "What's her name?"

"Joanne Woodward."

"If she were better looking, she might make it in the movies. She's a blonde, right?"

"A natural."

"I hate to break the news to Miss Woodward, but blondes are on the way out. Marilyn is starting to self destruct. When she goes, that will be the end of all her clones, dames like Jayne Mansfield and Mamie Van Doren. Those bitches will be buried in the same grave as Marilyn. Those blonde bombshells of the 40s are fading too if not completely over the hill. Lana Turner, a total cunt. Betty Grable, a nice gal but who wants nice gals? Veronica Lake, a total psychotic. Since you're dating Woodward, does that mean you're partial to blondes? Ever seen a redhead down below where the wind don't blow? It's quite a sight."

"There have been a few," he said boastfully, still resenting her suggestion that he might be a fag. "The gals come and go. I can't keep track of them, much less the color of their pubic hair."

"That's very interesting," she said. "At least I now know you're like me. You like to fuck around. I think you and I can heat up this fucking picture. Of course, I'll have to audition you."

"I'm sure we can get Curtiz to set up a screen test."

"Fuck Curtiz. Fuck that kind of screen test. There's only one way I audition my leading men." She shifted her eyes to the staircase leading up to her bedroom. "You said you weren't a fag. Here's your chance to prove it."

"You mean, you want me to make love to you?"

"No, asshole!" she said, standing up on wobbly legs. "I want you to fuck me."

***

Meeting with Vampira, Paul told her of how he'd been sucked into the private world of Susan Hayward. "'Fuck him right out of me,' was what she shouted to me in the middle of our tumble last night. I didn't know if she were talking about her divorced husband, Jess Barker, or Howard Hughes, who'd dumped her."

Paul claimed that he'd never had such violent sex with a woman. "She clawed my back and told me if I didn't satisfy her she'd tear it off. When she locked her legs around me, I felt like a trapped beast."

"You poor baby," Vampira said, not really meaning that.

"It was violent sex and I had the climax of my life," he told her. "If Susan calls me again, I'll come running, but I'll eat my Wheaties first."

The very next day Michael Curtiz phoned to tell him that "the red-haired bitch is off the picture. She doesn't want to play boozy singer. I should have sent a man to fuck the cunt, not a little girly boy like you."

"Thanks for the vote of confidence," he told Curtiz. With yet another star abandoning *The Helen Morgan Story*, he was beginning to have second thoughts about playing the male lead. His attorney had warned him that he didn't dare risk suspension by bolting from the picture, for which he was under contract. "Remember, you've got a wife and three kids stashed somewhere to support."

"Don't remind me," Paul said.

When Hayward turned down the role, Martin Rackin came to Curtiz. "Now who are you going to cast as a broken-down alcoholic singer?"

Curtiz thought for only a second. "Judy Garland."

"My God," Rackin said. "How obvious. We should have gone to her as our first choice. But, first, we've got to determine that she's in any condition to play the part."

Curtiz called Paul the following week. "Judy Garland's our Helen Morgan. She's just been cast and wants to see you. Saw you as girly boy in that Jesus Christ piece of shit. She's not sure you have balls enough to play tough gangster."

"Sounds like another casting couch call for me," he told Curtiz. "Do I have to fuck every broken down broad in Hollywood to get in this picture?"

Later that afternoon, he told Vampira, "As you know, screwing these legendary broads is one of my goals, but I don't want Curtiz to know that. Judy's a bit ripe, but she's always been at the top of my list. She's still a hot number. One day I'll pen my memoirs, and I need something to write about. To say I married an unknown actress and

Judy Garland
Sending Judy
Over the Rainbow

205

had three kids by her and then shacked up with Joanne won't sell one fucking copy."

"Go to it, big boy," Vampira advised, "and send Judy over the rainbow."

Arriving at Judy's house, he found her alone and a bit intoxicated. Did all screen legends drink in the afternoon? She no longer looked like Dorothy in *The Wizard of Oz*, but she still possessed a certain allure and a charm that he found mesmerizing. He didn't know if he were looking at the real Judy or the reel Judy. Instead of actually seeing what she looked like today, he envisioned her in all those Technicolor MGM movies from the 1940s.

"I once met Helen Morgan," she said. "Of course, I was a mere babe at the time, part of an act called The Gumm Sisters. Don't you love it?"

As the afternoon deepened, and as he and Judy talked, he realized how very different she was from Susan Hayward, who had absolutely no sense of humor. Judy, in contrast, had a quick wit and a gift for self-satirization. She was, in fact, the single most fascinating woman he'd ever encountered.

"I'm sure you've read all about me," she said. "Who in hell hasn't? The pills, the booze, the failed marriages. My being broke all the time. My being temperamental on the set or not showing up for work at all. My getting fired from gigs like *Annie Get Your Gun*."

"I don't believe what I read in the papers."

She giggled. "In my case, it's all true, but don't hold that against me. Clouds always get in my way." She moved over and joined him on the sofa. "But I'll change for this picture with that psycho bastard, Curtiz. I want to play Helen Morgan opposite you. I like you, kid. You and I can pull off this picture. Make it a big hit. I don't know you, but I feel there's a definite chemistry between us." She gently ran her hand across his cheek. "You like a woman on occasion, don't you?"

"Are you kidding?" he asked in astonishment. "I don't know what rumors you've heard, but I adore women, on all occasions. I adore you."

She kissed him gently on the lips. "If you do, and I think you're telling the truth, I want you to take me dancing tonight. I love to go dancing."

***

Two hours and five drinks later at the Cocoanut Grove, Paul sat with Judy at a secluded table. She seriously discussed why she wanted to do *The Helen Morgan Story*. "It gives me a chance to sing and be a dramatic actress." She clutched her throat. "My voice is my curse. I got cast in all those frothy musicals, but what I really wanted to be was a dramatic actress. Play Laurette Taylor's part in *The Glass Menagerie*. I could do that. Makeup could age me a bit." She uttered a little laugh that sounded like suppressed hysteria. "Of

206

course, these days it wouldn't take much makeup to age me."

"Judy, you can do anything," he assured her. "Musicals, drama."

"You bet your left nut I can," she said. "Mickey Rooney and I are the most talented performers ever to walk through the gates of MGM. Hell, I could have become the most dramatic actress in the world, if those fucking bastards like Louis B. Mayer had given me a chance." She looked at her empty glass and then gazed into his blue eyes. "Order me another drink, sugar. The night's still young."

It was at that moment that a strikingly handsome man with a beautiful blonde danced by their table. He looked vaguely familiar. Suddenly, Paul realized he was staring into the eyes of Robert Stack, whom he hadn't seen since the war years.

Robert came to an abrupt stop. "Paul, Paul Newman? I can't believe it. And out with my favorite gal, Judy herself. Hi, Judy." He bent over and kissed her on the lips, as he let go of the blonde beauty. The blonde leaned over and kissed Judy on the cheek.

"Paul Newman, meet the one and only Lana Turner," Judy said. "And, Robert, why did you stop calling?" She faked a mock jealousy as she eyed Lana. She turned to Paul. "This sultry goddess here steals all my men."

"Nice to meet you, Paul," Lana said, "and, Judy, you know I don't take your men. It was you who shacked up with one of my husbands." She was referring to the musician Artie Shaw.

Switching from Judy to Paul, Lana extended her hand. "You almost got to make love to me."

"Have I lost my chance forever?" he asked smugly, taking in her beauty. He glanced furtively at Robert, also taking in his beauty. He felt awkward, not knowing what to say to him. He managed a "Long time, no see, buddy." It was back to Lana. "Exactly what did you mean about that making love thing?"

"You may not know this, but I was originally thought of for the Virginia Mayo part in *The Silver Chalice*."

"Maybe you could have saved that turkey," he said.

"Listen, I've got an idea," Robert said, looking at Paul. "Why don't you gals indulge in a little girl talk while Paul and I go see a man about a horse and maybe step out into the garden for a cigarette to share a few wartime memories?"

Walking in the garden with Robert, Paul came to a stop and faced him in the moonlight. He'd lost his boyish glow of the 1940s, but had matured into a strikingly handsome man. "I've

Lana Turner
Bad but beautiful.

been meaning to look you up ever since you became a movie star, but I'm sorry I didn't get around to it," Robert said. "You look terrific." He leaned closer to him. "Still my cute little sailor boy with that adorable butt?"

"Cute little sailor boy is now a man in his thirties," Paul said.

"You still look sweet sixteen to me," Robert said. "Remember, I'm six years older than you. Now gimme a kiss and let's join the ladies. But, first, you've got to promise to spend the weekend with me."

"You've got yourself a deal," man" Paul said. "I'm not the innocent little sailor any more. I've learned a few tricks. This weekend I'm going to make you my bitch."

Robert joined Judy at table, while Paul asked Lana for a dance. On the floor, he whispered to her, "Wait until the gang back in Shaker Heights hears I danced with the glamorous Lana Turner."

"Someday maybe you'll be my leading man," she whispered back. "With all the privileges that entails."

"That would be a dream come true," he said. "After all, Tinseltown is the Dream Factory."

Robert and Judy had joined them on the dance floor. Judy broke from Robert and cut in on Lana, who was immediately swept away in Robert's arms.

Now it was Judy whispering in Paul's ear. "Way back when dinosaurs roamed the Earth, Ida Koverman, a PR agent, arranged for Robert to date me. She thought we made a lovely couple for photographers. But after a few fucks, he drifted away. When I sing about the man who got away, I think of Robert. I didn't know you knew him too."

"From our Navy days," he said. "He was my instructor."

"Knowing Robert's reputation, I can just imagine what he instructed you to do." She laughed as he whirled her around the dance floor. When the orchestra played a slow number, she snuggled up close to him. To his surprise, he felt a deft hand unzipping him. Before he knew what was happening, Judy was inside, expertly feeling the family jewels. She performed this stunt with any number of handsome young men over the years, as Robert Vaughn related in his 2008 memoir, *A Fortunate Life.*

"Don't mind me," she said, noting his embarrassment. "I like to check out what I'm getting. That way, there will be no unpleasant surprises when your pants come off later in my bedroom."

***

Driving from Los Angeles to Palm Springs, Paul got to know Robert Stack, the lover he had loved but hadn't really known much about in the

1940s. During the long drive, Robert had a chance to talk about himself, and for the first time Paul realized he'd been born into Hollywood royalty, his parents on the A-list, entertaining everybody from Edward G. Robinson to Will Rogers.

Not only that, but Robert was one of the best friends of John F. Kennedy and had hung out with him and seduced beautiful girls with him when the young Kennedy's father, Joseph, was ambassador to England.

"I supported your buddy Kennedy for vice president when he tried, but failed to get on the Stevenson ticket," Paul said. "I once worked for the Adlai Stevenson campaign."

"I predict that Jack will be president one day. Would you like to meet him? He flies into town every now and then. I arrange dates for him with beautiful actresses. All he has to do is look at a gal and she tumbles into his bed."

"Sounds like my kind of guy," Paul said. "Sure, I'd be glad to meet him. Set it up. Does he swing both ways like us?"

"Not really," Robert said. "But he's got this best friend, Lem Billings, who's gay. I know Lem. They met back in 1933 and have been together ever since. I think he lets Lem suck him off now and then, but that's about it."

"I'd like to screw his wife," Paul said. "That is one hot woman. I'd marry her if she'd propose to me, or else let me be her lover. With her husband screwing around so much, she's probably lonely on many a night."

"I saw Jackie before you did," he said. "I'm first in line."

"Not that I'm jealous," Paul said, "but are you seeing any guy in addition to all the hot women you're balling?"

"Just one right now," Robert said. "Brad Dexter."

"I just met him the other day at Peggy Lee's place," Paul said. "He's bisexual too? He didn't strike me that way."

"You'll find that all actors in Hollywood are bisexual—and that's not much of an exaggeration," Robert said. "Putting on makeup turns us into girly men. I met Brad after he was coming down from a big affair with Tyrone Power. They did *Untamed* together. Brad and I met when we filmed *The House of Bamboo* together. The day we met, I told him, "You've had Marilyn Monroe, so why not me? After MM, I'm the next best thing in town."

"I'm one of the lucky guys who's had both of you hot bitches."

In Palm Springs, Robert drove Paul to a secluded villa. "A gay guy I know—he's in love with me—lets me stay here anytime I want. Thank God we have the place to ourselves this weekend."

An hour after arriving, both of them were in bed but agreed to a siesta before getting down to heavy maneuvers. "It was just like old times," Paul told Vampira when he returned to Los Angeles. "We picked up right where we left off back in the days when the Japs were bombing everything that moved in the

Pacific."

"You guys getting married?" she asked, eager to hear every detail of their off-the-record weekend.

"Not at all. With Robert, it's always going to be a sometimes thing. It's like eating caviar. You don't want to devour it every day."

***

As he pulled into the driveway of Joan Crawford's home, Paul was filled with trepidation. He'd almost given up hope of ever becoming one of Crawford's leading men, but he was going to give it one last try. After all, she *was* Joan Crawford, or at least she used to be.

She'd called him the day before, reaching him through Warner Brothers. She'd invited him over to see her, claiming, "I have this incredible script that could be a career maker for you, even better for you than *Somebody Up There Likes Me*." Bait like that he couldn't resist.

Throwing open the door herself, Joan was immaculately groomed and made up. Dressed all in white, she looked as if she'd spent many hours preparing to receive him.

Shown into her immaculate living room, which was all in white, including the carpet, she offered him a drink. Like the other movie legends he'd met, she obviously liked her booze.

The beginning of the afternoon was all business. She'd been sent a script called *Autumn Leaves*, the story of a typist who marries a younger man only to discover he is mentally disturbed and already married.

"I have a copy of the script," she told him, handing him one. "Let's read our parts together. I think you'd be ideal as my lover in the film."

Before beginning the reading, she looked at her mantle on which her Oscar rested. She'd won it for the 1945 *Mildred Pierce*. "Baby over there is going to have a brother after we make this picture."

As he read the screenplay with her, he found his role had some dimension. The male part was not that of a screaming maniac from an asylum. It had a lot of nuance and subtlety. After reading the script, he told her he

Joan Crawford & Cliff Robertson
The Falling Autumn Leaves

wanted to do it.

"I'm getting a lot of scripts for an older woman with a young lover these days," she said. "But I think this is the best I've seen. The script beautifully portrays the desperation and loneliness of an aging woman seeking love. We can do it without overacting. Play it down a bit. I can help you through the mad scenes. After all I did a lot of research before filming *Possessed*."

As the sun began to set in the West, Crawford became edgy as if in tears. "You're young and beautiful. I was young and beautiful once."

"You are still beautiful," he said reassuringly.

"But no longer young. I've had to keep reinventing myself. I don't want to become a joke in fag circles like Bette Davis and Tallulah Bankhead. I want to continue to be taken seriously as an actress. *Autumn Leaves* is my big chance."

"Miss Crawford, I'm your man," he said with a sexy smirk on his face.

"I hope you mean that in more ways than one," she said, assuming the mask of the carnival girl she'd played in *Flamingo Road*.

"Indeed I do, as you shall soon see." He got up from the sofa, putting down the script, and walked toward the armchair in which she was sitting.

Two weeks later, he called Janice Rule. "You got your chance to work with Crawford. Looks like I never will."

"Why so?" she asked.

"I've had it with the bitch. I just read in the papers that Cliff Robertson has been cast opposite her in *Autumn Leaves*. She promised the part to me. Yes, the same Cliff Robertson who played *me* in *Picnic* on screen. If I ever meet up with this fucker, he's going to lose a few front teeth."

"Forget Crawford," she urged. "You'll be a bigger star than she ever was. Actually, you weren't her first choice. Originally she took the script to Brando. He turned her down, claiming, 'I don't do mother-son pictures.'"

A few years later, when asked about Paul, Crawford said, "Paul Newman has the potential of becoming a magnificent actor if he ever gets through this complex he has about playing boy-macho."

***

As it turned out, Jack Warner had the final word on who was to play Helen Morgan. When Curtiz went to his office to tell him that Judy Garland was available, the studio chief said, "So what? I'm still recovering from her making *A Star Is Born* for us. I've called Ann Blyth. Without checking with you, I gave the role to her."

Throughout their careers, both Paul and Steve McQueen were known for seducing their leading ladies. Such was not the case when Ann Blyth was cast

211

in the title role of *The Helen Morgan Story*. The star had gotten along beauti-fully with the temperamental Joan Crawford on the set of *Mildred Pierce*, but she found working with Paul difficult. "He was playing this cocky bastard both on and off the camera," she reportedly said, although this remark cannot be verified. There was no love lost between the two stars.

As Crawford's bitchy daughter in *Mildred Pierce*, Ann had also been directed by Curtiz. She was a singer herself and had trained for opera, which did not fit into Morgan's throaty torch song style. Gogi Grant was hired to dub Ann's voice for such numbers as "Body and Soul" and "Don't Ever Leave Me."

Knowing her career was coming to an end with the death of her type of musical, Ann told Paul on the last day of the shoot, "Why not go out playing the piano-sitting, kerchief-holding, liquor-swilling torch singer with a train wreck of a personal life?" She would later remember him as "gorgeously smirking" throughout the film.

Curtiz, who could not resist delivering a final insult to Paul, said, "Newman, if I direct a film—call it *Lusty Lips*—I'll cast you as the cocksuck-er."

While *The Helen Morgan Story* was being edited, Rackin and Curtiz were horrified to learn that Playhouse 90 had cast Polly Bergen as Helen Morgan in a teleplay of virtually the same subject matter. To their horror, the teleplay even bore the same name as their big-screen version. The teleplay of *The Helen Morgan Story* was broadcast for the first time on May 16, 1957. Polly delivered a brilliant performance as the doomed torch singer and even won an award. "Who will want to go see our movie when they've already watched it for free on TV?" Rackin asked.

Rackin's point was well taken. The big screen version reached movie houses six months later—on October 5, 1957. One of its advertising slogans trilled "NO STAR EVER CLIMBED SO HIGH, NO WOMAN EVER FELL LOWER."

Regrettably, *The Helen Morgan Story* marked the end of Ann Blyth's film career. She ended her status as a movie star with a box office bomb. Blasted by the critics, she faded into film history.

A.H. Weiler, writing in *The New York Times*, dismissed the film as "about as heart-warming as an electric pad." Paul was

Paul Newman & Ann Blyth
Going out with a bomb

denounced as a "one-dimensional but grotesque and unbelievable character."

Paul recalled seeing Ann in the 1970s on TV, advertising Hostess Cupcakes.

"Hollywood should have done better by her," Paul told Joanne.

"Forget her," his wife said. "Hollywood should have done better by me."

***

A day after the wrap-up of *The Helen Morgan Story*, Paul reported for work on his third loan-out to Metro-Goldwyn-Mayer. Like *Somebody Up There Likes Me*, the "soaper," *Until They Sail*, set in New Zealand during World War II, would also be produced by Charles Schnee and directed by Robert Wise.

It was the story of four love-starved sisters, deprived of their men who'd gone to war. The sisters were played by a stellar cast that featured Jean Simmons, Piper Laurie, and veteran actress Joan Fontaine, who was in the twilight of a luminous career which, in the 1940s, had included the romantic suspense film *Rebecca*. The fourth sister marked the debut of a fourteen-year-old blonde-haired model, Sandra Dee.

The award-winning playwright, Robert Anderson, had adapted *Until They Sail* from *Return to Paradise*, a story by James Michener.

On the first day of shooting, Paul told Joan Fontaine that "this is really a woman's picture, more suited to you than to me. The picture belongs to you ladies. I was hired as window dressing."

"There's nothing like a well-dressed window," she said, "to lure the ladies in."

He'd been cast as Captain Jack Harding, a loner who found solace in the bottle after a broken marriage. He told Robert Wise, "For me, this character is an easy slide to home base, a slice of my own life. I, too, am escaping to booze to deal with a marriage that's breaking up even as we speak. Right now I'm staring at the bottom of that bottle."

Until They Sail was another of those "overpaid, oversexed, and over here" WWII stories about horny American soldiers disrupting the private lives of local women. In most cases, these war dramas were set in England. What made *Until They Sail* unique was that Wise used the more exotic setting of New Zealand.

Paul had been enthralled with Anderson's emotional drama, *Tea and Sympathy*. "He walked a tightrope between realism and sentimentality," Paul said. Years later, with just a touch of regret in his voice, Paul said, "Of course, the fucker did a lot more for Steve McQueen in *The Sand Pebbles* than he did for me." He was referring to the hit drama released in 1966.

213

On the second day of the shoot, Charles Schnee, the producer, approached Paul. He was rather blunt. "Since you're still a relative unknown, we're counting on Jean Simmons to carry the box office," he said. "She's hot right now after appearing in *The Robe*. Of course, she's used to having Brando as her leading man." He was referring to her starring roles opposite Brando as Napoleon in *Desirée* and in the musical *Guys and Dolls*.

"After playing Rocky, this is pretty lightweight stuff for me," Paul said.

"In Hollywood, if you want to keep working, you can't always appear in gritty dramas. Romantic fluff has its place too. The important thing is that Wise and I can turn you into a romantic hero at the box office. You'd fit better into that role than either Monty Clift or Brando."

"I'm not sure that's what I want to be," Paul said.

"Who gets what they want in Hollywood?" Schnee asked. "Didn't you see my picture, *The Bad and the Beautiful*?"

Until They Sail brought Paul together with the red-haired Piper Laurie, who had toiled in fluffy programmers or else out-and-out garbage for all of the 1950s. Her studio hadn't used this fine actress properly. "You and Ali-Baba sure heated up the sands," Paul said, upon meeting her. He was referring to the "desert sandals" romps she'd made with Tony Curtis. "And you sure looked prettier than that talking mule, Francis."

He'd never taken her seriously as an actress until he'd seen her emoting in their current picture. Even so, both his talent and hers would be far better employed in *The Hustler* in which they co-starred for a 1961 release.

Paul attended the screening of *Until They Sail* with Vampira and Tony Perkins. After leaving the movie house, he said, "All I had to do was be sexually aroused from time to time with Jean Simmons. In case she ever wondered what that hard thing pressing against her was in our love scenes, it was my erect dick."

In his final appraisal, he claimed that after *Somebody Up There Likes Me*, *Until They Sail* "was a dismal comedown for me. Hollywood has a way of making an actor's balls smaller in each picture. Even if an actor clanks them big time in his debut picture, he'll eventually get his low hangers snipped off. Of course, I was castrated in my first picture. Castrated again in *The Rack*. Restored to full testosterone in *Somebody*. And now

Paul Newman & Jean Simmons
"Oversexed, overpaid, over here."

once again snipped."

After retiring to a café with Tony and Vampira, Paul said he dreaded what the critics would say. "Surely, they're not going to compare me to Brando again."

He was wrong. Writing in *Films & Filmings*, Kay Collier claimed "Paul Newman is gentler and less rugged than Brando, but his acting has the same arresting power."

Bosley Crowther in *The New York Times*, had a different perspective. "The genuine tugs at the heart are few and far between in this bittersweet and basically restrained chronicle. Unfortunately, there is a good deal of introspective soul-searching before this narrative arrives at its sad and happy endings."

Until They Sail ultimately flopped at the box office. "Even Newman's baby blues couldn't lure the women away from those TV boxes," Wise lamented. "We should have stripped him down more and shot the film with him half naked. That day will come for movies, I predict."

Back at the café with Vampira and Tony, Paul swore them to secrecy about an ongoing drama that evolved after the film was wrapped.

Although he'd worked on the film with three beautiful adult women, each of whom might have entertained a pass from him, it was the fourteen-year-old Sandra Dee who caught his attention.

It all began, according to Paul who was both amused and horrified, when he heard someone shouting at him through the open window of her dressing room.

"Mr. Newman, Mr. Newman," Sandra called, "Would you like to see my body?"

***

When Sandra Dee extended an invitation to Paul to view her body, he told her, "Yes, I'd like to, but there are laws against it."

When she explained the situation, he dared enter her dressing room against his better judgment. In the film, *Until They Sail*, the young actress/model was supposed to age from twelve to eighteen. To make her look older with a more rounded figure, the makeup department had devised an inflatable rubber suit for her to wear under her clothing. He was captivated by this child-woman who sat across from him. She was a perky, doll-like creature with champagne-colored corn-silk hair.

"Isn't it wiggy that we're appearing in the same film together?" she asked.

"Wiggy?" he asked. "That's a new one on me."

"I've been meaning to tell you," she said. "Ever since I saw your picture, I think you're the handsomest boy in Hollywood."

"Honeychild, I was born in 1925," he said. "I'm no boy. When were you born? Yesterday?"

"Don't put me down," she said. "I was born in 1944. I'm mature for my age. I don't like things kids my age go for. Rock and roll makes me nervous. Who needs Elvis Presley when they've got Paul Newman?"

"You ain't exactly got me yet," he said. "Besides, even if you were the right age, I already have a girlfriend."

"You mean Joanne Woodward?" she said. "That old thing. She's also ugly. Old and ugly. What a combination. Young and beautiful sounds better to me."

"You are beautiful all right," he said. "And you're dying to grow up, aren't you?"

"Oh, yes," she said. "When I reach sixteen, Butch is going to get me a four-seater T-bird."

"Is Butch your boyfriend?"

"No, silly, I don't have a boyfriend. At least I didn't until you came along. Butch is the name I call my mother."

"I'd better get out of here," he said. "You're jailbait."

"I'm at that awkward age," she said. "Too old to be a girl, too young to be a woman. Boys my own age are stupid. I like older men. Ever since I started going to the movies, I've had crushes on older men. All of them married or between marriages. William Holden. Ronald Reagan. Cary Grant. Clark Gable."

"A couple of those guys could be your grandfather," he said.

"I'm dying to become a woman," she said. "I want to experience life. I've got this awful crush on you, and I nearly fainted when I heard I was going to be in a movie with you."

"You seem breathlessly thrilled by it all," he said. "Like you're just discovering life."

"I am just discovering it, and I want you to be my guide," she said.

"I feel like I'm talking to Alice," he said. "And she's just dropped into Wonderland." He rose from his chair. "I've got to get out of here before someone calls the cops."

She stood before him. "Look into my eyes," she commanded.

He obeyed her, taking in a set of the most liquid brown eyes he'd ever seen.

"What color are they?" she asked.

Sandra Dee aged 14:
"Mr Newman, Mr. Newman, do you want to see my body?"

216

"Brown."

"Not blue, like yours," she said. "You have the world's most beautiful blue eyes. I want to have babies with blue eyes. So, to make babies, I've got to find a man with the bluest of blue eyes, not brown like mine."

"You're crazy," he said, backing away. "What makes you think I'm going to father your babies, much less give them blue eyes? I'm not sure you even know how babies are made."

"I'm not exactly sure, but you're the man to teach me how to make babies," she said. "I'm pretty god damn sure of that."

"What a little nymphet you are," he said. "I don't want to be one of the guys telling you to go home and after you grow up, come back to me. But that's what I'm going to do. You're not only young but innocent. I know you need to find out about the birds and bees. But I'm no teacher."

"Don't judge me by the pig-tailed innocent I'm playing in this film," she said, moving toward him. "My stepfather, Eugene Douvan, started fucking me when I was eight years old. He married my mother just to get close to me."

At that point, as Paul was later to tell Vampira, he was prepared to walk out the door of that dressing room and never see Sandra Dee again. "But when I heard about the sexual abuse from some bastard, when I saw how vulnerable she was, I figured I could at least be a big brother to her. "When she came to me, I took her in my arms and held her. She was sobbing hysterically."

That late afternoon, with a rubber body suit lying on a chair beside them, Paul began one of the most secret—and also, one of the strangest—relationships of his life. Nothing he'd ever experienced had quite prepared him for the likes of Sandra Dee.

***

Abandoning the Chateau Marmont, Paul moved with Joanne Woodward to a rented house in Malibu, which for an idyllic period they would share with Gore Vidal and his constant companion, Howard Austen. Their landlord, and the owner of the house, was none other than Shirley MacLaine.

Paul's marriage to Jackie had all but expired at this point. It waited only for the divorce papers to be filed. "Joanne has won her man," Lee Strasberg privately told members of the Actors Studio in New York. "But will she ever really have him? Paul likes to share himself with other admirers."

As for Paul's little children, he had nothing publicly to say about them. To friends, he expressed his fears. "I don't think my son Scott really digs me. He resents me far more than I did my own father."

The author, Christopher Isherwood, who had recently dined with Tennessee Williams, claimed that the playwright was "bubbling with jealousy" over Paul's decision to live with Gore. "I am certain that when Joanne is away, Gore is pawing those golden inches and sucking him dry," Tennessee, as reported by Isherwood, said. "Do you think Gore could resist Paul walking around at that beach house, in a pair of tight-fitting jockey shorts, coming downstairs for his morning coffee? Paul drinks a lot. It's inevitable that seduction is going to take place one night when the moon goes behind a cloud. Ask any gay man. The difference between a straight sailor and a gay sailor is a six-pack."

The unorthodox ménage of Newman/Woodward/Vidal/Austen escaped serious scrutiny in the press, but was the hottest news racing along the Hollywood grapevine. This was not the first time this bizarre quartet had been gossiped about. Once again, there was much speculation about the various sexual combinations the household might pursue. Even a four-way orgy was suggested, with Paul as the main object of communal desire.

Paul, no stranger to orgies after Robert Francis introduced him to Tyrone Power, dismissed such talk to his friends.

In his memoir, *Palimpsest*, Gore addressed the rumor of a sexual tryst between Paul and himself. "I should note here that over the years, I have read and heard about the love affair between me and Paul Newman. Unlike Marlon Brando, whom I hardly know, Paul has been a friend for close to half a century, proof, in my psychology, that nothing could ever have happened."

The logic or lack thereof of such a statement could be challenged. The world has long been peopled with fifty-year friendships that began as youthful love affairs.

Among the great literary feuds of the 20th century, the names of Gore Vidal and Anaïs Nin surface near the top. At the time of Gore's occupation of the Malibu house, he was still on speaking terms with Anaïs, the fabled diarist.

A *femme fatale*, at least in her own mind, Anaïs was a woman of mystery and passion, known for extravagant sexual exploits which included a torrid affair with Henry Miller and his wife, June. She was not known at the time for her bicoastal life where she had a husband stashed in New York and a younger husband in Los Angeles.

"She was liberated decades before female liberation," said the male chauvinist author, Norman Mailer. "I never let her seduce me that day she came on to me at a party in Greenwich

Joanne & Paul
An unorthodox ménage

218

Village. She got Jack Kerouac instead."

In the 1940s, the much older Anaïs had formed a friendship with young Gore that for a while had the intensity of a rocket taking off before its inevitable plunge to Earth. "We are the two *narcissi* of the Forties," Gore later recalled.

Reunited with her younger husband in Los Angeles, Anaïs drove alone to the Malibu house that Gore was sharing with Paul and their lovers, Howard and Joanne. Invited to lunch, she was eager to find out what was going on, as she was still gathering "portraits" for her as-yet-unpublished diaries, which in time Kate Millett would refer to as "the first real portrait of the artist as a woman."

Arriving at the Malibu beach house, she warmly embraced Howard and Gore. Gore introduced Anaïs to his roommates, Paul and Joanne. The diarist would later dismiss both of them as "starlets."

She told this author that Joanne was "a Southern belle lacking in grace and charm, the very antithesis of Tennessee's Blanche DuBois. I *am* Blanche DuBois. Not this actress, this Miss Woodward. She could be cast, perhaps, as a gum-chewing waitress at a burger drive-in, one on roller skates carrying trays of milk shakes."

She was far more intrigued with Paul, whom she described to novelist James Leo Herlihy, when he was lobbying to get Paul to star in *All Fall Down*, a movie role with similarities to the character Paul played in *Hud*.

"Newman is just as much of a narcissist as Gore is," Anaïs told Herlihy. "But he disguises it completely, and, like the most skilled of actors, puts up a mask to confuse the world. I suspect he will go far in an industry that is all about illusion."

"There is no self-awareness in this handsome young man at all," she claimed. "He is an obvious homosexual, but does not dare admit that to himself. He's a selfish rogue while pretending to be benevolent, supporting all the right causes. He has a facile charm but no depth. In spite of the hot sun out here, he already knows that California is a cold, harsh land. He does not want it to hurt him. So what will he do? What must he do? He will inflict emotional pain on others, therefore avoiding the pain of having the blows strike him first."

"I predict he'll have a miserable life in Hollywood," she said. "Beneath all of his swagger, I suspect there is a sensitive man lurking

Anaïs Nin
"What is a man
without dreams?"

somewhere there. He can't be frank with himself. It's obvious that he can't have a dialogue between his own flesh and his true spirit. He has no soul, or, if he does, it is hidden behind the package of surface beauty that he presents. I advised him to write down his dreams and try to analyze them, or get help from an analyst. I even volunteered to help him myself, but he rejected me. Amazingly, he told me, 'I don't dream.' What is a man without dreams?"

"His whole life is a deceit, a cover-up, and I join him in that," she said. "I, too, as you well know, am torn between two lovers. This balancing act has made me a mistress of deceit myself. Liars need to keep track of what they say. I have a secret *Book of Lies* that I write in daily. That way, I can remember what I told one lover and what I told another."

"I feel sorry for Newman because he will never be what he wants to be," Anaïs said. "If he wants to be a movie star, then he has to be as fake and artificial as Marilyn Monroe. He has to become a sort of dream figure for the women of America. American women are shallow. They always go for the superficial. They make gods and goddesses out of cardboard caricatures. I predict Newman will turn into a cardboard figure. There will be no reality to him. He *can't* be real."

"He's moving into a world foreign to him," she said. "He'll be an alien in Hollywood, as if he's landed from another planet. We'll never know who Paul Newman is, because he doesn't know himself. Perhaps one harsh, brutal morning, when the world tumbles in around him, he'll look into the mirror and see himself for the first time. But it will frighten him. He'll immediately reach for that mask to put on again, the one that conceals him from himself."

"While pretending to be one thing, which he isn't, he'll live a secret life in the shadows," she said. "He'll grab pleasure where he can find it and then flee from it back into this fake celluloid world. A tragedy, really. But, this is, after all, Lotusland."

Later, when Herlihy confided Anaïs's analysis of Paul to the author, Darwin Porter, Herlihy said, "I don't know if I learned anything about Paul Newman from listening to her. But Anaïs was not clever enough to conceal her own deceit. She was actually attracted to Newman, but could not admit that to herself. From the way she talked about him, I felt she wanted to add him to her stable of young men. But knowing how hopeless that was, she chose to trash him instead, the way she did Gore Vidal in her diary."

Ultimately, Herlihy himself faced "trashing" in an Anaïs diary, part of a perceived betrayal which led to a lifelong feud and which added, perhaps, to the events leading up to Herlihy's suicide at the age of 66 in 1993. But as it happened, many young men who did not satisfy Anaïs's libido ended up getting portrayed as impotent homosexuals in her diaries or novels.

***

Two weeks later Anaïs accompanied Joanne and Paul, along with Howard and Gore, to The Mocambo to hear "The Little Sparrow," French *chanteuse* Edith Piaf, singing with a passionate intensity. Even though she was an object of veneration in France, there were no other patrons that night for her Los Angeles appearance.

"She sang only for us," Anaïs later said. "Her voice, as always, was poignant, haunting. If a nightingale could speak, it would have the voice of Piaf. In Paris and New York, I always identified with Piaf. Both of us are women who cannot live without love."

During her performance, Piaf sang nearly all of her songs to Paul, gazing dreamily into his blue eyes. "I got the feeling from the look in her eyes that she was falling in love with me," he said. "After all, she's known for collecting beautiful young men as her lovers."

Later Piaf joined them at table, explaining that American audiences didn't know how to accept her. "Americans and I aren't the same breed," she said. "Since I'm French, they expect me to come out adorned with sable, furs, and sequins, like a showgirl at the Moulin Rouge. The curtains open, and there I stand in my little black dress. Marlene Dietrich I'm not."

"You are Piaf," Paul told her, "and that is real and more genuine than all the fake furs and all the glamour queens in the world."

She leaned over and kissed him on the lips for his compliment.

As the happy quintet was departing for the night, Piaf discreetly slipped Paul a note. In private, he read it.

"Call me," she wrote, giving her private number. "I will sing 'La Vie en Rose' only to you. You're like a young Brando."

"I never called," Paul would tell Eartha Kitt weeks later. Eartha knew Piaf from the days she had spent in Paris. "I'm not opposed to screwing some legends of the silver screen. I'm not even opposed to screwing Piaf, but it's not my cuppa. She's such a midget. But when she compared me to Brando, that was it!"

Edith Piaf
"Sadness fades so quickly"

Brando had told Paul that he'd seduced Piaf in Paris after he'd gone there at the end of his Broadway run of *A Streetcar Named Desire*.

Despite the fact that Paul had no intention of seducing Piaf, she was, after all, Edith Piaf, and he didn't want to ignore her invitation completely.

221

He wrote a note and personally delivered it to her hotel, leaving it with the front desk.

> *"Dear Mme Piaf,*
>
> *I am sure there are many songs you could teach me. One sunny day in Paree, we'll stroll along the Seine together, hand in hand. There will be new neighborhoods to discover for the first time. Montmartre. Montparnasse. The city will be as fresh, as new as a dewdrop on a ruby red rose. And if that trip to Paree never comes to be, we can still have joy in our hearts. The most glorious journeys are those only dreamed. Your eternal, devoted fan.*
>
> *Paul Newman."*

He added a postscript:

> *Voilà, jolie petite,*
> *Il ne fault (*sic*) pas pleurers (*sic*)*
> *Le chagrin va si vite;*
> *Laisse-moi m'en aller.*

He made a copy of the note and let Vampira read it. "That's beautiful," she said. "But I didn't know you spoke French."

"I don't," he said. "I asked a French waiter in a restaurant to add something romantic at the bottom."

"And you sent it to her, not knowing what it means?" she asked.

"Well, it seemed like a good idea at the time." he said.

Worried later that he'd inadvertently insulted her in French, he returned to the restaurant and asked the waiter for a translation.

"Monsieur, I am not a poet," the waiter said. "I stole the words from a French song. Here, I'll write them down for you in English."

> *Listen, my pretty one,*
> *You mustn't cry,*
> *Sadness fades so quickly;*
> *Let me go my way.*

***

"Why haven't I heard from you?" asked one of the world's most famous

222

voices. It was Judy Garland. "I'm not a leper you know. I'm fucked up but it's not contagious."

She wanted to talk for half the night. After an hour, she was only getting started. Hoping to end her long, rambling, drunken monologue, Paul agreed to slip away the following afternoon and see her.

"Good," she said, before ringing off. "I'll make sure we have the house to ourselves."

The next afternoon when Paul drove up to Judy's house, he hoped that Sid Luft was in New York, or shacked up in some motel in Palm Springs with one of his prostitutes. He also hoped Judy didn't have any children running around the house.

Judy answered the door and ushered Paul into her foyer, where he was introduced to Nunnally Johnson, a writer-producer-director for 20th Century Fox, and his wife, Dorris. After a handshake and pleasantries, the Johnsons were out the door. Judy, wearing slacks and a man's white shirt, ushered Paul into her living room.

"Before we get down to commando tactics, I want to share a script with you," she said. "It's called *The Three Faces of Eve*. It's based on a book written by two shrinks. It's about this dame from Georgia who's got not two but three multiple personalities. I know *The Helen Morgan* thing didn't work out, but there's a great role in Eve for you. The part of her husband. Warners makes plenty of dough renting out your hide. Those bastards will gladly lend you to Fox."

The next hour and a half was spent reading the script.

When they finished, he told her, "It's a fabulous part for an actress. My role's not so great but not bad either. But I see Oscar on it for a woman who can tackle the role of Eve."

"That's amazing," she said, her face lighting up. "Orson Welles, God knows why, read the script and said the same thing. You know, of course, that Orson was an old fuck buddy of mine?"

"Actually I didn't know that," he said, smiling. "But I'm sure I can sell the news to *Confidential*."

Standing over him, she reached for his hand. "I can't go dancing with you tonight. The kids are going to arrive around eight o'clock." She checked the clock. "That gives us at least two hours alone. Sid's in New York trying to arrange a booking for me at the Palace. We're all alone. You lucky boy."

"We are indeed," he said, "and I know how lucky I am. I've got a confession to make. I got a hard-on watching you in *Meet Me in St. Louis*. I wanted to be the guy, not that wimpy Tom Drake, who took your virginity."

"Honey, I lost that a long time ago to Spencer Tracy when I was fifteen, give or take a year," she said. "Now come along upstairs."

223

When Paul shared the latest Judy story with his friends, he said, "When we hit the sack, she delivered a great line."

"Tell us," Tony Perkins said.

"She asked me, 'Do you mind if we give each other blow-jobs before we get around to Number Two?'"

***

Paul borrowed the script from Judy, but did not rush home and show it to Joanne. She was in negotiations to do a low-brow version of John Steinbeck's *The Wayward Bus* so he didn't bother her with it.

He wanted Gore to read it, since he respected his literary opinion. He was also hoping Gore would write some pages to beef up his character as Eve's husband, in case he got the part. He could take the revisions to the director.

Reportedly, Gore approved the script, but also suggested it would be a star vehicle for Joanne.

When Joanne was presented with the script, she claimed that her mother had already read the book and had called her, urging her to go for it. "I told mother I didn't have a chance at a star part like that. Fox will want a big name. The most obvious candidate Fox can come up with is Susan Hayward."

"Would you believe Judy Garland?" Paul said. "She's been offered the role."

"She could probably do it if she can hold herself together," Joanne said. "But if Judy does it, Fox will have to call it *The Five Faces of Eve*."

A week later, back at Judy's house, Paul encountered a very different actress who'd changed her mind about *The Three Faces of Eve*. She informed him that she'd talked it over with Sid Luft, and that he was adamantly opposed to her appearing in "this tacky little film noir that no one will go see. He told me I could break records in Vegas. Make tons of money."

Over a drink, Judy talked more candidly about why she was turning down the role of the ordinary Southern housewife, given to splitting headaches and fainting spells as she switched personalities.

"I fear I have all of Eve's characteristics in myself," she confessed. "I think playing this gal could tip me over the deep edge. The role terrifies me. I identify too strongly with the character. There are no songs to sing. They want me to lose thirty pounds. I don't know if I can do that. I'm not going to do it, even though I'll put in a good word for you if you still want to play Eve's husband."

"We'll see," he said, not wanting to commit himself. He was eager to rush out of her house and inform Joanne that the part had become available, but he thought better of it. She might become suspicious as to why he knew so much

224

about what was going on in the life of Judy Garland.

"Actually I've decided to do another movie, and there's a great part in it for you," she said. "The Gentleman Caller."

"You mean Tennessee Williams' *The Glass Menagerie?*" he asked.

"No silly, I've been asked by General Teleradio—you know, Howard Hughes' old RKO—to do a remake of *Alice Adams*. I'll take the Katharine Hepburn role, of course, and you can be Fred MacMurray."

"I don't know," he said. "Tampering with a classic…"

"I'm sure before the night ends, I will have convinced you," she said, moving closer to him on the sofa.

Later, Paul would share a confidence with Frank Sinatra, perhaps seeking his affirmation. Frank found the story amusing and passed it along the grapevine.

"Newman told me," Frank said to Peter Lawford, "that he was learning something about seducing movie legends. There is no foreplay. They spend most of the night talking about their beauty or how wonderful they looked in their latest picture. Then, when they're ready to get plugged, they demand it. A man is virtually ordered to rise to the occasion whether he's in the mood or not. The only hope for my future is that Joanne Woodward doesn't become one of the great legends of Hollywood. It'll be the end of our romance. I want to fuck legends just to get another notch in my belt. I don't want to marry one of these creatures."

Nunnally Johnson told a reporter that, "As so often happens, dear, dear Judy is obviously not going to do Eve. She won't even return my calls. Once again, clouds got in her way. She'd rather get laryngitis in the dry desert air of Vegas than play Eve. I've offered the part to Susan Hayward."

As Paul would later tell Vampira and Tony Perkins, "I've been out here on the coast long enough to learn to play the dirty games. Joanne must never find this out, but I'm going to sabotage Nunnally Johnson's choice of a star."

***

"We meet again," Susan Hayward said, ushering him into her parlor for a long, lingering kiss. "After our last night together, I thought I would see more of you."

"I've been busy," he said.

"Was it as good for you as it was for me?" she asked.

"The best," he assured her.

It was different at Susan's from what it was at Judy's. Time lodged together in bed for wild sex preceded a script reading.

Fully satisfied sexually, he was back in her living room where he spent at

225

least an hour talking and drinking before he got around to the real reason he was here. "I read that Nunnally Johnson has offered you the lead in *The Three Faces of Eve.*"

"So, that's why you're here," she said, getting up and slamming down her glass as she rose to her feet.

He was appalled that she might already know he wanted Joanne to get the role.

"You didn't come here to make love to me," she said. "You came here to get my approval to cast you as Eve's husband in the film."

"It never occurred to me," he said. "I haven't read the script. But I do want to appear in a picture with you. You said we might. There's nothing wrong with that."

"You're a bullshitter, but I'll overlook that for a moment. All actors are bullshitters. I should know after all those years with Jess Barker, the stinking bastard."

When he managed to calm her down, she rejoined him on the sofa. "First, if I'm to star in this piece of shit, it's got to be in Technicolor. No more black-and-white pictures for me. Let's face it: my mane of red hair is the most famous in the history of Hollywood. Why would I want to conceal that fact in black and white?"

"Why indeed?" he asked.

"Let's read the script together," she said.

At the end of their reading, she said, "I can do something with this, but, frankly, I'm worried. It would take a tremendous commitment on my part. On *I'll Cry Tomorrow*, I worked myself into a nervous breakdown. I felt suicidal. I don't want to go through that hell again. On some days I started crying at eight o'clock in the morning and kept crying all afternoon. That's how emotionally wrecked I was."

"Frankly, Susan, I don't think this cheap little film noir is worth your taking a chance. It could cost you your life."

"Long before you got here, I was thinking the same thing," she said. "I don't think I could risk it."

"Then there's the problem of having to play three different women all in one body," he said. "That's hard to pull off. It could invite ridicule."

She walked into her den and came back with yet another script. "It's called *I Want to Live*. Read it."

He read a tragic and harrowing tale of the executed criminal and prostitute, Barbara Graham, the story of the first woman ever sent to the gas chamber in California. If anything, *I Want to Live* would be an even more strenuous role for Susan to play.

He chose to deliberately lie to her. "After putting down the script, he took

226

her in his arms. "Baby, this script has Oscar written all over it. No actress but Susan Hayward can play Barbara Graham."

"Do you really believe that?" she said. "You're not bullshitting again?"

"Not at all! Robert Wise is going to direct. Look what he did for me. You'll be in great hands." And, then he told her the biggest lie of all. "And through it all, I'll be there for you. That's a promise."

An hour later when he kissed her goodbye and walked out her door, he felt "like a dirty rotten heel," as he told his friends.

***

Paul kept his promise and continued to see Susan until she finally made that call to Robert Wise, telling him that she was "much too fragile" to take on a challenging role like *The Three Faces of Eve*.

With Susan out of the picture, Paul no longer took her calls. He told Tony Perkins, "That fiery redhead is more vampire than Vampira. She's a bloodsucker. She'd also snip off a man's nuts while he was sleeping peacefully."

With Susan off the picture, the pathway was cleared for Joanne. But Nunnally Johnson had other plans. He sent the script to three different stars—Jennifer Jones, June Allyson, and Doris Day.

"Shit, piss, and hell!" Paul said. "All these same actresses were up for *The Helen Morgan Story*."

One by one, each of these screen legends turned down "the little film." In desperation, Johnson sent the script to Carroll Baker. She, too, turned it down. Johnson finally placed a call to Joanne herself. "Would you consider the role?" he asked.

"You've found your gal," she said. "I won't even have to fake a Georgia accent. I'm from Georgia. Pot likker talk comes naturally to me. Would I take the part? I'd cut off my mother's tit for a chance to play Eve."

The next day, Joanne gladly surrendered her role in *The Wayward Bus* to Joan Collins, the British bombshell.

"If Warren Beatty is to be believed, Collins is the hottest piece in Hollywood," Paul told Tony Perkins. "I've started thinking seriously about calling her up one night and feeding her the pork."

At that point, neither Paul nor Joanne knew that both of them would soon be appearing in a film with Joan Collins.

***

Susan Hayward
Feeling suicidal

227

"Paul, this is Natalie Wood," came an enticing voice over the phone. "Remember me? After all, we starred together in the greatest Biblical film of all time. Cecil B. DeMille, eat your heart out."

"My little pussycat," he said. "When you grew up, I had planned to deflower you. Now I hear it's too late for that."

"I hope you're not opposed to sloppy seconds," she said in her most flirtatious voice.

"I've been known to go that route on a dark, moonless night," he said. "But I have a feeling you're calling me for some reason other than to get into my pants."

"Getting into those tight pants of yours is only one of my dreams," she said. "I just got the news from Warners. You've been cast opposite me in *Marjorie Morningstar*. It's a love story. Don't you think we should start practicing our scenes right now?"

He was stunned at the news and was familiar with all the pre-publicity this film had received in the press. So far, no one at Warners had bothered to tell him what his next assignment was. He had to learn it from Natalie.

Marjorie Morningstar, the story of a "Jewish princess" rebelling from her parents and coming of age in New York City in the 1950s, had been a best-selling novel by Herman Wouk. When Jack Warner acquired the rights to the novel, which had been published in 1955, he announced that only Elizabeth Taylor could play the lead. He had planned to borrow her from MGM, but that studio had another picture for the star. Warner then decided that only Audrey Hepburn could play the part, but Paramount had other ideas.

Natalie had read the novel and announced that it was a role "I'm destined to play." She practically broke down the door to Warner's office. When she emerged from that heated session, the studio chief agreed to give her a screen test. Natalie even met with Wouk, but the novelist told Warners that she was not his concept of Marjorie Morningstar.

The director, Irving Rapper, conducted the screen test and pronounced Natalie's performance as brilliant. He called Jack Warner, "You have your Marjorie Morningstar." Rapper even showed the test to Wouk, who changed his mind about Natalie.

In spite of such endorsements, the producer, Milton Sperling, announced that he was going to launch a nationwide hunt for an unknown actress to play Marjorie. He compared such a launch to David O. Selznick's search for an unknown to play Scarlett O'Hara in *Gone With the Wind*.

Natalie was furious, having thought the part was hers. Once again, she barged into Jack Warner's office without an appointment. "Forget that God damn nationwide search," she told him. "You're fucking looking at Marjorie

Morningstar. If I have to suck your dick to get the part, I will."

The hardened veteran of many a confrontation with a movie star, including the formidable Bette Davis, was shocked at her language. From Joan Crawford, he would expect such talk. But such words coming from Natalie took him by surprise, since he still regarded her as a child star. He went over the head of his producer and ordered that Natalie be cast in the part. "If she's got that much fire in her belly, she'll be better than all the other actresses."

When Rapper asked Warner who he wanted to cast as the male lead, he said, "Throw Newman in the role. The fucker is taking a thousand a week from my pocket and not earning it."

Natalie had been given the script before Paul. Driving to her home that night, he was unaware of all the behind-the-scenes negotiations leading up to the final casting. He couldn't wait to see what kind of role he'd be playing. Unlike Natalie, he hadn't read the novel.

Before heading out, he told Gore and Howard, "I wonder what new shit Jack Warner has come up with for me. After *The Silver Chalice*, I don't trust anyone at Warners. I did better when they lent me out and made big bucks off my baby blues."

Natalie greeted him at the door and kissed him with a certain passion on the lips. Settling himself comfortably on a sofa, he took the drink she offered and together they read the script.

Paul found that his role as Marjorie Morningstar's summer romance was cardboard-flat and lackluster. Concealing his utter contempt for the script, he told Natalie, "You'll be great in this movie." He made no mention of himself. "There's probably an Oscar in it for you."

He couldn't bear to tell her the truth, because she'd worked and lobbied so hard for the part.

"It will send my career into the heavens," Natalie predicted.

He'd save his negative review of the project for when he talked it over with Joanne and Gore the next day.

After reading the script with Natalie, the talk between them got personal—or "down and dirty," as he'd later confide to Janice Rule when he went over the details of that night.

Natalie told Paul that she'd wanted him to be "the first to do it," but that her mother had a different idea.

"Your mother?" he asked, astonished.

Natalie Wood & Gene Kelly
What might have been for Paul

229

"She decided it was going to be Nick Adams," she said. "You know him. You met him with Dean on the set of *Rebel*. Even though I was only fourteen, mother decided that Nick was the guy to teach me 'the ways of the world,' as she put it. She said that although she could trust Nick to be gentle with me, she couldn't trust some of my other boyfriends."

"I thought Dean kept Nick Adams fully booked," Paul said.

"Are you kidding?" she asked. "Dean has so many people to fuck during the course of any given day that it leaves plenty of time for Nick to screw around too."

She wanted another drink.

"Isn't teenage drinking against the law in California?"

"Fuck that," she said. "I'm pretty grown up, and in the privacy of my own home."

He poured that drink, thinking Natalie was growing up too fast.

"I'll show you just how grown up I am," she said, walking over to a desk in the hallway and removing a sheet of paper. She handed it to him. "Read my list of future conquests, and then don't question where my mind is."

He read:

PAUL NEWMAN
ELVIS PRESLEY
RAYMOND BURR
NICKY HILTON
DENNIS HOPPER
TAB HUNTER
JOHN IRELAND
ARTHUR LOEW JR.
SCOTT MARLOWE
STEVE MCQUEEN
AUDIE MURPHY
LANCE REVENTLOW
FRANK SINATRA
STUART WHITMAN

"Thanks for putting me at the top of the list," he said. "I'm flattered. I noticed the names of James Dean and Nicolas Ray are missing."

"Been there, done that," she said.

"As for Elvis, I guess he heads the list of a lot of teenage gals," he said.

"I'm going to have him," she said. "I'm very determined. Both Nick Adams and I plan to fuck Elvis when he comes to Hollywood. He wants Nick to take him to all the haunts where he hung out with Dean. The way I figure

230

it, if he wants to hang out with Dean's boy, why not Dean's gal?"

"It looks like our friend from Memphis is gonna be one busy fucker," he said. "By the way, I didn't see Robert Wagner on that list."

"He's a bit of a bore," she said. "After hanging around with Jimmy Dean and Nicholas Ray, R.J. is just like white bread."

"But you gotta admit, this R.J. of yours is a beauty," he said.

"Takes one to know one," she said, stroking his cheek. "Maybe he'll go for you if you think he's so beautiful. Give him a call one night."

"Not my scene," he said, hoping to change the subject.

"I've got this bright idea," she said, jumping up from the sofa. "I've shown you my list. Now show me your list."

"Is this a show-and-tell night?" he asked. "I've never compiled a list."

She went over to that hallway desk and returned with a notebook. "Time's wasting."

A little drunk, he decided to play her game. At the top of the pad, he scrawled in very large letters the name of NATALIE WOOD.

"I know that already, silly," she said. "Go on. Give me more names."

He thought for a minute and then began to write:

LANA TURNER
AVA GARDNER
RITA HAYWORTH
ELIZABETH TAYLOR
AUDREY HEPBURN
GERALDINE PAGE
JANICE RULE
JOAN COLLINS

She studied the list carefully. "I noticed that Marilyn Monroe and Grace Kelly are both missing."

"Been there, done that." He glanced at his watch. "It's getting late," he said. "Way past your bedtime."

"The night's still young," she said.

And so are you," he said, reaching for her. "I'll tuck you in. You know what tuck rhymes with?"

"Indeed I do," she said, moving toward him and cuddling herself in his arms.

"There's a reason I want to get it on with you," he said. "I believe you will seduce Elvis, and I want to have you before he spoils you for all other men."

The next day Paul shared his adventures with Natalie with Tony Perkins and Vampira. But conveniently, he forgot to tell Joanne Woodward the details of his evening.

Later, he told both Gore and Joanne that he was turning down the role he'd been offered in *Marjorie Morningstar*. "You'll go on suspension," Joanne warned him, "and you need the money."

"I'll face the music," he said. "I'm not doing that picture—and that's that."

***

During the shooting of *The Three Faces of Eve*, word was seeping out that Joanne was delivering an Oscar worthy performance. But the star herself had her doubts, telling Gore and Paul that, "I think this could be the end of my career."

Eve was the first film to explore the subject of multiple personalities, although mental illness itself had been brilliantly depicted by Olivia de Havilland when she appeared in *The Snake Pit* (1948). Paul heard that his possible role as Eve's husband had gone to David Wayne, always competent, never a star. Lee J. Cobb was cast as one of Eve's psychiatrists. Orson Welles turned down the role, preferring to devote his attention to *A Touch of Evil*.

When Paul was invited to see the first rushes, he told Gore, "Joanne breathes life into all three women. Each gal has a distinct personality. My

Paul Newman's Illustrated Wish List of Anticipated Hollywood Conquests

Ms. Turner

Ms. Gardner

Ms. Hayworth

Ms. Taylor

Ms. Hepburn

Ms. Page

Ms. Rule

Ms. Collins

232

favorite is when she plays Eve Black, a whore. If Oscar is awarded on merit, she'll get it."

"You know by now that Oscars are never awarded on merit," said the cynical Gore. "If that were true, you'd already have one for *Somebody Up There Likes Me*."

When he wasn't before a camera, Paul was guzzling beer day and night, reading film scripts ("why aren't they any good?"), and fretting over a possible nuclear war. He consistently turned down interviews. "The only aspect of my private life I'll discuss is what kind of underwear I have on and whether or not I sleep in the nude. As for who I sleep with, that's nobody's god damn business but my own."

With Joanne absorbed almost day and night in her difficult film role in *The Three Faces of Eve*, Paul had a lot of free time. He spent a weekend with Robert Stack at the Palm Springs villa. Somehow word got out about that weekend, and the news made the gossip circles throughout Hollywood.

To his private weekend gathering, Robert had invited not only Paul but Brad Dexter. The Hollywood grapevine had it that there had been a three-way orgy at the desert villa.

Paul often talked privately with certain close friends about his affairs, but he remained tight-lipped after returning from Palm Springs that weekend. *Confidential* got word of the weekend and was hot on the trail of the story.

Paul had very briefly met the former husband of Peggy Lee, and it was believed that he was immensely attracted to the ruggedly masculine star.

Without Peggy Lee, Brad was enjoying a reputation as a menacingly handsome actor who loved to play screen heavies. "They're always the best-written characters."

Paul was spotted two weeks later having lunch with Brad at a secluded restaurant in Santa Monica. He was also seen at a gym engaged in a boxing match workout with the actor. Brad had been a member of the boxing team at the University of Southern California and later became a Golden Gloves light heavyweight.

After his failed marriage to Peggy Lee, Brad told the press, "I doubt if I'll ever get married again." He would later marry two more women, one in 1971 and another in 1994.

Brad became known in Hollywood for having affairs with his leading men, including Tyrone Power, Yul Brynner, and Robert Mitchum. A room service waiter once walked in on Mitchum and Brad in bed with Gloria Grahame.

His close friendship with Brynner was once the scandal of Hollywood. In later life, Brad spent a lot of time with Frank Sinatra, who had become one of his closest friends.

"It's always been a mystery to me why Paul refused to tell any of his friends what was going on between Brad Dexter and himself," Vampira said. "Why the secrecy? He let us know what was happening with his other secret relationships. Brad seemed someone special, someone he didn't want to talk about. The two men conducted their affair—or whatever it was—like a Back Street relationship, definitely something to be ashamed of."

The only person with any credibility who discussed Brad's relationship with Paul was Miss Peggy Lee herself. She once confided in Frank Sinatra and Rosemary Clooney that she'd pursued Paul and tried to get him to become her next husband. "He turned me down," she confessed. "But when my ex called him, Paul always came running. I guess Brad had something between his legs that I don't. Hell, what am I saying? I know the fucker has something between his legs. I married him."

On the set of *Exodus* in 1960, Paul's co-star, the bisexual Peter Lawford, pointedly asked him why he was "hanging out with the former Mr. Peggy Lee."

"He's teaching me Serbo-Croatian," was Paul's enigmatic reply. Although born in Nevada, Brad was the son of parents who'd moved there from Yugoslavia. He'd learned to speak Serbo-Croatian as his first language.

"I think Paul became very jealous when Brad more or less dropped him and started hanging out with Steve McQueen when those guys appeared together in *The Magnificent Seven* in 1960," Vampira said.

"I asked Paul about that new relationship, and he seemed bitter but tried to mask his jealousy," she said. He answered me with a smirk. "The film is badly titled. "In Brad's case, it should be called *The Magnificent Eight and a Half.*"

***

While *Three Faces of Eve* was being edited at the studio, Joanne was rushed into another movie, *No Down Payment*, in which she'd appear with an all-star cast, including Sheree North, Jeffrey Hunter, Tony Randall, Patricia Owens, and Barbara Rush.

The director, Martin Ritt, feared tension on the set between two of his co-stars, Jeffrey Hunter and Barbara Rush. Formerly married, the couple had divorced in 1955. A former assistant to Elia Kazan, Ritt was bouncing back in his career as a director, having been blacklisted as a suspected Communist sympathizer throughout most of the

Brad Dexter
Serial seducer

1950s.

Jeffrey Hunter, who'd co-starred with Joanne in *A Kiss Before Dying*, was frankly jealous of Paul and his success, although for the most part, he concealed it.

An extraordinarily handsome young man, who'd been born in New Orleans, Jeffrey was known for his beautifully piercing eyes. Those eyes would lead to his getting cast as Jesus Christ in the 1961 remake of *King of Kings*.

Hunter had met Paul before and became re-acquainted with him when he'd appeared on set of *No Down Payment* to observe a day's shooting. The jealous actor would later spread unattractive gossip about Paul.

Cameron Mitchell, another co-star in the film, observed what was going on. Hunter later told him that Paul came on to him seductively, but in a very subtle way.

"Knowing I was friends with Robert Wagner, Newman suggested that we might get together for a workout or else spend a Sunday at the beach at Venice," Hunter said. "It was obvious to me that Paul had a crush on Robert Wagner, and he wanted me to bring Bob along on one of these jaunts. He also wanted me as part of the package. Everything he suggested—the gym, the beach—would involve our stripping off some or most of our clothes."

"I led him on, just to see how far he'd go," Hunter claimed. "He went far but avoided an out-and-out proposition. I think he had too much pride for that. You can't help feel sorry for guys like Newman. They have too much to lose if they make one false step. Look what *Confidential* did to Tab Hunter. They can't go after what they want, like when a man sees a pretty gal. When Joanne Woodward came up, Newman became all macho. He'd brought cold beer to the set, but Martin Ritt refused to let us have any. Newman drank alone. He was sad in many ways. Having to pretend to be what he wasn't. But most of us Hollywood hunks in the 1950s had to do that."

***

Joanne was right. With a wife back East and three kids to support, Paul could not risk suspension from Warners. According to his contract, he had to accept whatever role the studio offered him.

When word reached him that Paul had rejected the script of *Marjorie Morningstar*, Jack Warner

Joanne:
One Woman, Three Faces
"The end of my career?"

235

went into a screaming rage. "Who in the fuck does this little Jew bastard think he is? Bette Davis?" He called the legal department and had them send a special delivery letter, notifying Paul of his impending suspension.

But Warners never carried through on that threat. Paul was saved when 20th Century Fox called Warners, asking to borrow Paul to appear in a film, *The Long, Hot Summer*. The picture would co-star Joanne Woodward. Since Warners was paying him only $1,000 a week, the studio could get a lot more for him on a loan-out to Fox. The threatened suspension was revoked, as Warners went for the money Fox held out.

"Hitler danced a jig of joy at the fall of France," Paul told Gore, "and I did the same when I heard I'd be starring with Joanne."

Paul called Jackie and told his wife that he was going to fly to Clinton, Louisiana to "soak up local color" before filming began. When he did, Jackie confronted him with the newest spin on his affair with Joanne, in much the same way she'd scolded him for his too close relationship with James Dean. Apparently, Jackie viewed Joanne as a greater threat than Dean.

"I need the money," he told her. "I can't turn down the picture. They'll put me on suspension. You of all people know I have hungry mouths to feed."

"Fears of suspension didn't stop you from turning down *Marjorie Morningstar*," Jackie allegedly told him. "You couldn't be anxious to do this movie because the great Miss Woodward is in it, could you?"

"You don't understand," he protested.

"I understand more than you know," she reportedly said, or at least that's what Paul told his friends.

After telling him that she was taking their two daughters—"and your rebellious son Scott"—back to live with her parents in Wisconsin, she put down the phone.

At long last, he told Joanne that his marriage was over. "I tried straddling the fence for years, but I just fell off that fence into the briar patch. The next few months of breaking up my family are going to be hell for me, but I've got to get through it."

He reported all this conflict to Janice Rule, begging her to be supportive of his decision.

"Let's face it," she said bluntly. "In your heart you left Jackie Witte years ago. Now you're free to commit to Joanne. Does all this mean you'll be settling down

Robert Wagner (left)
with **Jeffrey Hunter**
A pass not intercepted

with just one woman in your life? Or, are you going to continue to be a whore having a lot of fun?"

He paused a long moment before replying. "I'll go on my wicked ways until 1975. At least 1975. The way I figure it, that's when I'll settle down except for a few harmless crushes."

***

He had many misgivings after reading the script of *The Long, Hot Summer*. Ostensibly, it was based on the amalgam of two short stories by William Faulkner. Paul, however, secretly believed that Fox was ripping off *Cat on a Hot Tin Roof* with another variation of a steamy Southern drama. The stage play of *Cat on a Hot Tin Roof* had opened on Broadway's Morosco Theater in March of 1955, running for a blockbusting 694 performances. Tennessee Williams had promised Paul the lead, but he'd lost out to Ben Gazzara. Grace Kelly, originally slated to play Maggie the Cat, had bowed out of the play because she had a royal wedding on her mind. Her part eventually went to Barbara Bel Geddes; with the role of Big Daddy going to Burl Ives.

"Fuck it!" Paul said, angered that he had not been offered the Broadway role of Brick in *Cat on a Hot Tin Roof*. "I'll get to play a Brick-like character before MGM even starts filming *Cat*."

The casting of *The Long, Hot Summer,* might have caused elation at Paul's Malibu household, but there was only sadness at his home back East. It can be assumed that Jackie was well aware of her husband's ongoing affair with Joanne Woodward—the press certainly kept her informed. News of the illicit relationship had been frequently leaked to tabloid gossips.

Before he left for filming in the Deep South, Paul had one final tale to share with Tony and Vampira. Song-and-dancemaster Gene Kelly had called him and asked him to lunch. Meeting in a restaurant along Sunset Strip, Gene had thanked Paul for turning down *Marjorie Morningstar*.

Gene had ended his long bond with MGM in 1957. He told Paul that "they aren't making a lot of musicals today, especially the ones I used to star in. Both Fred Astaire and I are shopping around for dramatic parts. Pickings are lean. I saw Judy Garland the other day. She's also opting for dramatic parts. Both Judy and I know what time it is, at least by the MGM clock."

Gene Kelly
Hand on knee, traveling north

Paul revealed to his friends that the more Gene talked to him, the closer his hand under the table moved up from his knee toward his crotch.

"Nothing was said," Paul said. "It's like Gene was talking one way above the table and doing something else under the table. I didn't stop him. I knew he was bisexual and had had an affair with Vincente Minnelli. Gene was terrific in *Singin' in the Rain*. I felt I owed him one. I fully expected him to ask me to check into a hotel with him that afternoon. But guess what?"

"You went with him," Tony said.

"Not at all," Paul said. "I might have if he'd asked me. After all, he *used* to be Gene Kelly. But he didn't ask. At the end of the lunch, which he paid for, he thanked me again for turning down that dumb picture. Then he shook my hand like we were concluding a business deal. I stood watching him drive away from the parking lot. I never expect to see him again. Hollywood is one queer place."

"Are you just finding that out?" Vampira asked. "If you want to see weird, just look at me. How many dames do you know who are a vampire?"

Paul, Scott (age 5), and **Jackie**
A bumpy ride for a dysfunctional family

Chapter Seven
Changing Partners & Other Loves

Leaving his complicated love life behind him, Paul without Joanne boarded a plane for New Orleans. At that crucial point in his life, with a divorce pending, he did not want to be photographed getting off a plane with Joanne.

In the empty seat beside him rested the screenplay of *The Long, Hot Summer*, the creation of the husband-and-wife writing team of Harriet Frank and Irving Ravetch. He also had copies of two short stories by William Faulkner, *The Spotted Horses* and *Barn Burning*, on which the script was based, and he carried Faulkner's novel, *The Hamlet*, which included scenes that had also been worked into the film script.

Even though the screenplay took place in Mississippi, the director, Martin Ritt, had selected the towns of Clinton and Baton Rouge in Louisiana as backdrops.

Paul wanted to arrive two weeks before the film crew to soak up local atmosphere. "I decided I had to turn this Yankee boy from Ohio into a Mississippi redneck." To do that, he planned to hang out in the local bars and pool halls. Amazingly, though he was touted as Hollywood's hottest rising male star, not one of the redneck barflies recognized him. At one point, he asked a burly bartender, "Don't they show movies in this briar patch?"

When asked what he did for a living, he told them that he was a former boxer, a line no doubt inspired by his impersonation of Rocky Graziano. "Even before landing in Louisiana, I already knew how to drink more beer than any redneck in Alabama, Louisiana, or Mississippi combined," he said.

Temporarily left behind in Hollywood, Joanne had to face an embarrassing question or two from reporters. In the wake of her appearance in *The Three Faces of Eve,* interest in her had increased because of the rumors that she'd become an Oscar contender. She was bluntly asked by a reporter if she planned to marry Paul if he got a divorce. Her response was vague. "I've always maintained that if a marriage doesn't work out, divorce is inevitable." Her statement was baffling, since millions of people have stayed in bad mar-

239

riages without getting a divorce.

She was also queried about her living arrangements. She told reporters that she was looking for an apartment to share with Joan Collins. A reporter from *Variety* seemed astonished. "Joan Collins? I didn't know Woodward was that kind of dame. After all, Collins out here is known as 'the British Open.'"

In *The Long, Hot Summer*, producer Jerry Wald was hoping to create a new screen team to replace the aging Spencer Tracy and vintage Katharine Hepburn. Even though Paul and Joanne weren't in the same league as Tracy and Hepburn, they were formidable challengers for the role of Hollywood's next dynamic duo.

Paul shared something in common with Tracy and Hepburn. All three actors were bisexual. Joanne was not a member of that switch-hitting league, although her remark about moving in with sexpot Collins caused some minor speculation.

"At least with my newly acquired cornpone-and-molasses accent, I won't be compared to Marlon Brando," Paul told Ritt. "No one would consider Brando for this role."

Actually, Paul was wrong. What he didn't know is that originally, Ritt had wanted to cast Brando and his *On the Waterfront* co-star, Eva Marie Saint, in the film, figuring they would be magic at the box office in a return bout.

Saint had to bow out because she became pregnant, and Ritt had turned to Joanne, with whom he'd worked in her most recent film, *No Down Payment*. Paul had not even been Ritt's second choice for the role of Ben Quick. After Brando's rejection, the director asked Robert Mitchum to play the part of Ben. He, too, rejected the script.

Producer Jerry Wald told Fox executives that "I fully expect Newman to be a road show version of Brando in this film. It's like the Mark of Zorro on him."

When Gore Vidal, in Hollywood at the time, was asked about the casting, he privately told friends, "Joanne is a real actress. Paul is a movie star. It will take years for him to turn into a real actor *and* a movie star." It is not known if the news of that remark ever reached Paul.

Cocky and seemingly amoral, Ben Quick in the movie is an alleged pyromaniac, accused of burning barns. He arrives in the small Southern town of Frenchmans Bend and goes to work for

the bullying patriarch, Will Varner, as played by Orson Welles. Like Paul himself, Welles was Ritt's third choice after both Edward G. Robinson and James Cagney had turned down the role.

Varner sees Paul as a "big stud horse, good for breeding," feeling he might inject some new blood into his weak family. Cast as Clara, Joanne plays an uptight, sexually repressed schoolteacher with her hair arranged into a very tight bun. Her boyfriend is played by Richard Anderson. Paul, as Ben Quick, tells her, "If you're saving it for him, honey, you got your account in the wrong bank."

Cast as Welles' weak son, Jody, Tony Franciosa, who'd just married Shelley Winters, was appearing with Lee Remick as his flashy trollop wife, Eula.

As the mistress of Welles, Angela Lansbury, playing Minnie Littlejohn, gave her usually brilliant performance, although Ritt did not use her enough.

During the first week of shooting, Welles and Paul were still speaking. "I'm flat broke," he told Paul. "I owe everybody. I even had to accept a $10,000 check from Rita Hayworth. Fox is giving me $150,000 for the role, and that's all the money I have in the world. The IRS is on my ass day and night."

For some reason not known, Welles by the second week had turned on Paul. "I detest Newman," the corpulent actor told Ritt. "Another Method actor. Give me a real actor like Joseph Cotten any day."

Paul weighed in with his own opinion of Welles. "It's like shooting a film with the devil."

Ritt and Welles clashed over every scene. Welles was battling not only the Louisiana summer heat, but a serious weight problem, which made it difficult for him to get around. His makeup ran in the blistering sun. He told Ritt that he hated the script, calling it "something Tennessee Williams might dash off after a long weekend of getting stinking drunk and gangbanged by three hustlers."

Even though he fought constantly with Welles, Ritt admitted Welles was giving a brilliant performance. In his scenes with Paul, viewers would later claim that they could "almost smell all that testosterone."

Scene-stealing Welles was "Big Daddy" at his best, evoking the character in

Orson Welles
Oligarch Lost in the Swamp

Cat on a Hot Tin Roof. "This was vintage Welles," Ritt claimed. "He was clammy, blustery, a fat cat with a bullfrog voice, jowly, bullying, overly brutish, domineering, and, finally, castrating."

Welles was only forty-three at the time he shot the film, although he could well have played a sixty-year-old without benefit of makeup.

One day when Ritt could stand this oligarch no more, he drove Welles into the swamp on a pretense. He lured him out of the car and sped away. From the depths of that sweltering den of snakes and mosquitoes, Welles had to find his way back to the set. After that, Ritt became known in Hollywood as "the lion tamer of Orson Welles."

When he saw the first rushes of Joanne and Paul emoting, Ritt was thrilled. "This is not movie acting," he wired Fox executives. "This is bona fide passion." The director claimed that Paul had a "great fuckability quotient."

On screen and off, the two lovers were creating an alchemy of fireworks—or "lightning bugs on a summer night," as one viewer of the rushes put it. In spite of the creaky melodrama of the plot, Ritt knew he was creating a Southern fried masterpiece.

Joanne, a Georgia girl herself, perfectly depicted a coyly seductive belle with hot pants. Ritt ordered Paul to take off his shirt and expose a sculptured, pumped, and ripped physique worthy of Michelangelo's *David*. The director predicted that women in movie theaters across America would swoon when Paul stripped down.

"In one scene I even made Paul strip down to his jockey shorts," Ritt said. "Gay guys in the audience will jerk off under their overcoats."

Paul and Joanne, absorbed in their own love affair and threatened with the possibility of a messy divorce, did not endear themselves to other cast members. Lansbury noted that Hollywood's most famous unmarried couple spent most of their off-camera time alone.

On weekends, Paul would take Joanne to New Orleans, where, in an antique store, they came upon a large brass bed that had been salvaged from a local bordello once frequented by Louisiana's dictator, Huey Long. Years

Paul and Joanne
Lightning bugs on a summer night

later, when Tennessee Williams saw the bed, he tried to purchase it from the Newmans for his Key West house.

Paul warned Ritt that "If my dressing trailer is rock 'n rolling, take the advice of that Marilyn Monroe film, *Don't Bother to Knock*."

Night after night, Paul agonized over having to divorce Jackie. Joanne had already experienced the pains of divorce as a child when her parents separated, and she didn't want to be portrayed in the press as the "home-breaking other woman." Nevertheless, she told Ritt, "I can't live without him."

Privately, Lee Remick was rather disdainful of both Paul and Joanne, although she showed great respect for them during public interviews. Privately, she spoke more bluntly with Ritt. "Just who are these two stuck-up snobs?" she asked. "They think they're such hot shit. Fuck them. I'm going to be First Lady one day."

Ritt looked astonished at her revelation, which she did not explain. She was obviously referring to her ongoing affair with a young Robert Kennedy. For years she entertained the illusion that he would divorce Ethel, leave his big family, and marry her.

The weather continued to be unbearably hot, and then a hurricane hit, shutting down production.

"Joanne and Paul were the only people on the set who took advantage of that hurricane," Ritt said. "They holed up for five days and nights. How can one man, even Paul Newman, fuck so much? At one point you'd think he'd come up for a breath of fresh air. No, not that one."

After the hurricane passed over, another hurricane descended in the form of Shelley Winters, Paul's friend and confidante from the Actors Studio. She'd heard that her new husband, Tony, was "balling some of the southern belles," and she wanted to investigate personally.

The first person she encountered was Ritt himself. "You bloody cocksucker," she greeted him. "You promised me that Lee Remick role." Ritt fled back to his own trailer to escape Shelley's fury.

As always, Shelley bonded with Paul. "Lee Remick thinks she's hot shit because she's fucking a Kennedy. Well, I fucked Adlai Stevenson."

Shelley Winters, Tony Franciosa
Invitation to a three-way

According to Ritt, but not confirmed by another source, Shelley at one point invited Paul to slip away with her and join her in bed with Tony. "You must be getting tired of all that southern poontang." During their marriage, Shelley and Tony became known for inviting a beautiful woman or a handsome young man into their bed.

"You did all right joining Marlon and me," Shelley reminded Paul. "Tony's an even better lover."

Paul turned down her invitation, though assuring her that Tony was "one cute guy."

Welles, however, was not impressed with Tony. He asked Shelley, "Why did you marry this string of linguine?"

"It's not linguine," she said. "More like an Italian salami."

It took five days to shoot the barn-burning scene. There was even a scene of a posse chasing a white man for a change. After the last week in November of 1957, Ritt wrapped the film, after congratulating the entire cast, including Welles himself.

When Paul flew out of New Orleans, he was unaware of how important-ly the director would factor into his later career. Nor did he know that he'd work again one day with screenwriters Ravetch and Frank.

Embracing him, Ritt assured Paul that his reviews would be terrific, and so they were. *Time* called Paul's performance "as mean and keen as a crack-le-edged scythe." Bosley Crowther, writing in *The New York Times*, found that "behind Paul's hard blue eyes lay the deceptions of a neo-Huey Long." *Variety* claimed that Paul slipped "into a cracker slouch with professional ease."

Paul would not win an Oscar for his performance as Ben Quick, but he did walk away with the Best Actor Award at the Cannes Film Festival on the French Riviera.

***

After months, even years, of ago-nizing over a divorce, the problem was solved for Paul at the completion of *The Long, Hot Summer*. Jackie finally came to realize that she'd lost Paul forever and filed for the divorce herself.

Hollywood gossips had salivated, waiting for messy details and embar-rassing revelations. Most of the gossip mavens of the day, including Hedda Hopper, were aware that Paul led a dou-ble life. Laws of libel had prevented

Sweating out a long hot summer
Arriving with a bag of tricks

them from writing about Paul's secret life.

But if Paul, along with his numerous affairs with both men and women, had been exposed as part of a courtroom hearing, the "Tabloid Teddies and Tillies" would have been free to blast Paul with "Second Coming" headlines. Undoubtedly, this exposé would have destroyed his promising career.

Jackie made few demands, caused little fuss, and seemed to want to make a divorce from Paul as easy as possible. She reportedly told a friend, "The secret's out. When that Mississippi film is released, the whole world will see my husband making love to Joanne Woodward."

Paul flew alone from New Orleans to Mexico where the divorce would be granted.

"Jackie Witte was married to Paul for years; she fucked him; she bore him three children. Like the gentleman he was, he paid up." Those comments came from Jerry Wald, the producer of *The Long, Hot Summer*.

The divorce of Paul and Jackie remains shrouded in mystery even today. Jackie retained custody of their three children. Reportedly, she received a "lifelong financial settlement." The terms were apparently satisfactory to her, and she never again took Paul to court or challenged the terms of the settlement.

Paul was granted rights to visit with his children on weekends and in summer. Because of his incredibly busy schedule making films, he would not always be available to take advantage of those rights.

Years later, he said, "My children never lost the pain of my divorce from Jackie, especially Scott. He was older and seemed to almost hate me for deserting his mother. Joanne turned out to be a good mother, not only to the children we had together, but to the ready-made family I brought into our marriage."

As a new year, 1958, rolled around, Paul at long last was a free man. He could marry Joanne, a dream he'd cherished for so long.

But Janice Rule claimed that Paul, after a night of heavy drinking, called her. "Now that I can marry anybody I want to, I suddenly don't want to marry anybody, with the possible exception of you. I want to be free."

"You're just getting cold feet," she said. "It happens to the best of us."

In the morning Janice proved to be right. He went ahead with his long stalled plans to marry Joanne. "But I'll carry the guilt of abandoning my wife and family until the day I die. If one's happiness is based on causing unhappiness to others, how solid can that relationship be?"

"I think I'll wake up one day and regret I ever married Joanne, like I feel now about having married Jackie," he predicted. "I don't think I'll be a great father. If she's to stay married to me, she's going to have to be a very understanding wife and overlook a lot of my crap. I know well-meaning friends will come to her in the future with tall tales about me. If our marriage is going to work, she's going to have to keep me on a very long leash. I'm one of those selfish dogs. Every time I see a fire hydrant, I want to piss on it."

In the short time leading up to his second marriage, Paul, from all reports, decided to stage a last hurrah. He began to date another woman, a stunning blonde from the Southwest, perhaps Arizona. Her identity isn't known, but she towered at least six inches over him. And Lita Milan was about to enter his life.

Sal Mineo still had him staked out, and Tony Perkins had become a permanent fixture. Marilyn, on the rare occasion that he saw her, was a sometimes thing.

Sandra Dee, on learning of Paul's upcoming marriage to Joanne, went public with her disdain for Paul's choice of an upcoming wife.

"I hate Joanne Woodward," she dared tell the press. "How could any man as good-looking as Mr. Newman stoop so low as to hang out with a Georgia woman like that. You know what I call Miss Woodward? Bessie."

***

While *The Long, Hot Summer* was being edited at Warner Brothers, Paul and Joanne signed a contract to appear in a teleplay together, *The 80-Yard Run*, a Playhouse 90 Production. The 90-minute drama was adapted for TV by David Shaw from a short story by his celebrated brother, the novelist Irwin Shaw.

Aired on January 16, 1958, the show also starred Richard Anderson, who had played Joanne's boyfriend in *The Long, Hot Summer*. Once again, Anderson was cast as Paul's love rival.

Darryl Hickman, a well-known actor in the 1950s, was also cast in the drama. He was the child star of the 1930s and 40s, trying to jump-start his career after he'd dropped out of Hollywood to enter a monastery, but decided that the life of a monk was not for him.

Evoking in some small way the character of Brick that Paul would soon play in *Cat on a Hot Tin Roof*, he was cast as Christian Darling, a former college football star reliving his glory days when he scored a legendary 80-yard run in the 1920s.

**Paul's Mystery Blonde
from Arizona**
A last hurrah before marriage

That achievement had won him his 15 minutes of fame. But after the crash of 1929, he finds himself unemployed, broke, and turning to the bottle.

In contrast, his wife, Louise Darling, as played by Joanne, is a fast-rising star on a fashion magazine.

After a whirlwind teenage romance, Paul's character finds his marriage disappointing and coming apart. In some ways, the character conjured up his failed marriage to Jackie Witte, which had just ended.

Franklin Schaffner, the director, shot some sequences at the UCLA football stadium. At the end of the shoot, Schaffner had only high praise for Paul. At the time of his working with Paul, his great hit, *Planet of the Apes*, lay in his future. Paul claimed that Schaffner was "one of the most creative minds in early television."

Joanne, never one to suppress an opinion, found the script "dramatically weak," suggesting the teleplay might have been acted out in just 30 minutes. Yet some TV critics claimed that Paul gave his best performance to date as the fallen football hero. The teleplay must have evoked memories of his own attempt to become "Saturday's Hero" in front of adoring football fans back in Shaker Heights.

Quick to capitalize off an opportunity, executives at Fox purchased a commercial during the airing of the teleplay, hawking *The Long, Hot Summer* with joint appearances by Paul and Joanne.

Once hailed as the Golden Boy of live television in the 1950s, Paul was starring for the last time in a live TV drama. In the future, he'd often appear in dramas or comedies on TV, but these would be re-runs of his movies.

The teleplay had a typically 50s ending, as Paul redeems himself and takes a modest job as a football coach at his own alma mater. Joanne abandons her life as an overachiever and gives up her promising career to join "the man she loves." This teleplay was broadcast years before the launch of women's liberation.

The host of Playhouse 90 was veteran actor Mickey Rooney, once the world's box office champion. When he'd been thirty, he'd evoked Golden Age Hollywood. Both Paul and Joanne admired Rooney as one of the most talented stars to ever grace the screen. But at the time they met him, Rooney and his career were in an inevitable decline. He was trying to bring back his heyday of the Andy Hardy films by shooting *Andy Hardy Comes Home*, a box

Paul & Joanne in an 80-Yard Run
Last Call as TV's Golden Boy

office failure. One critic noted, "This latest Andy Hardy film is too bland to even be considered camp."

***

After more than five years, the ricochet romance of Paul Newman and Joanne Woodward ended in marriage. The date was January 29, 1958. Uncharacteristically for them, they chose glitzy Las Vegas as the venue, marrying at Hotel El Rancho, not far from the gambling tables.

Only three days before, Paul had turned a ripe thirty-three although he didn't look it. Joanne was still twenty-seven, with another birthday staring her in the face.

In front of a Nevada judge, they at long last became man and wife. Paul designated Stewart Stern as his best man, with Joanne anointing Ina Bernstein, her manager, as maid of honor. Entertainers from the casino hotel witnessed the marriage. They included Sophie Tucker, comedian Joe E. Lewis, and singer Eydie Gorme, who had married another singer, Steve Lawrence, only the month before. At the end of the ceremony, Sophie, "the last of the red hot mammas," stepped up in front of Paul and said, "Lay one on me, big boy, and make it a wet one."

A publicist at Joanne's studio falsely claimed that the couple had fallen in love while shooting the teleplay, *The 80-Yard Run*. In Hollywood, after reading that piece of fluff, a jealous Joan Crawford pronounced it "pure bullshit. And to think the bitch that got him was named after me. He'd be better off sticking with the real thing."

Deserting Las Vegas, Mr. and Mrs. Paul Newman flew to New York where they checked into a small hotel in Greenwich Village for a few days. They were seen in coffeehouses, and Paul, often without Joanne, hit a few bars for mugs of cold beer.

On a number of occasions, his good looks brought some whistles from gay men as he walked down the street. One antique dealer claimed Paul bought a small wooden chest from him. "His eyes are really blue," he said. "The bluest I have ever seen. He might convert me. Up to now, I always went for boys with brown eyes."

Rod Steiger told friends at the Actors Studio, "It's about time they got married. You can't spend the rest of your life slipping in and out of hotel rooms, although in Paul's case I'll bet he continues to do just that."

Flying to London for the final stage of their honeymoon, Joanne and Paul joined Gore Vidal and Howard Austen. "All four of them should have gotten married," remarked one British journalist. "What a friendly quartet they are, and we must not speculate any more than that."

What only a few close friends in Hollywood were privy to, and what the British press didn't know, was that Joanne was four months pregnant as she began her honeymoon.

Mr. and Mrs. Paul Newman were registered at the prestigious Connaught Hotel. With Gore as their guide, they set out to explore London. "I got my education from Gore," Paul later said. "He knew everything about everything. He made Hampton Court come alive for me with all sorts of juicy tidbits about scandals from yesterday. He is the best tour guide in the world, especially when it came to court intrigue."

After that, Joanne and Paul rented a car to explore some of the English countryside. The honeymooners returned to London to stay with Howard and Gore at a mews house on Chesham Place. A spooky English butler named "Tattersall" was there to assist them. Joanne thought he looked like "he just stepped out of a Dickensian novel." Paul said, "at least he's not named Jeeves."

On February 20, a letter arrived for Gore from his mother, Nina Vidal. In that letter she attacked Howard as a "faggot Jew," and blamed Gore for all the troubles in her life. Before his glittering guests arrived from the theater world, Gore sat down and wrote his mother a letter in response. "I'll never see you again as long as you live." He was a man of his word.

The letter from Nina was unknown to Paul when he greeted Gore's guests, who included Kenneth Tynan, the influential and controversial theater critic.

"I had an affair with Marlon Brando," Kenneth said, "and I'd like to have one with you too. Otherwise, I have no basis to compare you two."

"What about our body of work?" Paul asked.

"That's important," Tynan said, "but I need more."

"Okay, I'll take you into the bathroom and give you a full mouth kiss—but that's it," Paul said.

At that point Claire Bloom interrupted them. "You miserable fuck!" she said to Tynan before turning her back and walking away.

"I get this all the time," Tynan told Paul. "I panned her performance in *Duel of Angels*."

"I hope you had kind things to say about her co-star, Vivien Leigh, because I hear Larry Olivier is showing up here tonight."

"Oh, Larry," Tynan said. "He's completely harmless. Larry and I go way back, intimately so. Now let's you and I go to the bathroom for that promised kiss."

At the party Claire spent most of her time talking to Joanne. A friendship was developing.

Paul chatted briefly with Ralph Richardson, before moving on to John Gielgud, who'd been drinking.

"I hear that in the film, *Gigi*, Louis Jourdan, that divine Frenchman, shows an impressive package in tight pants," the distinguished actor said. "I'm dying to see the movie. What's your opinion about actors showing package on camera or on the stage?"

"I think it definitely detracts from the performance," Paul said. "Surely, as an actor, you wouldn't want to do that."

"As an actor, I don't have much package to show."

A tap on his shoulder and Paul turned around to stare into one of the most famous faces in the theater, Laurence Olivier himself. Directing him to a quiet corner of the room, Olivier and Paul bonded as intimately as did Joanne with Claire Bloom.

Somehow, through the grapevine, Olivier seemed to know about Paul's secret involvement with Marilyn Monroe, and he wanted to exchange opinions about the blonde bombshell. The stately actor had completed *The Prince and the Showgirl* with Monroe.

"The press has gone into great detail about my involvement with Miss Monroe," Olivier said, "so I won't bore you with a rehash. She is clearly two people. Total enchantment on the one hand, horribly rude and inconsiderate on the other. She thought I was just using her for box office, and in a way she might have been right about that."

"Finally, I came to my wit's end," Olivier continued. "I was appalled at her constant lateness, her lack of professionalism, and the annoying interference from Paula Strasberg who was trying to direct her performance. At one point when she asked me for my guidance, I told her, 'Just be sexy—that's all that's required of you.' It was terrible of me to say such a thing, but my poor nerves had taken their final beating. Needless to say, we did not have an affair.

Sir John Gielgud
England's stateliest homo

Kenneth Tynan
Secret kiss in the loo

Sir Laurence Olivier
Lacerating Marilyn

Vivien asked me about that."

"And just how is your fantastically talented wife?" Paul asked. "I admire her so much."

"She's in Hollywood meeting with George Cukor," Olivier said. "That reminds me. I have some news for you. George Cukor's agreed to direct the film version of *Cat on a Hot Tin Roof.* He wants Vivien to play Maggie the Cat. Cukor has two candidates in mind to play Brick."

"Please don't keep me in any more suspense," Paul said.

"First choice, Montgomery Clift," Olivier said. "Second choice, Paul Newman."

"I always get Clift's sloppy seconds," Paul said. "At least Tennessee hasn't asked Brando to play the role."

"Vivien is very excited at the prospect," Olivier said. "She's done very well playing Southern damsels. She definitely feels a third Oscar is in order with this script. Incidentally you must promise to see her when you fly back to the coast. She wants you to take her out to dinner."

"A date with Scarlett O'Hara," Paul said. "How could I turn that down?"

"I'll give you the details," Olivier said. "She'll be expecting you."

As Olivier went to find Gore's toilet, Tynan passed by, overhearing the conversation. "It'll be more than dinner. You'll have to fuck her as well. And thanks for that open mouth. You're good, but now I want more. Do you think your dick is long enough to reach the back of my throat?"

"That's for me to know, and you to never find out," Paul said before walking away to greet Peter Ustinov. The distinguished actor shook Paul's hand and took his arm and led him over to the far end of the living room for a chat. "Have all the stately homos of the London theater been making a play for you tonight?"

"As a matter of fact, they have," Paul confessed.

"Don't worry, my child," Peter said. "You're the new kid on the block. These lads have had Richard Burton and all the others. They are starved for fresh meat from America. If you're interested, Tynan gives the best blow-jobs, but Olivier is better at taking it up the ass. Forget Gielgud. He'll demand that you come three times before removing your penis from his devouring lips."

***

Joanne's pregnancy had not been noticed by anybody, with the possible exception of Claire Bloom. One night Paul and Joanne had gone to The Salisbury, the original gin palace, a pub near Leicester Square that attracted English stage stars. The travel writer, Stanley Haggart, had written, "In its cut-glass mirrors you can see reflected the Olivier of yesterday and of tomorrow."

251

After arriving back at the Chesham Place house, Joanne began to complain of stomach pains. Gore summoned a doctor to the house, who told Paul that his new wife was in the process of a miscarriage.

Transferred to St. George's Hospital, Joanne lost her child with Paul, but remained in the hospital to recover from the ordeal.

Very reluctantly, Paul had to leave her side and fly back to Hollywood to begin work on a picture. Gore and Howard were due in New York, and they too had to tell her good-bye.

Feeling abandoned, Joanne was delighted when her new friend, Claire Bloom, came to call on her every day and bring flowers. As Fred Kaplan related in his biography of Gore, "It was a terrible end to a lovely honeymoon."

When Paul returned to Hollywood by himself, it was speculated that his marriage had ended in disaster before it had even begun.

Claire Bloom had a private reason to be sympathetic to Joanne's plight. After the actress and her lover, Rod Steiger, a friend of both Paul and Joanne, had returned to New York from a vacation in Sicily, she found herself two months pregnant. Ever the gentleman, Steiger offered to marry her, the ceremony taking place in the office of the sheriff at Malibu. Unlike Joanne, Claire carried her pregnancy to term giving birth to a daughter, Anna.

***

Paul had already played Billy the Kid in Gore Vidal's teleplay. Retitled *The Left Handed Gun*, Gore had crafted it as a sort of Greek tragedy, with modern overtones, into a full-length film script.

Arthur Penn, a young Turk from TV land, had already directed Paul in Hemingway's *The Battler* for TV. Both Penn and producer Fred Coe had also husbanded Paul through Gore's original teleplay of *Billy the Kid*.

Penn was given a modest budget of $700,000, and he was ordered to shoot the film in only twenty-three days.

For the setting of the town of Medaro, and to trim costs, he used old sets from the 1939 epic, *Juarez*, which had starred Bette Davis and Paul Muni.

Anxious to make good in his first feature film, Penn rode the cast without mercy. Paul admitted to Gore that he felt "disconnected" from the character of Billy the Kid in this revi-

Claire Bloom
And Steiger's baby makes three

252

sion of the original teleplay. He was, in essence, shooting a different script.

For months, Gore and Paul had struggled to get a studio to agree to make the movie, finally receiving the green light from Warners. Amazingly, the studio was holding out for a happy ending. "That's like filming *The Saga of Abraham Lincoln*, having him skip his date with destiny at the Ford Theater, divorce Mary Todd Lincoln, and ride on off into the sunset in Kentucky with his all-time love, Joshua Fry Speed," Paul said.

The brass at Warners didn't like the implicit homosexuality they found in the original version of *Billy the Kid* by Gore. "When movie-goers hear that Newman is playing a fag cowboy, they'll stay away in droves," predicted Jack Warner.

Paul didn't seem to have a struggle playing gay. As a liberal, he'd always taken a stand for homosexual rights, claiming, "Ever since I was a kid, I've never been able to understand attacks on the gay community."

Even its title, *The Left Handed Gun,* carried a double meaning. In some parts of America decades ago, left handed was a code word for being gay. The young gunslinger was actually right handed.

Leslie A. Stevens III, a playwright working on his first feature film, was called in to adapt Gore's original script. He shifted the plot from a repressed homosexual intrigue into more of a surrogate father-son drama, muting the Freudian subtext before its final release into movie houses. In Stevens' version, Billy is depicted as "half boy, half man," coming to regard rancher Tunstall (as played by Colin Keith-Johnson) as a father figure. The "half man" part of Paul's character gets to deliver "the cojones" line of the movie. "I don't run. I don't hide. I go where I want. I do what I want."

A Navy brat, born in Washington D.C., Stevens would, in time, create the cult TV series, *The Outer Limits* (1963-1965).

In his playful way, Paul nicknamed Stevens' script, *The Left Handed Jockstrap.* The adult Western was filmed on location in Santa Fe, New Mexico, which involved another separation from Joanne, with many more such absences to come in the future, one lasting six months.

"Anybody can have an ideal marriage," Laurence Harvey, a future costar of Paul's in *The Outrage*, one remarked. "That is, if they remain separated for most of the year. It worked for me."

Penn later claimed that Paul "Method-

Paul as Billy the Kid
"Playing Gore Vidal's fag cowboy"

253

acted his way through the entire film." At one point Paul curls up into a ball on the floor, a scene and acting style that Penn found "pure James Dean." In an ironic twist, Dean had once expressed an interest in starring in a possible film version of *Billy the Kid.*

"Through it all," Paul confided to Fred Coe, "I feel Dean could have done a better job than me in this film. That thought is driving me crazy. Tonight I'll have to have six extra beers."

One reason Paul wanted to make good in this film was financial. Still drawing that $1,000 a week salary from Warners, he also for the first time stood to collect 14 percent of the profits.

Penn turned out to be a clever, even experimental director, creating a black-and-white movie that was cutting-edge, at one point employing slow motion and vision blur in a death scene.

***

In *The Left Handed Gun,* Hurd Hatfield was cast as "Multrie," a journalist and a sort of mysterious commentator remarking on the events taking place. His character seems to interpret Billy the Kid as a "star outlaw," an anti-hero with the power to enchant movie-goers.

Hurd disliked his role, finding his character an epicene figure holding a handkerchief to his nose. "It's obvious that I'm in love with Billy the Kid," he later said.

Meeting Paul for the first time, Hurd came up to him and shook his hand. "You should have been cast as Dorian Gray, not me," said the New York actor. "I never thought of myself as a great beauty, and I still don't know why I got the part. But with your baby blues and that Roman coin profile, you would have been sensational."

Hurd was talking about his infamous appearance as the star of *The Picture of Dorian Gray* (1945), the film version of Oscar Wilde's novel. The role made him a star, not his portrayal of a Chinese peasant, along with Katharine Hepburn, in the forgettable *Dragon Seed*, his first film, in 1944.

"I've spent the rest of my life regretting accepting that Dorian role," Hurd claimed.

"I thought you were splendid in the picture," Paul assured him. "Why the regrets?"

"It's hard to explain," he said. "I became very unpopular in Hollywood after making the film. I guess the picture was too weird, a bit *avant garde* for its time. All that decadence. It's obvious that I was playing a bisexual, actually a homosexual. Suddenly, after the film was released, no one would return my calls. I was a leper in Hollywood. You should be thankful they've removed

254

the gay aspects from *Billy the Kid*, or at least tried to. Whatever you do in your future career, *don't play gay*. It will destroy your image."

Fred Coe, the producer, always claimed that Hurd and Paul had a brief fling during the filming of *Billy the Kid*. He is the only source for that, even though he claimed that Hurd admitted it directly to him. Neither Hurd nor Paul, nor any other cast members, have spoken out on the subject. Coe was a man of truth and integrity, not given to exaggerations or lies. He was possibly telling the truth.

If the two handsome men did have a brief affair, as was rumored, it was only a passing thing, having little importance other than relief of a temporary passion.

"They were two good-looking guys," Coe said. "Paul was bisexual and Hurd was completely gay. When two forces like that come together, it's not surprising something came of it. Hurd was seen on occasion coming and going from Paul's dressing room. I hope those two had a good time."

Both Paul and Hurd had a bond between them. Each of them maintained a handsome and relatively youthful appearance well into their seventies. Hurd said it was because, "I don't drink; I don't smoke, and I exercise every day." Paul said he maintained his looks because "I drink and I exercise every day."

In the years ahead, and on the few times Hurd and Paul would encounter each other, each actor checked out the other's face. "My God, you haven't changed a bit." That line was almost a joint refrain the two men exchanged. They would joke about the portrait each of them had hiding in the attic, a reference to Wilde's *Dorian Gray*.

"Oh, God," Paul told Hurd, "let that portrait get as many wrinkles as it wants to, but keep them away from my face."

***

The sultry, even fiery, Lita Milan was cast as Celsa in *The Left Handed Gun*. Coe felt that in the movie *Billy the Kid*, the hero had hung out with too many cowpokes, and Lita's character was created for a diversionary romance, even though Celsa in the film is already married to a good-natured locksmith (Martin Garralga).

The daughter of a Polish homemaker and a Hungarian fur salesman in the Flatbush section of Brooklyn, and originally named Iris Lia Menshell, Lita shot like a rocket into the film world of the mid-1950s before disappearing forever.

Hurd Hatfield
"I hate Dorian Gray."

255

A wild and lovely young woman, she had a smoldering beauty. "She drew men to her like moths to a flame," said Fred Coe. "One of those moths was Newman himself. He showed that even though he was just launching a married life once again, he had no intention of staying faithful to Joanne. It was obvious that he did not want to be trapped into a monogamous relationship. Let's face it: He fucked everybody during his first marriage. How could such a hot, desirable guy reform overnight? He didn't want to feel trapped."

Lita had been a Las Vegas showgirl and model before getting cast as a spitfire *señorita* in *The Ride Back* in 1957.

In any biographical sketch of Lita, there appears this line: "She had a passionate affair with Paul Newman during the filming of *The Left Handed Gun*." Unlike some of his affairs, Paul did not share details of this short-lived romance with Lita to his confidants. Perhaps he felt embarrassed to do so because the fan magazines were filled with glowing tributes to his marriage to Joanne.

On the set, Lita amused both Paul and Coe with stories of the road she traveled on her way to Hollywood. "I dreamed of being a movie star," she said. "But my parents back in Brooklyn were dead set against it. I got as far as Las Vegas, where I ended up playing a slave girl in Shan Varr's revue at the Thunderbird. He's that East Indian dancer."

Along the way to her horizon, there was an encounter with Ralph Meeker,

Sultry Lita Milan in THE LEFT HANDED GUN

Left photo: **Lita Milan** rolling in the Hay with **Paul** both on and off the screen

Insert: Would-be Dominican dictator **Ramfis Trujillo** with **Lita**, his *esposa*

Right photo: Billy the Kid's *puta* and "**The Evita of the Caribbean**"

Paul's rival from *Picnic*, and a run-in with Kirk Douglas, Paul's friend.

Along with 14 other beautiful actresses, Lita had been chosen as a WAMPAS Baby Star of 1956. She was pictured in a magazine getting advice from Ginger Rogers. Paul asked her, "Exactly what kind of advice did Ginger give you?"

"She told me to fuck my way up the Hollywood ladder," she said. "That, she said, would virtually guarantee my success."

After the shoot, Paul apparently never saw Lita again.

One afternoon he agreed to meet Steve McQueen at a cheap hotel in Long Beach. Inside the sweaty bedroom, where a Bible rested on a night stand, Steve told Paul, "I've got every horny woman in Hollywood trying to get me to fuck her. I'm only one man. I need a break, a different kind of action now and then. You're the kind of change I have in mind."

During the course of the night, Steve confessed that he was involved in a torrid affair. "She has that peasant girl kind of beauty. In bed, we sizzle like steaks on the grill." He called such encounters "fuck flings."

"What's the name of this sugartit?" Paul asked. "Sounds like I'd go for her myself."

"Lita Milan," he said.

Paul was stunned, but masked his surprise.

Lita and Steve were filming *Never Love a Stranger* at that time.

He told Paul, "When I check into some seedy hotel room, and there's a red neon light flashing outside the window all night, my dick grows an inch or two."

"Is that why you had me meet you at this dump?" Paul asked. "And exactly what is that fucking neon red sign advertising."

"Chinese take-out."

In only a short time, after she met Ramfis Trujillo, Lita would abruptly drop both Paul and Steve. Ramfis was the dashingly handsome son of the dictator of the Dominican Republic, Rafael Leonidas Trujillo y Molina. She was introduced to Ramfis at the Mocambo when she went out one night with Zsa Zsa Gabor, Porfirio Rubirosa, and Kim Novak.

Her torrid romance with Ramfis led to marriage and the abandonment of her movie career. After the assassination of the dictator Trujillo in 1961, Ramfis tried to seize power in the D.R. But, along with Lita, he was forced to flee the country, going into exile in Madrid. There went Lita's dream of becoming "the Evita Peron of the Caribbean."

The darling of the yellow tabloid press in Madrid, rivaling the coverage of Ava Gardner, Lita lived with Ramfis until his death in 1969, following complications from a car accident.

In its bastardized, watered-down version, with bad editing, *The Left Handed Gun* opened in New York on May 7, 1958, to disappointing box office.

Film critics were waiting with poison pens. The reviews were devastating, as New York writers didn't know what to make of "these television boys venturing into feature films." The reference was to Fred Coe and Arthur Penn. "Poor Mr. Newman," wrote Howard Thompson in *The New York Times*. "He seems to be auditioning alternately for the Moscow Arts Theater and Grand Old Opry, as he ambles about, grinning and mumbling endlessly."

One radio reviewer was particularly venomous. "For this type of role," he claimed over the air, "We need to resurrect James Dean from his grave. Maybe Marlon Brando could have pulled it off, certainly not little Paul Newman. A midget off screen, a midget on screen."

Not every critic attacked the film. Writing for *Time Out*, Tom Milne called it, "A key stage in the development of the Western."

In spite of its initial box office failure, Paul, in later years, spoke kindly about the film, calling it "way ahead of its time and still a classic in France." Gore himself continued to be disappointed at the way his script had been butchered and rewritten. He called it "a movie that only someone like the French could praise."

Even though he and Paul remained friends, Gore still expressed his resentment of the way Paul handled the film when he wrote his autobiography, *Palimpsest*. "Paul, no tower of strength in these matters, allowed the hijacking to take place." He was referring to Penn's ordering a rewrite of his script, as Paul stood by, not uttering a word of protest.

Sometime during the 1970s, John Calley became head of production at Warners. He'd been intrigued by the critical reappraisals of *The Left Handed Gun*, particularly of Penn's own assessment that if his original version had not been edited so poorly, *The Left Handed Gun* would rank right up there with Gary Cooper's *High Noon*.

He called Penn and asked him to re-edit *The Left Handed Gun* into the original version he had wanted. But when a search was made in the archives at Warners, it was discovered that the unused footage had been junked.

Hollywood's fascination for sagas about the American West continued. As late as 1989, Val Kilmer would star in an all-new interpretation entitled *Gore Vidal's Billy the Kid*. Of the fifty or so films made about the life of this psychotic gunslinger, Kilmer's was the most accurate in adhering to the actual events in The Kid's life—a greater, more artful, and more historically accurate depiction than either of Paul's previous interpretations on television and on the big screen.

Ironically, in the wake of Paul's second attempt to play Billy, Marlon Brando would star in *One-Eyed Jacks* in 1961, his character also based on the notorious Kid.

"The Mark of Zorro is indeed on me," Paul said upon seeing *One Eyed Jacks*. "I can't escape the curse of Brando. My wife even had to go make a film with him. Don't get me wrong, I love Brando dearly. When he calls me, I come running. Even after all this time, I still find him mesmerizing. But there are times on a bad hair day when I think I will always live in his shadow."

Arthur Penn once said, "Some day, film historians will have to judge *The Left Handed Gun* on its own merits."

That judgment came down in 2004, when film critic David Thomson wrote of Paul's portrait of Billy the Kid as "the intellectual's noble savage."

Otherwise, Thomson was skeptical of Paul's "blue-eyed likability. He seems to me an uneasy, self-regarding personality, as if handsomeness had left him guilty. As a result, he was more mannered than Brando when young, while his smirking good humor always seemed more appropriate to glossy advertisements than to good movies."

***

After purchasing the film rights for *Cat on a Hot Tin Roof*, Metro-Goldwyn-Mayer considered George Cukor as its possible director. But from the beginning, there were problems with the script. The explosive Tennessee Williams drama about a neurotic Southern family dynasty had enthralled Broadway audiences with its homoerotic subtext. Nonetheless, the studio felt it had to "laundry" this Pulitzer Prize-winning drama before it "went out to be viewed by every little homophobic town in America."

At first, the film's producer, Lawrence Weingarten, felt that Cukor might know how to make the script acceptable to mass audiences, in spite of (or perhaps because of) the director's own homosexuality.

The director was initially intrigued by the project, thinking it might be the proper vehicle to lure Vivien Leigh back to the screen. She was obviously too old to play Maggie the Cat, but Cukor was persistent in his choice of a star. Ever since he'd cast her as Scarlett O'Hara in *Gone With the Wind*, he'd always wanted to work with her again, but never had the chance.

When Paul returned to Hollywood after his honeymoon in London, Cukor invited him to dinner to meet Vivien Leigh, although he had not been actually signed to play Brick, the drama's protagonist/hero.

Paul seemed near the top of the casting line-up, but there were other considerations. He'd heard that Montgomery Clift had turned it down because he

259

did not want to play a character who was a closeted homosexual. "Too close to home," Monty told his brother Brooks.

In a red dress and with a minimum of makeup, Vivien seemed to cast a spell of enchantment over the night. He found in her fragile voice a combination of flirtatious Scarlett O'Hara and a doomed Blanche DuBois.

"My enemies claim I'm washed up in Hollywood," she said. "Not at all. I've been waiting for the right script to lure me back. I've always thought of myself as a stage actress, but I've done all right in films as well."

"All right?" he answered. "Two Oscars and countless great roles. I'd say that was more than just 'all right.'"

"You're such a darling man," she said. "I must taste you before the night ends."

"Taste me?" he asked puzzled. "You mean taste as in sampling caviar."

"That's Vivien's way of saying she plans to seduce you before the rooster crows," Cukor said.

As the trio settled in for a talk about how to bring *Cat* from the Broadway stage to the big screen, Paul noticed that Vivien was visibly shaking. She reached for Cukor's hand. "Oh, dear heart," she told him, "I'm terrified of taking on such a challenging part." She turned her focus to Paul. "As George knows, I get exhausted at times. There are spells of depression that descend. I call them ghosties. When I'm both tired and depressed, I'm a mess. I felt I must warn you."

"I think we can see it through," he said, reaching for her other hand.

"You give me such comfort," she said.

"I never got a chance to direct Vivien," Cukor said. "Here's my chance. It may never come again."

"You can be my Rhett Butler," Vivien told Paul.

"I've always thought of myself as more the Ashley Wilkes type," he said.

She paused for a moment of reflection. "I think you're right. Brick is more Ashley than that God-awful Rhett. You are Ashley. On second thought, you are Ashley with none of the brute qualities of Rhett. After all, Ashley was the love of Scarlett's life."

"I've always wanted to ask you a question," he said. "May I?"

"Not a Scarlett question," she said, with a mild protest. "I positively loathe talking about *Gone With the Wind*."

Vivien Leigh
"Did Larry have you first?"

260

"It's something else," he said. "Did you resent Marilyn when she took over your role in *The Prince and the Showgirl*? I know you did the part on the stage."

"Not at all," she said. "I never viewed Marilyn as a threat. As for a possible affair with Larry, it was out of the question. Poor Larry wouldn't know what to do with a woman like that. I decided during the shoot that if anybody was going to seduce Marilyn, it would be me."

"You and Larry seem to have the kind of marriage I had hoped for," Paul said. "But I fear Joanne is the jealous type."

"Regardless of how many lovers I take on, I've always remained under the spell of Larry Boy," she said. "But sometimes it causes a problem. If I bring a boy home, it's not certain whether he'll sleep with me or with Larry. This pattern of behavior began when I brought Marlon home when we were filming *A Streetcar Named Desire*. Larry wanted Marlon first."

***

Shortly before dawn, Paul woke up in Cukor's guest bedroom. He reached for Vivien, but found the space in bed beside him empty. He switched on the lamp on the nightstand, its light casting a forgiving glow across the room.

Standing nude at the window overlooking the pool, she glanced back at him. "The night is such a thing of terror for me. Thank you for sharing it with me. You keep the ghosties away. They follow me everywhere, even across the ocean to America. Darling, I have to ask you something."

"Fire away," he said.

"What a quaint American expression," she said. "So militaristic." She walked over and reclaimed her flimsy nightgown which had been draped across an armchair. "When you were fucking me, did you think of me or did images of Scarlett race through your head?"

"I cannot tell a lie," he said. "I thought of Scarlett. But you *were* Scarlett. I was thinking of you."

"The key word there is were," she said.

"I'm sorry," he said. "I couldn't erase that image from my mind."

"No man ever can," she said, "especially American men. I have an apology to make to you as well. When you brought me to that divine climax, I apologize for screaming out Larry's

George Cukor
A question of homosexuality

261

name."

***

In the week that followed, Pandro S. Berman was brought in for the debate over the film script of *Cat*. During his tenure as chief at RKO, he'd overseen Cukor's cross-gendered allegory, *Sylvia Scarlett*, starring Cary Grant and Katharine Hepburn. It had been a box office disaster, so Berman immediately took a dim view of having Cukor direct the Tennessee Williams play.

Berman told Lawrence Weingarten that if he weren't careful, Cukor would turn *Cat* into "a fag piece."

Berman became exasperated when Cukor announced to the press that the movie, like the play, would have to deal up front with the issue of homosexuality.

"Who in hell does this queer think he is?" Berman asked Weingarten. "We're not allowed to even mention the word homosexual in a movie. What does Cukor want? A flashback, showing Brick sucking off Skipper in their football heyday. Fire Cukor!"

The battle heated up between Cukor and MGM. Finally, the director withdrew. He told Louella Parsons, still the reigning gossip maven, that he could not maintain the integrity of Williams' play because of the censorship being imposed on its film adaptation. "I am not sure the public will like this play or understand it," Cukor said. "But I just couldn't do an emasculated version, and I don't see how the movie itself could be properly presented."

With Cukor off the picture, so went the casting of Vivien. Weeks later, after it was announced in the papers that Elizabeth Taylor would be starring as Maggie the Cat, Vivien placed a call to Paul. "Elizabeth replaced me in *Elephant Walk*, so why not *Cat on a Hot Tin Roof*?" she said.

"No one could ever replace you," he said. "You're an original."

"You were so nice to send those flowers over to me the following morning," she said. "So many men I pick up—gardeners, garage mechanics, whomever—just give me a pat on the ass the next morning and say, 'Thanks for the memory, Scarlett.'"

***

For their living quarters, the newly married Paul and Joanne initially rented a house in Laurel Canyon in Hollywood. They also rented an apartment in the East 80s in Manhattan. "We're East Coast folks," Paul told a reporter.

His three children occasionally visited Paul and "Auntie Joanne." When Scott arrived at the Laurel Canyon house, he expressed his disappointment when he found they had no swimming pool. "I thought all movie stars had pools," he said.

Paul told him, "We're not movie stars, we're actors."

At this point in their lives, the Newmans were still pinched for money. Paul continued to draw his $1,000 a week salary from Warners, but a lot of that went for child support and alimony payments to Jackie. Joanne was taking home only $500 a week before taxes.

In just a few short months, Jackie herself arrived with her children in Los Angeles, eventually settling into a modest house in San Fernando Valley. Once, when Paul came to pick up the kids, Scott angrily confronted him. "You should never have left my mother to marry some whore."

When news reached the Newman household that Joanne had been nominated for an Oscar for *The Three Faces of Eve*, Joanne didn't seem impressed. She showed a lack of respect for the Academy of Arts and Sciences, suggesting to the press that many factors went into deciding who got the Oscar. "It's so rarely based on who gave the best performance," she claimed.

On Oscar night, 1958, as a side show to the more compelling drama associated with the Best Actress award, Paul and Joanne were asked to present a minor award, that of Best Editing. After the envelope was opened, the prize went to Peter Taylor for his work on *The Bridge on the River Kwai*.

The tension built as the evening progressed. Joanne was up against some formidable competition. She faced Elizabeth Taylor in *Raintree County*, Anna Magnani in *Wild Is the Wind*, Lana Turner in *Peyton Place*, and Deborah Kerr in *Heaven Knows, Mr. Allison*.

When her name was finally read, she forgot all about her bad-mouthing of the Academy, as she rushed to the stage to accept her Oscar from John Wayne. She burst into tears of joy, telling millions of people that, "I've waited for this moment since I was nine years old."

Still nursing her crush on Paul, a cynical Joan Crawford sat in the audience, an aging relic of Hollywood's Golden Age. Once she'd attacked Marilyn Monroe's wardrobe. Now she turned her fury onto Joanne, claiming that "she's set back Hollywood glamour twenty years by making her own dress." She was referring to Joanne's homespun creation in green satin and velvet.

Privately, Joan told friends, "For the life of me, I can't see what Newman sees in that Woodward creature. He could be shacked up with

Oscar Night:
John Wayne and Joanne
"The Last of the Great Broads"

some of the biggest names in Hollywood. I'm sure Ava Gardner or Lana Turner would go for him. But, no, he prefers this Georgia redneck and her feedsack dress."

After seeing the movie, its original inspiration, Christine Costner Sizemore, writing in her 1977 autobiography, *I'm Eve*, revealed that she had 26 multiple personalities, not just three. She also charged that Dr. Corbett Thigpen, the author of *The Three Faces of Eve*, had forced her to sign over all rights to her story. "As a result, I received nothing from either the book or the Woodward film."

The day after Joanne received her Oscar, Paul received a call from Susan Hayward. "You dirty, rotten, cocksucking son of a bitch," she said into the phone. "You tricked me. You wanted the part for your ugly little girlfriend." She slammed down the receiver.

In the weeks that followed the Academy Award presentations, and Joanne's triumphant win over far better established stars, Hollywood insiders predicted she was headed for a glorious career in films.

That would not happen, although she'd make an occasional film, often with her husband. Ironically, many of the Newman/Woodward films would bomb at the box office.

As Crawford observed the Newman marriage as the years went by, she said, "I think he's an insecure male—very sexually confused as well—and can't stand having another big star in the family. I'll tell you what happens to insecure male movie stars. When an actor is married to a star bigger than he is, he can't get a hard-on any more. I was married to Philip Terry, and I know what I'm talking about. Take the case of Jane Wyman and Ronald Reagan. After she won her Oscar for *Johnny Belinda*, Reagan was so intimidated by her greater fame and talent that he couldn't get it up any more for her. Jane told me that herself when I was advising her to drop Rock Hudson because he was gay. At first she didn't believe that. The poor fool had developed this almost obsessive crush on Rock, whose heart lay elsewhere."

After that Oscar win, Paul and Joanne became the talk of Hollywood, and they would remain a hot topic of gossip and speculation for years to come.

Not only Janice Rule, but many other stars who didn't even know the Newmans, weighed in with an opinion. Paul called Joanne "The Last of the Great Broads." That caused Bette Davis to sneer. "I thought that title belonged to me."

As the marriage, launched under somewhat tawdry circumstances in Las Vegas, endured, Paul was constantly asked if he were tempted to stray. After all, he knew or had worked with some of the most desirable women on the planet. He always had a pat answer. "Why go out for hamburger when you've got steak at home?"

Crawford wasn't impressed with that response. "What a clever thing to say, but how true is it? First, I think Woodward is hamburger, not steak. As for Paul, he dines out frequently, and on the most succulent filet mignon, from what I hear."

As Paul waited for MGM to decide if he'd be cast in *Cat on a Hot Tin Roof*, an offer came in for Joanne.

The box office receipts had been so profitable for *The Long, Hot Summer* that 20th Century Fox decided to revisit the Gothic Deep South. Producer Jerry Wald and director Martin Ritt once again cast Joanne, this time in William Faulkner's 1929 novel, *The Sound and the Fury,* which some critics considered one of the hundred greatest of the 20th century.

Screen writers Irving Ravetch and Harriet Frank were hired again for another Faulkner adaptation. From their typewriters came a plodding tale of a girl seeking independence from her strict Old South family rule.

In the wake of his big screen success in *The King and I* in 1956, Yul Brynner was cast as the lead. Lana Turner was originally offered the third lead but turned it down because it was not a star part. The role went to British actress Margaret Leighton. Ethel Waters also signed on. *The Sound and the Fury* would be her last motion picture.

Lana had another reason to turn down the role. She was pursuing bigger game in the Hollywood jungle. Richard Brooks, the director of the oncoming *Cat on a Hot Tin Roof,* called her. "It's almost certain that you're going to play Maggie the Cat," he told the star. "We want you to come in for a reading with Paul Newman. He's one of the stars who's up for the role of Brick."

"I'd be thrilled to play Maggie the Cat," she said. "Me, Lana Turner, in a Tennessee Williams drama of the Old South. Vivien Leigh did just swell with Tennessee. I can do the same. Who would have thought it? I'd adore playing opposite that divine Paul Newman. But who is his competition? He'd be perfect for the role. Don't tell me Ben Gazzara."

She was referring to the actor who originated the role on Broadway.

"You're not going to believe this," Brooks said. "Elvis Presley."

"You've got to be kidding," said an astonished Lana. "Lana Turner and Elvis Presley starring in Tennessee Williams' *Cat on a Hot Tin Roof.*"

"A distinct possibility," Brooks told her. "But you've got the billing wrong."

***

Lawrence Weingarten, the producer of *Cat on a Hot Tin Roof,* loved to dine out on stories about Old Hollywood. Born in Chicago in 1897, he would eventually win the Irving G. Thalberg Memorial Award, presented by

Katharine Hepburn at the 46th Annual Academy Awards in 1974. Weingarten was married for many years to Thalberg's sister, Sylvia.

Weingarten was full of Hepburn and Spencer Tracy stories, since he'd produced both *Pat and Mike* (1952) and *Adam's Rib* (1949). He told marvelous Jean Harlow stories, having produced *Libeled Lady*, back in 1936, months before her untimely death.

But, according to Richard Brooks, the director of *Cat on a Hot Tin Roof*, no story rivaled Weingarten's tale about Paul Newman and Elvis Presley. Some claim the story is apocryphal, but both Brooks and Weingarten always insisted it was true.

Elvis was always trying to break away from Col. Tom Parker's influence and show that he was a bona fide actor capable of performing in high drama, even a Tennessee Williams play. "No one can play a Southern boy like Elvis Presley," the singer said. As a member of the audience, he'd seen the Broadway version of *Cat on a Hot Tin Roof* on three different occasions, watching Ben Gazzara perform opposite Barbara Bel Geddes as Maggie the Cat.

Elvis believed "the part has my name on it. So far, they turn the cameras on me and let me sing 'Let Me Be Your Teddy Bear.'" He was referring to the 1957 movie, *Loving You*. "I can't go on forever shaking my butt at a group of screaming teenage gals. I want to show the world I'm a serious actor."

Without Col. Parker's permission, Elvis called Brooks and Weingarten, telling them, "I'm your Brick, and I won't even have to fake a Southern accent."

Although at the time both director and producer were considering Paul for the role, the idea of casting Elvis with Lana Turner had their eyeballs registering dollar signs at the box office.

After dark on Good Friday, 1958, Lana, or so it was believed by such Hollywood insiders as Frank Sinatra and Howard Hughes, had fatally stabbed her gangster lover, Johnny Stompanato, with a carving knife. The mob boy had also been the lover of Lana's best friend, Ava Gardner.

Lana's teen-aged daughter, Cheryl Crane, took the blame for the stabbing, admitting her guilt. But those in the know met the claim with scepticism. To this day, Cheryl insists that she was the one who thrust the knife into

Elvis Presley
"A piece of perversion"

the gangster's stomach.

Unless Cheryl makes a deathbed confession, the actual truth may never be known, although various sources, including Sinatra himself, claimed that Lana confessed the murder to him. Peter Lawford, Lana's longtime friend and former lover, also made the same claim.

Far from damaging Lana's career, the notoriety surrounding the case stimulated a morbid rebirth of interest in Lana, increasing her box office clout, especially if teamed with Elvis. As Brooks himself so colorfully put it, "Elvis is the biggest thing in America since God invented baby shit."

If Elvis would make himself available, Brooks was willing to "throw Newman under the bus."

But when Col. Tom Parker heard that his breadwinner was conducting secret negotiations without him, he nearly had a stroke. "No man had a greater temper than Parker," claimed Bud Godsell, who once worked for the show business entrepreneur.

"I don't know what I'm gonna do with my boy," Parker told Godsell. "He's always trying to get cast in a drama by one of those faggot playwrights. First, Bill Inge. Now, Tennessee Williams, the biggest queer who ever walked across a Broadway stage. Now get this. Folks tell me that the character Elvis wants to play in this fucking piece of shit is a repressed homosexual. My Elvis playing a homosexual. I think at times he's trying to destroy the career I created for him."

"As long as I'm still able to smoke a cigar, there is no way in hell that my Elvis is going to appear in this piece of perversion," Parker said. "God made a man and a woman. He gave a man a dick and a bitch a hole. God's intention was to have a man stick his thing in the cunt and make babies. It was not God's intention to stick his thing up another man's ass. Assholes are made for shitting, not fucking. There is no way in hell that Elvis is going to appear in this crap."

In the end, Parker prevailed. Elvis had to bow out of the movie. The Colonel would approve of future scripts for his star, some of which included *Girls! Girls! Girls!* and *Viva Las Vegas*.

Elvis did get to team with a major star of the past when he appeared with Barbara Stanwyck in *Roustabout* in 1964. But even that was a disappointment to Elvis, since he'd wanted to costar with Mae West instead.

Even though Elvis was off the picture, Paul didn't know that when Elvis called him. "Hey, kid," Elvis addressed Paul, "I hear you and I have both got our hearts set on playing Brick in *Cat on a Hot Tin Roof*." Even though Elvis called Paul a kid, Paul had actually been born ten years before the King of Rock 'n' Roll.

"May the best man win," Paul told Elvis, astonished that he was actually speaking to him on the phone.

"That would mean me," Elvis said. "Back in Memphis, guys have a way of deciding who gets the prize. I want you to come over to my house tonight, and we'll settle this shit once and for all."

"You mean duke it out?" Paul asked.

"Something like that," Elvis said. "I'll put one of my boys on the phone, and he'll fill you in on how to get here."

Paul was vastly intrigued at this bizarre invitation. "There's no way in hell I'm not going to show up," he said.

Elvis welcomed Paul into his home like a dear friend. There seemed not the slightest sense of rivalry between the two men. "I thought about one contest we could have tonight," Elvis told Paul. "We could invite Marilyn Monroe over. We'd each throw a fuck to her and let her decide who's the best man."

"That would be too easy for me," Paul said, with a smirk on his face. "You know I'd easily win that round."

"Don't be too sure, ol' boy," Elvis said. "Okay, then I'll come up with another game."

"What's that?"

"Later, later," Elvis said, "after we've both consumed a lot of beer. I hear you're a world-class beer drinker."

"That I am," Paul said. "But you know I'd win in any beer-drinking contest."

"You got that right," Elvis said. "I'm not that much of a soggy bottom. Let's talk a while before the fun and games. Get to know each other. I understand you used to pal around with James Dean."

"Indeed I did," Paul said. "He was one of my best friends."

"I never got to know him, but I thought he was one hell of an actor. Is it true he was homosexual?"

"I've heard reports," Paul said.

"Cut the bullshit," Elvis said. "You probably fucked him, but that's your business. I'll make a little confession. I'm about the straightest dude that ever walked the planet. But if that fucker had ever called me, I'd come running to his bed. Just to see what it was like if for no other reason. I guess you'd say I have this obsession with Dean."

"We all did, but it's time to turn the page."

If the story is to be believed, Elvis around midnight got up and invited Paul into his garden. He had been surprised earlier when he'd asked the direction of the toilet twice. "I need to piss away some of the suds," Paul said.

"Hold it for just a little bit," Elvis had urged.

Following Elvis into the moonlit garden, Paul said, "Do you mind if I piss on your flowers since your toilet must be stopped up?"

"Actually, I invited you here for a pissing contest," Elvis said. "In Tennessee when two men in a bar get into a fight over a girl, they can beat the shit out of each other. Or else go out back and see who can piss the farthest. That's why we're here now. Whoever can throw the longest arc of golden showers wins the role of Brick. Deal?"

"You're on," Paul said. "Let's whip it out. I'm raring to go."

Weingarten claimed that Paul later revealed that he won the pissing contest that night, but that Elvis was gracious in defeat. "I had the advantage," Paul said. "My dick hangs longer than his."

Paul was shocked when Weingarten told him that Col. Parker wasn't going to let Elvis do the picture. "The part is yours."

"Then why did Elvis put me through that contest? What's going on here?"

"I guess King Creole just wanted to see you take a piss."

***

Even though Paul turned out to be the greater pisser, Elvis apparently was not impressed. Brooks later claimed that Elvis called him with some casting ideas of his own.

"The boy who can play Brick, other than myself, is Jack Lord," Elvis said. "He's my favorite actor in all the world. I hope you saw him in *Cat* on Broadway. He was far better than Ben Gazzara, and he'll be a hell of a lot better than Paul Newman. Trust Elvis on that one. Newman's quite a pisser. Say hello to him from Elvis." He put down the phone.

Eventually, in spite of Elvis's advice, Brooks cast Paul. Lana needed work and grew impatient waiting for MGM to cast her. She contracted to do another picture instead.

In a huddle in the executive offices at MGM, the "suits" decided that the perfect Maggie the Cat was already on their own lot. "Get Elizabeth Taylor on the phone," Weingarten ordered his secretary. "We'll send the flag up the pole and see if she salutes it."

Discreetly, through the studio, Lana arranged a luncheon meeting with Paul. She spoke with him briefly before setting up the rendezvous, asking that he tell no one about his meeting with her.

Over lunch at an off-the-beaten track restaurant in Laguna Beach, Lana arrived with her blonde hair concealed by a scarf and her eyes covered by a pair of large sunglasses. She was visibly shaken, and her eyes kept darting around the room as if she was expecting someone.

Over a cocktail, she confessed as to why she was being so secretive. She pointed out two men in casual sports attire dining at a nearby table, defining them as members of a 24-hour security squad paid for by Howard Hughes in the wake of Johnny Stompanato's death. Mobster Mickey Cohen, a friend of Stompanato's, never believed that Lana's daughter had stabbed his friend. He was convinced that the murderer was Lana herself. He vowed revenge.

"They're not planning to kill me," Lana said. "Cohen is plotting something worse. I received an anonymous letter. That letter writer claimed that one day when I least expect it, somebody is going to throw sulfuric acid in my face. If that day ever comes, I will commit suicide. Without my beauty, I'm ruined. I would be nothing. I wouldn't be able to face the world. I wouldn't even be able to face my own image in the mirror."

He tried to assure her as best he could that it was only an idle threat. Later he would tell Richard Brooks that Lana was on the verge of a nervous breakdown, and he doubted very seriously if she could have held up under the strain of playing a difficult role like Maggie the Cat.

He advised her to drive to Palm Springs with her security guards and hole up there for a few months. "This thing will blow over," he assured her. "Some new scandal will come along, and Hollywood gossips will forget all about you and Johnny Stompanato."

She told him she couldn't retreat from Hollywood. "It's financial," she said. "I desperately need the money to carry on. My legal bills have taken all my hard-earned cash."

He understood her plight and was sympathetic, yet blamed her in some way for having taken up with a low-life like Stompanato in the first place. "How in hell did you ever hook up with a sleazeball like that?" he asked, while eating a fruit salad.

"It was all Ava's fault," she said. She was, of course, referring to Ava Gardner, another screen legend who loomed in Paul's future.

"I was very lonely and depressed one night," she said. "I hadn't gotten over Tyrone Power and his dumping of me. Sometimes Ava and I share boyfriends. We often pass a particularly good lover on to each other. She gave Johnny my phone number, and he called me one night, asking if he could come over."

She leaned in closer to him. "I shouldn't be telling you this, but Johnny told me he had something in common with the Oscar. I asked him what he meant. He said, 'Go measure the length of that Oscar. When you do, you'll know exactly what I have in common with Oscar. It drove Ava crazy, and she wants you to enjoy some of the fun.'"

"I've heard a lot of lines guys use in coming on to gals, but I must admit that's an original," he said.

After lunch and over two more cocktails, Lana told Paul how much she had wanted to play Maggie the Cat. "My great fear is that I'm a bit too old for the role, but makeup and good lighting would have covered up a lot.

"You're still beautiful and will always be," he assured her. "You are a very sexy woman, perhaps the sexiest who ever graced the screen. You and Ava. What a pair!"

She leaned over and kissed him lightly on the lips. "Ever since I thought I'd be working with you on *The Silver Chalice*, I've wanted to appear in a movie with you. I thought both of us would be dynamite on the screen. I still think that. I've always regarded you as the heir apparent to all those great stars like Tyrone, Errol Flynn, Clark Gable. You're different, of course. You're a more modern type of star and also the star of tomorrow. I predict that by 1970 your reputation will have equaled any of those men I named."

"Talk like that some more and I'll fall in love," he said.

"If you like blondes so much, I wish you'd married me and not your darling Joanne Woodward."

"Then I could never be myself," he said.

"What do you mean?"

"I'd be forever known as Mr. Lana Turner."

She laughed to dismiss such an idea. "You're joking, of course. The world will be talking about Paul Newman long after Lana Turner is a forgotten memory of soldiers who fought in World War II."

Since he'd learned that she wasn't able to appear as Maggie the Cat, he was impatient to learn why she'd wanted to meet with him. Finally, he asked her.

"Ever since I met you on your date with Judy Garland," she said, "I've

At the Airport: **Lana Turner**, **Johnny Stompanato**, and **Cheryl Crane**
Lana's gangster lover had a date with destiny.
But which of these two women really stabbed him?

been wanting to get to know you. Not today, but tomorrow I think a property is going to come along that would be ideal as a Lana Turner/Paul Newman vehicle. Of all the actors in Hollywood, you are the one I'd most want for my leading man."

"I'm flattered," he said. "You were always my dream girl."

"And dreams do come true, at least sometimes," she said, rising from the table.

After lunch, Paul followed Lana in his car. Her two guards were driving her to a private villa, owned by Howard Hughes, where she planned to spend the weekend. She'd invited him by for an afternoon swim . . . or whatever.

He didn't know how the preliminaries would go, but, as he'd later relate to Richard Brooks, "We got down to business right away. No sooner were we inside the door than she was in my arms."

"I think Lana is desperate," he said. "At one point, when we were in bed, I held her. She was trembling like a leaf. In a very plaintive voice, she said, 'Please, don't ever leave me.'"

***

A series of bizarre events occurred almost in succession in Paul's life. As he'd later tell Vampira, "Mother told me there would be days like this."

In response, she delivered her usual refrain, "Welcome to Hollywood."

Invited by Robert Stack to his villa retreat in Palm Springs, Paul arrived to greet his long-time friend. With a certain excitement, Robert told Paul, "*He's* here. He's in the back room entertaining a visitor."

"Exactly who is here?" Paul asked. "Brad Dexter?"

"No, my buddy Jack Kennedy," he said. "He's in the guest room with one of my favorite gals. She's married. He's married. You're married. What does a wedding ring mean in Hollywood anyway?"

"A wedding ring is just a license to screw around and make a hasty retreat claiming you're a married man," Paul said.

"You got that right, baby," Robert said. "Now gimme a kiss before they emerge from their den."

In bathing suits, Paul was sitting with Robert having a beer when Kennedy came out of the back bedroom. He was fully dressed in a suit and tie. All smiles, he shook Paul's hand firmly as he was introduced, but glanced nervously at his watch.

"I'd like to sit and chat," Kennedy told Paul, "but I'm very late as it is." He gave Paul another handshake. "Great meeting you. Give me a raincheck. I'd like to get together with you sometime."

Paul assured him he'd be eager for that to happen, and told him he'd been rooting for him in 1956 when he'd sought the vice presidential nomination, losing to Estes Kefauver, a liberal Democrat from Tennessee.

"My Boston accent worked against me," Kennedy said. "America still prefers a redneck in a coonskin cap."

An aide arrived to tell Kennedy that he had to leave at once for the airport. He thanked Robert for his hospitality, and seemed to disappear almost as quickly as he'd entered the pool area.

"So who's the babe he's shacked up with?" Paul said.

"That's for me to know and you to find out," Robert said smugly.

It was almost an hour before Kennedy's bed partner emerged. Paul was shocked to see Janet Leigh, dressed in a conservative business suit, enter the pool area. Mrs. Tony Curtis herself seemed in a bit of a rush, but she was warm and gracious to Paul. "Maybe we'll make a movie together one day, sweetie," she said, leaning over to give him an air brush kiss on the cheek. The movie, *Harper*, still lay in their future.

During her brief chat with Paul and Robert, Janet made it clear that she was in Palm Springs stirring up grassroots support for Kennedy. She claimed she'd fallen in love with him when he appeared at the 1956 Democratic Party Convention in Chicago. "I was so disappointed when he lost the vice-presidential bid to Kefauver. But all of us, including Pat and Peter, are vowing that will be the last election he loses." She was referring to her friends, Peter Lawford and his wife at the time, Patricia Kennedy, JFK's sister.

Janet said she had to go, but before she left she secured promises from both Robert and Paul that she could count on them for generous contributions when Kennedy actually announced for the presidency in the months ahead.

After she'd gone, Robert asked Paul, "Do you think he has a chance?"

"No," Paul said. "He's too sophisticated, too young, and too urbane. And, from what I hear, too prone to scandal. Besides, his old man carries too much baggage. Not only that, he's a Catholic. America hasn't grown up enough to elect a Catholic to the White House. But I liked him. I'll support him if he makes the run. Of course, I'd like to meet him again if that chance ever happens. Mostly, I'd like to meet Jacqueline Kennedy. If I had a woman like that at home, I wouldn't be leaving her while I chased after Janet Leigh. Even Joan Crawford and Lana Turner have told me

Psycho star **Janet Leigh** Hysterical over JFK

273

they've had affairs with him. What's his game plan? To seduce every major star in Hollywood?"

He could if he wanted to," Robert said. "I've pimped for him. There's not an actress yet who's turned him down. Gene Tierney, June Allyson, Peggy Cummins, Arlene Dahl, Marlene Dietrich, Zsa Zsa Gabor, Susan Hayward, Sonja Henie, Audrey Hepburn, Hedy Lamarr, Jayne Mansfield, Marilyn Monroe, Lee Remick, Jean Simmons, even Blaze Starr and Tempest Storm."

"Blaze and Tempest?" Paul asked in astonishment. "You mean, the strippers?"

"One and the same."

"What's he got that we don't have?" Paul asked.

"It's not dick size, I can assure you," Robert said. "It's his personal charm and magnetism. The ladies lap it up. I met his close buddy, another womanizer named George Smathers, that senator from Florida. He told me that, 'No one is ever off-limits to Jack—not your wife, your sister...not even your mother.'"

***

In New York for a brief visit, Paul had a reunion with Sal Mineo, who was still complaining that Paul didn't see enough of him. Paul later recalled, "Of all the actors I've known, I never met anyone who enjoyed being a movie star more than Sal. He enjoyed being a movie star even more than Lana Turner, who practically invented the term."

Sal invited Paul to spend the day with him in Mamaronek, outside New York City in Westchester County. Sal had purchased Mary Pickford's old 20-room mansion overlooking Long Island Sound for $200,000. Director D.W. Griffith had shot part of *Birth of a Nation* at the estate.

Before Paul's visit, Yul Brynner had just left. A very young Sal had appeared on the Broadway stage with Brynner in *The King and I*. "He likes to fuck young boys and older actresses," Sal claimed. "He even named some of his conquests for me—Tallulah Bankhead, Ingrid Bergman, Anne Baxter, Joan Crawford, Judy Garland, Marilyn Monroe, and, of course, Marlene Dietrich. Right now, Yul is flying to Paris to smoke opium with Jean Cocteau. He's become fast friends with the French faggot."

"Now, now," Paul cautioned him, "let's not use that word."

"Forgive me," Sal said. "It's a holdover from my vocabulary in the Bronx."

Sal invited Paul to go for a swim in the Sound. He'd purchased two bathing suits for them—one white with red polka dots, the other white with blue polka dots.

"I hope all those photographers from your fan magazines aren't hiding in the bushes to take our picture," Paul said, slipping into the suit.

During the course of that afternoon, Paul learned that Sal the movie star was taking in $300,000 a year. The news made Paul eager to start thinking of ways he might get out of his own contract at one thousand a week with Warner Brothers.

Back at the mansion, Paul said, "All my relatives are in the Bronx tonight, visiting family. We've got the place to ourselves. I'm going to barbecue hot dogs out back for our dinner."

"Let me make the cole slaw," Paul said. "I discovered a secret way to make it. It'll be the best you ever had."

"You're the best I ever had," Sal said, moving in on Paul.

Sitting out with Paul in the backyard after dinner, Sal regaled him with stories of his adventures in Hollywood—some quite improbable, others more believable. The most startling piece of information passed along that day was that mobster Mickey Cohen, who had been threatening Lana Turner, had offered Sal $10,000 "to fuck my ass. That gangster likes a little boy ass along with his string of gun molls like Liz Renay, that Marilyn Monroe clone."

"Did you take Cohen up on his offer?" Paul asked.

"Why not?" Sal said. "He got off in just five minutes. Ten Gs for five minutes work isn't bad."

"Not at all," Paul said. "It takes me ten weeks to make that much money."

During the course of the evening, Sal claimed that he was being stalked by film actress Gloria Grahame, who was two years older than Paul. A familiar face in film noir dramas, she'd won an Oscar for Best Supporting Actress in 1952 for *The Bad and the Beautiful*.

During her marriage to director Nicholas Ray, he'd caught her in bed with his then thirteen-year-old son, Anthony Ray. Years later, in 1962, she would scandalize Hollywood and damage her career when she ended up marrying Anthony, her former stepson, eight years after her divorce from his father, Nicholas. In time she would have children with both father and son.

Sal Mineo
In the footsteps of Mary Pickford

"What can I say?" Sal said. "This aging blonde sexpot likes young guys. Everywhere I go, she seems to show up. I think she believes all that shit written about me in fan magazines—that I'm girl crazy. Yeah, I'm girl crazy all right.

If only my fans knew I was getting plowed by Yul Brynner, Paul Newman, and Mickey Cohen."

Sal told him that when Dick Clark on his *American Bandstand* show ran a contest called "Why I Want to Have Dinner with Sal Mineo," more than 28,000 eager applications poured into the show in less than three days.

"All of us live in a fantasy world out there on the coast," Paul said. "Now get me another beer. The fan magazines even think I'm a faithful husband."

"That'll be the day," Sal said.

Before he departed from Mamaronek the following morning, Paul was presented with a miniature of himself in oil. "I did it from a film still when you played Rocky," Sal said. "The portrait I did of Abraham Lincoln is much better, but I thought you'd find this more amusing."

Paul studied the painting carefully. Sal had drawn him without his boxing trunks. "You fucker," he said to Sal. "You could have made it an inch or two longer."

"I did it from memory since I didn't have you to pose for me," Sal said, moving in on him.

"Watch it, kid," Paul said. "I'm an old man. After last night, you drained me to the last drop."

"I like to leave 'em satisfied," Sal said. "Now don't hold out on me. Nature has a way of replenishing these things."

On the train back into Manhattan, Paul picked up a fan magazine with Sal on the cover. It had been abandoned by a departing passenger.

The feature on Sal was headlined, "The Women in Sal Mineo's Life." Calling him Hollywood's Junior Casanova, the article claimed that swarms of teenage girls flock around Sal whenever he appears in public. "Can he fight them off?" the article asked. "If you're Sal Mineo, it's not easy."

***

Catalyzed by his bit part in *Somebody Up There Likes Me*, Steve McQueen and his career were climbing the Hollywood ladder at a dizzying pace. He'd been signed for a role in the TV series *Wanted Dead or Alive*, and critics were comparing him to Humphrey Bogart and Gary Cooper.

"At least that's better than comparisons I get to Marlon Brando," Paul said. Friends noted that he seemed jealous of McQueen, who one critic called "the Kool Kat's answer to John Wayne on the prairie, bow legs and all."

Word reached Paul that McQueen was fighting with everybody—the script writers, the producers, his sponsors, even wardrobe. He rejected their "starchy" cowboy outfits and showed up instead in scruffy clothes and an old cowboy hat that had once blazed across the West topping the head of

Randolph Scott.

McQueen took on Ronald Reagan himself, arguing with and even screaming at him about a script submitted for Reagan's *General Electric Theater.*

"Steve McQueen is one of the biggest shits I've ever come across in show business," Reagan told his friend William Holden.

"That's funny, because I once said the same thing about Yul Brynner," Holden said.

Meeting with McQueen for lunch in a New York restaurant, Paul asked him, "What is this I hear about you? You've become as temperamental as Bette Davis. Is that true?"

"The talk from cunts," McQueen said. "I've been around Hollywood long enough to know that some men out there have bigger cunts than women. I'm not trying to be popular. Even my horse, Ringo, tried to attack me. I'm trying to be a star making quality movies. Is there anything wrong with that?"

"Go for it, boy," Paul urged.

During the course of their meal—Steve rejected two hamburgers before the waitress got his order right—he gave Paul some career advice. "Keep your second wife barefoot and pregnant like you did your first wife. That way you'll have the little woman waiting at home frying the chicken while you're out doing whatever in the fuck you want to do."

After lunch, Steve invited Paul for a drive in an XK-SS Jaguar he was trying out. He called it "The Green Rat."

Paul later recalled to his friends, "It wasn't a drive. It was a race to dare death. He made James Dean and Monty Clift look like safe drivers. When Steve took off, anyone on the road had to get out of his way."

As a harbinger of Paul's own future interest in speed, McQueen drove like "The Madman of Le Mans." He seemed to keep the accelerator pressed to the floor and not even know where the brake was. He lurched the car from one side of the road to the other, passing other cars, with his brakes squealing every time he had to slam on them suddenly.

Amazingly, without ever getting stopped by a patrolman, he eventually got Paul to Montauk at the extreme eastern tip of Long Island.

"You got a place out here?" Paul asked. He had never been told where they were going.

"No, I don't need one," McQueen said.

Steve McQueen
Breaking and Entering

"These are mainly second homes for most people out here. Most of them are empty on weekdays. I'll just borrow a place, one that looks like a cozy nest, perhaps with some booze, a full bar and cold beer in the fridge for you."

Paul wanted to protest but didn't. He'd made headlines before, charged with drunk driving on Long Island. NEWMAN AND McQUEEN NABBED IN HOUSE ROBBERY. Paul could just see tomorrow's headlines.

"Like a fool," he later told friends, "I followed Steve up through someone's beautiful garden at the rear of a house. It overlooked the water. It would have been the perfect honeymoon cottage."

"I used to be a thief," McQueen said. "I was even jailed for it. I still know how to break into a house."

As the afternoon chilled, McQueen made a fire for them in the living room. Sitting in front of the fireplace, McQueen talked of his dreams. "I know I'm going to become the biggest star in Hollywood, the biggest box office attraction in the world. I can feel it in my gut."

"You're rising fast," Paul said.

"But I've got a problem," McQueen said. "In the years ahead, I view you as my major competition."

"It's highly likely we'll be up for some of the same parts," Paul said, accurately predicting their future.

"There's a way to avoid this," McQueen said. "You and I should team up and make buddy movies in the future when we have star power. Of course, there will be a cunt or two in the background. You gotta have pussy running back and forth so audiences won't think we're a pair of fags. But I want to do man-on-man action movies with you. I'm even dreaming of a script where we play rival race car drivers."

"You've got yourself a deal, good buddy," Paul said. "Let's become the John Wayne and Gary Cooper of the 1970s."

"That's for tomorrow," McQueen said. "Tonight we have some unfinished business. Long time, no see, partner."

***

When Paul visited Brando in his New York apartment, he found the actor in a bitter mood. Because the temperamental star had walked out on *The Egyptian*, he'd been forced to take a cut in salary to avoid a potential lawsuit. Consequently, for his role in *The Young Lions*, he'd contracted, against his will and as punishment from the studio, for a fee of only $50,000. During their meeting, Brando expressed fury about how his costar, Monty Clift, was pulling in a reported $750,000 for his role in the same film.

As the afternoon deepened, Brando discussed his love/hate relationship with Montgomery Clift, Brando comparing its dynamics to the emerging relationship between Paul and McQueen.

"We admire each other, and, yes, there's some love there," Brando told Paul. "Yet Monty and I hate each other at times."

"It's very strange, but I often feel the same way about Steve," Paul said. "I'm drawn to him but at the same time I resent him."

"You want to know Monty's reaction to *Guys and Dolls*?" Brando asked. "He told me that all he saw on the screen was this big, *big*, big, fat ass! What did McQueen think of your performance in *The Left Handed Gun*?"

"Not much," Paul said. "After he saw the movie, he had only one reaction—that he planned to fuck Lita Milan. Okay, I'll be completely honest. In this Western series he's doing on TV, he's a better star in an oater than I am. In some ways, he has more talent than I do, and I suspect he'll surpass me in the Hollywood rat race."

"I'll be truthful, too," Brando said, "for a change. I think Monty did a better job in *A Place in the Sun* than I did in *A Streetcar Named Desire*. I even voted him to win the Oscar. That's how fair I am about judging talent."

Brando surprised Paul when he told him about the debate at Fox over casting the third male lead in *The Young Lions*. "The studio wanted Tony Randall, that homophobic faggot," Brando said. "I told Dmytryk I wouldn't work with Randall."

He was referring to Edward Dmytryk, one of the original Hollywood Ten, who'd served a prison term for his refusal to testify before the House Committee on Un-American Activities in its witch hunt for communists in the entertainment business.

Marlon Brando
A Sympathetic Nazi?

"I told Fox they should borrow you from Warners for the role," Brando claimed. "But they turned down my casting idea and went for Dean Martin of all people."

"That guy needs a good role to help him break away from the Jerry Lewis stereotype," Paul said.

"I didn't feel so bad when Deano told me he was getting only $25,000 for the picture," Brando said. "Just half of my salary. You've got to see *The Young Lions*. I make the Nazi I play a tragic hero."

"You're making a Nazi a sympathetic hero on the screen?" Paul asked. "How daring. I've got to see how you pull this

279

one off. You've played Napoleon. The next thing I know you'll be bringing a cuddly Hitler to the screen."

"For that smartass remark, I'm going to punish your butt," Brando said. "You deserve it."

"We did shit like that a long time ago," Paul said. "Let's leave it as a memory."

"Who in the fuck are you talking to?" Brando asked. "I let go of an ass only when I'm finished with it—and not a moment before. Okay, if you don't want to fuck, let's do some nude wrestling. Take off your clothes."

"I guess I can do that," Paul said. "But no funny stuff."

Later that night when Paul met Shelley Winters for dinner, he confided to her, "The inevitable happened."

"He pulled the same stunt on me one night," Shelley said. "The brute is into nude wrestling with both men and women. He calls it foreplay. He always comes out the winner in the end."

"What an apt expression," Paul said, as they both broke into laughter.

***

Tony Perkins was also living in a New York apartment, plotting his next career move. A part-time maid answered the door to Tony's apartment, inviting Paul in and ushering him down a long corridor to a room in the rear. "Come on back," Tony called to him.

When Paul came into a brightly lit dressing room, with a stage mirror encased in light bulbs, Tony was seated applying blood-red lipstick. He was dressed in beads and spangles like a 1920s chorine.

"What on earth?" Paul asked. "Until now, I never knew you're a transvestite."

"I'm not," Tony said. "I'd kiss you but I just applied my lipstick."

"Now it can be told," Paul said with a smirk. "Tony Perkins wants to be a chorus gal in a 20s musical."

"Something like that," he said, standing up and raising his dress so Paul could better examine his showgirl legs.

Inviting him back into the living room up front, Tony linked his arm with Paul's. "Great to see you again," Tony said. "As always, you're looking fabulous. All that beer drinking never seems to take its toll."

Paul came to Tony's rescue as he wobbled shakily in his stiletto heels.

In the living room, Tony asked the maid to bring Paul a cold beer. "Billy Wilder dropped in the other day with a synopsis of a new script he's planning to shoot. He wants me to appear as one of the stars. It's called *Some Like It Hot*, and it's a comedy set in the 1920s. There's talk that Marilyn Monroe might star in it."

Tony admitted that "it's a great part," but claimed that his agent, Herman Citron, had advised him not to appear in women's clothing again after his star turn in *The Matchmaker*. "Herman thinks my appearing in drag might get me laughed off the screen." The actor's dressing up as his demented mother in *Psycho* still lay in his future.

He explained to Paul how, in *Some Like it Hot,* the two male stars witness the Chicago Valentine's Day Massacre. To flee from the scene of the crime, they dress up in drag as showgirls and join an all-girl band heading for Palm Beach.

"If you've called me here to try out for the other drag role, forget it," Paul said. "That's not the macho image I'm cultivating."

"No, silly," he said. "Wilder wants Sinatra for the other male role."

"Frank on the screen in drag?" Paul said. "I loved his *Sunset Blvd.*, but Wilder must be out of his fucking mind. There's no way in hell that my rival for the title of Blue Eyes is going to dress up in drag onscreen. Cary Grant, maybe, but he's probably too old for the part. Why not your buddy boy, Tab Hunter? He's still pretty enough. You and Tab in drag would provoke more whistles than Marilyn Monroe, at least from the gay fraternity."

After Paul complimented Tony three times on how fetching he looked dressed as a woman, Paul read the brief synopsis of the plot for *Some Like It Hot* while Tony retreated to the dressing room. The actual script hadn't been finished yet.

When Tony came back dressed in street clothes, Paul told him, "This thing, especially with Wilder directing it, has the makings of a really hot comedy. With Monroe in it, I think it could be a hit. I mean, *big*. You sure you don't have the balls to do it."

"I'm too afraid," Tony said. "Too many people between Broadway and Hollywood are discussing my homosexuality. I've got to be careful. I live every day with the fear of exposure. Look what happened to Tab."

He was referring to a devastating *Confidential* exposé that had outed Tab as a homosexual. In the wake of that exposure, once-loyal fan magazines such as *Teen Life* were not only predicting Tab's downfall, but eagerly anticipating it.

Over dinner, Tony didn't seem much interested in Paul's career, but was filled with news and adventures

Tony Perkins
In fear of *Confidential*

281

of his own recent accomplishments. As the career of his lover, Tab Hunter, floundered, Tony had blossomed into a major star thanks to some recent releases. He'd even been nominated for a Tony for his appearance in Thomas Wolfe's *Look Homeward, Angel*.

Tony was never pleased with his work, however, and he expressed disappointment over all of his films, even though he had enjoyed working with Shirley Booth in *The Matchmaker*. "She's my favorite actress," Tony told Paul. He also revealed that *The Matchmaker*, in its original conception, had been shaped as a vehicle to reteam Spencer Tracy with Katharine Hepburn. It would later, of course, become the inspiration for Carol Channing's Broadway musical, *Hello, Dolly!*

"I hated working with Sophia Loren in *Desire Under the Elms*," Tony said. "She hogged the camera." He warned Paul never to make a film with her, but he would ignore this advice. "They call Loren The Roman Rocket," Tony said. "She can blast off in another direction."

During the filming of *This Angry Age*, Tony had been intimately linked with his French director, René Clément. It had co-starred Silvana Mangano, called "the Italian Rita Hayworth" and Alida Valli, another Italian beauty once hailed as "the new Garbo."

"Those gals are neither Garbo nor Rita," Tony said to Paul. "I spent my time in Rome shacked up with Tab when he drove down from Germany, and later with Rock Hudson when I welcomed him to Cinecitta Studios."

Tony told Paul that he was considering doing first a play, and then a film version, of F. Scott Fitzgerald's *This Side of Paradise*. This turned out to be just a dream.

He also wanted to do a remake of *Destry Rides Again*, the film classic that had starred Marlene Dietrich and James Stewart. That would never happen either, although Andy Griffith would star in a Broadway play of the same name.

According to Tony, James Cagney wanted him to appear in *Shake Hands With the Devil*, the role eventually going to Don Murray, who'd scored a bull's eye with Marilyn Monroe in *Bus Stop*. Delmer Daves had also offered Tony the lead in a film called *Parrish*, the part eventually going to the blond, blue-eyed heartthrob, Troy Donahue.

In spite of all these offers, Paul later said that Tony "made a horrible mistake" in agreeing to play a brave young fugitive in *Green Mansions*, opposite Audrey Hepburn as a wood nymph. Paul told friends, "Both stars were horribly miscast, and I couldn't sit through the thing."

Back at Tony's apartment, Paul found the actor deeply troubled, as always, by his homosexuality. He feared that Dorothy Kilgallen, "The Voice of Broadway," was about to expose the "Three Ts" in her column.

"Tony Perkins, Tab Hunter, and Timmy Everett."

Paul had read that Timmy was scoring a big success starring in Elia Kazan's production of *The Dark at the Top of the Stairs*, by playwright William Inge. After a lover's quarrel between Timmy and Tony over Tab, Timmy had attempted suicide by slashing his wrists. He recovered from the attempt, but Tony never came to visit him in the hospital.

"My God, man, you've got chorus boys threatening suicide over you," Paul said. "I've heard of lady killers. You're the boy killer."

"If someone falls in love with me, and I'm not always there for them, that's their fucking problem," Tony said.

"Thank God I never fell in love with you," Paul told him. "But you're a great piece of ass."

"I'll always be there for you, baby cakes," Tony said.

Two nights later, when Paul shared dinner and the episode with Janice Rule, she offered a grim assessment: "I don't think Tony will ever accept his homosexuality. It will probably destroy him one way or another."

***

When Paul returned to Hollywood, he decided to ignore the many telephone messages left by his "stalker," the underaged Sandra Dee. He had heard that the older singer, Bobby Darin, had taken an interest in Sandra and that she'd probably moved on to her next adventure. He was wrong.

Within less than a mile from the MGM parking lot, Sandra popped up from the back seat of his car like a Jack-in-the-Box. "SURPRISE!" she shouted at him.

He nearly ran the car off the road. "How in hell did you get in my car?" he asked, flashing anger.

"I bribed a guard," she said. "All I have to do is flash my brown eyes, and the world is mine." He ordered her into the front seat but pushed her away when she tried to kiss him.

En route to taking her to her own home, he ordered her to get over him. "I'm married to Joanne," he told her, "and I'm going to stay married to her. There has never been anything between us, and there will never be anything between us."

She burst into tears, and he tried to comfort her, deciding it was a useless endeavor. He parked a block from her home, as he didn't want to be seen pulling into her driveway. "Now get out of this car and never get in it again," he sternly told her. "Do you get that?"

"I'll get out of the car today," she said, her face a mask of steely determination. "But I want to put you on notice. I plan to have you. And when I plan to have you, I mean just that. You're not getting away from me." As she got out of the car, she looked back at him. "God, I hate Joanne Woodward. I wish she were dead, so you could be mine and mine alone."

***

Around midnight, Paul was awakened by a call from Richard Brooks. "Forget Grace Kelly. Forget Vivien Leigh. Forget Lana Turner. We've got a new Maggie the Cat. I've just returned from a late-night meeting. At long last, it's final. The contract is signed. Miss Elizabeth Taylor is your Maggie. No doubt she'll soon be meowing after you."

"Not as long as Mike Todd is still alive," was his immediate response.

Chapter Eight
Hot Cats & Sweet Birds

Hollywood gossip columnists buzzed with excitement when the news was finally announced that Elizabeth Taylor, then at the peak of her sultry beauty, would co-star with Paul Newman, then at the peak of his male flash, in Tennessee Williams' Pulitzer Prize-winning Broadway play, *Cat on a Hot Tin Roof.*

"When the man with the glacial blue eyes meets the girl with the eyes of a spring violet, the great movie romance of the century will surely unfold," one columnist wrote. "How can two such sex symbols resist the magnetism of each other?" The writer didn't even mention that Elizabeth was madly in love with her husband, showman Mike Todd, and that Paul had recently married Joanne Woodward after years of agonizing delay.

Shooting commenced on March 12, 1958, and Elizabeth showed up on the set to meet the cast. Coming together with Paul for the first time, she said, "You're more beautiful in person than on the screen, if such a thing is possible."

"You took the words out of my mouth," he said. "Surely you are the most beautiful woman in the world, maybe in the universe for all I know."

"Your flattery will get you everywhere," she said. "If I were naming a perfume after you, I would call it *Temptation.*"

"If I were naming a perfume after you, I'd call it *Enchantment.*"

"Come on, kids, break it up," said the film's director, Richard Brooks, who was standing with them. Elizabeth felt comfortable working with the director. He'd helmed her through *The Last Time I Saw Paris* in 1954, when she'd starred opposite the homosexual actor, Van Johnson. Brooks would later marry one of Elizabeth's best friends, her fellow British actress, Jean Simmons.

Before introducing Elizabeth to the rest of the cast, Brooks invited Paul and her to lunch in the MGM commissary. She was fresh from the shooting of

Raintree County with Monty Clift. Paul was eager to hear stories about his former friend and how he'd held up during the completion of the film in the wake of his accident.

"Had Monty accepted the role of Brick, he would be standing here with you today instead of me," Paul reminded her.

"Had Grace Kelly not run off and married a prince, Maggie the Cat would be blonde—and not me." She said, "By the way, that Oscar Joanne took home belonged to me." She flashed her famous smile to indicate she was joking. "Tell your bitch when you get home that if she steals another Oscar from me, I'll cut off her right tit."

"We got your gracious note, congratulating Joanne on her win." Paul said. "It meant more to her than all the other congratulations she received. But I'll take your advice. I will personally see that Joanne never takes the prize from you again."

Elizabeth leaned over and gave him a gentle kiss on the lips. "I know you're a man of your word, and I'll hold you to that promise."

In the words of Brooks, Elizabeth "behaved like a queen" during her interactions with her fellow cast members.

Burl Ives was cast as "Big Daddy," the patriarch of the Southern Pollitt family. As the film begins, he's the only member of his clan who hasn't admitted he's dying of cancer as his dysfunctional family gathers around him for last rites.

Ironically, Burl Ives was only one year older than Jack Carson, who played his older son, Gooper, and only sixteen years older than Paul, who was cast as his morose (but preferred) younger son, Brick.

The brilliant lesbian actress, Judith Anderson, was cast as Big Momma, with Madeleine Sherwood playing Gooper's social-climbing, child-bearing wife, May. Her quintet of "no neck monsters" stampede roughshod at regular intervals amid the antiques and fine carpets of the Pollitt mansion.

The clan has gathered to watch Big Daddy fade from life. Gooper wants his father's millions and the plantation for himself, his breeding wife, and her kids.

Over lunch in the MGM commissary, Richard Brooks delivered disappointing

Paul Newman and Elizabeth Taylor
Temptation meets *Enchantment*

news to Paul, who had assumed that the original plot and original theme of Tennessee's play would be transferred directly to the big screen.

The director told him that MGM executives had rejected the first draft of his script. In that version, Paul (Brick) confesses his homosexuality to Elizabeth (Maggie the Cat), informing her that he doesn't make love to her because he's still in love with his dead friend, Skipper. He goes on to confess that he blames himself for Skipper's suicide.

In the earliest draft of the script—later destroyed—Brick even confesses his homosexuality to Big Daddy. The men reach an understanding about both of their "sexual perversions," Big Daddy confessing that he used to "fool around" with some farm boy in the barn loft when he was a teenager growing up in redneck Mississippi.

To elicit their sympathy during his conflict with MGM, Brooks told Paul and Elizabeth that it wasn't the first time he'd seen a script "castrated" because of its references to homosexuality. Brooks had published a novel in 1945, *The Brick Foxhole*. It was a large success, telling the story of a group of Marines who pick up and then murder a homosexual serviceman. The novel was a stinging indictment of intolerance.

Brooks eventually sold his novel to be filmed, and in the ensuing conversion to the big screen, the ill-fated victim was recast as a Jew, and he died at the hands of an anti-Semite. Released in 1947, the film had been retitled *Crossfire*, and it starred three actors named Robert—Young, Mitchum, and Ryan, respectively—with sultry Gloria Grahame as the female lead.

"You've got to understand my dilemma," Brooks said. "The Production Code doesn't even allow us to mention the word homosexual on the screen."

At this point they were joined by James Poe, a writer who was working with Brooks to adapt the Williams play for the screen. Elizabeth already knew Poe because two years previously, in 1956, he had worked with Mike Todd on the script of *Around the World in Eighty Days*. Both Poe and Brooks remain the major source of inside information about the relationship of Elizabeth and Paul that occurred during the tragic complications associated with the filming of *Cat on a Hot Tin Roof*.

Director Richard Brooks
"Castrating scripts"

Brooks waited until their lunch was nearly over to deliver the punch line. In many scenes during the early part of the film, the script called for Paul to appear topless, wearing only the bottom of his pajamas. He'd have to hobble around on a crutch, having broken his leg one gung-ho drunken night while running the hurdle at his old alma mater. He was trying to recapture his days of football glory which he shared with his friend Skipper, for whom he is still in deep mourning, trying to drown his sorrow in the bottle.

In the filmed, watered-down version of *Cat*, Maggie lies to the family, especially Big Daddy, asserting (falsely) that she is pregnant. In the final stages of the script, Brick, as played by Paul, backs her up in her lie. He is seen throwing his pillow to a position beside Maggie's on the bed. The movie comes to an end as they are about to have a "horizontal reconciliation," with the implication that he will penetrate her and that they will actually make that baby whose birth has already been publicly announced by Maggie. As part of the film's happy ending, previous wrongdoings and misunderstandings fade away.

At the end of the lunch meeting, Paul turned to Brooks and Poe, saying, "I'll leave it up to you guys to show this shit to Tennessee."

Brooks tried to salvage the luncheon with at least some good news: Whereas originally MGM had opted to shoot the picture, budgeted at two million dollars, in black and white, Brooks and Mike Todd persuaded the studio to shoot it in Technicolor, if for no other reason than to show off the beautiful eyes of the two leading stars.

That afternoon, back in his dressing room, Paul received a phone call from Gore Vidal. He'd been working at MGM on a script for *Ben-Hur*, a remake of the famous 1925 silent film that had starred Ramon Novarro.

Gore informed Paul that Sam Zimbalist, MGM's studio chief, had wanted Paul to play Ben-Hur. "I nixed that idea," Gore said. After *The Silver Chalice*, I told the guys that there was no way you'd ever appear on the screen again wearing a cocktail dress showing off your skinny legs." Instead, the role went to Charlton Heston. Ironically, Zimbalist himself died in 1958, on location in Rome during the filming of *Ben-Hur* of a stress-induced heart attack provoked by the making of that film.

The early rapport established between Paul and Elizabeth did not last through the rehearsals. "She is totally lifeless working with me," he told Brooks. "We have no chemistry at all. She's holding back."

When the actual filming began, and after Paul had seen the rushes, he revised his opinion of Elizabeth. "The moment the camera is turned on her, she becomes radiant," Paul said. "She's a much better actress than I ever imagined. I've never seen anything like it. She's a true film actress, not appropriate for the stage."

From the very beginning, Brooks was pleased with Paul's work on the screen. "Even though we were forced to remove a lot of the motivation from Paul's character, he pulled it off with his cool detachment cast opposite the hot-to-trot Maggie. In spite of the weakness of the script, Paul would succeed in making Brick a creditable character, if not always properly motivated."

Mike Todd showed up on the set one day, introducing himself to Paul. He, too, had seen the rushes and he thought Elizabeth "has never been better." He made no comment on Paul's performance.

"I completely changed my mind about her," he told Paul. "I didn't want her to play Maggie the Cat. I even flew her to London to see Kim Stanley when she was appearing as Maggie in the West End. I took Elizabeth backstage and tried to get Kim to convince her that the role was not for her."

"And why not?" Paul asked. "She's great as Maggie."

"I know that now," Todd said, "but originally I had one serious objection. I said, 'No one's gonna believe that any man—even if gay—would turn down the chance to fuck Elizabeth Taylor.'"

After only a few days of shooting, Elizabeth developed a severe head cold. She was running a dangerous fever and had to be sent home in a limousine. Brooks and Paul learned the next day that her illness had developed into pneumonia.

Executives at MGM were anxious for Elizabeth to complete *Cat*, for which she was being paid $125,000, according to the terms of her contract. But that contract was running out and slated to expire on June 1, 1958. After that, it was speculated that Elizabeth could command far more money on her next picture, at least $350,000, perhaps a lot more.

Paul was still on his small salary. In a surprise move, Warners had asked MGM only $25,000 for loaning him out as the star of *Cat*. In contrast, Tennessee Williams was getting $450,000 for the screen rights.

Brooks was the first to inform Paul that he'd have to shoot around Elizabeth until she recovered enough to come back onto the set. "I know her," he said. "She's very fragile, a woman of delicate health. I feared something like this might happen. A head cold was bad enough, but pneumonia could threaten her life. I've just come from a meeting at MGM. They're so worried that

Elizabeth Taylor with **Michael Todd**
Not-so-lucky Liz

289

Elizabeth won't be able to finish *Cat* that they've called Carroll Baker's agent to see if she could be made available."

"I don't think it'll come to that," Paul said in astonishment.

"Let's face it: Elizabeth could die," Brooks said. "I've always had this intuition. I can smell death in the air."

***

On March 22, 1958, Mike Todd, along with a pilot and co-pilot, took off in a torrential rain storm from Burbank in a private, twin-engine Lockheed Lodestar he'd nicknamed *Lucky Liz*. The plane, as it came to be, was anything but lucky.

Ironically, Elizabeth was supposed to have been on that flight, but had to remain bedridden because of her illness. The virus that had infected her ended up saving her life.

In another irony, although Todd had invested $25,000 to install a lavender-colored bedroom aboard *Lucky Liz*, he'd shelled out only $2,000 to improve the aircraft's anti-icing system. The bedroom money should have been spent on the anti-icing system.

Todd was flying to a testimonial dinner at the swanky Waldorf-Astoria in New York where he'd been pre-announced as the guest of honor. A few hours after takeoff, *Lucky Liz* crashed into the Zuni Mountains of New Mexico. Todd and his pilots were killed on impact, their bodies charred beyond recognition. *Lucky Liz*'s impact with Earth occurred at 2:40am, local time.

The producer's gold wedding ring was retrieved from the wreckage and returned to Elizabeth in Beverly Hills. At 6am in California, Elizabeth had not slept all night. She was waiting for the phone call from Todd that he had promised when the plane landed in Albuquerque.

It wasn't until 8:30am that Elizabeth was told of Todd's death. She became hysterical. Clad only in a see-through nightgown, she tried to flee from her home. Had she succeeded, she'd have faced a barrage of reporters, photographers, and TV newsreel crews. Doctors restrained her and sedated her. She was carried up the steps and returned to bed. Ironically, Debbie Reynolds, married at the time to Eddie Fisher and still on good terms with Elizabeth, had arrived at the house to take charge of Elizabeth's children.

A steady stream of well-wishers, including Samuel Goldwyn, also arrived at Elizabeth's house throughout the day.

It was on Day Two after the plane wreck that Paul was allowed into the house. Amazingly, one of the first persons he encountered in the crowd downstairs was Greta Garbo, coming down from Elizabeth's bedroom upstairs. She did not know Paul but recognized him immediately. "Go upstairs and offer her comfort. I did what I could," Garbo told him.

Mounting the stairs, Paul knocked on her door. There was no answer. As he turned, he spotted a photographer trying to conceal himself behind the open door of an adjoining bedroom. He confronted the photographer and demanded that he leave. As security later learned, the photographer had planned to barge into Elizabeth's bedroom and snap a picture of the grief-stricken widow, which no doubt would have appeared on the front covers of tabloids across the country.

After the photographer was evicted from the premises, Paul returned to Elizabeth's bedroom and knocked again. This time Elizabeth herself opened the door. She stood before him in a sheer nightgown.

When she saw him, she fell into his arms, and he guided her back into the room, where he gently returned her to bed, covering up her nudity.

Without makeup and with no sleep for the previous two nights, she looked at him, her violet eyes bloodshot. In spite of her pain, she remained beautiful. She reached for him. "Don't ever let me go," she said, her voice barely a whisper. Those words eerily evoked what a frightened Lana Turner, under threat from the mob, had once uttered to him.

Through tear-streaked eyes, she told him that "Mike had a premonition about that flight. Before he left my bedroom that night, he returned five times and kissed me right on the lips even though I had pneumonia."

Elizabeth and Paul talked for an hour, a session Paul later shared with Brooks. Fearing she wouldn't be able to return to the film set of *Cat*, he desperately wanted to assess the emotional condition of his star.

"I was always the strong one in any relationship I ever had," she confessed to Paul. "Even with my parents and certainly through my marriages. But when Mike came along, I surrendered myself to him. He made the decisions. He was my shield against the world. I was his vassal. He solved all my problems. He loved me as no man has ever loved me. I was his. Without him, I have nothing."

On a wild impulse, he blurted out, "You have me." Later, he would tell Brooks that he didn't really know why he'd said that. "The words just came out."

"Stay with me tonight," Elizabeth whispered in his ear. "I can't stand to be

Elizabeth with her brother, **Howard Taylor, Jr.** at Mike Todd's funeral "Day of the Locust'

alone. Mike slept here by my side. Last night I kept reaching out for him, finding nothing. No one."

"I'll be here for you," he promised.

If Brooks is to be believed, Paul told him that he made love to Elizabeth that night. "It was not a love of passion but a love of comfort," Paul allegedly told his director. "She needed me. My human warmth."

He also told Brooks that "I came to my senses the moment I left her house. I couldn't replace Todd in her life. I have a life of my own. A wife. Kids. I feared I'd horribly misled her. I can't be the next Mr. Elizabeth Taylor. I just can't."

Brooks assured him that he should feel no guilt for what he had done. "You were just tending to a desperate woman's needs."

The next day Elizabeth placed three frantic calls to Paul on the set, but he didn't return those desperate pleas to speak to her.

Paul only grimaced when he learned the news of Mike Todd's funeral, a savage outpouring of hysterical fans evocative of the novel, *Day of the Locust*, by Nathanael West.

He heard that souvenir hunters had ripped the black veil that covered her face and had even yanked whole strands of her hair from her scalp. Security guards could not control the mob. Elizabeth finally escaped to a waiting limousine.

On April 14, Elizabeth returned to the set of *Cat on a Hot Tin Roof*. Embarrassed, Paul left his dressing room to greet her. There were no recriminations. She kissed him gently on the lips. "Thanks for being there for me when I needed you," she said. Her charm under duress made him feel like a heel, as he later told Brooks.

Having lost at least twelve pounds, Elizabeth in her grief looked more stunning than ever. She requested a private lunch with Paul. There was no talk of love. She seemed to be very practical. "I have to get back to work," she told him. "There are bills to be paid." After Mike's assets are liquidated and his debts paid, I'll receive only $13,000 from his estate."

Once again, he offered his sympa-

Above: **Debbie Reynolds** with then-husband **Eddie Fisher**
Below: **Eddie Fisher** with then-wife **Elizabeth Taylor**

The best of friends, the worst of friends

thy. Her response startled him. "He's not dead," she said, her face a mask of steely determination. "I know he parachuted to safety. He'll be found any day now wandering the badlands of New Mexico. I refuse to believe that he's dead."

Eddie Fisher, Paul learned, seemed to be at Elizabeth's house every night. He had been Todd's best friend. Paul could not forget his marital obligation to Joanne, but it appeared that Eddie had conveniently forgotten that he was married to Debbie Reynolds. In fact, "Debbie & Eddie" were widely identified throughout the media as "America's sweethearts."

Brooks told Paul that Elizabeth had made a startling confession to him during the final days of the filming of *Cat on a Hot Tin Roof.*

"I feared that a scandal was brewing, thanks to Elizabeth spending so much time with that Fisher boy," Brooks said. "I confronted her. I don't want to sound greedy, but I was afraid fans would stay away in droves if news got out that Eddie had become the surrogate Mike Todd in her life—yes, including the fulfillment of marital duties."

The next day Brooks shared with Paul Elizabeth's response. It was a shocker, and we have only Brooks' word for this.

"I've known for months that Eddie is in love with me," Elizabeth allegedly told Brooks. "Even Mike knew that. He just dismissed it as a harmless flirtation. 'What red-blooded man on the planet wouldn't fall for Elizabeth Taylor?' he used to say. "I fear I've developed an attachment far more scandalous than Eddie Fisher. I think I'm falling in love with Mike Todd Jr."

***

Except that he was the son of her late husband, Mike Todd Jr. might have made a proper new husband for Elizabeth. At least they were in the same age bracket: Todd Jr. was 28 when his father died, Elizabeth a ripe 26.

He spent hours telling her about his dream of Smell-O-Vision. That dream became a reality in 1960

Left to right:
Eddie Fisher, Mike Todd Jr., and E.T.
Forbidden Love

with the release of *Scent of Mystery*, starring Peter Lorre and Denholm Elliott.

During every screening, smells released from tiny tubes beneath the viewer's seat assaulted the nostrils with the scent of roses, a woman's perfume, the odor of grape juice, even pipe smoke. Critics dismissed it as a gimmick, and Smell-O-Vision was never again associated with a feature-length film.

Quite by chance, the author of this biography, in Ireland in the mid-1970s with travel writer Stanley Haggart, once encountered Todd Jr. in a Dublin pub. He'd come in for a glass of gin and ended up having quite a few.

Todd, Jr., spoke frankly about his failed dreams of becoming a big-time showman like his father. During the course of the evening, and after his sixth gin, he admitted that he had once fallen in love with Elizabeth. "I was the one who pulled away," he admitted, "because I knew our marriage—which would have been possible only after I divorced my-then wife Sarah—would have destroyed Elizabeth's career. Look what happened to another Oscar winner, Gloria Grahame, when she married her stepson, the son of Nicolas Ray."

Todd Jr., after suffering for years from diabetes—he even had one leg amputated—eventually died on May 5, 2002 in Ireland, the victim of lung cancer.

Back in 1958, Todd Jr.'s then wife, Sarah Jane Weaver, rescued him from the clutches of Elizabeth. Eddie Fisher then abandoned his then-wife, Debbie Reynolds, and rushed to fill the role of Mike Todd Sr.

Throughout the remainder of the filming of *Cat on a Hot Tin Roof*, Paul provided Elizabeth with strong moral—but not physical—support. Their moment of intimacy, conceived and executed at perhaps the worst moment of her life, seemed to have been relegated to a far and distant memory within both of their brains.

In later years, Elizabeth expressed gratitude to Paul for his good manners during the conclusion of the shooting of *Cat*. "He was most courtly to me," she told friends, "a real gentleman. If I were about to have a nervous breakdown, he was by my side, guiding me through a scene."

"I think Elizabeth gave her greatest performance in *Cat*," Paul later claimed. "She turned out to be a real trouper."

That was his public position. Privately, he told Brooks, "I really wish I was a free man. In all my life, I never wanted anything as much. To be the man lying in bed with Elizabeth Taylor when she woke up in the morning. Those violet eyes gazing into my baby blues."

***

At long last and once again, Paul felt he would escape comparisons to Brando after *Cat* was released. The first review he read, however, was by

Penelope Houston, appearing in the *London Observer*. She claimed that Paul had "the look of a sulkier Brando, which seems, if anything, a little too strong for Brick."

Paul remembered with horror the day he sat in a viewing room with Brooks and *Cat*'s playwright, Tennessee Williams. He cringed throughout the screening, and Paul kept shifting nervously in his seat. When the screening was over and the lights came up, Tennessee rose to his feet.

He looked first at Paul. "You looked fabulous without your shirt," Tennessee said. "One tasty morsel." Then he turned to Brooks. "You emasculated my play. You bastard! I'm going to urge the public to stay away from it." Then he stormed out of the studio.

On September 20, 1958, when *Cat* opened in theaters around the country, Elizabeth was sternly being denounced as "the other woman." Tabloid fodder for the press, she was accused of breaking up the marriage of America's so-called sweethearts, Debbie Reynolds and Eddie Fisher. Assuming that modern-day Debbie Reynolds has some powerful lawyers lurking in the background, the true story of Reynolds/Fisher marriage probably won't be told until both parties have departed.

But instead of seguéing "notorious Liz," as she was called, into box office poison, publicity generated by the illicit romance had movie-goers lining up around the country to gaze upon "this Jezebel."

Cat was nominated for Best Picture, Best Adapted Screenplay (in spite of Tennessee's assault), Best Director, Best Actor (Paul himself), and Best Actress (in spite of the negative press out there on Elizabeth).

At the Academy Awards, Paul faced stiff competition from Sidney Poitier in *The Defiant Ones* and Tony Curtis, also in *The Defiant Ones*. It can be assumed that two nominees for the same picture cancel each other out. Therefore, Paul had to measure up against David Niven in *Separate Tables* and Spencer Tracy in *The Old Man and the Sea*.

Niven, playing a bogus war hero and child molester, walked off with the Oscar. Paul modestly admitted to friends, "I didn't deserve the win this time. Maybe next time."

Ironically, Elizabeth lost to Susan Hayward for *I Want to Live*, a script that Paul had urged Susan to make. That was not because he really wanted her to do it, but because he wanted her to reject *The Three Faces of Eve* so Joanne could get the role.

Since he'd lost the Academy Award, that left the Newman-Woodward household with only one Oscar resting on their mantelpiece.

Instead of Beverly Hills, the Newmans preferred to purchase a former coaching house in Connecticut. The property dated from 1780, and it was set on three acres of fruit trees with a trout stream running through.

When in New York, Paul chose not to arrive anywhere by chauffeured limousine, as did such visiting stars as Lana Turner, who was still calling him. Wearing a Tam O'Shanter and goggles, he buzzed around the city *incognito* on a motor scooter painted red.

As for Joanne's Oscar, thieves in the late summer of 1976 broke into the Newman home in Connecticut and made off with it. The police eventually found it and presented her with her Oscar in a mock ceremony honoring her performance in *The Three Faces of Eve* once again.

In 1958 Joanne, under contract to 20th Century Fox, and Paul, still under contract to Warners, were hot properties. "Either of them, more or less, could have their pick of roles," claimed producer Lawrence Weingarten. "But in a fit of madness, Joanne gave in to Paul's demands to do a comedy, *Rally 'Round the Flag, Boys!* Maybe Paul had drunk too much beer that day."

For his services, Paul was paid $1,750 a week, although Warners took in $7,500 a week for lending him out. When Warners later made an annual review of his salary, Paul was notified that in the future he would be making $2,000 a week.

This screwball comedy and suburban farce was based on Max Shulman's best-selling novel. Filmed in CinemaScope, it was the story of a community, Putnam's Landing in Connecticut, that got into an uproar over a projected missile base.

The old-time director, Leo Carey, was assigned to the project. A veteran of scads of comedies, Carey had directed the best silent films of Stan Laurel and Oliver Hardy, and he'd also helmed everyone from The Marx Brothers to W.C. Fields.

Paul later learned that the film had first been offered to Frank Sinatra, Deborah Kerr, and William Holden. "At least Carey didn't offer it to Brando first," Paul quipped.

In mid-June of 1958, just before filming began, Paul and Joanne clashed with Carey. For the second female lead, Carey wanted Jayne Mansfield, but Joanne and Paul held out for their friend, Joan Collins.

"Blondes are funny," Carey told them. "Not brunettes." Nonetheless, because of the star power of the Newmans, he was forced to drop Mansfield and go with the British import.

At the time, Carey was considering Mansfield for the third lead, the blonde bombshell had just scored a hit in the film, *Will*

Joan Collins with **Paul**
Modeling lingerie in
Rally 'Round the Flag, Boys!

296

Success Spoil Rock Hunter? When Carey called her to tell her she'd lost the part, she shot back, "Tough shit! I could have shown that Newman boy what it's like to fuck a real blonde. There's one problem, though. I heard he's Jewish, and I usually don't like to be penetrated by men with cut meat. I like my hunks with a little foreskin like Mickey Hargitay, Ronald Reagan, Frank Sinatra, and John F. Kennedy."

To make *Rally 'Round the Flags, Boy!*, Joanne herself had turned down the role of the luckless floozy in *Some Came Running* (1958), the MGM melodrama starring Sinatra and Dean Martin. Reportedly, for reasons of her own, Joanne did not want to co-star with Sinatra. The juicy role went to Shirley MacLaine, who would later co-star with Paul in the disastrous *What a Way to Go!*

At the time she showed up to film the *Rally 'Round the Flag* movie, Collins was known as "The Dime Store Liz Taylor." In the movie, she played a neighbor, who turns her dark and roving eye on Paul, cast as Joanne's husband, in this splurge of slapstick.

With Natalie Wood, Paul had drawn up a list of possible conquests for seduction among the sexpots of Hollywood. Joan had been on that list. But when she became a family friend, especially of Joanne's, he struck her name from the list.

Paul told Carey, "Joan's close friendship with Joanne took the fire out of my hard-on." Collins had actually met Paul earlier in the 1950s at a party at the home of a millionaire playboy. On that night, she'd encountered not only Paul, but Marlon Brando and James Dean. Each actor was attired in tight-fitting blue jeans and eating juicy hamburgers.

"Marlon was the sexiest," Joan later called, "Jimmy the moodiest and most brooding. P.L. was the most handsome and charismatic." Close friends of Paul's often called him P.L. His middle name was Leonard.

Collins once weighed in on rumors about Paul's promiscuity. "I believe he was totally faithful to Joanne in the many years of their love affair in spite of the fact that every starlet (and some stars) threw their caps at this charismatic, blue-eyed actor." At least that was Collins'

Joan Collins *Rallying!*
Ablutions for the dime-store Liz Taylor

297

public opinion. What she really thought is not known. By "stars," she may have been referring to Lana Turner, Judy Garland, Susan Hayward, Ava Gardner, and Elizabeth Taylor.

Carey and Collins had no love for each other. She later called him, "an old Hollywood has-been who seemed to have had a sense of humor bypass."

Collins liked the Newmans both socially and professionally. She had accompanied them to the Academy Awards presentation when Joanne had won the Oscar for *The Three Faces of Eve*.

Collins recalled that during the making of the film, Paul created the most delicious salad dressing, "which made the boring lettuce taste marvelous." He would later, of course, share that salad dressing with the world. "I was lucky enough to have been one of the guinea pigs who got to try that dressing out."

She later regretted turning down Paul's request to put her own image on the label of Newman's Own Virgin Lemonade—"for the obvious irony it lent."

She said that at the last party she attended with Paul late in life, the guests played a morbid game of suggesting their own epitaphs. With a beer in hand, Paul rose to his feet and quipped, "Here lies Paul Newman who died a failure because his eyes turned brown."

When Paul filmed scenes with Collins, she was amazed at his incredible intake of beer on the set. In one scene, he was actually drunk when he had to swing from a chandelier. A heavy drinker herself, she asked him if he ever got a hangover.

"Sure I do," he said, "but I take a cold shower when I wake up, then a hot, one, then another cold one, and then I dip my face in a tub of ice for five minutes. You gotta try it!" He also confessed that he did hundreds of push-ups and sit-ups every day.

She later recalled that in one madcap scene with Paul, she tripped and her ass came into intimate contact with Paul's face. He quipped, "Angela Hoffa [the name of her character], I'd know that face anywhere." The crew burst into hysterical laughter.

Once again Paul bared his skinny legs when Collins catches him alone in a hotel suite without his pants.

Other than Collins, Newman, and Woodward, Carey had assembled a talented cast, notably including Jack Carson who had just filmed *Cat on a Hot Tin Roof* with Paul. A shrewd and talented actor, "Jack could have played Paul's role in his sleep," Carey claimed. "Paul struggled day and night to get it right."

When Carson sat with Carey watching the rushes, he delivered an early critique at Paul's attempt at comedy. "Newman is full of hot shit," Carson told Carey. "The pukey, yellow, runny kind."

Carey agreed with Carson. "Newman plays it too broad," he said. "In some scenes he should be more subtle. I should force him to sit through some Jimmy Stewart and Cary Grant movies. At least Jerry Lewis won't have to lie awake feeling threatened by the competition."

Carson performed his own scenes flawlessly, playing an oafish Army officer who at the end of the picture is fired into space in a rocket.

Carey was much more impressed with Joanne's performance as Newman's wife, comparing her take on screwball comedy to that of the late Carole Lombard, Clark Gable's former wife.

In some scenes, Dwayne Hickman stole the picture. He was cast as a caricature of an American teen, spoofing Brando's black-jacketed motorcyclist in *The Wild One*.

Of all the cast, it was the doe-eyed, beautiful blonde, Tuesday Weld, who caught Paul's eyes. Cast as "Comfort Goodpasture," Tuesday played a nubile high schooler. "But with Sandra Dee waiting in the wings for me, and growing up every day, I'd better lay off," Paul said. "Besides, Joanne is here hawk-eying my every move."

Later in life, Tuesday starred with Steve McQueen in both *Soldier in the Rain* and *The Cincinnati Kid*. Paul later said, "I hope ol' boy Steve did the honors for me. I missed out on that one. Tuesday Weld is one delectable piece, and she looks hot to trot."

When Paul saw the completed film, he admitted to Carey, "I was weak. Joanne was more forceful. I loathed myself in it."

Time magazine seemed to agree with them, claiming the picture "fizzles like an overheated bottle of pop."

***

On the verge of buying out his contract with Warner Brothers, Paul agreed to make one final film for the studio that had held him in bondage for such a long time. He later said, "I had to make *The Young Philadelphians*. They had me trapped, but I knew from the start the picture was going to be a disaster."

What he really wanted to do was appear in a drama on Broadway early in 1959, playing Chance Wayne, the controversial hustler in Tennessee Williams' *Sweet Bird of Youth*. Even as Paul was shooting *The Young Philadelphians*, he was secretly meeting with

Some movie exhibitors claimed that this poster depicted fornication.

Tennessee to discuss his role in the play and possible actresses who might star with him. The playwright had originally wanted Marlon Brando and Tallulah Bankhead to star in his play, but both stars turned him down. "There's that Brando once again," Paul said, "One day I'm going to turn down a role and let Brando take my sloppy seconds."

Based on a novel, *The Philadelphians*, by Richard Powell, the film told the story of a bright young lawyer climbing the ladder of success. The long-time director, Vincent Sherman, had assembled an impressive cast. He'd once been known for seducing his leading ladies, including Bette Davis and Joan Crawford.

Lined up to co-star with Paul were Barbara Rush, Alexis Smith, Brian Keith, Billie Burke, and Robert Vaughn.

Paul took delight in meeting Burke, the Good Witch Glinda from *The Wizard of Oz*. In 1914, she married theatrical impresario Florenz Ziegfeld, soonafter realizing that both of them had a desire for chorines.

Paul was also cast opposite another bisexual actress, Alexis Smith, who played a married woman in the film. She had to pretend she had the hots for Paul. "She was about as attracted to me as Eleanor Roosevelt was to Jerry Lewis," Paul later recalled.

Barbara Rush was the genuine straight female of the film. At first Paul was prepared to dislike her, dismissing her as "mere window dressing," but he came to respect her talent which had often been buried in programmers, including such films with Rock Hudson as *Taza-Son of Cochise*.

Still Paul resented her, but didn't want to tell her why. Who he resented was actually her former husband, Jeffrey Hunter, whom she'd divorced in 1955.

Paul told Vincent Sherman, "If that God damn Hunter doesn't stop telling everyone he knows that I made a pass at him, I'm going to stick a fourteen-inch black dildo up his much overused asshole. He's the one getting plugged—not me. He thinks that by gossiping about me, it'll take the heat off himself."

As a footnote, Adam West, the future campy Batman, played a socialite in the film. On screen and on his wedding night, he proves impotent and commits suicide. "Sherman had the good taste to get rid of that West guy right away," Paul later said.

Brian Keith, who specialized in playing

Jeffrey Hunter with
Barbara Rush
"The threat of a 14-inch dildo"

300

gruff guys with a soft spot, also annoyed Paul. The actor had recently starred in a film, *Dino*, with Sal Mineo who played a troubled teen.

Somehow Keith had heard gossip about Paul's involvement with Sal, and he spread the word. "When I once visited Sal's dressing room during the shoot of *Dino*, I saw that he'd pasted six pictures of Newman on the wall, all shirtless," Keith told Sherman.

Perhaps Keith resented his role in *The Young Philadelphians* where he'd been cast as Paul's father, even though he was only four years older than Paul. "What is it with this stuck-up prick, Newman?" Keith asked Sherman. "I know he's had at least two facelifts. Sex symbol, my asshole. I bet my prick is twice the size of anything this aging Romeo has hanging."

Of all the stars in the film, Paul bonded more with Robert Vaughn, who was cast as his alcoholic ex-college buddy. In the film, when Robert is falsely indicted on a charge of murder, Paul agrees to defend him.

Paul even agreed to a screen test, but warned Vaughn that "I'll be off camera." Their big scene together was when Paul, playing a corporate lawyer, visits Vaughn in jail. The two actors had stayed up the night before, rehearsing for their big scene together.

To research his role, Vaughn, playing a Korean War vet and Main Line alcoholic, visited Skid Row, hanging out with winos who'd lost all hope. This diligence paid off. That year, Vaughn was nominated for an Academy Award for Best Supporting Actor.

On seeing the final cut, Paul detested his performance. "It's pure soap opera. I could have called in my performance."

Even so, *The Young Philadelphians* was the only film that Paul made for Warner Brothers that showed a profit.

***

On "the hottest day in the summer" of 1958, Paul arrived at the offices of Jack Warner. The studio chief had asked his employee, Ira Thomas, who took shorthand, to record the exchange between the two of them.

It was because of her later "loose lips sink ships" revelations that we know of that now notorious dialogue that took place between Paul and the studio chief.

Before Paul arrived for a show-

Robert Vaughn with **Paul Newman**
Hanging out with Skid Row bums

down, Warner had told Ira, "Not since Miss Bette Davis have I had to deal with such a temperamental star. The kid has hated every script we ever sent him. I want you to record every 'God damn' and every 'fuck you' he says. As for me, I plan to keep smiling through the entire interview and treat the scumbag faggot with great respect. I promise, even when things heat up, I won't call him a cocksucker. If he sat in my seat, Louis B. Mayer would call the prick a cocksucker. I must not lose any patience with my fellow Jew. But before this day ends, I predict I will have taken this blue-eyed pipsqueak to the cleaners where he's going to face the hottest pressing iron of his wasted life."

Confronting Paul that day, Warner did not challenge him about all the rumblings he'd heard about Paul's discontent. One of his associates had even told Warner that Paul referred to him as "fuck-face." The studio chief confessed he'd been called worse by his own brothers. "Fuck-face is a new one, however. Usually I'm known as 'the fucking Jew bastard.' Bette Davis even told me that she suspected my prick is so short that I wet my pants every time I take a piss. She claims that my little hose doesn't hang far enough from my zipper to do the job. I told her, in one of the few times I was not a gentleman, that I suspected her cunt was so big that men have to insert their entire heads, ears and all, in her vagina to bring her satisfaction."

"Now, now, Mr. Warner," Ira said. "Now, now. Let's not forget I'm a lady."

"Sorry," he said.

Ira, who made many revelations about the stars at Warner Brothers after she'd safely retired, claimed that Paul entered the office of Jack Warner, "his face a red purplish glow. He was obviously primed for a fight. But Mr. Warner disarmed him almost immediately. Using Joan Crawford's famous line, Mr. Warner had told me in advance, 'I've dealt with bigger shits than Paul Newman.'"

Warner was known for a skilled negotiating tactic whereby he immediately threw his victim off guard by making a startling revelation. As soon as Paul was seated before him, Warner surprised him by saying, "I just saved your career yesterday, though it cost me a bit of money. Not only that, I saved the career of your bitch."

"Don't call her that," Paul protested.

"Why not?" he asked. "The word is too good for her? I've called Bette Davis, Joan Crawford, Olivia de Havilland, and countless other broads bitches. These are women with far more talent than your wife."

"Okay, okay," Paul said, growing impatient. "Sure, Joanne can be a bitch at times, but that's not why we're here. And just how did you save our careers. This I've got to hear."

302

"*Confidential* was about to expose you and Woodward," he said. "They have evidence that you're a secret faggot and that she's a lesbian. That you married each other to serve as each other's beards. I paid them off to the tune of $20,000."

"That's about what I get from making a film for you or for a loan-out."

"You don't have to pay me back," Warner said. "My treat."

"You know, of course, that that *Confidential* reporter is a fucking liar. Joanne and I are very much in love."

"I know nothing of the sort," Warner said. "And I don't give a fucking nickel what kind of arrangement you two New Yorkers have with each other. I envy you. I only wish my wife was as understanding. From what I hear, you plug any hole available, and you don't inquire about the your victim's gender. But let's not talk about indiscretions. Let's get down to business. What's on your mind?"

"Why is it that ever since I set foot in this hell-hole you've given me every rotten script that has come along, beginning with *The Silver Chalice*? If there's a good role, you see that I don't get it. You've thrown nothing but shit at me."

Jack smiled. When exchanges became heated, he always sat back and smiled. It was part of his negotiating technique. He knew that Mayer, in contrast, would have been screaming by now.

"I haven't given you a really challenging script because you can't handle it. You're too limited as an actor. I've worked with the best of them, or at least seen their work at other studios. Paul Muni, now that's an actor. Bogie, James Cagney, Edward G. Robinson. I did pretty well with a guy named Marlon Brando. Surely you've heard of him."

"Let's stop the games," Paul said. "You've held me in bondage long enough. I want out of my contract."

"But you've got three years left," Warner protested. "I'm entitled to use you in whatever crap I come up with. Three years. After that, you'll be too old for romantic parts. I know that you were born in 1925. You were practically a middle-aged man when you arrived in Hollywood. You still look good, although if I were a homosexual, I'd probably go for the Errol Flynn type, not you. I must admit the fags and the ladies go for you when you take off your shirt. To me you look a bit puny. Believe me, Hollywood is filled with thousands of aspiring actors with greater chests than yours."

Paul rose to his feet. "How much do I have to cough up to escape from Warner's?"

"Just half a million meager bucks."

"I had twenty thousand in mind," Paul said. "Fifty thousand at the most."

The phone rang, and Ira answered it for him. "My God," she said. "It's Mae West on the phone."

"You've got to be kidding," Warner said. She's still alive. She used to be big."

"She's got this script," Ira said. "I heard she's shopping it around studio by studio."

"Okay, I'll take her call." Warner was the epitome of charm and graciousness as he picked up the phone. "My Little Chickadee, so good to hear from you."

Before launching into his talk with a fading star, he turned to Paul. All smiles had evaporated. "It's half a million—or else!"

Paul stormed out of the office, driving over to speak to his new agent, Lew Wasserman, a celebrated figure. Before their hour-long meeting ended, the shrewd Wasserman had advised him to go for it, although he promised to call Warner personally to see if he'd go down in his demands. "I know Warner, however, and once he utters a figure, his pride will force him to stick to it."

Before leaving the agent's office that day, Wasserman assured Paul that at the very minimum he could get $250,000 for his next picture if he broke the contract. He even held out the figure of $350,000. "In no time at all, you'll be able to pay Warner back."

"Get me out of that God damn contract," Paul said, standing up. "Let all of Hollywood know that from this day forth, Paul Newman is his own man. I'm on the auction block. For sale to the highest bidder." At the door, he looked back sternly at Wasserman. "Don't send over any more shitty scripts. I'm a star now, and I want only the pick of the litter."

***

Asked to comment on his return to Broadway, Paul said, "You wake up in the middle of the night and find yourself drenched in sweat. You have this terrible fear that your fraud will be discovered, and you'll be back in the dog kennel business. That's why it's good to work on Broadway as well as Hollywood. You know you'll get the hell kicked out of you once in a while, but if you don't you'll fall back on a lot of tried-and-true tricks an actor always has stashed away in his pocket."

Paul had just signed a contract to appear on Broadway in *Sweet Bird of Youth*, the latest play by Tennessee Williams, who was then riding the crest of a wave of success before entering a long decline in the 1960s.

Unknown to Paul at the time, Tennessee had first shown the play to Marlon Brando. After reading the script about the doomed hustler, a gigolo to a faded movie star, Marlon flew to Key West to discuss his possible appearance on the stage. He later dropped out when he learned that producer Cheryl Crawford and director Elia Kazan really wanted "pretty boy Newman" in the role.

Marlon later regretted that he didn't pursue the role of Chance Wayne more aggressively. "I know more about hustling than Newman," he said. He also regretted not having appeared in *Cat on a Hot Tin Roof* opposite Elizabeth Taylor. "I know more about being a homosexual than Newman," he said. "It's very clear to me that Tennessee modeled Alexandra del Lago after Tallulah. I surely know how to appear opposite Tallulah better than Newman. Besides, I hear my prick is bigger than his."

For the role of Alexandra Del Lago (aka Princess Kosmonopolis), Tennessee first offered the part to his dear friend, Anna Magnani, whom he'd visited in Rome. Producer Cheryl Crawford, later said, "Tenn must have been on something at the time. Magnani is all wrong for the part. The role calls for an American star, and the Hollywood Hills is full of women who can play has-been actresses. Lana Turner, Ava Gardner, Rita Hayworth, Lauren Bacall, and the beat goes on."

Magnani had never viewed a Paul Newman film, and she demanded to see an image of him. Frank Merlo, Tennessee's longtime companion, found a publicity shot of Paul and presented it to the Italian diva. She studied it seriously for a moment and then ripped it to shreds. "No! No! No!" she shouted at Tennessee. "I can't play with this man. There is no poetry in his face."

After Magnani wisely turned down the role, Tennessee presented it to Tallulah. After all, he'd written the part with her in mind. She read the script and told Tennessee that she'd seriously consider it. Immediately she wanted to know what actor would be cast as the gigolo opposite her. "Not Marlon Brando!" she yelled at Tennessee, puffing furiously on a cigarette. "I will never work with that bastard again. Do you know what he did during my long monologue in *The Eagle Has Two Heads*? He turned his back to the audience and urinated against the scenery."

"That's our Marlon," Tennessee said. "He can urinate on me any day he wants. No, it's not Marlon. I want that divine creature, Paul Newman, to play Chance opposite you. His golden velvet body was designed by God herself to grace pink satin sheets."

"I must meet this Apollo," she said. "I've only seen one of his movies, *Cat on a Hot Tin Roof.* After seeing him shirtless, I decided I must have him. After all, I went to Hollywood with only one purpose in mind—not to make those stupid movies I did, but to fuck that divine Gary Cooper. Why don't you arrange for me to meet God's new wonder? Have you had him yet, *dah-ling*?"

Tallulah Bankhead
"I must meet this Apollo."

"Not yet, Princess," he said, "but Bill Inge has. If Inge can get Newman, so can I. I'll place a hundred dollar bet with you that before *Sweet Bird* ends its run, I will have had him."

"You're on, *dah-ling*" she said. "I like bets. My whole life is a bet. Right now I'm betting against the clock. What type casting *Sweet Bird* will be for me. A fading has-been of an actress. Look at me, *dah-ling*. I *used* to be Tallulah Bankhead."

To his friends at Actors Studio, Paul recalled his first meeting with Tallulah. Upon being introduced to Paul by Tennessee, she went right to the point. "How big is your cock, *dah-ling*."

"That's for you to find out later tonight," Paul said.

"A promise I will hold you to," she said. "Come on in, dear one. I'm already seven drinks ahead of you pansies."

"I'm not a pansy," Paul protested. "I'm a happily married man."

"Oh, please, *dah-ling*, people are eating," she said. "Sit down and tell me all about your divine self. I'm especially interested as to why you haven't put out yet for my devoted friend here. After all, he wrote your greatest part in that *Cat* movie, and I think you'd owe him one."

Trying to be as sophisticated as this worldly pair, Paul looked over at Tennessee. "I do owe you one," he said. "But you can only have me from the neck down—and not tonight." He glanced toward Tallulah. "It appears that I'm going to be booked up this evening."

For three hours, Tallulah amused Paul and Tennessee with her quick wit and drunken charm.

"Oh, God, *dah-ling*," she said. "I've had everybody from Hattie McDaniel to John Barrymore. I struck out with Ethel Barrymore, however. When I propositioned her, she slapped my face."

As she went on and the drinking continued, she said, "I've tried several varieties of sex. The conventional position makes me claustrophobic, and all the other positions give me either a stiff neck or lockjaw."

By one o'clock both Tennessee and Paul were ready to leave. As they rose to bid her good night, Tallulah urged Tennessee "to run along into the night, *dah-ling*. I know you're meeting up with this new kid on the block—Warren Beatty, I think that's his name. He's going to appear in Bill Inge's *A Loss of Roses*. He also wants to audition for you. Good luck tonight. This Warren Beatty sounds divine."

Paul started to leave with Tennessee but Tallulah possessively grabbed his arm. "Not you, *dah-ling*. Tonight you're going to experience first hand what brought such enchantment to Sir Winston Churchill."

***

Tallulah later claimed she'd turned down the role and the chance to star opposite Paul because she'd already committed to do *Crazy October*, a play written by her friend James Leo Herlihy. Even though the playwright graciously offered to tear up her contract, she said she felt that "would not be right. If anything *dah-ling*, Tallulah is loyal to her friends," she said.

The role went to Geraldine Page, Paul's close friend from the Actors Studio.

Years later, Herlihy told the author of this biography, "I think Tallulah was afraid to go on the stage as Alexandra Del Lago. Tennessee had modeled the character on her, and she would have been better in the part. Let's face it: Tallulah is a debauched, drug-addicted ex-film queen, and Geraldine is not."

"With Paul Newman and Tallulah Bankhead starring in the same play, those two would have had theater-goers lined up for blocks," Herlihy predicted. "Incidentally, did you know that Tallulah, Tennessee, and myself all got our fifteen minutes of ecstasy with Paul? It was strictly a one-night stand for all of us. Notably, he never returned to any of our beds for a repeat performance."

One afternoon at the Actors Studio, Paul told Rod Steiger and Lee Strasberg, "In Tennessee's play, I'm a male whore. Guess who is giving me tips on how to play the character? Steve McQueen. In his teenage years, he had a lot of experience selling his meat to guys."

For the play, Kazan had assembled what was perhaps the most talented cast on Broadway during its 1959 season. Although she'd been considered too young for the part, Geraldine settled beautifully into the role of Alexandra Del Lago.

Even during rehearsals, she electrified the cast with her interpretation of this boozing, washed-up actress. Vain, insecure, and desperate, she played it with raw emotion, and she would well deserve her Golden Globe for Best Actress in a Drama.

Diana Hyland played Heavenly Finely, Chance's former girlfriend. In the play Chance takes Alexandra Del Lago back to his hometown in Florida to hook up with Heavenly again.

Before leaving town, he'd infected her with a venereal disease, forcing her to have a hysterectomy.

Heavenly is the daughter of Boss Finley, a brutal figure who rules the town. The role was played on the stage by veteran actor Sidney Blackmer. Rip Torn, who would later take over the role of Chance, was cast as Boss Finley's son and Chance's avowed enemy.

Torn and Geraldine would marry in 1963, a union that lasted until her death in 1987.

In a brilliant performance, Madeleine Sherwood was cast as Boss Finley's discarded mistress. Bruce Dern, who became a great drinking buddy of Paul's, was cast in a small role.

Making some excuse to Kazan and presumably to his family, Paul flew to San Juan for a long weekend with Tennessee. Both the actor and playwright were world-class drinkers, and they shared a deluxe suite together at El Convento Hotel. One old-time retainer there remembered them checking in.

Once when asked during an interview, Tennessee, as predicted, denied their weekend together. "I have never auditioned actors that way," the playwright claimed, although his statement wasn't true. "Besides, Paul Newman is too big a star to lie on the casting couch." Tennessee, of course, was referring to Paul's career-advancing moves in the earlier 50s when he became involved with both Bill Inge and Joshua Logan.

Frank Merlo revealed to Tennessee's friend, Stanley Haggart, and the author that one night during "pillow talk" Tennessee confessed that he had indeed serviced Paul one weekend. "I knew it would be my one and only chance to have him, and I took advantage of it, just as I did with Marlon way back in those early days in Provincetown."

Although Frank and Tennessee were lovers, they had an open relationship and talked about their lovers with each other. Paul sometimes spoke to his confidantes, but he never mentioned that San Juan weekend with his friends, so far as it is known.

"Let's just call it *The Lost Weekend*," he told Kazan upon his return. Paul was referring to a film Ray Milland made in 1945, where he'd won an Oscar for playing an alcoholic.

Tennessee also told Frank that after their weekend together, Paul warned him. "Now, God damn it, the next time you have a great part, you come to me, not Marlon Brando. Who's the man, baby?"

In his memoirs, *Elia Kazan, A Life*, the director didn't seem to know that Paul, his male star, existed

Paul as hustler
Chance Wayne
"Your body is designed
for satin sheets"

in *Sweet Bird of Youth*. But privately he told Tennessee that "Newman was too much of a pretty boy for the part. I'm going to dye his hair red to make him look more sleazy, and I'm also going to order him to get his hairline shaved. I want audiences to see him with a receding hairline. That will make him look over the hill. After all, he's playing a gigolo past his prime."

Initially Kazan had wanted Paul but after the first week of rehearsals he began to have his doubts. He feared that Paul was not adequately portraying the vulnerability of Chance. Then Kazan came up with a plan, although he knew it'd be brutal on the actor. He never gave Paul one compliment for his work, although he praised almost everything Geraldine did.

Years later Kazan confessed to Tennessee that he'd deliberately "cold-shouldered" Paul throughout the rehearsals.

"Chance Wayne is terribly insecure, uncertain of his mankind, possibly gay, and afraid of tomorrow. By destroying his self-worth, I'll make Newman a more believable Chance Wayne on opening night," Kazan said.

In spite of the brutal treatment during rehearsals, Paul had only kind words to say about Kazan, who had so intimidated him. "Kazan has broad shoulders, and his invention, patience, and imagination are extraordinary," Paul later said. "Not once did the man who'd directed Brando compare me to him, and for that I was God damn grateful."

Before opening night, Paul tried to hide his private time with Tennessee from Kazan, but he did make one confession. During one drunken night, he'd gone to bed with Geraldine Page. "I was always planning to do it, but we finally committed the horrible sin. We're both Method actors. We felt it would make our characters more believable if we knew each other as David knew Bathsheba."

Kazan congratulated him on his good judgment. Unknown to Paul, the director was not the best person to keep a secret. After Kazan's appearance before the House Committee on Un-American Activities, where he outed fellow Communists, Brando had nicknamed him "The Squealer." Kazan liked to discuss the private sex lives of stars he'd directed, including not only Brando but James Dean as well.

On March 10, 1959, *Sweet Bird of Youth* opened on Broadway at the Martin Beck

Paul Newman with **Geraldine Page**
Playing a male whore to a debauched actress

Theater. The play had a shattering climax when Boss Finley's goons come to seek their revenge on Chance for deflowering Heavenly. Led by Rip Torn, the bully boys of the Old South descend to castrate Chance, so he'll never again ruin the life of another young woman.

Even though Paul played a heel, there were tears in the eyes of some first-nighters when he delivered his climatic line. "I don't ask for your pity, but just for your understanding—not even that—no, just for your recognition of me in you, and the enemy, time, in all of us."

On opening night, Paul truly staged a *coup de théâtre.*

***

Paul received his best reviews to date in Tennessee's play about lost youth. So far, not one review has surfaced in which his acting was compared to that of Marlon Brando. Had he become his own man as an actor at last?

As the play became more deeply entrenched within its run, Paul received many visitors backstage, many of them world-famous stars. But on April 8, 1959 the most blessed visitor arrived in the form of an infant. Elinor Teresa Newman was born and named for two of her grandmothers. Paul and Joanne insisted on calling her "Nell." Paul was now the father—proud or otherwise—of four children, all of whom were girls except Scott.

Although he'd tried to bond with Scott over the years, father and son remained rather distant from each other. Scott adored his mother, Jackie, more than he did his father.

Scott always seemed to feel that Paul had betrayed his family "by shacking up with that Southern magnolia."

One of Paul's strangest visitors was an aging former hustler who sent Paul a note backstage inviting him to have a beer with him after the show. "I was the guy Tennessee based the character of Chance Wayne on," the note read.

Tennessee Williams
"Servicing" Chance Wayne

Paul was intrigued enough to allow the stage manager to show the man backstage. When Paul opened the door to his dressing room, he encountered a no-longer young man who looked unkempt, a kind of over-the-hill Tab Hunter. Somehow the years of heavy drinking and a wasted life had taken a toll, but, even so, Paul saw the remains of the hustler's former beauty.

He shook Paul's hand. "I'm Mitch Parker," he said. Once, when Frankie and Tenn

310

broke up, I filled in. Back in those days I could get a hundred a night."

Paul invited him across the street for a beer, and the two men talked until the bar closed down. He believed Mitch's story, and the former hustler had several snapshots taken of his life with Tennessee.

"I was actually castrated," he said. "That's where Tenn got the idea. It wasn't on the orders of a political boss. Back then, I let men do me for money, but I screwed gals on the side. I once got caught. That was in a town down on the Panhandle. The husband and some of his friends kidnapped me and took me to an abandoned cornfield where they cut my balls off. I had broken up with Tenn at that time. I wrote him begging for him to send me some money, but he never answered. I read in the paper about the play. It sounded familiar. I knew I was Chance Wayne. I never shacked up with a movie star, but I told Tenn about the year I lived with this rich woman in Boca Raton. She had once been a great beauty, but time had passed her by. I just know you're playing me."

"And well I might be," Paul said. It was getting late. Paul slipped him a one hundred dollar bill and watched him disappear down a rainy street in the Broadway district.

As he watched him go, he speculated on the fate of Chance Wayne at the end of the play. To him, the Chance Waynes of the world just seemed to disappear in the vastness of the American wasteland, perhaps escaping into an early death.

***

It was Tennessee who brought Ava Gardner to see the play. Perhaps imitating Ernest Hemingway, the playwright had always wanted to see Ava cast in one of his plays. Although somewhat pleased in the main with Geraldine Page's performance, he felt Ava would bring a "tragic loveliness" to the character of Alexandra Del Lago. He'd not been too happy that Geraldine was playing the role with a harpy's screech and looked rather blousy. He felt that the film version should present his character as a greater beauty, albeit faded.

At the end of the play, Ava told Tennessee that the role of Alexandra Del Lago "hits me in the belt. Did you base this character on me? I'm called a man-hungry movie star. I'm virtually retired now and certainly a has-been. That pill-popping and heavy drinking comes close to having been inspired by the life of Ava Gardner. The whole world knows that I ripped off Rita Hayworth's life in *The Barefoot Contessa*. Now it's time I got roasted."

Even so, she wanted to meet Paul Newman. "He's like so many men I've loved temporarily, then had to discard and move on to the next one."

Meeting Paul, she found him enchanting. "When you took off your shirt,

311

I swooned. I always wished Frankie had a better chest. All of his growth went into his cock."

He'd already been warned that Ava had a "potty mouth," so he wasn't at all surprised to hear that line coming from what he viewed as one of the most beautiful creatures on Earth. In some ways, he found her beauty more arresting than that of Elizabeth Taylor herself, or so he would claim later to his friends.

Tennessee invited Paul and Ava to join him in a little hidden tavern in the Broadway district where actors often gathered after curtains fell.

"So what did you think of our little drama tonight?" Paul asked Ava.

She was not a woman to mince words. "I'm from North Carolina, honey, a real Tarheel. We call a spade a spade. There's some pretty strong stuff here— a male whore, drug addiction, alcoholism, racism, venereal disease, and castration. That castration thing was a bit over the top. I shuddered to think America's reigning male sex symbol might be losing the source of his power."

"It gives me nightmares just to think about it," he said. "I find myself touching the family jewels every night just to see that they're still there."

"You need a beautiful woman to fondle them to reassure you that you're indeed still intact."

Tennessee later claimed he was rather insulted by Ava's critique. But in some ways she evoked the appraisal of Henry Popkin in the *Tulane Drama Review*.

"Williams now seems to be in a sort of race with himself, surpassing homosexuality with cannibalism, cannibalism with castration, devising new and greater shocks in each succeeding play. It is as if he is trying to see how far he can push the Gothic mode of playwriting."

Ava very accurately predicted that the writing would have to be cleaned up for the screen. "The day will come when Hollywood can present realistic drama. I want to be the first actress to use the word 'fuck' in a major motion picture, but Elizabeth Taylor will probably beat me to it, since every third word that comes out of her lovely lips begins with F."

Tennessee, who knew Hemingway only briefly from Key West, quizzed her about working on the adaptation of his novel *The Sun Also Rises*.

She spoke eloquently of the "last days" of Errol Flynn and Tyrone Power who had co-starred with her in the movie. Both stars would meet early deaths, Power in 1958, Flynn in 1959.

Ava Gardner
"A tragic loveliness"

312

Ava told Paul and Tennessee that she'd dated both Power and Flynn back in the Forties. "When they showed up on the set of *The Sun Also Rises*, both of them looked like old men. They had prematurely aged. You know, of course, they used to be lovers."

"I didn't know that," Paul said.

"They must have made a lovely couple," Tennessee said. "I think they were the most beautiful men I've ever seen on the screen." He flashed his famous grin at Paul. "That is, until this divine creature came along."

"Flattery has already gotten you everywhere," Paul quipped.

Quick to pick up on the innuendo, Ava said, "Oh, I see. You two fellows already know each other."

"Don't worry," Tennessee said. "The passage will not appear in my memoirs."

"Half of my lovers, including Howard Hughes and Peter Lawford, were secret cocksuckers," she said. "Rory Calhoun, when he wasn't fucking Lana or Marilyn, told me that what Hollywood needs is more good cocksuckers."

Tennessee laughed, but Paul did not. In some way, as he'd later confess, Ava was one of the most outspoken women he'd ever known. She far topped his wife in giving her candid opinions.

"Flynn especially was a spectacular wreck, not a magnificent wreck," Ava said. "He was far too gone to be magnificent at anything. I should know. We tried it again one night for old time's sake. Forget it."

"You'd be perfect for the role of a lost exile from Hollywood," Paul said, abruptly changing the subject.

"Oh, darling," she said, "I fear I am indeed Alexandra Del Lago and don't really need to play her in a movie."

"Perhaps some time with me would convince you," Paul said.

At that point, Tennessee jumped up from the table. "I'll pay the tab and leave you two love birds. He's good, Ava. Enjoy." He kissed both Paul and Ava on the lips before wandering into the night like some lost feathered bird.

No one knows for sure what transpired that night, because Paul and Ava, at least in this case, didn't indulge in Monday morning quarterbacking after Saturday's game. Tennessee, however, always maintained that they connected, at least for a one-night stand. "It must have been a lovely coupling," Tennessee said, "the world's most beautiful woman, a bit past her prime, coming together with the world's most beautiful man."

In spite of their night together, Paul did not convince Ava to play Alexandra Del Lago, so they could at least continue their love-making on screen. He did tell Elia Kazan that Ava Gardner "is one of the world's most fascinating creatures. She *is* Venus." He might have been referring to her 1948 film, *One Touch of Venus*.

In 1964, Ava finally agreed to do a Tennessee Williams film, *The Night of the Iguana*, based on his Broadway play which had starred Bette Davis as Maxime Faulk. Davis had appeared in a wig so bright red she could have been mistaken for Lucille Ball.

Tennessee was intrigued with the idea of Ava playing opposite Paul as the lecherous, defrocked priest.

Over dinner at a Hollywood tavern, Ava expressed her reluctance to follow Bette Davis' stage interpretation of the role.

Ava told Paul and Tennessee that she had once met Davis when she was checking into a hotel in Madrid. "I rushed up to her and introduced myself. I told her how enthralled I was to meet her. She looked at me skeptically, almost like a queen eyeing one of her subjects. 'Of course, you are,' she said to me before walking on."

Paul showed a strong interest in the role opposite Ava, but his prior commitments did not match the shooting schedule. Eventually, the role went to Richard Burton instead.

Finally, for the 1972 release of *The Life and Times of Judge Roy Bean*,

---

The Life and Times of Judge Roy Bean

An illustrious cast on a bad hair day:
Paul (upper left) **John Huston** (upper right), **Tony Perkins** (lower left), and **Tab Hunter** (lower right)

314

Paul and Ava came together in this First Arts Production directed by John Huston and co-starring Victoria Principal.

The film was significant for another reason. It brought Anthony Perkins back for a reunion with two of his former lovers—Tab Hunter and Paul himself.

On the set, Ava told Paul that she'd regretted turning down the role of Alexandra Del Lago. "We would have made a great team," she predicted.

Cast as Lily Langtry, mistress to the English king Edward VII on a holiday in America, Ava and Paul reunited as long-lost friends on the set. A photographer snapped their picture sitting together, his head cradled in her ample bosom. Huston jokingly told the crew that Paul and Ava were bosom buddies.

Ava's truce with Paul had the life of a sickly butterfly. When she invited him back to her hotel room for the night, he told her, "I'm an old married man and faithful to my wife these days."

That infuriated Ava. "That will be the day," she screeched at him.

"The second time around with Paul didn't pan out," Huston said. "She became even more furious when word reached her that Paul had called her 'predatory.'"

After her scenes were shot, she told her old friend Huston, "Paul Newman is one of my least favorite actors in all of Hollywood. Believe me, I've known all the shits, but he's the biggest shit."

"Ava, dear one, Marilyn sang it all. 'We all lose our charms in the end.'"

"Fuck you!" Ava said, before disappearing inside a limousine to take her back to Los Angeles.

***

Lana came back into Paul's life when she became one of the many actresses flying into New York to see and evaluate Tennessee's new play. There weren't that many great parts for aging actresses, and Lana wanted to see if she felt comfortable doing the role before making a play for it back in Hollywood. "After all," she told Tennessee, "MGM owes me a few favors. I practically saved them from bankruptcy in the 40s."

Over a drink at Sardi's before the curtain went up on *Sweet Bird of Youth* that night, Tennessee and Lana laughed

Ava Gardner as **Lily Langtry**
Love is never better
the second time around

315

about his former days at MGM when he'd been assigned to work on the screenplay of *Marriage Is a Private Affair* that was set to star her. Although he fretted for days over the project, he ultimately could not relate to the plot, joking to friends that he was working on a "celluloid brassiere for Miss Turner."

"What happened to you at MGM?" Lana asked Tennessee.

"The studio heads finally decided that I was not going to produce a screenplay for you," Tennessee told her. "They then assigned me to a scenario about Billy the Kid. That was more Gore Vidal's fantasy—not mine. Then they asked me if I wanted to create a scenario starring Margaret O'Brien. I told them where they could shove Little Miss Margaret. Finally, MGM and I parted ways."

"Finally, MGM and *I* parted ways, too," Lana said. "But I may come back if I get cast in your *Sweet Bird*."

Throughout the performance of *Sweet Bird of Youth*, Tennessee noted that Lana studied Geraldine's every movement and expression "like a hawk."

Lana told Tennessee she'd loved the play but, like her best friend, Ava Gardner, she feared it would have to be "cleaned up" for film audiences.

She was all charm and grace when Tennessee escorted her backstage for a reunion with Paul. Right in front of Tennessee, she kissed Paul. It was a long and lingering open-mouthed kiss that forced her to repair her makeup in front of Paul's dressing room mirror.

"I'm in New York all alone," she told Paul.

He wasn't sure where her other lovers—or could there be a husband?—were. He'd lost track of her many entanglements. "I need someone by my side at all times," she said. "I'm so dependent on a man. But aren't most women like me?"

"I can definitely assure you that most women aren't like Lana Turner," Paul said.

"I've always been alone," Tennessee said, not revealing his many companions over the years. "I have always depended on the kindness of strangers I meet along the way."

It was agreed that Tennessee would take both of them to dinner at Sardi's before retiring for the night. Lana wanted

Lana Turner with her old flame
Ronald Reagan
"A celluloid brassiere" from Tennessee

to go dancing later, and Paul agreed to be her escort.

At Sardi's later in the evening, all heads turned as Lana walked in with Paul on one side, Tennessee on the other.

This famous trio did not talk about *Sweet Bird*, but listened to a startling sexual confession by Tennessee. He claimed he was going to Cuba.

"You'd better stay out of there," Paul warned him. "You could be kidnapped and held for ransom."

"If that's what it takes to meet Fidel Castro, I will take that risk," he said. "I've got this powerful crush on Fidel Castro. I dream at night of getting raped by him. If it takes a kidnapping for me to meet my idol, I'm willing to take that risk."

This was no idle boast on Tennessee's part. His friend, Meade Roberts, once claimed, "Tenn wanted to be kidnapped by Castro—also by Ché Guevara, another one of his fantasies. He'd had the hots for them when that pair was still outlawed and hiding in the Sierra Maestra, kidnapping Americans for ransom. Tenn thought very seriously about getting himself into a situation like that—*anything* to meet Castro."

Lana told Tennessee that she found the idea ghoulish and feared for his safety. Later she'd tell Paul that she thought the playwright might possibly be insane.

"Like all great artists," he countered.

After dinner with Tennessee, Lana, in a limousine with Paul, went to a night club uptown. As the stunningly beautiful couple entered, a hush fell over the patrons. She looked gorgeous, sheathed a clinging white evening gown that was slit high up the side and low down the front. Her blonde hair was cropped short.

Dancing in Paul's arms, she told him, "Everybody is looking at us. We'd make a fabulous pair on the screen."

"Everybody is looking at *you*," he corrected her. "To attract attention, I think I'll have to take off my jacket, shirt, and undershirt."

"Later, darling," she whispered into his ear.

Paul did not share details of his later visit to Lana's hotel suite. He'd seduced her before, finding her clinging and desperate.

Even though he didn't give a blow-by-blow description of what happened

Guerilla fighters **Ché Guevara** and **Fidel Castro** Tennessee's fantasy kidnappers

that night between Lana and him, he did share an intimacy two nights later when he had a drink with Tennessee.

"As I was leaving her suite the following morning, she held me close and delivered a shocker. 'You may not know it now,' she said to me, 'or even tomorrow. But one day in the not-so-distant future you are going to become my next husband. Note I said next and not last husband.' With that tantalizing remark, she shut the door in my face."

***

Paul was stunned when he received a note from the stage door security guard. He was used to beautiful movie stars arriving backstage to greet him, often on the pretense of wanting to appear as Alexandra Del Lago in the movie version. He told Frank Sinatra when he came to visit one night that he felt that many of these glamorous stars "are just coming backstage to hook up with me so that they can fuck me."

Sinatra laughed at the remark, telling him that an entire lineup of screen queens, ranging from Joan Crawford to Ingrid Bergman, had arrived at the stage door to greet the new sensation of Broadway, Marlon Brando, when he appeared in *A Streetcar Named Desire*.

"Fuck those broads who appeal to you and tell the rest of them to go home and use a dildo," was Sinatra's advice.

One note that arrived was the most startling of all. Not from a women, it was from Elvis Presley. Once again.

Was he still bitter over not being allowed to appear as Brick in *Cat on a Hot Tin Roof*? Intrigued, Paul told the guard that he'd meet Elvis when the curtain went down. In a return reply, Elvis told him that he'd be waiting outside in a white limousine, its windows darkened so that fans could not peer inside to discover him.

After the show, one of Elvis' "boys" opened the back door of the limousine and ushered Paul inside where Elvis was waiting, swigging blackberry brandy directly from the bottle. "Haul your ass in here, kid," Elvis said. "I'll take you for a ride."

"Another pissing contest?" Paul asked. "Don't tell me you want to play Chance Wayne in the movie."

"No more pissing," Elvis said. "You won that round. We've got some serious business to talk over tonight. And, yes, MGM has offered me the role of Chance Wayne. Fuck what Col. Parker says. I'm gonna play that male whore. As a film star, no one takes me seriously considering the shit I do." He swigged more from the brandy bottle. "But that day is gonna change."

"Actually I think you might be great as a hot-headed redneck male prostitute," Paul said.

"Thanks for the compliment," Elvis said. "Hal Wallis wanted me to appear in *The Rainmaker* with Katharine Hepburn and Burt Lancaster. I was set to do it, but the deal fell through. All the serious roles I've been offered I never got to do. That scumbag Parker saw to that. He sabotaged every deal."

In the suite of the king of rock and roll, Paul confronted a much more mature and rather bitter Elvis, not the man he'd encountered before. He continued swigging the blackberry brandy, but he was also popping pills. Paul suspected the drug was Seconals, viewed as relatively harmless in the late 50s.

Years before, Elvis had been considered quite the Southern gentleman, but the star tonight was snapping orders at his staff. He was rude and flashing a bad temper, but not at Paul, whom he continued to treat with respect.

"Col. Parker is a bloodsucker," Elvis claimed, "and he's virtually ruined my film career with junk movies. This time, thanks to Chance Wayne, I'm gonna defy the fucker."

"I got to ask you," Paul said. "Why am I here? I have no control over casting. If you want the part, you've got it. You're the hottest thing in town. I think you opposite Ava Gardner would be the biggest grosser of the year."

"Ava Gardner," he said. "I've never fucked her. Frank Sinatra told me he'd cut off my dick if I plunged into that succulent pussy."

"This time no pissing," Paul said. "If you want the role, it's yours. I'd love to play Chance Wayne on the screen, but it's yours for the asking."

"That would make me a heel," Elvis said, before turning to one of his boys from Memphis. "It's time my best friend here and I did some serious drinking. Get us a pitcher, asshole. We're ready to start chug-a-lugging screwdrivers."

Elvis turned his attention to Paul again, where his voice became softer. "I'd be a fucking son of a bitch if I took something you wanted," Elvis said, standing up and starting to pull off his clothes. "That's why I'm here to make a deal with you. I just learned that MGM is willing to pay you $350,000 for starring as Chance Wayne. Elvis is going to offer you $350,000 for NOT being Chance Wayne. You can find an even better script that will also pay you $350,000. That means you can double your money. Sounds God damn fair to me."

He continued to strip down to his jockey shorts. "I'm not trying to turn you on, although I know you go for the boys. My masseur has arrived. I'm taking youth treatments. Would you believe I'm starting to sag a little bit here and there. After all, I was born in 1935."

Elvis Presley
Trespassing
on the family jewels

"Want to hear an even sadder story?" Paul asked. "I was born ten years before that."

Two of Elvis' boys wheeled in a hospital bed with a curtain around it. They were followed by a masseur who looked a bit effeminate. "I know Fido here doesn't look like much of a man, but he's got the most skilled hands of any masseur in America. He's from Haiti. A High Yaller."

The mulatto smiled at Paul and motioned for Elvis to go behind the curtain. Pulling down his jockey shorts, Elvis stepped inside and apparently got up onto the bed. From behind the curtain, he continued to talk to Paul, who sat on the sofa enjoying the best screwdriver he'd ever tasted in his life.

After fifteen minutes of conversation, Paul heard Elvis scream, "You god damn cocksucking faggot." He stormed outside the curtains, knocking the masseur in the face. The masseur fell to the floor as a nude Elvis, boasting a semi hard-on, started kicking the young man in his ribs.

Two of Elvis' boys suddenly appeared and restrained him. "Get that faggot out of here! He was trying to jerk me off." A third member of Elvis' boys emerged with a red silk robe which he slipped on. "Better give him $10,000 to buy him off so the queer won't sue me."

And then the screen goes black. Two hours before the next performance of *Sweet Bird of Youth*, Paul was relating the story about his encounter with Elvis to Geraldine and Kazan.

They were interrupted, and Paul never finished his story of what had happened earlier that evening with Elvis.

In panic, Tennessee Williams came rushing down the aisle. "I'm dying!" he shouted. "I've just come from my doctor. He says I have inoperable cancer. I'm dying! This is the last play I'll ever write."

This was the beginning of fifty such outbursts from the playwright, each announcing his imminent death, until inevitably that day of doom arrived.

***

After the fantastic success of *The Three Faces of Eve*, Joanne continued her losing streak by making *The Fugitive Kind*, co-starring Marlon Brando and Anna Magnani. To a small Key West movie theater, the author of this biography accompanied Tallulah Bankhead and Tennessee Williams to a showing of the film. At the end of the screening, Tallulah rose to her feet and boomed in a voice loud enough to be heard in the back row, "TENNESSEE, THEY'VE MADE A PERFECTLY AWFUL MOVIE OUT OF A PERFECTLY AWFUL PLAY."

Without uttering a word, Tennessee ignored Tallulah and left the theater. That night, he didn't show up for a dinner staged in her honor. She flew back to New York without a reconciliation with him. Weeks would go by before he returned her calls. "Like a loving puppy dog, Tennessee would always return to Tallulah's side for more punishment," recalled novelist James Leo Herlihy.

Originally Tennessee in 1940 had offered his play, *Battle of Angels,* to Tallulah, but she had rejected it and denounced it. Even so, a friendship had formed. In time, Tennessee would take *Battle of Angels* out of mothballs and rework it under the more pretentious title of *Orpheus Descending.* The movie producers insisted on changing the title to the more commercial *The Fugitive Kind.*

For his role in the movie, Brando was offered an almost unprecedented million dollars. When he contracted to do the role because he desperately needed the money, Brando told the director, Sidney Lumet, "I'll have to eat a shit sandwich made by Tennessee Williams himself." Paul, however, envied the paycheck since the part would have gone to him had Brando rejected it.

In a touch of irony, Paul had once performed in a scene from *Battle of Angels,* playing the sexy drifter, Val Xavier (Brando's role), which had led to Paul's acceptance as a player at the Actors Studio.

Joanne shocked audiences—what few there were—when she appeared on the screen playing an alcoholic nymphomaniac with white pancake makeup and kohl-rimmed eyes. She would later claim, "Hated the movie, loved Anna."

There was no love lost between Brando and Joanne. Brando was rude and uncooperative. At one point Joanne complained to Lumet, "There's nothing there for me to reach out to. He's a complete blank regardless of how much money he's hauling in for this turkey."

Perhaps Brando was punishing Joanne because of her marriage to Paul. For reasons known only to Brando at the time, he was furious with Paul. Carlo Fiore, Brando's best friend, later speculated that he knew the reason for Brando's discontent.

For the first time, many movie reviewers were no longer regarding Paul as Brando's clone. One reviewer, in praising *Cat on a Hot Tin Roof,* claimed that "Paul's performance is far greater than Brando, with all his mutterings and mannerisms, would have been in the role." According to Fiore, Brando feared that Paul would soon surpass him.

"To piss off Newman," in the words of Fiore, Brando spread the

Left to right: **Anna Magnani, Marlon Brando,** and **Joanne Woodward** in *The Fugitive Kind.* Spreading vile rumors

321

rumor that he was "shacking up" with Joanne during the filming of *The Fugitive Kind*. There isn't the slightest clue that this was true. "Marlon loved making Newman squirm," Fiore said.

It was rumored that Joanne had dated Brando briefly in 1953. Both Tennessee Williams and his companion, Frank Merlo, claimed that Paul had told them during the stage run of *Sweet Bird of Youth* that he suspected that Brando had at some point in the early 50s seduced his wife.

"For some reason this thought tormented him, even though he was unzipping all over Broadway at the time," Merlo said. "Paul felt the gander could play around and have his fun in the barnyard but that the goose should stay home nesting on her eggs."

By the time Brando was playing opposite Paul's wife, the intimacy between Brando and Paul had faded into something akin to a youthful indiscretion. However, they would remain superficial friends for years to come, especially when they bonded together to march for civil rights.

The Fugitive Kind, as predicted, flopped at the box office, signaling a long, slow, steady decline in Brando's career, which, except for a few shining moments, would see one disaster piled on top of another. Paul could not gloat too much, because a long string of box office disasters, mixed with some memorable hits, also awaited him.

Whatever Paul thought of *The Fugitive Kind*, and chances are it was unfavorable, he kept his critique to himself. He turned down a reporter's request for a "review of" Joanne emoting with Brando. As she moved forward into her second pregnancy, Joanne stated her lofty ambition to the press. "I want to be the best actress in the world. The best wife. The best mother."

***

Sweet Bird of Youth ran on Broadway for 375 performances.

Paul recalled his last performance as Chance Wayne at the Martin Beck. "I remember my last night going to the theater. I swallowed two jiggers of honey for energy and my throat. I felt completely exhausted. I must have been in the hot shower for thirty minutes. I broke down and started crying like a baby. It came to me: I'd never say Tennessee's words again. I'll never have that kind of quiet near the end of the third act. Never that specific kind of quiet, as a hush came over the theater."

Toward the end of the run of *Sweet Bird of Youth* on Broadway, Paul signed to do the film, *From the Terrace*, eventually released in 1960, for $200,000. During the day in New York he would be filming, but at night he'd return to Broadway to appear on stage as Chance Wayne.

Once again, Paul traveled back to the fictional setting of Philadelphia for his role of David Alfred Eaton, who moves from Philadelphia to the canyons of Wall Street, climbing the ladder of success as his marriage crumbles.

Starring with him was both his on-screen and off-screen wife, Joanne. Already they were becoming known as the husband-and-wife team of the screen, although they did not like to be known as such.

Playing his "true love" in the film, Ina Balin appears as a mysterious page in Paul's off-screen life. She is remembered mainly today for co-starring with Elvis Presley in his 1969 film *Charro!*

Paul felt she was a sympathetic soul, and he shared much in common with her, especially when it came to helping children.

On the first day Paul met Balin, she revealed a bit of trivia about his own career. Before Gene Kelly and Natalie Wood signed for *Marjorie Morningstar*, it was originally slated to star Paul Newman and Ina Balin.

"Those two got on beautifully together during the making of *From the Terrace*," director Mark Robson recalled. "It was obvious to me they were attracted to each other, but with Joanne around I don't think anything came of it. At that time in his life, Paul was playing a game with his buddy, Steve McQueen, to see how many of their leading ladies each of them could seduce."

Robson speculated that had Paul not already been married to a woman he loved, he might have found in Balin a soulmate who shared his goals and dreams.

In 1970 Balin toured Vietnam with the USO. This would be the first of many trips she'd pay to this war-torn part of the world. She was there during the fall of Saigon in 1975 when she aided in the evacuation of orphans. Eventually, she would adopt three of these homeless children.

In 1990, when Balin was dying from pulmonary hypertension, Paul drove to visit her in New Haven, Connecticut, a secret, personal journey.

Robson also said that Paul seemed embarrassed when George Grizzard showed up on the set one day to appear in his role as Lex Porter. "I'd heard those two guys had been an item in New York," Robson said. "But they were totally professional together. In spite of the depth of their intimacy, they behaved more or less like two college alumni coming together. Yet I sensed the tension between them."

Ina Balin with **Presley** in *Charro!*
From Paul's soulmate to
"Arms around Elvis"

Paul renewed his acquaintance with writer Ernest Lehman, who'd written *Somebody Up There Likes Me*. Paul told Robson he found the script "creaky."

Although he struck out with *From the Terrace*, Lehman over the course of his screenwriting career received six Academy Award nominations.

Paul also complained about Robson's "weak direction. He was a bit full of himself."

Robson had reason to gloat, having been nominated for an Oscar for directing *Peyton Place* with Lana Turner and again the following year winning the same honor for directing Ingrid Bergman in *The Inn of the Sixth Happiness*.

Playing Paul's alcoholic mother, veteran actress Myrna Loy stole every scene she was in. The first day she arrived on the set, she found her dressing room bare, but flowers kept arriving in Paul's dressing room all day. She would later recall the nadir of her career.

"While Cary Grant and Clark Gable romanced Grace Kelly and Sophia Loren on the screen, I mothered Paul Newman in *From the Terrace*. It's a man's world."

Paul joined her for lunch, showing her his greatest respect. "My dear," she said, "there was a time back in the 1930s when I was the biggest female movie star in America. Today that seems like a distant dream."

At the end of filming, Paul approached Myrna, giving her a long, lingering kiss, which rather surprised the crew looking on. She told him, "After today I guess I'll sit by the phone hoping it will ring."

After *From the Terrace*, she would wait around nine years for another movie role, when she returned to the screen in *The April Fools*, released in 1969.

When Paul saw the final cut of *From the Terrace*, he was not pleased with his performance. "What else is new?" he asked. "I'm not pleased with any of my screen performances." Usually her own harshest critic, Joanne was more favorably disposed to her screen appearance. She told friends, "I looked like Lana Turner. That day will

Myrna Loy
"I remember it well..."

never come again."

The film was essentially another soap opera, but it did fair returns at the box office. Once again Paul had to read in *The New Yorker* that in the lead role he "is a dead ringer for Marlon Brando, complete with built-in pout."

***

When they did return to Hollywood, Paul and Joanne rented a house from Linda Christian, who at the time was called "the world's most seductive woman."

Linda is noted today for being the first Bond girl. She appeared in a 1954 TV adaptation of the James Bond novel *Casino Royale*.

Seduced by Errol Flynn, she later married his lover, Tyrone Power. In Linda's garden stood a nude statue of herself.

Meeting briefly with Paul, Linda joked about her tabloid reputation. "When it comes to men, I'm always the pursuer. Only once have I failed to interest a man. Cary Grant."

"Gay, perhaps?" Paul asked.

The Newmans settled into the house with their daughter, Nell. "Another baby's in the oven," Paul told friends.

[While Paul was filming *Sweet Bird of Youth*, Melissa Newman would enter the world on September 17, 1961, Paul's fifth child and his second daughter with Joanne.]

In the long gestation period it took to bring Tennessee's play, *Sweet Bird of Youth*, to the screen, Paul received a call from Orson Welles. It surprised him because the talented director/actor had made his distaste for Paul known during the filming of *The Long, Hot Summer*.

Speaking to Paul, Welles was at his most charming. It soon became apparent that he was shopping for the proper vehicle in which to star his former wife, Rita Hayworth. "She'd make the perfect Alexandra Del Lago," Welles predicted. "The screen requires a softer, gentler Del Lago, not that brash harridan Geraldine Page played on the stage."

In some ways, Paul agreed with him. When Welles invited Paul and

The Battling Newmans:
Joanne confronts **Paul**
"I looked like Lana Turner."

Richard Brooks, the upcoming director of *Sweet Bird*, to Rita's house, Paul eagerly accepted, although Welles explained that he would not be present at the gathering.

Paul had always wanted to meet Rita, as she'd long been on his A-list of stars he planned to seduce. When in the Navy, he'd had a pin-up of her pasted to his locker door. In some ways, he found Rita far more enticing than Ava Gardner, a comparable beauty.

When Rita graciously received Brooks and Paul into her home, he was struck by how different she was from her screen image as best showcased in the 1946 *Gilda*. She was dressed simply in slacks and a blouse and wore little makeup.

Time had been a bit cruel to the Love Goddess of the 1940s, a vivacious, sexy, and desirable woman known for her sunny smile and the come-hither glint in her eye. In many ways, today's Rita would be perfect as a fading movie star. She *was* a fading movie star.

During their time with Rita, Paul and Brooks met a realistic, straight talking woman without the glamorous moves of Lana Turner, who could never stop playing Lana Turner even when the cameras were turned off for the night.

If anything, there was something very wholesome about Rita, in spite of her bizarre marriages, not only to Orson Welles himself, but to Prince Aly Khan. He'd read that after her divorce from the Argentine singer, Dick Haymes (whose marriage had lasted from 1953 to 1954), she'd married producer James Hill. But Hill was nowhere in sight.

Paul complimented her on her performance in *Pal Joey*. "Do you know that Mae West was originally offered the part?" she said. "Mae probably could have done it better."

"I doubt that," Brooks said.

Linda Christian. landlady to the Newmans Home runs with Errol Flynn and Tyrone Power, strike-outs with Cary Grant

Brooks and Paul talked about Rita appearing in *Sweet Bird of Youth*, but later when the two men discussed it together, they expressed their beliefs that she didn't really want to appear as the fading actress, but had been cajoled into meeting with them because of Welles. Still in love with Rita, he was trying to jump-start her dying career.

Her reddish auburn hair looked as lustrous as ever, but she was smaller than she appeared onscreen. Her maid kept supplying her with highballs, and Paul matched her drink for

326

drink. Brooks held back.

"As Alexandra Del Lago, I can be what I am, a fading star," she said. "I might as well let it all hang out. Somehow people seem to think I'm as old as Joan Crawford and Bette Davis. I started so young—that's why they think that.

"*You Were Never Lovelier*," Paul told her, evoking the title of her 1942 movie.

"Thank you, dear," she said. "I've had a lifetime of compliments, but now they fall on suspicious ears. I know what I look like. I know what time it is. Like Alexandra Del Lago, I, too, am battling that old enemy, time."

"Would you be our Alexandra?" Brooks asked.

"Let me think about it." She turned to Paul and took his hand, holding it up to her cheek. "This beautiful man here and I could light up the screen, like Glenn and I did in *Gilda*." She was referring, of course, to her frequent co-star, Glenn Ford.

The maid came back into her living room with three more highballs, but when she started to hand a drink to Brooks, Rita motioned for her not to. "If you have to go, I understand," Rita said. Brooks did not have to leave so soon. "I'd like Paul to remain behind. We can sit in my garden and talk about appearing on the screen together. It'll give us a chance to discover each other. I think in this role I can show the world I have some depth. All my life Rita Hayworth has had only a few good moments, everything else was about image."

At the door, she kissed Brooks on the cheek. "Thank you for coming, dear one," she said. "We'll see if this offer leads to anything." He noticed that she was holding Paul's hand at that point.

"Well, you two take care," he said.

Brooks was the source of information about the meeting between Paul and Rita, and the director knew nothing of what happened after he left. Paul never confided in him. In a few weeks, Metro-Goldwyn-Mayer rejected the idea of casting Rita.

Brooks' last memory of Rita was her standing with Paul at the doorway and looking into his eyes. Her gaze was penetrating, yet somehow suspicious. Her final statement was somewhat enigmatic. He would remember it for years.

"Before the night is over, I must convince Paul I'm not *Gilda*."

Rita and **Orson** headed for divorce
"You were never lovelier."

327

***

It would not be until 1962 that *Sweet Bird of Youth*, in a "castrated" version, reached the screen, starring Paul Newman and Geraldine Page. Repeating their Broadway roles were Rip Torn and Madeleine Sherwood. Ed Begley contracted to play Boss Finley in the film version, as did Shirley Knight to appear as Heavenly, the girlfriend. The very talented character actress, Mildred Dunnock, was assigned to the role of Heavenly's Aunt Nonny, who is sympathetic to Chance.

Signing a contract to appear as Chance Wayne in the film, Paul made his best financial deal yet, getting $350,000 for his performance, plus a percentage of the take. He'd finally arrived on the A-list of movie stars, where he would remain for a very long time.

Because of studio pressure, Richard Brooks was forced to water down the original script, just as he'd been ordered to do in *Cat on a Hot Tin Roof*. Instead of a castration, Chance suffered a beating at the hands of Boss Finley's goons.

Instead of being infected with a venereal disease, Heavenly undergoes an abortion instead. The biggest change, and one that infuriated Tennessee, was the happy ending Brooks added to the film. Heavenly and Chance run away,

Paul as an international star in *Sweet Bird of Youth*
Decadence knows no borders

presumably toward a happy future, although that hardly seems likely after what has come down before.

Sweet Bird of Youth, advertised as HE USED LOVE LIKE MOST MEN USE MONEY, premiered on March 21, 1962. Unlike the play, the vanilla film version of Tennessee's drama bombed, as audiences stayed away in droves. For the most part, film critics panned the movie. But when it came time for Academy Award nominations, *Sweet Bird*, in spite of its flaws, was not ignored.

The film brought Academy Award nominations for some of its actors, including Geraldine Page as Best Actress in a Leading Role. She would lose that year to Anne Bancroft, who appeared in *The Miracle Worker*. Shirley Knight was nominated as Best Actress in a Supporting Role. But it was Ed Begley, nominated as Best Actor in a Supporting Role, who walked off with an actual Oscar.

It took more than a quarter of a century for *Sweet Bird of Youth* to open in a theater in London's West End. It premiered on July 8, 1985, at London's Haymarket Theatre. Lauren Bacall, formerly known as "Bogie's Baby," played the role of Alexandra Del Lago. She was certainly typecast as a faded film actress.

In a foolish decision, Elizabeth Taylor in 1989 agreed to star as Alexandra Del Lago in a remake of the film. She captured none of the nuances of Geraldine Page and gave one of the flattest on-screen characterizations of her career.

Casting actor Mark Harmon as Chance made the few viewers who watched the 1989 version of *Sweet Bird* realize just how good Paul and Geraldine had been in the original, both on stage and on the screen.

***

In Los Angeles, a call came in to Paul shortly before midnight. "This is Otto Preminger," came the famous Viennese voice. "You are one lucky boy. I've just decided to cast you as a great hero, a Hagannah leader, Ari Ben Canaan. You will lead the Jews to the Promised Land."

Paul started to say something, but Preminger cut him off. "Not now. Be in my office at ten o'clock tomorrow morning. By the way, don't bring Joanne Woodward to Israel with you. I've already cast your co-stars. Many choice specimens for you to fuck." He slammed down the phone.

Three faces of **Alexandra Del Lago**

Left to right: **Lauren Bacall, Geraldine Page,** and **Elizabeth Taylor**

Chapter Nine
The 4-H Club:
The Hustler, Hud, Harper, & Hombre

Temporarily abandoning her own career, Joanne, along with Paul and their baby daughter, Nell, flew to Israel for the filming of *Exodus*, sections of which would eventually be shot in Cyprus.

The director, Otto Preminger, had heard rumors about Paul's private life. He quipped, "Miss Woodward is no doubt protecting her own interests. Maybe she doesn't trust Newman in the desert with all those hunks I've cast in the film—Sal Mineo, John Derek, Peter Lawford, and George Maharis. Each one of those guys is a homosexual's dream. With Eva Marie Saint, there is no sexual threat. She and Paul are old friends—good chums—from way back, nothing more. I'd bet my left nut on that if I hadn't already lost it to a quack surgeon."

Later, Preminger would claim, "All the gay boys in my film, or should I call them switch-hitters, were after Newman. They circled him, like sharks wanting to devour a tasty meal. Fortunately, he brought Woodward along as a security guard."

Before leaving for Israel, Preminger had negotiated with Lew Wasserman, Paul's agent, who wanted $200,000 for his client. "Too high," Preminger said. "I'll give him half."

"Fine," Wasserman said, without further negotiation. "It's a deal."

The novel by Leon Uris had been a bestseller. Rights to the film were originally purchased by MGM for $75,000. Fearing an Arab boycott of MGM films because of its pro-Israeli stance, MGM finally turned the property over to Preminger. As an independent producer, he would be relatively immune from a threatened Arab boycott. The story depicted the plight of Jews who had to fight their way to sail from Cyprus to Israel on a ship called *Exodus*.

In Tel Aviv, Preminger handed a copy of the finished script to Paul. The director told him that he'd launched the project with Uris himself but had to fire him. "He was hopeless. A novelist writes dialogue to be read. A scriptwriter writes dialogue to be heard." Preminger than hired Dalton Trumbo, the blacklisted writer.

Like Ben Hecht, Trumbo was one of the notorious "Hollywood Ten." He was forced to write under various pseudonyms to avoid the blacklist.

Later, when Trumbo's version of *Exodus* was released, Uris denounced it to the press. "That dictator [meaning Preminger] ruined my book."

The morning after he'd read the finished script, Paul confronted Preminger with six pages of suggestions. He'd done that with each of his previous directors, and the technique had been successful in implementing changes. But it didn't work with Preminger.

Paul had extensively rewritten passages of dialogue uttered by his character, who in the movie falls in love with an American nurse and befriends an Arab.

"Very interesting suggestions," Preminger said to Paul, without even reading them. "If you were directing the picture, you would use them. As I am directing the picture, I won't use them." He tore up the sheets of paper handed to him by Paul, dropping the shattered bits at Paul's feet.

"Fucking Nazi," Paul later told Peter Lawford.

In Tel Aviv, Preminger introduced Paul to Prime Minister David Ben Gurion. Paul also met Golda Meier and General Moshe Dayan, members of the ruling Labor Party. They told Paul how disappointed they were with the script, objecting to Israelis being portrayed as terrorists. Preminger countered their argument by claiming that during the birthing of a Jewish state in 1947, violence had been inevitable.

From New York, Sal Mineo had called Paul in Los Angeles before his flight to Israel. "Here I am, a WOP from the Bronx, playing a Jew," Sal said. "I hope no one finds out I'm not circumcised."

"Your secret is safe with me," Paul said.

Sal protested Paul's commitment to bring Joanne on location. "Here is my chance for us to have some time alone together. With her tagging along, my

(Above, left to right): **Sal Mineo, George Maharis, John Derek,** and **Peter Lawford**
In praise of bisexual men.

332

plans are now fucked."

"Too bad," Paul said. "She's determined. She knows that men stray when wifie is away."

"I know nothing about any wives," he said. "To me, a girl is someone to grab hold of only when a photographer from a fan magazine is nearby."

"See you in Israel," Paul said, hanging up.

In the movie, Sal had been cast as Dov Landau, a seventeen-year-old survivor of the Warsaw Ghetto and Auschwitz who had been "used" by the Nazis.

In the movie's most controversial scene, Sal tells his interrogators what the Nazis did to him. "They used me. They used me like you use a . . . a . . . woman."

Hope Bryce Preminger, Otto's wife and the costume coordinator on *Exodus*, called Paul "a cold man. He was remote from the minute he walked onto the set and remained icy throughout the entire shoot. On the plane from Cyprus to New York after the film had been shot, he told Otto, 'I could have directed the picture better than you.' Could you imagine saying that to Otto Preminger of all people?"

Jill Haworth, making her film debut in *Exodus* at the age of fourteen, later said, "At a certain point deep into the filming, Paul would not even take direction from Preminger. Paul was more or less directing himself, and that led to some regrettable mistakes."

When Paul wasn't needed on the set, he and Joanne toured Israel. "We were trailed by dozens of people wherever we went," he said. "You might have thought we were Marc Antony and Cleopatra returned from their tombs. These fans acted like they'd never seen movie stars before, which was probably true. To make matters worse, Joanne could not find the proper blonde dye. The roots of her hair were turning black. A God-awful state for a 'true' blonde."

Paul's biggest insult in Israel came not from Preminger but from Mrs. Ben Gurion. Right to his face, she said, "For a Jew boy, I don't think you're all that pretty. We have far more handsome boys right here in Israel. I don't know why Preminger cast you in the lead when we have many home-grown actors who would have been better suited for the role."

Months later, when the controversial film was released, the Arabs, as predicted, dismissed it as Zionist propaganda. Critics also dismissed Paul's performance as "stiff," "wooden," and "lacking in depth and emotion." Even so, it grossed more at the box office than any of his previous movies.

The New York Times had kind words, calling it "a

Otto Preminger
A "Nazi dictator"
in Israel

dazzling, nerve-tingling display that rips the heart." Britain didn't interpret the picture as breathlessly, however, since that country's soldiers were depicted as anti-Semitic.

One reviewer wrote that Paul's role should have been played by Charlton Heston, not Newman. "At least the fucker didn't say Marlon Brando," Paul quipped.

Variety weighed in with this: "Technically, Paul Newman gives a sound performance, but he fails to give the role the warmth and deep humanity that would give the character distinguished stature." That review more or less summed up the opinion of most of the world press.

Of all the actors in *Exodus*, including its director, only Sal Mineo emerged triumphant. He received an Academy Award nomination as Best Supporting Actor for his role as the bitter Jewish boy who joins an Israeli terrorist group.

The final word on Paul's appearance in *Exodus* was uttered by Joanne in London. She told a TV reporter for the BBC, "Paul can't stand to talk about *Exodus*. Or even think about it."

***

Some aspects of the private relationship between Paul and John Derek during and after the making of *Exodus* remain clouded in mystery. On several occasions in the city of Haifa at the Hotel Zion during the filming of *Exodus*, Paul was spotted leaving Derek's bedroom. Interpreting the role of Taha, an Arab, Derek was cast as a *mukhtar*, a life-long friend of Paul's character, Ari Ben Canaan.

When word first reached insider Hollywood that Derek and Paul might have become an item, in spite of Joanne's highly visible presence during the shooting of *Exodus*, many people could not believe it. After all, John Derek was a certified womanizer, and is remembered today not so much for his movie roles, but for being the husband of such beautiful actresses as Ursula Andress, Linda Evans, and Bo Derek.

Adela Rogers St. Johns, the columnist, was far more sophisticated in these matters than her rivals, Louella Parsons and Hedda Hopper. She weighed in on the possibility of an affair between Derek and Paul. "All the big-time womanizers in Hollywood, including Clark Gable and Errol Flynn, even Howard Hughes, always had a pretty boy locked up in the closet somewhere," she claimed.

John Derek
Matching motorcycles

It wasn't until years after the release of *Exodus* that some of the behind-the-scenes maneuverings were revealed. Paul was not the source. In the 1950s, he had shared a number of his private experiences with close friends like Eartha Kitt and Janice Rule.

"At one point, Paul just clammed up," said Tony Perkins. "I felt free in talking about my private life with him, but he was no longer forthcoming with details about his affairs. He remained my friend, but I obviously had lost a confidant."

It was Sal Mineo who first revealed what had happened during the filming of *Exodus*. "Paul just dumped me the moment he set eyes on John Derek," claimed Sal Mineo in an apartment in New York's Chelsea district. "It made me wonder what Derek had that I didn't have."

Sal confessed that for the duration of the filming, and in an attempt to make Paul jealous, he turned to the bisexual actor, Peter Lawford, the brother-in-law of John F. Kennedy. This Rat Packer, an on-again, off-again friend of Frank Sinatra, began an off-the-record affair with Sal that would last for about three convoluted years.

"I still loved Paul," Sal told the author, "but Peter was making love to me at night. And Peter was the Nijinsky of oral artists."

At first revealed in Darwin Porter's *Katharine the Great*, a biography of Katharine Hepburn, John Derek, then known as Derek Harris, had once hustled men. One of his clients had been Spencer Tracy, Hepburn's long-time bisexual companion. Derek had been born the son of writer/director Lawson Harris and bit actress Dolores Johnson.

Derek had shot like a cannonball to short-lived stardom when he played an incarcerated juvenile delinquent on death row in Columbia's *Knock on Any Door* (1949), opposite Humphrey Bogart.

Long after the end of their involvement with *Exodus*, Paul and Derek would remain bosom buddies. As late as 1969, a maid had discovered them in a motel in eastern Oregon one morning when she walked in on them, claiming that she had found them making love. She had tried to sell her tale to scandal magazines, but there were no takers.

Paul had escaped to Oregon that summer. He was hanging out with loggers and getting "the lay of the land" before filming *Sometimes a Great Notion*, based on the novel by Ken Kesey, who'd recorded the saga of an Oregon logging family.

The son of a dairy farmer in Colorado, Kesey was a novelist much admired by Paul, who had wanted to appear in a film based on his first novel, *One Flew Over the Cuckoo's Nest* (1962). A counter-cultural icon, Kesey viewed himself as "the missing link" between the Beat Generation of the 1950s and the hippies of the late '60s. "I was too young to be a beatnik," he said, "and too old to be a hippie."

The actual film as we know it today would not be shot until 1970, on scenic locations near the Oregon towns of Lincoln City and Newport, on the watersheds drained by the Siletz and Yaquina Rivers.

That previous summer, Paul had rented a retreat in western Oregon on a little peninsula that shot like a finger into the Pacific. He and Derek spent many a bucolic evening together in Oregon.

During the day Paul could be seen working with loggers, preparing himself for his upcoming role. In the late afternoon, Paul and Derek were observed on matching motorcycles roaring through the countryside.

That summer in Oregon Paul resumed his heavy drinking—consuming not just beer but large amounts of vodka as well. He and Derek were spotted in various local taverns.

Following examples established by James Dean, Paul was taking wild and reckless chances on his motorcycle. In one accident, he was injured so badly he had to be flown to Los Angeles for X-rays. Back in Oregon, he resumed riding his cycle, even though he had one foot in a cast. At a breakneck speed, he had yet another accident. Amazingly, his already injured foot wasn't damaged further.

When the filming of *Sometimes a Great Notion* began, Paul had to take over both the film's direction and its starring role when he became disappointed with the early rushes directed by an inexperienced director, Richard Colla.

Paul had veteran actor, Henry Fonda, to costar with him in the film, playing his cranky old father. In spite of their utter lack of chemistry during the filming of *The Long, Hot Summer*, Paul cast Lee Remick to play his wife.

She later recalled, "Newman, like Steve McQueen, was known for seducing his leading ladies. I can assure you that this is one leading lady who never slept with him. He turned me off."

"The one big scene I had in the movie was a love bout with Michael Sarrazino, who played Leland Stamper, Paul's half brother in the film. There was nudity in my love scene with Michael. But Newman cut it before release. Thank God I played that scene with Michael instead of Newman. There was no way I wanted to get in bed jaybird naked with Newman. The film in its second release was retitled *Never Give an Inch*. That would have been an appropriate title for Newman's relationship with me."

At long last, Paul got to work with Richard Jaeckel, with whom he'd had an affair in the 1950s. Richard Jaeckel was flown from Los Angeles to Oregon to appear as his cousin in the film. His character plays a drowning man who is trapped under a fallen tree in the water.

Originally, George Kennedy, no great beauty, had been cast in the role. But Paul nixed the idea. "If I'm gonna spend three days shooting an extended kissing scene with another guy, it's gonna be Richard Jaeckel. He's one good looking mother fucker, and I always promised him we'd work together. I'd throw up if I was forced to go lip to lip with George Kennedy."

Paul was referring to the most dramatic scene in the movie. As the tide is rising and Jaeckel's character is about to drown, Paul breathes gulps of fresh air to blow into Jaeckel's lungs. It's really a kissing scene, Paul's only mouth-to-mouth encounter with another male on screen.

Henry Fonda claimed that "Jaeckel and Newman kissed each other for hours." Then he turned catty. "I think those two continued to practice that scene late at night long after the cameras had shut down for the day."

When one suspicious Hollywood reporter encountered Jaeckel and asked him about his prolonged mouth to mouth with Paul, the stocky actor said, "Paul saw me playing football one day on the beach with friends in Malibu. He thought I had the right build for the part of a logger in the North Woods."

For his work in kissing Paul, Jaeckel received an Academy Award nomination. "Nice work if you can get it," Jaeckel said.

In spite of the critical and financial failure of *Sometimes a Great Notion*, Paul still believed in the film. According to friends, when the Academy Award nominations were announced, he was furious. In spite of the overwhelming odds against him, he still expected an Oscar not only for Best Actor but also for Best Director.

"Who do these upstart new actors think they are?" Fonda said upon hearing this. "Paul Newman is no Erich von Stroheim."

One wonders what Fonda meant: When *Notion* was released in 1971, Paul could hardly be called "new" in Hollywood. Yet Fonda thought so little of *Sometimes a Great Notion* that he didn't even mention it in his memoirs.

"Paul Newman and Jane [a reference to his daughter Jane Fonda] should do a film together," Fonda said. "The director could strip them down for most of the film. With those two naked on the screen, they might attract some sort of an audience."

Paul Newman with
Richard Jaeckel
"If I must kiss a man..."

***

In 1961 Elizabeth Taylor seriously considered starring in the tiresome two-character piece, *Two for the Seesaw*. The play by William Gibson had been a medium-sized hit on Broadway for 750 performances between 1958 and 1959 when it had starred Henry Fonda and Anne Bancroft.

For its mutation into a movie, the producers

wanted a bigger box office name than Bancroft for the female lead, and they turned to Elizabeth who entertained the idea. Robert Wise, who'd directed Paul in *Somebody Up There Likes Me*, suggested that he would be ideal as the sullen, self-hating Nebraska lawyer who gets involved with the eccentric "born victim" character of Gittel Mosca.

By reteaming Elizabeth and Paul, Wise was perhaps hoping to repeat the success of their first pairing in *Cat on a Hot Tin Roof*.

Paul went to see the play and found it mildly amusing, although he felt that the man's role was weak and that Elizabeth, playing a dancer living in Greenwich Village, would steal the film. The prospect of appearing with Elizabeth again intrigued him, as he'd always believed she was not only one of the world's most beautiful women but one of its most fascinating.

Elizabeth had never left his life, as he had encountered her randomly as the years had passed. Usually these encounters were disastrous. Paul had looked on helplessly as Elizabeth had mired herself in her marriage to Eddie Fisher. Paul had referred to her mating with Fisher as a "mess."

The 1960s had arrived and Fisher's career was faltering. He was even talking of becoming his wife's producer, evoking unfavorable comparisons to Mike Todd, a real producer.

Connecting with Elizabeth in a private meeting, unknown to either Joanne or Fisher, Paul had a frank talk with Elizabeth, assuring her that he'd be honored to work with her again.

Most of that time was spent talking about Eddie Fisher. Janet Charlton, the columnist, had jokingly revealed that Elizabeth was threatening to write a memoir devoted to Fisher. Charlton claimed that Elizabeth was calling it *Louse*, and in her confessional "she might even claim that Fisher is impotent."

At this time Paul had yet to make *Sweet Bird of Youth*. Elizabeth startled him by confessing that only two weeks previously, she'd met with Tennessee and that he'd practically begged her to play the aging movie star has-been, Alexandra del Lago, in *Sweet Bird of Youth*.

Of all the actresses considered, Elizabeth was the last person Paul would have cast in the role. He told her so. "You're at the peak of your power and beauty," he said. "No fan will believe you in the part unless you put on thirty pounds and paint wrinkles on your face.

"Perhaps you're right," she said.

Instead of gaining weight, Elizabeth had been on a crash diet. Joseph Mankiewicz, who'd directed her in *Suddenly Last Summer*, in which she'd starred with Katharine Hepburn and Monty Clift, had told her that her upper arms looked like "a bag of dead mice." She was so horrified that she went on a diet the next day after a night of getting drunk and cursing Mankiewicz.

Speaking confidentially with Paul, she admitted that her marriage to

Fisher had been "the biggest mistake of my life."

When she met Paul, Elizabeth was still bitter over her loss of an Oscar for her role in *Suddenly Last Summer*. She contemptuously referred to Katharine Hepburn, her co-star, as "a fucking dyke." Hepburn had also been nominated for an Oscar, which meant that she'd split the vote with Elizabeth, thereby paving the way for a win by the French actress, Simone Signoret, who took home the Oscar by default for *Room at the Top*.

Paul had not met privately with Elizabeth for quite a while. He'd always seen her with her people. Such was the case when she invited him to the Desert Inn in Las Vegas to catch Fisher's act during a two-week engagement.

Paul later told his associates that Fisher was "shamelessly exploiting Elizabeth," insisting that she sit at the ringside table. "Fans were coming to see Elizabeth, not Eddie," Paul claimed. He sings all his numbers to her, and she blows him kisses."

That night Paul was also invited to the Sands Hotel where his friend, Kirk Douglas, was celebrating his seventh wedding anniversary to his second wife, Anne—a union that would continue for at least another 50 years, despite well-publicized infidelities on his part. Frank Sinatra arrived with Marilyn Monroe. Paul tried to talk to Sinatra, but he seemed distracted.

To Paul's dismay, Marilyn was incoherent. He wasn't certain that she even knew who he was.

She'd swallowed so many pills, which she'd consumed with a massive intake of alcohol, that she was actually drooling. Paul took a napkin and wiped the slobber from her mouth.

When Sinatra took to the stage to sing a tribute to Kirk and Anne Douglas, Marilyn disrupted his act. Sitting at ringside within reach of the stage, she pulled off one of her high heels and started pounding the stage. Sinatra signaled his handlers to remove Marilyn from the room.

Paul followed the guards, who carried Marilyn to her hotel room. After the guards had left, he stripped her down and put her to bed. She was still mumbling incoherently, denouncing Joe DiMaggio for some alleged insult in a recent phone call.

When she seemed to be sleeping peacefully, he slipped out of the hotel.

The next morning, suffering from a hangover, he received a phone call from Marilyn, who had apparently recovered from the previous evening.

She cried into the phone. "I called Frankie, but the bastard won't speak to me. He said I made a spectacle of myself last night and embarrassed the hell out of him."

"He'll get over it," Paul assured her. "Sinatra's made an ass of himself on many a night. He can't hold that against you."

"You're sweet," she said. He turned down her invitation to make love to her that morning. But he did accept her invitation to visit her at a mansion in Beverly Hills the following week. She didn't tell him who owned the estate, but she said she was in residence there for a week, and she wanted to meet with him there.

She told him that she had read a "dynamite" script, and that she'd suggested to its producer, Jerry Wald, that she wanted Paul to co-star with her in the production.

He pressed her for details, but she refused to divulge any insights, claiming they would read the script together when he came to visit her the following week in Los Angeles.

"At long last," Marilyn predicted, "us two beauties will be up there lighting up the screen as it's never glimmered before. That is, if both of us aren't too drunk to play our roles."

***

A few hours later, he received an invitation from Elizabeth. Having discovered that he was having an affair with a Las Vegas showgirl, she'd had a knock-down fight with Eddie Fisher, and she had kicked him out of her suite.

"What a *schmuck!*" Paul said. "He's got Elizabeth Taylor in his bed, and he's running around with some cheap hooker."

When Paul arrived at her suite, a maid directed him to Elizabeth's bathroom. There he was startled to find her in a bubble bath. She invited him to take off his clothes and join her. She told him that she liked to make love in the tub, claiming that it alleviated her back aches. "When Eddie can get it up, he fucks me in the tub and it seems to help. So let's go for it, big boy."

We're left only to imagine the outcome of that encounter. What we know was pieced together with a cackle by Tennessee Williams one night in Key West when the playwright told his guests what he'd learned about that Las Vegas trip from both Paul and Elizabeth.

"When she told me about Paul, she also informed me that she wouldn't be appearing in *Sweet Bird of Youth*. That is fine and dandy with me—my grandfather used to use that expression," Tennessee told his drunken dinner guests. "But actually, Ava Gardner would probably be more effective in the role of Alexandra Del Lago."

The novelist, James Leo Herlihy, a guest at Tennessee's dinner party, assured Tennessee that "there are dozens of fading actresses living in the Hollywood Hills who'd give their left tit for a chance to play that role. You might even consider Geraldine Page herself."

The leading role of Gittel in the film version of *Two for the Seesaw* eventually went to Shirley MacLaine, cast opposite Robert Mitchum. Anne

Bancroft later said, "I'd have given anything to make the movie of that, but it got away from me."

Ironically, Elizabeth had also been the first consideration to star in the film version of *The Miracle Worker*. United Artists had wanted Arthur Penn, the director, to "dump" Bancroft in favor of Elizabeth. He held out, claiming that only Bancroft could handle the role of Annie Sullivan, as she'd already demonstrated so brilliantly in the Broadway play.

***

Two for the Seesaw almost cost Paul his chance to film *The Hustler*, one of his most memorable roles. Because of delays with *Cleopatra*, Elizabeth was not free to accept the female lead in *Seesaw*, and the role, as mentioned, was eventually awarded to Shirley MacLaine, with Robert Mitchum accepting what would have been Paul's role.

While still filming *Cleopatra*, Elizabeth contacted Paul, claiming how sorry she was that they would not appear in *Two for the Seesaw*. She sent her love and promised that she'd get together with him "the next time I have a severe backache."

She held out the hope that they would still reteam on the screen when a great script came along. "If you find roles for us in the right property, don't walk. Come running."

In a few short years, Paul would see a play on Broadway that he believed would make a perfect joint vehicle for Elizabeth and himself. It was Edward Albee's controversial *Who's Afraid of Virginia Woolf?*. That play also starred George Grizzard, the actor with whom Paul had had a fling several years previously. But Paul did not go backstage that night to congratulate George on his performance.

Paul felt that the part of a dysfunctional academic and his embittered wife would be idyllic for him and Elizabeth, a refreshing change of pace from roles with which they'd previously been associated. He called her, and she came to the phone at once.

With a certain eagerness, he told her about the play, asking if she'd had a chance to see it yet. "Yes, as a matter of fact, I have," she told him. "You'd be terrific in the part—I just know it. But it's too late. Richard and I have already signed contracts to star in it."

She, of course, was referring to her husband,

Elizabeth Taylor
How to cure a backache

341

Richard Burton. "Next time, cute stuff," she said. "Our day on the screen will come, I just know it."

Bitter at the rejection, he said, "Let's make sure it's sooner than later. Otherwise, we'll end up playing grandpa and grandma."

***

After a series of critical and commercial disappointments, Paul needed a good strong role. He told his agent, "I've got a lot of mouths to feed, and I need a hit—a box office bonanza."

His wish came true when director Robert Rossen chose him to play a pool shark, "Fast Eddie" Felson in *The Hustler*, based on a novel by William Tevis.

The Hustler would be the first of four movies that Paul made in the 1960s, each of whose names began with an "H." These included *The Hustler*, *Hud*, *Harper*, and *Hombre*.

Paul looked forward to working with Rossen, who had scored a big hit with Broderick Crawford in *All the King's Men* in 1949. Rossen, who was dying at the time from a terminal illness, was staging a kind of Last Hurrah with *The Hustler*, and he desperately wanted it to be a great picture.

After reading the script, Paul felt he could play a loser like Fast Eddie on his self-destructive path.

For Paul's back-up team, Rossen had assembled a formidable cast. Jackie Gleason was cast as Minnesota Fats, who was hailed as the greatest pool player in fifty states. Piper Laurie, freed from those horrible Technicolor "Westerns in the sands" pictures of the 1950s, was cast as Eddie's girl, Sarah Packard. The role had been offered to that "lavender blonde," Kim Novak, but she'd rejected it.

After he'd signed the contract, Paul learned that he was not the only actor who'd been considered for the role of Fast Eddie. Unknown to him, Frank Sinatra had originally optioned the novel, acquiring the film rights. But as it happened, Sinatra didn't like the finished script, claiming "it has too many pool halls, not enough raw emotion."

The part was then offered to Jack Lemmon, who turned it down.

Jackie Gleason with **Paul Newman**
Minnesota Fats vs. Fast Eddie

Cliff Robertson, always Paul's rival for roles, tried to convince Rossen that he was right for the part of the pool shark, but Rossen wasn't convinced. The director continued to consider other actors.

On several occasions Rossen had mentioned Paul as the possible lead, but had dropped the idea when he'd learned that Paul had signed to act in *Two for the Seesaw*. When Paul unexpectedly became available, Rossen called him at once, touting what a great role Fast Eddie would be for him. After mulling it over, Paul agreed. Regrettably, Rossen had promised another actor the lead but had not yet signed him.

On the set Paul had a reunion with Piper Laurie, who had co-starred with him in *Until They Sail*. The actress hadn't worked in four years, and *The Hustler* marked her return to the screen.

Rossen later said that he felt "Piper and Paul had great respect for each other. Paul was known for seducing some of his leading ladies, but I don't think he scored with Piper. Now Ronald Reagan and Piper—that's another story."

Paul found George C. Scott, also cast in the movie, a formidable personality. He'd scored a big hit in *Anatomy of a Murder*, and seemed headed for stardom as one of the most dynamic, uncompromising new talents to hit the screen in years. With his gravelly voice and stern features, he was cast as Paul's cool, smarmy promoter, for which he'd receive an Academy Award nomination. He became the first actor to go on record as refusing the nomination.

Paul bonded with Gleason, and even challenged him for a real-life game of pool. A world class pool player, Gleason handily won. Paul had gotten a little cocky and had overestimated his ability as a player.

To prepare for his role as Fast Eddie, he'd worked with the world champion pool player, Willie Mosconi, learning the fine art of the game. In the film, close-up shots of Mosconi's hands would be used.

Rossen directed that *The Hustler* be shot in New York within a context of seedy hotel rooms and dark pool halls. Paul later said, "Both Rossen and I knew we were making a great movie. I gave it my best. The character of Fast Eddie was foreign to me, but I inhabited his skin."

Even before the film was

Paul Newman with **Piper Laurie**
"reality instead of dreams"

officially released, word had spread that the picture was a winner. Fearing bankruptcy, 20th Century Fox, its producer, was desperate for a hit. The making of *Cleopatra*, starring Elizabeth Taylor, had driven them to a very high cliff. In spite of the early good reviews of people who'd seen rushes of *The Hustler*, Fox executives were still worried about box office. "All that pool hall crap will turn off female viewers," predicted one chieftain.

Just before the official premiere, Richard Burton had hosted a midnight screening of *The Hustler* for the cast of various Broadway shows. Paul's fellow actors, including those from the Actors Studio, gave him rave reviews. The actual world premiere was held in Washington, DC, on September 25, 1961.

Critic Roger Ebert wrote that *The Hustler* is "one of the few American movies in which the hero wins by surrendering, by accepting reality instead of dreams."

Paul came up with his own review. "It's a film that hits you in the gut with a punch that knocks you out."

The Hustler opened to good box office throughout the country. On the decline for decades in America, the art of playing pool came back into vogue.

Early in 1962 it was announced that *The Hustler* had been nominated for Oscars for Best Picture, Best Actor (Newman himself), and Best Director among other nods.

On the night of the Academy Awards, Paul was a heavy favorite. Both Maximilian Schell and Spencer Tracy were competing for the Best Actor award for their joint appearances in *Judgment at Nuremberg*. Historically, two frontrunners nominated as Best Actor (or Actress) in the same picture will tend to cancel each other out.

The honor of announcing the Oscar winner for Best Actor went to Joan Crawford, the nemesis of Joanne Woodward. One reporter noted Paul's reaction as the names were read. "He was a ball of fire and looked like he was about to break free of his skin. It was obvious: he really wanted that Oscar."

When Schell's name was read by Crawford as the winner, "Paul masked his pain and broke into that cheesy grin of his," the reporter claimed.

Paul would later tell *Playboy*, "I was really hurt by the loss." As compensation, he would win the British Academy of Film and Television Award as Best Actor. *The Hustler*, in the British sweepstakes, would emerge as Best Picture.

Ever the gentleman, Paul did not want to appear as a sore loser on Oscar night in Los Angeles. He went backstage and congratulated Schell. "Many Oscars await you in your future," Schell assured him. "This was my only chance—I just know it."

In contrast to Paul's impeccable behavior, Joanne did not experience her finest hour. She even refused to speak to Schell. Those who stood near her claimed she "threw a fit" upon hearing Crawford announce Schell's name. Joanne was heard cursing and crying.

"How awfully tacky of her—and so typical," Crawford said upon learning of this, using the opportunity to deliver yet another attack on Joanne. "She'll never work in this town again after the spectacle she's made of herself. She's also ugly to boot. I can't see what Paul Newman sees in her." Crawford was repeating her familiar refrain.

Speaking strictly off the record later that evening at a party attended by Rosalind Russell and Jennifer Jones, Crawford said, "It's true that many homosexuals marry ugly women. The poor dears are so delighted that anyone will marry them that they dutifully stay at home while hubbie is out turning tricks at night."

Even though Paul emerged from *The Hustler* as a full-fledged Hollywood star, he still hadn't reached the pinnacle of "Top Ten" at the box office. That position, among others, was reserved for actors who included Elizabeth Taylor, Rock Hudson, and Doris Day.

Even so, producers from all over the world were trying to cast him as the male lead in their films.

Federico Fellini didn't want Paul for *La Dolce Vita*, but his producers did. Paul wisely turned down the role, knowing he was wrong for it. The part went instead to Fellini's friend, Marcello Mastroianni, playing the tabloid reporter who sees his life as worthless in shallow Roman society, but is unable to change it.

Paul's career would soar in the 1960s. The other artists who'd worked on *The Hustler* didn't fare so well. Gleason was never again offered a Grade A film role. Piper Laurie left the screen until 1976 when she came back with the hit movie, *Carrie*. Robert Rossen died in 1966 at the age of fifty-seven, after having completed one final picture, *Lilith*, two years previously.

After *Lilith*, Rossen lost interest in directing. During the making of the film, he'd had several grueling conflicts with its star, Warren Beatty. "It isn't worth that kind of grief," he told reporters, announcing his retirement. "I have nothing to say on the screen right now. Even if I never make another picture, I've got *The Hustler* on my record. I'm content to let that one stand for me."

Right before his death, he said, "At long last, Paul Newman is a star in his own right. In the future Marlon Brando will be accepting roles that Paul has turned down—not the other way around."

***

If one fast-forwards nearly a quarter of a century, to the mid-1980s, Paul would finally get his Oscar for Best Actor, in 1987, but there would be near-misses along the way. He'd be nominated for *Absence of Malice* in which he was directed by Sydney Pollack and cast opposite Sally Field. Paul had won the role by default after Al Pacino had dropped out.

Filmed in Miami, *Absence of Malice* was released in 1981. Henry Fonda, nearing the end of his life, was awarded the Oscar for *On Golden Pond*, a picture he'd made with his daughter, Jane Fonda, and Katharine Hepburn.

Paul almost got lucky again when he filmed *The Verdict*, released in 1982 and directed by Sidney Lumet. Paul was considered the heavyweight favorite, but the prize for Best Actor went instead to Ben Kingsley for *Gandhi*.

While filming *The Color of Money,* Paul learned that he was to be awarded an honorary Oscar by the Academy of Arts and Sciences. He was not thrilled, viewing an honorary Oscar as a consolation prize for stars who'd never won the real thing for a single performance. Even so, he was in good company. Honorary Oscars had previously been awarded to Charlie Chaplin in 1928 (the first ever); Greta Garbo (in 1954); Cary Grant (in 1969); Barbara Stanwyck (in 1981); and Kirk Douglas (in 1995). Paul told friends, "The Academy gives honorary Oscars when you're washed up."

Paul was furious and was about to announce that he would not accept the award, but Joanne prevailed on him to go for it. He reluctantly agreed but refused to attend the ceremonies in Los Angeles.

Accepting the award for him was Sally Field, who asserted onstage that Paul was "at the height of his career."

Back East, after the ceremonies, Paul quipped, "I'm grateful this award didn't come wrapped as a gift certificate to Forest Lawn. At least I now have a nude boyfriend to present to Joanne's Oscar." He was referring to the Best Actress Award Joanne had won way back in 1958 for *The Three Faces of Eve.*

Pool Sharks
Cruise with **Newman**
Young Bull vs. Old Bull

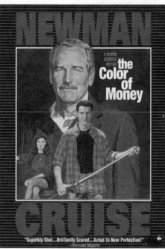

With his Honorary Oscar wrapped and in the mail to him, Paul resumed work on *The Color of Money*, a sequel to *The Hustler*. He'd be playing Fast Eddie Felson again. But in this new version, Paul, cast as an aging pool shark, finds a younger, greener version of himself. He decides to promote this hot shot kid for a chance at the bigtime.

Cast as Vincent Lauria, Tom Cruise in the film is eager to lay claim to Fast Eddie's throne. Cruise's girlfriend in the movie was Mary Elizabeth Mastrantonio, who had appeared as Al Pacino's doomed, coke-snorting sister in *Scarface* (1983).

Paul had met Cruise before when the young actor had auditioned for the role of Howard Keach in Paul's 1984 release of *Harry & Son*. Paul had rejected the rising star for the role, awarding it to Robby Benson instead.

The director of *The Color of Money*, Martin Scorsese, had seen Cruise in his film, *All the Right Moves* (1983) and thought he'd be ideal as Vincent, Paul's younger partner. The director later admitted that the only reason he'd signed on for *The Color of Money* was as a means of financing his upcoming production of *The Last Temptation of Christ*.

Immediately previous to his agreement to film *The Color of Money* with Paul, Cruise had filmed *Top Gun*, which would eventually open to sensational box office around the country. The press went wild over the Newman/Cruise casting. Many stories were filed about the screen mating. "The Sex Symbol of the 50s and 60s Meets the Sex Symbol of the 80s," headlined one story. A reporter even suggested that Paul himself had been "something of a Tom Cruise in the 1950s."

Cruise had been eager to work with both Scorsese and Paul. "When the director first called me," he told the press, "it was like getting a call from John Ford, Howard Hawks, and Orson Welles."

Long before he became famous on movie sets for his dictatorial control tendencies—nicknamed "Cruise Control" by other film industry workers—Cruise arrived on the set rather humble. At first he called both Scorsese and Paul "Sir." Finally, it was Paul who broke through to him, telling the uptight young man to call him Paul.

"He treated us with the same reverence the Chinese show their elders," Paul later said. "He made me feel like an old man making his last film. But we soon got over that, and he became one of my newest, but

Tom Cruise
"The kid has balls"

347

one of my best friends."

When he signed on, Cruise was no pool player. To prepare himself for the role, he showed amazing dedication. After seven weeks of training with pool hall sharpies, Cruise became so skilled at the game that he could keep up with the pros. Except for one trick shot, he was able to play pool on camera. Far from being jealous of Cruise's accomplishments, Paul bragged to the press about the young actor's newly acquired skill.

Even as a friendship developed, the old man of the screen and cinema's rising new star displayed a competitive edge in their emerging relationship. Paul was painfully aware that whereas he'd been born in 1925, Cruise had been born 37 years later, *before* the Fourth of July, in 1962.

It had to be obvious to Paul that his widespread identification as a sex symbol, with which he had always been uncomfortable, was being passed on to another man. "My God," he said one day to Scorsese, "I'm sixty years old."

"I know how old you are," Scorsese said. "The whole world knows how old you are."

Newman hugging Cruise:
And showing him *The Color of Money*

"And Tom is so young," Paul said. "I could be his father."

"If you started early enough, maybe even his grandfather."

"Don't remind me," Paul said, walking away.

News of the bonding of Paul with Cruise quickly reached both the press and the gossip circuit. A.E. Hotchner, Hemingway's biographer, and one of Paul's best friends, weighed in on the "Freudian father-son thing."

Paul's own son, Scott, had died by the time he met Cruise, and in some ways Paul had become a surrogate father to the young actor. Cruise himself had shown signs over the years that he was seeking a substitute for his own absentee father.

Paul quickly made Cruise his

Newman and Cruise ready for battle
Sex symbol of the 50s
meets sex symbol of the 80s

protégé, informing the press that he admired "Tom's courage. We've competed both on- and off-screen but that's good for both of us. It makes better actors out of us."

On the set, a reporter asked Paul about his developing relationship with Cruise. "It's like the story of an old bull and a young bull," Paul said. "These two bulls were walking together on a ridge when they spotted a herd of cows down below. Young bull says to old bull, 'Let's run down and hump one of those cows.' Old bull says to young bull, 'Naw, let's walk down the hill and jump 'em all!'"

In one "vanilla" biography of the younger actor, a paperback quickie called *Cruise Control* by Susan Netter, she speculates that Paul, in addition to being a surrogate father to Cruise, provided a role model for him too. She quotes Cruise as saying, "Paul lives a normal life. He's got several businesses, a wife, a family. That's good for me to see."

"In Paul Newman, Tom recognizes a true modern Renaissance man, one who could give not only to his family but to the less fortunate of the world at large," Netter claimed. "He also saw a man who, even though one of the favorite actors of the century, was not limited by acting or fame."

Shelley Winters, Paul's on-again, off-again friend and confidante, laughed at all the copy being written about Paul functioning as Cruise's role model.

"Paul Newman is not the candy ass the press makes him out to be," she claimed. "He's as much a Child of the Devil as I am. The only difference between us, morally speaking, is that I don't have millions to donate to charities. I can hardly keep myself afloat."

"I know Paul very well," she said, speaking privately and not for publication. "I'm sure he's drooled over Cruise's chestnut brown hair, those dancing hazel eyes, and that handsome, clean-cut American profile, very masculine. At Paul's age, drooling is about all he can do, I would imagine. All my hot men of yesterday have grown too old, or too fat in Marlon's case, to cut the mustard any more. Men are different from us blonde bombshells of the '50s. Some of us gals will be carrying on into our eighties . . . or beyond."

Shelley was not alone in thinking that Paul was sexually attracted to Cruise. At every Hollywood cocktail party, and in every gay bar from the New York islands to the California coast, there was speculation that Paul was having a torrid affair with Cruise. This appears to be mere speculation. No "smoking gun" has ever emerged.

However, everyone who worked with them, or encountered them in some capacity, had a story to relate. Whether that story was true didn't seem to matter to those eager for details, even if they'd been fabricated.

An attendant at a stock car stadium, where Paul and Cruise had raced that day, claimed he saw the two men showering together after a sweaty run. "They weren't doing anything other than washing off their grime," the attendant claimed. "I checked out each of their equipment. Newman wasn't staring at what Cruise had hanging and vice versa. Men routinely check out other men in the shower. If there was one thing I observed that day, it was that both men were going out of their way to keep their focus at eye level."

The attendant could have made up the story. Even so, it fell within the realm of possibility.

Perhaps Paul did check out Cruise, as he later claimed. "The kid has balls. He's going to become the next great legend of Hollywood." On the other hand, perhaps Paul was speaking symbolically about Cruise's *cojones*.

Another famous director, the controversial Oliver Stone, who had directed Paul in two films, predicted "a blazing future for Tom. He could become the next Paul Newman."

Some critics felt Cruise should have appeared more competitive with Paul on screen. "His pool shark toughness was diminished every time he looked at Newman," wrote one critic. "Through the film Cruise looked like he had a schoolgirl crush on Newman. The awe-struck actor should have played the role with a touch of greater hostility."

Cal Culver, the porno star who'd wanted to appear opposite Paul in the homosexual love story, *The Front Runner*, told a gay magazine that he, too, had heard all that talk about the romance of Cruise and Newman. "I didn't believe a word of it," Culver said. "To my knowledge, I was the last man on earth Newman ever had sex with, and that was in the late '70s. If Newman and Cruise had met in 1955, and both had been born in 1925, I bet there would have been fireworks. If a video had been shot of those two men, both young and in action back then, more guys would have seen them than went to my *Boys in the Sand*. When Newman was having sex with me, he wasn't . . . how can I say this diplomatically? He wasn't always sailing at full mast."

In a mock ceremony at the end of the shooting of *The Color of Money*, Paul placed a paper crown on Cruise's head. "You're the new Prince of Players," he told the young man. "I'm going to retire. After watching you dance around in your jockey shorts in *Risky Business*, I knew my day had come. With my skinny legs, I could never have pulled that one off."

It was Paul who introduced Cruise to his pet sport and hobby, stock car racing. One afternoon Paul rented an entire racetrack so that he and Cruise could practice. Both of them squeezed into the same race car.

"I loved going out with Paul to race," Cruise later said. "We spent hours and hours together doing just that. I have always loved fast cars and motorcycles. I wanted Paul to get me into stock car racing, and he did."

One reporter claimed that after Paul introduced Cruise to stock car racing, "He went from Cruise Control into Overdrive in just a few short months."

350

That statement is rather ambiguous. It perhaps meant that Cruise became more of an egomaniac after the testosterone buildup of the racing track.

In the years ahead, long after *The Color of Money* was wrapped, Paul and Cruise would continue to see each other. He was a frequent visitor at the rambling house that Paul and Joanne occupied in Westport.

Paul claimed that Cruise told him he wasn't going to let fame and fortune go to his head. "I don't know what's coming tomorrow," Cruise said. "That's the exciting part. I can't wait to find out what surprises are in store for me."

"Oh, you'll have a few," Paul predicted.

What Paul didn't predict was that in 1987 he'd win the Oscar for *The Color of Money*. By 1986 he'd given up hope for winning a real Oscar, something he considered distinctly more prestigious than the honorary Oscar he'd hauled in.

In the Best Actor race, Paul faced a less than formidable posse: Bob Hoskins for *Mona Lisa*, William Hurt for *Children of a Lesser God*, James Woods for *Salvador*, and Dexter Gordon for *'Round Midnight*. As defined by Joanne, whose family had perfected a secret recipe for making lemonade, the lineup of competitors for the award was akin to "weak lemonade." Paul was definitely the front runner.

From his base in Connecticut, Paul had asked Robert Wise, who had directed him in *Somebody Up There Likes Me*, to accept the Oscar for him in "the unlikely event I actually win." As Paul told friends, "I never planned to show up for the awards because I can't stand one more humiliation. I know I'm going to lose. Some dark horse will probably walk off with Oscar once again."

A drunken Bette Davis, making a spectacle of herself, swept onto the stage. The program called for her to introduce Robert Wise, who would then pay tribute to Paul. But Davis spent all of the allotted time telling millions of TV viewers who Robert Wise was.

Nervous and somewhat flustered, and reacting to signals from the TV crew to wrap things up, Wise hurriedly accepted the statuette in Paul's name, and then beat a hasty retreat from the stage. In its aftermath, the presentation emerged as more of a tribute to Wise than to Paul.

Wise later told reporters, "Newman should have won for the film I directed him in—*Somebody Up There Likes Me*. I'm sorry it took so long."

Paul later joked to the press. "With this baby in my pocket, maybe now I can find work. How appropriate that Bette Davis made the presentation. She claims she nicknamed the statue Oscar because its ass reminded her of her first husband. So, in honor of that guy's ass, I accept."

***

351

Back in Hollywood during the 1960s, Paul moved deeper into another decade of filmmaking. Those ten years would spawn some of his greatest successes, as well as some of his film career's most stinking bombs. Trouble lay ahead, both professional and personal. New seductions lay on the horizon, along with permanent breaks from old-time friends and confidants.

One alarm was sounded when a call came in from Robert Rossen, who had directed Paul in *The Hustler*.

"We've got a problem, at least a potential problem," Rossen told Paul. "Can you come to my office at two o'clock? A woman—more of a girl—is going to be here. I want you to talk some sense into her."

"Is this a looming paternity case?" Paul asked. "All big-time movie stars get them, and I guess my time has come. Should I bring a lawyer, and why is the bitch contacting you?"

"Just show up," Rossen said. "Everything will become clear at two o'clock."

Rossen was being so mysterious that at first Paul decided not to go. But curiosity won out, and he drove to Rossen's office at two o'clock where he was ushered in.

To his surprise, Sandra Dee, dressed in a woman's gray business suit with pink stripes, was seated in a chair opposite Rossen's desk. Taken by surprise, he leaned over to kiss her, finding her unresponsive. She didn't make eye contact. Had her crush on him vanished?

Prior to their meeting, Sandra had married the singer, Bobby Darin, in 1960, and her career had peaked the year before with the release of *A Summer Place*, a romantic film she'd made with Troy Donahue. Her name would be forever linked with that dreamy movie, in which she and Troy had fallen in love to Max Steiner's memorable theme music.

Darin had met Sandra when he was twenty-four and she was eighteen. Three months later they were married.

Rossen got down to business fast. "I've just learned through Sandra here that Darin is going to sue us over *The Hustler*?"

"On what grounds?" asked a startled Paul.

"Before you became available, I more or less entered into an agreement with Darin to play Fast Eddie Folsen. When you became available, I didn't sign his contract but offered you the role instead."

"That happens all the time in Hollywood," Paul said. "What's his case?"

Sandra turned to him and made eye contact for the first time. "Three top lawyers in a Los Angeles firm think Bobby has a powerful case. Bobby plans to pursue your asses, and he may take home millions. He thinks Fast Eddie was the role of a lifetime, and you've denied him his chance."

"Why are you here?" Paul demanded to know. "You're not his lawyer."

"Bobby doesn't know I'm here," she said. "I came to warn both of you what Bobby is planning to do. My motive? I was hoping you guys would meet with Bobby at our house and reach some sort of financial settlement before going to court."

Rossen turned to Paul. "Sandra requested that you be at this meeting although ultimately I think this is a decision that 20th Century Fox's lawyers will have to decide."

She rose to her feet. "If that's what you want, so be it. The papers will carry news of Bobby's lawsuit against you guys in the morning."

"Just a minute," Paul said. He would later tell Rossen that he had to re-evaluate Sandra on that day. "She's one tough cookie," Paul said. "Not the virginal little gal I met on the set of *Until They Sail*."

Rossen said that Paul volunteered to drive Sandra home—"or some-where"—that day. "Half of Hollywood had known for years that Sandra had a crush on Paul. I summoned Paul to my office hoping he might calm her down. I think he did."

As for the threatened lawsuit, it never materialized. Right before he died, Rossen, at the home of the California multi-millionaire Gordon Howard, told the author of this biography that the Fox lawyers, after careful consideration, felt Darin did indeed have a case against them. In an attempt to avoid litiga-

(Left to right:) **Paul Newman, Bobby Darin, Sandra Dee**
A question of adultery

tion, they secretly agreed to give him $150,000 in cash so he wouldn't have to report it on his income tax.

Bobby accepted the offer, and the case was closed, one of many such cases in the history of Hollywood "that was just swept under the carpet," according to Rossen.

The director didn't know the outcome of Paul's relationship with Sandra. "We never discussed it again. The whole thing was messy, and the less said about it the better."

The conclusion of the Dee/Newman relationship was revealed years later by Lana Turner, a friend of the author. She had been a "mother confessor" to Sandra when they'd made *Imitation of Life* and *Portrait in Black* together.

"Sandra told me that she'd always wanted Paul to be the man who took her virginity," Lana said. "That didn't happen. But after that meeting in Rossen's office, Paul drove her down to Laguna. At long last that deflowering that Sandra had anticipated took place."

Having another drink, Lana said, "I think Sandra was a bit disappointed. You know, you can want, even anticipate something for so long that when it finally happens you don't want it anymore. With Sandra's marriage to Bobby, her passion for Paul had begun to fade. I had the same thing with Tyrone Power. He dumped me and months later called me and wanted me back. We came back together for one night, but it wasn't the same. I had turned the page, moved on."

Lana claimed that Sandra in the years ahead occasionally met Paul "for a roll in the hay, but it was no great thing. Paul was still in love with Joanne, and she loved Bobby, but they didn't love their spouses to the point they wouldn't have sex outside the home. The sex between Sandra and Paul might have been a little better if both of them weren't drunk whenever they went to bed together. I should know. I've been made love to by drunks all my life. I told Sandra she should try Paul in the morning when he's sobered up. But apparently she never took my advice."

Information about Paul's relationship with Sandra always remained a not-so-well-kept secret in Hollywood. An item or two about them occasionally appeared in a column, mostly in the underground press. The established star and the fading star, so far as it is known, were never seen in public.

Over the years, Paul tried to see Sandra whenever she called him as she engaged in her nightmarish battle against booze, pills, depression, and anorexia.

Paul did tell Martin Ritt, "Imagine being Sandra Dee. You're not even thirty, and you're still blonde and perky and you're washed up, even though you used to be America's sweetheart."

Lana claimed that Sandra never loved Paul, although she was still drawn

354

to him. "I think he was more of a father figure to her than a lover. She always loved Bobby even though she divorced him in 1967. They stayed together until he died in 1973. He was only thirty-seven. She came to my house and was almost suicidal, so I know she still loved him."

"At one time, I asked her what went wrong in the marriage," Lana said. "She told me, 'Bobby went to see me when I played *Gidget* on the screen. He fell in love with Gidget and married her. But I grew up and became Sandra Dee, and he never expected that. My first mistake was in becoming Sandra Dee. I should have stuck with my original name, Alexandra Zuck."

Sandra never provided details about her relationship with Paul. However, in 1991 when she was appearing in a play, *Love Letters*, with John Saxon, she spoke to a reporter. "One of the great mistakes of my life was falling in love with happily married men like Paul Newman. I'll say no more about that."

***

Marilyn Monroe's breathless voice came over the phone. Paul hadn't heard from her since Las Vegas, although Hollywood was buzzing with rumors of her involvements with both Kennedy brothers, John and Robert. There was the hint of secrecy in her voice. She claimed that she was calling from a "secure" phone, as her own residence had been bugged.

"Paulie," she said, "I've missed you. Have you also missed your baby?"

"Of course, I have," he said. "Anyone who has been with you will miss you forever."

"You're so sweet, the sweetest lover I've ever had. Joe is so brutal and Arthur so cold."

She was, of course, referring to husbands Joe DiMaggio and Arthur Miller. He didn't dare ask her about the Kennedys.

She told him that she couldn't talk long on the phone, but wanted to meet him tomorrow afternoon at a mansion in Beverly Hills. She claimed she was hiding out there running from the mob. He was completely baffled as to her link with the mob. But he agreed to meet her at the appointed time.

"Tell no one about our getting together," she said, "especially your wife. I've learned the less wives know about their husband's affairs the better."

Arriving at a mansion owned by God knows who, Paul was ushered in by a black maid and out onto a patio where Marilyn in a white bikini awaited him. She jumped up and ran toward him, giving him a sloppy wet kiss.

Over lunch, where she nibbled and Paul ate lustily, she told him a highly edited version of what was going on in her life.

"Bobby wants you to play him in a movie based on his book, *The Enemy Within*."

355

He just assumed that Bobby referred to Robert Kennedy, the Attorney General of the United States.

"It's about Jimmy Hoffa and the mob," she said. "Bobby wanted me to contact you because he wants you to star in it."

"I'd be honored," Paul said. "I'd like to meet with him to discuss it."

"That's not possible right now," she said. "We have to be careful. People are spying on us, watching our every move. Jerry Wald is negotiating with Bobby for the screen rights. I want to co-star in the movie with you."

"I haven't read the book yet," he said. "Is there a strong woman's role? Sounds like a man's picture to me."

"There isn't a strong woman's part as of yet, but Jerry has promised to write in a role for me. Bobby has agreed. I want to play a tough prosecutor in a business suit who, arm in arm, works with Bobby to bring Hoffa to justice. With me in the picture and with you as Bobby, we can virtually guarantee box office. Besides, I'm tired of those dumb blonde movies. I want to sink my beautiful teeth into a strong, hard political drama like Frankie did." She was no doubt referring to Frank Sinatra's appearance in *The Manchurian Candidate*, an upcoming release she'd seen at a special screening in Las Vegas.

At one point, Marilyn ordered the maid to bring Paul a bikini. "Make it as revealing as possible," she instructed her maid right in front of Paul.

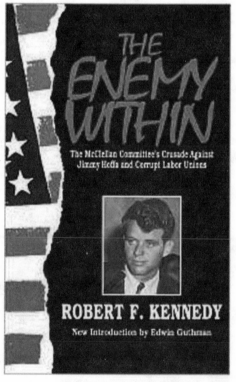

Before the afternoon ended, Jerry Wald arrived on the scene and was ushered into the pool area. "I spotted Marilyn, topless, at the far end of the pool," he later said. "She was making out with a man in a white bathing suit. I thought at first that it was Bobby Kennedy. After all, we were here to discuss *The Enemy Within*. I cleared my throat and moved closer. The man rose to his feet. I was stunned. It was Paul Newman. I'd wanted to meet with him to discuss his starring in the picture."

Marilyn hardly needed to introduce Wald to Paul. He was well known to both the Newmans. Paul only hoped that Wald would be discreet the next time he encountered

Joanne. He'd produced *No Down Payment* with her as well as *The Sound and the Fury*. Not only that, but he'd also produced *The Long, Hot Summer*. In a touch of irony, he was about to produce *Hemingway's Adventures of a Young Man*, in which he'd cast Paul, and also *The Stripper*, a film in which he'd cast Joanne.

Wald was long familiar with Marilyn as well, having produced her *Clash by Night* (1952) with Barbara Stanwyck and *Let's Make Love* (1960).

During their talk, Wald later claimed that Marilyn never put on her top in spite of his presence. "It was very distracting trying to talk to Paul with Marilyn's breasts exposed," Wald later recalled. "When she got up to go upstairs to get dressed, I quizzed Paul about everything that had happened before I got there. He'd confided in me before. He gave me a complete account, but was puzzled about how I was going to create a strong role for Marilyn in a movie devoted to Bobby and the mob. 'Who is Marilyn going to play?' Paul asked me. 'Jimmy Hoffa?'"

"Scriptwriters can work wonders," Wald assured him. "Besides, Bobby demands that we create a role in the movie for Marilyn. He owes her a favor or two."

"I can well imagine," Paul said.

Wald later discussed privately with friends why *The Enemy Within* was never made. The studio, 20th Century Fox, began to receive death threats, no doubt from some shady members of the Teamsters' Union. Wald claimed that he was warned that if the movie were made, "it'll be your last picture." The producer also claimed that he was told that movie houses showing the film would be bombed.

"Both Marilyn and Paul also received death threats," Wald said. "Marilyn had many reasons to fear the mob—but that's a story for another day—and *The Enemy Within* loomed as another nail in her coffin."

"That role for Marilyn never got written," Wald said. "It was just as well. With her in the picture in a totally made-up part, it would have thrown off the focus of the film anyway. Her relationship with Bobby was deteriorating rapidly. Also, Paul pulled the plug. He was very concerned with

Marilyn with the **Kennedy Brothers**
A not-so-happy birthday greeting

357

those death threats, and was very anxious that no harm come to his family. The final blow came when he read the first draft of the film script and rejected it. He called it a piece of shit. I don't know why he was so violent in his objection. He'd made shit before."

Pierre Salinger, the press secretary at the White House, privately told friends that "Bobby was furious when Newman rejected the role to play him in *The Enemy Within*. And Bobby was a guy to hold a grudge. He even sent Paul a note under the letterhead of the Attorney General. It was short, not sweet. FUCK OFF!!!"

Wald said that with Paul off the picture, he turned to a rising young actor, Jack Nicholson. "With makeup, Jack could be made into a more convincing version of Bobby Kennedy than Paul ever could."

Like so many projects in Hollywood, the film died a slow death. It just drifted into oblivion. Everybody—Paul, Marilyn, Bobby—was caught up in a different agenda. And each of their lives was changing, quickly and dramatically.

Wald's own life was also about to change for all time. He exited the world in the summer of 1962.

***

Before he was felled with a stroke, Joseph Kennedy, the President's father and the former ambassador to England, worked behind the scenes to get *The Enemy Within* launched as a film. The elder Kennedy was long a veteran on the Hollywood scene, going back to the silent era when he'd romanced screen vamp Gloria Swanson.

When *The Enemy Within* fell through as a project, the former ambassador turned his attention to getting a film launched called *PT 109*, which documented young JFK's heroic pursuits in the Pacific during World War II. For months Old Joe had launched a relentless public relations campaign to get his son's exploits—real or exaggerated—before the widest possible public.

Although he didn't want to play Bobby Kennedy in *The Enemy Within*, Paul was intrigued with the idea of playing JFK in the American campaign in the Pacific. It brought back memories of Paul's own less-than-heroic service in the Navy.

Using his connection with JFK's close

Cliff Robertson
Sinks PT 109 for Paul

friend, Robert Stack, Paul arranged a meeting between the President and himself when JFK flew into Los Angeles. The President had a very rushed schedule, including a rendezvous with Marilyn Monroe. Out of loyalty to Stack, Kennedy agreed to meet with Paul, but he could only grant him an audience of fifteen minutes.

The Secret Service ushered Paul and Stack into Kennedy's suite, where the relatively young, handsome president greeted Paul warmly and embraced his longtime friend, Stack. Paul was only mildly surprised when the two men kissed each other on their cheeks a total of four times.

Kennedy talked briefly about his wartime mission, which he hoped the film would dramatize. "You're handsome enough to play me," Kennedy said to Paul. "Everybody in the press writes about how good looking I am. Actually, the best looking guy in the family was Joe Jr. He had not just me, but my brothers beat on all counts. Dad was going to run him for president if he hadn't been killed."

He was referring to Joseph P. Kennedy Jr., the eldest of the nine children born to Joseph and Rose Kennedy. The President's brother died on August 12, 1944 in a doomed flight during World War II known as "Operation Aphrodite."

Paul later told friends that he was almost certain that the role of JFK was his. The next day the President called Stack with the bad news. "I don't want Newman to play me," JFK said to Stack. "Definitely not. There are two problems here. First, Newman is far too old for the part. Maybe if they did a movie about Dad, that would be different. Actually, Jackie wants Warren Beatty in the role. You know how she's always getting crushes on movie stars. There's another reason. I hesitate to bring it up. Newman looks too Jewish, not Irish at all. He just wouldn't do. Convey my apologies to him, would you?"

The popular singer, Ed Byrnes, was considered, even Peter Fonda, before the Kennedys decided on Cliff Robertson. As for playing a twenty-six year old JFK, Robertson was born in 1925, the same year as Paul. On hearing that his "forever competition," Robertson, had contracted for the part, Paul was furious.

He got over his anger when he actually saw a screening of *PT 109*. "What a disaster!" he said. Actually, he'd walked out of the film about half an hour before it ended.

***

Marlon Brando came up with what he viewed as a hot property for his Pennebaker Production Company. It was called *Paris Blues*, and he felt that the role of the female lead would be ideal for Marilyn Monroe, his on-again, off-again lover. For a week or two, she was convinced, throwing herself into the project and believing Brando's promise to take her on a voyage of discovery to the Paris he'd known after he left the Broadway production of *A Streetcar Named Desire* in the late 40s.

But a month or two later, Brando woke up and decided he didn't want to appear in *Paris Blues*. During the time it took him to make up his mind, Marilyn had already "turned the page," as she called it, signing to do *The Misfits*, a play with script by Arthur Miller. It would reunite her with Montgomery Clift and introduce her to Clark Gable, upon whom she'd had a crush since she was a teenage girl. For Gable and Monroe, it would be their last film.

As adverse as he was to accepting Brando's "sloppy seconds," Paul agreed to play the lead in *Paris Blues*, especially since Brando had already cast Joanne Woodward as the female lead before Paul signed on.

In 1960, Mr. and Mrs. Newman flew to Paris to begin location work on their next disastrous film together. It would be their fourth picture together. *Paris Blues* would also be Paul's second picture with director Martin Ritt.

Even before the picture was shot, *Paris Blues* cost Paul a once-valuable relationship. In Paris, Eartha Kitt met privately with him, a rendezvous apparently unknown to Joanne, who may never have known about the close bond between Eartha and Paul that dated back to both of their involvements with James Dean.

Eartha desperately wanted to play *Paris Blues'* fourth lead—the part of a black woman named Connie Lampson. There were very few good roles for black women in those days, and Eartha thought that by playing her, she could win an Academy Award as Best Supporting Actress.

In response to her pleas for the part, Paul told her that he could not control casting, and that Brando himself had decided on casting Diahann Carroll opposite Sidney Poitier, who was Diahann's lover both on and off the screen, even though both of them were married at the time.

Eartha was furious, accusing Paul of not doing her "this one favor" in spite of her long-standing relationship with him as his confidant. "I was always there for you, and now I ask you to be there for me—and

...betrayed

360

you're not."

He apologized to her but said there was nothing he could do. The last he saw of her was as she rushed to the sidewalk and hailed a taxi to make a speedy exit from his life.

It is entirely possible that Eartha, one of the best sources of information about the private details of Paul's life during the 1950s, would not have been so outspoken about him to her friends if he'd come through for her.

But since he didn't, she spoke openly and frequently about his private relationships with both men and women that she'd been privy to. In Key West, she once said, "What you see up there on the screen is not the real Paul Newman. He doesn't believe in friendship like I do. I would do anything for my true friends. He wouldn't give them air in a sealed jug."

***

In *Paris Blues*, Paul played Ram Bowen, an American trombonist, who was living an ex-pat lifestyle with his black friend, as played by Sidney Poitier, the first African-American actor to attain A-list status in Hollywood. They are enjoying the bohemian lifestyle until two American tourists show up, Joanne Woodward and Diahann Carroll, who temporarily disrupt their lives.

The film explored racism and passion, neither one very well. It's more like a romp through gay Paree. Paul was forced to deliver lines like, "Baby, I love

The Newmans in Paris, in love
Kentucky oysters doing their job

music morning, noon and night—d'ya dig?"

Just as he'd learned to play pool from the experts, Paul also worked with trombonist Murray McEachern, who had played in Benny Goodman's orchestra, to teach him how to be a jazzman.

Arriving in Paris in the middle of winter, Joanne rented an apartment for them in Montmartre, as she was intrigued by the fact that Picasso had once lived there. The two-story rental was cold and dark. Even so, Paul could be seen by his neighbors in the little courtyard of the rental, cooking steaks for his wife and himself.

In Paris, Poitier claimed that his role of Eddie Cook, an ex-pat jazzman, was one dimensional. Carroll, who had starred opposite Poitier in Otto Preminger's *Porgy and Bess* (1959), found her role more challenging.

At one point, Martin Ritt considered making the film very daring, at least by the standards of the day. He wanted to have the script rewritten to make Paul lovers with Carroll, Joanne lovers with Poitier. The producer, United Artists, nixed the idea.

Paul was an amateur compared to the musical greats Ritt had rounded up, none more notable than Louis Armstrong and Duke Ellington.

After only two weeks of shooting, Paul complained to Ritt, "Joanne and I are playing second fiddle to the musicians."

In the beginning, Paul had said, "We have a surefire winner here," but his enthusiasm quickly diminished.

The author, at his favorite hangout in those days, *Le Café des Deux Magots,* on the Place St. Germain des Prés, spotted Paul and Joanne at a sidewalk table. She was drinking some sort of cocktail, and Paul was enjoying quite a few beers. They seemed very much in love, almost as if they were on a honeymoon. There were no other actors or actresses in *Paris Blues* to complicate Paul's love life.

To the Parisians, they did not look like movie stars. In those days Paris was used to stars arriving

Diahann Carroll with **Sidney Poitier**
Feeling guilty...an adulterous romance

like royal visitors. Paul was dressed in blue jeans and a shabby sweater, and Joanne looked like a housewife from western Kansas. No one seemed to recognize them except yours truly who chose not to invade their privacy, at least for that one afternoon.

The author also encountered the Newmans again one night dining at Haynes, a Harlem-inspired restaurant on rue Chauzel. Their dining partner was Louis Armstrong, who had come here to fill up on barbecued spareribs, corn on the cob, and "Kentucky oysters." The diners recognized Satchmo but, again, didn't seem to know who the Newmans were. Paul stuck to ordering beer that night, but Satchmo preferred bourbon. "I drink the brown stuff," he told Haynes.

Big, burly Haynes, who hailed from the Deep South, U.S.A., was the owner of this American outpost. He presided over the Newman table, even serving them his old-fashioned homemade apple pie for dessert.

Upon its lackluster release, the editors of *Cue Magazine* nailed *Paris Blues* accurately as "self-consciously socially significant—a loosely amoral, romantically dreamy-eyed casually inter-racial, pseudo-realistic tale of music and music-makers, of love, conflict, boys-grab-at-girls, dope, tragedy, and raucously wild music, and all so slickly fricasseed and illogical as to add up to a Frenchified fairy tale that fobs off criticism."

Paris Blues opened across the United States on September 27, 1961, two days after *The Hustler* opened. Audiences ignored the former, flocking to the latter.

With the completion of *Paris Blues*, he had finally paid off his $500,000 debt to Warner Brothers. "Free at last," he shouted, ordering a keg of beer to celebrate throughout the night.

***

After campaigning with Joanne for Gore Vidal's unsuccessful run for a Congressional seat from New York State, Paul flew back to Hollywood. Both Paul and Joanne had signed to appear in films with the sensitive young actor, Richard Beymer, hers called *The Stripper*, based on the William Inge play, *A Loss of Roses*.

In a move opposed by his agent, Paul had agreed to appear with Beymer in *Hemingway's Adventures*

Joanne *The Stripper*
Bursting balloons

of a Young Man (1962), a script penned by A.E. Hotchner, Paul's friend and neighbor in Westport. Martin Ritt signed on once again to direct Paul. Another of Paul's friends, Jerry Wald, signed on to produce the picture for 20th Century Fox.

As a punch drunk, fifty-five-year-old pug, Paul reprised his 1955 appearance in the teleplay, *The Battler*, based on Hemingway's autobiographical stories of "Nick Adams." At the time, Richard Beymer was being groomed as "the new Paul Newman." He'd been designated as the lead.

No longer cast as a pretty boy, Paul was heavily disguised to look like a battered old boxer who'd seen too much of life on the wrong side of the tracks.

He shocked his fans when he appeared on the screen with gargoyle make-up and using a hoarse voice.

Ritt later claimed that Dan Dailey, Betty Grable's song-and-dance partner of the 40s, made a pass at Paul during filming. Dailey appeared in the film as a drunken press agent. The pass was not intercepted.

It was Paul himself who made a pass when he met a beautiful young girl named Sharon Tate. As he was advising her to become a full-time actress, Beymer approached. Paul quickly realized that she was Beymer's girlfriend, and he backed off. Beymer himself also urged Sharon to pursue an acting career.

At the time he met Paul, Beymer was shooting to fame for his role as Tony in *West Side Story*, the one film for which he is most remembered today. He told Paul he'd hated his appearance in *West Side Story*. "I was sort of caught up in my own web of illusion."

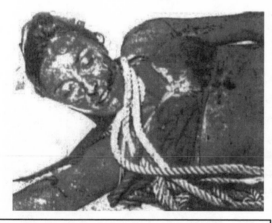

Sharon Tate
Date with destiny

364

Sharon told Paul that she and Beymer were being flown to Verona, Italy, where they would film some concluding Hemingway stories in the actual locale of his World War I adventures when he was an ambulance driver.

As Nick, played by Beymer, is recovering from a wound in the hospital, he falls in love with his nurse, as played by Susan Strasberg.

Sharon was excited about going to Italy where she would appear as an extra and where she would meet Susan, who also encouraged her to become an actress.

Years later, on August 9, 1969, Paul was horrified when he received a phone call from his friend Steve McQueen. Sharon, eight and a half months pregnant and the wife of Roman Polanski, had been murdered in her home, along with four others. The massacre, it was later learned, was committed by Charles Manson and members of his cult. Steve added a chilling note, "I was supposed to have been a guest at that party."

More tragic news was on the way. Hemingway himself wrote the film's opening and closing narration and was scheduled to utter it himself. But the cast and crew, while filming a segment in Verona, Italy, received a blow. On July 2, 1961, "Papa" had committed suicide at his home in Ketchum, Idaho.

The film failed at the box office. *The New York Herald Tribune* claimed that Paul's performance was "essentially a caricature that fails to capture Hemingway's compassion for the indomitable in a man seemingly in the last ditch of defeat."

***

Paul had known Susan Strasberg, the daughter of Lee Strasberg, since she was a young girl breaking out as an actress on Broadway. Over the years he'd still remained close to her father and the Actors Studio, but he had never paid much attention to Susan.

But when she arrived on the set of *Hemingway's Adventures of a Young Man*, he paid close attention to her.

Richard Beymer
A promise unfulfilled

Susan had gone through a tumultuous love affair with Richard Burton and had not yet entered into her doomed marriage to the handsome actor, Christopher Jones.

Paul had always found her a "Jewish American princess," but meeting her on the set of the Hemingway picture, he encountered a more mature and alluring Susan. She had no scenes with him, but was going to Verona, Italy, to play Beymer's nurse in the film.

Since both Paul and Susan knew Marilyn Monroe, their initial talk focused on her, but Susan also spoke about her father and Method acting. Their talk grew so animated, he invited her out, claiming it was "purely social, merely friendship."

She told him that she expected no more "from a happily married man."

At a party in New York in 1977 that the author had taken her to, Susan admitted that her brief fling with Paul was "nothing more, nothing less. We both were a bit bored. I was between engagements. He was experiencing a dry period if you know what I mean. We both weren't that interested in being committed to one person one hundred percent. Our souls were too adventurous for that."

She claimed that over her first drink with Paul, she confessed that she'd never gotten over Richard [a reference to Burton], and that she'd developed a crush on Alain Delon.

"Alain is so beautiful," Susan told Paul. "Just like you."

"I was a little drunk that night, and I got flirtatious," she told the author. "I told Paul, 'I hope you're beautiful all over.'"

He looked around the café. "Do you want me to prove it to you right now and take off all my clothes?"

"Later, darling," she said. "I'll conduct a complete inspection."

"A promise I'll hold you to," he said.

She later claimed, "It was very satisfying, a release of passion and pent-up frustration. I liked Paul but I wasn't going to fall in love with him. No way. He was a married man. I never had any problem sleeping with married men— that hardly makes me a whore. In the theater, no actor—or actress for that matter—is ever faithful to their lover or spouse. That's not how it's played. Marilyn herself— my surrogate sister—told me that being faithful to a partner is like missing out on half the fun in New York."

Susan Strasberg
...a release of passion

Susan called Paul on another occasion when Fox invited her to fly to Los Angeles to promote *Hemingway's Adventures of a Young Man*. Both Paul and Susan agreed that it would not be discreet to be seen together, so they slipped away somewhere private.

"It was a seedy motel out in San Fernando Valley," she said. "But I had fun. I felt I was being very naughty. In some way, I was competitive with Marilyn at the time. She had so

366

many lovers and I didn't have all that many. I was jealous of her conquests. She'd had Paul Newman, and I wanted him so I could brag to her."

At the time of her California visit, Susan was dating—of all people—the bisexual actor Cary Grant. "Paul was flabbergasted. 'Couldn't Grant be your grandfather?' he asked me. I guess he could. I was introduced to Grant by his former lover, Clifford Odets. I knew all about the gay thing."

Don't tell me that Paul Newman wasn't interested in gossip," she said. "He wanted to know all about my brief affair with Cary. There wasn't much to tell. We went to bed only one time, and he couldn't rise to the occasion. He broke down and cried. This famous actor. He told me his great dream in life was to have a child of his own. Of course, he later married Dyan Cannon, and he did produce a child, his one and only, Jennifer. I told Cary that if I ever have a daughter, I'll name her Jennifer too."

On March 14, 1966, Susan, in honor of her old commitment, named her daughter Jennifer Jones, as she'd promised. The father was Christopher Jones, whom she'd married the year before.

"Paul was always a great friend of the Actors Studio," Susan claimed, "but I saw him very infrequently in the years ahead. We never referred to the times we did it. It seemed so unimportant. While we were still together, we did discuss the Elizabeth and Burton thing that was making headlines around the world. I told Paul, 'For years I've had to compete against Marilyn. Now I have to compete against Elizabeth. What chance does a girl like me have competing against Marilyn Monroe and Elizabeth Taylor? God must be a very bad person to force a girl to face such competition.'"

"You'll find someone," Paul assured her.

"Actually, I have," she told him.

"Who's the lucky guy?" he asked.

"Paul Newman, but he's taken."

***

About three weeks before her death on August 5, 1962, Paul received an urgent call from Marilyn Monroe, who wanted to meet with him privately in a room at the Chateau Marmont, their former hangout.

Rushing to her side, he encountered an unkempt Marilyn wearing no makeup and looking her worst from another sleepless night.

Because Paul confided the events of that late scorching morning in Los Angeles to Janice Rule, we know some details about the last time Paul met with Marilyn.

He'd never seen Marilyn filled with such self-pity. She was lashing out at Hollywood and all the people who'd used her, especially John and Robert

Kennedy.

"They won't return my calls," she told Paul. "I leave messages for them everywhere. I thought I was more, but—guess what—I turned out to be just another piece of ass to them. Figure that. What a fool I was. Can you believe I was so stupid? At one point in my relationship with each of them, I actually believed their promises about leaving their wives for me. Bobby will be with Ethel until the day he dies, and Jack will be with Jackie."

At one point, according to Paul, Marilyn pulled the sheet from her body and stood up on wobbly feet beside her bed. She was completely nude. At the window, she pulled back the draperies, letting in the sun which was soaring toward its noon-day high.

Even in her disheveled state, Paul found there was a loveliness about her, a moody melancholy that hung in the air. She turned from the window and commanded him "to look at my body."

"I haven't been able to keep my eyes off it," he said.

"You're kind," she said. "A real sweet man. Just like Peter Lawford. He's a good guy too. A little mixed up in the head, but who isn't?" The telephone rang but she warned him not to pick it up. Returning to bed, she crawled under the sheets. "Call room service. I need some champagne."

After Paul had tipped the waiter, he sat on the edge of Marilyn's bed, sipping a tulip-shaped glass of champagne with her. "The bubbly soothes my nerves." She talked as if she were drugged.

He said little that day, letting her do most of the talking.

"Fame's a bitch, isn't it?" she asked. "You've handled it so much better than I have. I've fucked up everything, my whole life. My career's in shambles. After I got fired from *Something's Got to Give*, no studio will hire me again."

"Are you kidding?" he asked. "When you pull yourself together, you're going to come back bigger than ever. The whole world loves Marilyn Monroe."

"As I said, you are so sweet, Paulie. My life would have been so different had I hooked up with you. You're strong like a man should be. You're dependable. If I'd married you instead of Arthur and Joe, I'd be the Queen of Hollywood today." She leaned toward him to kiss him on the lips. "And you'd be the king. The former king of Hollywood is dead, after all. I killed him!"

She was referring to Clark Gable, with whom she'd starred in *The Misfits* shortly before his death. "I put him through so much shit on that picture, I shortened his life."

"He died of natural causes," he assured her. "You're not to blame."

"If only I could believe that," she said. She moved closer to him. "Hold me. I need strong arms around me. A man's arms. Paulie's arms."

After he'd embraced her for a long time, she broke away. "I want you to run away with me," she said, desperation in her voice. "We'll leave Hollywood behind. Perhaps go to Mexico. You can get a divorce there and marry me. I want to be the next Mrs. Paul Newman."

"I'm already married," he said. "I not only have a wife, but children, responsibilities. I'm a breadwinner. As tempting a romantic adventure it is, running away with Marilyn Monroe is out of the question."

"I thought your marriage is just a cover," she said. "Not a real marriage."

"It's real all right," he said, standing up. He felt the heat of the day. "Don't they have any air conditioning in this fleabag?"

"I turned it off," she said. "If the heat is too much for you in this room, you can leave. Get out! You're rejecting me too, just like the Kennedys."

"I'm not rejecting you," he said. "I just can't give up the life I've built and run off to the border with you. What would we do?"

"I won't bother to tell you, because it's not going to happen," she said. "I thought I could call on you, and you'd rescue me. I see that you won't. I'm on my own. I've always been on my own in Hollywood. They took my youth, used me. I'm on the way to becoming Alexandra Del Lago in that movie of yours, *Sweet Bird of Youth*. A has-been at thirty-six. Maybe when I'm fifty they'll book me into Vegas. I'll face a sea of gray staring back at me as I sing 'Diamonds Are a Girl's Best Friend.'"

"Listen, I don't want to leave you like this," he said. "I can get help for you. I know this clinic up the coast. A lot of stars use it. I'll drive you there and check you in and visit you whenever I can. When you come out of that place, you'll be a new woman. A more mature Marilyn will take Hollywood by storm. Your greatest roles are ahead of you."

"I know we live in fantasyland, but cut this fantasy shit. That's not going to happen. I'm finished in this town. You're going to rise to the top—not me. Not Marilyn. With all the silly movies I've left behind, all those dumb blonde parts, I'll become a footnote in Hollywood history. I won't even be a legend like Jean Harlow unless I die young."

"That's fool's talk and you know it," he said. "You can bounce back. You've had setbacks before."

Misfits **Monty Clift, Marilyn Monroe,** and **Clark Gable**
"...betraying Monty, betraying me"

369

She rose up in bed, baring her breasts. "I'm cleaning house, baby. My so-called mentor, Paula Strasberg, is on her way back to New York with a one-way ticket. Bobby and Jack are gone. I don't ever want to see Sinatra again. Dr. Greenson's going to go. I'm even going to get rid of Mrs. Murray."

She was referring to Dr. Ralph Greenson, her analyst, and Eunice Murray, her housekeeper.

She looked up at him, as if seeing him for the first time. "Didn't I tell you to get out of my room."

"I didn't think you really meant it." he said.

"I meant it!" She shouted at him. "Get out. Monty told me how you treated him and mocked him for losing his beauty in that accident."

Monty Clift, following his disfigurement in his car accident, had also starred with Marilyn in *The Misfits*. "You know I never did anything of the sort," Paul said. "Monty's lying."

"Like hell he is," she said. "For all I know you'll leave my bedroom and tell the world you encountered Marilyn Monroe, the broken down old hag."

She picked up an alarm clock from her nightstand and threw it at him. He ducked before heading for the door. "I'm going, but I have to warn you: I won't come back."

"That's the only good news I've had today, you bastard," she said. "Just as sneaky as Sinatra. I'm calling a press conference. I'll denounce the Kennedys, and I'll denounce you. I'll tell them you've spent more time fucking me than you did Joanne Woodward. That will be the end of Hollywood's most idyllic couple. You only pretend to like women anyway. Sinatra and I talked about it in Nevada. He's always known that you're a fag."

He opened the door and walked down the hallway. He was devastated, but felt he could talk to no one with the possible exception of his secret friend, Janice Rule. He kept telling Janice that if the acting didn't work out, she should become a psychiatrist to the stars.

***

Marilyn's press conference didn't happen. She was found dead—suicide or murder?—before she could "blow the lid off this rotten country," as she'd threatened.

Paul's marriage was left intact, but upon hearing the televised news of Marilyn's death, he was devastated. He could not share his grief with his wife.

Paul threw himself into his work, thinking he'd found the perfect vehicle in a script presented to him by his friend and partner, director Martin Ritt. It was a Western of sorts, and it was based on the novel, *Horseman, Pass By*, by Larry McMurtry.

370

"Of course, the title's got to be changed," Ritt warned Paul. After several title proposals, including *The Man with the Barbed Wire Soul, Hud Bannon,* even *Coitus on Horseback,* the movie was officially entitled *Hud.*

The screenplay had been adapted from McMurty's novel by Irving Ravetch and his wife, Harriet Frank Jr. Paul was already familiar with this husband-and-wife's screenwriting skills. They had previously adapted William Faulkner's works into screenplays for both *The Sound and the Fury* and *The Long, Hot Summer.*

Paul wanted to start shooting right away. He'd be playing a world-class villain. He was so anxious to prepare for the role of a self-centered libertine that weeks in advance of shooting, he flew to Claude, Texas, to soak up atmosphere. He even became adept at wrestling a pig in the mud.

Hud was an arrogant, brash, and unscrupulous cowboy who devoted his life to "booze, broads, and barroom brawls," when not joyriding in his pink Cadillac, cruising for trouble.

The film depicted a conflict of three generations. Playing the elderly rancher-father, Homer, was Melvyn Douglas, an old-time romantic leading man who'd starred with such legends as Greta Garbo. In contrast to Hud's rotten character, he is deeply principled.

Also living on this Texas ranch is Hud's teenaged nephew, Lonnie, played by Brandon De Wilde. He was cast as the son of Hud's deceased brother, Norman, who was fatally injured in a car wreck caused by Hud's recklessness. Both Hud and Lonnie are attracted to Alma (Patricia Neal), the family's middle-aged housekeeper. Her memorable line, as spoken to Hud, is, "I've done my time with one cold-blooded bastard. I'm not looking for another."

Hud responds, "Honey, don't go shootin' all the dogs 'cos one of them's got fleas."

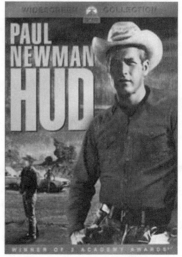

In the novel, the Patricia Neal character had been that of a black maid, but the producers in 1963 were not daring enough to go there. "It's dangerous enough that Hud does not find redemption at the end of the movie," one executive said. "Clark Gable used to start out as a bad guy, but he always found redemption in the final reel."

The plot thickens when Homer buys some cheap Mexican cattle infected with hoof-and-mouth disease. He plans to destroy the herd but Hud wants to dump the cattle on another unsuspecting rancher. Lonnie has a challenging role, as he is torn

371

between his adolescent adulation of Hud and his loving respect for his grand-father.

Unknown to Ritt and perhaps even to Paul, Brandon later claimed, "I played Lonnie as gay."

Arriving two weeks before actual shooting began, Brandon De Wilde, referring to himself as "hot and horny," checked into a seedy motel in Amarillo. The staff there had seen his memorable performance in the classic Western, *Shane*, released in 1953 and starring Alan Ladd.

The hotel manager believed Brandon when he claimed he had made arrangements to "bunk" with Paul. The tall Texan showed Brandon to Paul's room and unlocked the door, giving him a spare key. "You're gonna have to practically barricade the door. Gals have been swarming around this motel at night, hoping to get their chance with Newman."

Information about what happened between Paul and Brandon in Texas is attributed to the novelist James Leo Herlihy. He'd befriended Brandon when the young man had starred in the film versions of two of his works, one based on Herlihy's play, *Blue Denim*, another his novel, *All Fall Down*. Ironically, Herlihy's novel bears some resemblance to *Hud*. In *All Fall Down*, Brandon worships Warren Beatty, not Paul Newman.

Brandon De Wilde, born in Brooklyn in 1942, always appears on those lists of Hollywood bisexuals compiled by the likes of in-the-know observers such as Bill Dakota. He was a very experienced twenty-year-old when he first encountered Paul.

According to Herlihy, as related to him by Brandon, Paul turned the key to the door of his motel room to encounter a naked Brandon waiting for him in bed on top of the covers. "What took you so long to get here?" Brandon asked a startled Paul.

"What in hell are you doing in my room?" Paul asked.

"You do like to get down to business fast," Brandon said. "If you must know, I've been waiting half the afternoon to suck the cock of Paul Newman."

"Get out!" Paul said. "Or I'll call the manager and have you thrown out."

"No need for that," Brandon said, rising from the bed and moving toward Paul. "But before I go, *Baby Want a Kiss*." Without knowing it, Brandon was parroting the title of a Broadway play in which Paul would even-

Paul with Patricia Neal
"...cold-hearted bastard"

tually star.

As Brandon told Herlihy, "when I moved in on Paul, his resistance lasted about five seconds. His tongue was down my throat before I knew it. After that, I knew I had him, especially when I reached down below to find my cowboy rock hard."

Brandon had been exceptionally beautiful as a child, especially as a seven year old in 1950 when he made his Broadway debut in Carson McCullers' *The Member of the Wedding*.

Twelve years later he'd grown into a strikingly handsome, almost irresistible young man. As Brandon told Herlihy, "Even straight men want to fuck me."

As a prelude to sex with Paul, Brandon told him that Martin Ritt had instructed him to play his role of Lonnie as "hero-worshipping and blindly idolizing my no-good uncle. You are a Method actor. Well, I want to give The Method a try. We can begin with my idolizing you right tonight."

According to Brandon's account, Paul pronounced him "Hot as a firecracker—that's about the best sex I ever had. You leave no orifice unexplored."

Brandon didn't just "go the homo route." He told Herlihy that he often had to seduce two or three girls a day "just to keep from going crazy."

His nights preceding the arrival of the *Hud* crew in Texas, and during the filming, were spent with Paul. When they tired of each other, they went cruising for "hot Texas gals," in Brandon's words. "The pickings were easy. Half the women in and around that part of Texas flocked to get a look at Paul Newman. These women, married or unmarried, followed him around, with me trailing behind."

"Women were trying to climb through the transoms at that seedy motel," Paul later recalled. "One night I emerged buck naked from the shower, and I spotted this coed at the transom staring down at my dick."

"It wasn't a case of if we were going to make out that night," Brandon told Herlihy. "It was a case of which bitch we wanted that night. Often Paul and I fucked the same lucky bitch. When she left, we turned on each other for even hotter times."

It was rumored that during the shoot of *Hud*, one married man threatened to kill both Brandon and

Brandon De Wilde, Melvyn Douglas, and Paul Newman
Three generations in conflict

373

Paul for "violating" his wife.

Paul later told Ritt, "Our boy Brandon is a sex maniac. I've never seen anything like it. He's hot to trot day and night. He's a boy nympho. I have a hard time keeping up with him. I'm seventeen years older than the kid."

"I don't know how you guys face the camera in the morning," Ritt said. "I hear you spend all nights chasing booze and broads."

"Something like that," Paul said. "Something like that."

At the end of the shoot, Brandon told Paul, "Don't think it's over between us. I'm going to be tracking you down every chance I get. Once you've had Paul Newman, you can't get him out of your blood."

Back in Los Angeles, Paul confessed his affair to Janice Rule. He had taken to calling her "my mother confessor."

"What should I do? Drop him? Kick him out of my life? That's what I want to do. But that's not what I plan to do."

"I know that," she said. "You don't even have to tell me."

"The kid gets real low down and dirty," he said. "He's got all these tricks. God knows where he learned them. He told me he started having sex with both men and women when he was only nine years old. It's like he was born in a brothel."

"Maybe he's reached a little patch of your brain where depravity lives," Janice said. "We all have it. Even I, sweet cakes. I've never told you half the things I'm up to. Go for it. Slip away and be with Brandon whenever you can. But don't tell another soul. Before Brandon leaves your life, and he will one day, you'll find out what Paul Newman is really like."

"That may be true," he told her, "but do I want to face who I really am? Up to now I've been content to live with the image I project to the public."

***

On May 28, 1963, *Hud* held its premiere in New York City. In the weeks ahead, as it opened in cities across America, Paul enjoyed his box office success. "Maybe Hollywood will forget my failures," he said.

On the night the Academy Awards were presented, Melvyn Douglas won for Best Supporting Actor, beating out Bobby Darin in *Captain Newman M.D.* Patricia Neal car-

Brandon De Wilde
Paul's party favor

ried off an Oscar for Best Actress in a Leading Role, but Paul once again lost the Oscar as Best Actor.

But despite the loss, with his cruelly curled lips, his aw-shucks grin, and authentic calluses on his hands from roping steer, Paul had captured hearts across America playing an anti-hero. For the role, he'd developed the cowboy's lope and a Texas accent. Posters of Paul in tight-fitting blue jeans that revealed the outline of his cock vied for sales with Marilyn Monroe at her sexy best.

Paul lost his Oscar to his co-star in *Paris Blues*, Sidney Poitier, for his very appealing performance in *Lilies of the Field*. "I voted for Sidney," Paul told the press in New York the night of the Oscars. He'd decided against flying to Los Angeles to face another humiliating loss. Privately, he told friends, "That fucking Oscar belonged to me. No one in the history of movies ever played a cad with as much charm as I did in *Hud*."

***

"After the release of *Hud*, Paul was at the top of the heap in Hollywood," Martin Ritt claimed. "He could have almost any property he wanted. The question remains, why did he then select a series of disastrous films that only tainted his image? Even his most ardent fans didn't go see some of the rotten movies he made. For my role in any of his poor selections, I sincerely apologize to the movie-going public who had to shell out their hard-earned cash to see shit."

"Paul was getting involved in politics," Ritt noted. "Civil rights, all that stuff. He became bitterly disillusioned when John F. Kennedy was assassinated in Dallas. I think he was getting bored with his marriage. He really didn't take to the role of a father, although he kept having kids. Another daughter would be on the way. He was still battling Scott. I think he was also becoming bored with film making, but he pressed on. Frankly, I think he needed another big-time affair. But Marilyn was dead and there was no one to replace her. And Grace Kelly was having affairs with men far younger than Paul."

"He was drinking pretty heavily at the time, but that was hardly news," Ritt said. "He'd been drinking since the '40s, from what I heard. In some ways, Paul wan-

Sidney Poitier receives Oscar (1963) from **Anne Bancroft**.
Paul bites the dust for *Hud*

dered into the '60s a lost, lonely boy. He wasn't a boy any more, except he acted like one at times, especially when he got together to raise hell with Brandon De Wilde. Paul was moving into his forties and facing middle age."

"He longed for the return of the '50s, but they were gone and Hollywood was changing," Ritt said. "He spoke a lot about James Dean and the wild times they'd had. But Dean was long gone too. Paul's dream gals of the '40s—Lana Turner, Rita Hayworth—were already on their third face-lift. He was indulging in quickies like that thing with Susan Strasberg. But I don't think he found those flings very satisfying. Hollywood in 1963 just wasn't the Hollywood Paul walked into in 1953."

"Yet, through it all, the terrible, tumultuous '60s would bring Paul some of his biggest hits and successes, making up for those bombs he also made in that decade," Ritt said. "There would be a lot of compromises on the road to his horizon."

Hud
Chasing windmills
& trying to sell diseased cows

Chapter Ten
Winning Some but Losing More

"I'm not one to talk, considering the career choices I've made, but Paul Newman launched a series of downers in the '60s that could have destroyed a lesser star," said Shelley Winters. She was talking to her table mates at Downey's Restaurant in New York.

Paul's former lover, Susan Strasberg, once said, "If you went to Downey's, you didn't need to read gossip columns. There you found out everything that was happening, and to whom." The author agrees with her assessment, having gone there regularly throughout the 1960s.

Seeing that she'd captured the attention of her table, Shelley went on, giving a command performance. "When Paul and Brando weren't in Hollywood making all those turkeys, they campaigned for civil rights. My former husband, Tony Franciosa, even joined them, marching into the rotgut belly of redneck Alabama. Burt Lancaster, another one of my beaux, hooked up with them on some occasions. I've got a new spin on those guys marching for civil rights."

"All of these guys, including my ex-husband, are bi's," she claimed. "Away from their wives, spouses, boyfriends, girlfriends, whomever, they spend more time making out than marching. Those pricks were screwing around big time—hot-to-trot, star-struck gals, impressionable boys, you name it."

"Paul told me that in Gadsden, Alabama, Brando invited him to join him in his hotel room," Shelley said. "He was shacked up with a teenage brother and sister. If I got the story right, these siblings were black. Paul claimed he turned down the invitation, but you never know. Have you ever met a man yet, especially an actor, who told the truth about his sex life?"

"One mayor in Alabama, at least according to Paul, threatened to throw both Brando and Paul in jail," Shelley said. "He was going to order the sheriff to have a photographer present while Paul and Brando were strip searched.

Those pictures would surely have made the underground press."

"Maybe all those celebrities—Tony Curtis, Charlton Heston, Sammy Davis Jr., Harry Belafonte, Lena Horne, James Garner—did some good for civil rights. I really don't know. A lot of people resented celebrities arriving in these small redneck towns. In Paul's case, it was another excuse he had to be away from home. If I hear one more story about how faithful Paul Newman is to his wife, I'll puke all over this table."

***

Those turkeys that Shelley was referring to were lined up one after another, easy targets for critics to shoot down. First came *A New Kind of Love* (1963), followed by *The Prize* (1963), *What a Way to Go!* (1964), *The Outrage* (1964), and *Lady L* (1965).

Paul didn't want to make the Paramount picture, *A New Kind of Love*. But Joanne did, and she could be very persuasive.

Paul waited two decades later to give his impression of the film to a reporter from *Time* magazine. In an interview, he recalled:

"Joanne read it and said, 'Hey this would be fun to do together. Read it.' I read it and said, 'Joanne, it's just a bunch of one-liners.' And she said, 'You son-of-a-bitch. I've been carting your children around, taking care of them at the expense of my own career, taking care of you and your house.' And I said, 'That's what I said. It's a terrific script. I can't think of anything I'd rather do.' This is what is known as a reciprocal trade agreement."

After reading the script, he told the director and author, Melville Shavelson, that "The only reason Joanne wants to make this thing is to be seen on the screen in expensive French lingerie. After making *The Stripper*, she thinks she's Marilyn Monroe."

In contrast, Joanne told Shavelson, "It's the dirtiest script I've ever read—I love it!"

Shavelson had lined up a formidable supporting cast, including the beautiful Eva Gabor along with the talented but deadpan Thelma Ritter, who always stole every scene she was in, even when appearing with Bette Davis in *All About Eve*. Other talented

Brando (center) with **Paul:**
Speaking out for civil rights
A proposed strip search

378

character actors included Robert Clary and George Tobias.

More stunning than any of the actors were the costume designs. The lesbian, Edith Head, who'd dressed most of the big stars from Bette Davis to Mae West, was in charge of wardrobe, with access to many original designs by Christian Dior and Pierre Cardin.

Even though he signed the contract, Paul knew better. "It was against my better judgment," he told the director. "Let's face it, we're not Doris Day and Rock Hudson."

Paul came up with that opinion long before Judith Crist, writing in the *New York Herald Tribune*, more or less echoed the same opinion. She added, "They're not Day and Hudson—and shouldn't aspire to be."

When Joanne signed on to this clunker, her career had lost its speed. Hollywood had almost forgotten that she'd once won an Oscar. After the failure of *The Stripper*, she was hoping for a box office bonanza.

She told the press *A New Kind of Love* was a "fast-moving comedy," but it dragged on for 110 minutes. One critic called the film "interminable."

On the plane to Paris, Paul's character meets Samantha Blake (as played by Joanne), a dull, drab career girl. Love-starved Samantha, in hopes of attracting Paul, does an ugly duckling-to-swan conversion, subsequently appearing as a sultry blonde in a wig and *haute couture*. In her reincarnation, Paul mistakes her for a high-class hooker.

Paul did prevail upon his buddy, Frank Sinatra, to sing the title song, but by doing so Paul set himself up for a critic's potshot. "Sinatra is the only one in the film who has show business talent, with the possible exception of Thelma Ritter. Who wouldn't love Ritter in anything?"

One of Paul's lines in the movie gave critics a field day. His character, a newspaper columnist, Steve Sherman, says: "It must be a new kind of love. They ought to bottle it and call it 'instant stupid.'"

It became obvious during the filming that Eva Gabor, youngest of the notorious Gabor sisters, was making a play for Paul. "He is the best-looking man I think I've ever seen," Eva said, "and I've just learned he's got Hungarian blood in him. No wonder I am so attracted to him." She was speaking to Shavelson.

Reportedly Joanne had to warn Eva that "Mr. Newman is taken. In case you

"The dirtiest script I've ever read."

didn't know, I'm his wife."

Behind Joanne's back, Eva told Shavelson, "Paul is divine but that Woodward creature is a bitch! Also, *dah-link*, you should have let me design that blonde wig of hers. It's hideous on the poor creature."

Years later, at a dinner party thrown by Merv Griffin for twenty-four guests, Eva was asked if she'd managed to seduce Paul while making the film.

"Of course, I did, *dah-link*," she said. "You didn't think that Woodward creature could safeguard a handsome hunk like that twenty-four hours a day? I'm very experienced. I've been seducing other women's husbands for years."

A somewhat skeptical Zsa Zsa asked her, "Did you really seduce Newman, or are you just claiming that?"

"Let me put it this way," Eva said. "If I did not seduce him, I would claim my conquest anyway. After all, *dah-link*, I've got a reputation to maintain. So have you, Sister Dear."

A refreshing moment came in the film with the appearance of Maurice Chevalier as himself. Publicly, Paul presented a smiling face to Chevalier. Privately, he told Eva Gabor, "Marlene Dietrich goes around Hollywood claiming that Chevalier is impotent. She also claims that in spite of Chevalier's homophobic remarks, he's gay himself."

By the time *A New Kind of Love* premiered on October 30, 1963 in New York City, Paul and Joanne had been dethroned as the idyllic couple gracing the covers of fan magazines. The world wanted a duo more notorious and found it in Richard Burton and Elizabeth Taylor, following their scandals during the making of *Cleopatra* in Rome. As a screen couple, Paul and Joanne retired until they made *Winning* in 1969.

***

Freed of studio constraints, including his contractual bondage to Warner Brothers, Paul could pick and choose among "Grade A" film projects. With director Martin Ritt, he formed Jodell Productions, based on the names of their two wives, Joanne and Adella. With John Foreman, his former agent, he established the Newman-Foreman Company.

Despite all this clout and new power, he foolishly chose to star as a drunken, womanizing novelist in *The Prize*, a sort of Hitchcockian thriller written by Ernest

Eva Gabor
Boasting of seduction

380

Lehman, who had penned *North by Northwest,* later filmed with Cary Grant.

Metro-Goldwyn-Mayer was hoping for another box office bonanza like *North by Northwest*. But two elements were missing from *The Prize*: Alfred Hitchcock and Grant.

The Prize was based on Irving Wallace's novel which had sold more than 100,000 copies in hardback. Even though he'd starred in it, Paul later admitted that he'd never read the novel. He had a nostalgic soft spot for Lehman, who had written *Somebody Up There Likes Me*, although the scriptwriter had failed him in *From the Terrace*.

Throughout the shoot, Paul had an easy working relationship with Mark Robson, who had helmed him in *From the Terrace*. Cast opposite such temptations as Elke Sommer, he managed to keep his jockey shorts on throughout the shoot.

He later said, "I had more fun making *The Prize* than any movie I've made so far. I mean just plain fun. I raced to the studio in the morning to try all sorts of inventions on the screen. It was a real challenge." Perhaps it was too much of a challenge for him. Many reviewers felt the role called for a Cary Grant, or at least a David Niven.

In trying to build suspense, the film also played for laughs, especially when Paul finds himself at a nudist convention. Some Paul Newman fans claimed that the only reason they went to see the film was to watch their hero cavort around half nude in a towel.

Even at his age and in spite of all that beer drinking, Paul still had the body for the nude caper. In one scene that caused gasps from certain members of the audience, he appeared in jockey shorts, revealing a promising mound.

Don F. Reuter, author of *Shirtless!*, a beefcake book devoted to Hollywood actors,

Paul, a true Prize
"A male body for the ages"

Critics referred to Paul's appearance in this movie as his most exhibitionistic beefcake film to date.

Micheline Presle with **Paul** in
The Prize
Fleeing from a nudist colony

referred to Paul as "a male body for the ages. Possessing an almost perfect body, Newman's lean, muscular, tanned physique set a standard for male bodies that was rarely if ever equaled, let alone surpassed. Of his dozens of films, such as *The Prize*, many offer glimpses of what some could call a body sculpted by some divine being."

Paul wanted to have his character wear a beard throughout the film, thinking it would add credibility to his role as a prize winning novelist. Producer Pandro S. Berman, who had also produced *Sweet Bird of Youth*, nixed the idea. He reminded Paul that Clark Gable's worst flop was *Parnell*, in which "he'd foolishly hidden his face behind a beard." Berman went on to say, "If I decide to let Paul drop his towel during the nudist convention sequence, I'll also insist that he shave off the hairs on his ass."

With his clothes on, Paul diminished his sex appeal by appearing in horn-rimmed glasses. Even so, Elke Sommer seemed to devour him on screen like a tasty smörgåsbord.

In this implausible story set in Stockholm during the annual Nobel Prize awards, Paul has to solve the mystery of the kidnapping of a Nobel scientist and his replacement with a look-alike, as played by veteran actor Edward G. Robinson, who received $75,000 for the role.

In Stockholm, authorities objected to the script, claiming it cheapened the integrity of the Nobel Prize.

Allegedly, Paul based his characterization—or tried to—on the controversial renegade author, Norman Mailer. Encountering Mailer at a party in New York, the novelist told him, "I heard you played me in *The Prize*. If you'd really played me, you could have won an Oscar. After seeing this turkey, I told people you weren't playing me. I thought you were more Gore Vidal than me. Perhaps Truman Capote. You girly men just can't seem to get it right." With a drink in hand, a drunken Mailer turned and walked away, heading for the bar.

Although *The Prize* would ultimately be disappointing at the box office, it opened in New York on Christmas Day, 1963, attracting a brisk Yuletide business.

In spite of the bad movies, 1963 had been a good year for Paul in that exhibitors named him Number Nine among the Top Ten box office stars of the world. He'd never made the list before.

Except for the well-perceived perform-

Edward G. Robinson
escaping the poison pen of critics

382

ance of Edward G. Robinson, reviewers sharpened their pens for their attack on Paul and *The Prize* in general.

Arthur Knight in *The Saturday Review* labeled it a "mélange of claptrap melodrama and purply passion," suggesting that *The Prize* be retitled *Dr. No in Stockholm*. Judith Crist, in the *New York Herald Tribune*, stated bluntly that Paul "seems intent on living down whatever artistic reputation he has earned."

Bosley Crowther of *The New York Times* suggested that the story "might happen at a bathing beauty contest—but please, not at the Nobel Prize affair!" At least Elke Sommer's generous physical endowments, especially her protruding breasts, met universal approval.

***

All Hollywood was confused as to why Paul would accept a minor role in a minor comedy, *What a Way to Go*! The studio was familiar, 20th Century Fox, which had purchased the rights to this J. Lee Thompson production, with a screenplay by Betty Comden and Adolph Green.

Now it can be told: Fox originally wanted Elizabeth Taylor in the lead role of Louisa Benson, an eccentric millionairess who marries, in rapid succession, five husbands. "Type casting," Hollywood wags said, when learning of Elizabeth's interest in this satiric comedy.

Even before Elizabeth was considered, the role was initially offered to Marilyn Monroe, months before her death. One of the sets used for a Hollywood mansion was originally created for Marilyn and Dean Martin in her unfinished film, *Something's Got to Give*.

Ever since *Cat on a Hot Tin Roof*, Paul had been eager to work with Elizabeth again on screen. "Every man has a fantasy woman of his dreams," said Janice Rule. "For Paul, that was Elizabeth. She was everything Joanne Woodward wasn't: incredibly sexy, even dangerous, more glamorous than any woman should be, earthy, vulgar, the forbidden fruit of a thousand boudoirs. A man might go to bed with his wife while dreaming it was Elizabeth Taylor beneath him, assuming he practiced the missionary position. I didn't blame Paul one bit. If I were a man,

Paul appears with his former landlady,
Shirley MacLaine
Devoured by a machine

383

I'd pursue Elizabeth Taylor myself. She was Cleopatra. She was Catherine the Great. She was Eleanor of Aquitaine. She was Queen Bess. But, mostly, she was Helen of Troy."

Paul had already signed the contract to appear in *What a Way to Go!* when he learned that Elizabeth had dropped out and had been replaced with his friend and former landlord Shirley MacLaine. She was hoping to repeat her success in Billy Wilder's *Irma La Douce* (1963).

MacLaine was at a high point in her career, the sixth box office attraction in America, following Doris Day, Jack Lemmon, Rock Hudson, John Wayne, and Cary Grant. "And my leading men in the film were not chopped liver," MacLaine said. "There was Robert Cummings, who lived on vitamins; Dean Martin, who lived on Scotch; Dick Van Dyke, who lived on comedy; Paul Newman who lived; Robert Mitchum, who lived on life; and Gene Kelly, who lived on the perfection of song and dance."

Frank Sinatra was originally slated to play one of the husbands in *What a Way to Go!* But Darryl F. Zanuck at Fox balked at the singer's demands. Gregory Peck was then asked to play the part but he turned it down. Finally, Robert Mitchum agreed to accept the role.

Of all the cast members, Paul most enjoyed meeting Fifi D'Orsay. He was fascinated by this star of yesterday, listening for hours to tales of her life, including details about her torrid affair with Greta Garbo.

Earlier in her career, D'Orsay had played the quintessential Parisian coquette. At one point off-screen she was seen singing "Yes! We Have No Bananas" in French to Paul. She'd once sung the song at the Folies Bergère in Paris.

Although born in Canada, D'Orsay was known as "the French Bombshell." But she told Paul that when Ralph Edwards, in front of a camera on the set of his TV show, *This Is Your Life* (1952), presented her with a round-trip plane ticket to Paris, she cashed it in for money.

The writer-lyricists Comden and Green had fared better when they participated in the cinema masterpiece, *Singin' in the Rain* (1952). This usually talented pair went a little haywire in creating Paul's character.

Allowed to wear a beard for the first time, Paul was cast as the second of MacLaine's five husbands. Paul played Larry Flint, and for the third time he returned to Paris for his setting. A painter by night, he is a taxi driver by day.

His role was ridiculous, even outrageous. He invents a machine that converts music into paintings, which makes him rich. However, he eventually falls into the machine and is devoured.

MacLaine later said that "it was a delight working with Edith Head and her $500,000 costume budget, with seventy-two hairstylists to match the gowns, and a three and a half million dollar gem collection loaned out by

Harry Winston of New York. Pretty good perks, I'd say."

The movie was slaughtered by the critics and performed badly at the box office, even though today it's defined as something of a cult classic.

Since Paul appeared in only one fifth of the film's running time of 111 minutes, he didn't have to endure the full onslaught of the critical attacks. *The New Yorker* noted that "Paul Newman makes his obligatory appearance stripped to the waist—an odd trademark for a gifted man."

As one reviewer noted, "Paul Newman should give up his dream of becoming the next Cary Grant, a goal he will never reach. He'd better return to being Paul Newman on the screen, or else he may have no more career left in spite of the success of *Hud*."

Joanne wasn't doing much better, signing with director George Englund, Marlon Brando's close friend, to direct her in *Signpost to Murder*, a cheap thriller released in 1964. Joanne was cast opposite that handsome hunk, Stuart Whitman, who was coming down from an affair with Natalie Wood. Bushy browed and cleft-chinned, Whitman had a face that looked lived in, and he specialized in macho roles.

Later, all Joanne could remember about the film was that she was shooting a scene when the cast was notified that John F. Kennedy had been assassinated in Dallas.

***

Arm in arm, Paul arrived with Tennessee Williams at Tallulah Bankhead's swanky apartment on East 57th Street. Once again, the great playwright wanted to hear Paul and Tallulah read scenes from one of his Broadway plays, in this case, *The Milk Train Doesn't Stop Here Anymore*. The play's first Broadway run, though brilliantly acted by Hermione Baddeley, had flopped. Producer David Merrick, for reasons known only to himself, had agreed to bring it back to Broadway.

The Tallulah whom Paul

Tab Hunter with **Talullah** in *Milk Train*
"Us swamp bitches don't go in for hand kissin'."

385

remembered was very different from the one who sat before him this night. She'd once possessed a gaudy sensuality and even a kind of sultry sexiness. Those elusive qualities had vanished. What he saw sitting opposite him was an old lady beginning the last few precious years of her life.

In elephant-gray silk pajamas, Tallulah showed off a horribly burned hand. "A package of matches exploded, *dah-ling*, when I was lighting my cigarette."

Paul later recalled, "I was staring at a tiny little old lady smoking incessantly as if she were trying to hasten her own death. She mumbled most of her words, and her face seemed to have aged twenty years since I'd last seen her. That battered face of this once-celebrated beauty was haggard and drawn. She was a grotesque version of Alexandra Del Lago. Dissipated. Debauched. Perhaps Tennessee knew what he was doing casting Tallulah as Flora Goforth, an ex-Follies girl in a frantic denial of her imminent death."

Both Tennessee and Tallulah, uneasy allies for a change, urged Paul to accept the role of Christopher Flanders, the "Angel of Death," an enigmatic poet who arrives on Flora's doorstep to help her soul make the crossing to the other side.

Paul was willing to listen to these two towering icons of the theater, even though he knew instinctively that their glory days were behind them.

After her third drink with the two men, Tallulah yelled out "Cunty!" as a means of summoning her maid.

From the rear emerged a woman who looked exactly like Hattie McDaniel in *Gone With the Wind*, an actress with whom Tallulah had had a notorious affair. The maid brought a tray of conch fritters, Tennessee's favorite from his days of living in Key West. Before the housekeeper excused herself, Tallulah planted a big sloppy wet one on her large lips.

Tallulah spent the next half hour attacking the British director, Tony Richardson, who had been hired by Merrick to direct his resuscitated version of *Milk Train*. "He doesn't really want me," she protested to Tennessee. "The son of a bitch claimed he really wants Katharine Hepburn. I know Kate. I've even gone down on her a few times. Hell will freeze over before Kate Hepburn agrees to play this role of a decaying hedonist."

Throughout most of the evening, Tennessee remained almost stoic, and Paul sat mesmerized at the spectacle he was witnessing.

Before the night ended, Tallulah seemed to rise up and out of her decaying flesh. She promised that with Paul at her side on the stage, "I will make one grand exit from the theater. It will be my finest hour as Flora Goforth. I plan to give a legendary performance. As the bearded poet, this divine Paul Newman creature here will get even more spectacular reviews than he did in *Sweet Bird of Youth*."

At this point Tallulah rose to her feet. "Where is that bird?" she asked, raising her badly burned hand in the air. "Where have you gone, sweet bird? The sweet bird of my youth. It is said that youth is wasted on the young." She turned and stared into each of their eyes. "Miss Tallulah Bankhead never wasted one God damn fucking day of her youth."

As Paul and Tennessee were ushered to the door, there was no sexual invitation. Tallulah with some unknown person had no doubt performed her last sexual act. Paul later told Tennessee that evening that he suspected that "the candle that burned at both ends" which Tallulah always compared herself to has flickered out.

Over drinks Tennessee urged Paul to accept the role. "With help from both of us, Tallulah will rise like the phoenix from the ashes to deliver a performance that will compare with what Laurette Taylor did in my *The Glass Menagerie*."

Kissing Tennessee good night, Paul promised to call him the next day with his decision. He kept his promise, but rejected the possibility of his involvement with the reprise of *Milk Train* as part of the telephone call. Tennessee was very disappointed.

Two weeks later Tennessee contacted Paul, telling him that Richardson had wanted to cast his friend, Tony Perkins, in the role—that is, "until he met Tony's lover, Tab Hunter. Richardson fell for Tab big time."

"Tab Hunter co-starring with Tallulah Bankhead on Broadway?" Paul asked in astonishment. "Every queen in America will fly in for this one. I can just see the opening night audience."

"Tab always regretted turning down the opportunity to replace you in the role of Chance Wayne in *Sweet Bird of Youth*," Tennessee said. "In some way, he's making up for that lost opportunity by taking the role you turned down."

"I wish him luck," Paul said, "but I've got to be absolutely honest with you. Tallulah should not subject herself to a Broadway play. She needs to be in a nursing home with twenty-four hour supervision. You can prevent this disaster from happening."

"I am determined," Tennessee said. "You have to be a tough old bird to make it in the theater. Tallulah and I are tough old birds. We will show the world." He put down the phone.

The Milk Train Doesn't Stop Here Anymore opened at the Brooks Atkinson Theatre on January 1, 1964. Tallulah played to her screaming queens in the audience, and somewhere along the way Tennessee's ruminations on death got lost in the footlights.

The audience's loudest guffaws and most raucous laughter occurred just after Tallulah told Tab onstage, "Us swamp bitches don't go in for hand kissin'."

387

In August of 1964, in Atlantic City, New Jersey, Paul attended the Democratic National Convention, supporting President Lyndon Johnson in the mistaken belief that he'd end the war in Vietnam.

After the convention, during a weekend in Georgia, a fan spotted Paul walking the streets of Savannah with Brandon De Wilde.

Back in New York, and back to business, both Paul and Joanne signed to appear in the same two-act comedy, *Baby Want a Kiss*. Starring in the play with the Newmans was James Costigan, Joanne's former "fiancé" from the 1950s. Presented by the Actors Studio, it opened at the Little Theater in New York on April 19, 1964.

Perhaps after all his failure in comedy, Paul had learned a lesson or two, getting some of his best reviews in the play's four-month run. Director Frank Corsaro deftly guided Paul through any awkward moments on the boards.

Both Paul and Joanne played Hollywood stars—talk about typecasting. Paul was cast as "an aging juvenile," Joanne a "fading ingénue."

In the play—we trust not in real life—they can't stand each other. Paul's character of Emil at one point even makes homosexual advances toward Charlie, the third character as played by Costigan.

Howard Taubman of *The New York Times* took a dim view of this gay scene. "In the scene where Newman proposes at great length to the author (Costigan), he is like an actor who has wandered into the wrong theater. And you wish you had, too."

Paul was cast as a homosexual hiding in the closet with his marriage serving as his "beard." That raised speculation throughout the theater world. Was Paul actually playing his true character?

The Newmans signed an Equity minimum deal for which they were each paid $117.50 per week. They weren't in it for the money, but to help the Actors Studio.

John Chapman of the *New York Daily News* dismissed the play as "more fun for those who are in it than those who were at

Author **James Costigan**
supporting spoiled movie stars,
with Paul making homosexual advances

it." In spite of such put-downs, the play earned a tidy profit of $150,000.

Baby Want a Kiss would mark Paul's last appearance in a Broadway play.

"What gives with these two?" asked a Broadway columnist. "Why do they keep squandering their considerable talents on worthless properties?"

***

It is not known how much, if anything, actor Ben Gazzara, knew about Paul's relationship with Janice Rule. Of course, he was aware that both of them knew each other, as they'd appeared on Broadway in *Picnic* in the '50s.

Many sources claim that Gazzara had turned down the film role of Brick in *Cat on a Hot Tin Roof* that he'd originally created on the Broadway stage.

That is hardly the case. In his 2004 memoir, *In the Moment: My Life as an Actor*, he stated that when he learned that Paul had been cast as Brick in the film adaptation, it was hard for him to digest. "I'd created that role, lost the character, struggled and suffered to re-create him, and now a stranger to the play and the character of Brick would inherit what I'd done to bring Brick to life. It broke my heart. Never had I been so devastated in my career."

Gazzara had married Janice, the actress, singer, dancer, and eventually, psychoanalyst, in 1961. The tawny-haired beauty had been a confidant of Paul's ever since she'd played Madge on stage in William Inge's *Picnic*, but the relationship, at least according to Janice, had never been physical. That was about to change.

Originally, Janice had been drawn to Ralph Meeker, the sexy male star of *Picnic*. "I liked Paul's mind, but I infinitely preferred Ralph's body," she told the author at Downey's Restaurant in New York.

Janice claimed that her relationship with Paul turned sexual around the time she'd co-starred in a Freudian Western, *Invitation to a Gunfighter* (1964), with Yul Brynner.

"My affair continued on and off for quite a while with Paul. Of course, there were others, including Marlon Brando when we made *The Chase* in 1966. Ever since Paul and I starred in *Picnic*, there had always been sexual tension between us, but we resisted it until one night when we went at it.

Ben Gazzara with **Barbara Bel Geddes** in Broadway's
Cat on a Hot Tin Roof
"Never have I been so devastated."

Although I was married to Ben at the time, I was only too willing to join Paul in bed. I'd always been curious. We were so compatible that both of us decided that we should have married each other and not the partners we'd chosen."

Unlike ordinary mortals, Janice did not interpret adultery as the biggest sin in the world. After all, she'd been married to the writer Robert Thom when she began an affair with Ben Gazzara during their appearance together in *Night Circus*. On stage, Gazzara had to play a scene, "kissing her full, soft mouth during our love scenes," and one thing led to another. He confessed that their scenes together "aroused me as much as it did her. A torrid love affair soon followed."

In his memoir, Gazzara confessed that one night he walked in on his wife and another man. He caught them in the act. Word spread along Broadway that the man in question in coitus was none other than Paul Newman himself.

There is no strong evidence that the man was Paul. If it were, it would have been ironic that the actor who'd replaced Gazzara in the film version of *Cat on a Hot Tin Roof* was now replacing him in his wife's boudoir as well.

Friends (or enemies) of Janice often speculated about why she was so open in discussing her relationship with Paul after they broke up. Tony Perkins said, "Janice revealed too much, told too much, spilled too many of Paul's secrets."

There is a possible explanation. Janice developed a nerve condition that sent pain racing up and down her left arm. Her friends said it was almost more than a human could tolerate. No doctor seemed to know the cause. Based on prescriptions written by one of the finest neurologists in New York, Janice began taking Percodan, hoping that would bring relief. Eventually, she became addicted.

To deaden the pain even more, she mixed vodka with the drug. Gazzara claimed that the combination "altered her personality. Where once she had been simply opinionated, now she was strident. Where once she had been passionate, now she was loud."

There came a time when Janice would tell almost anything, providing graphic insights into her own life, including specifics about her brief affairs with Marlon Brando during their filming of *The Chase* and with Burt Lancaster

Janice Rule
"I should have married Paul."

during their filming of *The Swimmer*. "Janice even gave us penis sizes," Tony Perkins claimed.

Tired of sitting around waiting for the phone to ring, Janice studied at the Los Angeles Psychoanalytic Institute with the intent of eventually becoming a psychoanalyst. Perhaps she turned to psychiatry for insights into her own emotional problems.

The details are lacking, but it is almost certain that word reached Paul that Janice was supplying friends with details about his intimate relationship with her. No doubt he was horrified.

"One day he was just not there for me," she confessed. "He didn't return my calls. It took me a while to realize that he was seriously pissed off. All that vodka and Percodan loosened my tongue. I was never a great one for keeping secrets. It is odd that I chose the profession of psychoanalyst. In time, I learned to keep my trap shut. But I admit I was loose-tongued for quite a while. I made a lot of enemies for my indiscretions, and I paid the price."

She claimed she really loved Paul, both as a friend and a lover. "We promised each other than we'd be friends for life. But in show business, those lasting relationships are hard to maintain because you're torn in different directions. In such a world where the husband and wife are separated for long periods of time, it's not only hard to maintain fidelity to your spouse, but to keep loving the same person. Basically, in spite of my marriages, I often fell in love with whatever man I was with. That is, until I woke up the next morning."

"My biggest regret in life is that I did not divorce Ben and marry Paul. Of course, he always returned home to Joanne regardless of how much he strayed. She must have known things were going on. After all, she's a brilliant woman, which was evident when she first appeared on Broadway with us in *Picnic*. Perhaps the secret for the success of their marriage was that she gave her husband a very long leash."

"Without being outrageous, we might compare Paul's marriage to Joanne to the Queen of England's marriage to Prince Philip," Janice continued. "One of the Queen's relatives, I don't remember which one, was quoted as saying, 'Her Majesty doesn't demand fidelity from Philip. She demands loyalty.' Maybe that was the case between Paul and Joanne. In the end, regardless of what had gone down with him the night before, he was always there by her side for those important moments in life. How I wish my life had been different. How I wish that I'd had a man to stand by me through thick and thin. Often I was out there on a thin limb, dangling in the wind."

"I once wrote Paul a heartfelt letter apologizing for betraying him," she said. "I prayed he'd read it and get back to me. Then we could jumpstart our relationship once again. But I never heard from him. There was only a deafening silence between us. It was over."

***

Both Martin Ritt and Paul owed a film to Metro-Goldwyn-Mayer. Ritt was intrigued by the classic 1950 movie by Akira Kurosawa called *Rashomon*. Known for its multiple perspectives in relating a single moment in time, with conflicting versions, as told by different witnesses, of a single historical episode, it was later adapted for the Broadway stage by a husband-and-wife writing team, Michael and Fay Kanin. The play starred Rod Steiger and Claire Bloom, both friends of the Newmans. For the Newman/Ritt film production, Michael adapted the play, transferring the setting from feudal Japan to old Mexico.

The filmscript, originally entitled *The Rape*, presented four conflicting versions of the truth. Rashomon has even entered the English language as a word describing a situation characterized by multiple conflicting or differing interpretations.

Paul's original instinct was correct. He rejected the role of the Mexican bandit and alleged rapist, Juan Carrasco, proposing to Ritt that it would be an ideal vehicle for Marlon Brando. Paul was no doubt influenced by Brando's performance in the 1952 film directed by Elia Kazan, *Viva Zapata!*, in which Brando had portrayed the Mexican revolutionary Emiliano Zapata, in a script by John Steinbeck.

Initially, after Brando read the script, he told Ritt, "I love it." Even so, although the debut of shooting was rapidly approaching, he wouldn't commit to the project.

The producer of *The Outrage*, A. Ronald Rubin, claimed that when Paul heard how much Brando liked the script, he changed his mind and wanted to play Carrasco after all.

On accepting the role, his fifth movie with Ritt, Paul said, "My character is an absolute primitive, which I had never played, with an entirely different sense of movement and an accent I'm not familiar with. I did it because it was a challenge. I didn't think I could pull it off, but I was sporting enough to give the thing a try."

Paul facing off with **Laurence Harvey**
"A King to my Queen."

Ritt had signed an all-star cast. Claire Bloom contracted to repeat her role on Broadway as a frontier woman who's the victim of the alleged rape. The British actor, Laurence Harvey, was signed to play her husband, who dies as part of the film's plot. Paul reunited with Edward G. Robinson, with whom he'd worked in *The Prize*. He also encountered Albert Salmi, playing the sheriff.

Perhaps to escape the responsibilities of being a husband and the father of a brood whose numbers were beginning to resemble the Brady Bunch, Paul fled to Mexico for two weeks prior to the beginning of the actual shooting. His announced reason was to learn the language, study the customs of the land, and familiarize himself with the manners of *mexicanos*. At that, he would not be entirely successful. The blue-eyed boy from Shaker Heights was never entirely convincing as a Mexican *bandito* and rapist.

At the first hotel he stayed at in Mexico, Paul met a startlingly handsome, eighteen-year-old bellhop, who called himself "Pepe." He'd previously lived for two years in Detroit and spoke a badly accented English. Paul would later claim he "stole" the accent he adopted for *The Outrage* from Pepe.

In Mexico, the green-eyed Pepe and Paul showed up together at many a sleazy cantina, drinking lots of *cerveza* with tequila chasers.

Paul was so entranced with this Pepe that he flew him to additional location shooting in Arizona, where on the few occasions he introduced him to anybody, he was referred to as Paul's "language consultant." One of the actors Paul introduced Pepe to was the bisexual English star, Laurence Harvey.

Harvey seemed entranced by both Paul and Pepe. One night when Harvey went on a drinking binge with Paul, he asked him, "Would you be king to my queen for the night?" Paul rejected the generous offer. Harvey had once extended a similar invitation to John Wayne.

During the first week of the shoot, Paul's friend, Rod Steiger, sent him a telegram. Perhaps Steiger was slightly jealous of Paul for re-creating the role he'd originated so successfully on Broadway. "Welcome to my part," Steiger wrote. "I bet I was better in it than you will be. Here's hoping you fall up against a cactus and get thorns in your ass."

As Paul told Ritt, "Dear ol' Rod can be downright hostile sometimes. It wasn't the friendliest of greetings."

Although the film was shot in black and white, Paul showed up on the set wearing brown contact lenses, which made his eyes tear. Later, when his image came onto the screen, some members of various audiences laughed at seeing him in his latest re-incarnation. In buckskin chaps and large jangling spurs, Paul wore a sombrero over his matted hair and a poncho draped across his shoulders.

Although his hair was a black wig, the stubble on his face was authentic.

393

The fake nose was not.

On reflection, Ritt later said, "Every time Paul veered from his screen image, he hatched a turkey."

During the shoot, Albert Salmi orchestrated a reunion of sorts with Paul. Both of them seemed to have a Pandora's box of shared memories that each of them wanted to keep closed.

Over the years, Salmi, who had not retained his ruggedly handsome look of the '50s, frankly told friends that he was jealous of Paul for becoming the star that he was. "Producers and directors conspired to take the big roles from me," Salmi claimed. As time had gone by, Salmi continued to work, but in minor roles such as playing a cowboy in TV westerns like *Gunsmoke*.

Salmi maintained a smoldering resentment of Paul for the rest of his life. Even so, Paul embraced the actor when his final scenes were shot and wished him well in his life.

In spite of the chill, Paul continued to hear of Salmi's work in the years to come. Paul was saddened to learn of Salmi's death in 1990.

At the age of sixty-two, he died tragically as part of a murder-suicide in Spokane, Washington. Separated at the time from his second wife, Roberta Pollock, Salmi fatally shot her with a .25 caliber pistol. Then, with a different weapon, a Colt .45, he then shot himself in the heart. Days went by before the police discovered their bodies on Monday, April 23.

Ironically, Salmi had been writing his memoirs in the weeks and months before his death. He'd told friends that he was devoting an entire chapter to Paul Newman. When the unfinished manuscript was discovered after Salmi's death, it appeared that he'd burned most of his material on Paul.

"From what I hear now, Newman's a nice guy and does a lot of good for people," Salmi said. "I don't want to reveal to fans what a snake in the grass he really was."

When filming *The Outrage* on location in Arizona came to an end, Paul gave Pepe one thousand dollars, but refused to bring him back with him to Los Angeles.

To the rescue came Harvey, who flew with Pepe to New York. Three months later Pepe was seen on the arm of Tennessee Williams arriving at a cocktail party. Harvey and Tennessee were friends.

Harvey, in Los Angeles a few months later, had seen the final cut of *The Outrage*. The always outrageous actor told Paul, "You had me tied to a tree

Albert Salmi
Murder before suicide

394

throughout most of the film. It would have been more appropriate if you'd raped me instead of Claire Bloom."

"Dream on!" Paul told him, giving him a quick kiss on the lips. "That's just a hint of what you'll never get."

"You bloody sod," Harvey said. "English actors are so much more cooperative than you Yanks."

"Even more so than young Mexican boys called Pepe?" Paul asked.

"*Touché!*"

Holding its premiere in New York on October 7, 1964, *The Outrage* went into limited release nationwide, playing to diminishing audiences.

Critic Judith Crist compared Paul to a "junior grade Leo Carrillo, spitting and spewing and wallowing in dialect and playing the villain, the lecher, the social outcast, the lover and the coward to the hilt for his own very private edification."

Comparisons to Brando surfaced once again, much to Paul's humiliation. "Brando," in the words of one acid critic, "fitted comfortably into the role of a Mexican revolutionary. Apparently, as Newman confessed to one reporter, 'I came close to crawling out of my skin as Juan Carrasco.' A truer self-assessment by an actor is unlikely to be heard any time soon."

The film would ultimately flop, but twenty years later Paul was still making the claim that it represented "some of my best work."

In Mexico City, when it premiered, both the public and critics greeted Paul's impersonation of a *mexicano* with ridicule. One critic wrote, "We have plenty of home-grown rapists who could have done the role so much better. Why did the director have to turn to a blue-eyed gringo from Ohio to play Juan Carrasco?"

***

Perhaps Metro-Goldwyn-Mayer's original cast choices, Tony Curtis and Gina Lollobrigida, could have saved *Lady L*. Although shooting had begun on the film, with George Cukor directing, MGM shut it down long before its completion. The bad script was left to gather dust in MGM archives until the late autumn of 1964 when Carlo Ponti revived it. He wanted his wife, Sophia Loren, to star in the picture opposite Paul Newman. A deal was struck between Ponti and MGM.

Ironically, the joint casting of Paul with Loren had been announced earlier for a screen version of Arthur Miller's controversial play, *After the Fall*, an intensely personal view of Miller's experiences during his marriage to his former wife, Marilyn Monroe. The version with Newman and Loren was never made.

Paul had met Peter Ustinov in England, and was impressed when this super-talented man signed on to write the screenplay of *Lady L* based on a novel by Romain Gary. Ustinov even agreed to direct the picture.

"What was my dear old buddy, Paul, thinking?" Tony Perkins asked. "Accepting a role as a bomb-toting French anarchist at the turn of the century? Talk about miscasting!"

Loren, also horribly miscast, came off better than either of her male co-stars, which also included the perennially suave David Niven.

"Paul liked a lot of the plot when I presented it to him," Ustinov said, "especially when he seeks refuge in a bordello. He saw his role of Armand as a French Robin Hood. He also liked playing against type as a bank robber. But somehow the project just didn't make Jell-O."

Ustinov cast himself in the movie as the visiting Prince Otto.

Ponti convinced Loren to play the girl who delivers the laundry to a brothel in Paris, then ends up marrying into the British aristocracy, becoming Lady L. Although she'd risen from the back streets of Naples, Loren by then already sounded like Oscar Wilde's Lady Bracknell, so she didn't need any language lessons for the role.

A lot of the difficulties Ustinov encountered involved the script itself, even though he'd written it. MGM executives were alarmed by the scenes that were to take place in a brothel. Today that would be a no-brainer, but, because of the pervasive censorship that still existed as late as the 1960s, it was a potential pitfall.

Loren reportedly ridiculed Paul's insistence that he wear a mustache in the film. He finally won out "by beating Ustinov to a pulp."

Ustinov despaired after the first two weeks of directing Paul. "He wants to talk over every motivation hour after hour," the actor said. "He needs this the way a car needs petrol. I had to steel myself to be worn out by hours of Method conversation about interpretation. I was groggy at the end of one of our sessions. Sophia just waited there as patiently as I did, saying 'when is he going to stop?'"

Gore Vidal claimed that Joanne feared that Paul might stray from home and hearth as an after-affect of those love scenes with the legen-

Paul with Sophia Loren in Lady L
No chemistry, on or off the screen

396

darily voluptuous Loren. But intimacies between them never came to be.

Loren was no more attracted to Paul than she was to Marlon Brando, with whom she would co-star in *A Countess from Hong Kong*, directed by Charles Chaplin.

"Sophia just didn't get off on these so-called American sex symbols," Ustinov later recalled. "She might have been flirtatious with Cary Grant, but I don't think that romance ever got off the ground. I think she preferred a man like Rossano Brazzi, her co-star in *Legend of the Lost*."

Lady L was shot in France, Switzerland, and at Yorkshire's famous Castle Howard in Northeast England. "I couldn't help but notice that Newman kept himself amused with a series of young ladies, some rather beautiful," said Niven. "I doubted all those rumors about his being gay. The evidence pointed otherwise."

Of course, Niven said the same thing about his notorious former roommate, Errol Flynn, whom he always maintained was straight in spite of overwhelming evidence to the contrary.

At one point, Ustinov nearly had a nervous breakdown. He told Niven and others, "There is just no on-screen chemistry between Sophia and Paul, and they are supposed to be lovers."

Niven, perhaps joking but with a ring of sincerity, suggested that "Newman should fuck Loren and get her to fall madly in love with him. Then those two will light up the screen."

Ustinov later claimed that it was he, not Niven, who suggested to Paul that he seduce Loren, as Joanne had feared. But nothing ever came of it. Loren told Ustinov that she found "this American uncouth and vulgar. Let him go back to his beer drinking. He doesn't even appreciate the glory of wine."

Loren uttered that remark on the same day that she'd asked Paul how he attached his false mustache.

Before walking away, he replied, "Sperm."

After taking a beating from the press in both Britain and the United States, Paul said, "Anything wrong with *Lady L* is the fault of one man and one man only. The villain is Paul Newman. I have very American skin. When I try to move inside the skin of a foreigner, I flop."

"It was indeed a flop, although I came out looking good," Ustinov chuckled. "Of all the Newman films, this one seems least likely for a big revival."

Lady L premiered in 1965 in England but its release was delayed in the United States until May of 1966. MGM in Los Angeles was not pleased with the picture, but they had good reports of Paul's role in *Harper*, which they predicted would be a big success. The release of *Lady L* was delayed until all the rave reviews came in for *Harper*. Then *Lady L* was released. It never managed, however, to cash in on Harper's success.

Paul celebrated his fortieth birthday on the set of *Lady L* in Paris, but he didn't look middle-aged, more like thirty-two.

Paul had something else to celebrate and that was the birth of his sixth and final child. Nicknamed "Clea," Claire Olivia Newman was born on April 21, 1965.

To regain her figure after "birthin' babies"—a line, of course, from *Gone With the Wind*, Joanne took up ballet to bring shape back to her shapely figure. She would be the mother of not only her own three daughters, but on occasion Scott and Paul's daughters with Jackie Witte.

As for Paul, he boasted to friends like Geraldine Page, "I've fathered six children, and I never changed a fucking diaper."

***

One afternoon, in an unexpected move, Paul went to the phone at the studio to receive an important call. He recognized the voice at once. It was that of the lonely princess in *Roman Holiday*, the child woman *Sabrina*, the party girl of *Breakfast at Tiffany's*.

It was Audrey Hepburn.

Her director, Stanley Donen, had said, "Audrey's magnetism is so extraordinary that everyone wants to be close to her. But she places a glass barrier between herself and the world. You can't get behind it easily. It makes her remarkably attractive."

She was lowering the glass wall for Paul and inviting him to meet privately with her. "You must tell no one," she cautioned. "Certainly not my husband, Mel." She was referring, of course, to actor Mel Ferrer, with whom she was involved in what she referred to as an "emotionally sterile" marriage.

Because of her secretary, personal assistant, and hairdresser, Freddie Stellars, who spoke extensively to the press after his dismissal from Audrey's inner circles, we know some of the details of what transpired over the next few weeks between Paul and this very private, mysterious actress of high chic.

Invited to her hotel suite, Paul was excited at the prospect of seeing her again. Her name symbolized elegance, grace, and style. She'd captured his

Audrey Hepburn
Breaking the glass barrier

398

heart in *My Fair Lady* and *Funny Face*, and she remained an elusive target on his A-list of women he hoped to seduce.

When Paul arrived at her suite, he was greeted by Freddie, who volunteered his services to get Paul a cocktail and even volunteered to restyle Paul's hair, giving him a new look for the 60s if he wanted it. Paul accepted the drink but turned down the restyling.

The suite looked surprisingly homelike. Freddie explained that Audrey always arrived anywhere she was going with twenty trunks. These trunks contained family pictures, her favorite possessions, drinking glasses, even flower vases. She would unpack all of her possessions and place them about the suite. She even traveled with her own bed linens and quilts.

Within ten minutes, Audrey emerged from her bedroom. Doe-eyed and pencil thin, she was as ravishingly beautiful off the screen as she was on. She greeted him with that heartbreaking lilt in her voice and kissed him on both cheeks in the French style. "I so admire you," she said. "I've longed to see you without others around us."

"I don't just admire you, I worship you," he said, bending down to kiss her delicate hand.

"I can worship you, too," she said provocatively, even flirtatiously, but later for that." What transpired over the next few hours and days is seen entirely through the perspective of Freddie's memory.

He maintained that during her reunion with Paul, Audrey threw down a gauntlet of challenge to the actor. Both of the stars were children born in the '20s, and Audrey feared that as Hollywood moved deeper into the '60s, each of them faced the prospect of becoming irrelevant if they didn't change with the times and accept the New Age that was dawning.

"I'm thirty-seven," she said.

He rushed to assure her that she didn't look her age.

"Neither do you look your age, but time will catch up with us. That's why I've asked you here. I want you to read a script." She signaled to Freddie to bring the script to Paul. "It's called *Two for the Road*. It's a complete change for me. A new image. And the leading male role is divine, ideal for you."

She briefly outlined the plot to him. In its most sim-

Albert Finney with **Audrey Hepburn**
in *Two for the Road*
Threats from a pissed-off husband

399

plistic form, it is the story of a bickering couple reminiscing about their twelve years of marriage. In the plot, they are trying to save their marriage.

"We would shoot it on the French Riviera," she said, her eyes dancing with glee. "Four glorious months away from husbands or wives, our responsibilities behind us. I've been on the verge of a nervous breakdown. I'm sure you need rejuvenation in your life. I think our working together . . ." She paused. "Or even playing together would become one of the highlights of our lives."

"Do you think teenagers would go for it?" he pointedly asked her. "They seem to be the arbiters of taste at the box office these days."

"I think everybody will go for it," she said. "It'll attract audiences of all ages. I'm taking a big chance. The role goes against my public image. In the film I'm even acerbic at times. Our bedroom scenes together will be rather frank." She almost blushed when she said that, at least according to Freddie.

"I'm eager to hop in bed with you," he said. "On the screen, naturally."

"Audrey held out that film script to Paul like Eve the apple to Adam," Freddie said. "But she was dangling more, so much more. She was seducing him. If she'd given the greenlight, he would have risen from the sofa and carried her rail-thin body into the bedroom and locked the door behind them. But that wasn't Audrey's way. She toyed with a man before seducing him."

Freddie claimed that during Audrey's stay in Los Angeles, Paul returned on five separate occasions. "How can I put this diplomatically? Those visits were conjugal. Of course, they weren't exactly married, but after her first night with Paul, I think Audrey fell in love. She always fell in love spontaneously, like that fling with William Holden."

"There was one big problem," Freddie recalled. "Paul was not seeing the real Audrey. He saw only Holly Golightly or one of her screen images. In the short time he knew Audrey, he failed to sort out the *real* from the *reel*."

"How do these quickie romances end?" Freddie asked himself. "In this case, with a whimper. I never knew Paul Newman well enough to know what he was thinking. He called Audrey's suite one day and got me on the phone. Audrey was out seeing someone. He told me that he'd read the script of *Two for the Road* and was rejecting it. He said he'd have a messenger return his copy later in the day."

"Audrey will be back at five," Freddie said. "Wouldn't you like to speak to her personally?"

"No," Paul said, "I'm leaving town. Just tell her the best dreams are those only dreamed." He put down the phone.

Freddie said it was his awful duty to break the news to Audrey. "When I told her, she cried all night. I think she was really beginning to fall in love with Paul. She was a waif-like creature, always willing to give away her heart to the wrong man."

"By dawn, when I went to deliver breakfast to her, she seemed to have recovered," Freddie said. "In some ways, in spite of her vulnerability, she could rally and be made of steel when the situation called for that."

With Paul out of the picture, Stanley Donen cast Albert Finney in the role. In the South of France, Audrey and Finney had a torrid romance until her husband, Mel Ferrer, arrived on the scene.

"Her husband threatened to divorce her if she continued her romance with Finney," Freddie claimed. "He told her that he would cite adultery as the motivation for his divorce action and name Finney in the suit. Then he delivered the final blow. He said that after the divorce he'd take their son, Sean, away from her. Audrey collapsed and gave in to him. Ever since they'd been married in 1954, he'd always coasted on her fame. She even got roles for him. I was glad when she divorced Ferrer. I never liked him anyway."

"In the years ahead," Freddie said, "she spoke only lovingly of Paul. One night when we were having a quiet drink together, she said, "I fear the youth culture of America is making me *passée*. That's not the case with Paul. He keeps reinventing himself and bouncing back."

***

Bounce back from his string of box office disasters is exactly what Paul did in 1965 when Warner Brothers asked him to read a script based on the novel, *The Moving Target*, by Ross Macdonald. The film that evolved from this novel would move Paul back to superstar status. It would also mark his return to Warner Brothers, the studio that had caused him so many disappointments and frustrations. But this time he was warmly received by management.

Jack Warner, whom Paul called "the second greatest vulgarian I've ever known," showed up personally on the set to welcome Paul back to the studio. The terms he proposed to his former boss were tough, $750,000 for his upfront salary, plus ten percent of the gross after $7.5 million. Amazingly, Warner, a hard bargainer, accepted these terms. Before leaving the set that day, Warner sent best wishes to Paul's wife, whom he referred to as "Joan."

The original name of the detective in the novel was Lew Archer, but Paul wanted it changed to Harper because of the success he'd enjoyed with movies that began with H, notably *The Hustler* and *Hud*. Ultimately, producers Jerry Gershwin and Elliott Kastner decided to call the film itself *Harper*.

When producers Gershwin and Kastner met with Paul, Kastner suggested that Paul play the role of Harper "as a man with big balls."

In accepting the role, Paul was following a long tradition established by such film veterans as Humphrey Bogart in *The Maltese Falcon* (1941).

To evoke the memory of Bogie, Warner had hired "Bogie's baby," his former wife, Lauren Bacall, to play opposite Paul.

William Goldman's script was taut and to the point. "Like a drink?" the sultry Bacall asks Paul.

"Not before lunch," he says.

"I thought you were a detective."

"New type."

His dialogue with Janet Leigh, playing Susan, his ex-wife, was equally brittle.

"What do you want from me?" she asks.

"A few kind words," he says.

"Anything else?"

"Anything I can get?"

Paul played Harper as hard-boiled, cynical, and stylish. He later claimed he modeled his persona on Robert F. Kennedy.

On the day of Paul's opening shot, the director, Jack Smight, told Paul that Frank Sinatra had been Warner's first choice for the role. "At least it wasn't Marlon Brando," Paul said. Ironically, Sinatra would get his own chance at playing a detective the following year when he made *Tony Roma*.

On the set, Paul had a reunion with Robert Wagner, who had been cast in a minor role as Allan Taggers. The world had changed since the early 1950s. Wagner's star was dimming, and so was his once startlingly beautiful appearance. When he made *Harper*, he was merely handsome, but no longer "Stop the Press."

In days of yore, Paul reportedly had had a crush on Wagner and wanted to look like him, but that was no longer the case. Both actors, each of whom had enjoyed the favors of Natalie Wood, were friendly on the set and would soon star in a picture together.

But despite their nominal friendship, there had always existed a certain professional rivalry between Paul and Wagner. Actually Wagner had coveted Paul's role in *The Hustler*, and was very upset when he'd lost the part. Paul promised to make it up to him when the next good script came along. He was instrumental in getting Wagner cast in *Harper*, although the role was not a real star part.

Jack Warner objected to Paul's choice. Wagner remembered Paul going to bat for him.

Paul Newman as Harper
"A man with big balls."

402

"Paul is quite formidable when he's on your side," he recalled. "The part in *Harper* was made for me. For the first time, I got some damn good reviews."

Playing an airline pilot, Wagner is involved with a junkie nightclub singer as played by Julie Harris, a friend of Paul's from their days at the Actors Studio.

Paul also had a reunion with his former confidant of the 1950s, Shelley Winters. She was cast as a once-gorgeous but now alcoholic former starlet, Fay Eastbrook. "I'm playing myself," she told Paul before giving him a sloppy wet one.

In a strange footnote to movie history, Paul's first wife, Jackie Witte, called him and asked for a small part in the film. Cast as Mrs. Kronberg, she was billed as Jacqueline de Wit. Since they still had three kids, Paul and Jackie had remained on speaking terms for the sake of the children.

Janet Leigh and Paul had met several times previously, including once during a chance encounter when she was sleeping with John F. Kennedy. They came to know each other more intimately on the set of *Harper*. Janet told the press, "When Paul looks at you with those blue eyes of his, he commands you to look at him and listen. He *makes* you respond to him. That's the basis of his sex appeal."

"Janet should know," Shelley Winters, years later, told the author. "She was sleeping with him—lucky gal. But I got there first a long time ago."

In addition to intimacies with Kennedy and her husband, Tony Curtis, Janet had slept around, having participated in previous flings with partners who included Peter Lawford and Tarzan, Lex Barker, who went on to marry Lana Turner. At one point Janet had even been involved with the gangster Johnny Stompanato who was stabbed to death one night at Lana's home, allegedly by her daughter, Cheryl Crane.

During the course of the filming of *Harper*, Paul was surprised to learn that Janet had married a student, Kenneth Carlyle, when she was only fourteen years old. The marriage was later annulled.

Pamela Tiffin, who'd been cast into a minor role in the film, had made a memorable film debut in Billy Wilder's *One, Two, Three*, opposite James Cagney. She had nothing but praise for time spent working with Paul. She was less enthusiastic about Joanne Woodward,

Paul feeding **Shelley Winters** in *Harper*
"Janet Leigh, not me, was sleeping with him."

who had appeared on the set one day. Tiffin claimed that Joanne didn't have a sense of humor, but her marriage to Paul seemed to "be a working one—steady, not capricious, not flighty."

Paul, however, was fun-loving and amused by Janet. "Paul used to confide in me, but during the making of *Harper*, he turned all his attention to Janet," Shelley said. "Those two used to slip away for hours in his dressing room when they weren't needed on the set."

Though *Harper* was made after Paul filmed *Lady L*, it was released in the United States two months before his bomb with Sophia Loren.

After *Harper* was released, Paul got rave reviews. Rose Pelswick in the *New York Journal-American* called it "about the best performance of his career."

But not all critics were pleased. Pauline Kael, writing for *The New Yorker* disagreed, calling Paul's performance the worst since *The Silver Chalice*.

Paul would reprise his role of *Harper* when he made the far less successful *The Drowning Pool*, released in 1975, and starring, of all people, Joanne Woodward. Unlike the original *Harper*, Paul's second time around as the cynical detective was reviewed as "a dull, dreary, and hackneyed pseudo-thriller clunkily directed."

When Steve McQueen saw *Harper*, he called Paul. "Of all the film roles you've made, this one had Steve McQueen branded on it. You should have sent the script over to me, you fucker. I would have been better in it than you."

"The only thing you can do better than me is suck cock," Paul said.

"I'll plug your ass for that remark," McQueen said before hanging up.

***

Paul often followed a hit movie like *Harper* with a disaster. Such was the case when he signed on to film *Torn Curtain* at Universal. He was eager to work with its producer and director, Alfred Hitchcock. The screenplay by Brian Moore was a dull and plodding Cold War so-called thriller.

In a surprise move, Paul was cast opposite Julie Andrews, the daughter of musical hall entertainers and one of the great singers of her age. *Torn Curtain* came in the wake of her incredible international successes with *Mary Poppins* and *The Sound of Music*. She certainly had a "backseat" to Paul in this Hitchcock film, but her name on the marquee attracted far more business than this film might have otherwise.

Paul was cast as Michael Armstrong, an American atomic scientist who passes himself off as a defector to East Germany, where in this guise he hopes to gain deadly secrets to bring back to the West.

Actually Hitchcock wanted to cast his stars of *North by Northwest*, Cary

Grant and Eva Marie Saint, as the film's key players. But Grant told the director, "I'm too old," and the studio vetoed the possibility of Eva Marie, preferring Andrews because of her box office appeal.

Hitchcock constantly referred to Andrews not by her name but as "the singer." When Universal wouldn't cast Eva Marie Saint, Hitchcock ironically proposed yet another singer for the role: Doris Day. He'd been impressed with her acting in *The Man Who Knew Too Much* and had even worked a song, 'Que Sera, Sera,' into the plot. That song became a worldwide hit.

"Doris can pull this caper off," Hitchcock said. "Not Miss Mary Poppins."

He knew from the beginning that the casting of Paul with Andrews was wrong, but he was nonetheless forced to follow the studio's dictates. When the film was finally released, Archer Winsten of the *New York Post* nailed the problem. "Newman simply doesn't add up as a nuclear physicist. Maybe he was *Harper* too recently and was too good in it. And Julie Andrews doesn't resemble in any way the assistant to a nuclear physicist. She has been too much the Baroness and *Mary Poppins* or even an Americanized Emily, to fit this chore."

Julie Andrews with Paul in *Torn Curtain*
No Doris Day, no Cary Grant

At the age of sixty-six, Hitchcock was nearing the end of his career, and he'd begun to regard movie making "as a very dull task indeed, especially with the actors of the '60s." When the director saw the first rushes, he knew there was no chemistry between his stars. "In a laboratory it would be the equivalent of mixing plain water (Newman) with plain water (Andrews). Maybe I should have Andrews sing something from *My Fair Lady*. That she can do."

In the first version of the script, Paul was supposed to be a homosexual. The plot, very roughly, had been based on England's notorious Burgess-MacLean spy

Unmarried lovers:
Paul in bed with Mary Poppins
Denounced by the Legion of Decency

case of the '50s, where those two lovers defected to Russia.

Guy Burgess and Donald MacLean were British officials, one an intelligence officer, the other a diplomat, who spied for the Soviet Union, betraying Western secrets to the Russians during the Cold War.

Reportedly, Paul balked at playing a gay spy, and the script was rewritten.

"There's no way that Newman can play a homosexual," Hitchcock told Universal executives. Obviously, he hadn't seen Paul's stage role in *Baby Want a Kiss* or his film, *Cat on a Hot Tin Roof.*

Originally Paul had said, "You bet your sweet ass I'd like to work with Hitchcock." But tensions arose between the two men before shooting even began. When the director invited Paul to his home for a formal dinner, Paul showed up in clothes more suited to a fishing trip. When Hitchcock presented vintage wine from his cellar to his guests, Paul said, "Make mine *cerveza*. I'll get the beer myself." He headed to the kitchen and emerged with a bottle of beer, which he preferred to drink right from the bottle, refusing a glass or mug.

As a Method actor, Paul kept demanding that Hitchcock provide him with more motivation for his character. By the second week of the shoot, Hitchcock's patience was wearing thin. When confronted with yet another question about his character's motivation, Hitchcock replied icily, "Mr. Newman, your motivation is your salary." The director turned his back on Paul and walked away.

At one point an exasperated Hitchcock told an associate, "My attempt to direct this gentleman is impossible. Why is he concerned with the motivation of his character all the time? He presents endless memos to me about script changes. It's all a waste of time. He will end up playing just plain Paul Newman, as he's done in every film he's ever made. He has no range at all."

In an interview with *The New York Times*, Hitchcock made a widely circulated comment. "The most difficult things to photograph are dogs, babies, motorboats, Charles Laughton (God rest his soul), and Method actors." Under his breath, he said, "I have one such actor in mind. But don't print his name."

For years, it was widely and clearly understood, and in some cases virtually written into his contract, that Paul would agree, when requested by a director, to display his sculpted physique during the filming of a movie. In *Torn*

Paul murdering **Ludwig Donath**
What's this Method acting shit?

Curtain, Hitchcock flirted with the idea of male nudity. He conceived a scene of Paul in the shower. A plastic curtain protected Paul's privates from the viewing public. Actually, he was protected in another way. The curtain doesn't obscure the fact that he's in the shower wearing underpants.

Paul was in great pain during the filming, as he'd recently suffered a motorcycle accident on Sunset Boulevard. He sustained such severe burns on his legs and left hand that skin grafts were needed. His primary physician predicted that he would never again regain use of his left hand. When not on the set, Paul was in his dressing room gripping a wet towel, an exercise he hoped would make his hand functional again.

Paul took to drinking heavily during the final weeks of shooting. He snapped at his wife and assistants around him. "It was obvious," Andrews recalled, "he was very unhappy during the filming."

Andrews hated the script, but was thrilled to work with Paul and Hitchcock. Paul got star billing over her, but she was paid $750,000 against ten percent of the gross. This was a larger cut than Paul was getting. A big hunk of the five million dollar budget for *Torn Curtain* went to Paul and Andrews, certainly not into the poor production values.

The film opens with a love scene in bed between Paul and Andrews. Paul and Andrews are not married, which brought condemnation from the Legion of Decency, which attacked *Torn Curtain* as "morally objectionable" because of its implications of premarital sex. The Legion issued an awkwardly worded statement declaring, "Parents should be aware that the 'Mary Poppins' image of the female lead (Julie Andrews) shattered in this film cannot serve as any criterion of the film's acceptability for their children."

During the course of the filming, Paul tended to focus his ire on the director, not at Andrews. He announced that "she's the last of the great dames." Even so, no friendship developed between them, certainly no romance, as had been the case with some of his other leading ladies."

Andrews later said, "I did not have to act in *Torn Curtain*. I merely went along for the ride. I did it just for the privilege of working with Hitchcock. But why is he so afraid of women?"

Paul's comment on the film was very brief. "I dislike it!"

***

Escaping from the clutches of Hitchcock, Paul at forty-two contemplated his next move. Tony Perkins said, "He continued to cheat Father Time. Of course, those baby blues were framing a wrinkle or two, but he still looked thirty-four. Somehow he never got a beer gut, although his consumption was amazing. Those saunas, that health diet, and that daily plunge of his handsome

407

face into a bucket of ice water kept him forever young."

As Paul moved deeper into middle age, his love life dimmed. The only person he was known to see outside his marriage was Brandon De Wilde, a friendship that was conducted in the strictest of privacy, away from family and friends.

Paul told Martin Ritt that he wanted to star in a buddy movie with Brandon, "probably a Western." Ritt was instructed to find the right script as a vehicle for the two of them. "That little boy in *Hud* is growing up," Paul said. "He's all man now."

The script Ritt came up with didn't have a role for Brandon, but it had a star part for Paul. *Hombre* became another one of his "H" films. Ritt would both produce and direct the movie from the screenplay by the husband-wife team of Harriet Frank and Irving Ravetch, writers who had served Paul so well through their authorship of *The Long, Hot Summer* and *Hud*. "They are my tried-and-true cohorts," Paul said. "A winning team."

Based on an Elmore Leonard novel, *Hombre* cast Paul as the stoic John Russell, an outcast figure who had suffered racial prejudice even though he was Caucasian. Paul would play an anti-hero. He'd done so in the past and would again in his future, but this role would be his most extreme in that genre.

"I was attracted to the script because Brando had taught me to appreciate the plight of the American Indian," Paul said. "*Hombre* was not your typical Western. We didn't need to kill off all the Indians in this film. It was a plea for tolerance, and the need for both the Indian and the Caucasian to come together and to cooperate for their mutual benefit."

He was challenged by the role of a white man reared by Apaches, a loner who feels he belongs to neither race. As he did for most roles, Paul moved through the Southwest, often with Brandon at his side, learning as much as he could about Apache culture.

While Brandon and Paul roamed the desert, Ritt was lining up an extremely talented cast of players, notably veteran actor Fredric March, one of the greatest. The other stars included Richard Boone, Cameron Mitchell, and Diane Cilento. Once again, Paul would be cast in a movie with the beautiful Barbara Rush.

Paul as *Hombre*
A Caucasian raised by Apaches

Hombre appears to be an update to John Ford's classic 1939 *Stagecoach*. Paul's character finds himself in Arizona riding inside a stagecoach back in the 1880s. He's traveling with a group of whites, and their stagecoach is attacked by bandits. Paul's character of Russell becomes their only hope for survival. Originally the passengers had been disdainful of him because of his upbringing with Indians.

Of all of Paul's films to that point, *Hombre* contains the smallest amount of dialogue for him. He must convey his character to audiences through mannerism and action.

Sean Connery visited the set to meet with his then-wife, Diane Cilento. By coincidence, Connery at about the same time was filming *A Fine Madness* (1966) with none other than Joanne Woodward.

Reportedly, Paul asked Connery, "How do you manage in a marriage when the husband is a far bigger star than the wife? When you're hot shit and she's what is known as a highly respected actress."

"You don't," Connery told him. "Divorce is inevitable."

Indeed Mr. and Mrs. Sean Connery divorced in 1973.

Hombre would be the last film that Paul would make with Ritt. They parted as friends.

When *Hombre* was released in 1967, critical reaction was generally favorable.

The review of Joseph Gelmis in *Newsday* exemplified the mixed reception the film received in some media.

"In *Hombre* the H is silent and so is Paul Newman," wrote Gelmis. "He's strong and silent and mean. If he has more than a page of dialogue in the film, it would be a surprise. *Hombre* has less impact than his previous gallery of H films—*Hud, Harper, The Hustler*. I liked *Hombre*. It is rough, funny, exciting. But I couldn't take it very seriously. Newman's blue-eyed Indian, a Caucasian raised by Apaches, is somehow implausible, even when he is being his most nasty, inscrutable, or even violent. The heroic gesture at the end of the film is unbelievable, or, at least, out of character."

The picture was not a commercial success.

Brandon De Wilde
Riding side saddle with Paul

***

Before the reviews were in for *Hombre*, Warner Brothers, a studio he once despised, sent Paul a script that he read three times in one night.

When morning came, he announced, "This is the role I was born to play. It may be the defining film of my career. It's called *Cool Hand Luke*. The only other actor in Hollywood who can play it better than me is Steve McQueen. But there's no way in hell that I'm gonna let Steve grab hold of this baby. It's mine!"

Paul in the desert with **Diane Cilento**
"How does Sean Connery do it?"

Sean Connery:
An unexpected visitor
"Divorce is inevitable"

Chapter Eleven
Cool Hand Luke Meets Butch Cassidy

Paul rejected Columbia's offer to star with Steve McQueen in Truman Capote's *In Cold Blood* (1967), although these two rivals would probably have generated headlines in their portrayal of "cold-blooded killers. The roles went instead to Robert Blake and Scott Wilson. Both McQueen and Paul later regretted turning down these juicy parts.

Paul found the script for *Cool Hand Luke* more thrilling, figuring that he could top his almost classic anti-hero appearance in *Hud* with this existential tale of a free-spirited convict on a chain gang in the Deep South. As was the case with many of the roles he'd been offered during the course of his career, Paul emerged as "a sloppy second," the role having been originally offered to Telly Savalas.

Jack Lemmon had even considered playing Luke, since his company, Jalem Productions, was producing the film.

Gordon Carroll was slated to produce *Cool Hand Luke*, with newcomer Stuart Rosenberg as the director. Donn Pearce authored the screenplay based on his own novel. Pearce had served two years on a chain gang, and *Luke* was based on his personal experiences. Unhappy with some aspects of the script, the director called in Frank R. Pierson, who had co-scripted *Cat Ballou* (1965), as part of a much-needed rewrite.

One night Paul received a surprise phone call. He immediately recognized the voice as emanating from Miss Bette Davis. She'd been offered the role of Luke's mother, a brief cameo appearance. "Miss Davis, it's an honor to speak with you," Paul said, trying to show as much respect as possible.

She cut to the chase. "Tell your director, one Mr. Stuart Rosenberg, that I'm not going to play your mother in this chain gang picture. As far as I'm concerned, chain gang movies died in the '30s." With the abrupt announcement, she hung up the phone.

Paul always wondered why Davis called him to deliver this pronouncement and not the director himself. After all, he had nothing to do with casting. The mother role eventually went to Jo Van Fleet, who'd won a much deserved Oscar for her appearance with James Dean in *East of Eden*.

Bette was even more cryptic years later when Joanne Woodward, living in Connecticut, encountered her, a fellow resident. Joanne invited her to come by the Newman home for a visit. "Why?" asked Bette before going on her way.

Upon seeing Paul again, Van Fleet kissed him on both cheeks. "I didn't get to play your mother in *East of Eden*. Now's my chance. What a fine son I have. If only I were a few years younger, it'd be incest."

For his actors in *Luke,* Rosenberg rounded up a strong supporting cast that featured both George Kennedy and Dennis Hopper.

Once again, Paul was co-starring with Strother Martin, with whom he'd worked in *Harper*.

Ironically, Richard Davalos was also cast. Paul had lost the role of one of the brothers in *East of Eden* to Davalos. "No hard feelings, pal," Paul said, shaking the hand of Davalos. "In either case, Dean would have sucked us up like red eye gravy."

In the film, Paul as Luke Jackson was sentenced to two years on the chain gang for unscrewing the tops from a series of parking meters. Naturally he'd been drunk at the time, as the movie so plainly demonstrated. Carrying Method acting too far, Paul was actually tanked up on beer when this sequence was filmed.

Defining his character "the ultimate rebel and non-conformist," Paul faced his most difficult scene in *Cool Hand Luke* when he had to eat fifty hard-boiled eggs in one sitting.

Jo Van Fleet
It could have been incest.

Miss Bette Davis
"I don't play mothers."

Several sources claim that Paul actually ate all those eggs depicted in the film. An assistant director, Hank Moonjean, who'd worked with Paul on other films, told the truth about this sequence.

"He would bite an egg and chew on it, and after the cut, he would spit it out. We had buckets all around him. This went on egg after egg. As for that 'full stomach,' Paul could contort his stomach so that he looked bloated."

When not needed on the California set of *Cool Hand Luke*, Paul was often spotted driving around the countryside in a blue Mercury convertible with Brandon De Wilde.

The two men were often seen in several taverns soaking up beer. In one sleazy joint, an aging bartender, who never went to the movies, asked Paul, "What do you do for a living?"

While filming *Cool Hand Luke*, Paul was offered the lead role in the allegorical fable, *The Swimmer*, by John Cheever. William Holden and Glenn Ford had turned it down. After Paul rejected it, Burt Lancaster put on a tight-fitting, revealing bathing suit and steered *The Swimmer* into a box office disaster.

Cool Hand Luke helped generate some of Paul's best reviews, leading to Paul's nomination for the fourth time as Best Actor by the Academy. George Kennedy was also nominated as the year's Best Supporting Actor for his role as well. The Oscar, that year, however, went to Paul's long-time friend, Rod Steiger, for his role in *In the Heat of the Night* in which he'd played a bigoted Deep South cop.

Even though he'd failed once again to win an Oscar, Paul received a consolation prize—the Golden Globe Award as the "World's Favorite Actor."

The most famous line from *Cool Hand Luke* is, "What we've got here is a failure to communicate." It was listed as number eleven on the American Film Institute's list of the 100 most memorable movie lines.

***

Hank Moonjean had previously worked on three films with Paul—*Until They Sail, Cat on a*

George Kennedy with **Paul**
in *Cool Hand Luke*
Chickening out over eggs

Hot Tin Roof, and *Sweet Bird of Youth*.

During the filming of *Cool Hand Luke* in the San Joaquin region near Stockton, California, Moonjean noted a strange new passion of Paul's. "He would sit at the first banquette table in the motel's dining room, with oil and all sorts of herbs in front of him, trying to concoct a new salad dressing. I'd walk by and he would say, 'Sit down and try my new salad dressing, Sport!' I once saw Paul adding water to his concoction and I said, 'You're not supposed to use water in an oil dressing. That's just not done.' How wrong could I have been? Paul has made a fortune with his salad dressings, and all profits are given to various charities."

Paul finally got that salad dressing right. In a most unlikely partnership, he teamed up with his close friend in Connecticut, A.E. Hotchner, Hemingway's biographer, and launched what became a multi-million dollar food industry.

"We did everything wrong," Hotchner recalled. "We did just the opposite of what the experts told us to do. Actually, we started with virtually no capital in the bank—a couple of bumbling amateurs trying to fish with no bait in a sea of sharks. It's one thing to want to put a bottle of salad dressing on supermarket shelves, but quite another to get it there."

The business had actually begun during the Christmas season of 1977 when they bottled the salad dressing in old wine bottles and presented it to friends and neighbors in Westport. The dressing became so popular that the following year Paul and Hotchner bottled it and sold it in local markets.

Each of the men put up $20,000 as capital, although experts in the food business warned them that they should be prepared to lose a cool million the first year of operation.

Slowly Paul and Hotchner lined up a marketing strategy, hiring a marketing firm in Port Washington, New York, and a bottler in the Boston area. Operating out of a cubbyhole in Westport, the two men did not advertise the business they launched in 1982. Word of mouth launched them, and soon bottles of salad dressing were selling out, the demand outdistancing the supply.

Otherwise, 1982 was a sad year for Paul, as he lost his mother, Theresa. She died of cancer, having lived some thirty years longer than her husband.

Their spaghetti sauce, Fra Diavolo or

Cool Hand Luke
The ultimate rebel

"Devil's Brother," followed the salad dressing, and it, too, became a big success. Paul then launched his favorite food—popcorn, calling it Old Style Picture Show Popcorn. By 1987, he'd launched Newman's Own Old-fashioned Roadside Virgin Lemonade. He mockingly claimed that the virginity of Joan Collins was restored after she drank four quarts of his lemonade.

A world class beer drinker, Paul wanted to market his own kind of beer until Joanne nixed the plan.

Once again Paul returned to the Roman toga, an outfit he'd shunned since the release of *The Silver Chalice*, to pose for a mock-up bust for Newman's Own Caesar Dressing.

At the end of 1983, their little Salad King, Inc., made a profit of nearly $300,000. "It's tacky for an actor and writer to be making money in the food business," Paul told Hotchner. "Let's give it all away to them what needs it."

From Guam to Greenland, consumers bought Paul's products, with his smiling face on the label. The charities to which they contributed ranged from the Actors Studio to the American Foundation for AIDS Research. Their donations to foreign countries ranged from Haiti to Vietnam.

One of Paul's greatest charitable achievements was to launch a camp for children suffering from cancer or AIDS. Although it was located in the northeast corridor of Connecticut, its theme and architecture evoked the Wild West. The groundbreaking ceremony occurred around Christmas in 1986, the camp being built around a forty-eight acre lake.

A.E. Hotchner
"Fishing in a sea of sharks"

By the late spring of 1988, the Hole in the Wall Camp opened. The first cancer-stricken children arrived that summer at the camp whose name had been inspired by the hideaway of the motley crew of thieves led by Butch Cassidy and the Sundance Kid in Paul's classic film with Robert Redford.

Nothing in the camp reminded children of the hospitals where they'd previously spent a lot of their time. Of course, Paul had to build an infirmary with a staff of volunteer doctors, but he disguised it, calling it the O.K. Corral.

After the founding of a multi-million dollar empire, Paul told a reporter, "I can only say that if someone told me twenty years ago that I'd have my face on a bottle of salad dressing, I'd have got them committed. But it's turned out in a way that we've never, ever expected."

Surveying reports of all the millions he's contributed to charities over the years, he said, "From salad dressings all blessings flow."

***

Paul often followed a hit movie with a disaster. Such was the case when he shot *The Secret War of Harry Frigg* for Universal.

The plot, such as it is, revolves around five Allied generals held prisoner in an Italian villa during World War II. Known for engineering daring escapes, Harry Frigg, as played by Paul, is brought in to smuggle out the brass.

But he delays his mission when he falls for Sylva Koscina, who played a beautiful countess. She is, in fact, the best thing to look at in the movie, not Paul's awful mugging in yet another attempt at comedy.

Paul's director, Jack Smight, had directed him in *Harper*, but this time around, Smight seemed lost.

In the film Paul had a reunion with actor James Gregory, with whom he'd worked in *The Desperate Hours* back in 1955.

He told Gregory, "I've grown bored with acting. I need the money, but the scripts I'm getting suck. The more I try to perform, the more I keep repeating tricks I've already exposed to the camera. I might take up directing."

Paul ridiculed Gregory for his appearance with Elvis Presley in the 1967 musical *Clambake*, and he chastised him for "being a Benedict Arnold. I can't believe you made *PT 109* with that jerk, Cliff Robertson. I was supposed to play Kennedy. I got double-crossed on that one."

Brandon De Wilde was seen on several occasions on the set, laughing when Paul called his character of Harry Frigg, "Henry Fuck." Brandon had very little to say to cast and crew, but stayed in Paul's dressing room, waiting for his return.

"It was obvious to me that Paul was banging Brandon," said Jack Smight to Gregory and some other members of the cast who'd seen the young actor hanging around. "Till then, I didn't believe those rumors. But after *Harry Frigg*, I believed them. Just like the impressionable teenager he'd played in *Hud*, Brandon clearly idolized Paul. I felt Paul was taking advantage of the kid. But I guess Brandon was old

Paul with **Sylva Koscina**
Deadlier Than the Male

enough. I was a little worried, so I had my assistant check the kid's birthdate."

"He was born in 1942 so I was no longer afraid that Paul might be brought up on a child molestation charge," Smight said. "Hell, I suddenly realized he must be at least 25, maybe 26. I figured if he'd been around for a quarter of a century, he knew what he was doing. Brandon was free, white, and twenty-one, although I hear it's not politically correct to say that anymore."

When Brandon wasn't around, Paul paid close attention to his lovely co-star, Sylva Koscina. Born in 1933 of Greek and Polish descent, Sylva was from Zagreb, Yugoslavia, but grew up in Italy. In 1967, just before meeting Paul, she'd played a lesbian assassin in *Deadlier Than the Male*, but was best known for being the leading lady of Steve Reeves in two Hercules films, or for playing "herself" in Fellini's *Juliet of the Spirits* (1965).

Harry Frigg was shot mostly in the Los Angeles area, though scenes in the so-called Italian villa were filmed in the Sierra Madre, to which the crew journeyed.

One day when he wasn't needed on the set, Paul drove into the desert with Sylva. After he'd returned the next day, he'd nicknamed her "My Cactus Flower."

She was rhapsodic about the American desert. "I've never seen colors quite like it," she said to Gregory. "That particular orange, that special gold, the silver sky that can turn red at times. Paul found quartz crystals for me. He bought me a piece of turquoise jewelry."

"He took me to this cantina where we had chicken tacos," she said. "I'd never eaten them before. They were served with refried beans. Why do cooks need to refry beans? You'd think once would be enough."

"Once was hardly enough for Sylva," said Gregory. "During the rest of the shoot, she seemed mad about the boy. She couldn't keep her hands off him. If only their chemistry on screen had been as good as their chemistry off screen."

Since Paul and Gregory's friendship went way back to the dawn of their respective careers, Paul could talk to him in a confidential man-to-man style. He told Gregory that, "I've fallen in love with the gal's tits. I could suck on them for hours. I got so worked up I dove into her like a torpedo launch."

But when the filming of *Harry Frigg* ended, Paul's passion fizzled just as quickly as it had flared. Sylva didn't understand what another star, Ronald Reagan, called "Leadingladyitis." Stars fell in love with each other during a shoot. When the film was wrapped, "those louses went back to their spouses," to paraphrase Marilyn Monroe's song.

"Sylva was heartbroken," Gregory claimed. "He seemed so fine and decent a man that I can't believe he won't return my calls," Sylva said.

"Paul will never leave Joanne Woodward," Gregory predicted. "Maybe for a few weeks or even months at a time, but not forever. Better get over him. Why don't you call Warren Beatty? I hear you're his type. Or Steve McQueen. Everybody is his type. Why not call Brandon De Wilde? I'm told that when he's not with Paul, he seduces two or three women a day."

"Men!" said Sylva in disgust. "Why do we really need them?"

***

No longer associated in a working partnership with Martin Ritt, Paul joined with John Foreman, his former agent, to create the Newman-Foreman Company. Its corporate mission involved producing movies as well as finding "world class properties" in which Paul could appear as the star. They spent considerable time appraising and buying scripts that would appeal to Paul's growing numbers of international, and not just American, viewers.

As he moved deeper into the changing culture of the '60s, he witnessed old-fashioned supper clubs in Los Angeles biting the dust, including such once-famous names as Mocambo and Ciro's. The Cocoanut Club at the Ambassador Hotel was fading into legend, as had Clark Gable and the many movie stars who'd made the club famous. The defunct Romanoff's, once a favorite hangout of Bogie, had become The Jazz Suite.

When Paul by chance encountered Ava Gardner one night, she noted that the times were changing. "Can you believe it?" she asked Paul. "I always said Frank would end up with a boy—and so he did." She was, of course, referring to Sinatra's new love interest, Mia Farrow.

Impressed by a private club in Beverly Hills called the Daisy, Paul decided to join backers to create The Factory, which eventually evolved into a major rival. Co-investors in that project included such rat packers as Peter Lawford and Sammy Davis Jr., along with Anthony Newley and Pierre Salinger, who had been John Kennedy's press secretary during his years in the White House.

The men found an abandoned building at 652 North La Peer Drive in Los Angeles. The site dated from 1929 when William Fox, the studio mogul, constructed it as a camera company. During World War II, the building had been converted into a bombsight factory.

If you didn't know where you were going, you could have easily driven by The Factory without knowing it. Its plain façade was identified only with a black awning and a red flag emblazoned with a monkey wrench. A clue to its fame would be the steady stream of stars arriving in Rolls-Royces. Each of them paid $1,000 in annual dues.

Inside, except for the people, the scenery hardly improved. Windows were covered in chicken wire, and Paul himself purchased the cheap, rickety tables at various Flea Markets.

The nightly crowd, which might include Sonny and Cher or Barbra Streisand, melded blue jeans with tuxedos. After surveying a sea of scantily clad dancers, including Hollywood's most beautiful girls, Paul quipped, "All we need now is to install beds."

On any night Paul showed up, often with Brandon De Wilde, he headed for the bar in the rear, which contained four pool tables, one covered in red felt for the ladies. There he and Brandon, relatively unmolested by this hip crowd, could play game after game of pool.

"I thought I was witnessing a replay of *The Hustler*," Sinatra said after he dropped in to check the club out. He later headed for the second floor where he frugged with Mia Farrow to a live band called "The Nudies."

Warren Beatty showed up with his girl *du jour*, and Paul's longtime friend, Tony Perkins, still struggling with his homosexuality, appeared with female companions, hoping he could go straight. Before the night ended at dawn, Tony often dumped his female companion and made off into the bright light of morning with one of the waiters.

Each of the waiters was decked out in dungarees and blue denim work shirts. "Before The Factory closed down, Tony got around to balling most of us," said James Duval, one of those waiters. "All the waiters had wanted to score with Newman, but we struck out. That De Wilde was like a bodyguard protecting him. Jealous little bitch."

"The people who dig The Factory are going to dig it forever," said Sammy Davis Jr. How wrong he was.

The Factory, highly successful throughout most of its short life, soon faded into dust, as revelers rushed to a newer hot spot, The Candy Store, whose part owner was Tony Curtis.

Deserting his own club, Paul himself often migrated to The Candy Store, sometimes accompanied by Brandon. On other nights, Paul could be seen just driving aimlessly around Los Angeles with Brandon in his Volkswagen with its Porsche engine.

He and Brandon often stopped in at bars. Paul would request that the bartender serve him his beer in

Frank Sinatra, Dean Martin, Peter Lawford, and Sammy Davis, Jr.
Rat Packers' pool night at Paul's Factory

an unopened bottle. He'd take the "church key" attached around his neck like a dogtag and open the beer. At one point, Brandon was overheard chiding him, "When you're really cool, you'll learn to open that fucking bottle with your teeth."

In one bar, Rawhide, a heckler came up to Paul when he was standing with Brandon drinking beer. "Hey, Newman, take off those sunglasses and let me stare into those baby blues." Paul was so infuriated that he slugged the intruder. Brandon restrained him.

Later, Paul gave the man five one-hundred dollar bills, asking him not to press charges for assault and battery.

"He's not a violent man," Brandon told Henry Slager, the club's owner. "Sometimes he can't stand for strangers to intrude aggressively into his space. He's a very private person."

***

An executive at Paramount delivered the bad news to Paul. The only way the studio would consider his latest film project, *Rachel, Rachel*, was if Shirley MacLaine starred in it. "I know you want a job for your wife—and God knows she needs a hit after her last two films bombed. Neither *A Fine Madness* nor *A Big Hand for the Little Lady* rang any bells at the box office, in spite of her co-stars, Sean Connery and Henry Fonda. So what do you say?"

"I'm out of here," Paul said. "It's Joanne or no one." He put down the phone.

At MGM, Paul was told, "Frankly, the story is too downbeat. No one's gonna pay good money to see this shit. It's just not commercial. Now if you wanted to show me a script by Tennessee Williams and a contract to star Elizabeth Taylor, then we'd show some interest."

The statement turned out to carry a certain irony. In a 1968 release, *Boom!* Elizabeth Taylor and Richard Burton, along with Noel Coward, had signed on to do a screen adaptation of the playwright's disastrous *The Milk Train Doesn't Stop Here Anymore*, in which Tallulah Bankhead and Tab Hunter had had such a dry run on Broadway that was mercifully brief.

At Columbia, another executive told Paul that, "It's been so long since Woodward's had a hit that she's become a footnote in Hollywood history. As for those films you two made together, I'd rather suck rotten possum eggs than sit through one of them."

Before hanging up, Paul angrily said, "You may not know this, sucker, but possums don't lay eggs."

At Universal, Paul was told, "This dud has about as much appeal as Jerry Lewis starring in *Hamlet*."

Agent John Foreman had sent Joanne a novel by the Canadian author Margaret Laurence called *A Jest of God*. Immediately recognizing the scope and potential of the project, Joanne tried to get Paul intrigued by the novel. At first he seemed reluctant to read it until she insisted.

It was a grim tale of a 35-year-old school teacher, living with her overbearing mother (Kate Harrington) and desperate to find a man to love her. She has become almost spiritually ill from the lack of love in her life.

The unhappy pair lived above a funeral parlor. Their undertaker husband/father had died. Before doing so, he had already engraved his daughter's name on the family gravestone.

To adapt the novel, Paul turned to a family friend, Stewart Stern. Despite the passage of years, Stern was still riding high over his scripting of James Dean's *Rebel Without a Cause*, although he was experiencing a career slump at the time. His friendship with the demanding Newmans almost didn't survive the scriptwriting session.

Stern complained that Joanne virtually wanted to see the script written her way, and Paul, in contrast, often had a different way of seeing things. "We had a lot of catfights at that home in Connecticut," Stern later said. "I didn't think the film would ever be made. At one point I stormed out of their house, never planning to return. The matter was resolved when Paul showed up at my house in a Nazi uniform. Giving me a Nazi salute and a Heil, Hitler!, he proclaimed, 'I'm the boss.'"

The scene that caused a screaming match was one associated with a depiction of Rachel, in bed, masturbating. Each member of the trio believed that the masturbation scene was important to the drama, but Stern, Joanne and Paul each had a different idea about how it should be depicted on the screen. The argument centered on what position Joanne as Rachel should be in when she "pleasures herself." A prone position or otherwise? That was the question.

The script, of course, was eventually finished and shopped from studio to studio. With a female star of unreliable box office potential and no "bankable director," each major studio in Hollywood rejected it.

Paul had listed himself as the producer. But when he saw that *Rachel, Rachel* had no backers, he announced that he would direct the picture. After all, he'd studied directing at Yale University, and it had long been his dream to

Paul directing *Rachel, Rachel*
"I'm a virgin, use vaseline."

get behind the camera instead of in front of it.

With himself as the director, his dreaded nemesis of yesterday, Warner Brothers, agreed to back the project with a modest budget of $700,000. Any money spent over that amount would have to be paid for out of Paul's own pocket.

At Warners, he'd found a sympathetic soul in Kenneth Hyman, who wanted to make artistic films, hiring Sidney Lumet, for example, to direct the 1968 *The Seagull*, based on the Chekhov play.

There was also a poison pill clause in the contract. According to the contract he'd signed with Warner Brothers, Paul agreed to make two films for Warners at half his salary. Joanne also agreed to make a film for Warners at a greatly reduced salary.

If he'd signed on with a studio as an actor, he could haul in one million, a far cry from the $1,000 a week he was paid when filming *The Silver Chalice*. As a director, he agreed to take no salary at all. *Rachel, Rachel* was a true labor of love.

"They really had us over the barrel," Paul said, "so we reluctantly said okay. That's how committed we were to filming *Rachel, Rachel*."

Cleverly Paul had written into his contract that if the creative management team at Warners changed, he would not have to follow through with his two-picture commitment. When Hyman left the studio soon after signing on for *Rachel, Rachel*, the Newmans were freed from that "slave agreement," as they called it.

At one point it was decided to shoot the film in some barren California town, but Paul opted instead to film in Danbury near his own Connecticut home. He signed his brother, Arthur Newman Jr. as associate producer, and even cast his daughter, Elinor, in the drama. Billed as "Nell Potts," she was to play Rachel as a young girl.

James Olson, who had starred in Jack Garfein's *The Strange One* in 1957, signed on to play Rachel's lover, an old high school friend who returns to town and seduces her before mov-

A terribly intense **Paul** directing **Joanne**
Telling her how to be a spinster

ing on. Estelle Parsons, riding high as an Oscar winner for her appearance in *Bonnie and Clyde*, with Warren Beatty and Faye Dunaway, signed to play Rachel's friend, a lesbian schoolteacher who makes advances toward her.

Paul also hired Frank Corsaro, who had directed the Newmans in *Baby Want a Kiss* on Broadway.

When asked why he'd decided to direct, Paul said, "Why be a violinist if you think you can conduct?"

On the first day of the shoot, Paul assembled cast and crew telling them, "I'm a virgin. So be gentle when you penetrate and use plenty of Vaseline."

In dark sunglasses and a ripped T-shirt, Paul with a Schlitz always in his hand set out to direct Joanne. He'd found acting in a film meant spending many boring hours sitting around, but directing was another matter. "I was kept busy with one problem after another," Paul recalled. "They even came to me when the delivery man didn't arrive with the pizzas for our lunch."

During the filming, Paul and Joanne seemed to have some shared vocabulary unknown to the rest of the crew. He'd order her to "thicken it" or "pinch it," and she intuitively seemed to know what he was talking about.

A reporter visiting the set asked Paul if there were any friction between Joanne and himself while he was directing her. "Oh, yeah," he said. "We had several spats and squabbles—big ones. There are never little ones in our family. But it had nothing to do with work on *Rachel*. In that sense, Joanne and I never had one harsh word in that entire period. It was really amazing. The reason we got along is that artistically at least, we trust each other."

When asked later why he'd been so successful in his first major venture as a director, Paul quipped, "I went barefoot and never washed my shorts during the entire shoot. I had piss stains all over them."

Dede Allen, who had previously edited both *The Hustler* and *Bonnie and Clyde*, worked hand-in-glove with Paul every day. It was later claimed that Allen was the real director of the picture, and that the honors eventually associated with the film should have gone to her, instead of to Paul.

The film took only five weeks to shoot but eight months to edit. Both Paul and Joanne were pleased with the final results. Joanne, reportedly, felt that she'd done her best work since *The Three Faces of Eve*.

At the finish, Joanne told reporters, "I just wish Paul could direct every movie I'll do again."

Joanne even compared Paul's directorial gifts to the Swedish director, Ingmar Bergman. Unfortunately, a neophyte reporter wrote "Ingrid" instead of "Ingmar."

After the strain of production, Paul was off to Florida "for some heavy drinking and speedboat racing."

"I'm having a boys' night out," he told a reporter he encountered in

Daytona Beach. He was later seen checking into a suite at the Breakers Hotel on Palm Beach with one Brandon De Wilde.

In Florida, he was informed by his partner, John Foreman, that offers for him to direct pictures were pouring in from all over the world.

On most occasions, the Newmans shunned the press, but for the purpose of promoting *Rachel, Rachel*, both stars made themselves available. Paul was very revealing in his comments, exposing that the real reason he'd signed on as a director was to provide a proper showcase for his wife's talent, something Hollywood producers had rarely been adept at doing.

"Joanne really gave up her career for me," Paul said. "To stick by me. To make our marriage work. That's one of the reasons I directed this film with her." He might have said, "That's the only reason I directed *Rachel, Rachel*."

He told *Playboy* that Joanne had turned down major film work to stay with him and their six children, three, of course, from Paul's first marriage. "She's done this to the detriment of her career, I'm afraid, but it's helped keep us together. Without her, I'd be nowhere, nothing."

The film made a modest profit of $8 million, but won almost universal approval from the critics.

Writing in *The Saturday Review*, Arthur Knight claimed that Joanne "recalls Helen Hayes and Barbara Stanwyck in the films of the thirties—actresses with a similar intensity and range—and suddenly we realize how much has been lost in the name of underplaying or 'cool.'"

William Wolf in *Cue Magazine* admitted that Paul as a director didn't set the industry afire, but "shows a truth-seeking directness that stamps the film with conviction and honesty."

His co-star in *Hud*, Patricia Neal, called him after seeing the film. She'd suffered a massive stroke in 1965, which affected both her memory and her speech. She congratulated him on *Rachel, Rachel*, a film in which she would have been ideally cast before her stroke. Suddenly, she asked, "Who are you, anyway?"

The Golden Globe Awards gave Paul its Best Director in a Motion Picture Award, and presented a similar award to Joanne as Best Motion Picture Actress.

However, Paul was ignored when the nominations for the Academy Awards were announced in Hollywood. *Rachel, Rachel* received four nominations, however, for Best Picture, Best Actress (Joanne herself), Best Supporting Actress (Estelle Parsons), and Best Adapted Screenplay (Stewart Stern).

There were no winners. Paul felt he'd been humiliated by the Academy once again. "There's a God damn prejudice against me, and I think I know the reason why. It's because I prefer to shun Beverly Hills and live in New

England."

Ironically, Patricia Neal competed with Joanne in the Oscar sweepstakes, Neal having scored a win in the film *The Subject Was Roses*. Both Joanne and Patricia lost to Barbra Streisand for *Funny Girl* and to Katharine Hepburn in *The Lion in Winter*. For the first time in its history, the Academy declared a draw—so both Hepburn and Streisand walked away with Oscars.

Even though he did not get that Oscar, Paul in 1966 was named the World's Favorite Actor at the thirty-third annual Golden Globes banquet, sharing the honor with his female counterpart, Natalie Wood. "That's not all they shared that night," Martin Ritt claimed. In 1967 Paul was nominated Best Actor of the Year by the National Association of Theatre Owners.

Paul triumphantly told friends, "Now Marlon Brando licks the dingleberries off my ass, not the other way around."

***

Turning down lucrative script offers, Paul in 1968 became a political activist somewhat in the style of Marlon Brando. He was disappointed at the presidency of Lyndon Johnson, and infuriated that "he'd pulled a double cross" and accelerated the Vietnam War. When maverick senator Eugene McCarthy of Minnesota announced that he would run against Johnson, Paul called the senator and enlisted in his cross-country campaign.

At first Paul felt that McCarthy didn't have a chance. But then the returns came in from New Hampshire, showing that McCarthy could best Johnson by running on an antiwar platform.

On the campaign trail, Paul faced a lot of opposition from people who didn't want a movie star telling them how to vote.

Supporters of Nixon attacked him verbally. He always had an answer for them. "I'm a citizen. I'm a father. I'm a voter. I have the same concerns as yourself. I'm speaking as a citizen—not a movie star."

In New Hampshire, a Jaguar dealer lent Paul the use of a car on weekends. He later learned that the same car was made available for Nixon on Tuesday and Wednesday.

Finding this out, he left Nixon a note:

"DEAR MR. NIXON. YOU SHOULD HAVE NO TROUBLE DRIVING THIS CAR. IT HAS A TRICKY CLUTCH. PAUL NEWMAN."

When the press found out, Nixon was gracious in his response. "He may think I'm a lousy politician, but I think he's a fine actor."

Privately, Nixon fumed. Perhaps that's why Paul ended up as number nineteen on the president's notorious enemies list. That list was made public in 1973, and Paul viewed it as "my crowning achievement."

From the lush countryside of Connecticut to the barren wastelands around Omaha, Paul stumped tirelessly for McCarthy, a man whose "courage and convictions" he greatly admired.

"This is my kind of town," Paul claimed when arriving in Milwaukee. "I've drunk so much beer in my time I've put Milwaukee on the map." Of course, that comment was a mere quip and not meant for publication.

Paul also popped up in Oregon, New York State, and Indiana. On some of those long trips from home, he was accompanied by Brandon De Wilde, who never appeared at any rallies in public with Paul, but often shared his hotel room later in the evening.

In Albany he was met with campaign workers, who greeted him with cornbeef sandwiches and plenty of cold beer. His taste for *cerveza* was, by that time, well known.

He drew his biggest audiences on college campuses, but was not adverse to speaking to factory workers from the tailgate of a truck in the Detroit area.

On the campaign trail, he encountered his friend, Myrna Loy, and other stars he'd made films with, including Lauren Bacall.

Paul was often uneasy during some of his public appearances. As long as he was speaking from a prepared text, he seemed confident. But he often bombed with his answers to off-the-cuff questions. His main issue was the war, and he showed an appalling lack of familiarity with the other issues of the day.

He also grew increasingly uncomfortable with the demands his fans made, based on his status as a movie star. As he explained to the *New York Sunday Times* magazine.

Eugene McCarthy
"Bring my husband home"

Richard Nixon
"A tricky clutch"

426

"When a Mrs. Jones marches up to me for an autograph, I'm supposed to immediately stop what I'm doing, whether it's eating dinner, playing with the kids, or making love to my wife. I'm supposed to say, 'Oh, sure, Mrs. Jones, I'll smile for you. I'll take off my sunglasses, then I'll put them back on.' The whole thing is ridiculous!"

The race heated up when Johnson announced he would not run for re-election. But McCarthy would not be a shoo-in for the nomination. The ever-popular Robert F. Kennedy joined the race for the nomination.

Immediately, a number of A-list Hollywood entertainers backed Kennedy, including Shirley MacLaine, Sammy Davis Jr., and Peter Lawford. Still miffed at the Kennedys, Sinatra announced that he'd cast his vote for Hubert Humphrey. Paul and other stars, including Dustin Hoffman, stuck with McCarthy.

At one point, Scott Newman joined his father on the campaign trail in Cleveland, but quickly dropped out when a Nixon supporter crushed a lemon pie in his face. "Politics is your bag," he told his dad. "It's not for me."

In a move viewed as not very bright, Paul urged the public to boycott his films as an "act of conscience" against the war in Vietnam. Similar pleas for a boycott of their own films were issued by Jon Voight, Arlo Guthrie, Dennis Hopper, Peter Fonda, and Alan Arkin. Ironically, these stars actually owned a percentage of the films they were asking the public to boycott.

Paul attended the now-notorious Democratic National Convention in Chicago in '68. He was a delegate from the state of Connecticut, and was often photographed, standing alongside playwright Arthur Miller, Marilyn's ex.

Throughout the convention, Paul was horrified, especially at the violence occurring on the streets outside. He later reported that the convention "sickened me in my gut. When it was over and Humphrey emerged triumphant as the Democratic Party's designated presidential delegate, only Sinatra was happy. I just knew we'd lose to Nixon."

This was the infamous convention where Gore Vidal and William F. Buckley were moderators for ABC. When Vidal suggested that Buckley was a crypto-Nazi, Buckley shot back, "Now, listen, you queer. I'll sock you in your goddamn face."

Gracious in defeat, Paul told the press, "I feel I'm the better man—win, lose, or draw—for having been a part of this campaign." That quote was published in *The New York Times*.

After the defeat of the Democratic ticket in 1968, Gore Vidal urged Paul to enter politics, suggesting that he run first for Senator from Connecticut and follow it up with a bid for the presidency. The idea on the surface seemed preposterous to most political observers, but Paul considered it seriously for a few weeks. Finally, he rejected the idea, "I don't have the arrogance, and I don't have the credentials."

One drunken night in Connecticut, Paul called his friend, Tony Perkins. "God damn it, I've changed my mind. I'm gonna run for president of the United States against Nixon in 1972. And I'm going to start campaigning tomorrow morning, beginning in New England. Before election year comes, I will have visited every state. Stay tuned for my announcement in the morning."

When no announcement came the following morning, Tony called Paul. "What happened?"

"I woke up, sobered up, and chickened out," was the response.

***

In New York City, Joanne had made an appearance, telling listeners that she wanted them to vote for McCarthy "so I can bring my husband back home. Since he discovered politics, I never see him anymore."

Joanne's remark in New York set off speculation in print about the Newmans' so-called idyllic marriage. "Were the couple really as in love as they seemed?" asked writer Susan Netter. "Even if they were, could the marriage survive the pressures of show business and the separations and temptations presented by not only one but two movie careers? Besides all that, Newman was one of the handsomest male actors around. All he'd have to do would be to wink one of those devastating blue eyes and hundreds of women would come running. Joanne was pretty enough, but she'd had three kids in seven years, gossips noted, and everyone knew what *that* could do to your figure. Could a woman really feel sexy and desirable and in the mood for fun and romance with all those kids underfoot?"

Alice Tucker, a writer for the short-lived *Hollywood Screw*, a notorious underground magazine that surfaced in the late Sixties, even published an article about Paul's "alleged" bisexual lovers. She ran beefcake pictures of Paul with some of his bedmates of yore, including Steve McQueen, Marlon Brando, Montgomery Clift, James Dean, Tony Perkins, and Sal Mineo.

In one of her most outrageous and unproven claims, Tucker reported that Paul had a tumultuous romance with Christopher Jones, the charismatic young actor—"the new James Dean"—who had been married to Susan Strasberg.

After that sleazy little tabloid ran a scandalous article about Frank Sinatra, it was rumored that he had *Hollywood Screw* shut down. How he managed to do that is not known.

Paul once summed up his marriage, claiming, "It's not always fine and dandy. We're two different people with very different attitudes to things, very different ways of seeing life. Even so, I think the marriage has a certain thickness to it. We go through bad periods, like any couple."

One author speculated that Joanne must have heard about Paul's "quickie, meaningless affairs" with some of his leading ladies or superstar sexual predators like Ava Gardner and Lana Turner.

"Joanne's a very smart woman," Tony Perkins once told Shelley Winters. "She must know about them. Paul's first wife found out about that James Dean thing. Joanne is a lot smarter. She must have known all along that her husband also liked guys. How could she not know? I don't know how much she reads the underground press, but 'well-meaning' friends had to tell her about the rumors. She'd be living blind if she didn't know."

Susan Strasberg remembered that Paul's adulterous romances with both women and men were one of the principal topics of gossip at that show biz hangout, Downey's Restaurant in New York. "People who slept with Paul didn't keep it a secret. Marilyn, for example, told me all about her affair with Paul. Brando did too. With my father and myself, Paul talked openly about his bisexuality, claiming 'I am not ashamed.'"

***

Every straight or bisexual male has his fantasy woman. For Paul, he still considered Elizabeth Taylor one of the most enchanting women of her time. But, as he'd once told intimate friends, "Jacqueline Kennedy is the most desirable woman on the planet. Our Helen of Troy."

After her brother-in-law, Robert F. Kennedy, announced that he was going to run against Eugene McCarthy for the Democratic nomination for president, she placed a discreet call to Paul.

He was thrilled to be speaking to her and hearing that famous voice that in some way reminded him of Marilyn Monroe. He agreed to meet her in the bar of the Hotel Carlyle in Manhattan—the same hotel where John F. Kennedy had had sexual trysts with Marilyn Monroe.

The sale of her home in Georgetown in Washington, DC, had allowed her to purchase a Fifth Avenue apartment, but despite that, she chose to meet Paul at the Carlyle Hotel, perhaps as some kind of symbolic assertion of her independence.

Of his many involvements with famous personalities, Paul's short-lived link with Jackie is clouded in the most mystery and the subject of the most speculation. A doorman reported that Paul arrived at the appointed time of eight o'clock in the evening and was seen leaving the following morning around 8:30, hailing a taxi and quickly disappearing. He wore dark sunglasses and a hat. The sunglasses were familiar; the hat was not. Even so, the staff

Marlon Brando   **William Holden**   **Paul Newman**

at the Carlyle recognized him and spread the word. The story was too good, too hot to keep to one's self.

Susan Strasberg claimed that within days, the story was making the rounds of Downey's Restaurant, where it quickly spread through the grapevine to Washington and on to Hollywood.

The only recognizable name who spoke openly about the night Paul spent with Jackie in her hotel suite was Truman Capote, her treacherous friend. In Tennessee Williams' New York apartment, Capote claimed that Jackie had confessed to him "only some of the details of that night."

Capote made his claims in the presence of Tennessee himself, Margaret Foresman (an editor on *The Key West Citizen*), Stanley Haggart, and the author of this biography. Capote is an unreliable source, but he often knew truths unknown even to insiders.

Jackie loved gossip, and in Truman Capote she'd found a soulmate. He not only was the untitled gossip queen of America, but believed that gossip as *reportage* would become "the literature of the future."

Capote claimed that one night he and Jackie, drunk on champagne, named the three movie stars they'd most like to seduce. For Capote, the size of a certain appendage seemed to dominate his selection of John Ireland, Steve Cochran, and Rock Hudson.

As her desirable stars of choice, Jackie named Marlon Brando, William Holden, and Paul Newman, claiming, "I've already attained two-thirds of my goal." At that time, she was referring to Brando and Holden, not Paul, whom she was yet to meet.

From what Capote claimed, a sketchy report has emerged. He said that over drinks he'd discussed Paul with Jackie.

In a secluded corner of the bar at the Carlyle, Jackie in dark sunglasses greeted Paul. He kissed her on both sides of the cheeks. She casually pointed

| Rock Hudson | Steve Cochran | John Ireland |

to a man in a dark business suit sitting a few tables away. She told him that he was a member of the Secret Service assigned to guard her. "He's also my lover," she allegedly told Paul. If he were shocked, he masked it effectively. He even assumed that she might be joking because it was unbelievable that she'd be this frank with him.

Upon his arrival, he'd presented her with a porcelain rose, which was investment enough for him, even though he'd heard she would spend as much as $100,000 on an antique snuff box.

That night Paul met Jackie, he encountered a very different woman from the brave widow he'd read about in the press. Sitting opposite him was a flirtatious and attractive woman, with a mischievous gleam in her eyes, not the brave widow of a slain American president.

When she'd had enough champagne, Jackie could become outrageous, not the "steel butterfly" so often depicted on camera.

One night at a White House gala, when she'd had more than her share of the bubbly, Jackie took off her shoes and danced and flirted with every handsome man in attendance, much to the annoyance of her husband who hawkeyed her every move. Perhaps she was paying him back for his own sexual trysts with his woman *du jour*.

A minor friend of Jackie's, Paul Mathias, the New York correspondent for France's *Paris-Match* Magazine, summed her up. His assessment later appeared in *A Woman Called Jackie* by C. David Heymann. In Mathias' words, the former First Lady "was the tease, the temptress of her age. She perfected the art, she invented it. She was Miss Narcissist, perpetually searching mirrors for worry wrinkles and strands of prematurely gray hair. She didn't worry about growing old, she worried about looking old. Within 18 months of JFK's assassination she had two dozen of the world's most brilliant and important men dangling like marionettes, dancing at her fingertips, most of

431

them very married, very old, or very queer."

In Paris, Aristotle Onassis told a reporter, "Jackie is too young and too vibrant a woman to spend her life maintaining the Camelot legend. It is time for her to come down from that pedestal and do something very, very indiscreet, like marrying Truman Capote."

Even John Kennedy told associates that "Jackie is known for developing crushes, like on Warren Beatty. But she's very fickle. They don't last long. She becomes bored quickly."

From what Capote learned, Paul spent a good part of the evening hearing about the Kennedys. Although Jackie was very supportive of Bobby, and urged Paul to switch his allegiance, she was highly critical of Rose Kennedy. "She'll eat a juicy steak for lunch and serve the rest of the table hamburgers, even hot dogs. To save money, she orders the chef not to make desserts, even bread pudding from stale bread."

One speculation she may have shared with Paul that night was her belief that her husband would not have been re-elected. "His indiscretions had become so plentiful, so well known, that they would have made headlines during the campaign and would have destroyed him."

During the course of the evening, she revealed to Paul that former Democratic presidential candidate Adlai Stevenson had pursued her after the death of her husband in Dallas.

Alone in her suite with Paul, she spent at least an hour or two extolling the virtues of Bobby Kennedy. She claimed that she personally knew Eugene McCarthy but also believed that he was a one-issue candidate. "The war," she reportedly said, "that God damn Vietnam War." She warned him that there were other issues of the day, including the war on poverty. "Bobby can offer hope to the downtrodden that McCarthy can't. He's a candidate whose stand on the issues, not just the war, is all-encompassing. He can save this nation from itself. That is, if he can save himself from an assassin's bullet. They've killed one Kennedy in this country. They might strike again." Supposedly, she never revealed who "they" were.

The most provocative line of the evening, if Capote is to be believed, is that Jackie confided to Paul that she'd never been able to satisfy her husband sexually. "Perhaps I can change that state of affairs with you tonight," she may have told him.

At least for one night Jackie may have convinced Paul to switch his political alliance. But in the sober light of morning, when he left the hotel, he remained in McCarthy's camp. He later

Jackie Kennedy Onassis
Miss Narcissist battling time

432

told Tony Perkins, "I faced more temptation that night than did Antony when he met Cleopatra."

Of course, when Bobby Kennedy was assassinated in June of 1968—allegedly by Sirhan Sirhan—Paul's support of Jackie's brother-in-law became a moot issue.

Howl!, a scandal sheet emanating from New York City's East Village that flourished for only two months during hippiedom's "Dawning of the Age of Aquarius," was the only newspaper, if that's what it could be called, that carried the rumor. The headline, as were all that short-lived paper's headlines, was rather blunt: PAUL NEWMAN FUCKS JACKIE O.

***

Weeks after his defeat, McCarthy called Paul to thank him for his support. He also revealed a shocking detail. He was planning to leave his wife, Abigail, after nearly a quarter of a century of marriage. "We were just sticking together to get through the campaign and into the White House. If elected, we planned to live together in the White House but in different bedrooms."

McCarthy was a man of his word. After talking to Paul, he separated from his wife in 1969, although he never divorced her. The senator was not alone. He engaged in an affair with Marya McLaughlin, a CBS news correspondent, until her death in 1998.

McCarthy died in 2005 at the age of 89. Suffering from Parkinson's disease, he lived in a retirement home in Washington.

His future attempts at running for president failed, particularly in 1972 and 1976. Today he is often confused with the anti-Communist fanatic, Senator Joseph McCarthy.

"Although they had the same last name, no two men could have been more different," Paul claimed. "I was proud to work for Eugene for a cause I believed in. There would be other causes in my future, for which I'd stick my neck out."

***

In his next film, *Winning* (1969), about race car drivers, Paul was cast as "a boozing, workaholic, womanizer."

"Typecasting," said Eartha Kitt when she read about the film in *Variety*. At that point, her devotion to Paul was considerably diminished.

Once again in this John Foreman production for Universal, Paul would be cast opposite Joanne along with their long-time friend, Robert Wagner. Originally slated for a television presentation, it was turned into a feature film

433

when the Newmans signed on. Critics later wondered what Joanne was doing in this picture. It was hardly her finest role. Perhaps she joined just to work with Paul.

Paul's character was Frank Capua, an ace auto racing driver, who meets a divorcee (Joanne) and her teenage son (Richard Thomas). His major rival, Wagner, playing Luther Erding, has an affair with Paul's wife. Rumors that this actually happened in real life have proved mere gossip, or else tantalizing speculation. But at least on screen Paul caught Wagner in bed with Joanne.

Paul was placed in the awkward position of having to give Wagner "points" about how to make love to his wife. Privately, he told John Foreman, "I didn't want this to become an XXX-rated picture, so I didn't tell him how to hit all of Joanne's hot spots."

For Foreman, *Winning* would be a loser. It was no *Harper*, and certainly no *Butch Cassidy and the Sundance Kid*.

"Long before Joanne met Paul, I pushed her off a building in *A Kiss Before Dying*," Wagner said. His memory of time sequences may be a bit off. He added, "She forgave me for murdering her—I was playing a psychotic—and we've remained friends for a lot of years. They live in Connecticut, and I'm in California, or Aspen, but we stay close."

Long over his crush on Wagner, Paul claimed, "If I'm in the trenches, this is the guy I want next to me."

Wagner was a bit saddened when Paul announced his retirement from acting in 2007. But he noted, "I would bet you that if a great part comes along that Paul likes, and it's something he would be great in, he'll take the tap shoes off the wall and go into his dance."

Before filming on *Winning* began, Paul, along with Wagner, began to prepare for his role as a race track driver. He studied at the Bob Bondurant School of High Performance near Santa Ana in California. In just two weeks he could lap 142 mph in Indiana, the site of "The Indy," the toughest, fastest, longest (500 miles), and the most hazardous event in the world of sports car racing.

The most spectacular moment in *Winning* actually was a newsreel, showing a seventeen-car crash scene at the track in 1966.

To add verisimilitude to *Winning*, a number of real race car drivers appeared on screen, including Bruce Walkup, Roger McCluskey, Dan Gurney, Tony Hulman, Bobby Grim, and

Paul in race car drag
An obsession with *Winning*

434

Bobby Unser.

For this $7 million feature film, Paul was given one of his best deals yet, a $1.1 million upfront salary, plus a percentage.

Insured by Universal for $3 million, Paul refused to use a double for the most dangerous race sequences.

The film was almost a forecast of the future marriage of Joanne and Paul. Her character, both on and off the screen, would be threatened and torn apart by Paul's obsession with his "career" as a race car driver. On the set she objected to Paul's refusal to use a double, and she also opposed his getting involved in such a dangerous sport that might, in a flash, remove him as her husband and the father of his five daughters and one son.

During the filming of *Winning*, his old friend, Steve McQueen, called him when *Variety* ran a story that he, McQueen, was now number one at the box office. "Hey, it's lonely at the top, old pal, old buddy. Come for a motorcycle ride with me in the desert. I'll fuck you in the sands until you get cactus up your ass."

"Dream on, faggot," Paul said.

Although they talked "dirty" to each other, each man, though a screen rival, still maintained a deep and abiding love and respect for each other. Paul continued to like McQueen so much he would even invite him to join him as an investor in a new production company in the immediate years ahead.

Only a year later, Paul called McQueen in revenge, when *Butch Cassidy and the Sundance Kid* made him number one at the box office again. "How does it feel to be dethroned, old buddy, old pal? And to think you could have been riding in the saddle with me if you'd signed on as Sundance."

"You might be number one at the box office—at least for 1969—but my dick is bigger than yours, and there's not a God damn thing you can do about that, fucker," McQueen said. "Say, kid, since you're now the Queen of the Box office, let's get together for some beer. I'll let you feel it under the table so you'll know what a real man is like." With that invitation, he put down the phone.

First Artists Production Company was launched in June of 1969 with Barbra Streisand, Sidney Poitier, and Paul. In 1971 Steve McQueen joined the trio. Although the company would have such hits as *Butch Cassidy and the Sundance Kid*, they would also release duds at the box office, including *WUSA* (1970), in which Paul would co-star once again with Joanne along with old friends Laurence Harvey and Tony Perkins. In WUSA, Paul played a cynical drifter who becomes a DJ for an ultra-Right Wing Louisiana radio station.

The new production company also released the flat and rather boring *Pocket Money* (1972), in which Paul co-starred with Lee Marvin. In this tepid Western, Paul played a debt-ridden cowboy who gets mixed up with shifty

Marvin, a con man goof ball.

When *Winning* was released, it got a fairly good critical reception, William Wolf writing in *Cue Magazine*, "Newman and Woodward are zooming in stature as a film world couple. They are doing it without leading private lives that catapult them into headlines. Their own special ingredient is *talent.*"

Leo Mishkin in the *New York Morning Telegraph* noted that one scene alone, with the two of them sitting in a garden rocker, drinking beer out of cans, "comes as close to their own marriage, I suspect, as could be depicted in a fictional motion picture."

Sometimes critical of Paul, Judith Crist in *New York* found that "Howard Rodman's screenplay and dialogue have more clichés and cornball phrasing than the telephone booth has Smiths and Joneses. But since Paul Newman and Joanne Woodward could, for my money, just stand there and read the telephone book—who's to quarrel?"

Joanne reportedly said, "Paul should never have made *Winning*. His life has been at risk ever since."

In the years that remained before him, before he officially entered old age, Paul became so consumed with the race circuit atmosphere that it replaced acting as his main endeavor. "Was he trying to prove something to himself or to the world?" Tony Perkins privately asked his friends.

A drunken McQueen was once asked if his interest, and that of Paul's, in sports car racing expressed a death wish. "Death wish?" he asked, puzzled. "Why should we have a death wish? Either of us can fuck anybody in the world we want. All we have to do is call 'em on the phone, and they come running. There have been rumors about Paul and me, about most actors. There have even been suggestions that we're not masculine. Out on those race tracks, we show those faggot reporters who's the man, baby."

"I'm stoned on racing cars," Paul said. "For me, it's a natural high. I don't need pot. He compared his love of racing to a dog. "Like a terrier, I keep gnawing at it. Just trying to get my car to go faster and faster. Before I took up racing, I had never done anything more dangerous than ride my motorcycle in New York."

Paul's favorite racetrack was Lime Rock in his native Connecticut.

He relished this man's world and escaped to it whenever he could, which was most of the time. "He loved that world of macho guys, seedy beer taverns, and even seedier motels, the kind that are built around racetracks," said Bruce Broyhill, a race car driver. "What even married men do at these places—booking a hooker for the night, making it with another man—stays there. When morning comes, they return to wives, lovers, or whatever. We on the racing circuit aren't Hollywood gossips. We don't tell everything we know. We accepted Paul like one of the guys, figuring what he did was his own God damn business. I never saw what all that Hollywood bullshit about Paul was about. But then I'm no judge. I'm color blind. I don't see blue. To me, the world is gray."

On the circuit, Paul began so enamored of certain race car drivers that he sometimes invited them to what he called his "fuck flat," a reference to his apartment on New York's East Side. Marlene Dietrich became known for her scrambled eggs, but Joanne, according to all reports, made the "world's greatest caviar omelet.

In referring to his abode as a "fuck flat," there is no suggestion that Paul ever brought sportsmen there for any other reason than to be entertained by meeting Joanne and served a great breakfast.

Naturally, those homosexual rumors that dogged Paul for all of his life, at least until he got too old to be the subject of speculation, surfaced anew among his racing buddies. Paul was said to have had several affairs over the years with drivers, mechanics, or "track pals." Although homosexuals in the most limited and silly view are known as hair dressers or decorators, many gays are among the world's top athletes. Perhaps for the thrill, many of them are drawn to sports car racing, basking in all that male testosterone and camaraderie.

Another driver, Johnnie Brentwood, recalled Paul winning a chug-a-lug contest in a dusty backwater in Utah. Sometimes we'd go out back and engage in pissing contests with him. Newman claimed he once beat Elvis in a pissing contest, but I didn't quite believe that. Elvis, to me, is the King of all Pissers."

Sam Posey, one of the "kings of the tracks," praised Paul as "one of the finest endurance racers in the world. A born talent for getting the most out of a car without fucking up the engine."

As Paul's racing intensified, in spite of his years, he was often asked if he'd abandoned movies. "Not at all. Right now I'm working with Hemingway's biographer, my good pal, A.E. Hotchner. I'm going to play Don Ernesto on the screen." That film was never made.

"If I had it to do over again, I would have become a professional sports car racer in my twenties," Paul told reporters in Indiana.

When another reporter pressed him for more details about why he liked to race, Paul quipped, "It's a kick in the ass!"

Sometimes Joanne in a wide-brimmed hat and sunglasses would show up for one of Paul's races. Perhaps they had a mutual agreement. If she attended the race track, he'd have to take her to a ballet performance.

Paul told reporters, "Joanne thinks sports car racing is about the silliest thing there is. It is also very scary to her. She reminds me I could get killed. I tell her I could get killed driving on any American highway. Even crossing the street."

It was apparent at times that Joanne missed her husband and perhaps became overwhelmed with the responsibility of caring for their brood while he was away racing. Once or twice she let her frustration spill out, particularly one afternoon when she quipped, "It's not always easy living with Sam Superstar."

Then a reporter asked her, "What is it like to live in Paul Newman's shadow?"

"I have to dwell there," she reportedly said. "He gives off such a glow I'd be blinded if I didn't have a good old shade tree somewhere."

In 1972, at the age of forty-seven, when most car drivers were retiring, Paul officially became a professional racer. In the future, he would try to limit his adventures into acting to the winter months so he wouldn't miss the summer racing season.

Driving a Porsche 911S, Paul engaged in a 12-hour endurance contest in Sebring, Florida. He was sometimes seen racing a Triumph TR-6. But in 1974 it was a Datsun that brought him two national championships. By 1975 he had formed his own racing team, using his initials of PLN.

As could be predicted, the inevitable accidents occurred, some of them life threatening.

In a Datsun 510, he faced a close call in July of 1977 in Garrettsville, Ohio. Competing in the Sports Car Club of America Race, a fellow driver lost control of his car. Hurled through the air, he landed on top of Paul's Datsun. Miraculously, both drivers, including Paul, escaped with only minor bruises. When the other car crashed through Paul's roof, it was his helmet that saved him.

The other driver, Robert Dyson of Poughkeepsie, New York, reported that he had never heard curse words like that coming from Paul when he finally escaped from the wreckage. "Maybe he learned those words while serving in the Navy in World War II."

That same year (1977) Paul wasn't intimidated by his crash. In Florida during the Daytona 24-Hour Endurance Race in April, he drove Clint Eastwood's Ferrari and came in fifth in a tight race.

For his sponsors, Paul endorsed Budweiser, a beer he knew only too well, and the Nissan Motor Company.

Paul became so proficient as a race car driver that he, along with the Datsun factory team, won all four of the Sports Car Club of America races. At one of the most dangerous race courses in the nation, at Watkins Glen, New York, he even set a record.

Until the death of his son, Scott, in 1978, Paul had been a rather conservative driver on the race track. But following Scott's death, his race track friends reported that he began to drive more dangerously, taking more chances and not always following proper procedures.

"He was reckless, a dare devil," reported another driver. "At one time some of us speculated that he had a suicide wish."

Following Scott's death, Paul entered two of the world's most dangerous races, one at Daytona Beach in Florida, another at Le Mans in France.

The Daytona race was a complete failure for Paul. Only ten minutes into the race, his Porsche started rattling, and he was forced to pull off to the side, dropping out for the duration.

Le Mans was a different race. He had been relatively unmolested by fans and photographers in Florida, but in France it seemed like all the paparazzi turned out in full force. Even when he went jogging on the 300-acre estate of the Marquis de Vesins, photographers jumped out from behind trees to snap his picture.

For the 24-hour race in Le Mans, Paul teamed with Dick Barbour and Rolf Stommelen, the latter an ace German driver. This was a true endurance race, as they faced torrential rain and hazardous road conditions. But Paul and his teammates rode to glory in second place, he in command of a red Porsche 935 twin turbo. At his peak, he reached an impressive speed of 220mph.

As an actor in 1979, his record wasn't as impressive. For Robert Altman, he filmed *Quintet*, a bleak, futuristic story about an Ice Age world, in which some reviewers saw homosexual overtones in the script.

When Paul was introduced to President Jimmy Carter, he decided to talk about car racing. "Southern men really like the race track," Paul said. But he was surprised when the President showed no interest in the subject. He also seemed bored with Paul's pontifications on the nuclear threat. But what really excited Carter was when he began to ask Paul about the movie colony and filmmaking.

The President must have been impressed with Paul because he later appointed him a public delegate to a special session on disarmament at the United Nations. Paul sat with Senator George McGovern, who had unsuccessfully run for President against Nixon.

William F. Buckley, who had publicly insulted Paul's friend, Gore Vidal, now lambasted Paul. "Maybe Mr. Carter thinks that Mr. Newman will so confuse the Soviet delegates that they will dismantle their entire intercontinental missile system. More likely, they will determine that the farce at the United Nations isn't worth one more conference with Paul Newman."

Even as he moved out of middle age and into senior citizen material, Paul by 1985 had set ten new track records. Behind the wheel of what he called "my monster," a turbo-charged Datsun 300ZX, at speeds of 192 mph, he'd win four national and five divisional auto sports car racing honors.

On one occasion, at Riverside International Speedway in California in May of 1987, his brakes failed as he was speeding at the rate of 140mph.

Finding an escape route, he managed to slow the vehicle down to 60mph before crashing into a wall. His car, according to a newspaper report, was "pretzeled," yet he escaped relatively unharmed with only minor bruises.

Riding with another driver on a track outside New Orleans, he hit a rut and his car skidded on two wheels. The speeding car turned over onto its right side, but Paul and his companion managed to escape with only minor injuries.

When Paul raced his last car, he looked back on his achievements, a staggering eight national titles, plus 107 victories in races against far younger drivers.

***

In 1974 Patricia Nell Warren published a novel, *The Front Runner*, that today is a classic in gay literature, having sold more than ten million copies. Although more than that, the novel is the story of a cross-country coach, Harlan Brown, who, at an obscure New York college, falls in love with a young Olympic runner named Billy Sive, the affair leading to disaster.

The plot very tenderly and with great sensitivity explores the developing love relation between the ex-Marine track coach and his openly gay athlete. *The Front Runner* became the first contemporary novel about gay love to be listed on *The New York Times* bestseller list. In publishing, it became known as a cross-over novel, meaning that it appealed to straight readers as well as gay ones.

It was Paul's producer, John Foreman, who first read the novel, buying a copy at the airport and reading it on his flight to London. When he returned to Los Angeles, he sent Paul a note. "Do we dare?" the note asked. As a whimsical postscript, he scribbled, "I know you still look devastatingly young and gorgeous, but I had you in mind for the coach, not the young front runner."

Paul read the novel that weekend and was intrigued at the prospect of bringing an openly gay love story to the big screen. He ordered his staff to acquire film rights to *The Front Runner*.

But within a few weeks, he began to have serious doubts. The director, George Roy Hill, reminded Paul, "No one will believe Paul Newman playing a homosexual." Hill seemed to forget that Paul had already played gay, both on the screen, though heavily masked, in *Cat on a Hot Tin Roof*, and on stage in *Baby Want a Kiss*.

To make the story work, the onscreen chemistry between Paul and the actor playing Billy

PATRICIA NELL WARREN

the**Front Runner**

A NOVEL

THE MOST CELEBRATED GAY LOVE STORY EVER

20th Anniversary Edition

Sive had to be idyllic. Ever since he'd made *Butch Cassidy and The Sundance Kid*, followed by *The Sting*, he and Redford had promised each other that they'd both be on the lookout for the perfect script in which they could co-star again, hopefully as successfully as they did in their two previous ventures together.

Reports still exist that Paul wanted Robert Redford to play Billy. However by the mid-1970s Redford had entered middle age—after all, he was born on August 18, 1937—although he didn't look it. Because of Redford's age, some sources claim he was never considered by Paul for the role. Actually, he was.

At that time in Redford's career, and with the right kind of makeup, almost twenty years, or at least fifteen, could be removed from his face.

"One night," Foreman claimed, "perhaps when he'd had too much beer, Paul talked with great enthusiasm about playing love scenes on screen with Redford. Perhaps he knew in his heart that's the only way he could make love to Redford—that is, in front of a camera." Foreman was well aware of Paul's bisexuality.

It cannot be confirmed, but Paul sent Redford an early draft of the movie script for *the Front Runner*. If legend is to be believed, Redford read the script and rejected it outright. "There is no way I'm going to appear on the screen with you, playing a homosexual."

Redford, or so it was said, had been deeply troubled over his gay-bisexual role in *Inside Daisy Clover* and didn't seem inclined to play an openly gay athlete. Throughout his career, Redford has never been the supporter of gay rights to the degree that Paul was.

"I don't know what Redford's problem is," wrote reporter Barry Devlin upon hearing of Redford's rejection of *The Front Runner*. "For those who could see with any sort of open mind, both Redford and Newman had already played homosexual lovers in *Butch Cassidy and the Sundance Kid* and in *The Sting*. With that in mind, look at *The Sting* again and decide for yourself."

Paul may have had his feelings hurt at so abrupt a rejection. Nonetheless, he didn't hold a grudge against Redford. That Christmas he sent him a paperweight containing sparkling blue eyes in porcelain. It was inscribed simply FORGET ME NOT.

Perhaps to counter the sentimentality of Paul's gift, Redford sent Paul a wrecked

Cal Culver
Losing the race

Robert Redford
"I'm not Newman's boy"

Porsche. To get back at him, and perhaps embarrassed at the sentimentality of his earlier gift, Paul shipped Redford two boxes of toilet paper with Redford's face illustrating every sheet.

"Paul's wooing of Redford, such as it was, was about as successful as Joan Crawford's attempt to seduce Bette Davis," said Foreman.

With Redford removed from consideration, Paul conjured up his own choice for Billy. "The Front Runner," at least for a few weeks, was Richard Thomas, the young actor who'd played his son in the race car picture, *Winning*.

Then for a brief time, Paul considered Robby Benson, who had starred with him in *Harry and Son*. Foreman reminded Paul that Benson had been nominated for a "Razzie Award" after his dreadful appearance in that film. Foreman also warned Paul that neither Benson nor Thomas were handsome enough for the part. "Billy should be blond, blue eyed, and gorgeous, Robert Redford in 1962, in other words."

"As if to answer a maiden's prayer" [Foreman's words], a picture and resumé arrived from Cal Culver. Foreman rushed it to Paul. It was what Paul had been dreaming of, a photograph of a young, beautiful, and sexy Robert Redford reincarnate. Except, as both Foreman and Paul learned, Cal Culver carried a certain baggage.

Under the name of Casey Donovan, Cal had appeared in *Boys in the Sand*, a landmark film in gay pornography in the 1970s. Born in 1943, he was five years younger than Redford, but looked much younger than that.

In addition to evoking images of Redford, Cal also suggested Guy Madison, Troy Donahue, and Tab Hunter at the peak of their beauty.

With Foreman beside him, Paul watched a screening of *Boys in the Sand*. Both men agreed that the handsome young actor was stunning. A question was raised. Would Cal's previous appearances in porno ruin him for mainstream films? Foreman thought not. "He has a large gay following, maybe millions have seen *Boys in the Sand*, and that would only increase box office for us. Straight audiences, however, would not have seen *Boys in the Sand*, and could not possibly care."

"Fly him to Hollywood," Paul said. "I'd like to meet this angel."

It can't be ascertained exactly what Paul was expecting when he first met Cal, but perhaps it was not the well-educated actor and model who appeared before him. Cal was not only charismatic, but articulate and full of grace and charm. "He was a knockout," Paul told Foreman the next day.

In Key West in the late 1970s, Cal told the author of this biography that, "I seduced Newman the first night we got together. It was the easiest thing I've ever done. I'm a take-charge kind of guy, and I just moved in on him. He put up no resistance at all. To judge by the moans, I gave him great sex. As for me, I've had better. But he *was* Paul Newman, and I was thrilled to submit to the casting couch. Of course, it became a question of just who was casting whom on that casting couch."

"I had described myself to Newman as Robert Redford's younger brother," Cal claimed, "and he seemed to agree. For one month, I was in Hollywood, with Newman paying all my bills. The only offkey note was one night when we were going at it, and he called me 'Robert.' I didn't like that, but I forgave him. After all, it was I who had been promoting the image of my own similarity in looks to Redford's. What could I expect?"

"We had great times together," Cal recalled. "Newman convinced me we were going to make the movie, and that we'd actually appear nude on the screen together—no full frontals, of course. He seemed to be looking forward to it."

"I was bouncing around up there in the clouds," Cal claimed. "In spite of my porno background, I wanted to go legit. After all, I'd appeared on stage with Ingrid Bergman. This was going to be my big breakthrough role. I even told myself that I might allow myself to fall in love with Newman, although another actor, Tom Tryon, had his stamp on me."

Tryon had been the star of Otto Preminger's *the Cardinal* (1963).

"Late one morning," Cal recalled with a certain bitterness, "the sky fell in on me. I came down from the clouds. Newman called shortly before noon. I was still asleep, groggy from the previous night. I fell down from the clouds. He told me that he had abandoned plans to film *The Front Runner*, and that our relationship was over. Before hanging up, he also told me that a check was in the mail. He put down the phone and that was it. End of my big, silly dream."

"I was devastated," Cal said. "Newman's check never arrived but John Foreman called me. I came by his office where five thousand dollars in one hundred dollar bills was waiting for me. That's a hell of a lot more than either Liberace or Merv Griffin gave me for similar services. I flew to Miami knowing it was all over for me. Eventually even Tom Tryon didn't want me any more. It was back to hustling and porno. I was, after all, known as the gay Adam."

"Quite by chance I ran into Paul one night in New York," Cal said. "I thought he'd ignore me, but he didn't. He stopped and chatted for a minute or two, apologizing that *The Front Runner* didn't work out for either of us. I suggested that he might like to come back to my apartment for a drink, but he turned me down. He told me that his affairs were over, that he was going back to settle down in New England. 'Everyone who's been a whore has to get out of the profession sooner or later—and that goes for you too, kid.' Those were his last words to me."

443

On the Sunday of August 10, 1987, Cal died of a lung infection associated with AIDS. Jay McKenna, writing in *The Advocate*, called him "the first widely embraced gay symbol to appear during the post-Stonewall years."

Years later, Paul claimed he regretted not making *The Front Runner*. "I made *Slap Shot* instead, and who cares about that fucker today? Had I made *The Front Runner*, it could have been a landmark—a turning point, really—in the history of cinema. Too bad I didn't have the balls. Cal Culver and I would have become the screen's new romantic lovers." He hesitated. "In the Greek tradition, of course."

***

All of Hollywood buzzed with the news. At 20th Century Fox, it was announced that Richard D. Zanuck, head of production, had just paid a record high of $400,000 for a script entitled *The Sundance Kid and Butch Cassidy*, its original title. William Goldman, the scriptwriter, had spent six years researching the lives of these two legendary train robbers, drawing some of his material from the archives of the historic Pinkerton Detective Agency.

The speculation was that this film was conceived as a spoof of all Westerns ever made. It was to be a comedy but with plenty of action and gunfights, including one fatal sequence where Butch Cassidy and the Sundance Kid take on the Bolivian army. Soldiers trap the outlaws after they flee into exile in South America.

Actually, the saga of Butch and Sundance had first been recorded on film way back in 1905 at the dawn of motion pictures. Butch and Sundance weren't gunned down until 1911. Reportedly, the real Butch and Sundance risked arrest to attend a screening of this early film, which was inspired by their own notorious lives.

Surmising that despite the passage of time, the saga of the two outlaws was still fresh in the public's mind, the screenwriter had spent six years polishing the story of these two legendary bandits.

Richly accessorized with a sense of nostalgia, the script conveyed the poignancy associated with the lives of Butch Cassidy and the Sundance Kid. At the dawn of the 20th Century, the Old West of legend was dying out. Notorious outlaws and bank robbers like Billy the Kid were becoming a thing of the past.

Word spread across Hollywood that the roles of Butch Cassidy and the Sundance Kid, scheduled for a 1969 release, would be plums in the year's pudding. Zanuck was firm in his choice of stars, wanting Marlon Brando to play Butch Cassidy and Warren Beatty to play the Sundance Kid. "Brando's career is in a slump, and I just know he'll go for this part," Zanuck said. "Let's

444

face it: he's done Westerns before. He can handle himself in a saddle. And, after the release of *Bonnie and Clyde*, Beatty's a hot piece of shit. He can guarantee box office even if Brando can't pull it off any more."

George Roy Hill, the director who had just completed *Thoroughly Modern Millie* (1967), had agreed to direct the Butch Cassidy film, but he wasn't thrilled with either of the designated actors.

John Foreman, who had just produced *Winning* with Paul and Joanne, also agreed to produce the Sundance and Butch film.

Over the years, sources have reported that Zanuck was unable to locate Brando, and, after a few weeks, gave up on him as a possible star of this upcoming western. That is simply not true. Brando was in New York at the time, and he read the script on the same day he received it, according to his longtime friend and confidant Carlo Fiore.

"Marlon could be shrewd about many things," Fiore claimed. "He saw some possibilities in this film, but only if Fox would agree to make the picture the way he conceived it."

"It's a love story of two men," Brando said. "Butch and Sundance are lovers. In fact, I envision a scene in which they are depicted buck-assed naked in bed together. If I play Butch, I'll be the top. Sundance will be my bottom."

Fiore made the claim that it was Brando, not Fox, who called Paul Newman with the suggestion that he should go for the role of Sundance.

"Would you like to star in an adult fairy tale?" was Brando's opening invitational line to Paul.

"You mean about two gay guys?" was Paul's immediate question. "I've played a homosexual before, but I don't know if the world is ready for a big screen version."

"Butch and Sundance are practically living in each other's crotches," Brando claimed. "We'll get naked together, like we used to, except this time it'll be on the screen. And we've got to show an ass shot here and there. You have a very nice ass if I recall. Of course, mine's getting a little big for on-camera exposure."

"I see the fade-out like one of those romantic movies of the '30s and '40s," Brando continued. "After kissing each other—maybe a little tongue or a whole lot of tongue—you and I will go out in a blaze of gunfire and glory."

Without the approval of either Hill or Zanuck, Brando sent Paul a copy of the script, which he read immediately. Goldman had written the screenplay for *Harper*, and Paul was impressed with his writing, although he often wanted to make changes in his own character's dialogue.

Paul placed a call to Zanuck, claiming, "I might be interested in playing the role of Sundance."

Zanuck later reported, "I was all ears. The screen team of Newman and

445

Brando was a thrilling suggestion. Besides, I wasn't getting anywhere pitching the role of Sundance to Beatty." At that time, Zanuck hadn't heard that Brando wanted to turn the script into a love affair between the two outlaws, with "hot man-on-man sex."

Beatty had been sent the script, but he was wavering, claiming at one point, "It's too much like *Bonnie and Clyde*. I don't want to be forever trapped in gangster or *bandito* roles."

Beatty made a lot of demands which Zanuck didn't like. If he'd accepted the role, he might have been offered as much as three and a half million dollars.

Paul would agree to do the part for $750,000.

Beatty called the director, Hill, and informed him that, "I don't feel like getting on a horse and riding around."

Hill had never wanted Beatty in the first place, and was glad to hear that. "If you don't want to ride a horse, why don't you take a walk." In anger, Hill then hung up the phone.

In a bad career move, and in lieu of opting for a role in the *Sundance* project, Beatty moved closer into the orbit of director George Stevens. Their property of choice for film development was the ill-fated Elizabeth Taylor movie, *The Only Game in Town*, an oddly old-fashioned saga about a gambling addict/pianist and a showgirl sharing an apartment in Las Vegas.

If Brando had signed on to the *Sundance* project, Paul would have played Sundance. If Beatty had signed on, Paul would have appeared as Butch. "It really didn't make any difference to me which role I played," Paul later said. "Both parts were equally terrific."

But Brando, for reasons known only to himself, suddenly bolted from the proposed cast and refused to return calls from Zanuck. "At the moment, I'm just too tired to make another God damn movie." He called Paul and told him of his decision to withdraw his name from the roster of candidates. "Why don't you get Steve McQueen to play Sundance?"

The studio had other ideas than McQueen.

Jack Lemmon, who had made a 1958 movie called *Cowboy*, came to mind. At that time, *Butch and Sundance* was more of a comedy script than it later became. Lemmon rejected it, claiming, "I don't like spending all that time on a horse." He also had a scheduling conflict with another film, *The Odd Couple* (1968).

For a brief two weeks, Zanuck considered offering the role of Butch to Dustin Hoffman. He was particularly impressed with his acting in *The Graduate*, which had made Hoffman a big star.

Paul called both Zanuck and Hill and abruptly withdrew his name from consideration. "After bombing in *The Secret War of Harry Frigg*, I've decided comedy is not my bag."

"You don't understand," Hill protested. "The situations created by Goldman are comedic, not the part of the Sundance Kid."

Paul agreed to reconsider. "I'll get back to you. Don't call me. I'll call you."

In two weeks, Paul called both Hill and Zanuck. "I'll appear in your picture. But I've changed my mind. I want to play Butch instead of Sundance."

Both the producer and the director quickly agreed, before launching a search for the Sundance Kid. In the rumor mill of Hollywood, word reached all out-of-work actors, desperate for a part, that as a result of Paul having committed to playing Butch Cassidy, the role of the Sundance Kid had become available.

***

John Derek was only a year younger than Paul, and still in fine shape. Paul hadn't seen the actor in several months but knew that his career was in decline.

When Derek reached Paul on the phone, Paul immediately proclaimed him "the stud of Hollywood. Ursula Andress—not bad. I haven't caught *Nightmare in the Sun* yet, but I want to see it. So you're a director too."

Paul was no doubt referring to *Once Before I Die* (1966), which marked Derek's directorial debut.

"Those nudes you shot of Ursula for *Playboy* were hot stuff," Paul said.

"Wait until you see my *Childish Things* with Linda Evans," Derek said. "I direct Linda in it. She's hot, man. Up there with Ursula."

"John," Paul said, "I know you well. You didn't call me to talk over all the hot pussy you're getting. You want to play the Sundance Kid, and you want me to go to bat for you at Fox."

"How is it you're able to read my mind?"

"You'd be great as the Sundance Kid," Paul claimed. "Really great. Two handsome fuckers on the screen like us. I promise you. You'll be my candidate."

"You really mean that?" Derek asked.

"Of course, I do," Paul said. "Have I ever lied to you about anything?"

"Not that I know," Derek answered. "Maybe we exaggerate the size of our dicks to each other."

"But if I don't get it for you," Paul cautioned, "will you be seriously pissed and break off with me?"

"Not at all. I've been around Hollywood since the war years. At least Derek Harris, my former billing, has. I know how the game is played. If Richard Zanuck fucks me, I'm out, and I know you can't do anything about it."

447

They ALL wanted to Sundance
for Paul Newman's BUTCH

John Derek	Sal Mineo	Steve McQueen	Brandon De Wilde

Marlon Brando	Jack Lemmon	Warren Beatty	Dustin Hoffman

Above:
Scott Newman
A father/son
collision

Immediate left:
Katharine Ross
with **Paul**
on a bicycle not
built for two

"Let's have lots of beer together, and some day I want you to do some wilderness travel with me," Paul said. "How about it?"

"Ever since *Exodus*, I've been your man. All you have to do is call."

"I'll hold you to that promise," Paul said.

Indeed he would. John Derek remained Paul's friend in spite of his disappointment when he lost the role of the Sundance Kid to Robert Redford.

Derek told his friends that Paul used his influence to try to get the coveted role for him, but it was the director, George Roy Hill, who nixed him, not Zanuck.

Months later when Hill was questioned about that, he told Zanuck and others that he didn't remember Paul ever bringing up Derek as a possible Sundance. "I don't know how I could have forgotten something like that. It didn't matter if Paul backed Derek for the role or not. I would never have cast him. Frankly, I think he's just another pretty boy. But he sure knows how to get the ladies. He must have a ten-inch dick . . . or something."

***

According to the novelist, James Leo Herlihy, Brandon De Wilde and Paul ended their relationship over a fight they had about casting the role of the Sundance Kid. Ever since the shooting of *Hud*, they'd been conducting a secret friendship, often at clandestine places.

Paul, of course, was married during his years-long relationship and so was Brandon. Both men were bisexual and didn't let the women in their lives prevent them from carrying on a love affair. In 1963, Brandon had married Susan M. Maw. They'd had a son, Jessie De Wilde, but by the time of the casting of the Sundance Kid, that marriage was coming unglued.

"Brandon was in love with Paul," Herlihy said. "Even when the kid broke up with me, we remained friends until he died. I went from being his secret lover to father confessor. I would have preferred the lover role, but Newman beat me out."

"From the beginning, Brandon was always being the one hurt in his relationship with Newman," Herlihy said. "He was seriously pissed off that he was the only one of the four principal players not nominated for an Oscar for *Hud*.

"Brandon desperately wanted to play Sundance, and he felt Paul had the power to secure the role for him," Herlihy claimed. "I don't know exactly what happened. Those two guys had a bitter fight. I think Brandon could have played Sundance and pulled it off beautifully. Obviously Newman didn't think so. For all I know, he had already committed to Redford."

"Our young friend was convinced that the Sundance Kid role would have

449

gotten him the Oscar he was denied in *Hud*," Herlihy said. "All I know is that after that fateful night when Brandon tangled with Newman, it was all over between them. I gathered Brandon punched Newman. When he called me the following day, he was so depressed he sounded suicidal. All through the years, ever since my *Blue Denim*, Brandon had dreamed of major Hollywood stardom, the kind Newman obtained. But the kid never got there."

"I felt sorry for him, and I always took his side when he'd pour out to me his hurt feelings about the way Newman was neglecting him," Herlihy said. "He once told me, 'All I am to Mr. Box Office is a piece of hot boy ass. He never treats me like an equal. My marriage is breaking up. I wasn't happy in it anyway. I didn't want to live life as a totally gay man, although I would have if Paul had asked me to be with him all the time. He never will, though. He's much too fickle. Regardless of the great times we have together, he always wants to return home to Mama."

Brandon, of course, was referring to Joanne Woodward. "At times he couldn't even stand to repeat her name, because he blamed her for standing in the way of his happiness," Herlihy said.

During the final years of his life, Brandon accepted a series of second-tier stage roles, when he could find them, and dabbled with the idea of breaking into the music industry. During a 1965 holiday in The Bahamas, he'd watched as Paul McCartney wrote the song, "Wait," during the filming of the Beatles movie, *Help*.

Yet despite encouragement from a Beatle, Brandon never followed through on his music and soon became bored with it.

By the late 60s and early 70s, in lieu of any big movie roles, Brandon was accepting second- and third-tier stage roles whenever he could find them. In Denver he was appearing in the play, *Butterflies Are Free*. While driving to the theater one night, he was killed in a car crash in Denver's suburb of Lakewood. To avoid a head-on collision with a drunk driver, he swerved his car and crashed into a construction truck parked on the side of the street. Pinned under the wreckage of the massive truck, he lay there dying before an ambulance arrived after a thirty minute delay. He died three hours after his arrival into the emergency room of Denver University Hospital.

It was the evening of July 6, 1972. Brandon was only thirty years old.

Herlihy heard the news of Brandon's death over the radio. "I was shocked. He was still so young, so beautiful. To me, he would always be the blond, blue-eyed Joey in *Shane*. In *Shane*, he idolized that strange gunman played by Alan Ladd. In real life he idolized the bastard played by Newman in *Hud*. I don't know what Newman did the night that Brandon died, but he had to be hurt by the news. He must have cried. Even though he disappointed Brandon at the end of his life, they had had some good times together. I think they truly loved each other. It was a wicked night for me to hear of Brandon's death. The next morning I felt the world was a much less hospitable place without Brandon around."

Brandon's body had originally been buried in Hollywood, but his parents later had his remains transferred to Pinelawn Memorial Park in Farmingdale, Suffolk County, New York. Frederick De Wilde never recovered from the death of his beloved son. He died in 1980. His wife, Eugenia De Wilde, lived until 1987.

The only known reaction from Paul was reported to Herlihy by his friend, Tony Perkins. The actor revealed that Paul had admitted that he'd journeyed to Pinelawn Memorial Park and placed a porcelain white rose on the grave of Brandon. That rose was later stolen.

"I stayed at the grave all afternoon and talked to Brandon," Paul confessed to Tony. "It was our goodbye. It was our closure. He'd meant a lot to me, and the likes of him will never be replaced in my life. He would have made a great Sundance Kid. I know that now. Like the Sundance Kid, Brandon delivered up the greatest gift of all to the Gods: An unfinished life."

***

By 1969, Sal Mineo's once vibrant career as a teenage star had virtually come crashing to an end. His young fans, mostly high school girls and gay boys, had grown up, the young women retreating with their husbands to the suburbs of the 1950s to raise children. A new generation had taken over, and new stars had emerged.

Born in 1939, Sal was no longer convincing as a teenage heartthrob.

In 1968, Sal was 29 when word went out that Paul was searching for a Sundance Kid. Soon after, Sal renewed his friendship with Paul, which he'd broken off when they'd filmed *Exodus* together and Paul had spent more time with John Derek than he did with Sal. Since then, both Paul and Sal had moved on to other lovers. Even so, Paul agreed to meet privately with Sal in Los Angeles.

Sal wanted to be the Sundance Kid, hoping it would revive his career. With Wayne Newton (of all people), he'd starred in *80 Steps to Jonah*. Audiences stayed away in droves. He didn't fare much better in the Cinerama presentation of *Krakatoa, East of Java*, the climax being the eruption of the Krakatoa volcano. Actually, the volcano was west of Java.

At the premiere of *Krakatoa*, Sal stood up halfway through the screening and yelled, "This is the worst piece of shit I've ever seen," according to his biographer, H. Paul Jeffers.

Fleeing bill collectors, having squandered the hefty paychecks of his

451

teenaged years, Sal met Paul in a restaurant and bar. Reportedly, Paul was shocked at how much Sal had aged. When Sal met Paul, the 1950s, Sal's heyday, was dead and gone.

Sal told the author of this biography that during his reunion with Paul, he did everything in his power to ingratiate himself with his former lover. "He turned a deaf ear to me," Sal said. "It was over. I knew when I invited him to go away with me for the weekend that he wouldn't go. I even reminded him of the size of my dick, but even that didn't turn him on."

"Paul was not the man I'd known when I caught up with him in 1968," Sal said. "He'd been the golden boy of the 50s. Everybody was after him in those days. He was a real hell-raiser. Now he seemed older, more mature, like he'd settled down. In the '50s both Paul and I could have anybody we wanted. And we did. He still could get, more or less, what he wanted, but somehow he didn't seem that interested in hot sex any more. I mean, I'm sure he still got off with somebody, but not everybody, if you know what I mean. He was no longer classified as one of Hollywood's bad boys. The Paul I encountered that night was rapidly becoming an American icon, and I was deep along the road toward becoming a has-been."

"I did something that night I'd never done before," Sal claimed. "I literally begged Paul to get me the role of Sundance."

"Paul said the part called for an All-American type with blond hair and blue eyes," Sal said. "I told him the fucking part could be rewritten, that we'd be great on the screen together. He wouldn't listen. He wouldn't budge an inch. I reminded him that he'd once told me he'd loved me. I remember him looking at me, with that strange, quizzical look of his. 'How many years ago was that, Sal?' he asked. He had me on that one."

"Finally, I took my cheapest shot, Sal said. "I told Paul, 'James Dean would want us to star together in *Butch Cassidy and the Sundance Kid*. Come on, Paulie: let's make the picture for Jamie."

"Now James Dean," Paul said. "What a guy! Dean would be perfect as the Sundance Kid. If Dean were alive, I'd see that he got cast in a moment's notice."

"That infuriated the shit out of me," Sal said, his eyes exploding with fury. "I knew then that Paul wouldn't get me a fucking job as the water boy. I stormed out of the restaurant. In front of everybody, I called him a faggot asshole."

Sal paused a long time before he agreed to finish the story. "I did something I'm not proud of even to this day. After my exit from Paul's life, I didn't know if he'd ever speak to me again. From his son, Scott, I got his private number and called him late one night. I told whoever picked up the phone that it was about his son. A matter of life and death. It wasn't Joanne Woodward.

I think I was speaking to one of Paul's daughters. She brought Paul to the phone right away. Otherwise, I don't think he would have received my call."

"He came onto the phone very alarmed," Sal said.

"What is it?" Paul asked. "Where's Scott? What's happening? Tell me."

"Okay, you asked for it," Sal said. "Right this minute he's lying under me taking the pounding of his life. I'm feeding him my nine and a half inches just like I fed it to dear old dad. He's squealing like a pig. Can you hear him squeal?"

Paul slammed down the phone.

"After that night, Scott fell in love with me," Sal admitted. "I never loved him. I'm not sure I even liked him. But when I screwed Scott, I was really fucking Paul Newman. He could have rescued my career and made me a star again. When it really counted, he turned his back on me. Up in the Bronx, when that happens, we get our revenge in one way or the other. Since beating the shit out of Paul Newman wasn't really an option, I did it my way."

In 1969 when Sal could find no movie work, he turned to the stage in both California and off-Broadway in a gay-themed prison drama, *Fortune and Men's Eyes*. In California, he attracted sold-out gay audiences by his nude appearance in a prison scene in which he rapes a young Don Johnson.

In spite of that brutal ending to their friendship, Paul was said to be shocked when he learned about Sal's murder on February 12, 1976. On his way home from a rehearsal of James Kirkwood's *P.S. Your Cat Is Dead*, Mineo was stabbed to death in a deserted alleyway in back of his apartment building in West Hollywood.

He was stabbed through his heart and lived for only a few minutes after the attack. His murderer much later was identified as a pizza deliveryman, Lionel Ray Williams, who was sentenced to fifty years in prison for killing Sal and committing ten robberies in the area.

***

Butch Cassidy and the Sundance Kid were not the only two most coveted male roles in Hollywood at the time. When it was announced that director John Schlesinger

Sal Mineo: Misfortune and Men's Eyes
P.S. Your Star Is Dead

had acquired the rights to the James Leo Herlihy novel, *Midnight Cowboy*, many actors vied for the roles of a naïve Times Square hustler, the heavily endowed Joe Buck and his sidekick "Ratso." Joe Buck was hailed as "the sexiest role of the year," and the part of Ratso was viewed as a character role so stunning that one was "guaranteed" to win an Oscar.

Originally and ironically, it was Sal Mineo himself who was the first star to read the novel. He flew down to meet with Herlihy in Key West. Although interested in acquiring the rights, he, of course, did not have the financing. As he told an interviewer, "the book's fuckin' fantastic, man."

He spent the weekend in Key West. Herlihy admitted to the author that he had sex with Sal. "He was like a firecracker. Paul Newman might kick him out of his bed, but Sal could put his shoes under my bed any night he wants."

When the author of this biography expressed amazement that Sal thought he could play Joe Buck, Herlihy quickly corrected him. "No, no. no. Sal wants to play the streetwise Ratso. The kid's from the Bronx. He'd be terrific as Ratso. He's hip enough to realize that my novel is really the love story of two men, Ratso and Joe Buck."

Regrettably for Sal, the role ultimately went to Dustin Hoffman, who delivered one of the most brilliant performances of his long career.

Warren Beatty was the next to weigh in. At the height of his sexual allure, he wanted the juicy role of Joe Buck for himself. Beatty had appeared in Herlihy's *All Fall Down*, which had been based on his first novel.

James Leo Herlihy
"Sizing up" Paul Newman

Herlihy thought Beatty would be ideal as Joe Buck. Of course, the ultimate decision lay with Schlesinger, the director, who turned Beatty down. He told Herlihy that Beatty was too well known and too sophisticated to play the naïve hustler, who arrives in New York to sell his sexual favors to women.

In New York, Paul contacted Herlihy through Arnold L. Weissberger, a famous theatrical attorney who represented such clients as Marlene Dietrich and Elizabeth Taylor. Herlihy was astonished to receive the call and agreed to meet Newman at his little bachelor pad in the East Village, a walk-up with the bathtub in the

454

kitchen.

"I'd always had a certain resentment of Newman," Herlihy confessed. "I used to think that *Hud* was a bit of a rip-off of my novel, *All Fall Down*. My movie had starred Brandon De Wilde and Warren Beatty. *Hud*, of course, had also starred Brandon but with Paul Newman this time. *Hud* did very well at the box office, *All Fall Down* did not. I have to admit I was rather jealous of the success of *Hud* over my own work."

"Newman was all charm and graciousness when he walked up to my little hippie pad," Herlihy said. "'Mr. Newman' became 'Paul' after a few beers. He had that winning smile that captivated me at once. I could really go for him, and I think he knew that. He talked a lot about my character of Joe Buck. We both understood that the character I wrote about was a lot younger than Paul."

"Paul came up with a slightly different interpretation of the movie character Joe Buck," Herlihy said. "He believed that if Joe Buck planned to hustle older, rich women, these ladies wouldn't want to be seen out in public with a young Buck but with an older, well-preserved Buck. 'No fifty-five-year-old woman wants to show up at a party in New York with a man young enough to be her son . . . or her grandson,' Paul told me. He had a point. I realized that a man like Paul would be more convincing as a New York stud than some young kid who just got off the Greyhound bus from Texas."

"I was rooting for Paul before the night was over, but I hadn't a clue as to what John Schlesinger would think," Herlihy said. "At the time Paul was also up for Butch Cassidy. He couldn't seem to make up his mind which role he really wanted. A real cowboy like Butch Cassidy or a *faux* cowboy like Joe Buck. In some ways, I think he wanted to do both pictures. He wondered if *Midnight Cowboy* could be delayed until he finished shooting Butch Cassidy. I didn't know about that."

"Throughout the evening, Paul and I had been sizing each other up," Herlihy said. "I'd heard that he was bisexual, and I made it clear I wanted some action. I didn't have to come out and proposition him. We were too subtle for that, even though both of us were drunk. When I invited him to spend the night, he readily agreed. And when we both decided we'd be more comfortable if we pulled off our clothes, the night was ours."

"We liked it so much that we went at it again the next morning," Herlihy claimed. "I thought we were so hot together, both drunk or sober, that he'd surely call again. He never did. Paul seemed to have lost interest in both Joe Buck and me by the following day. However, there's a footnote to the story. He gave the novel to his friend, Tony Perkins. That weekend the *Psycho* man himself called me. He'd read the novel, and now *he* wanted to play Joe Buck."

"As far as my love life was concerned, I thought I'd died and gone to gay heaven. First, Sal Mineo. Then Paul Newman. Then Tony Perkins. Too bad I never got to audition Warren Beatty. My friends, Tennessee Williams and Bill Inge, thought Beatty—and Newman, too—belonged in the pantheon of Greek Gods."

***

When Herlihy came together with Tony Perkins, he encountered an actor who desperately wanted to play Joe Buck. He feared that he'd be destined to play *Psycho* remakes unless he dramatically changed his image with the movie-going public. "Joe Buck is the kind of cowboy character who can do that for me," Tony said.

Herlihy had avidly followed Tony's career ever since he saw him on Broadway in *Tea and Sympathy*, where he played a student accused of being gay. But after Alfred Hitchcock cast him as the rail-thin, quivering wacko in *Psycho* (1960), he was forever identified as Norman Bates.

"I found my soulmate in Tony," Herlihy claimed. "Both of us were a little mad, but we brought out the best in each other. The first night I met him in Key West, I took him to Tony's Bar. We were both high on pot. I found out Tony wanted to be a singer. He stood up in front of a roaring crowd and sang 'Midnight Swim.' The guys loved him, and so did I later in that evening."

"Tony talked about Paul Newman all the time," Herlihy claimed. "Year after year throughout our long drawn-out, on-again, off-again affair. He seemed obsessed with Newman, and measured his success on the screen—or lack of it—with that of Newman's. Newman had obtained the stardom that Tony wanted, and he resented it, even though he continued to maintain a long friendship with both Newman and his wife."

Tony relayed to Herlihy all of the details of his early affair with Paul in the '50s. "He's just as gay as I am, but he won't come out of the closet. He uses that so-called great marriage of his to conceal his true desires." In spite of that criticism of Paul, Tony also lived deep in the closet throughout most of his life as well.

John Schlesinger would not even consider the concept of Tony Perkins playing Joe Buck for more than a few seconds. "It's about the worst casting idea I've ever heard," Schlesinger told Herlihy. "Norman Bates as Joe Buck! You guys have been smoking too much pot."

Despite his disappointment over losing the role, Tony and Herlihy remained friends, getting together in secret and going to out-of-the-way gay bars in New York.

Tony continued to sleep around and kept Herlihy abreast of his many affairs. His relationship with Tab Hunter had long ago ended, and he pursued famous bed partners only rarely, having a torrid affair with Rudolph Nureyev, the ballet dancer. For the most part, he preferred hustlers, beautiful young Thai men, and lots of tall, thin Broadway male dancers.

"Tony was kinky," Herlihy admitted. "He'd pay guys to climb through his bedroom window, tie him up with a rope, and rape him."

Author Truman Capote, who knew Herlihy only casually, chastised him for hanging out with Tony. "Personally I don't like blood even though I wrote *In Cold Blood*," Capote told Herlihy. "Tony's a sadist. He likes to see blood. I mean, he *is* Norman Bates."

Herlihy himself had not seen such aberrant behavior in Tony, but he'd heard stories.

Later in life, Tony came to Herlihy and asked the writer if he'd help him pen an autobiography. "Random House will give me a hundred thousand bucks for every dick I say I sucked." He never went through with the plan and finally turned down all offers for a personal memoir. His former lover, Tab Hunter, however, did agree to write the story of their love affair, but only after Tony had died.

Tony told Herlihy an amazing story: When Paul got him a role in the 1972 *The Life and Times of Judge Roy Bean*, Paul had grown tired of listening to Tony rant about how much he wanted to go straight. Responding to Tony's expressed intentions to "become heterosexual," Paul urged him to have an affair with Victoria Principal, who was also starring in the movie. "Don't knock it until you've tried it."

Paul pointed out to Tony that he'd had very satisfactory relationships with both men and women. "Each one is a different thrill in its own way. Instead of getting off on soft breasts, you learn to dig a hard chest, or vice versa. Instead of a hole to plug, you get plugged. The thrills are there in either case."

Tony took Paul's advice and seduced Victoria Principal, who would go on to become a household word when she starred in the long-running CBS nighttime drama, *Dallas*, from 1978 to 1987.

As Tony later admitted to *People* magazine, his meeting with Principal produced a "spontaneous combustion" and launched a four-day sex binge. "I was a virgin before I met her," admitted the forty-year-old actor.

Victoria Principal
A four-day sex binge

Tony Perkins
"The sadist likes blood."

"In claiming virginity, he seemed to have forgotten all the dozens of men he'd slept with," said Herlihy, "including me. I can personally testify that Tony was no virgin when he met Principal."

Tony's biographer, Charles Winecoff, claimed that after Tony's cherry-popping sex binge with Principal, the actor "became a real man."

In his attempt to go straight, he married Berinthia ("Berry") Berenson, an American photographer, actress, and model, on August 9, 1973. She was the granddaughter of fashion designer Elsa Schiaparelli. The union produced two sons, actor/musician Oz Perkins (1974) and folk/rock singer/songwriter Elvis Perkins (1976).

Even throughout the course of his marriage, Tony would continue his intimacies with male prostitutes on the side, according to Herlihy. It was from one such prostitute that he acquired AIDS.

In 1990, he sued the *National Enquirer* for writing that he'd tested positive for the AIDS virus. But, to his horror, he found out that the tabloid was right. A lab technician had sold the results of Tony's blood test to the paper. Tony did have AIDS, from which he would die two years later.

His widow, Berry Berenson, was among the passengers aboard one of the airliners that was deliberately flown into the north tower of the World Trade Center by terrorists on September 11, 2001.

Paul never wanted to speak of Tony or the disaster that occurred to his widow. He referred to both deaths as tragedies and preferred to conceal his memories of his long friendship with the troubled actor whose fear of exposure helped seal his own doom.

***

There was a footnote to the casting of *Midnight Cowboy*, the role that Paul briefly coveted, as did Tony Perkins.

Schlesinger told Herlihy that all his casting plans had been tossed out the window when Elvis Presley called. "This guy wants to play Joe Buck."

Herlihy thought Elvis in this truly serious role might be a sensation. "I

Elvis Presley
Wanting to play
"a fag cowboy"

Jon Voight & Dustin Hoffman
X-rated Best Picture of the Year

458

can just see Elvis walking down Times Square dressed as a cowboy hustling his dick. The public would go wild."

But within two weeks Schlesinger called Herlihy again. Once again Col. Tom Parker had intervened. "There's no way I'm gonna let Elvis play a fag cowboy," Col. Parker told Schlesinger. "Sometimes I think my boy doesn't have enough sense to come in out of the rain. No wonder, he's doped up all the time." Then Col. Parker slammed down the phone.

Finally, Schlesinger "turned down all applicants" [his words] and cast Jon Voight into the role of Joe Buck. Herlihy was hardly delighted but had no vote or veto power in the actual casting.

In the film, Ratso and Joe Buck argue about cowboys, Ratso claiming that, "Cowboys are fags." Joe counters, "John Wayne is a cowboy. Are you calling John Wayne a fag?"

In a touch of irony, both Voight and Hoffman would eventually be nominated for a Best Actor Oscar for their roles in *Midnight Cowboy*, each losing out to none other than John Wayne himself for his performance in *True Grit* (1969). *Midnight Cowboy* as a film, however, would become the first X-rated movie ever to win a best Picture of the Year Oscar. Schlesinger carried away the Best Director Oscar.

As for *Butch Cassidy and the Sundance Kid*, the film was nominated for both Best Picture and Best Director, but would lose both. For their roles as Butch Cassidy and the Sundance Kid, Paul and Redford would be ignored by the Academy but not by the movie-going public Paul had predicted the film might take in as much as $50 million. Soon after its release, it doubled that figure and continues to make money to this day.

***

Even after *Midnight Cowboy* was cast, Richard Zanuck still hadn't decided on the actors he wanted for *Butch Cassidy and the Sundance Kid*. He told director George Roy Hill that Steve McQueen should be offered the role of Sundance. "Newman and McQueen are two of the world's biggest stars. With those guys on the marquee, millions around the world will flock to see them. Of course, there will be a problem with top billing. They're both number one."

It was then that Hill proposed his own idea of who should star as Sundance. "I personally prefer Robert Redford," he told Zanuck. "I've known him since '62. I know what he can do. He'd make the best Sundance of any other actor in Hollywood."

Hill then pointed out to Zanuck that "Redford will cost Fox only half as much as McQueen."

Zanuck was not impressed with Redford's string of failures at the box office. "My mind is set. It's Steve McQueen and Paul Newman, or else the picture might not be made." He sounded threatening.

Zanuck told executives at Fox that McQueen is a "born screen cowboy," citing his role in *The Magnificent Seven*, which he'd made in 1960. He contacted McQueen and sent over the script.

Three days later, McQueen called. "I'm your Sundance. Draw up the contract. I don't work cheap. Remember that."

For years Paul and McQueen had discussed appearing in a film together, and the roles of Butch and Sundance now seemed to provide that chance. In talks night after night, they became so fired up over the movie's possibilities that Paul proposed that they acquire the rights to the script themselves, putting up $200,000 from each of their own pockets. McQueen rejected that idea.

The question of billing kept coming up, McQueen demanding top billing but Paul refusing to give up his star status. Fox intervened when they heard of this argument and proposed a staggered but equal billing.

After endless debates with himself, and after reaching an agreement with Paul to appear opposite him, McQueen, suddenly and impulsively, turned down the movie offer. "There's no way in hell that I'm gonna play Newman's bitch," McQueen told the stunned executives at Fox. He had finally figured out that *Butch Cassidy and the Sundance Kid* was the story of a love affair between two homosexual outlaws.

When Paul and McQueen finally did work together, in the disaster movie, *The Towering Inferno*, released in 1974, that concept of shared but equal billing was used in the posters. That 20th Century Fox film would also include Paul's son, Scott, in a small role, along with William Holden, Faye Dunaway, Fred Astaire, Susan Blakely, Richard Chamberlain, Jennifer Jones, Robert Vaughn, Robert Wagner, and future jailbird O.J. Simpson.

With McQueen out of the running as a candidate for the Sundance Kid, Hill again pressed Zanuck with the idea of casting Redford. The producer was dubious, but agreed to go along with the idea. Hill then called Paul, telling him that Redford would be ideal cast opposite him. Without missing a beat, Paul said, "The next time you have a role as a Wall Street lawyer, cast Redford. There's no way in hell I'm going to appear in this fucker with Redford. It's not his thing."

To consider Redford for Sundance is a waste of time," Paul told Hill. "He's a good-looking mother fucker, though. If I were a gay boy, which I'm definitely not, I'd fuck him. And he's got blue eyes, just like mine."

Up to then, Paul had seen only two films in which Redford had starred. *Barefoot in the Park* (1967) had been a hit, but Paul credited the success of the movie to its playwright, Neil Simon, and to its female star, Jane Fonda.

He also sat through *This Property Is Condemned* (1966), starring Redford

460

and Natalie Wood, who developed a crush on the handsome star. It was loosely based on a one-act play by Tennessee Williams. After watching Redford emote, Paul said, "I've appeared in two of the best plays Tennessee ever wrote. Redford has appeared in the worst."

It was Joanne who finally convinced Paul to cast his vote for Redford. In a complete about-face, Paul phoned Zanuck. "I'm convinced. We should go for Redford. Goldman practically created the part for him."

"You have yourself a co-star," Zanuck said.

"Who's going to play the girl?" Paul asked.

"We're thinking Katharine Ross," Zanuck said. "She was great in *The Graduate*. Hill has the hots for her."

"Actually I promised Susan Strasberg I'd put in a plug for her," Paul said. "Consider that promise of mine fulfilled. Just between us guys, I don't know if it matters who plays the girl. The part is incidental. I don't know if movie audiences will get it or not, but this is the story of a love affair between two guys. Just ask Brando."

***

When Hill finally introduced Paul to Redford, the director said, "It was love at first sight on Paul's part. Redford seemed to hold back and reserve judgment. Perhaps he suspected there might be a casting couch involved. I had no idea if he'd heard stories about Newman. Surely he must have known that Newman slept with some of his leading ladies . . . and leading men. Newman seemed mesmerized by Redford and his good looks in spite of those bumps on his face. Those two guys came together joking and bantering. Newman's chemistry was bubbling right away. It took Redford a while to work up combustion. The way I figured it, if Sundance and Butch were in love with each other, then Newman and Redford were the dudes to bring 'Out' two outlaws on the screen."

Rumors swirled around Hollywood, romantically linking Paul with the handsome, blond-haired Redford, the screen's new matinee idol in the making. With Joanne safely tucked away in London, Paul spent as much time with Redford as he could.

Hill spread the rumor that Paul's "blue eyes danced" when Redford came into view. There was one problem with these rumors and speculations. No one can be absolutely sure, but Redford and Paul never became an item. Redford was straight, Paul was not.

"I think Paul was too much of a gentleman to put the make on Redford," Hill claimed. "If Redford had just winked at him, Paul would have jumped into bed with the guy. But I don't think that ever happened. Knowing Redford

461

as I came to know him, I can bet my balls that it didn't happen. Maybe in Paul's mind, but that was the extent of it."

Early in production, a fundamental disagreement arose. Redford didn't like to rehearse but Paul did. "I ended up rehearsing," Redford said. "After all, Paul was calling the shots on this one."

After their initial explosion of chemistry, Paul began to see more characteristics in Redford he didn't like. No matter what or when the appointment was, Redford showed up late. Since Paul learned his screen pal was left-handed, he suggested to Hill that he re-title the script, *Waiting for Lefty*.

Hill disliked tardiness more than any other director. Fortunately, he never worked with Marilyn Monroe. Paul recalled that once, to pay Redford back for being late, "Hill took him up in his airplane. Scared the bejesus out of Redford."

What made production difficult during the short twelve-week shoot was Paul's fear of horses. "He was always afraid that one of those horses would kick him in his balls and ruin his married life . . . or whatever," Hill said.

Paul and Redford made the screen versions of Butch and Sundance lovable figures, with very little in common with their historical antecedents. The real Butch Cassidy had been a ruthless, desperate, and destructive outlaw, Sundance a cold-blooded, trigger-happy killer. Paul and Redford imbued their screen characters with a rakish charm and a reckless bravado, thereby appealing to rebellious young audiences of the late '60s.

During the filming, Redford and Paul managed to bond together partly because of their shared enthusiasm for fast cars and racing. And their camaraderie managed to survive in spite of Paul's frat boy humor. "He tells the worst jokes," Redford said. "And that wouldn't be so bad if he didn't keep repeating them over and over."

During the shoot, Redford more or less stayed on the sidelines, as Hill and Paul battled over scenes. Even Goldman was called in to settle an argument about the script.

Their most heated argument came over a segment in the movie that came to be known as "the Bledsoe scene." The argument became so heated that production was shut down for the day.

The scene involved a meeting between Butch and Sundance with Sheriff Bledsoe, played by Jeff Grey, an old friend who warns both outlaws that "you're gonna die bloody and all you can do is choose where."

Paul wanted it to be the last scene in the movie before their escape to New York. Hill violently objected, feeling the scene and the information it contained had to appear sooner.

By the following morning, Hill and Paul had made up and shooting continued.

However, Paul was not above exacting a minor revenge. He hired a studio grip to saw Hill's desk into two pieces.

Their disagreement over the Bledsoe scene percolated until the final day of the shoot. After viewing the final cut, Paul finally agreed that Hill had been right.

One of the most memorable events during the shoot was when Paul got to meet Lulu Betanson, the sister of the historical Butch Cassidy. She stayed on to watch a scene in which Butch kicks actor Ted Cassidy, playing "Harvey Logan," in the balls.

"My brother really did have blue eyes and a winning grin just like you do," Lulu told Paul.

Hill was a temperamental director, and he became known for kicking writers, producers, and even actors, including Katharine Ross, off the set.

But even though he fought frequently with Paul, the film's megastar was too big to be ordered off. At the time, Paul even had the power to persuade Zanuck to replace Hill in favor of a less feisty director. Paul said, "I fought with Hill, but I respected him too much to get him fired. So, we just duked it out."

In one of the film's most memorable scenes, Ross, without shoes, is precariously perched on the handlebars of that newfangled contraption, the bicycle.

She later told the press that she enjoyed shooting the silent, bicycle-riding sequence with the film crew's second unit rather than with her director. "Any day away from George Roy Hill is a good one," she said.

The trick bicycle riding sequence was also performed by Paul. Even a stuntman had turned that scene down, for which he was subsequently fired.

Following the release of *Butch and Sundance*, Ross was swept up in a whirlwind of fame that blew through her life in the late '60s when she became the symbol of beauty for the Woodstock generation.

In a touch of irony, Joanne's close friend, Cloris Leachman, was cast as a friendly prostitute in a short scene featuring Paul as Butch.

Bob Dylan refused to sing "Raindrops Keep Fallin' on My Head," the job going to B.J. Thomas who made the song a hit.

Deep into the picture, Paul came to realize that "we're making a masterpiece that will live down through the ages. They'll be showing this fucker a hundred years from now as the last great western ever made in Hollywood."

He cornered Redford, when he wasn't playing practical jokes on him, and told him, "Pal, you and I are going to become the Tracy and Gable of the '70s. I've seen the rushes. Our male camaraderie lights up the screen. It's obvious to anyone but a homophobic fool that we're in love with each other. On the screen, I mean."

In spite of such assurance, Paul was nervous about the final scenes in the film. He began to drink heavily, pouring Scotch on ice into a coffeepot to disguise his choice of beverage. At lunch he supervised the making of a gigantic salad, which he distributed to the other tables, where the crew ate.

The faces of Paul and Redford were so stunning that Hill often turned the cameras on each of them for close-ups. When Zanuck saw these rushes, he said to Hill, "What in hell! Do you think Paul Newman is Greta Garbo or something? So he's got blue eyes. So what?"

Throughout the movie, Paul is subtly muted and nimbly self-effacing, consistently underplaying, giving scene after scene to Redford.

Before he signed for *The Sting*, their next picture together, Paul was asked to reflect on Butch and Sundance. "It was a delight both to make and watch. Too bad we had to be killed off in the end. Butch and Sundance could have gone on in the movies forever."

Toward the end of the film, the outlaws, with Etta Place (Katharine Ross), head for Bolivia, thinking it would provide a source of gold for them. They soon learn that isn't the case.

Etta, as played by Ross, knows what's in store for her men, and she makes her exit so "I won't watch you die."

Caught in a cul-de-sac trap, Butch and Sundance face their end, battling Bolivian soldiers. In a freeze frame, the movie comes to its brilliant conclusion. Audiences don't have to watch the slaughter of what evolved into two of the screen's most notorious but most endearing "heroes."

The most famous scene in the film, the cliff top jump, was filmed not in Bolivia but at the Animus River Gorge near Durango, Colorado.

Paul and Redford landed safely on a ledge cushioned with a mattress seven feet below.

The wide-angled, distant view of the cliff jump was shot at the studio's Century Ranch near Malibu. Stunt doubles jumped off a construction crane, which was obscured by a matte painting of the cliffs. The cliff jump was later cited as one of the ten best stunts ever filmed.

"Newman and I got through the movie without killing each other," Hill later said. "But he's a control freak. Even Redford thought he was an arrogant snob at first. I have a word for Newman. We use it a lot on Hollywood sets. The word is prick!"

After working with Redford as Sundance, Hill later said, "Redford is a dangerous man to let loose on the streets. He has holes in his head. He should be arrested."

In spite of the difficulties, Paul would work with Hill again on *The Sting*, the 1973 hit that would bring him back to the screen with Redford. Once again, Hill hired an impressive roster of character actors, including Robert

Shaw, Charles Durning, Ray Walston, Eileen Brennan, and Sally Kirkland.

The story is that of two small-time Chicago con men who try to put "the sting" on a high roller from New York. The picture won seven Oscars, including Best Picture, Best Director (Hill himself), and Best Screenplay (David S. Ward).

Long after the release of *The Sting*, George Roy Hill would again star Paul in *Slap Shot* (1977), about a failing ice hockey team who finds success through the use of constant fighting and violence during games.

The film was attacked by critics for its foul language. "There is nothing in the history of movies to compare with this movie for consistent, low-level obscenity of expression," wrote Richard Schickel in *Time*. Paul's only comment? "Ever since *Slap Shot*, I've been swearing more. I knew I had a problem one day when I turned to my daughter and said, 'Would you please pass the fucking salt?'"

When Fox executives screened the first cut of *Butch and Sundance*, no one wanted to point out the obvious. Robert Redford was far better in the film as the Sundance Kid than Paul Newman was as Butch Cassidy.

Opening slowly at the box office in the autumn of 1969, *Butch Cassidy and the Sundance Kid* soon developed into a monster hit, as word of mouth extolled its virtues. After all his failures at comedy, Paul finally got it right. Never before and never again would his comedic persona light up the screen in such a way. Redford was the perfect foil for him.

Of course, Burt Bacharach's "Raindrops Keep Fallin' on My Head" and Paul's bicycle-riding sequence added greatly to making the film an entertainment wonder.

Over the ensuing decades many directors would try to steal the thunder of *Butch Cassidy and the Sundance Kid* in various films and plot devices, but none of these would ever equal the original.

Released in 1979, a prequel to the Newman/Redford film, *Butch and Sundance: The Early Days*, starred William Katt and Tom Berenger.

The public liked Paul as Butch and Redford as Sundance more than the critics. Pauline Kael headlined her review "The Bottom of the Pit," borrowing one of Etta Place's lines from the movie.

One of the harshest appraisals of

Butch Cassidy & The Sundance Kid
The West's most notorious
but endearing "heroes"

the film appeared in *Time* magazine, which charged that the two male stars "are afflicted with cinematic schizophrenia. One moment they are sinewy, battered remnants of a discarded tradition. The next they are low comedians whose chafing relationship—and dialogue—could have been lifted from a *Batman and Robin* episode. The score makes the film as absurd and anachronistic as the celebrated Smothers Brothers cowboy who played the kerosene-powered guitar."

TV Guide claimed that *Butch Cassidy and the Sundance Kid* "reinvented the Western for a new generation."

Throughout America, bedroom walls were draped with the famous poster of Butch and Sundance. The poster was in black and white except for two pairs of bright blue eyes. Redford joked that the film should have been called "Two Pairs of Blue Eyes."

Even as Paul was shooting his disastrous next picture, *WUSA,* Butch and Sundance would continue to rack up the largest gross of any Fox non-road show movie to date, making Paul America's number one box office attraction. The film would become the highest grossing Western in the history of motion pictures.

In the Oscar sweepstakes that year, *Butch Cassidy and the Sundance Kid* was nominated for Best Picture, Best Director, and Best Original Screenplay. In those categories, only screenwriter William Goldman took home the Oscar.

Launched by Redford at his Utah ski resort, Sundance, the Sundance Film Festival was named, of course, for his role in the film. Paul also named his Hole in the Wall Gang Camp for seriously ill children from the gang in the movie.

***

Sitting in the theater watching *Butch Cassidy and the Sundance Kid* was an eight-year-old Tom Cruise. In 2009 Cruise announced to the press that he planned to remake the film for United Artists.

"Paul gave me his blessing," Cruise claimed. "He would have wanted me to do it." That statement, of course, cannot be confirmed. Few superstars want lesser actors remaking their classics.

Even though Paul had been Cruise's close friend, he announced that he didn't want to play Butch Cassidy, but preferred the role of Sundance. For Butch, Cruise said that he hoped to cast John Travolta. Wags immediately claimed that the post-millennium version of Butch and Sundance, if it's ever remade, would be the Scientology version.

***

Robert Redford & Paul Newman   Tom Cruise   John Travolta

During the shooting of *Butch Cassidy and the Sundance Kid*, there was tension in the Newman/Woodward marriage over his heavy drinking. "She's nitroglycerine and I'm diesel fuel," Paul explained to George Roy Hill.

There was more trouble awaiting Joanne in her marriage, widely interpreted at the time the most enduring in Hollywood. That trouble arrived on the set of Butch and Sundance in a very shapely form. A cheesecake model and sometimes reporter, Nancy Bacon had posed for provocative pictures using the name "Buni." The curvaceous cutie had been hired to write a fluff piece on the production. Her first interview was with Paul Newman himself. That "interview," on and off, lasted for eighteen months. With Robert Redford reportedly serving as Paul's "beard," he launched a torrid affair with Buni.

Before she became a reporter, Buni had tried to become a movie star, cast first as Satan's Helper in the *Private Lives of Adam and Eve* and later, that same year, as a night club hostess in *Sex Kittens Go to College*.

Sometimes when not in front of the camera, she worked behind the scenes training big cats like Zamba or Clarence the Cross-eyed Lion. At one time she worked as a celebrity gossip writer for *Confidential*, the exposé magazine. She also became a romance novelist, creating potboilers like *The Love Game* and *Bayou Lady*.

In Mexico and even in Colorado, Buni became Paul's constant companion. In Cuernavaca, she shared Paul's hotel suite. Their illicit liaison continued even when Paul returned to Los Angeles, except these assignations took place in her apartment.

Those who want to actually read the indiscreet tales need only to turn to her gossip-filled biography, *Stars in My Eyes . . . Stars in My Bed*, originally published in 1980. Of course, it's hard to find a copy today since the autobiography is out of print.

Paul wasn't the only man upon whom Buni was bestowing her favors. It was in her tell-all memoir that she revealed her affairs with several famous actors, including Vince Edwards, Errol Flynn, Rod Taylor, Hugh O'Brien, and comedian Tommy Smothers. From 1963 to 1967 she was married to rock musician Don Wilson of "The Ventures." With her husband, she had a daughter, Staci Wilson.

According to Buni, after Paul reached a climax, he called it "heart attack time." Apparently, he did not always reach that desired climax. He wasn't getting any younger, and all that beer and Scotch drinking was sometimes or even often interfering with his lovemaking.

News of the affair spread rapidly across the Hollywood grapevine, no doubt reaching Joanne through some well-meaning "friend." Paul's heavy drinking during the time he played Butch Cassidy was problem enough for his marriage, but Buni may have proved too much for Joanne to handle.

By that time, Paul had already become famous for his pro-Joanne line, "Why go out for hamburger when I have steak at home?" Hollywood wags rewrote his line to say, "I've got steak at home, but I have to go out for my sizzling bacon."

It was Joyce Haber, the gossip columnist, who first broke the news to a worldwide public that the Newmans might be on the verge of breaking up. Writing for Syndicated Newspapers, she reported that "the Paul Newmans are living apart, according to friends, and will soon get a divorce," although she admitted that these were just "fascinating rumors, so far unchecked."

To counter her revelation, the Newmans took out a $3,000 half-page ad in *The Los Angeles Times*. It read:

"RECOGNIZING THE POWER OF THE PRESS, FEARING TO EMBARRASS AN AWESOME JOURNALIST, TERRIFIED TO DISAPPOINT MISS HABER AND HER READERS, WE WILL TRY TO ACCOMMODATE HER "FASCINATING RUMORS" BY BUSTING UP OUR MARRIAGE EVEN THOUGH WE STILL LIKE EACH OTHER."

It was signed: "Joanne and Paul Newman."

Although Buni may have dreamed the impossible dream, she realized that she could have only a Back Street affair with Paul. Nonetheless, she took pride when Paul one night deserted Joanne at a party and drove over to her apartment. On another afternoon he missed his airplane headed for New York "because he was in my bed." Joanne flew East without him.

On another night she recalled being at The Factory, a dance club in which

Paul had part ownership, and seeing him walk in with Joanne and all five of his daughters.

Eventually, Buni decided that she didn't want to carry on with an affair going nowhere. She lied to him, telling him that she'd met a man and had fallen in love with him. He hardly melted in front of her, but wished her all the best of luck. According to her memoirs, he did have one final request. "Could we get together a couple of times more before you do it?"

Buni took full responsibility for ending the affair, blaming it on his alcoholism. "I finally said to myself, I can do better than this. I told him, 'You're always drunk, and you can't even make love.'"

Buni was also rumored to be "more than friends" with the likes of President John F. Kennedy, his brother, Robert F. Kennedy, and such actors as Sean Connery and John Wayne.

She was once a roommate of Marilyn Monroe and also had close friendships with Elizabeth Taylor, Sharon Tate, Jayne Mansfield, and Judy Garland.

Although the general public still regards Paul as the most faithful husband in Hollywood history, insiders knew better. As Buni herself confesses, "We were hot and heavy. He was at my house almost every night. It was the worst-kept secret in Hollywood. People used to joke about it."

Upon Paul's death, and upon publication of a posthumous biography of him, headlines revealed what some called "Newman's Secret Mistress." Apparently, many of these newspaper editors didn't know the Newman/Bacon affair was about as much of a secret as the Monica Lewinsky/Bill Clinton blow-job in the Oval Office.

Buni, living today as a collage artist—and a very good one—in Washington State, told *The Enquirer* that she has no regrets about the story breaking once again after Paul's death. "As long as it's truthful, why not?" she asked. "That was the wild '60s."

After the breakup of his affair with Buni, Paul with suitcase arrived back at his house in Connecticut. "I'm home," he called out to Joanne emerging from the kitchen. "But, I must warn you, the fires of autumn burn on a very low flame."

He stole the line from a Gore Vidal play.

To restore their marriage, they

Nanci ("Buni") Bacon
Tired of steak, Newman turns to bacon.

469

THIS IS BUNI

These were Buni's Bosom Buddies

| Jayne Mansfield | MM | Elizabeth Taylor |

These were Buni's Jackrabbits

| Vince Edwards | Hugh O'Brien | Tommy Smothers | Rod Taylor | Errol Flynn | Paul Newman |

Here's MORE of Buni, with Lovers, Flings, or "Just Friends?"

(lower left to upper right)
Sean Connery, John Wayne, Robert F. Kennedy, John F. Kennedy, and covergirl **BUNI**.

A Buni with a taste for secret agents, cowboys, and philandering political brothers.

470

journeyed once again to London where they'd spent their honeymoon, much of it with Gore Vidal.

"For two people with almost nothing in common, we have an uncommonly good marriage," Paul told the tabloid press in London.

As for Joanne, she seemed to be getting tired of all that talk about what a sex symbol and box office sensation Paul was. "Look, he's forty-four, got six children, and snores in bed. How can he be a sex symbol?"

***

"Scott Newman spent the first five years of his life screaming in rage for having been born," Paul often said to friends. "He was unhappy throughout his short life. That libelous book on Joan Crawford by her adopted daughter, *Mommie Dearest*, took place in a child's playground compared to the struggles between Scott and me. I've always planned to use the story of our lives to inspire a film script one day, but I guess I never will—too personal." These words were spoken to John Foreman, Paul's producer, in the aftermath of Scott's tragic death.

Nervous and high-strung from birth, Scott grew into a hyperactive teenager who never forgave his father for deserting his family.

Lon Holden went to school with Scott and was his friend for a number of years. "Most kids would have been happy to have a big movie star for a dad, but not Scott," Holden said. "He was always bemoaning his fate. He took it real bad when his father left home to marry another woman. His two sisters seemed to adjust and accept, but not Scott. He developed a grudge against his dad that he never got over. I knew him for years on and off. Every time I saw him, he'd talk to me and ask about my life, but couldn't wait to launch into an attack on his dad."

"He was the most sensitive of the Newman children, including Joanne's brood," said Tony Perkins, who often visited the Newmans. He told novelist James Leo Herlihy that "Scott suffered from uncontrollable homosexual urges. I, of all people, know about that. One time out by the pool I had on this very revealing bikini. Scott was

"Father, dearest" **Paul Newman** with son **Scott**
"How can I compete against Mr. Superstar."

drunk and came on to me. There was no way in hell I was going to make it with Paul's son, and I flatly turned him down, even though I found him attractive. He stormed out of the house and never forgave me. He never wanted to be around me again. I guess he was too embarrassed."

If Scott resented his father and his success, he positively loathed Joanne, blaming her for destroying his parents' happy home. At times his rage against her became so extreme that he refused to speak to her for an entire year, although living temporarily under the same roof with his stepmother in their homes in Connecticut and California.

Once in Westport, an argument between Scott and Paul over money became so heated that Paul struck his son, a rare occurrence for him, since he did not believe in physical violence as a means of settling arguments. In fairness to Paul, he had been badgered all weekend and seemed to have boiled over in his fury and frustration with his son. Both father and son had been drinking heavily that weekend.

"I'm not going to raise another Hollywood brat!" Paul had shouted at Scott. "Instead of begging money off me, why don't you go out and earn some of your own?"

"You stingy, faggot asshole!" Scott had shouted at him.

That's when Paul bashed him in the face, bloodying his nose. Scott fled from the house and stayed away for four months, telling his friends what had happened between Paul and himself.

"How can I compete against Paul Newman?" Scott asked his girlfriend, Carol Studden. "He's handsome, he's rich, he's famous, he's adored. He has a certain talent although I'm a better actor. It's like he takes all the glory in the family and leaves nothing for the rest of us. What a greedy bastard."

Paul refused to give Scott a hefty allowance. "Peanuts is what I get from him," Scott said. "Not enough to buy a couple of beers on a Saturday night. Paul did send him to private schools, but Scott kept getting expelled. He always made poor grades and never applied himself—that is, if he showed up in the classroom at all. Often he didn't.

There was an attempt to go to college, but Scott dropped out. "What in the fuck do I care what Napoleon did? That was so long ago."

By the age of nineteen, Scott had grown into a six-footer, weighing 180 pounds. He told both his boyfriends and his girlfriends, "I'm bigger than my dad. Not just taller, but bigger in every other department as well." He never explained how he'd acquired such a measurement.

"From his late teen years and throughout his twenties, Scott continued to drown his sorrows in alcohol and drugs," said Wayne Edmonston, an occasional friend and drinking buddy. "I hung out with him sometimes, but I got tired of hearing him blame Paul Newman for everything that had gone bad in his own life. Often he didn't have money for booze or drugs, and begged money from his friends. Here I was making eighty-five dollars a week and lending ten bucks to the son of a multi-millionaire. You figure."

Scott always resented going back home to Jackie Witte in her modest house in San Fernando Valley outside Los Angeles. "Joanne Woodward gets to live like a movie star," he told his mother. "You're the mother of three of his children. You get to live like the wife of a grocery store clerk."

"It's just not fair," Scott protested to Jackie. "His three daughters with the Woodward bitch live far better than we do. He even bought one of them a fur coat. He seems to forget that we're his children too. We have to live like peasants, while his branch of the family enjoys all sorts of luxuries. We deserve more, God damn it."

He also told his mother, "When I was staying with the Newmans"—that's how he referred to Joanne and Paul—"a photographer wanted to come by and take family pictures. Super Star said no. he wants to hog all the glory for himself. How can I become famous if he won't let me get my picture in the paper?"

"Scott was deep into drugs and booze by the time he turned eighteen," said Billy Kramer, a former friend. "When drunk he got violent. He was always getting into fights, and he wasn't that good at it either. He always ended getting beaten up or injured. The guy loved danger. He took up skydiving. He liked fast cars like his father. Steve McQueen, perhaps to defy Paul Newman who wouldn't give him one, gave Scott one of his better bikes, but it was secondhand. He raced that motherfucker day and night until he got into an accident. It would be the first of many accidents."

At one point Paul tried to get Scott interested in the dangerous sport of racing cars around the track. Scott raced for about three weeks, but dropped out. A far more skilled driver, Paul won every race against his son. "I couldn't compete against him as an actor, and I decided I wasn't going to go up against him as a race car driver either. I told him I was going to stick to skydiving. That's something I did better than he did."

Scott became such a skilled jumper that the United States Naval Academy employed him as a parachute instructor. But after Scott didn't show up four days in a row, and didn't even call in sick, he was fired.

A breaking point between Paul and Scott came when Paul rejected Scott as a candidate to

Scott, accessorized for
The Towering Inferno.
A career not catching fire.

473

play opposite him in *Butch Cassidy and the Sundance Kid*. Paul went so far as to let Scott read the script with him, but he was not impressed with Scott's grip on the role of Sundance. "This could be a really big picture. You need more experience."

"How in the fuck can I get experience if no one, especially my father, will give me a break?"

"My father didn't help me become an actor at all," Paul shot back. "He was completely opposed to it. He even set up roadblocks. You should do it on your own. That way success will taste all the sweeter."

"I can't do it on my own," he said. "All doors are closed to me."

"I'll try to find something for you," Paul promised.

"Yeah, right!" In fury, Scott stormed out of the house. Before leaving he called back, "While you're trying to find something for me, why don't you go fuck yourself?"

After that confrontation, Scott was determined to make it on his own. In desperation, he once accepted a job digging ditches at a salary of three dollars an hour. "I was virtually working for food at the time," he later said.

In 1970 while Paul was in Oregon scouting locations for *Sometimes a Great Notion*, he and Scott had a reconciliation. Paul had gotten Scott a job working on the second unit crew of the film.

"The closest I ever came to knowing my father was when I visited him in Oregon," Scott told Joan Chandler, who'd been his on-and-off girlfriend for nearly two-and-a half years when he was a teenager. "I think John Derek had just left when he invited me up there. It came as a surprise. I don't know where Joanne was, or what was going on in his marriage, and didn't seem to want to talk about that. But for the first time in his life, he talked openly about his marriage to my mother," Scott said. "Since Sal Mineo had told me that my dad also went for men, I quizzed him about that, and he admitted it. He said many men go through stages like that, and it didn't mean anything. I think he lied to me about that, at least as far as he was concerned."

"It was on that trip that I began to see him just as a man and not as this mythical figure the press created," Scott said. "In many ways, he seemed just as fragile as I was. Somehow I felt better about myself knowing how flawed he really was. He said he couldn't really reveal to me who he was because he had never figured that out. 'Sometimes I take on the characteristics of the role I'm playing,' he told me. 'I want to be the good and perfect husband, and father everybody thinks I am. But, to tell you the truth, I think there's a lot of evil in me. My whole life has been an attempt to keep it bottled up inside me. Maybe that's why I drink so much.'"

At this point Paul rose to his feet, going to the kitchen. He soon returned with two cold beers. "Now tell me about yourself, son."

474

"You know, I've never heard you call me son before," Scott said. "Dad."

"I've never heard you call me Dad before either," Paul said. "Now tell me about yourself. I'm asking again."

"You know I can't tell you all the things that are in my black heart," Scott said.

"I know that, and in some ways I don't really want to know. That's why we'll never be a son and his dad."

"Guess not," Scott said. "But the sun is high in the sky. We can at least go fishing."

"That we can, kid."

Paul later admitted that "I was a good father to Scott only in flashes. Most of the time I was afraid to approach him, not knowing the level of hostility on any given day."

He made that statement while filming *The MacKintosh Man* in 1973 to director John Huston. The film was an espionage thriller, but the public had seen it all before. In the film, Paul co-starred with James Mason, who would play a strange interlude in Paul's life in 1978.

When Paul was cast in the disaster movie, *The Towering Inferno*, he did manage to secure a small role for Scott as a nervous fireman. But Scott ended up working for the most part with Steve McQueen, not Paul. One critic, on viewing Scott's appearance, wrote, "The part is so small it is hard to assess potential, but Scott has obviously inherited his father's good looks."

Paul himself tried to recapture the box office clout of *The Towering Inferno* when he signed to do *When Time Ran Out*, released in 1980. But, by then, Scott had already spent two years in his grave.

In this other disaster film, the story of an active volcano threatening a small South Pacific island resort, Paul was cast opposite William Holden and Jacqueline Bisset. When Holden, by then a fading star, expressed his sympathy to Paul over the loss of his son, Paul turned from him and walked away after saying, "Let's not speak about it, okay?"

Paul was hopeful that "the box office on *When Time Ran Out* will be miraculous." It was not. After *The Towering Inferno*, lightning didn't strike twice. "The only disaster in this film was at the box office," wrote one critic.

At the time he made *The Towering Inferno*, Scott was living by himself in a rented apartment in Los Angeles and going to acting school. He told a reporter, "Paul Newman has everything. I have not one cent. Not even money to pay rent." He constantly borrowed.

Kathy Cronkite, the daughter of the legendary television newscaster Walter Cronkite, attended acting classes with Scott at the time. Both were children of famous parents, and as such they had "that special bond" between them.

"Scott didn't give a damn about acting classes," she later said. "Sometimes he didn't show up at all. If there was a rehearsal, he most likely would miss it. I thought he was only pursuing acting because it was his father's business. He didn't seem to take the profession very seriously."

In 1974, after filming had been completed on *The Towering Inferno*, Scott got into a drunken brawl at Mammoth Lake, a ski resort town in California. He was arrested and handcuffed, then placed in the back seat of a squad car to be hauled off to jail.

En route there, he kicked the officer who was driving the car, landing his boot on the back of the cop's neck. The policeman lost control of the car and ran into a snowdrift. No one was injured, but Scott was charged with felonious assault with a deadly weapon-in this case his boot—and resisting arrest.

At police headquarters he was locked up, Scott was given one phone call. He didn't want to utter a plea for help to his father, but he had no one else to turn to.

Later, in reference to his reaction to Scott's arrest, Paul said, "You go into the kitchen and you get about three ice cubes and you chill a beer mug and you sit there and think for a while. Listen, there's not much you can do except offer what support you feel is required."

Paul was perhaps remembering his own arrest for drunk driving on Long Island back in the 1950s. It was front page news.

Joanne was terse in her response, "Scott should stand on his own two feet and stop being such an emotional drain on Paul."

Scott's arrest appeared on several front pages across the country. Paul complained about the press coverage. "The incident with him was blown all out of proportion. The accusation is always on the first page, the retraction on page nineteen."

Using his movie star clout, Paul persuaded the judge to reduce the charges to a misdemeanor with a thousand dollar fine and two years' probation.

In desperation after the arrest, Paul finally admitted the obvious. "I can't help him. He's beyond me. I reach out to him but find nothing there. There is no response. Only a zombie staring back at me."

He called for professional help, hiring Dr. Robert Scott of the Advanced Health Center in Newport Beach, California. The doctor had several sessions with Scott, later claiming that he "was terrorized by the idea of trying to be a professional actor like his father. The risk of failure scared the hell out of him. That's one of the reasons he turned to drugs and alcohol. There were more buried reasons, but I'm not at liberty to discuss them."

The alcohol treatment program that Scott underwent was not a success. But Paul was not willing to give up on his son. He turned to both medical doctors and psychiatrists to help save Scott.

In the office of one psychiatrist, who wants to remain nameless, Paul accepted the doctor's invitation to sit in on sessions with his son. "These were the most violent sessions I think I ever held with one of my patients," the doctor said. "Scott blamed his father for everything. He screamed and shouted and at one point threatened his father with violence. I could not help Scott because he was too far gone. A patient has to work with me and reach out to some extent. Scott wouldn't budge an inch from his fixed position. He put it plain and simple when he told Paul Newman, 'You ruined my life, you fucking bastard you. Someday, somewhere, I'm gonna kill you.' Those were his exact words to his father."

Finally, in desperation, Paul paid two psychologists to stay on call twenty-four hours a day to help Scott if he became suicidal or called out to them in any way.

After *The Towering Inferno*, Scott had used Paul's connection with George Roy Hill and Robert Redford, to get himself cast in a new movie called *The Great Waldo Pepper* (1975). Scott would be a bit actor and an aviator stuntman because of his experience with skydiving. Earlier Paul had turned down the lead, giving it to Redford.

Later Scott asked, "Did I get the job on my own merits—or just because I'm Paul Newman's son?"

In 1975 Paul praised Scott for his performance on *The Merv Griffin Show*. Merv himself said, "The kid's very likable. And handsome, too."

But in the months that followed, Paul had little praise for Scott. Their relationship continued to be "mercurial," an expression often used to tactfully describe the tension between them. "We were like rubber bands, one minute close, the next separated by an enormous and unaccountable distance," Paul claimed.

Scott again tried to make it on his own, taking acting lessons from coach Peggy Feury four times a week. Changing his name to "William Scott," he attempted to get gigs singing in small nightclubs in the Los Angeles area, but he had an untrained, weak voice.

He made some vague plan to cut a record with the singer Don McLean, who was known for recording "American Pie."

The only starring role Scott ever got was in *Fraternity Row*,

Scott Newman and **Robert Redford**
in *The Great Waldo Pepper*
Flying too close to the sun

477

released in 1977, but set in the hazing heyday of the 1950s at an upper-class college. The film opened and closed quickly.

"Every time I dream something will break for me, it turns into a nightmare," Scott told his friends as he sank deeper into despair. "But Super Star just goes on and on, even when he appears in a disaster. He bounces back and recovers quickly with a hit picture. Why can't some big break come my way? Super Star didn't go to Hollywood until he was around thirty. There's still hope for me I guess. By the time I'm thirty, maybe I will have made it too. *Maybe.*"

***

Shortly before he died, Scott was drunk and drugged, racing his motorcycle down Santa Monica Boulevard in Los Angeles, when he lost control and crashed into a parked car. He broke three ribs and suffered a cracked shoulder that left him in constant pain.

It was the worst motorcycle accident in Scott's tortured personal history. In the past, he'd walked away from accidents and fallen down flights of stairs with relative ease, gotten up, brushed himself off, and collected his paychecks for his work as a stuntman. He'd survived countless tumbles from stallions. He'd survived hundreds of jumps from airplanes during his skydiving heyday. Often, as a means of making the experience more thrilling, he'd open his parachute only at the last possible minute before certain death.

After his release from the hospital, he checked into the Ramada Inn in West Hollywood. He'd lost his apartment when he was evicted for failure to pay the rent. Night after night he lay awake in his bed at the Ramada, watching the blinking neon lights outside his lone window.

The pain from the accident remained constant. He accelerated his drinking, drugs, and pill popping.

Sometimes his depression would be so extreme that he'd call Dr. Mark Weinstein, the clinical psychologist who was on Paul's payroll. Dr. Weinstein would dispatch his young associate, Scott Steinberg, to go spend the night with Scott. Suicide was an obvious fear on the part of this medical team.

"Scott's demons were moving in on him nightly," claimed Carol Studden. "There was one drunken night he spent with his father that he couldn't shake. He told me all about it. He was in tears." Although he was never faithful to her, Scott had been dating Carol for nearly two and a half years. "When Scott came around, which wasn't every night, I was there for him. In some ways, we were more best friends than lovers. I didn't have any other boyfriends but he did. I knew about them. He sometimes told me the details, knowing I wouldn't judge him."

"The most shocking story he told involved Paul arriving drunk one night at that seedy Ramada Inn where Scott was staying," Carol said. "Scott said that Paul pounded on his door, and he let him in. According to Scott, they talked for around three hours. At one point, Paul taunted Scott, claiming, 'You'll never be the man I am.' This infuriated the hell out of Scott, and he attacked Paul on the bed. Both men, according to Scott, were undressed at the time because Paul planned to spend the night."

"Scott was very vague on the actual details," Carol said. "But the whole thing ended as a wrestling match between two drunks. Without really knowing what was happening, it turned sexual. Scott became aroused and attempted to rape his father. He claimed Paul did not put up any resistance. But looking into his father's accusatory eyes made him lose his erection. He couldn't go through with it. It was too vile."

"In the days ahead Scott had to face up to a truth he didn't want to face," Carol claimed. "Instead of hating his father, he might have been in love with him. In his attempted rape, he was trying to break through the cold barrier that had existed between them since the dawn of time. It was awful for Scott. He broke down and cried. He was all mixed up."

"He told me what Paul's final words were to him, as he stood at the door to that motel room, adjusting his clothes," Carol said. "'You're not even man enough to finish what you started back in that bed,' Paul told Scott. Trying to rape your own father is nightmarish enough, but to turn impotent in the middle of it didn't help Scott's ego. Maybe permanently damaged it. I tried to be supportive, but there was nothing I could do. Although hopelessly drunk and drugged, he went for a night ride on his motorcycle."

Carol said that on the day of his death, she'd invited Scott over but he chose instead to go to a friend's house to watch a football game. Once there, Scott downed eight Cuba libres while complaining of a severe pain in his shoulder and under his ribs as a result of that motorcycle accident.

His friend offered him eight Valium tablets. Scott refilled his glass with rum and swallowed five of them. Before leaving his friend's house that afternoon, he took the other three.

Scott's friend (not named in any accounts) drove him to the office of Dr. Mark Weinstein, who was on 24-hour call for Scott.

"Scott was too drunk to drive himself," the friend later said.

Once at Dr. Weinstein's office, Scott spent an hour attacking Paul, blaming him for "ruining my life." He also issued a violent attack on his stepmother, Joanne, blaming her "for trying to send me off to another world."

Unaware of the Valium and liquor that Scott had consumed, Dr. Weinstein gave him a sample bottle of the painkiller Darvon to relieve the pain of the motorcycle accident.

Dr. Weinstein then directed his assistant, Scott Steinberg, to drive Scott home and stay with him for the night. Perhaps this was tantamount to a suicide watch, although not specifically labeled as that.

Steinberg drove the patient to the Ramada Inn, where Scott had rented two adjoining rooms. Steinberg sat and talked to him as long as he could, but Scott was becoming incoherent. He went to his own room, and Steinberg heard him making a number of calls. It is rumored, but never confirmed, that one of these calls was to his father. Exactly what Scott said that night will never be known. It is assumed that it was a farewell call, although Paul never alerted the police. From that lack of action on Paul's part, it can also be assumed that he was not unduly alarmed that Scott might take his life that night.

Scott called two other friends with whom he'd taken to hanging out. Both John Rutfield and Barry Devon claimed he told them he was going away on a long trip and wouldn't be back for quite a while.

"He told us what great fun he'd had with us," John said. "Our times together had been happy times. He thanked us and just hung up—and that was that."

Apparently, John and Barry, both homosexual lovers, had been indulging in a three-way with Scott.

John later said, "Scott told us that he'd learned from Sal Mineo that Paul Newman as a young man had indulged in some three ways, once with Marlon Brando and an old-time actress. Scott said, 'If it's good enough for dear old dad, it's good enough for me.'"

Scott's final call was to Carol, whose invitation he'd turned down only hours before. "His speech was slurred, and I couldn't make out every word he said," she claimed. "For the first time in his life, he wasn't attacking his father, but Sal Mineo. He told me he'd been trying to get in touch with Mineo all night and that the 'arrogant prick'—his words—wasn't taking his calls."

"But your pal died two years ago," Carol told him. "He was murdered. Don't you remember that?"

"And just who are you, bitch?" he shouted at her through the phone line. "You only dated me because I'm Paul Newman's son. Admit it, cow. You wanted to date me hoping you'd get a chance to fuck him."

"That drunken insult was too much for me to take," Carol claimed. "I slammed down the phone on him."

After checking on him periodically, Steinberg claimed that Scott entered into a deep sleep, snoring loudly. When the snoring stopped, Steinberg checked his pulse. Scott was still alive.

But perceiving that something was gravely wrong, Steinberg called paramedics, and Scott was rushed to the hospital immediately. The hospital was just across the street.

Scott was pronounced dead on arrival at 1:07am on Monday, November 20, 1978.

An autopsy revealed that Scott had ingested excessive amounts of Valium, Darvon, Quaaludes, and cocaine. Apparently, while with Steinberg in the motel room, he'd gone into the bathroom and ingested the cocaine and Quaaludes.

As if to protect himself from accusations of negligence, Steinberg reportedly said, "What was I supposed to do? Go into the bathroom with him and help him take a crap?"

Because of these farewell calls, the case of suicide as opposed to an accidental overdose is a compelling argument. Scott left no suicide note, but, in hindsight, it appeared that his choice of a pathway to self-destruction had begun long before.

In the previous two years, following Sal Mineo's murder, Scott had told friends, "In many ways, I identify with Sal. He ended up a failure, even though he had had his moment of glory. I'll end up a failure too, except I never had a fucking moment of glory. I don't see what's left for me. There will be no big career. I need money all the time. What in hell am I supposed to do? Wait around another forty years to inherit the old man's money? Hell, if I know Paul Newman, he'll live to be a hundred if his heavy drinking doesn't do him in."

The phone call that Paul had been "expecting all my life" came through in the early morning hours, reaching him at Kenyon College, his old alma mater. To honor an old commitment, he was there directing a student play, *C.C. Pyle and the Bunion Derby*.

After receiving the news of Scott's death, he stayed up the rest of the night crying. "Those baby blues were all bloodshot the following morning," a drama student said. Paul told his actors that he'd stay on and open the play with them, although he'd have to interrupt rehearsals to fly to Los Angeles for his son's funeral. "I need all of you," Paul told the young cast. "I need this show. Be as rowdy as possible. Anything to distract me."

At midnight, some of the students showed up in clown costumes at Paul's hotel, where he greeted them at the door to his room. They offered him a case of Coors beer and a bottle of Jack Daniels, which he accepted. He opened the liquor bottle and gulped down a hefty drink. "I haven't touched the brown stuff in eight years. But tonight's my night. He held up the bottle and looked at it. "Welcome home, old friend," he told the bottle. Clair Bass, one of the drama students, claimed she saw a tear fall. He thanked them and shut the door.

The New York Times headlined its obituary, PAUL NEWMAN'S SON DIES OF OVERDOSE. One news report asserted, "Scott Newman spent his entire life trying to escape from the shadow of his famous father. He never did. That shadow was too wide, too dark, too threatening. Only in death did he free himself from it."

The newspapers kindly reported that Scott died from an overdose, but the suggestion of a possible suicide was clear in many reports from insiders associated with the situation. Carol Studden said, "I think Scott started committing suicide the day he was born."

Dr. Robert Scott told the press, "There was no competition between Scott and Paul Newman. They adored each other." The good doctor knew better.

In Los Angeles, Scott's funeral was a private affair open only to family members. Jackie Witte showed up with her new husband, who shared a brief handshake with Paul. Jackie and Joanne came face to face but had nothing to say to each other.

Scott's friends felt rejected and decided to hold their own services at Actors Studio West. Actor Alan Goorwitz and Burton Kittay showed up to honor Scott's passing. Goorwitz, along with Mimi Leder, even took out a memorial ad in *Variety*.

"He was only twenty-eight," Mimi said between sobs. "He had his life before him. If only he could have gotten over comparing himself to Paul Newman."

Dudley Monroe, an out-of-work actor, met Scott during the last three months of his life. "When he was sober, he had that wonderful Newman grin," Moore claimed. "When he was sober, he could also charm the pants off you, and I mean that literally. The rest of the Newmans are all hogs from what I hear. Only Scott, or so I'm told, had the sensitivity of a poet. A regular Byron or Shelley. He was the true artist of the family."

Reportedly, days after the funeral, Jackie Witte called Paul late one night and screamed at him, blaming him for Scott's death. That rumor, however, cannot be confirmed.

Right after Scott's death, Joanne told friends, "I realize how far I've faded from the public's view," she claimed. "The question used to be, 'Aren't you Mrs. Paul Newman?' But after all the publicity surrounding Scott's death, I was asked, 'Aren't you Scott Newman's mother?'"

In memory of Scott, the Newmans launched the Scott Newman Foundation at the University of Southern California in Pasadena. Scott's oldest daughter, Susan, was placed in charge of the foundation, whose aim is to alert grammar school age children about the dangers of drugs. "We didn't want Scott to have lived in vain," Joanne said.

To escape the memory of Scott's death, Paul threw himself into work. With director Robert Altman, he'd made the disastrous *Quintet*, released in 1979, and set during a future ice age. Apparently, he hadn't learned his lesson, as previously he and Altman had presented *Buffalo Bill and the Indians or Sitting Bull's History Lesson* to the public in 1976. In a one-line summary, that flop of a movie had dealt with Buffalo Bill's plans to put on his own Wild West side show, starring Chief Sitting Bull.

Paul broke his silence over Scott during the making of *Fort Apache: The Bronx* (1981). Steve McQueen had turned down the starring role. "It's all yours, baby," McQueen told him. After John Travolta turned down the co-starring role, the part went to Ken Wahl.

Watching Wahl act one day, Paul told his director, Daniel Petrie, "The role of Corelli would have been ideal for Scott. Too bad my son's not here to play the part. I should have gotten better roles for him. I could have."

***

In 1978, in the immediate aftermath of Scott's death, Paul sat on the beach, staring out at the ocean. Steve McQueen had called him earlier in the day and wanted to meet with him.

A grief-stricken Paul later told Tony Perkins and other friends, "Steve was one of the very first to be there for me. He knew what I was going through, and he wanted to spend the day at the beach with me. I found looking out at the vast ocean great therapy for me."

"We didn't say much to each other that day," Paul confided. "Steve sat on my blanket with his arm around me. He had some pot with him, and we smoked it. We both drank practically a case of beer. We'd been rivals in the past. Lovers, whatever. But somehow when we came together that day, all that was behind us. We'd emerged from it all—the fights over billing, whatever— as true friends."

"When Steve left that day, he kissed me on the mouth, and told me that he loved me," Paul told Tony. "I couldn't believe that. Words of love coming from Steve McQueen. I had to admit I truly loved the guy too. We were friends. Friends until the end. I hardly knew how close the end would be in coming."

Steve McQueen died on November 7, 1980.

Another strange revelation about that day Paul spent on the beach came from James Mason, the actor who had co-starred with Paul in *The MacKintosh Man*.

In the 1980s, Mason told the author of this biography that shortly after Scott Newman died, he received a surprise call from Paul. "We knew each other but we could hardly be called friends," Mason said. "He told me that after Steve McQueen had left him on the beach mourning the death of his son, he'd sat there for an hour or two crying."

"He said that right before the sun set, he heard the recorded sounds of Judy Garland coming from a nearby beach house," Mason said. "Judy was singing the music she recorded for *A Star Is Born*, that picture we made together. Paul told me that the most dramatic scene in that movie, at least for him, was when I walked into the sea to drown myself to escape from the despair and failure of my life."

"Paul confessed that he too considered committing suicide that day the same way I did in the movie," Mason said. "He told me that he felt that the best part of his life, his youth, was over. He also told me that he felt that his best work was also behind him. 'Every trick I know I've played out on the screen,' he said. 'There is nothing left for me to give my fans. I have to find another reason for living.'"

"Paul also confessed to me that his love affairs were also behind him," Mason said. "He told me 'they have all come and gone. Joanne, bless her, remains faithful.' He didn't see much future for himself that day. 'I'll end up sitting somewhere in a rocking chair on a back porch in New England dreaming about Marilyn Monroe and James Dean. They had the good taste to get out of life before age moved in on them.'"

"After giving suicide serious concentration, Paul rejected the idea," Mason said. He told me, 'I picked myself up, brushed off the sand, walked back to my car, and drove away.'"

"Before he did that, he actually spoke out loud to the ocean," Mason said. "He confided in me his last words to the sea. 'I told the ocean I was not ready for it to reclaim me, at least now,' he said. 'I'm going to head out and see what surprises the future holds for me. Before the final curtain, something will turn up. I just know it.'"

Paul Newman and **Joanne Woodward**
as *Mr. and Mrs. Bridge* (1990)

"I never ask my wife about my flaws. You don't want any woman to look under the carpet, guys, because there are lots of flaws underneath. Joanne believes my character in Mr. and Mrs. Bridge *comes closest to who I really am. I don't think so. But I learned a long time ago not to disagree. The film, incidentally, centers on sexual tensions of an aging couple."*

—Paul Newman

Epilogue

Even for movie legends, who seem timeless, human survival has its limits. In the Tennessee Williams play, *Sweet Bird of Youth*, in which Paul had starred, the playwright had warned against that relentless enemy, Time.

In one of Paul's last films, *Road to Perdition* (2002), in which he'd costarred with Tom Hanks, he made this comment when he was asked what it was like starring in a film in the 21st century. He was seventy-seven at the time.

"You can't be as old as I am without waking up with a surprised look on your face every morning. Holy shit! Waddya know? I'm still around. It's absolutely amazing that I survived all the booze and smoking, the cars, the career."

Best pal A.E. Hotchner paid a final call on Paul who had only days to live. Both men seemed to realize it would be their last visit with each other.

Their parting words:

HOTCHNER: "I'll be in touch."
PAUL: "It's been a hell of a ride."

Near the end of his life, a doorman in New York asked Paul how he wanted to be remembered.

His answer revealed how fleeting he felt fame was.

"I got this letter from a young man in California praising *Newman's Own Spaghetti Sauce*. He wrote, 'My girlfriend mentioned that you were a movie star, and I would be interested to know what films you've made. If you act as well as you cook, your movies would be worth watching. P.S. Are any of your movies in VCR?'"

After acting in more than 65 films over a period that spanned a half century, Paul Leonard Newman died on September 26, 2008 at his home in Westport, Connecticut. The cause of death was lung cancer.

In his final interview he said, "We are such spendthrifts with our lives. The trick of living is to slip on and off the planet with the least fuss you can muster. I'm not running for sainthood. I just happen to think that in life we need to be a little like the farmer, who puts back into the soil what he takes out."

His last known words, while sitting in his garden for a final time, were, "I thought I heard a meadowlark sing."

Director Martin Scorsese, on hearing of Paul's death, showed his obvious pain at the passing.

"The history of movies without Paul Newman is unthinkable. His presence, his beauty, his physical eloquence, the emotional complexity he could conjure up and transmit through his acting in so many movies—where would we be without him?"

A LION IN WINTER
1925-2008
REST IN PEACE

Selected Bibliography

Alexander, Paul. *Boulevard of Broken Dreams- The Life, Times and Legend of James Dean.* New York: Penguin Group, 1994.

Amburn, Ellis. *The Most Beautiful Woman in the World- The Obsessions, Passions and Courage of Elizabeth Taylor.* New York: HarperCollins Inc., 2000.

Andersen, Christopher P. A Star, is a Star, is a Star- the Lives and Loves of Susan Hayward. New York: Doubleday, 2008.

Andrews, Julie. *Home- A Memoir of My Early Years.* New York: Hyperion, 2008.

Arce, Hector. *The Secret Life of Tyrone Power.* William Morrow and Co., New York. 1979.

Ashley, Elizabeth & Firestone, Ross. *Actress- Postcards from the Road.* New York: M. Evans & Co., 1978.

Bair, Deirdre. Anais Nin- A Biography. New York: G.P. Putnam & Sons, 1995.

Baker, Carroll. *Baby Doll-An Autobiography.* New York: Arbor House, 1983.

Bast, William. *Surviving James Dean* . New Jersey: *Barricade Books*, 2006.

Berteaut, Simone. *Piaf- Her Story.* New York: Dell Publishing, 1973.

Bloom, Claire. *Limelight and After- The Education of an Actress.* New York: Harper and Row, 1982.

_____. *Leaving a Doll's House- A Memoir.* Boston: Little, Brown & Co. 1996.

Bosworth, Patricia. *Montgomery Clift- A Biography.* New York: Harcourt, Brace Jovanovich, Inc., 1978.

Brando, Marlon. *Brando- Songs My Mother Taught Me.* New York: Random House, 1994.

Braudy, Susan. *Who Killed Sal Mineo?* New York: Wyndham Books, 1982.

Bret, David. *Joan Crawford- Hollywood Martyr.* New York: Carroll & Graf, 2007.

_____. *Doris Day- Reluctant Star.* London: JR Books, 2008.

Burroughs Hannsberry, Karen. *Bad Boys- The Actors of Film Noir.* North Carolina: McFarland & Co., 2003.

Carlyle, John. *Under the Rainbow.* New York: Avalon Press , 2006.

Carroll, Diahann. *The Legs Are the Last to Go.* New York: HarperCollins, 2008.

Christian, Linda. *Linda.* New York: Dell Publishing, 1962.

Clarke, Gerald. *Get Happy- The Life of Judy Garland.* New York: Random House, 2000.

Coleman, Terry. *Olivier.* New York: Henry Holt & Co., 2005.

Cottrell, John. *Laurence Olivier.* New York: Prentice Hall, 1975.

Dalton, David. *James Dean- The Mutant King.* San Francisco: Straight Arrow Books, 1974.

Diederich, Bernard. *The Death of the Goat.* New York: Little Brown, 1978.

DiOrio, Al Jr. *Little Girl Lost- The Life and Hard Times of Judy Garland.* New York: Manor Books, 1975.

Downing, David. *Robert Redford.* New York: St. Martin's Press, 1982.

Edmonson, Roger. *Boy in the Sand- Casey Donovan.* New York: Alyson Books, 1998.

Edwards, Anne. *The Grimaldis of Monaco.* New York: William Morrow and Co., 1992.

_____. *Judy Garland-A Biography.* New York: Simon & Schuster, 1975.

_____. *Vivien Leigh- A Biography.* New York: Simon & Schuster, 1977.

Englund, Steven. *Grace of Monaco.* New York: Zebra Books, 1985.

Ferguson, Michael. *Idol Worship – A Shameless Celebration of Male Beauty in the Movies.* Sarasota: Starbooks Press, 1996.

Finstad, Suzanne. *Natasha- The Biography of Natalie Wood.* New York: Harmony Books, 2001.

_____. *Warren Beatty- A Private Man.* New York: Harmony Books, 2005.

Fitch, Noël Riley. *Anaïs- The Erotic Life of Anaïs Nin.* New York: Hyperion, 2008.

Frank, Gerold. *Judy.* New York: Harper and Row, 1975.

Frischauer, Willi. *Behind the Scenes of Otto Preminger.* New York: William & Marrow, 1974.

Gazzara, Ben. *In the Moment- My Life as an Actor. New York:* Avalon Press, 2004.

Giddens, Gary. *Satchmo – The Genius of Louis Armstrong. New York:* Da Capo Press, 2001.

Gilmore, John. *Live Fast-Die Young-Remembering the Short Life of James Dean.* New York: Thunder's

Mouth Press, 1997.

Given, Kevin. *Absent Friends: Paul Newman-An Overview of the Actors Films*. USA: KRG Publishing, 2008.

Glatt, John. *The Royal House of Monaco- Dynasty of Glamour, Tragedy and Scandal*. New York: St. Martin's Press, 1998.

Godfrey, Lionel. *Paul Newman Superstar*. New York: St. Martin's Press , 1979.

Grobel, Lawrence. *Conversations with Brando*. New York: Hyperion, 1991.

Guralnick, Peter. *Careless Love- The Unmaking of Elvis Presley*. Boston: Little Brown & Co., 1994.

_____. *The Last Train to Memphis- The Rise of Elvis Presley*. Boston: Little Brown & Co., 1994.

Hamblett, Charles. *Paul Newman*. Chicago: Henry Regnery Co. 1975.

Hamilton, Nigel. *JFK- Reckless Youth*. New York: Random House, 1992.

Harris, Warren G. *Natalie & R.J. – Hollywood's Star-Crossed Lovers*. New York: Doubleday, 1988.

Heymann, C. David. *Liz- An Intimate Biography of Elizabeth Taylor*. New York: *Birch Lane Press, 1995*

_____. *A Woman Named Jackie. An Intimate Biography of Jacqueline Bouvier Kennedy Onassis*. New York: Carol Comm. 1989

✓Hickey, Des & Smith, Gus. *The Prince- The Public and Private Life of Laurence Harvey*. London: Leslie Frewin Publishers Ltd., 2008.

Higham, Charles. *Orson Welles- The Rise of an American Genius*. New York: St. Martin's Press, 1985.

Hirsch, Foster. *Otto Preminger- The Man Who Would be King*. New York: Alfred A. Knopf, 2007.

Holden, Anthony. *Laurence Olivier- A Biography*. New York: Atheneum, 1988.

Holtzman, William. *Seesaw – A Dual Biography of Anne Bancroft and Mel Brooks*. New York: Doubleday, 1979.

Hopper, Hedda & Brough, James. *The Whole Truth and Nothing But*. New York: Doubleday, 1963.

Hotchner, A.E. *Doris Day- Her Own Story*. New York: William Morrow & Co., 1975.

Hunter, Tab & Muller, Eddie. *Tab Hunter- Confidential*. New York: Workman Publishing, 2005.

Jeffers, H. Paul. *Sal Mineo- His Life, Murder and Mystery*. New York: Carroll & Graf, 2000.

Jones, Max & Chilton, John. *Louis- The Louis Armstrong Story 1900-1971*. New York: Da Capo Press, 1971.

Kaufman, David. D*oris Day- The Untold Story of the Girl Next Door*. New York: Macmillan, 2008.

Kazan, Elia. *A Life*. New York: Doubleday, 1989.

Kelley, Kitty. *Elizabeth Taylor – the Last Star*. New York: Simon and Schuster, 1981.

_____. *Jackie Oh!* New York: Ballantine Books, 1979.

Kitt, Eartha. *I'm Still Here*. London: Sidgwick & Jackson, 1989.

Kotsilibas-Davis, James & Loy, Myrna. *Myrna Loy – Being and Becoming*. New York: Alfred A. Knopf, 1988.

Krampner, John. *The Man in the Shadows-Fred Coe and the Golden Age of Television*. New Jersey: Rutgers University Press, 1997.

_____. *Female Brando- The Legend of Kim Stanley. New York: Back Stage Books, 2006*

LaGuardia, Robert. *Monty- A Biography of Montgomery Clift*. New York: Arbor House, 1977.

_____& Arceri, Gene. *RED- The Tempestuous Life of Susan Hayward* New York: Macmillan, 1985.

Lambert, Gavin. *Natalie Wood- A Life*. New York: Borzoi Books, 2004.

Leigh, Janet. *There Really Was a Hollywood- An Autobiography* . New York: Doubleday, 1984.

Leigh, Wendy. *True Grace- The Life and Times of an American Princess*. New York: St. Martin's Press, 2007.

Levy, Emanuel. *George Cukor – Master of Elegance*. New York: William Morrow & Co., Inc., 1994.

Levy, Sean. *Paul Newman- a Life*. New York: Harmony Books, 2009.

Linet, Beverly. *Portrait of a Survivor-Susan Hayward* . New York: Berkley Books, 1981.

_____. *Star-Crossed- The Story of Robert Walker and Jennifer Jones*. New York: G.P. Putnam's Sons, 1986.

Lobenthal, Joel. *Tallulah! The Life and Times of a Leading Lady*. New York: HarperCollins. 2004.

Logan, Josh. *Josh – My Up and Down, In and Out Life*. New York: Delacorte Press, 1976.

Luft, Lorna. *Me and My Shadows- A Family Memoir*. New York: Simon and Schuster, 1998.

MacLaine, Shirley. *Don't Fall off the Mountain*. New York: Bantam Books, 1970.

Maddox, Brenda. *Who's Afraid of Elizabeth Taylor?* New York: M. Evans & Co. 1997.

Malden, Carla. *Karl Malden – When Do I Start? –A Memoir*. New York: Simon and Schuster, 1997.

McClelland, Doug. *Susan Hayward – Actress of Infinite Variety- The Divine Bitch*. New York: Pinnacle Books, 1973.

McGilligan, Patrick. *George Cukor- A Double Life.* New York: St. Martin's Press, 1991.

_____. *Alfred Hitchcock-A Life in Darkness and Light* . New York: Regan Books, 2003.

Meyer, John. *Heartbreaker- A Memoir of Judy Garland.* New York: Citadel Press Books, 1983.

Moonjean, Hank. *Bring in the Peacocks- Memoirs of a Hollywood Producer.* Indiana: Author House, 2004.

Morella, Joe & Epstein, Edward Z. *Brando- The Unauthorized Biography.* New York: Crown Publishers, Inc., 1973.

_____. *Lana- The Public and Private Lives of Miss Turner.* New York: Dell Publishing Co., Inc., 1982.

_____. *Paul and Joanne- A Biography of Paul Newman and Joanne Woodward.* New York: Delacorte Press, 1988.

Morton, Andrew. *Tom Cruise – An Unauthorized Biography.* New York: St. Martin's Press, 2008.

Munn, Michael. *Lord Larry- The Secret Life of Laurence Olivier.* London: Robson Books, 2007.

Munshower, Suzanne. *Warren Beatty- His Life, His Loves, His Work.* New York: St. Martin's Press, 1983.

Newman, Paul & Hotchner, A.E. *Shameless Exploitation – In Pursuit of the Common Good.* New York: Doubleday, 2003.

_____. *Newman's Own Cookbook.* New York: Simon and Schuster, 1998.

Newton Beath, Warren. *The Death of James Dean.* New York: Grove Press, 1986.

Newquist, Roy. *Conversations with Joan Crawford.* New York: Berkley Books, 1980.

Netter, Susan. *Cruise Control –The Unauthorized Biography.* New York: Perigee Books, 1988.

_____. *Paul Newman & Joanne Woodward- An Unauthorized Biography.* New York: Paperjacks, Ltd., 1989.

Nin, Anaïs. *The Diary of Anaïs Nin- Volume Five 1947-1955.* New York: Harcourt, Brace, Jovanovich, Inc., 1974.

O'Brien, Daniel. *Paul Newman.* London: Faber & Faber, 2004.

Olivier, Laurence. *Confessions of an Actor- An Autobiography.* New York: Simon and Schuster, 1982.

Oumano, Elena. *Paul Newman.* New York: St. Martin's Press, 1989.

Parker, John. *Warren Beatty-The Last Great Lover of Hollywood.* New York: Carroll and Graf, 1994.

Porter, Darwin. *Brando Unzipped.* New York: Blood Moon Productions, Ltd., 2006.

_____. *Howard Hughes: Hell's Angel.* New York: Blood Moon Productions, Ltd., 2005.

_____. The Secret Life of Humphrey Bogart- The Early Years (1899-1931). Blood Moon Productions, Ltd., 2005.

Preminger, Otto. *Preminger- An Autobiography.* New York: Doubleday & Co., 1977.

Quirk, Lawrence J. *The Complete Films of Joan Crawford.* New Jersey: Citadel Press, 1968.

_____. *The Kennedys in Hollywood.* Dallas: Taylor Publishing, 1996.

_____. *Paul Newman.* Dallas: Taylor Publishing, 1997.

_____. & Schoell, William. *Joan Crawford –The Essential Biography.* Kentucky: University Press of Kentucky, 2002.

_____. & Schoell, William. *The Sundance Kid- An Unauthorized Biography of Robert Redford.* Maryland: Taylor Trade Publishing, 2006.

Reed, Dr. Donald A. *Robert Redford- A Photographic Portrayal of the Man and His Films.* New York: Popular Library, 1975.

Reuter, Donald F. *Shirtless! The Hollywood Male Physique.* New York: Universe Publishing, 2000.

Richmond, Peter. *Fever- The Life and Music of Miss Peggy Lee.* New York: Picador, 2007.

Robinson, Jeffrey. *Rainier and Grace- An Intimate Portrait.* New York: Atlantic Monthly Press, 1989.

Roorda, Eric Paul. *The Dictator Next Door.* Durham & London: Duke University Press, 1998.

Sakol, Jeannie & Latham, Caroline. *About Grace- An Intimate Notebook.* Chicago: Contemporary Books, Inc., 1993.

Sanello, Frank. *Cruise- The Unauthorized Biography. Dallas:* Taylor Publishing Co., 1995.

Santopietro, Tom. *Considering Doris Day.* New York: St. Martin's Press, 2007.

Savage, LC Van. *Virginia Mayo- The Best Years of My Life* . Missouri: Beach House Books, 2002.

Schickel, Richard. *Brando- A Life in Our Times.* New York: Atheneum, 1991.

Server, Lee. *Ava Gardner – Love is Nothing.* New York: St. Martin's Press, 2006.

Shipman, David. *Judy Garland – The Secret Life of an American Legend.* New York: Hyperion, 1992.

Sinai, Anne. *Reach for the Top- The Turbulent Life of Laurence Harvey.* Maryland: Scarecrow Press, Inc., 2003.

Spada, James . *Grace- The Secret Lives of a Princess.* New York: Dell Publishing Co., 1988.

Spoto, Donald. *Laurence Olivier- A Biography*. New York: HarperCollins, 1992.

_____. *Enchantment- The Life of Audrey Hepburn.* New York: Random House, 2006.

_____. *Rebel- The Life and Legend of James Dean.* New York: HarperCollins Publishers, 1996.

_____. The Kindness of Strangers- The Life of Tennessee Williams. Boston: Little Brown and Co., 1985.

Stack, Robert. *Straight Shooting.* New York: Macmillan Publishing Co., 1980.

Stapleton, Maureen & Scovell, Jane. *A Hell of a Life- An Autobiography.* New York: Simon and Schuster, 1995.

Stephens, Robert & Coveney, Michael. *Knight Errant- Memoirs of a Vagabond Actor.* London: Hidder and Stoughton, Ltd., 1995.

Stern, Stewart. *No Tricks in My Pocket- Paul Newman Directs.* New York: Grove Press, 1989.

Stirling, Richard. *Julie Andrews – An Intimate Biography.* New York: St. Martin's Press, 2008.

Strasberg, Susan. *Bitter Sweet.* New York: J.P. Putnam's Sons, 1980.

Summers, Anthony. *Goddess- The Secret Lives of Marilyn Monroe.* New York: Macmillan, 1985.

Taraborrelli, J. Randy. *Once Upon a Time- The Story of Princess Grace, Prince Rainier and Their Family.* New York: Dell Publishing Co., 1988.

_____. *Elizabeth.* New York: Warner Books, 2006.

Thomas, Bob. *Clown Prince of Hollywood- The Antic Life and Times of Jack L. Warner.* New York: McGraw-Hill, 1990.

Thomas, Bob. *Joan Crawford- A Biography.* New York: Simon and Schuster, 1978.

Tynan, Kenneth. *Kenneth Tynan - Profiles.* New York: Random House, 1990.

Vaughn, Robert. *A Fortunate Life.* New York: St. Martin's Press, 2008.

Victor, Adam. *The ELVIS Encyclopedia.* New York: Overlook Duckworth, 2008.

Vidal, Gore. *Palimpsest – A Memoir.* New York: Random House, 1995.

Voss, Ralph F. *A Life of William Inge-The Strains of Triumph .* Kansas: University Press of Kansas, 1989.

Wagner, Robert J. & Eyman, Scott. *Pieces of My Heart- A Life.* New York: HarperCollins, 2008.

Walker, Alexander. *Vivien- The Life of Vivien Leigh.* New York: Weidenfeld & Nicolson, 1987.

Wayne, Jane Ellen. *The Golden Girls of MGM.* New York: Avalon Publishing Group, 2003.

_____. *The Leading Men of MGM.* New York: Avalon Publishing Group, 2005.

Windeler, Robert. *Julie Andrews – A Life on Stage and Screen.* New Jersey: Carol Publishing Group, 1998.

Windham, Donald. *Tennessee Williams' Letters to Donald Windham- 1940-1965.* Canada: Holt Rinehart, Winston, 1977.

Winecoff, Charles. *Split Image- The Life of Anthony Perkins.* New York: Penguin Group, 1996.

Winters, Shelley. *Shelley II- The Middle of My Century .* New York: Simon and Schuster, 1989.

Wood, Audrey & Wilk, Max. *Represented by Audrey Wood.* New York: Doubleday, 1981.

Wood, Lana. *Natalie – A Memoir by Her Sister.* New York: Dell Publishing Co., 1984.

Yann-Brice Dherbier & Verlhac, Pierre-Henri. *Paul Newman- A Life in Pictures. San Francisco:* Chronicle Books, 2006.

Zec, Donald. *Sophia-An Intimate Biography.* New York: David McKay, 2008.

Zeldis McDonough, Yona. *Who Was Louis Armstrong?* New York: Grosset and Dunlap, 1971.

Zinnemann, Fred. *Fred Zinnemann- An Autobiography- A Life in the Movies.* New York: Charles Scribner's Sons, 1971.

Index

493

494

496

497

502

504

BLOOD MOON PRODUCTIONS

Entertainment about how America interprets its celebrities.

Blood Moon Productions originated in 1997 as *The Georgia Literary Association*, a vehicle for the promotion of obscure writers from America's Deep South. Today, Blood Moon is based in New York City, and staffed with writers who otherwise devote their energies to *THE FROMMER GUIDES*, a trusted name in travel publishing.

Four of Blood Moon's recent biographies have been extensively serialized (excerpted) by the largest-readership publications of the U.K., *The Mail on Sunday* and *The Sunday Times*. Other serializations of Blood Moon's titles have appeared in Australia's *Women's Weekly* and *The Australian*.

Our corporate mission involves researching and salvaging the oral histories of America's entertainment industry--those "off the record" events which at the time might have been defined as either indecent or libelous, but which are now pertinent to America's understanding of its origins and cultural roots. For more about us, click on **www.BloodMoonProductions.com,** or refer to the pages which immediately follow.

Thanks for your interest, best wishes, and happy reading.

Danforth Prince, President
Blood Moon Productions

And its affiliate, the Georgia Literary Association

Salvaging the unrecorded
oral histories of America's "off the record" past

Entertainment you wouldn't necessarily expect
from America's Deep South

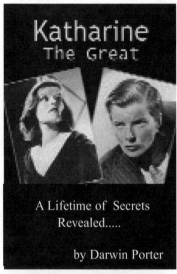

The drama of Steve McQueen's personal life far exceeded any role he ever played on screen. Born to a prostitute, he was brutally molested by some of his mother's "johns," and endured gang rape in reform school. His drift into prostitution began when he was hired as a towel boy in the most notorious bordello in the Dominican Republic, where he starred in a string of cheap porno films. Returning to New York before migrating to Hollywood, he hustled men on Times Square and, as a "gentleman escort" in a borrowed tux, rich older women on New York's Upper East Side.

And then, sudden stardom as he became the world's top box office attraction. The abused became the abuser. "I live for myself, and I answer to nobody," he proclaimed. "The last thing I want to do is fall in love with a broad."

Thus began a string of seductions that included hundreds of overnight pickups--both male and female. Topping his A-list conquests were James Dean, Paul Newman, Marilyn Monroe, and Barbra Streisand. Finally, this pioneering biography explores the death of Steve McQueen. Were those salacious rumors really true?

Steve McQueen   King of Cool   Tales of a Lurid Life
by Darwin Porter

ISBN 978-1-936003-05-1   Available December 2009   Hardcover $26.95

From the Georgia Literary Association,
in cooperation with the Florida Literary Association
and Blood Moon Productions

THE RENAISSANCE OF A CULT CLASSIC

You first heard about it in the 70s,
when it was the most notorious book
in Key West.   NOW IT'S BACK.

This is the book that satirized THE BOOK that changed the face of tourism in Savannah for all time.

MIDNIGHT IN SAVANNAH

BY DARWIN PORTER   ISBN 09668030-1-9   Paperback   **$14.95**

A saga of corruption, greed, sexual tension, and murder that gets down and dirty in the Deep Old South, this is the more explicit and more entertaining alternative to John Berendt's *Midnight in the Garden of Good and Evil.* .

If you've ever felt either traumatized or eroticized south of the Mason-Dixon Line, you should probably read this book.

"In Darwin Porter's <u>Midnight</u>, both Lavender Morgan ("At 72, the world's oldest courtesan") and Tipper Zelda ("an obese, fading chanteuse taunted as "the black widow,") purchase lust from sexually conflicted young men with drop-dead faces, chiseled bodies, and genetically gifted crotches. These women once relied on their physicality to steal the hearts and fortunes of the world's richest and most powerful men. Now, as they slide closer every day to joining the corpses of their former husbands, these once-beautiful women must depend, in a perverse twist of fate, on sexual outlaws for <u>le petit mort.</u> And to survive, the hustlers must idle their personal dreams while struggling to cajole what they need from a sexual liaison they detest. Mendacity reigns, Perversity in extremis. Physical beauty as living hell. CAT ON A HOT TIN ROOF'S Big Daddy must be spinning in his grave right now."   **EUGENE RAYMOND**

The author, Darwin Porter, a native Southerner, is co-author of ***The Frommer Guides*** to the City of Savannah and the State of Georgia. During his research, he formed some startling conclusions about the <u>real</u> Savannah, its most famous murder, and the sexual labyrinths of the Deep South.

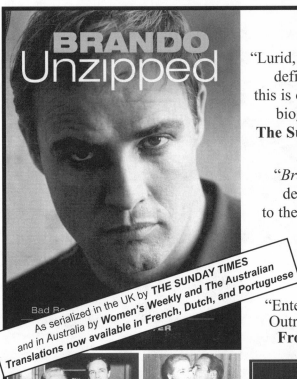

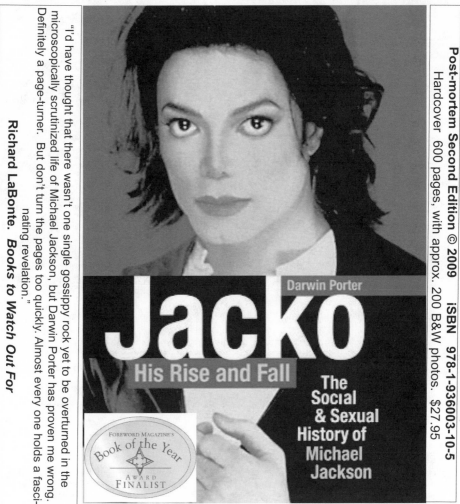

"I'd have thought that there wasn't one single gossippy rock yet to be overturned in the microscopically scrutinized life of Michael Jackson, but Darwin Porter has proven me wrong. Definitely a page-turner. But don't turn the pages too quickly. Almost every one holds a fascinating revelation."

Richard LaBonte. *Books to Watch Out For*

Post-mortem Second Edition © 2009 ISBN 978-1-936003-10-5
Hardcover 600 pages, with approx. 200 B&W photos. $27.95

Darwin Porter

Jacko
His Rise and Fall

The Social & Sexual History of Michael Jackson

FOREWORD MAGAZINE'S
Book of the Year
AWARD FINALIST

This is the world's most complete, most unbiased, and most comprehensive report on the scandalous life and enduring legacy of America's most eccentric musical genius--with the kind of even-handed reporting that no one else has even attempted. From investigative reporter Darwin Porter--the biographer who Unzipped **Marlon Brando** and brought **Babylon Back** to Hollywood

It illuminates the life of the Gloved One from cradle to grave, including insights into his fall from grace and latter-day attempts to revive his career. Published in the aftermath of MJ's tragic death in 2009, it provides often shocking insights into the artist's life, his tragic death, and its repercussions for the business and music industries. An award-winning finalist in Foreword Magazine's BOOK OF THE YEAR contest, this is unlike any other biography of the superstar ever written.

"Don't stop till you get enough. This is the story of the good boy turned rotten, or 'Peter Pan grows up.' Darwin Porter's biography of Michael Jackson is dangerously addictive." *The London Observer*

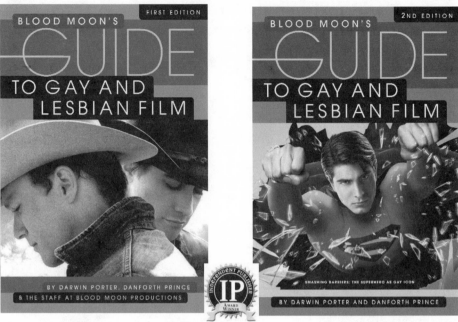

517

518

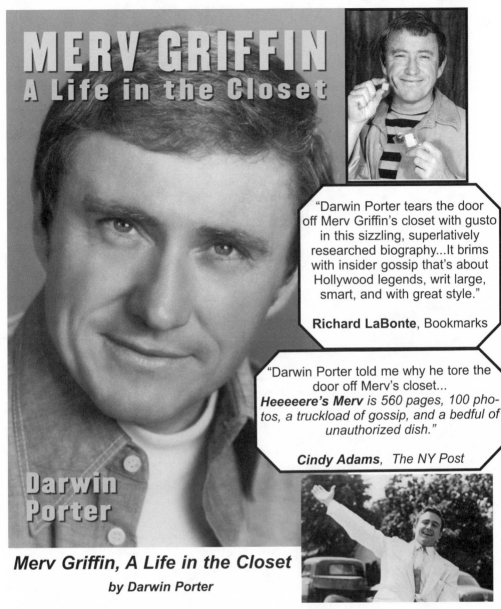

MERV GRIFFIN
A Life in the Closet

Darwin Porter

"Darwin Porter tears the door off Merv Griffin's closet with gusto in this sizzling, superlatively researched biography...It brims with insider gossip that's about Hollywood legends, writ large, smart, and with great style."

Richard LaBonte, Bookmarks

"Darwin Porter told me why he tore the door off Merv's closet... *Heeeeere's Merv* is 560 pages, 100 photos, a truckload of gossip, and a bedful of unauthorized dish."

Cindy Adams, *The NY Post*

Merv Griffin, A Life in the Closet
by Darwin Porter

Merv Griffin began his career as a Big Band singer, moved on to a failed career as a romantic hero in the movies, and eventually rewrote the rules of everything associated with the broadcasting industry. Along the way, he met and befriended virtually everyone who mattered, made billions operating casinos and developing jingles, contests, and word games. All of this while maintaining a male harem and a secret life as America's most famously closeted homosexual.

In this comprehensive biography--the first published since Merv's death in 2007--celebrity biographer Darwin Porter reveals the amazing details behind the richest, most successful, and in some way, the most notorious mogul in the history of America's entertainment industry.

HERE'S MERV like you've never seen him before.   Hardcover. 560 pages, with photos.   ISBN 978-0-9786465-0-9 **$26.95**

About the Author, Darwin Porter

This tell-all exposé of Paul Newman was authored by **Darwin Porter**, whose earlier portraits of **Merv Griffin, Marlon Brando, Humphrey Bogart, Katharine Hepburn, Howard Hughes,** and **Michael Jackson** generated widespread reviews and animated radio and blogsite commentaries worldwide. Some of Porter's biographies have been serialized to millions of readers in THE SUNDAY TIMES of London and THE MAIL ON SUNDAY.

Porter is also the author of *Hollywood Babylon-It's Back!*, a prize-winning anthology of celebrity indiscretion that was defined by some critics as "the hottest compilation of inter-generational scandal in the history of Hollywood," and "The Ultimate Guilty Pleasure."

Darwin was first introduced to Paul Newman by **Tennessee Williams** in 1959, when Darwin was functioning as the then-21-year-old bureau chief for the Miami Herald in Key West, Florida. From there, Porter began the compilation of a vast dossier on the early decades of Newman's private life from sources as diverse as playwright **William Inge**, author of the play *Picnic,* which launched Newman as a Broadway legend; **Richard Brooks**, whose screenplay for the film version of *Sweet Bird of Youth* was ruthlessly "castrated" by a studio that was determined not to release a film that was "too controversial"; actress **Geraldine Page**, who co-starred with Paul for hundreds of performances of *Sweet Bird of Youth;* novelist/playwright **James Leo Herlihy**, author of *Midnight Cowboy;* and dozens of other witnesses to Paul Newman's life and adventures.

Darwin is also the well-known author of many past and present editions of *The Frommer Guides,* a respected travel guidebook series presently administered by John Wiley and Sons Publishers.

When not traveling, which is rare, Darwin lives with a menagerie of once-abandoned pets in a Victorian house in one of the outer boroughs of New York City, with frequent excursions to California and various Frommer-related parts of Europe and the Caribbean.